# The Full Stack Development Book

# The Full Stack Development Book

By

Snehadeep Bhowmick

WhiteFalcon
Publishing

www.whitefalconpublishing.com

The Full Stack Development Book
Snehadeep Bhowmick

www.whitefalconpublishing.com

The contents of this book have been timestamped on the Ethereum
blockchain as a permanent proof of existence. Scan the QR code or
visit the URL given on the back cover to verify the blockchain
certification for this book.

Requests for permission should be addressed to
isnehadeep@gmail.com

ISBN - 978-93-89085-93-8

For Maa and Baba

and Debika

# FOREWORD

The book is written with the intent of making concepts understandable through simple language. The topics addressed in this book provide a primer around the fundamental concepts and prepares the reader for going deeper into the realm of full stack development.

The book is written in a way that encourages a reader to indulge in a *continuous read on a topic* and performing hands-on execution.

# READ ME FIRST

The history of web based application development usually required two types of engineering work, one obviously being the application programming part undertaken by a developer, and the other belongs to the provisioning of the infrastructure and deployment of the application. An application programmer's set of tasks is usually limited to the development environment and is further segregated into front-end and back-end development. The definition of a full stack developer is a programmer who can develop software for both client's end and also on the server side. For a generic mobile or web application, backend development involves building the server side software that ultimately handles the request from client app developed by a front-end developer. The realm of full stack development is a relatively new concept that entails a developer to be able to undertake the tasks of both front and back end development. This has become possible due to the evolution of the state of development toolsets, making them more robust and easy to use, and these modern tools enable a developer to build things in less time. Although, logically it made sense for a developer to be involved in both front and backend sections of an application development lifecycle, but it is only in recent times it has become feasible for an engineer to be specialised in both. For example, Firebase (not in the scope of this book) is an offering from Google that provides realtime database, authentication, cloud storage, etc. services ready to be used as backend assets of an application, thereby drastically reducing the hassle of creating a backend from scratch.

The traditional definition of full stack development does not include the array of other tasks that are present in the lifecycle of an app from development of front and backend, to ultimately deployment of the app. The deployment of an application requires the participation of a application/system engineer/architect who builds and manages the production environment. This book takes a leap toward all of those technologies that are most prominent in computer science in 2019, such that a developer is able to build not just the application but also the infrastructure.

The book starts off with the section on machine learning which is the most important invention in computer science of this century. Almost all applications are going to be re-written with and around machine learning methods. Therefore, for an application developer, it becomes the subject of highest priority to learn and implement in an app.

Next, is a section dedicated toward building a cloud infrastructure with Openstack. There are already cloud services available in the form of Amazon Web Services, Google cloud, Azure cloud, etc., but this book removes the abstraction from those services and takes an in-depth and hands-on tour through the underlying details of a cloud service by building a cloud infrastructure with Openstack.

Logging and log archiving is the key to how well an application is managed and so, Elastic stack takes care of that section in the third topic.

As search is a common attribute of most applications today, Elasticsearch provides a ready to use search engine.

This book takes an important walkthrough of DevOps practices with Ansible, bringing a developer closer to the work of a systems and application engineering.

The next section takes another important technology in recent times, the blockchain technology, and gives the reader a intuitive study on the subject for understanding its usage in applications.

The aforementioned backend programming, involving essentially server side code, is done with the Django framework and it is discussed in the next section of the book.

Using of containerised environment for development is among the best practices and so docker containers are discussed in the eighth section of the book.

Before actually developing a client side application, it is a good practice to go through a phase of mockup designs and prototyping. The section dedicated to UI/UX prototyping explains the usage of InVision Studio, an easy to use tool for prototyping.

For development of the frontend mobile app, the book uses a fairly new and easy native app development framework, FuseOpen, for both iOS and Android.

Lastly, the book again treads into the activities of application/systems engineering and discusses the application build and deployment lifecycle using CI/CD pipelines.

Therefore, the purpose of this book is to prepare a computer engineer with the knowledge on all those technologies that are necessary for building the complete application stack, with all its related facets. The book has plenty of QR codes which point to relevant online resources.

# CONTENTS

# SECTION 1

# Intelligence with
# Machine Learning

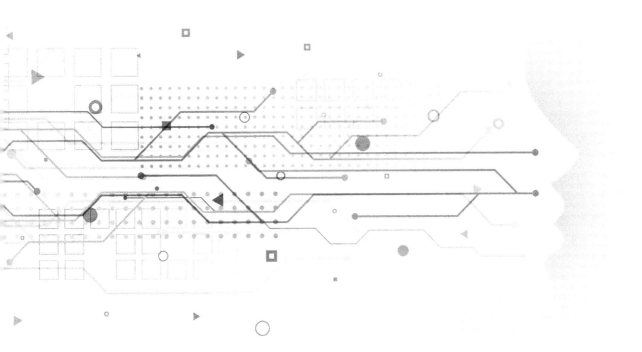

# Introduction

Since the inception of computers, programming has been the tool to encode logic, for accomplishing tasks with a computer. Up till by the end of 2018, there have been more than 700 programming languages according to Wikipedia. Programming languages belong to different programming paradigms and therefore they are used in specific use cases depending upon the characteristic of the problem that a program is trying to solve. That being said, the fundamental generalisation that we can do about a program, irrespective of the language with which it is written, is that, it is the set of arithmetic or logical steps written to encode a function or task. The accomplishment of the task, such as copying a data file between locations, is possible only through the knowledge about how it works, which then can be encoded into a computer program.

The concept of artificial intelligence has been there in computer science since the term was first introduced by John McCarthy in 1955. Over the years, computer science has had this two distinct concepts through which a task could be accomplished by a computer, one of which we already know as computer programming. The other one is through artificial intelligence. The intuition behind artificial intelligence as a concept can be described as the ability of a computer to accomplish a task, by making decisions on its own, without having to definitively encoding every single step, as in the case of programmed intelligence, in the form of a computer program.

The traditional method of building artificial/machine intelligence has been through writing computer programs that define a set of ground rules w.r.t. a particular use case, and it is these ground rules that gives the ability to a computer program, to decide on its own, about its actions for every event. Such artificially intelligent systems were comparatively difficult to build and had a moderate success rate.

Different from the traditional approach of artificial intelligence, a radically new method of machine intelligence was introduced in the form of 'Machine Learning' in 1959 by Arthur Samuel. This involved mimicking the function of learning through a statistical model and iterative improvement, unlike hard coding of rules. Machine learning has come a long way since then and has shown great potential. The progress in machine intelligence reached another milestone when the concept of deep learning was introduced in 1989 by Rina Decter. Deep learning is the method of bio-mimicking the functioning of a brain cell in its method of learning by using a new form of data structure called a neural network. In 2006, groundbreaking research done by Geoffrey Hinton and Yann LeCun were released, that solved a long standing unsolved problem of 'vanishing gradient' in training neural networks and finally paved the way for building artificially intelligent systems with excellent accuracy. We are going to discuss about both machine learning and deep learning in the next section.

As mentioned how machine/deep learning is different from traditional approaches of artificial machine intelligence, it has enabled the possibility of building intelligent machines faster with good accuracy, due to its nature of learning from experience and through training. Now, a program written to accomplish a task does not require hard coding of rules, but involves performing a series of fundamental steps, specific to the kind of the problem statement. The need for procedural programming is slowly heading toward becoming obsolete and machine intelligence is finally taking over. Although we have used the concept of artificial intelligence in describing the application of machine or deep learning, it is not limited to just that.

The paradigm of procedural programming is inclusive of all of the applications of computer programming and so, the method of task accomplishment through learning from experience is applicable for all use cases. A program that performs the 'sine' mathematical function of a value can be replaced by a machine learning program without requiring the knowledge about how the 'sine' function works. We will discuss how this is possible in the next section, but for understanding the implications of machine learning, it can be stated that all types of tasks that a computer program can accomplish, be it manipulating a picture as done in a photo-editing software, or performing some analysis on some big dataset, can be done with machine learning.

For a programmer, machine learning is a new technology that requires an understanding of some mathematical concepts just to understand the intuition behind the methods of machine learning. The first few questions that arise when discussing about machine learning are - Does machine learning involve writing of computer programs in the traditional sense?, How is a machine learning program different from our known programming methods and how is it able to accomplish all sort of tasks by performing a fundamental set of steps that is mostly common for all types of use cases?

The potential of machine learning is undeniable and as mentioned earlier, all applications will be rebuild or updated with machine learning components. Machine intelligence is the final frontier of computer science, and therefore stands out to be one of the most significant technologies that is required to be learnt.

# What is machine intelligence?

The intuition behind the term machine intelligence, is based upon the ultimate goal of computer science, in being able to make a machine work and make decisions on its own, without external intervention. Intelligence is all about information processing and a computer is such a machine that takes in input data, processes that data using the instructions given to it in the form of computer programs and produce an output. This ability of a computer to produce the desired result can be treated as intelligence of that machine. The definition of intelligence according to a dictionary is the ability to acquire and apply knowledge and skills. When a program is being written to solve a problem, say providing the output of the 'sine' function, what we are doing is, encoding the behaviour of the sine function based on the knowledge we have about it. The definition of skill is to be able to accomplish a task with expertise and obviously with an accuracy that fulfils the expected result. A program to find the sine of a value has the knowledge about the nature of the function encoded in it, and will perform the task without error, thereby establishing itself as a skilful executor of a task. Therefore, a machine that performs the sine function is an intelligent entity with respect to the relevant use case.

The understanding that we humans have about intelligence, is that it is something that is acquired through learning about a subject matter and empirical evidence. The way a human performs the sine function is by first learning about its characteristics and then applying the correct mathematical formula to yield the result. Although it may seem that our intelligence is different from that of a computer program because we have not encoded the algorithm for calculating the sine function in our brain, but in fact we did encode the sine function in our brain. The only difference in our case is that, we do it, not by writing a program for our brain. To understand this clearly, we have to expand a little on how learning works for humans. The general learning phase for a human involves memorising something in our brain and this is exactly what we have done when it comes to learning the sine function. The only difference between a human and a computer, regarding the knowledge of the sine function, is that, in case of a computer, all a programmer has to do is to correctly encode the sine function once, and it is able to function correctly from then on. Whereas, in the case of humans, we had to go through a learning phase to memorise the sine function formula, and the time taken in learning is dependant on the learning rate of a particular individual.

The process of learning involves iterating over a subject matter and with each iteration the understanding improves, till the subject matter is completely under the grip of a person. The best way to understand how the process of learning works is to contemplate about the way a baby learns about 'A for apple'. A baby has to read, write and hear repetitively the phrase 'A for apple' while pointing to the letter A and a picture of apple or using an actual apple. Usually babies have a slow learning curve and it takes multiple iterations in learning for the baby to correctly identify an apple among all fruits. During the learning phase of just the letter A, the brain is registering the shape of the letter A and the sound of the pronunciation for the letter and storing that information in the memory. We all very clearly remember how we all had to go through a lot of practise until we could write the letter A with precision. The same thing happens when learning the relation between the letter A and the fruit apple. The sound of the word apple and the shape and colour associated with the fruit is being registered in the memory. With each sincere iteration in practise, the impression of a lesson gets more prominent in a person's memory.

Machine learning takes inspiration from the very act of learning and applies in computer science. The whole idea about making a computer do something involves giving a definite set of instruction to the computer about a task. A computer neither functions on its own, nor does it learn on its own. Machine learning is about making a computer perform a task based upon the knowledge gained through training and participating in the very act of learning. Every task, say the performing of sine function or identifying the fruit apple, involves a statistic, when it comes to determining how well the knowledge has been acquired. In the first iteration, we acquire the least amount of knowledge about a subject matter. So, right after exposure to a subject matter for the first time, if an attempt is made to implement the task, say riding a bicycle, it will undoubtedly result in failure. With every trial, a rider gets better at it. This can be interpreted as the reduction in error percentage with every improvement in learning.

Before we tread any further in understanding the methods of machine learning, we must address an obvious question about why is it important for a computer to abandon the traditional method of functioning and take up this statistical method of learning. Taking the example of sine function is not an adequate use case to understand this, because it is obvious to us that writing a program and encoding the formula for sine function is straightforward. To understand this we will refer to computer vision, a branch of computer science that involves in interpreting information from an image data. Suppose there is a image of a basket of fruits, and it is the task of a computer to correctly identify the fruit apple among them if present. The traditional approach of computer vision is to write a program using special library such as OpenCV and define the characteristics of an apple. Here by characteristics we mean shape, size and colour of a common apple. A computer vision program is hard coded with rules about what properties define an apple and absence of what properties disqualifies a fruit from being identified as an apple. It must be kept in mind that all apples do not come as a perfect version of how apples are shown in pictures and their properties vary in a range. Some are less apple like, in terms of colour and shape, and sometimes can be mistaken for other fruits such as a pear in case of a green apple. Therefore, a good classification program that can identify an apple irrespective of the edge cases is quite a difficult job to build, not to forget, the fruit to be identified from a collection of other fruits involve considering the various orientations that it can have. A photograph of a collection of fruits, is a far more difficult use case than the photograph of a single apple, and so, a programmer has to take into account the fact that a fruit's visibility becomes obfuscated. A classifier program that works with precision across all these situations has been found not to be possible with our traditional approach in deciphering computer vision.

It must be understood, the term 'computer vision' is the implication of our attempt in making a computer understand the meaning of the real world around, through vision. Another relatable example of computer vision can be found in our smartphones or digital cameras. Every smartphone camera software has a facial recognition that makes a yellow coloured square perimeter whenever a face is visible in the picture preview. Here a machine, through computer vision software, has become smarter and is able to identify a person's face but it lacks the accuracy of a human. Machine learning is the result of our endeavour to make a machine become skilled as a human.

Taking the use case of computer vision, the fundamental difference between the methods of implementing, say, a facial recognition software, one through traditional coded rules for detection of features and the other through machine learning, is about how a computer is made to perceive data. As we mentioned earlier, the case of making a computer perform a sine function, the traditional approach of computer vision is also the same. To understand how data is represented in computer vision, we will use a further simpler use case called MNIST. MNIST is a large database of handwritten digits used in image processing. The non-machine learning way involves tracing the geometric features of a digit say, the number 8. The pixels in the image of the digit is compared to this trace of the figure 8. Here is a sample of the various styles in which the digit may be written -

$$8 \quad 8 \quad 8 \quad 8 \quad 8 \quad 8 \quad 8$$

Since these are handwritten, there will always be deformations compared to the actual shape of a digit. The accuracy is less by far when done in the non-machine learning way. This same task when done with machine learning, the pixel values of the image of a digit is taken into account. Say the image of the digit has N number of pixels. All these pixel values are stored in a matrix data structure represented with a 2D array. Each element of this 2D array corresponds to the pixel intensity. This array is now the input for our machine learning classification program.

We have mentioned that machine learning unlike procedural programming is comprised of a fundamental set of steps that are applicable for all types of problems. This means, the generic algorithm to build either a sine function or a digit classifier remains same. The principal algorithm behind machine learning is based upon linear algebra through the equation -

$$Y = Wx + C$$

This equation is the function that is used in learning. A function always takes an input data, performs some operations on that data, and produces new data as output. Now in the context of MNIST, let us first assume we have developed a function that correctly identifies a handwritten digit. Such a function would take an image data as input, perform its analysis and produce an output in the form of the corresponding digit's label. Here is a block diagram representing the MNIST digit identifier algorithm in action -

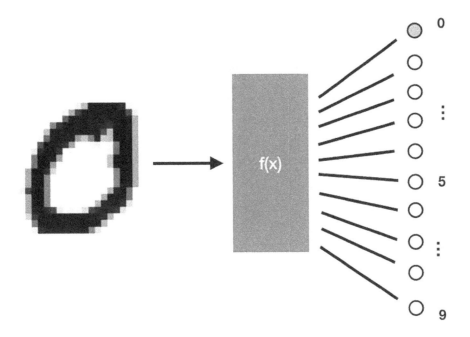

The analysis of the input digit is where the function f(x) is executing. The input digit represented in a 2D array is our x in the function Y = Wx + C. W is an array of weights containing random values within a range. With Wx, what we are doing is performing a matrix multiplication between the array of weights W and the array x. As our equation is right out of linear algebra, the array of weights W is basically the slope of a straight line. We will come to the relevance of using this equation shortly. For now let us concentrate just on the value produced by Wx and not on C, which is a constant and we will assume it to be set to 0 for now. The backbone of machine learning is linear algebra and so we will

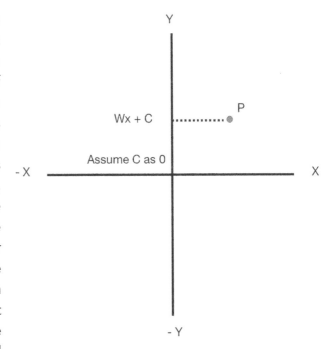

refer to a cartesian co-ordinate system. In our case, we require a 2D plane where the input x when multiplied with W, gives us the value for Y. So, starting with an instance of random weights in W we will get a point P on the 2D plane.

Suppose the input data is for the digit 0 and the point plotted for it is P with the instance of weights W. Now if we keep inputting more 0 digit inputs with the same instance of weights W, we will see no matter however each digit 0 is differing from other, all the plot points accumulate in a particular area in the plane. Here is such an example -

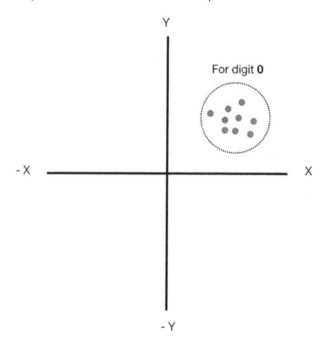

Similarly, plot points for other digits will also form such clusters of points. Here is another example of a few of them -

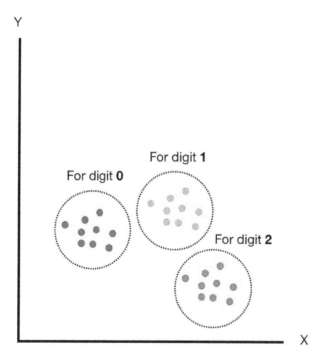

Each input digit is corresponding to a label and it is this label that we see in the block diagram we came across earlier -

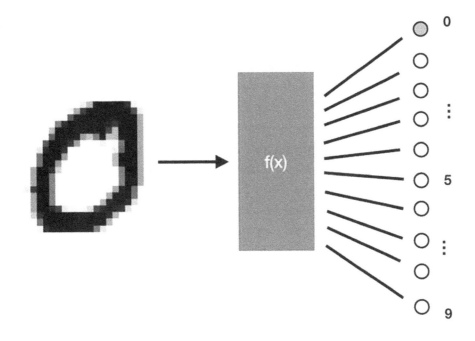

The digit labels are on the rightmost section as [0 … 5 … 9], with the intermediate ones omitted.

The fundamental intuition behind the machine learning method is that, any input, if converted into a plot points in a cartesian co-ordinate system, relations can be formed among those points and patterns will emerge from the way the function f(x) behave w.r.t. various input data.

This brings us to a very important question, which is, if we set out to build a function that does identification of handwritten digits or facial recognition or identifies the image of an apple or even performing the sine function, where is the definition of the algorithm happening? Up till now, we have discussed about converting input data into points on a cartesian co-ordinate system. The only function that we are using broadly, is Y = Wx +C, and so, the question arises how this single function is able to work in all the use cases?

With machine learning, the goal we set out to achieve is to build a universal function approximation engine. It means that our function f(x) will be able to represent and approximate the output of any function, by imitating the behaviour of that function. In order to understand how this imitation yields result, we will go back to the example of a child learning the letter A and how the human brain learns.

The human brain is made up neuron cells where information gets stored when new information comes along. These neuron cells are identical and so, whether we are learning to play chess or about the fruit apple, the fundamental way information gets stored is by formation of connections among neuron cells. A child learns about writing the letter A by imitating the shape of the letter. To a child, there is no relevance of the letter in the beginning and all the child is doing, is drawing the strokes that make up the letter. This information gets stored in the brain as strength of the connection between adjacent neurons. The strength of a connection among neurons is basically accumulation of ions. On the first iteration of learning the letter A, some feeble connections are formed among neurons. The connections keep getting prominent with more iterations and at the right balance of positive and negative ions, when a child is getting full marks for writing the letter A, this event of correctness is labelled in the brain as a successful acquirement of a skill. The concentration of ions can be expressed in terms of numerical value, and so, it can be concluded that information in the brain is basically the count ions per connection among the associated neurons. Therefore, learning is imitation.

Now coming back to the question of how using linear algebra we are imitating like the brain, we must rethink about how the input is being interpreted on a cartesian co-ordinate system and what the interpretation implies. As the brain is interpreting any information as collective strength of ions, the $Y = Wx + C$ function mimics the work done for storage of these ions in the form of weight values in W. To further understand the intuition behind the choice of this function and not any other function, we will take a look at the steps in machine learning. Every machine learning algorithm involves creation of a weights matrix W which is referred to as a 'model'. Similar to a human's learning process, in order to create an accurate model of a function, say facial recogniser, a lot of data has to be ingested by the algorithm. Say in case of MNIST, a lot of handwritten instances of the digit 0 has to be input, for learning the label 0. Before putting a machine learning model to work, it has to go through the training phase and testing phase. Say for building a model for the sine function, first training examples have to be fed into the algorithm. The training phase is an attempt by the algorithm to learn about the relation between the input and output. This is how a typical training dataset looks like -

| INPUT X | OUTPUT Y |
| --- | --- |
|  |  |
|  |  |
|  |  |
|  |  |

The general approach is to reserve at least 10% of the examples from the training dataset for testing phase, which has the same significance as we humans have with learning a subject matter and then taking exams to test our learning. Now to understand why we this particular equation $Y = Wx + C$ is chosen for learning, we have to imagine the entire superset of all possible skills that can be learnt mapped on a 2D plane.

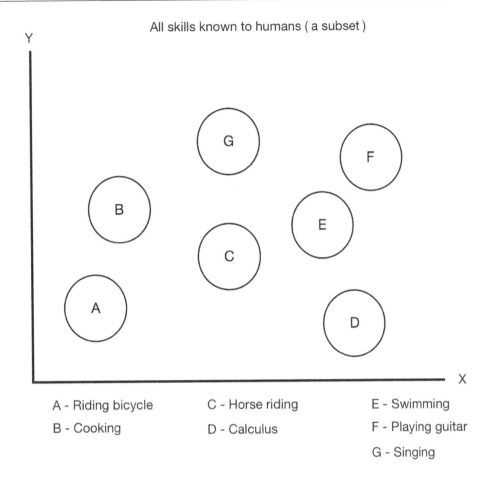

All skills known to humans ( a subset )

A - Riding bicycle    C - Horse riding    E - Swimming

B - Cooking    D - Calculus    F - Playing guitar

G - Singing

The above diagram represents such a 2D plane containing a subset of such skills. The regions of the plane enclosed by circles represent those values of Y w.r.t. Wx + C, that qualify as accurate attainment of a skill. Now let us visualise how the improvement with iterations can be mapped on this plane for a single skill, say playing guitar.

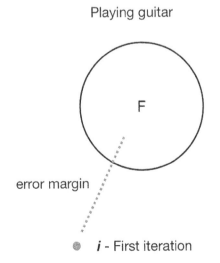

Playing guitar

error margin

*i* - First iteration

Obviously it is unlikely to hit the bulls eye right in the first iteration 'i', and so the above diagram is showing the error margin from skill domain F to the point plotted by the first iteration. The aim of acquiring a skill is about reducing the error margin such that the point 'i' belongs inside the perimeter of F.

Playing guitar

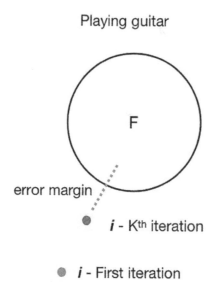

Therefore, a successful skill learning w.r.t. plotting points on a cartesian co-ordinates system, is about the translation of a point from an outlying region to the region defined by the skill. This translation requires the slope of the line passing through the point to be determined at each iteration and so, the simplest equation that enables us to do that is the equation -

$$Y = Wx + C$$

where W represents the slope in the scope of linear algebra.

The reason machine learning is referred to as a process of universal function approximation, is due the attributes of the learning process as we just discussed. The input for any task can be expressed as x for the equation $Y = Wx + C$, and therefore can be plotted on a co-ordinate system. The dimension of the co-ordinate system we used so far has been limited to just 2. In actual, the input data for the skill 'learning guitar' usually will be based upon various features such as strum rate, tone accuracy, pitch blending, etc. But it must be understood, that the attempt to make a computer learn a skill cannot be expressed as the attainment of a perfect value. Through practise we will see how there is always room for improvement and so, the term *approximation* is used to describe machine learning. Even intuitively, it is not possible to claim that someone is the best sprint runner, as there is always a possibility for someone to be better than Usain Bolt.

# Vectors and matrices

Machine learning relies heavily on the concepts of linear algebra, multivariate calculus, probability theory and statistics, and vectors, matrices. For this book, we will gently brush over some of these concepts. A computer system performs all sort of these mathematical functions for machine learning, using primarily vectors and matrices as the data structure. Therefore, we will gather a fundamental understanding upon matrices and vectors.

A vector as we may know, represents something that has both a magnitude and a direction, whereas a scalar representing only the magnitude. In linear algebra, a vector is represented as a m x 1 matrix called column vector -

$$x = \begin{bmatrix} x_1 \\ x_2 \\ \vdots \\ x_m \end{bmatrix}$$

and a 1 x m matrix called row vector -

$$x = \begin{bmatrix} x_1 & x_2 & \cdots & x_m \end{bmatrix}$$

The transpose of these vectors accordingly convert 1 x m to m x 1,

$$\begin{bmatrix} x_1 & x_2 & \cdots & x_m \end{bmatrix}^{\mathrm{T}} = \begin{bmatrix} x_1 \\ x_2 \\ \vdots \\ x_m \end{bmatrix}$$

and vice-versa.

As we may know there are two types of multiplication associated with vectors a *cross-product* and a *dot-product*. So, we will first understand the intuition behind these two types of products. First let us represent two vectors in a 2D space.

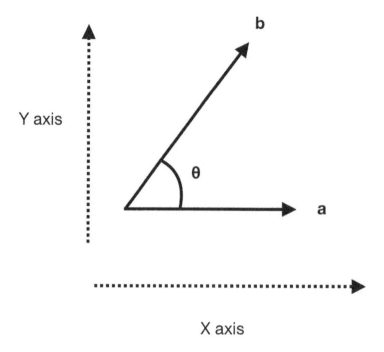

The result of a *dot product* is a scalar value which is the magnitude/length of the vector *a* multiplied by the magnitude of vector *b*. If the vector *b* is in the negative Y axis, the resulting value of dot product is also negative.

On the other hand, the result of a *cross product* is a vector which is perpendicular to the plane in which the two vectors a and b belong. It is calculated as the area of the parallelogram formed by the vectors, as shown in the diagram below -

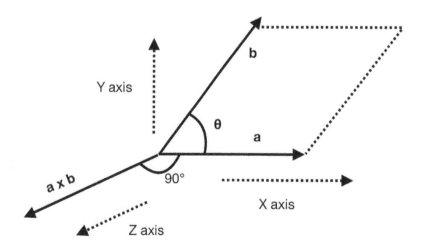

The length of the vector a x b, is equal to the area of the parallelogram marked by dotted lines.

A cross product with the matrix representation is as follows -

$$\mathbf{a} \otimes \mathbf{b} = \mathbf{ab}^\mathrm{T} = \begin{bmatrix} a_1 \\ a_2 \\ a_3 \end{bmatrix} \begin{bmatrix} b_1 & b_2 & b_3 \end{bmatrix} = \begin{bmatrix} a_1 b_1 & a_1 b_2 & a_1 b_3 \\ a_2 b_1 & a_2 b_2 & a_2 b_3 \\ a_3 b_1 & a_3 b_2 & a_3 b_3 \end{bmatrix}$$

$$\mathbf{b} \otimes \mathbf{a} = \mathbf{ba}^\mathrm{T} = \begin{bmatrix} b_1 \\ b_2 \\ b_3 \end{bmatrix} \begin{bmatrix} a_1 & a_2 & a_3 \end{bmatrix} = \begin{bmatrix} b_1 a_1 & b_1 a_2 & b_1 a_3 \\ b_2 a_1 & b_2 a_2 & b_2 a_3 \\ b_3 a_1 & b_3 a_2 & b_3 a_3 \end{bmatrix}$$

A cross product of two vectors is also called an *outer product.*

The matrix representation of vector dot product is -

$$\mathbf{a} \cdot \mathbf{b} = \mathbf{a}^\mathrm{T} \mathbf{b} = \begin{bmatrix} a_1 & a_2 & a_3 \end{bmatrix} \begin{bmatrix} b_1 \\ b_2 \\ b_3 \end{bmatrix} = a_1 b_1 + a_2 b_2 + a_3 b_3$$

$$\mathbf{b} \cdot \mathbf{a} = \mathbf{b}^\mathrm{T} \mathbf{a} = \begin{bmatrix} b_1 & b_2 & b_3 \end{bmatrix} \begin{bmatrix} a_1 \\ a_2 \\ a_3 \end{bmatrix}$$

Transposing a matrix A, converts the rows to columns and vice-versa, designated by $A^\mathrm{T}$. Transposing a matrix reveals various properties of a matrix such as symmetry, in which a square matrix when transposed, remains the same. In computer science, transposing a matrix for matrix multiplication is important for computational ease. In the context of computer graphics representation, an image is basically a matrix of pixel values and rotating an image is basically a matrix transpose operation followed by matrix reflection.

We have seen how vector products are done with transpose of matrices. Now we will understand the intuition behind the cross and dot product according to their respective formula.

The formula for dot product -

$$\mathbf{a} \cdot \mathbf{b} = \|\mathbf{a}\| \, \|\mathbf{b}\| \cos(\theta)$$

The name cos/cosine as we may know, is assigned to the ratio of the sides base to hypotenuse, in a triangle. The intuition behind dot product is to find how much one vector is in the direction of another vector.

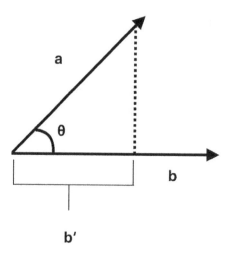

$b'$ is the length of the shadow cast by $a$ on $b$.

$\cos \theta = b' / \| a \|$
$\Rightarrow \| a \| \cos \theta = b'$

Therefore, $a.b = \| b \| . b'$, which means the dot product is basically the product of the magnitude of the vector $b$, with the magnitude of the portion of vector $a$, that is going in the same direction as $b$, i.e. length of the two vectors in the same direction.

When we want to find how much a vector is perpendicular to another, we use cross-product. The cross product is defined by the formula,

$$\mathbf{a} \times \mathbf{b} = \|\mathbf{a}\| \, \|\mathbf{b}\| \sin(\theta) \, \mathbf{n}$$

The name sin/sine as we may know, is assigned to the ratio of the perpendicular side of a right angled triangle to the hypotenuse. Unlike dot product, which produces a scalar, a cross product produces a vector due to $n$, which is a unit vector. For now, we will omit the $n$ vector and break down the formula for this product.

We know that, $\sin \theta$ = perpendicular / hypotenuse. The perpendicular in case of the two vectors $a$ and $b$ is marked by the dotted line $P$ in the following diagram -

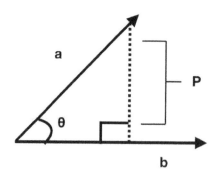

So according to the formula,

$sin\ \theta = P\ /\ \|\ a\ \|$
$=> \|\ a\ \|\ sin\ \theta = P$

As we stated that cross product lets us find how much the vector *a* is perpendicular to *b*, it can be done by casting a shadow of the vector *a* on a line that is perpendicular to *b*. Therefore, a cross product between *a* and *b* is,

$a\ x\ b = \|\ b\ \|\ .\ P$

and we can say that, the vector **a** is perpendicular to vector *b* by $\|\ a\ \|\ sin\ \theta$.

Multiplying the cross product with a unit vector n gives us a vector which is perpendicular to the plane and is equal to the area of the parallelogram formed by the vectors *a* and *b*.
Here is such a parallelogram formed by sides p,q,r and s.

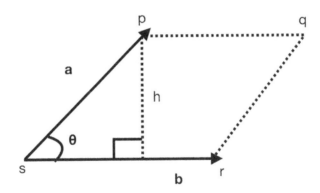

From the formula of area of a parallelogram,
Area = base * height
we can relate to the cross-product since the height *h* is $\|\ a\ \|\ sin\ \theta$ and base is $\|\ b\ \|$.

# Setup prerequisites

We are going to use Jupyter notebooks for coding machine learning algorithms. Here is an installer script for getting started with setting up of the environment -

All of the source code for the examples used in this book, are available here -

# Data preprocessing

In the introductory section of this machine learning chapter in this book, we formed the intuition about the machine learning, and there, we discussed how learning of a skill can be represented in a computer through the data structure used to store the weight values W. The purpose of training for a skill is to approximate the value for W, and this is referred to as training of a model. Therefore, a machine learning model is referred to the matrix data structure used to represent the weight values W.

Machine learning models cannot work with raw data sets. They have to be formatted. Before we get into the training process, we will have to prepare our datasets such that are devoid of inconsistencies that results in ML models that are inefficient in predicting.

Our dataset will be this tabular data that represents Country, Age and Salary correlating to the fact whether a person is willing to become a startup Founder.

We first upload this dataset to our jupyter environment as Data.csv

| Country | Age | Salary | Founder |
|---------|-----|--------|---------|
| France | 44 | 72000 | No |
| Spain | 27 | 48000 | Yes |
| Germany | 30 | 54000 | No |
| Spain | 38 | 61000 | No |
| Germany | 40 | | Yes |
| France | 35 | 58000 | Yes |
| Spain | | 52000 | No |
| France | 48 | 79000 | Yes |
| Germany | 50 | 83000 | No |
| France | 37 | 67000 | Yes |

Fig. 1

jupyter

Quit  Logout

Files   Running   Clusters

Select items to perform actions on them.

Upload   New ▾  ↻

| 0 ▾ ▮ / | Name ↓ | Last Modified | File size |
|---------|--------|---------------|-----------|
| ⬚ data_preprocessiong.ipynb | Running | 5 minutes ago | 2.33 kB |
| ⬚ Data.csv | | 29 minutes ago | 226 B |

We will be writing our code for pre-processing the dataset in the python notebook - data_preprocessing.ipynb.

First we import the following python libraries.

```
In [2]: import numpy as np
```

```
In [4]: import matplotlib.pyplot as plt
```

```
In [5]: import pandas as pd
```

*numpy* - This is a library that contains mathematical tools and used for scientific computations. It contains objects to work with N dimensional arrays, something that we would be requiring extensively for our machine learning purposes and also functions in linear algebra, random numbers etc.

*matplotlib* - We would want to visualise how our machine learning models are performing. This is a plotting library for graphically representing data-points.

*pandas* - This library contains data structures to for handling structured, formatted data such as *.csv files, database files etc.

Now that necessary libraries have been included, we will load the dataset into our program. As we know machine learning algorithm works with feeding X as input and the output generated is Y as predicted value. The dataset we are using, will be used to predict whether a person is likely to become a start-up founder, based on the parameters - Country, Salary and Age. Therefore, our X for the machine learning algorithm will be a 2D array of data where each row is of the form [Country, Salary, Age]. The corresponding Y will be the array 1D array containing values from Founder column of our dataset.

We first unpack the data we have in the Data.csv file using pandas library.

```
In [8]:  #import the dataset
         ds = pd.read_csv("Data.csv")
```

We want only columns 0,1 and 2 for X.

```
In [11]:  X = ds.iloc[:,:-1].values
```

The notation [ : , :-1 ] - This is a representation of 2D array [m,n] where m is row and n is column. The colon ':' at m represents all rows to be included and ':-1' means to include columns from index 0 to the last index (n-1) minus 1, where n is the number of columns.

Here is the content of X after loading data.

```
In [14]:  print (X)

          [['France' 44.0 72000.0]
           ['Spain' 27.0 48000.0]
           ['Germany' 30.0 54000.0]
           ['Spain' 38.0 61000.0]
           ['Germany' 40.0 nan]
           ['France' 35.0 58000.0]
           ['Spain' nan 52000.0]
           ['France' 48.0 79000.0]
           ['Germany' 50.0 83000.0]
           ['France' 37.0 67000.0]]
```

We take the entire column index 3 as our Y.

```
In [15]: Y = ds.iloc[:, 3].values
```

The content of Y.

```
In [16]: print(Y)
         ['No' 'Yes' 'No' 'No' 'Yes' 'Yes' 'No' 'Yes' 'No' 'Yes']
```

So we have loaded the data into arrays. Looking at the data in array X, we come across few tuples or rows, where it contains 'nan' as value. For example, rows 4 - ['Germany' 40.0 nan] and row 6 ['Spain' nan 52000.0]. This is because our dataset in Fig 1. had empty values for those tuples. When it is loaded with pandas library, it replaces the empty data points with 'nan'. The most important goal of pre-processing the dataset is to fix for inconsistencies such as this one, where our algorithm cannot make use of an empty data point. Our next step would be to replace the empty data points with values relevant to the dataset. This is a common case in statistics where missing values have to be replaced and its called *imputation*.

For imputation, we are going to use the sklearn python library.

```
In [*]: from sklearn.preprocessing import Imputer
```

We instantiate an Imputer object.

```
In [22]: imputer = Imputer(missing_values = 'NaN',strategy = 'mean',axis = 0)
In [23]: print (imputer)
         Imputer(axis=0, copy=True, missing_values='NaN', strategy='mean', verbose=0)
```

The Imputer constructor is fed the following parameters -

*missing_values* - Our dataset contains 'nan' as missing values. We will instantiate with 'NaN'.

*strategy* - 'mean' strategy replaces missing values with the mean among all the values of a particular type of data point. The other strategies are 'median' and 'most_frequent' which replaces values with the one that is most frequently used in the dataset.

*axis* -When set to '0', imputes data column-wise. When set ton '1', imputes data row-wise.

Now before we put the Imputer object to use, we are going to learn about Fitting in machine learning.

Fitting is a measure of how well a model generalises to provided data w.r.t to the data it was trained on. We are training a model to generate a curve such that it can be most similar to the curve that is generated by data points. When a model efficiently does predictions, it generates the data points, that lie very close or on the curve, we are trying to mimic with our model. This refers to how well the generated points, by our model, 'fits' on the curve or has been trained. So fitting a model with data is the act of training that effectively makes changes in the model based on the data.

```
In [27]:  imputer = imputer.fit(X[:, 1:3])
```

This step is for the purpose of replacing missing values from data set and so we provide our data points to the imputed object such that it learns from the data points and and puts in values at empty places, based on the 'mean' calculated from the data points. Here no such machine learning activity is happening but the imputed.fit() function is named so, in the general spirit of - feeding data to an object though a function call, that makes changes to the data. It is though not to be compared in ditto with the use of 'fit' keyword in function names, that we will come across later in the book. Our missing data occurs in the column indexes 1 and 2, so we use the notation X[ :, 1:3].

Now in order for the values to be replaced we have to execute another function.

```
In [29]:  X[:, 1:3] = imputer.transform(X[:, 1:3])

In [30]:  print (X)
          [['France' 44.0 72000.0]
           ['Spain' 27.0 48000.0]
           ['Germany' 30.0 54000.0]
           ['Spain' 38.0 61000.0]
           ['Germany' 40.0 63777.77777777778]
           ['France' 35.0 58000.0]
           ['Spain' 38.77777777777778 52000.0]
           ['France' 48.0 79000.0]
           ['Germany' 50.0 83000.0]
           ['France' 37.0 67000.0]]
```

Our data has been successfully replaced with values at missing places - ['Germany' 40.0 63777.77777777778] and row 6 ['Spain' 38.77777777777778 52000.0].

We are quite not ready yet to get started with training process with our data. Our input matrix or array still contains values that our algorithm cannot make sense of for performing mathematical operations. It is the column index '0' of X, that contains values -

```
In [32]: print (X[:, 0:1])

         [['France']
          ['Spain']
          ['Germany']
          ['Spain']
          ['Germany']
          ['France']
          ['Spain']
          ['France']
          ['Germany']
          ['France']]
```

These values are categorical data in our dataset since they can group our dataset. We can although categorise our dataset with Age range and Salary range as well but in this context it means numerical value in dataset. For our use case, we need to encode only for Country column. It consists of string values, and the term we use in machine learning paradigm for that is label.

```
In [33]: label_encoder = LabelEncoder()

In [34]: X[:, 0] = label_encoder.fit_transform(X[:, 0])

In [35]: print (X[:, 0])

         [0 2 1 2 1 0 2 0 1 0]

In [36]: print (X)

         [[0 44.0 72000.0]
          [2 27.0 48000.0]
          [1 30.0 54000.0]
          [2 38.0 61000.0]
          [1 40.0 63777.77777778]
          [0 35.0 58000.0]
          [2 38.77777777777778 52000.0]
          [0 48.0 79000.0]
          [1 50.0 83000.0]
          [0 37.0 67000.0]]
```

We create an object of the LabelEncoder class and invoke the fit_transform function on X[ :, 0]/X[ :, 0:1], our Country column. 'France' has been encoded to '0', 'Germany' to '1' and 'Spain' to '2'.

But, now that labels have been replaced by numbers 0,1 and 2, we have a problem at our hand. The purpose of encoding was to replace string values which are in no way related to each other, but the collating sequence of 0,1, and 2 evokes a relation that 'Spain' which is '2', is greater than 'Germany' and 'France'. We don't want our machine learning algorithm to regard this relation as a contributor to the prediction.

We need another form of encoding called One-Hot encoding.

```
In [37]:  from sklearn.preprocessing import OneHotEncoder
```

```
In [38]:  one_hot_encoder = OneHotEncoder(categorical_features = [0])
```

```
In [39]:  X = one_hot_encoder.fit_transform(X).toarray()
```

```
In [46]:  print ("%.0f %.0f %.0f %.0f %.0f"%(X[0,0],X[0,1],X[0,2],X[0,3],X[0,4]))

          1 0 0 44 72000
```

We created an object on OneHotEncoder class with the parameter categorical_features which defines the column index of the input data X, which needs to be transformed.

Our first row values have now become -

$$[1 \quad 0 \quad 0 \quad 44 \quad 7200]$$

The one-hot encoding has expanded column Country into three columns. The column index '0' represents 'France' when '1' is present as a value.

Similarly,

```
In [46]:  print ("%.0f %.0f %.0f %.0f %.0f"%(X[0,0],X[0,1],X[0,2],X[0,3],X[0,4]))

          1 0 0 44 72000
```

```
In [47]:  print ("%.0f %.0f %.0f %.0f %.0f"%(X[1,0],X[1,1],X[1,2],X[1,3],X[1,4]))

          0 0 1 27 48000
```

```
In [48]:  print ("%.0f %.0f %.0f %.0f %.0f"%(X[2,0],X[2,1],X[2,2],X[2,3],X[2,4]))

          0 1 0 30 54000
```

'Spain' is represented by '1' as value in column index '2' of X and 'Germany' is represented in column index '1' of X as the value '1'.

We have removed strings from X but we still have strings in Y in the form of 'yes' and 'no'. We do it the similar way as before.

```
In [64]:  Y_label_encoder = LabelEncoder()
```

```
In [65]:  Y = Y_label_encoder.fit_transform(Y)
```

```
In [67]:  print (Y)

          [0 1 0 0 1 1 0 1 0 1]
```

For Y, we do not need the one hot encoding as the values are all 0's and 1's.

The next step we will do is to split our dataset into X_train, X_test and Y_train, Y_test, where *_train and *_test represent training data and data on which the trained model is to be tested respectively.

```
In [75]:  from sklearn.model_selection import train_test_split

In [76]:  X_train, X_test, Y_train, Y_test = train_test_split(X, Y, test_size = 0.2, random_state = 0)
```

*test_size* - Can be a value between 0 and 1. Represents the proportion of data to split for test purpose.

*random_state* - Its just a seed value used for the random number generator.

All of the data in our dataset is now in a form where the algorithm can treat it as valid input for training. But, the data isn't quite in a range which would make the training process efficient. We are talk referring to the columns Age and Salary. These two are not in the same scale and it is this difference in scale that would make our training process to run longer and performance in predicting would also be affected.

The next step we are going to perform is called *feature scaling*, where the dataset is normalised to a common scale. The term feature is used to refer the input data because each value is to be perceived by the training algorithm as a feature or attribute that produces a certain Y.

This is our X_train training data before scaling.

```
In [36]:  print (X_train)

          [[0.00000000e+00 1.00000000e+00 0.00000000e+00 4.00000000e+01
            6.37777778e+04]
           [1.00000000e+00 0.00000000e+00 0.00000000e+00 3.70000000e+01
            6.70000000e+04]
           [0.00000000e+00 0.00000000e+00 1.00000000e+00 2.70000000e+01
            4.80000000e+04]
           [0.00000000e+00 0.00000000e+00 1.00000000e+00 3.87777778e+01
            5.20000000e+04]
           [1.00000000e+00 0.00000000e+00 0.00000000e+00 4.80000000e+01
            7.90000000e+04]
           [0.00000000e+00 0.00000000e+00 1.00000000e+00 3.80000000e+01
            6.10000000e+04]
           [1.00000000e+00 0.00000000e+00 0.00000000e+00 4.40000000e+01
            7.20000000e+04]
           [1.00000000e+00 0.00000000e+00 0.00000000e+00 3.50000000e+01
            5.80000000e+04]]
```

This is after scaling.

```
In [37]:  from sklearn.preprocessing import StandardScaler

In [38]:  std_scaler_X = StandardScaler()

In [39]:  X_train = std_scaler_X.fit_transform(X_train)

In [43]:  X_test = std_scaler_X.transform(X_test)

In [41]:  print (X_train)

          [[-1.          2.64575131 -0.77459667  0.26306757  0.12381479]
           [ 1.         -0.37796447 -0.77459667 -0.25350148  0.46175632]
           [-1.         -0.37796447  1.29099445 -1.97539832 -1.53093341]
           [-1.         -0.37796447  1.29099445  0.05261351 -1.11141978]
           [ 1.         -0.37796447 -0.77459667  1.64058505  1.7202972 ]
           [-1.         -0.37796447  1.29099445 -0.0813118  -0.16751412]
           [ 1.         -0.37796447 -0.77459667  0.95182631  0.98614835]
           [ 1.         -0.37796447 -0.77459667 -0.59788085 -0.48214934]]
```

All the values in our training dataset has been normalised to a range -2 to +3. Since, machine learning is in many of the cases based upon Euclidean distances between data points, our models will train faster and efficient. Here there are two things to notice in the above code snippet, we scaled our X_test training data with just the *transform* function of scaling object. This is because we applied the *fit_transform* function for scaling X_train, in which the scaler object is first fitted on the X_train dataset and then the transformation operation is invoked. We want our X_test dataset to be transformed based on the same fitting that we have for X_train.

We do not need to scale our dependant variable Y_train, Y_test for this dataset since this is problem where the dependant variable is categorical, meaning, the data fed into the model as X would point to a label, in this case a 0 and 1. We would although apply scaling on Y if this was a regression use case.

## Dummy variables

These are the extra variables or predictors that we add to our input dataset that act as an indicator for a categorical variable in the dataset. This is represented by a binary value.

In our dataset, *Country* is the independent variable or predictor which we replaced with three new variables, 'Spain', 'France' and 'Germany'. The *Country* variable is a categorical variable in the dataset as the values in *Country* can distinctly segregate or group our dataset. We substituted *Country* column with three new columns because of course there are three distinct values of *Country*. But should we have substituted *Country* by two variables if there were two distinct values for *Country*?

The answer is no.

As said, the purpose of a dummy variable is to act as an indicator for a value in the original dataset. Whenever a dummy variable is being introduced to a dataset, we have to keep in mind to avoid redundancies. The cardinality of the variables in input data should be necessary and sufficient, otherwise, with unnecessary dummy variables, gives rise to the *dummy variable trap*. As with the case with *Country* variable, if say there was only two values 'India' and 'China', we would not have required addition of any dummy variables. We already have done this in our current example with the dependant variable Y, where '0' is represented as 'No' and '1' for 'Yes'.

## Dummy Variable Trap

It is a scenario when independent variables are multi-collinear, such that two or more variables are highly correlated. In multi-collinearity, the value of one variable can be derived from the other. If we used Country1 and Country2 as the two dummy variables substituting Country, where the distinct values for Country is 'India' and 'China', we would be just duplicating the variable Country as Country2 = 1 - Country1.

We should always use one variable less than the number of dummy variables that can be created for each distinct value in a categorical variable. This brings us to a necessary reduction in the number of variables that is required in our dataset.

```
In [46]:  print ("%.0f %.0f %.0f %.0f %.0f"%(X[0,0],X[0,1],X[0,2],X[0,3],X[0,4]))

          1 0 0 44 72000

In [47]:  print ("%.0f %.0f %.0f %.0f %.0f"%(X[1,0],X[1,1],X[1,2],X[1,3],X[1,4]))

          0 0 1 27 48000

In [48]:  print ("%.0f %.0f %.0f %.0f %.0f"%(X[2,0],X[2,1],X[2,2],X[2,3],X[2,4]))

          0 1 0 30 54000
```

As you can see the index 0,1 and 2 represent the dummy variables for *Country*. We can get rid of any on of the indexes [0-2]. Our information will still be intact because, say we drop index '0' (France), the dataset can still represent France for '0' as values at indexes of 'Spain' and 'Germany'.

# Regression

Machine learning is about training a program to mimic a function or more accurately, to approximate a function. A function takes in values as input say, X and produces output Y, and for the task of predicting a Y that is closest to the desired value, the relationship between the independent variable X and the dependant variable Y should be understood by a machine learning model. This is what makes *regression* such a integral part of machine learning process because the job of our algorithm would be to learn and improve from the training data in approximating the best fitting regression line through a plot of the data points.

## *Simple Linear regression*

$$Y = mX + C$$

In this type of regression we have one independent variable and one dependent. Our training process involves adjustments to the values m - the slope of the regression line and C - the constant.

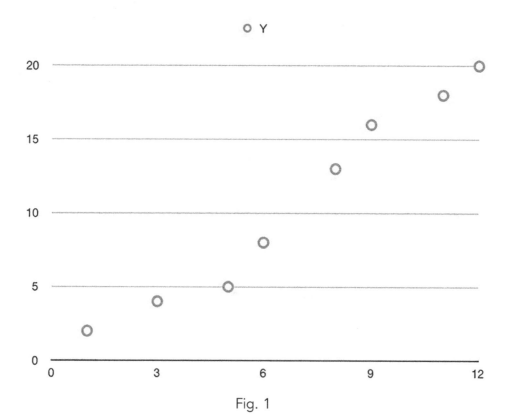

Fig. 1

Fig. 1 shows example plot of data-points. When we train our model, the aim will be to learn and adjust the slope of the the line that passes through the data-points such that ideally most points lie on or closest to the regression line. The value for C also plays a significant role as it the measure of where the regression line cuts the Y axis and thus it is estimated as well.

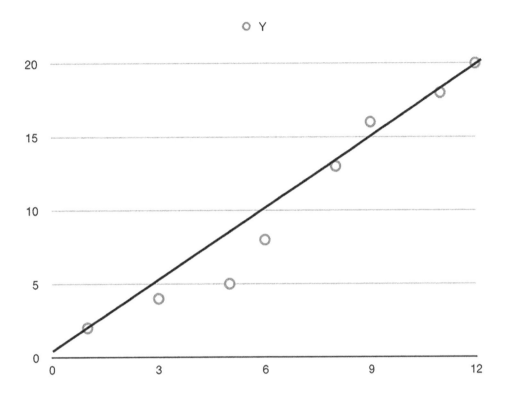

Here the best fitting line is the one in the plot above as four data-pints lie on the line. The line and the incidence of points on it or around it, is the representation of how good our model has been trained. For a well trained model, it should be able to predict a value for Y that lies close to or on the regression line, but that is again dependent on how much data has been fed to our training phase.

Next we are going to see how the machine learning algorithm actually teaches the model to generate a best fitting line through the *Ordinary least squares* method.

In the fig 3. we will name the eight data points starting from left as A through H.

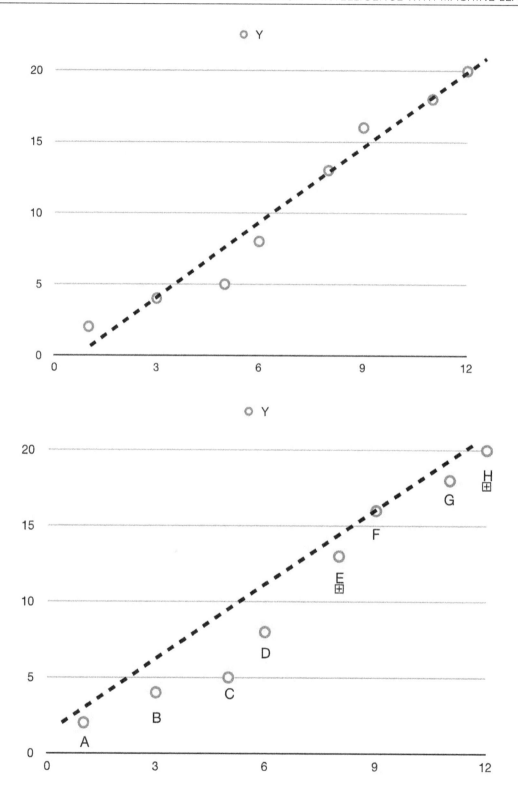

The least squares method works by drawing possible regression lines that places the data-points in close vicinity and recording the distance of the points from the regression line.

Then the sum of those distances are recorded for one such regression line. The same process of drawing regression lines and recording the sum of the distances is done w.r.t to all the points. Once, we have all the possibles sums, the line that has the least value is selected as the best fitting regression line.

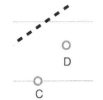

We will now train a model in with the dataset for the plot in fig 2.

| X | Y |
|---|---|
| 1 | 2 |
| 3 | 4 |
| 5 | 5 |
| 6 | 8 |
| 8 | 13 |
| 9 | 16 |
| 11 | 18 |
| 12 | 20 |

Fig. 2

We uploaded the dataset to jupyter and loaded the variables X and Y.

```
In [1]: import numpy as np

In [2]: import matplotlib.pyplot as plt

In [3]: import pandas as pd

In [4]: ds = pd.read_csv("Data_simple_linear_regression.csv")

In [13]: X = ds.iloc[1:, :-1].values

In [14]: print (X)

        [['1']
         ['3']
         ['5']
         ['6']
         ['8']
         ['9']
         ['11']
         ['12']]

In [15]: Y = ds.iloc[1:, 1].values

In [16]: print (Y)

        ['2' '4' '5' '8' '13' '16' '18' '20']
```

The dataset is split into training and test data and trained.

```
In [18]:  from sklearn.model_selection import train_test_split

In [19]:  X_train, X_test, Y_train, Y_test = train_test_split(X, Y, test_size = 0.2, random_state = 0)

In [21]:  from sklearn.linear_model import LinearRegression

In [22]:  l_regressor = LinearRegression()

In [23]:  l_regressor.fit(X_train, Y_train)
Out[23]:  LinearRegression(copy_X=True, fit_intercept=True, n_jobs=1, normalize=False)
```

And finally we predict with *l_regressor* model.

```
In [24]:  Y_pred = l_regressor.predict(X_test)

In [25]:  print (Y_pred)
          [18.25766871   7.91411043]

In [27]:  print (Y_test)
          ['18' '5']
```

Before we compare the Y_pred and Y_test values for accuracy in prediction we must remember that we used an extremely small dataset for our example. Our model predicted 18.25766871 as compared to the expected value 18. The prediction is over-estimated but very close to the desired value. The other predicted value is though a little more overestimated. This dataset was deliberately chosen as we now have the scope to experiment and see how our prediction accuracy changes if we change the parameters while splitting the dataset.

```
In [28]:  X_train, X_test, Y_train, Y_test = train_test_split(X, Y, test_size = 0.4, random_state = 0)
```

This is our prediction if we change the *test_size* to 0.4.

```
In [32]:  print (Y_pred)
          [18.17105263   8.06578947   4.69736842  19.85526316]

In [33]:  print (Y_test)
          ['18' '5' '4' '20']
```

Next we are going to visualise our results.

We use the plotting library that we imported to plot the training set results first.

```
In [113]:  #For training set
           plt.title('X vs Y')
           plt.xlabel('X')
           plt.ylabel('Y')
           plt.scatter(X_train.astype('int'), Y_train.astype('int'), color = 'red')
           plt.plot(X_train.astype('int'), l_regressor.predict(X_train), color = 'blue')
```

Out[113]:  [<matplotlib.lines.Line2D at 0x7f0cb19f3c50>]

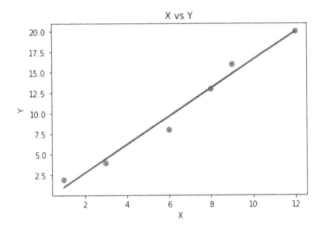

Now the plot with test set.

```
In [117]:  #For training set
           plt.title('X vs Y')
           plt.xlabel('X')
           plt.ylabel('Y')
           plt.scatter(X_train.astype('int'), Y_train.astype('int'), color = 'red')
           plt.plot(X_train.astype('int'), l_regressor.predict(X_train), color = 'blue')
           plt.scatter(X_test.astype('int'), Y_test.astype('int'), color = 'green')
           plt.plot(X_test.astype('int'), l_regressor.predict(X_test), color = 'yellow')
```

Out[117]:  [<matplotlib.lines.Line2D at 0x7f0cb18f9e10>]

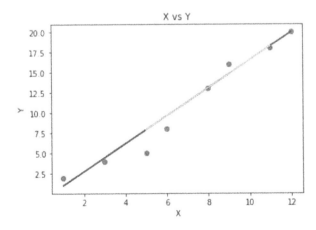

Assumptions of linear regression

a) Linearity
b) Homoscedasticity
c) Multivariate normality
d) Independence of errors
e) Lack of multicollinearity

Linear regression is the most basic form of regression and that is why not all kinds of data is suitable for reaping good prediction results. It is a necessary practise in machine learning to first plot the training dataset to visually form an intuition and decide which type of regression should be used. We will try to understand briefly, some of the major assumptions of linear regression.

*Homoscedasticity* - The assumption of homoscedasticity dictates that the error values or the residual values (actual - predicted) are same across all values of the independent variables in a dataset. The term means - having the same scatter and in such a dataset the distance of the residual points is about the same from the regression line. Here is a plot that qualifies as homoscedastic -

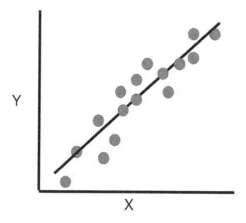

In contrast, a heteroscedastic dataset may look like -

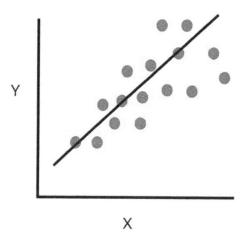

*Multivariate normality* - A dataset is multivariate normal when the linear combination of the independent variables is normally distributed. A normal distribution is a bell shaped frequency distribution curve and looks like the following -

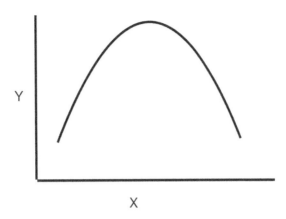

A dataset such as the following shall produce such a bell curve.

| No. of students | Marks |
|---|---|
| 5 | 60 |
| 10 | 65 |
| 12 | 70 |
| 15 | 75 |
| 20 | 80 |
| 15 | 85 |
| 12 | 90 |
| 10 | 95 |
| 3 | 100 |

*Multicollinearity* - It is state of high intercorrelations amongst the independent variables. It is a disturbance in the dataset and if present, then the model trained is not reliable. The major reasons for multicollinearity in dataset is due to improper use of dummy variables, something that we discussed previously. It also occurs when a variable is derived from some other independent variable(s) or when there is repetition of variables.

## Multiple Linear regression

$$Y = m_1X_1 + m_1X_2 + \ldots + m_nX_n + C$$

It is the same as simple linear regression but here the dependant variable is influenced by multiple input values of X and slope m. The significance of C is same as that in linear regression.

| R&D Spend | Administration | Marketing Spend | State | Profit |
|---|---|---|---|---|
| 165349.2 | 136897.8 | 471784.1 | New York | 192261.83 |
| 162597.7 | 151377.59 | 443898.53 | California | 191792.06 |
| 153441.51 | 101145.55 | 407934.54 | Florida | 191050.39 |
| 144372.41 | 118671.85 | 383199.62 | New York | 182901.99 |
| 142107.34 | 91391.77 | 366168.42 | Florida | 166187.94 |
| 131876.9 | 99814.71 | 362861.36 | New York | 156991.12 |
| 134615.46 | 147198.87 | 127716.82 | California | 156122.51 |
| 130298.13 | 145530.06 | 323876.68 | Florida | 155752.6 |

Here our dataset is expenditure details of 50 start-ups and our prediction job is to estimate the profit. We are going to dive right into building the model and predicting.

```
In [12]:  from sklearn.preprocessing import LabelEncoder, OneHotEncoder
```

```
In [13]:  label_encoder_x = LabelEncoder()
          X[:, 3] = label_encoder_x.fit_transform(X[:, 3])
          one_hot_encoder = OneHotEncoder(categorical_features = [3])
          X = one_hot_encoder.fit_transform(X).toarray()
```

```
In [14]:  #Remove the dummy variable trap
          X = X[:, 1:]
```

We have skipped over the data loading part which is same as before, the noticeable section in the above snippet is the use of *LabelEncoder* and *OneHotEncoder*.

The State variable in our dataset has string values which we encoded and then after applying the on-hot encoding on *State*, our dataset is replaced with three new columns for *State*.

```
In [20]:  print ("%.0f %.0f %.0f %.0f %.0f %.0f"%(X[0,0], X[0,1], X[0,2], X[0,3], X[0,4], X[0,5]))

          0 0 1 165349 136898 471784
```

The column indexes '0', '1' and '2' represent 'California', 'Florida' and 'New York' respectively.

We have the similar case of a dummy variable trap as discussed previously, which is the indexes '0','1', and '2'. Therefore, we will only include k - 1 variables for k dummy variables.

```
In [14]:   #Remove the dummy variable trap
           X = X[:, 1:]
```

The index '0' is removed. The training process is similar as before.

```
In [23]:   from sklearn.model_selection import train_test_split
           X_train, X_test, Y_train, Y_test = train_test_split(X, Y, test_size = 0.2, random_state = 0)
           from sklearn.linear_model import LinearRegression
           l_regressor = LinearRegression()
           l_regressor.fit(X_train, Y_train)
```

Finally, the the model has been put to prediction and here are the results.

```
In [24]:   Y_pred = l_regressor.predict(X_test)
```

```
In [25]:   print (Y_test)
           print (Y_pred)

           [103282.38 144259.4  146121.95  77798.83 191050.39 105008.31  81229.06
             97483.56 110352.25 166187.94]
           [103015.20159795 132582.27760816 132447.73845175  71976.09851258
            178537.48221057 116161.24230167  67851.69209676  98791.73374687
            113969.43533014 167921.06569552]
```

As we can see, the indexes '0', '8', '9' show very close predictions.

For our multiple linear regression we went in with all our variables after elimination of the dummy variable trap. But we have to bring about the consideration if all the variables were necessary as predictors. To test if a better result in prediction can be achieved for our dataset by possibly eliminating values we will go though a few statistical concepts first.

## Null Hypothesis

This is a statistical concept used to declare the non-relation between to measurable events. The hypothesis holds true till the non-relation exists. In case of an empirical evidence showing a relation between the events, the null hypothesis is rejected. For example, the statement "earth is not spherical, but flat", qualifies as a null hypothesis, as it suggests there is not relation between earth's shape and a sphere. Now an experiment showing results opposite of the claim, is regarded as the alternative hypothesis ($H_1$) being true and thus refuting the null hypothesis ($H_0$). The hypothesis through experiment has been nullable. A null hypothesis is tested versus the alternative hypothesis by running significance tests.

## P-value

For testing a null hypothesis for a statement such as, " earth is not spherical, but flat ", a significance level S is set at a value say - 0.4. P-value is the probability of closeness of the test results, to the statement supporting the null hypothesis. The significance level is the threshold for accepting or rejecting the null hypothesis. If the probability is less than the threshold level, the null hypothesis can be rejected.

We have the following ways to build a model for multiple linear regression.

a)  All variables included
b)  Backward elimination
c)  Forward selection
d)  Bi-directional elimination
e)  Score comparison

## All variables included

This is when we have the prior knowledge that all the variables are necessary for prediction and do not discard any of the independent variables.

## Backward elimination

It is a process of checking if a variable is necessary in prediction by first starting with all variables and then removing variables based on a test case. This test case is the p-value w.r.t the significance level set.

The algorithm -

Step 1:  Select a significance level stay in the model. Say S = 0.05 or 5%.
Step 2:  Fit the model with all predictors.
Step 3:  Consider the predictor with the highest p-value. If the p-value is > S, goto Step 4 else goto Finish.
Step 4:  Remove the predictor.
Step 5:  Fit the model with the current number of predictors after the elimination.
Step 6:  Goto Step 3.

## Forward selection

It is the process of inclusion of a predictor until the necessary and sufficient number of predictors are accumulated for the model.

The algorithm -

Step 1: Select a significance level stay in the model. Say S = 0.05 or 5%.
Step 2: Fit all possible simple regression models. Select the one with the lowest p-value.
Step 3: keep the variable(s). Fit all possible models with one extra predictor added to the one(s) already present.
Step 4: Consider the predictor with the lowest p-value. If the p-value < S, goto Step 3, else goto Finish (Keep the previous model).
Step 5: Goto Step 3.

## Bi-directional selection

This method is in a way a mixture of both forward selection and backward elimination and is computationally costlier.

The algorithm -

Step 1: Select a significance level to enter in the model, S_enter = 0.05 and to stay in the model S_stay = 0.05.
Step 2: Fit all possible simple regression models. Select the one with the lowest p-value (p-value < S_enter).
Step 3: Perform all the steps of backward elimination. Variables must have p-value < S_stay.
Step 4: Goto Step 2 until no new variables can be removed or added.

## Scope comparison

This is the most thorough approach and also the costliest.

The algorithm -

Step 1: Select a criterion for goodness of fit (e.g Akaike criterion).
Step 2: Contract all possible regression models (2n-1 combinations).
Step 3: Select the one with the best criterion.

Now we are going to see how the accuracy of predictions behave for backward elimination.

```
In [25]:  import statsmodels.formula.api as sm
```

```
In [30]:  X = np.append(arr = np.ones((50,1), dtype = int), values = X, axis = 1)
```

We added a new library as *statsmodels* and we appended an array of fifty 1's as the first column of our input X. This is because in the *LinearRegression* class, the constant C was by default added but in the backward elimination process we won't be using the *LinearRegression* class and so we have to deliberately add C as a column of 1's as initial value for C.

Refer to the steps of our algorithm for backward elimination method. The first thing we do is create a new matrix for our dataset on which we will perform the elimination process.

```
▶ In [31]:  X_minimal = X[:, [0, 1, 2, 3, 4, 5]]
```

We start with including all the column indexes 0 though 5 with the above notation.

We will execute the Step 2 of fitting the model all predictors using the ordinary least squares method. This is exactly the same as the regression we did for simple linear regression with least squares.

```
In [32]:  regressor_OLS = sm.OLS(endog = Y, exog = X_minimal).fit()
```

*OLS* is the function for ordinary least squares. *endog* and *exog* are the dependant variable and the observations respectively.

Next we have to know about the p-values for each of the independent variables before carrying out Step 3.

```
▶ In [33]:  regressor_OLS.summary()
```

Out[33]:

OLS Regression Results

| Dep. Variable: | y | R-squared: | 0.951 |
|---|---|---|---|
| Model: | OLS | Adj. R-squared: | 0.945 |
| Method: | Least Squares | F-statistic: | 169.9 |
| Date: | Sat, 18 Aug 2018 | Prob (F-statistic): | 1.34e-27 |
| Time: | 22:48:59 | Log-Likelihood: | -525.38 |
| No. Observations: | 50 | AIC: | 1063. |
| Df Residuals: | 44 | BIC: | 1074. |
| Df Model: | 5 | | |
| Covariance Type: | nonrobust | | |

|  | coef | std err | t | P>\|t\| | [0.025 | 0.975] |
|---|---|---|---|---|---|---|
| const | 5.013e+04 | 6884.820 | 7.281 | 0.000 | 3.62e+04 | 6.4e+04 |
| x1 | 198.7888 | 3371.007 | 0.059 | 0.953 | -6595.030 | 6992.607 |
| x2 | -41.8870 | 3256.039 | -0.013 | 0.990 | -6604.003 | 6520.229 |
| x3 | 0.8060 | 0.046 | 17.369 | 0.000 | 0.712 | 0.900 |
| x4 | -0.0270 | 0.052 | -0.517 | 0.608 | -0.132 | 0.078 |
| x5 | 0.0270 | 0.017 | 1.574 | 0.123 | -0.008 | 0.062 |

| Omnibus: | 14.782 | Durbin-Watson: | 1.283 |
|---|---|---|---|
| Prob(Omnibus): | 0.001 | Jarque-Bera (JB): | 21.266 |
| Skew: | -0.948 | Prob(JB): | 2.41e-05 |
| Kurtosis: | 5.572 | Cond. No. | 1.45e+06 |

The *summary* function show us a whole lot of information but for now we are going to focus only on the p-values. The significance level we fixed is 0.05 and we see x2 (dummy variable for state) has the highest p-value with 0.953 and so x2 has to be removed.

```
In [18]:  X_minimal = X[:, [0, 1, 3, 4, 5]]
```

```
In [19]:  regressor_OLS = sm.OLS(endog = Y, exog = X_minimal).fit()
```

We have eliminated x2 and fitted the model with the remaining predictors. This how the p-values have changed.

|  | coef | std err | t | P>\|t\| | [0.025 | 0.975] |
|---|---|---|---|---|---|---|
| const | 5.011e+04 | 6647.870 | 7.537 | 0.000 | 3.67e+04 | 6.35e+04 |
| x1 | 220.1585 | 2900.536 | 0.076 | 0.940 | -5621.821 | 6062.138 |
| x2 | 0.8060 | 0.046 | 17.606 | 0.000 | 0.714 | 0.898 |
| x3 | -0.0270 | 0.052 | -0.523 | 0.604 | -0.131 | 0.077 |
| x4 | 0.0270 | 0.017 | 1.592 | 0.118 | -0.007 | 0.061 |

At this iteration, x1 clearly has the highest p-value. Finally, we will be left with only the *R & D spend* predictor.

```
In [26]:  X_minimal = X[:, [0, 3]]
```

```
In [27]:  regressor_OLS = sm.OLS(endog = Y, exog = X_minimal).fit()
          regressor_OLS.summary()
```

|  | coef | std err | t | P>\|t\| | [0.025 | 0.975] |
|---|---|---|---|---|---|---|
| const | 4.903e+04 | 2537.897 | 19.320 | 0.000 | 4.39e+04 | 5.41e+04 |
| x1 | 0.8543 | 0.029 | 29.151 | 0.000 | 0.795 | 0.913 |

| Omnibus: | 13.727 | Durbin-Watson: | 1.116 |
|---|---|---|---|
| Prob(Omnibus): | 0.001 | Jarque-Bera (JB): | 18.536 |
| Skew: | -0.911 | Prob(JB): | 9.44e-05 |
| Kurtosis: | 5.361 | Cond. No. | 1.65e+05 |

## Polynomial regression

$$Y = m_1X_1 + m_2X_2^2 + \dots + m_nX_n^n + C$$

In this type of regression, we will be taking in account the powers of multiple variables and their coefficients in predicting Y. This is how a plot of a polynomial function looks like -

The use and advantage of polynomial regression comes from the ability to plot a regression line for functions that have a trend of increasing slope such as the one above. Such a type of regression is generally found in problems like share markets or global spread of disease analysis etc. A simple or multiple linear regression will not be able to provide good predictions as compared to the curvilinear data points generated by the function above.

The dataset we are going to use for our polynomial regression model is this level of an employee at a company and the expected salary.

| Position | Level | Salary |
|---|---|---|
| Business Analyst | 1 | 45000 |
| Junior Consultant | 2 | 50000 |
| Senior Consultant | 3 | 60000 |
| Manager | 4 | 80000 |
| Country Manager | 5 | 110000 |
| Region Manager | 6 | 150000 |
| Partner | 7 | 200000 |
| Senior Partner | 8 | 300000 |
| C-level | 9 | 500000 |
| CEO | 10 | 1000000 |

The data contains no polynomial terms as X is comprised of only column *Level* and thats why we add polynomial terms and visualise the regression line.

```
In [6]: from sklearn.preprocessing import PolynomialFeatures

In [7]: poly_reg = PolynomialFeatures(degree = 2)

In [8]: X_poly = poly_reg.fit_transform(X)
```

We start with adding only one polynomial term, and thats why degree = 2. This will add the term $X^2$ to the dataset.

```
In [9]: print (X_poly)
        [[   1.    1.     1.]
         [   1.    2.     4.]
         [   1.    3.     9.]
         [   1.    4.    16.]
         [   1.    5.    25.]
         [   1.    6.    36.]
         [   1.    7.    49.]
         [   1.    8.    64.]
         [   1.    9.    81.]
         [   1.   10.   100.]]

In [10]: print (X)
         [[ 1]
          [ 2]
          [ 3]
          [ 4]
          [ 5]
          [ 6]
          [ 7]
          [ 8]
          [ 9]
          [10]]
```

The revised dataset *X_poly* shows a new column for $X^2$ at index '2'. The dataset now has to be fitted into a linear regressor.

```
In [12]: l_regressor = LinearRegression()
         l_regressor.fit(X_poly,Y)

Out[12]: LinearRegression(copy_X=True, fit_intercept=True, n_jobs=1, normalize=False)
```

This is the regression line we get.

```
In [34]:  plt.title('Level vs Salary')
          plt.xlabel('Level')
          plt.ylabel('Salary')
          plt.scatter(X.astype('int'), Y.astype('int'), color = 'red')
          plt.plot(X.astype('int'), l_regressor.predict(X_poly), color = 'blue')
```

Out[34]:  [<matplotlib.lines.Line2D at 0x7f731ff42240>]

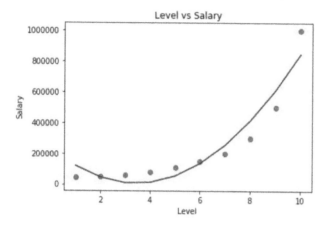

The plot was done with values of Y, predicted by our *l_regressor* model with a polynomial input of the 2nd degree. We should compare to a plot if generated by predicted values of non-polynomial terms.

```
l_non_poly_regressor = LinearRegression()
l_non_poly_regressor.fit(X,Y)
```

Out[57]:  LinearRegression(copy_X=True, fit_intercept=True, n_jobs=1, normalize=False)

```
In [58]:  plt.title('Level vs Salary')
          plt.xlabel('Level')
          plt.ylabel('Salary')
          plt.scatter(X.astype('int'), Y.astype('int'), color = 'red')
          plt.plot(X.astype('int'), l_non_poly_regressor.predict(X), color = 'blue')
```

Out[58]:  [<matplotlib.lines.Line2D at 0x7f731fcb5b70>]

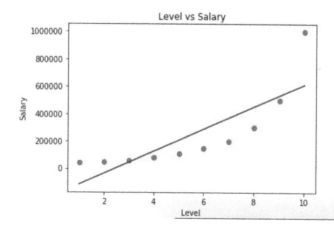

As we can see this prediction task for a model would be very poor if simple linear regression is applied.

Now we will try to plot an even better regression line by adding another polynomial term $X^3$.

```
In [59]: poly_reg = PolynomialFeatures(degree = 3)
```

We get an even better plot.

```
Out[62]: [<matplotlib.lines.Line2D at 0x7f731fc94978>]
```

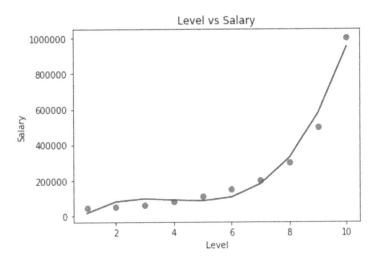

Now with degree = 4.

```
Out[66]: [<matplotlib.lines.Line2D at 0x7f731fd1a9e8>]
```

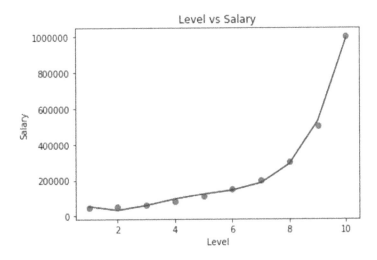

Our plot is getting more accurate as all of the data-points are touched by the regression line. We will try a step further with degree = 5.

Out[70]:  [<matplotlib.lines.Line2D at 0x7f731fdcbb00>]

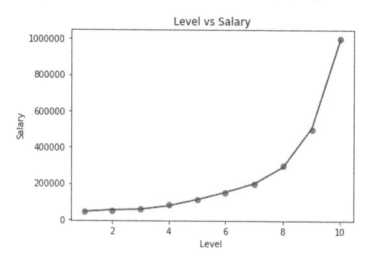

We can say our model should predict pretty well, and so lets put it to test. Say we have a use case where we have to estimate the salary of a 6.5 *Level* employee such that a new position has been added to the company for Senior regional manager.

In [75]:  l_regressor.predict(poly_reg.fit_transform(6.5))

Out[75]:  array([174878.07765172])

The model gives us an estimate for how much should be the salary set for the position.

Polynomial regression is non-linear, yet we may have the confusion for the reason of use of *LinearRegression* model here. It is because polynomial regression is regarded as a special case of multiple linear regression although it models non-linear relationships. The OLS (ordinary least squares) method does not know that $X_i^n$ is an polynomial term and treats it just as another variable.

One notable thing which we did not do in our program with our data-set, is, the step for feature scaling. The X and the Y are clearly not in the same scale, yet we don't require feature scaling because we have only one independent variable that does not required to be scale w.r.t to any other predictor variables. Also, we do not require to scale the *Salary* variable because in most of the regressors, feature scaling is an integral part.

## *Support Vector regression*

This is a type of Support Vector Machine (SVM) that does both linear and non-linear regression which is referred to as SVR. We have been performing our regression tasks on 2D planes, until now.

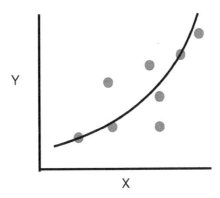

With SVR we will be performing regression on a higher dimensional space. Before begin to understand SVR, we should visit SVM just to get an understanding of how SVR differs from it. SVM is used for classification tasks in machine learning and we will have a dedicated section for that later in this book. In the coding section of SVR, which will come next, we will be using *SVM* model, so it is important that we have the intuition behind using *SVM* in regression tasks, clear. A classic data-point scatter for SVM look like this -

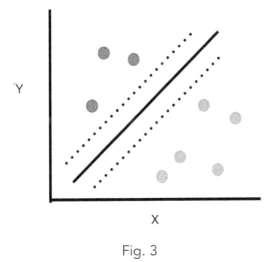

Fig. 3

The line separates the two classes of data-points and the distance from the line to the dotted line (margin) is managed by a hyper parameter called epsilon. We will discuss in details about it later in SVM.

In contrast to the example data-point scatter above, the scatter points on which we would be using *SVM* model would look something like this -

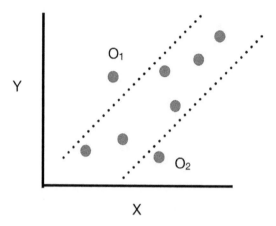

The *SVM* model when used for regression, the task consists of broadly two parts. In the above diagram, the data-points are evidently not arranged in a way depicting different classes as compared to fig. 3.

The SVM when used for regression do not divide two classes with a hyper-plane between margins on either sides, rather tries to place as many points within the margins. We chose to omit the hyper-plane in the above diagram as, although it would be present since its an SVM, but will not be relevant in understanding the SVR functionality of SVM. The outliner points $O_1$ and $O_2$ are taken in reference to adjust the value for epsilon.

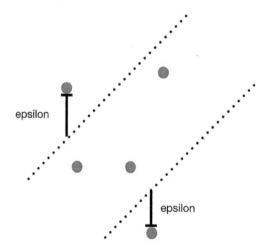

We will be describing the term hyper-plane and its significance later and for now focus on the second part of regression with SVM. In SVR each of the data-points have their own dimension.

For a point on 2D plane, a point is represented by of course (x,y), but with SVR, its (x,(p,q)). This isn't a proper notation, and the pythonic way of representing it can be like - [x, [p,q]], where [p,q] is y. SVR has usage of certain kernels that can project a point on the 2D plane into a higher dimension called *kernel trick*.

Here is the scatter for training and test points (green) on the 2D plane.

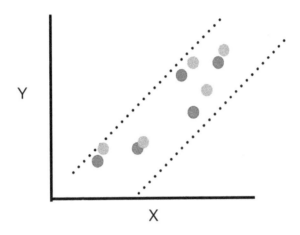

We will consider any one of the test-training pair of points and visualize in the Z plane.

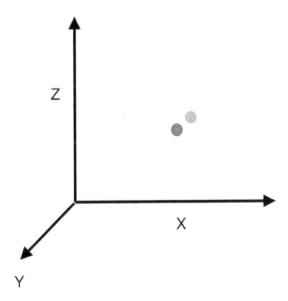

When the test and training points for all the data-points are projected on the Z plane, SVR can then perform linear or non-linear regression on them using the proper kernel methods.

## Decision Tree regression

In this type of regression we will be building models for classification problem statements. The data-points are sorted in the form of a tree data structure such that each intermediate node is a class criterion and the leaf nodes are the actual data-points. Here is a sample scatter plot -

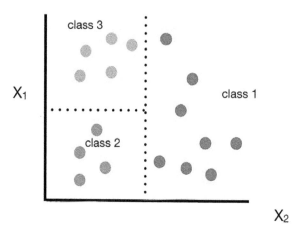

The dotted lines are not regression lines but logical separations for class inclusion criterion. The variables $X_1$ and $X_2$ are our independent variables. Since, this type of regression involves classification, it is obvious that we can be using decision tree regression on data-set where the dependant variable Y has values that can be segregated into classes like the on we had in Fig 1., where Y was either yes or no. In this type of regression, the average value of all the points in a class in taken and for predicting the class of a new data-point, it is allocated its respective class based on the comparison with these average values of classes.

We are going to apply the regression on dataset in Fig 2.

```
In [27]:  from sklearn.tree import DecisionTreeRegressor

In [28]:  regressor = DecisionTreeRegressor(random_state = 0)

In [29]:  regressor.fit(X,Y)

Out[29]:  DecisionTreeRegressor(criterion='mse', max_depth=None, max_features=None,
                    max_leaf_nodes=None, min_impurity_decrease=0.0,
                    min_impurity_split=None, min_samples_leaf=1,
                    min_samples_split=2, min_weight_fraction_leaf=0.0,
                    presort=False, random_state=0, splitter='best')
```

Now we are going to see if we get the prediction correct when we test with the data we used to train the model and see if it matches with the value for Y in the dataset. The first tuple is [1, 0, 0, 44.0, 72000.0], which is ['France', 44, 72000].

```
In [40]:  Y_pred = regressor.predict(np.array([[1, 0, 0, 44.0, 72000.0]]))
```

```
In [41]:  print (Y_pred)

          [0.]
```

| Country | Age | Salary | Founder |
|---------|-----|--------|---------|
| France  | 44  | 72000  | No      |

We can see our prediction is correct, as the data was -

    Also,

```
In [30]:  Y_pred = regressor.predict(np.array([[1, 0, 0, 45.0, 73000.0]]))
```

```
In [31]:  print (Y_pred)

          [0.]
```

Now we will apply this regressor to a dataset that may seem unlikely to be in the classification type of problem statement. The dataset provided in Fig 6. maps a *Level* of an employee to a *Salary*. Here Y's data-points are not distinct classes, but as decision trees are formed with classification criterion as intermediate nodes, the data-points in Y can be divided into distinct ranges each of 20,000.

    This is how the plot looks like -

```
In [9]:  X_grid = np.arange(min(X),max(X),0.1)
         X_grid = X_grid.reshape(len(X_grid),1)
         plt.scatter(X,Y, color = 'red')
         plt.plot(X_grid, regressor.predict(X_grid), color = 'blue')
         plt.xlabel("Level")
         plt.ylabel("Salary")
```

```
Out[9]:  Text(0,0.5,'Salary')
```

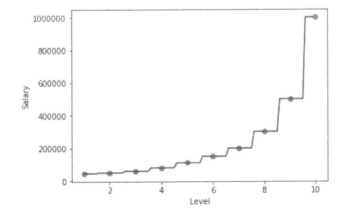

In previous plots, the regression lines where continuous but in this case, the plot is for discreet data-points. In this staircase plot, each steep edge followed by a horizontal top represents the intercept for the data-point in that class. The *X_grid* variable is used here to plot the x-axis with a higher resolution such that each class segment is subdivided 0.1 separations.

## Ensemble learning

With this method of regression we are going to have an introduction to ensemble learning. Ensemble learning is of the form where predictions from a collection of estimator methods (prediction algorithms) are used as base estimations for some algorithm that then makes the final prediction. It can be used for both regression and classification tasks. Multiple predictors trying to predict a single value will perform a better job than a single predictor in an ensemble setup. The reasons for difference in the actual prediction and ideal prediction are noise, variance and bias in a model. Ensemble learning helps to reduce the factors - variance and bias.

There are two families of ensemble learnings -

a)  averaging/bagging methods - The intuition is to build several estimators and then take the average of the predictions of those estimators to form a final prediction. Here, random sub-samples of the dataset is taken up by each estimator such that each model is little bit different from the other and since each estimator independently makes predictions, it reduces the error by reducing variance brought about by outliers in the dataset and also avoids *overfitting*. *Random Forest regression* is a form of bagging method.

b)  boosting methods - The intuition here is in contrast with averaging methods where predictors do not make estimations independently but sequentially, therefore predictors learn from the mistakes of the previous ones. The motivation is to combine the several weak models to produce a powerful ensemble. Here the focus is on weak learners (predictors with greater error percentage), and therefore the model is trained on the errors of the previous model with the caveat of overfitting, if the stopping criterion for learning is not optimised, as learning is faster in this method. Gradient Tree Boosting is one such example.

Overfitting - The aim of a learning algorithm is to reduce the error percentage in predictions. It may occur that a kernel focuses too much on reducing the error encountered for a data-point such that the resulting model becomes trained based on a special case. Suppose the dataset in Fig 6. has a datapoint where a Level 3 employee, whose Salary is although supposed be the range of 50,000 to 60,000, but has a Salary of 30,000 for reasons unknown. The kernel if fixates on that data-point and trains the model to inhibit the exception data-point, the kernel will be then over-training or over-fitting.

## Random Forest regression

The algorithm -

Step 1:  Pick random k data-points from the training data.

Step 2:  Build a decision tree based on the k data-points.

Step 3:  Choose the number of decision trees to be built and execute Step 1 an 2.

Step 4:  For each data-point make each one of the decision trees to predict a value of Y, and produce the result of the average of all the predictions made by the decision trees in the forest.

| Position | Level | Salary |
|---|---|---|
| Business Analyst | 1 | 45000 |
| Junior Consultant | 2 | 50000 |
| Senior Consultant | 3 | 60000 |
| Manager | 4 | 80000 |
| Country Manager | 5 | 110000 |
| Region Manager | 6 | 150000 |
| Partner | 7 | 200000 |
| Senior Partner | 8 | 300000 |
| C-level | 9 | 500000 |
| CEO | 10 | 1000000 |

Since, predictions are based on averages, the problem of overfitting is tackled easily as prediction for outliner data-points are unable to affect the average value.

We are going to use this regression technique on our employee *Level* versus *Salary* dataset.

```
In [5]:  from sklearn.ensemble import RandomForestRegressor

In [6]:  regressor = RandomForestRegressor(n_estimators = 10, random_state = 0)

In [7]:  regressor.fit(X,Y)

Out[7]:  RandomForestRegressor(bootstrap=True, criterion='mse', max_depth=None,
            max_features='auto', max_leaf_nodes=None,
            min_impurity_decrease=0.0, min_impurity_split=None,
            min_samples_leaf=1, min_samples_split=2,
            min_weight_fraction_leaf=0.0, n_estimators=10, n_jobs=1,
            oob_score=False, random_state=0, verbose=0, warm_start=False)

In [8]:  Y_pred = regressor.predict(6.5)

In [9]:  print (Y_pred)

         [167000.]
```

The prediction we get for a 6.5 Level employee is 1,67,000 and now we will employ the same dataset for *Decision Tree* kernel and compare the results.

```
In [5]: from sklearn.tree import DecisionTreeRegressor

In [6]: regressor = DecisionTreeRegressor(random_state = 0)
        regressor.fit(X,Y)

Out[6]: DecisionTreeRegressor(criterion='mse', max_depth=None, max_features=None,
                    max_leaf_nodes=None, min_impurity_decrease=0.0,
                    min_impurity_split=None, min_samples_leaf=1,
                    min_samples_split=2, min_weight_fraction_leaf=0.0,
                    presort=False, random_state=0, splitter='best')

In [7]: Y_pred = regressor.predict(6.5)

In [8]: print (Y_pred)

        [150000.]
```

The random forest regression certainly gives a better prediction over *Decision Tree regression* which predicts 1,50,000 but still *Polynomial regression* gave us the best prediction of on the same dataset.

```
In [75]: l_regressor.predict(poly_reg.fit_transform(6.5))

Out[75]: array([174878.07765172])
```

This gives us a good understanding of the clear difference in regression and classification tasks. As we know the dataset used here isn't quite the perfect candidate for classification task in machine learning, an for best results in predicting *Salary* can be found with continuous regressors such as the polynomial regressor.

The advantage of *Random Forest* regression over *Decision Tree* regression can be well understood by comparing the graphical plot of both.

The plot for *Decision Tree* regression

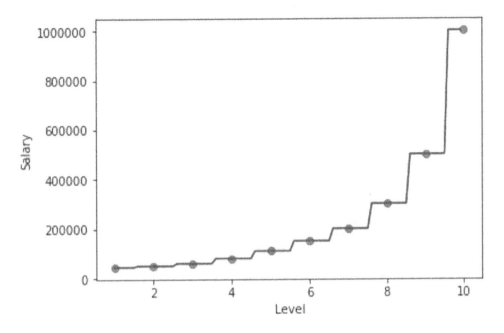

The plot for *Random Forest* regression

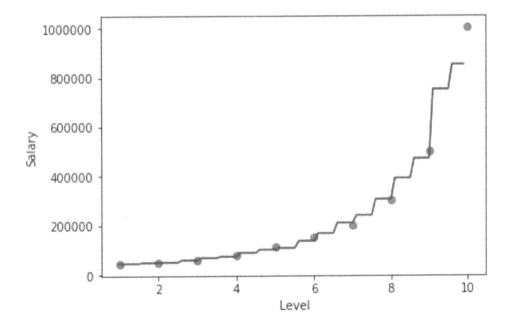

Random Forest regression creates more classes than the prior, thereby making the predictions fall into more granular ranges.

# Regression analysis

We have seen how the accuracy of predictions is dependant on having the necessary and sufficient predictor variables in a multi-variable regression. Earlier we used p-value as a metric to decide which variable is necessary for our models. Here is a reference of the model metrics that we used earlier -

In [33]: `regressor_OLS.summary()`

Out[33]:

OLS Regression Results

| Dep. Variable: | y | R-squared: | 0.951 |
|---|---|---|---|
| Model: | OLS | Adj. R-squared: | 0.945 |
| Method: | Least Squares | F-statistic: | 169.9 |
| Date: | Sat, 18 Aug 2018 | Prob (F-statistic): | 1.34e-27 |
| Time: | 22:48:59 | Log-Likelihood: | -525.38 |
| No. Observations: | 50 | AIC: | 1063. |
| Df Residuals: | 44 | BIC: | 1074. |
| Df Model: | 5 | | |
| Covariance Type: | nonrobust | | |

We used Ordinary Least Squares method for best fitting the regression line and reducing error in prediction by choosing the minimum of the squares of the residuals (difference between actual and predicted value). We are going to learn how the values $R^2$ and Adjusted $R^2$ are important metrics for measuring the performance of our multiple regression models.

### $R^2$

It measures how much error is eliminated when we use Least Squares regression. We use linear regression to predict Y w.r.t an independent value X. The regression gives the relation between X and Y, but if we were to predict Y without using regression on X, our best prediction will be w.r.t the average of Y such that the maximum error for a predicted data-point is $Y_i - Y_{avg}$.

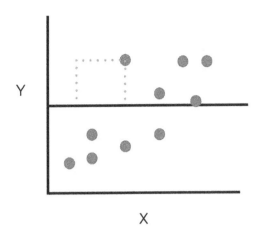

The square of only one residual is shown in the above diagram. Here the sum of the square of residuals be $SS_{avg} = SUM(Y_i - Y_{avg})^2$

Now when we estimate Y using regression, our regression line does not pass through the middle of Y and looks like -

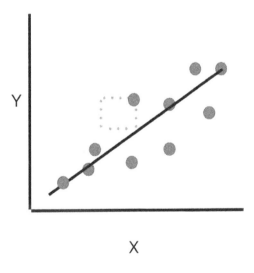

Here we can see the value square of the residual is lesser than that with the average line. Let the sum of the square of the residuals be $SS_{res} = SUM(Y_i - Y_{reg})^2$.

Finally the measure for $R^2$ is -

$$R^2 = 1 - SS_{res} / SS_{avg}$$

The closer the value of $R^2$ is to 1, the lesser amount of error is present in the prediction. As the value of $SS_{res}$ is reduced the greater will be the value for $R^2$. But $R^2$ alone cannot be regarded as a metric for good predictions. Let us look at the summary of the model we used OLS.

```
In [33]:  regressor_OLS.summary()
```

Out[33]:

OLS Regression Results

| Dep. Variable: | y | R-squared: | 0.951 |
|---|---|---|---|
| Model: | OLS | Adj. R-squared: | 0.945 |
| Method: | Least Squares | F-statistic: | 169.9 |
| Date: | Sat, 18 Aug 2018 | Prob (F-statistic): | 1.34e-27 |
| Time: | 22:48:59 | Log-Likelihood: | -525.38 |
| No. Observations: | 50 | AIC: | 1063. |
| Df Residuals: | 44 | BIC: | 1074. |
| Df Model: | 5 | | |
| Covariance Type: | nonrobust | | |

| | coef | std err | t | P>\|t\| | [0.025 | 0.975] |
|---|---|---|---|---|---|---|
| const | 5.013e+04 | 6884.820 | 7.281 | 0.000 | 3.62e+04 | 6.4e+04 |
| x1 | 198.7888 | 3371.007 | 0.059 | 0.953 | -6595.030 | 6992.607 |
| x2 | -41.8870 | 3256.039 | -0.013 | 0.990 | -6604.003 | 6520.229 |
| x3 | 0.8060 | 0.046 | 17.369 | 0.000 | 0.712 | 0.900 |
| x4 | -0.0270 | 0.052 | -0.517 | 0.608 | -0.132 | 0.078 |
| x5 | 0.0270 | 0.017 | 1.574 | 0.123 | -0.008 | 0.062 |

| Omnibus: | 14.782 | Durbin-Watson: | 1.283 |
|---|---|---|---|
| Prob(Omnibus): | 0.001 | Jarque-Bera (JB): | 21.266 |
| Skew: | -0.948 | Prob(JB): | 2.41e-05 |
| Kurtosis: | 5.572 | Cond. No. | 1.45e+06 |

There are five predictors during the first fitting, when value for $R^2$ is 0.951.

| Dep. Variable: | y | R-squared: | 0.951 |
|---|---|---|---|
| Model: | OLS | Adj. R-squared: | 0.945 |

Comparing with the $R^2$ when the number of predictors have been optimised to only one variable, there is a decrease in $R^2$ to 0.947, but the our model is much more improved. Therefore, considering the value of $R^2$ for the goodness of fit comes with the assumption of, the model with its coefficients and bias has been optimised. The limitations of $R^2$ are as follows -

1) Each time a new predictor is added to the model, during the Forward selection method, it increases the value of $R^2$. A model with more predictors may project a higher $R^2$ value, as we

see in Fig. 8. Therefore, a higher value for $R^2$ does not indicate that the model is adequate. It is possible to have a low $R^2$ value for a good model, and a high $R^2$ value for a model that does not fit the data.

2) If a model has too many predictors and higher order polynomials, the training process begins to model the random noise in data and giving way to the problem of Overfitting, and $R^2$ may have misleading high value.

## Adjusted-$R^2$

It is the metric that handles the limitations of $R^2$. When more predictors are added, $R^2$, is unable to adjust its value and it never decreases. This is a problem, as, it leads to adding unnecessary predictors and overfitting the model. It is necessary to have some indication whether the addition of a predictor is actually improving the model's accuracy. Adjusted-$R^2$ controls the degree of freedom for addition of predictors to a model, by introducing a penalising factor to the value of $R^2$.

| | |
|---|---|
| **R-squared:** | 0.951 |
| **Adj. R-squared:** | 0.946 |

The value for Adjusted-$R^2$ above when no predictors are eliminated, is clearly indicative of a better intuition for the error percentage than $R^2$. The final model contains only one predictor and the constant C,

| | | | | | | |
|---|---|---|---|---|---|---|
| **const** | 4.903e+04 | 2537.897 | 19.320 | 0.000 | 4.39e+04 | 5.41e+04 |
| **x1** | 0.8543 | 0.029 | 29.151 | 0.000 | 0.795 | 0.913 |

and, the value for $R^2$ gets tuned to be closer to Adjusted-$R^2$ as visible in the final model.

| | |
|---|---|
| **R-squared:** | 0.947 |
| **Adj. R-squared:** | 0.945 |

Here is the measure for Adjusted-$R^2$ -

$$\text{Adjusted-}R^2 = 1 - (1 - R^2) *(n-1 / n-p-1)$$

where n = sample size, p = number of regressors.

The ratio (n-1 / n-p-1) is the adjustment/penalizing factor, in which the value of the denominator decreases when p increases, and as a result the value of the ratio increases. When the product of increased ratio (n-1 / n-p-1) value with (1 - $R^2$) is deducted from 1, it accounts for a low value for Adjusted-$R^2$.

We used *OLS* regressor for getting the in details view of the various parameters, although the *LinearRegression* class also provides the value for $R^2$ through *score* function. We train the model with only the *R & D expenditure* X[ : , [ 3 ]] predictor,

```
In [68]: from sklearn.model_selection import train_test_split
         X_train, X_test, Y_train, Y_test = train_test_split(X[:,[3]], Y, test_size = 0.2, random_state = 0)
         from sklearn.linear_model import LinearRegression
         l_regressor = LinearRegression()
         l_regressor.fit(X_train, Y_train)
Out[68]: LinearRegression(copy_X=True, fit_intercept=True, n_jobs=1, normalize=False)
```

which gives the value for $R^2$ as,

```
In [69]: Y_pred = l_regressor.predict(X_test)
         l_regressor.score(X_test, Y_test)
Out[69]: 0.9464587607787219
```

and Adjusted-$R^2$ can be evaluated.


## Normalization

In the data preprocesing section we dealt with the necessaity of scaling the input before fitting using *StandardScaler* class. Although we can use the *normalize* parameter in all regression classes provided by sklearn library to scale the input.


## Regularisation

This is a technique in regression that constraints or shrinks the coefficients/weights such that it prevents overfitting. During fitting, the loss in prediction is evaluated by the sum of squares of the residuals and in order to minimise this loss, the weights/coefficients are adjusted by the cost function. If there is noise present in the training dataset then the model in order to learn from the loss w.r.t. the noisy data-points adjusts the values of the weights. The estimated weights won't generalise to predict future data. Through regularisation, the coefficients are reduced and this keeps the risk of overfitting in check.

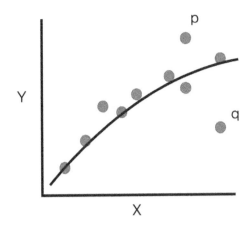

The above plot shows the presence of noise in the form of points p and q. In a situation where the the input values are scaled and the number of predictors have been chosen as minimal and necessary, such that the Adjusted-$R^2$ is indicative of a good fit, it is still possible that the model has been overfit. This may happen if the coefficients of any of the predictors is high than the rest. The predictors with high coefficient contribute to the overall prediction more than others. During training, the noisy data points attribute or boost even higher values to the coefficients that have comparatively high values from the rest. Regularisation penalties the coefficients by adjusting the magnitude of the coefficients to an optimal value and ultimately aims at reducing the variance of a model without substantially increasing the bias. There are various regression techniques that does regularisation such as Ridge regression, Lasso regression and Elastic net regression that we will be discussing shortly.

## Bias

A bias in an erroneous assumption in the model. Though training a model, an approximation is made about the actual function that the dataset represents and therefore a model will never be 100% accurate. A best fit model is where the value of the bias is well adjusted. A high bias will result in an *underfit* model such that the regression curve or line consistently misses the plot points during training and as a result the predictions are way off. The bias is represented as,

$$\text{Bias}\left[\hat{f}\left(x\right)\right] = \text{E}\left[\hat{f}\left(x\right) - f(x)\right]$$

Where E is the mean error between $\hat{f}\left(x\right)$, the function that gives the predicted value and $f(x)$, the function that gives the expected value.

## Variance

This is an error picked up a model due to sensitivity toward small fluctuations or noise in the training dataset. A high variance causes a model to *overfit*. The noisy data-points lures the training process to account for them and so it is necessary to have a simple model. Suppose, a quadratic model where $y' = mX + mX^2 + C$ has the following regression -

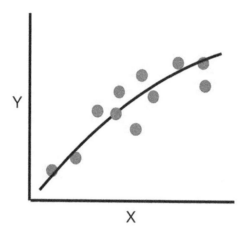

Adding complexity to the model by adding a cubic component $mX^3$ although would show the regression as more accurate to the training data but this in turn causes the model to overfit. Thus the variance of the model increases and the bias decreases.

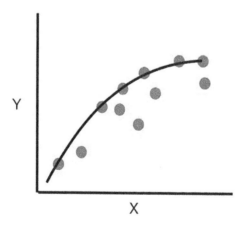

Therefore, the less complex a model is, the least is the tendency to overfit. The variance of a model is represented as,

$$\mathrm{Var}\left[\hat{f}(x)\right] = \mathrm{E}[\hat{f}(x)^2] - \left(\mathrm{E}[\hat{f}(x)]\right)^2$$

A good model is one where *bias* and *variance* has been adjusted to an optimum value and the dependence with model complexity is represented as the follows -

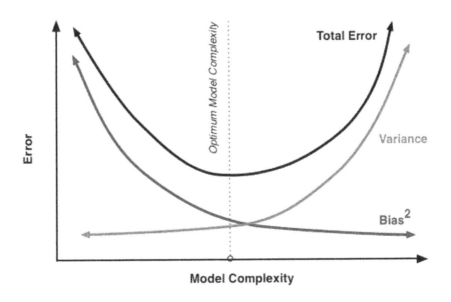

**Model Complexity**

## Ridge regression

This addresses some of the problems of OLS (ordinary least squares) method of residual evaluation, by imposing a penalty on the coefficients. The ridge regression regularises the coefficients by minimising a penalised sum of squares of errors. The cost function is given by -

$$\min_{w} ||Xw - y||_2^2 + \alpha||w||_2^2$$

Here the '|| ||' notation means SUM of all values and therefore the $\alpha||w||_2^2$ component is responsible for penalising the total loss provided by OLS, by adding the square of the sum of all the coefficients/weights in a model. This form of regression is useful in choosing predictors when there is a large number of predictors present. When a predictor is added its weight gets accounted in $\alpha||w||_2^2$, and therefore all the weights have to be recalibrate and reduced such that the error percentage remains at the desired threshold. This enables the choice of necessary predictors and helps to avoid multicollinearity. $\alpha \geq$ 0 is the tuning parameter and controls the magnitude of shrinkage i.e. the regularisation strength. The values of the weights approach toward zero but not absolute zero, as the value for $\alpha$ increases. Here is the sample coefficients for different values of $\alpha$ for a dataset of departmental store.

For α = 0.5

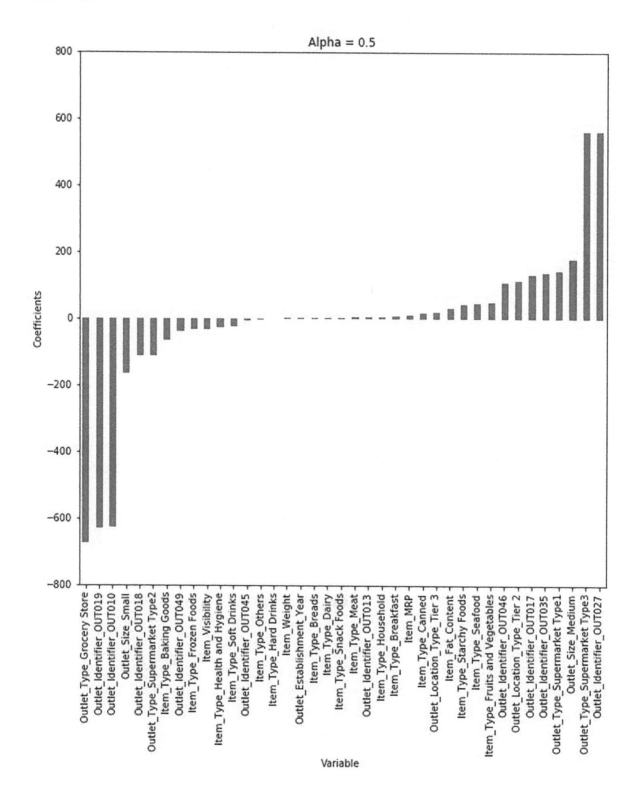

For α = 0.05

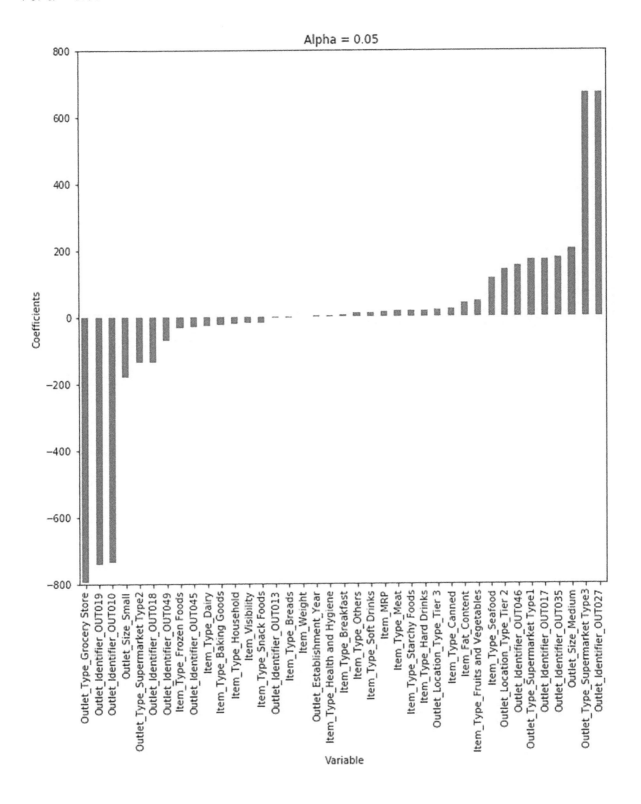

For α = 5

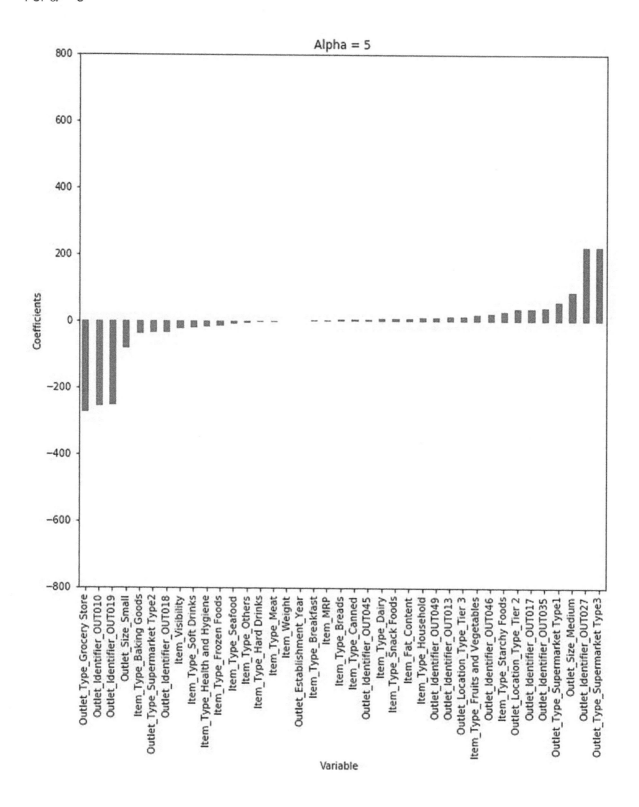

The measure for $R^2$ has to be checked for the changes in $\alpha$ and settle for the best value provided by $R^2$. The ridge regression is also called *L2 regularisation or norm.*

## Lasso regression

This is quite similar to ridge regression and is called *L1 regularisation.* It is a linear model that estimates sparse coefficients. Like the ridge regression, it too has a penalising component. The cost function is given by -

$$\min_{w} \frac{1}{2n_{samples}} ||Xw - y||_2^2 + \alpha||w||_1$$

The penalising component is not the square of the weights as was in the case of L2 norm, but sum of absolute weights. The change in $\alpha$ has different effect on the coefficients compared to L2, as in L1 the values are drastically reduced to zero.

For α =0.5

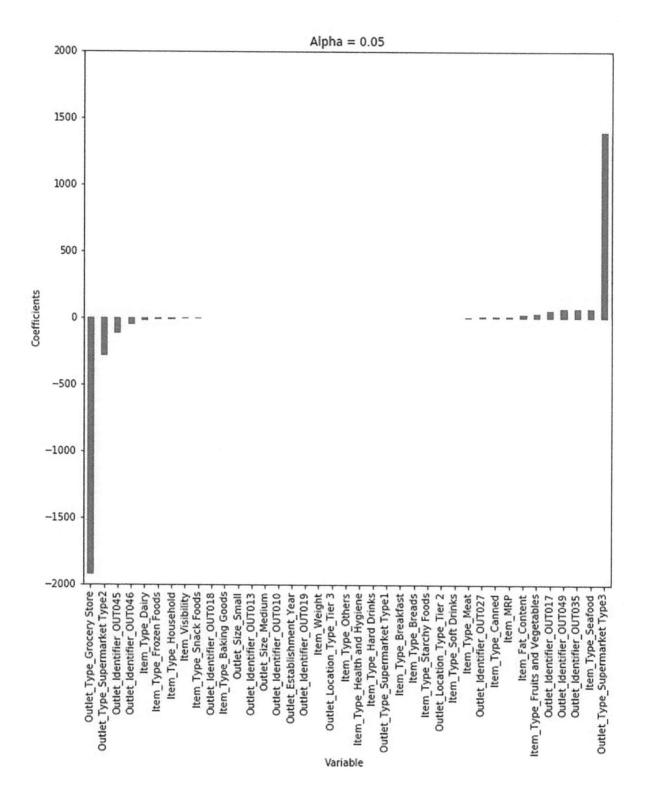

Therefore, lasso selects some features, the ones that participate most in the prediction, while reduces the others to zero enabling prediction for sparse coefficients and be useful in cases where there is a huge number of features/predictors present. The tendency of L1 regularisation to reduce predictors to zero, makes it act as a feature selector.

## Elastic net regression

This is a linear regression model that has both L1 and L2 prior/norm as regulariser. This combination allows for training a sparse model where only the necessary features are non-zero, but also the ability to regularise like L2 without reducing feature values to zero. This combination is of L1 and L2 is controlled by the *l1_ratio* parameter. The cost function is given by -

$$\min_{w} \frac{1}{2n_{samples}} ||Xw - y||_2^2 + \alpha\rho||w||_1 + \frac{\alpha(1 - \rho)}{2}||w||_2^2$$

$\rho$ is the *l1_ratio*. Elastic net is effective when there are a lot of independent variables in a dataset and the elastic net works by sampling groups of those variables to find which groups contain correlated independent variables such that they are a strong predictor. Unlike lasso, where the strongest predictor coefficients are reduced and the others are rendered zero, elastic net treats the predictive capability of variables in groups and also brings about the stability of L2 norm, where variables less important in prediction aren't reduced to absolute zero. Both $\alpha$ and $\rho$ have to be defined during training for controlling L1 and L2 penalties.

Suppose p and q are values assigned to L1 and L2 parameters such that $\alpha$ = p+q and $\rho$ = p/(p+q).

## Regularisation in detail

The lasso and ridge regression have powers to the penalising function - 1 and 2 respectively. The cost function $\min\left(||Y - X\theta||_2^2 + \lambda||\theta||_1\right)$ for lasso regression yields the following plot for $\lambda||\theta||_1$ -

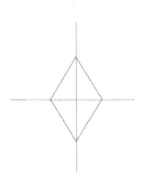

and the cost function $\min\left(\|Y - X(\theta)\|_2^2 + \lambda\|\theta\|_2^2\right)$ for ridge regression yields the following plot for $\lambda\|\theta\|_2^2$ -

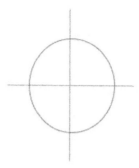

The change in degree of regularisation from 1 in lasso to 2 in ridge is not limited and can extend to higher degrees as the more generalised term to represent regularisation is - Lp. It has been stated earlier that the penalising term $\sum_i |\theta_i|^p$ is a sum of all the weights/coefficients, and when it is plot with the sum of residuals term $\|Y - X\theta\|_2^2$, it produces the following plot -

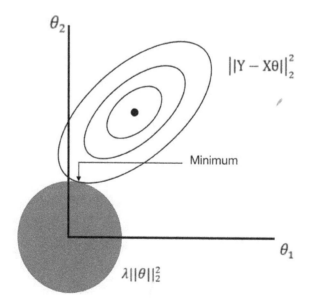

The above plot is representing L2 regularisation. With this diagram we can understand how the shape of the L2 regulariser given by the circle reduces the value of coefficients by intersecting at a tangent with the shape for sum of residuals shown by the ellipse. The point of intersection annotated as *Minimum*, lies above the axis.

The L1 regularisation on the other hand produces the following plot with the sum of residuals -

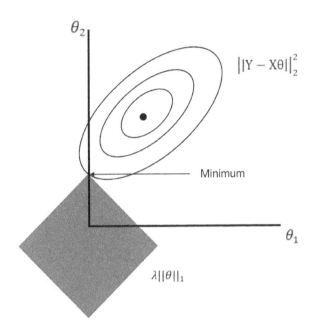

Here we see how the point of intersection (Minimum) lies on the $\theta_2$ axis. This is because the contour of $\lambda||\theta||_1$ has sharp corners and it is able to intersect the contour of $||Y - X\theta||_2^2$ on a point that lies on the $\theta_2$ axis. The $||Y - X\theta||_2^2$ term (sum least squares) being quadratic produces the residual contour as concentric ellipses.

The L1 regularization is able to reduce coefficients to 0 and a produce sparse vector because of the intersection point lying on the $\theta_2$ axis, whereas the contour of L2 regularizer being a circle, intersects at a point above the axis and therefore the minimum value is never 0.


## Comparing polynomial regression with ridge and lasso regression

In this section we will construct a program with functions dedicated to each of the types of mentioned regression and compare the change in coefficients upon regularisation.

The X dataset is generated as a values of angles converted to radians and Y is the *sine* of those angles.

```
#Define input array with angles from 60deg to 300deg converted to radians
X = np.array([i*np.pi/180 for i in range(60,300,4)])
np.random.seed(10)   #Setting seed for reproducability
Y = np.sin(X) + np.random.normal(0,0.15,len(X))
data = pd.DataFrame(np.column_stack([X,Y]),columns=['X','Y'])
plt.plot(data['X'],data['Y'],'.')
```

[<matplotlib.lines.Line2D at 0x7f307aeace48>]

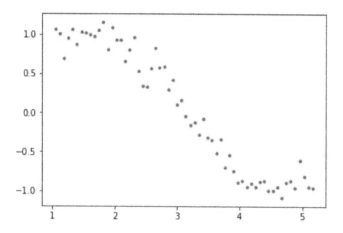

The *DataFrame* is a 2D tabular data-structure that has labelled axes.

The polynomial regression is to be done on the objective function with polynomial terms (predictors) up to the power of 15.

```
for i in range(2,16):
    colname = 'X_%d'%i        # Column name style - X_<power>
    data[colname] = data['X']**i
```

```
print (data.head())
```

```
          X         Y        X_2        X_3        X_4        X_5        X_6   \
0  1.047198  1.065763  1.096623   1.148381   1.202581   1.259340   1.318778
1  1.117011  1.006086  1.247713   1.393709   1.556788   1.738948   1.942424
2  1.186824  0.695374  1.408551   1.671702   1.984016   2.354677   2.794587
3  1.256637  0.949799  1.579137   1.984402   2.493673   3.133642   3.937850
4  1.326450  1.063496  1.759470   2.333850   3.095735   4.106339   5.446854

        X_7        X_8        X_9       X_10       X_11       X_12       X_13  \
0  1.381021  1.446202   1.514459   1.585938   1.660790   1.739176   1.821260
1  2.169709  2.423588   2.707173   3.023942   3.377775   3.773011   4.214494
2  3.316683  3.936319   4.671717   5.544505   6.580351   7.809718   9.268760
3  4.948448  6.218404   7.814277   9.819710  12.339811  15.506664  19.486248
4  7.224981  9.583578  12.712139  16.862020  22.366630  29.668222  39.353420

        X_14       X_15
0   1.907219   1.997235
1   4.707635   5.258479
2  11.000386  13.055521
3  24.487142  30.771450
4  52.200353  69.241170
```

The head() function of the DataFrame object returns the first 5 rows of the dataset.

In order to accommodate multiple plots, the dimensions of the plot image is configured in inches.

```
from matplotlib.pylab import rcParams
rcParams['figure.figsize'] = 12, 10
```

The definition for linear regression function -

```
def linear_regression(data, power, models_to_plot):
    #initialize predictors:
    predictors=['X']
    if power>=2:
        predictors.extend(['X_%d'%i for i in range(2,power+1)])

    #Fit the model
    l_regressor = LinearRegression(normalize=True)
    l_regressor.fit(data[predictors],data['Y'])
    y_pred = l_regressor.predict(data[predictors])

    #Check if a plot is to be made for the entered power
    if power in models_to_plot:
        plt.subplot(models_to_plot[power])
        plt.tight_layout()
        plt.plot(data['X'],y_pred)
        plt.plot(data['X'],data['Y'],'.')
        plt.title('Plot for power: %d'%power)

    #Return the result in pre-defined format
    rss = sum((y_pred-data['Y'])**2)
    ret = [rss]
    ret.extend([l_regressor.intercept_])
    ret.extend(l_regressor.coef_)
    return ret
```

Our aim is to perform polynomial regression with increasing number of predictors taken at a time, i.e. the regression function when invoked with power parameter set to 6, it will take the predictors labelled X, X_2, X_3, X_4, X_5, X_6. That is why the *predictors* list is updated with label names. The returned 1d array contains the residual sum of squares in *rss* along with the intercept and the coefficients of X. The *subplot* function breaks down the graph plot region into sub graph as we will show plots for multiple powers. The check for *power* in *models_to_plot* dictionary is to check if the plot is to be made for the specified *power*. Now on we will invoke the linear function -

```
#Initialize a dataframe to store the results
col = ['rss','intercept'] + ['coef_X_%d'%i for i in range(1,16)]
ind = ['model_pow_%d'%i for i in range(1,16)]
coef_matrix_simple = pd.DataFrame(index=ind, columns=col)
#Define the powers for which a plot is required
models_to_plot = {1:231,3:232,6:233,9:234,12:235,15:236}
#Iterate through all powers
for i in range(1,16):
    coef_matrix_simple.iloc[i-1,0:i+2] = linear_regression(data, power=i, models_to_plot=models_to_plot)
```

The linear_regression function is invoked for powers from 1 through 16 as we see in the snippet above and the result is stored in a *DataFrame* as well. The labels for rows and columns for the DataFrame object *coef_matrix_simple* is set with *ind* and *col*.

The resulting plot for the linear_regression function is as follows -

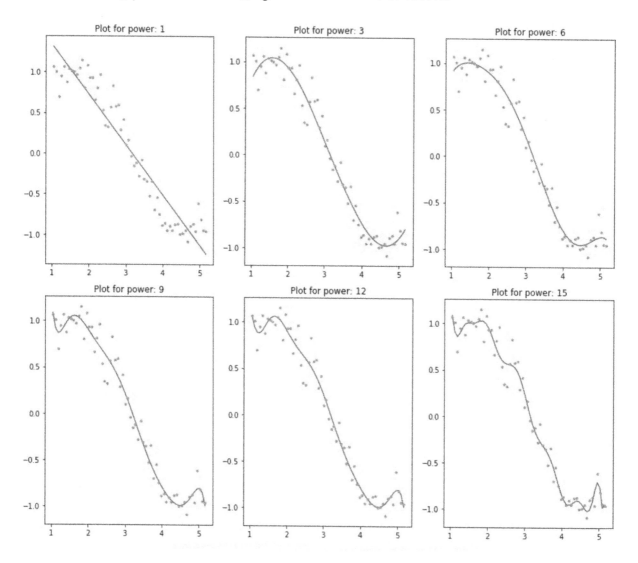

The *models_to_plot* dictionary stores the powers for which we want to get a plot as keys 1,3,6,12,15 and the value for each key is in the form xyz, where x is the number of rows in the subplot, y is the number of columns and z (1 - 6) is the (x,y) cell in which the plot is to be placed.

A snippet below shows the coefficient matrix formed by the data returned by linear_regression -

```
pd.options.display.float_format = '{:,.2g}'.format
coef_matrix_simple
```

| | rss | intercept | coef_X_1 | coef_X_2 | coef_X_3 | coef_X_4 | coef_X_5 |
|---|---|---|---|---|---|---|---|
| model_pow_1 | 3.3 | 2 | -0.62 | NaN | NaN | NaN | NaN |
| model_pow_2 | 3.3 | 1.9 | -0.58 | -0.006 | NaN | NaN | NaN |
| model_pow_3 | 1.1 | -1.1 | 3 | -1.3 | 0.14 | NaN | NaN |
| model_pow_4 | 1.1 | -0.27 | 1.7 | -0.53 | -0.036 | 0.014 | NaN |
| model_pow_5 | 1 | 3 | -5.1 | 4.7 | -1.9 | 0.33 | -0.021 |

Now in case of ridge regression we will check how the coefficient values get changed in with the change in alpha parameter which controls the strength of regularization and so unlike linear_regression function invocation as before, we will perform the regression with all the predictors.

Here is the function for ridge regression -

```
from sklearn.linear_model import Ridge
```

```
def ridge_regression(data,alpha, models_to_plot):
    #Fit the model
    r_regression = Ridge(alpha=alpha,normalize=True)
    r_regression.fit(data[predictors],data['Y'])
    y_pred = r_regression.predict(data[predictors])
    #Check if a plot is to be made for the entered alpha
    if alpha in models_to_plot:
        plt.subplot(models_to_plot[alpha])
        plt.tight_layout()
        plt.plot(data['X'],y_pred)
        plt.plot(data['X'],data['Y'],'.')
        plt.title('Plot for alpha: %.3g'%alpha)

    #Return the result in pre-defined format
    rss = sum((y_pred-data['Y'])**2)
    ret = [rss]
    ret.extend([r_regression.intercept_])
    ret.extend(r_regression.coef_)
    return ret
```

This function is invoked the same way as before.

```
#Initialize predictors to be set of 15 powers of x
predictors=['X']
predictors.extend(['X_%d'%i for i in range(2,16)])

#Set the different values of alpha to be tested
alpha_ridge = [1e-15, 1e-10, 1e-8, 1e-4, 1e-3,1e-2, 1, 5, 10, 20]

#Initialize the dataframe for storing coefficients.
col = ['rss','intercept'] + ['coef_x_%d'%i for i in range(1,16)]
ind = ['alpha_%.2g'%alpha_ridge[i] for i in range(0,10)]
coef_matrix_ridge = pd.DataFrame(index=ind, columns=col)

models_to_plot = {1e-15:231, 1e-10:232, 1e-4:233, 1e-3:234, 1e-2:235, 5:236}
for i in range(10):
    coef_matrix_ridge.iloc[i, ] = ridge_regression(data, alpha_ridge[i], models_to_plot)
```

The corresponding plot -

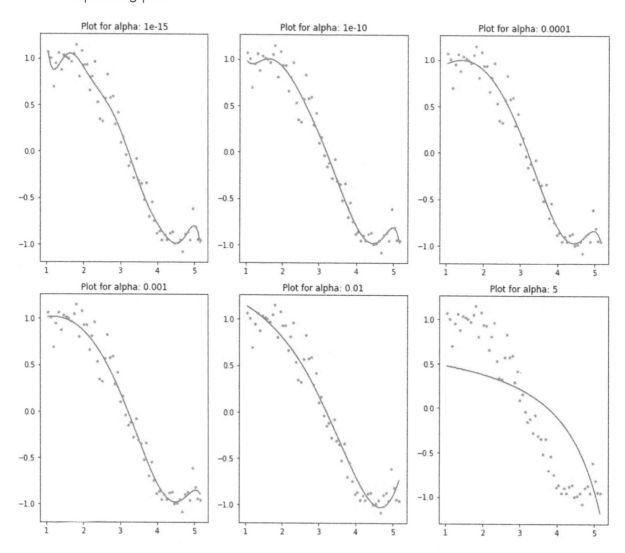

The alpha value 0.01 produces a good fit.

We will now investigate the changes in coefficients made by the alpha parameter.

| | rss | intercept | coef_x_1 | coef_x_2 | coef_x_3 | coef_x_4 | coef_x_5 | coef_x_6 | coef_x_7 | coef_x_8 |
|---|---|---|---|---|---|---|---|---|---|---|
| alpha_1e-15 | 0.87 | 94 | -3e+02 | 3.8e+02 | -2.4e+02 | 68 | -1.2 | -3.7 | 0.3 | 0.19 |
| alpha_1e-10 | 0.92 | 11 | -29 | 31 | -15 | 2.9 | 0.17 | -0.091 | -0.011 | 0.002 |
| alpha_1e-08 | 0.95 | 1.3 | -1.5 | 1.7 | -0.68 | 0.039 | 0.016 | 0.00016 | -0.00036 | -5.4e-05 |
| alpha_0.0001 | 0.96 | 0.56 | 0.55 | -0.13 | -0.026 | -0.0028 | -0.00011 | 4.1e-05 | 1.5e-05 | 3.7e-06 |
| alpha_0.001 | 1 | 0.82 | 0.31 | -0.087 | -0.02 | -0.0028 | -0.00022 | 1.8e-05 | 1.2e-05 | 3.4e-06 |
| alpha_0.01 | 1.4 | 1.3 | -0.088 | -0.052 | -0.01 | -0.0014 | -0.00013 | 7.2e-07 | 4.1e-06 | 1.3e-06 |
| alpha_1 | 5.6 | 0.97 | -0.14 | -0.019 | -0.003 | -0.00047 | -7e-05 | -9.9e-06 | -1.3e-06 | -1.4e-07 |
| alpha_5 | 14 | 0.55 | -0.059 | -0.0085 | -0.0014 | -0.00024 | -4.1e-05 | -6.9e-06 | -1.1e-06 | -1.9e-07 |
| alpha_10 | 18 | 0.4 | -0.037 | -0.0055 | -0.00095 | -0.00017 | -3e-05 | -5.2e-06 | -9.2e-07 | -1.6e-07 |
| alpha_20 | 23 | 0.28 | -0.022 | -0.0034 | -0.0006 | -0.00011 | -2e-05 | -3.6e-06 | -6.6e-07 | -1.2e-07 |

As we can see, with the increase in value of alpha parameter, the value of coefficients decreases. Comparing the coefficient values in the first and the last rows are the evidence of that.

Again with the increase in alpha, the residual sum of squares (rss) increases drastically.

Another noticeable thing is that, none of the coefficients are absolute 0, although being close to 0 as described graphically previously.

We will compare the effect of alpha on lasso regression and here is the function -

```
from sklearn.linear_model import Lasso

def lasso_regression(data, predictors, alpha, models_to_plot):
    #Fit the model
    lassoreg = Lasso(alpha=alpha,normalize=True, max_iter=1e5)
    lassoreg.fit(data[predictors],data['Y'])
    y_pred = lassoreg.predict(data[predictors])

    #Check if a plot is to be made for the entered alpha
    if alpha in models_to_plot:
        plt.subplot(models_to_plot[alpha])
        plt.tight_layout()
        plt.plot(data['X'],y_pred)
        plt.plot(data['X'],data['Y'],'.')
        plt.title('Plot for alpha: %.3g'%alpha)

    #Return the result in pre-defined format
    rss = sum((y_pred-data['Y'])**2)
    ret = [rss]
    ret.extend([lassoreg.intercept_])
    ret.extend(lassoreg.coef_)
    return ret
```

The lasso regression is invoked in the similar way -

```
#Initialize predictors to all 15 powers of x
predictors=['X']
predictors.extend(['X_%d'%i for i in range(2,16)])

#Define the alpha values to test
alpha_lasso = [1e-15, 1e-10, 1e-8, 1e-5,1e-4, 1e-3,1e-2, 1, 5, 10]

#Initialize the dataframe to store coefficients
col = ['rss','intercept'] + ['coef_x_%d'%i for i in range(1,16)]
ind = ['alpha_%.2g'%alpha_lasso[i] for i in range(0,10)]
coef_matrix_lasso = pd.DataFrame(index=ind, columns=col)

#Define the models to plot
models_to_plot = {1e-10:231, 1e-5:232,1e-4:233, 1e-3:234, 1e-2:235, 1:236}

#Iterate over the 10 alpha values:
for i in range(10):
    coef_matrix_lasso.iloc[i,] = lasso_regression(data, predictors, alpha_lasso[i], models_to_plot)
```

The plot generated -

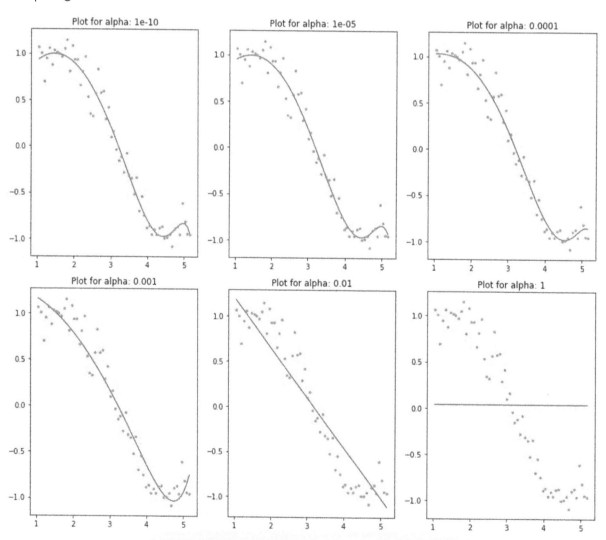

The coefficient matrix shall show us how the coefficients were effected.

| | rss | intercept | coef_x_1 | coef_x_2 | coef_x_3 | coef_x_4 | coef_x_5 | coef_x_6 | coef_x_7 | coef_x_8 | coef_x_9 | coef_x_10 | coef_x_11 | coef_x_12 | coef |
|---|---|---|---|---|---|---|---|---|---|---|---|---|---|---|---|
| alpha_1e-15 | 0.96 | 0.22 | 1.1 | -0.37 | 0.00089 | 0.0016 | -0.00012 | -6.4e-05 | -6.3e-06 | 1.4e-06 | 7.8e-07 | 2.1e-07 | 4e-08 | 5.4e-09 | 1. |
| alpha_1e-10 | 0.96 | 0.22 | 1.1 | -0.37 | 0.00088 | 0.0016 | -0.00012 | -6.4e-05 | -6.3e-06 | 1.4e-06 | 7.8e-07 | 2.1e-07 | 4e-08 | 5.4e-09 | 1. |
| alpha_1e-08 | 0.96 | 0.22 | 1.1 | -0.37 | 0.00077 | 0.0016 | -0.00011 | -6.4e-05 | -6.3e-06 | 1.4e-06 | 7.8e-07 | 2.1e-07 | 4e-08 | 5.3e-09 | |
| alpha_1e-05 | 0.96 | 0.5 | 0.6 | -0.13 | -0.038 | -0 | 0 | 0 | 0 | 7.7e-06 | 1e-06 | 7.7e-08 | 0 | 0 | |
| alpha_0.0001 | 1 | 0.9 | 0.17 | -0 | -0.048 | -0 | -0 | 0 | 0 | 9.5e-06 | 5.1e-07 | 0 | 0 | 0 | |
| alpha_0.001 | 1.7 | 1.3 | -0 | -0.13 | -0 | -0 | -0 | 0 | 0 | 0 | 0 | 0 | 1.5e-08 | 7.5e-10 | |
| alpha_0.01 | 3.6 | 1.8 | -0.55 | -0.00056 | -0 | -0 | -0 | -0 | -0 | -0 | -0 | 0 | 0 | 0 | |
| alpha_1 | 37 | 0.038 | -0 | -0 | -0 | -0 | -0 | -0 | -0 | -0 | -0 | -0 | -0 | -0 | |
| alpha_5 | 37 | 0.038 | -0 | -0 | -0 | -0 | -0 | -0 | -0 | -0 | -0 | -0 | -0 | -0 | |
| alpha_10 | 37 | 0.038 | -0 | -0 | -0 | -0 | -0 | -0 | -0 | -0 | -0 | -0 | -0 | -0 | |

It is clearly visible how lasso regression generates sparse vectors as coefficients have been reduced to 0.

# More regression techniques

### *Least angle regression* (LARS)

As we have discussed previously the various techniques of predictor selection in multiple regression such as Forward selection, Backward elimination, etc., LARS used another method of predictor selection for higher dimensional data (higher number of features). LARS although is similar to forward selection method, but tackles the greedy problem associated with forward selection.

We know forward selection starts with no features and keeps adding features based on their correlation strength till a point they are significant. But the forward selection method that adds a feature upon having a valid significance, continues to keep that feature and search for new features to add on top of it. The inclusion of a feature at a prior step does not ensure that it will continue to be useful. There may come a feature, which has more or similar effects to that of the prior selected feature such that adding the new feature yields no significant effect all together or it may even be redundant. This problem is tackled by the forward stage-wise regression.

In forward stepwise regression, the features are partially added with the option of removal. Each time upon feature inclusion, the tests are run to compare significance of added features.

LARS is an update to the forward stepwise regression with a haul over efficiency as the stepwise method is inefficient and time consuming. The LARS algorithm is similar to that of stepwise method, but instead of including variables at each step, it increases the coefficients of variables that are more correlated to the residuals.

The algorithm for LARS -

- Start with all the coefficients W equal to 0.
- Find predictor that $X_j$ that is most correlated with y.
- Increase the coefficient $W_j$ in the direction of the sign of its correlation with y. Take residuals on the way, r = y - y'. Stop when some other predictor $X_k$ has as much correlation as with r as $X_j$ has. The predictor that is most correlated with the residual forms the least angle with the residual, hence the name.
- Increase $W_j$ and $W_k$ in their joint least angle direction until another predictor qualifies based upon the same criteria.
- Continue until all predictors are in the model.

LARS is useful where the size of the features is a little more than the size of the dataset.

Here is the code for LARS regression with the same dataset used for polynomial regression before to calculate the salary of an employee w.r.t. the level -

```
X_poly
```

```
array([[1.000e+00, 1.000e+00, 1.000e+00, 1.000e+00, 1.000e+00],
       [1.000e+00, 2.000e+00, 4.000e+00, 8.000e+00, 1.600e+01],
       [1.000e+00, 3.000e+00, 9.000e+00, 2.700e+01, 8.100e+01],
```

```
from sklearn.linear_model import Lars
```

```
reg = Lars()
```

```
reg.fit(X_poly,Y)
```

```
Lars(copy_X=True, eps=2.220446049250313e-16, fit_intercept=True,
    fit_path=True, n_nonzero_coefs=500, normalize=True, positive=False,
    precompute='auto', verbose=False)
```

```
plt.title('Level vs Salary')
plt.xlabel('Level')
plt.ylabel('Salary')
plt.scatter(X.astype('int'), Y.astype('int'), color = 'red')
plt.plot(X.astype('int'), reg.predict(X_poly), color = 'blue')
```

```
[<matplotlib.lines.Line2D at 0x7f45048fffd0>]
```

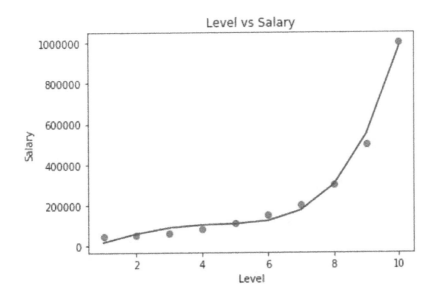

The R² value

```
reg.score(X_poly,Y)
```

0.9920421718638675

## *Bayesian regression*

In order to discuss about bayesian regression, we have to recap our intuition of linear regression. The generalised formula for linear regression is Y = wX + c, and we know how Y is an estimation based upon the coefficients w of input value X. The goal of linear regression is to find weights of w such that the changes in the weights interpret the changes in the response prediction Y. Therefore, the goal of linear regression is to find those coefficients that best interpret the data and reduce the error in prediction. A model trained with linear regression produces only a single estimate for the model parameters (weights or coefficients) as learnt from the training and therefore all the information about the model can only be drawn from a single state of the coefficients. This forms the basis of the significance of bayesian regression.

Bayesian regression aims for extending the limitation of a model trained with linear regression by providing a distribution of the possible values of the coefficients rather than single state of the coefficients at an instance. In Bayesian regression as from the name we may understand, a probability distribution is produced instead of point estimates in linear regression. The value for Y is not a single value but a probability distribution that form a *Gaussian distribution*. This probability distribution is a *posterior distribution*, which is basically the conditional probability of an event or in this case the value of the coefficients w and prediction Y evaluated on the knowledge from values obtained from training process. The term posterior in this context means estimating the probability after the training process. The posterior probability is expressed as -

$$P(w \mid Y,X) = P(Y \mid w,X).P(w \mid X) /P(Y \mid X)$$

Where P(w | Y,X) is the posterior probability distribution of the model parameters w.r.t. input X and output prediction Y of the dataset. P(Y | w,X) is the likelihood of the prediction Y and P(w | X) is the prior probability distribution of the model parameters given the dataset X during training.

The noteworthy point in learning about Bayesian regression is that we have talked less about the prediction Y' which is also expressed as a probability distribution, but more of the probability distribution of the model parameters (coefficients). This is because unlike linear regression, we now have a better knowledge about the model and we know how the range of coefficients values affect the prediction. The two major benefits of this type of regression is -

a) *Prior* - In order to predict an outcome, it is beneficial to have a prior knowledge about the probable model parameters rather than predicting based on just the value for X. This is not to be confused with training of a model. The training process sets the values of the coefficients which can be declared as the state of the model at an instance. Unlike linear regression, here a model is set at a state of coefficient values but in addition to that has a knowledge of how the coefficients were affected during the training process.

b) *Posterior* - The result of bayesian regression is a gaussian distribution of probabilities of model parameters based on the training dataset and the prior. The posterior gives us an estimation of how informed we are about the model.

The conditional probability expressed before can be written as -

```
Posterior = (Likelihood * Prior) / Normalization
```

We start with an initial estimate with the prior and as the model learns from more data, the model becomes more accurate. It is then, the *Likelihood* of a prediction is stronger and gains more significance over *Prior*.

For coding a regressor we will use the Bayesian ridge regression, which is basically a L2 regularised version.

```python
# Generating simulated data with Gaussian weights
np.random.seed(0)
n_samples, n_features = 100, 100
X = np.random.randn(n_samples, n_features)  # Create Gaussian data

# Create weights with a precision of 4.
lambda_ = 4.
w = np.zeros(n_features)

# Only keep 10 weights of interest
relevant_features = np.random.randint(0, n_features, 10)
for i in relevant_features:
    w[i] = stats.norm.rvs(loc=0, scale=1. / np.sqrt(lambda_))

# Create noise with a precision alpha of 50.
alpha_ = 50.
noise = stats.norm.rvs(loc=0, scale=1. / np.sqrt(alpha_), size=n_samples)

# Create the target
y = np.dot(X, w) + noise
```

The above snippet is for generating a dataset. The np.random.seed() method is for a seed value for reproducibility of the results. The randn() method generates a gaussian normal distribution dataset of size 100 and also having 100 features as set in variable n_samples and n_features. The Y of our dataset will be generated from this X and weights w. The method stats.norm.rvs() generates random variates. A random variate is basically the value of a random variable at any instance, and is subject to change. The weights list w[] is set with these random values. The intercept for the model named as noise is also set as a random value with rvs(). Lastly the Y is produced with a dot product on X and w.

```python
# Fit the Bayesian Ridge Regression and an OLS for comparison
bayes_reg = BayesianRidge(compute_score=True)
bayes_reg.fit(X, y)

lin_reg = LinearRegression()
lin_reg.fit(X, y)
```

We will compare both bayesian regression and linear regression, so both are trained.

```python
# Plot true weights, estimated weights, histogram of the weights, and
# predictions with standard deviations
lw = 2
plt.figure(figsize=(6, 5))
plt.title("Weights of the model")
plt.plot(bayes_reg.coef_, color='lightgreen', linewidth=lw,
         label="Bayesian Ridge estimate")
plt.plot(w, color='gold', linewidth=lw, label="Ground truth")
plt.plot(lin_reg.coef_, color='navy', linestyle='--', label="OLS estimate")
plt.xlabel("Features")
plt.ylabel("Values of the weights")
plt.legend(loc="best", prop=dict(size=12))
```

In the above snippet, we generate a plot to visualise the weights of bayes regression (bayes_reg) and linear regression (lin_reg) alongwith original values of weights w.

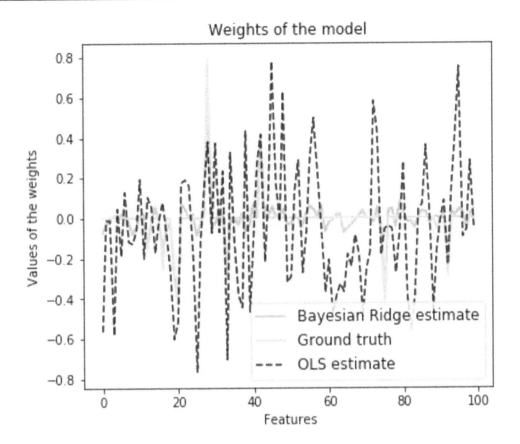

# Cost function

The previous chapters have introduced us to the preliminary concepts of data science in through various methods of regression. To summarise regression in its entirety, we can say that it is the process of approximating an object function by learning from a dataset containing the input and output to such an object function. Approximation therefore, comes with the obvious trade off with a portion of error. As we already know that, approximations are done using functions based on measuring Euclidean distances - Y = wX + C, training the values for w and C and reducing the error percentage in them, constitutes the objective. The objective function is also called the *hypothesis function* and we are going to interchangeably use it.

The minimisation of error between the result of hypothesis function and the desired result is expressed as a function - minimise(h(x) - Y)$^2$ known as squared error, where h(x) is the hypothesis function and Y is the desired result. This function when applied for all the tuples in the dataset, is called the mean squared error and expressed as -

$$J(\theta) = \frac{1}{m} \sum_{i=1}^{m} \left( h_\theta(x^{(i)}) - y^{(i)} \right)^2$$

Here $\theta$ is represented as the weights w. The expression $\frac{1}{m}$ is for calculating the *mean* of the squared error for all the **m** tuples in the dataset. In some places we may come across the mean to be calculated over $\frac{1}{2m}$. This is purely due to the ease of calculation, as calculating the minimum value of the function $J(\theta)$ is computationally faster for the 1/2 of $J(\theta)$. Therefore, we see how training a model involves optimising for the value of two functions - the objective function that approximates and the cost function, such that, accuracy of the objective function is inversely proportional to the cost function output.

We are going to delve a little deeper into understanding how these two functions are adjusted and for this we will be using the following $\theta$ based notation for variables -

*Objective function*

$$h_\theta(x) = \theta_0 + \theta_1 x.$$

## Cost function

$$J(\theta) = \frac{1}{2m} \sum_{i}^{m} \left(h_\theta(x^{(i)}) - y^{(i)}\right)^2.$$

The goal of the learning process is to minimise the output of the cost function using a method called *Gradient descent*. Let us see how the cost function plots w.r.t. the objective function.
Suppose we have a training set that plots the following data-points -

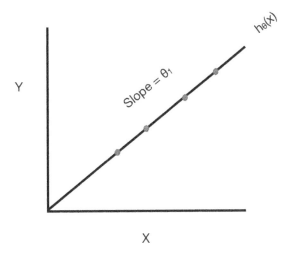

Here the regression line passes exactly through the plotted points with slope $\theta_1 = 1$, the intercept is $\theta_0 = 0$ and therefore the cost function is $J(\theta)$ i.e. $J(\theta_1) = 0$ with no error. A plot for the cost function is as follows -

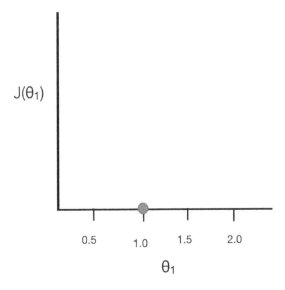

The above example is an ideal situation where there is a perfect fit for the regression line. For a real dataset, the process of fitting a regression line is iterative, starting with errors and approaching towards having an optimal solution with the least error.

Now here is a plot for data-points that are unevenly spread out.

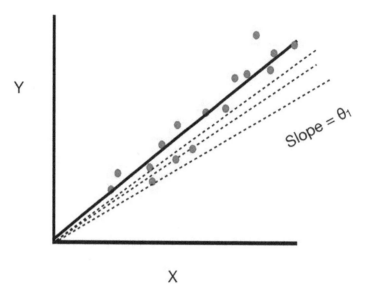

The linear regression techniques that we have learnt so far, have the same schematic of fitting a good regression line, which is, to start with a regression line corresponding to a starting value for $\theta_0$ and $\theta_1$, and approach toward a line that has least error. The dotted regression lines in the above plot, shows how the value for $\theta_1$ is adjusted to drawn the best fit regression line in solid black. On the first iteration, the regression line has the max error w.r.t. all the data-points, although it passes through one data point.

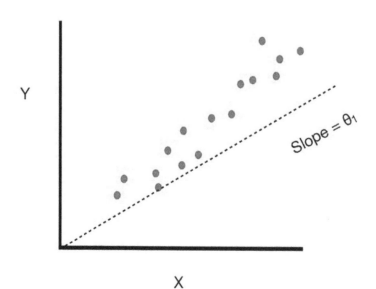

Now let us plot a fictional cost function for the above regression line.

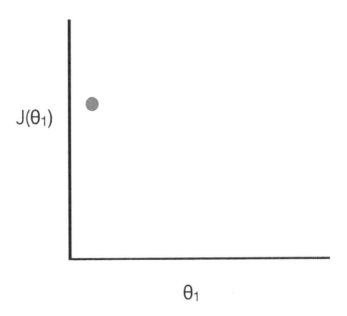

The plot of the cost function for the rest of the regression lines can be as the following -

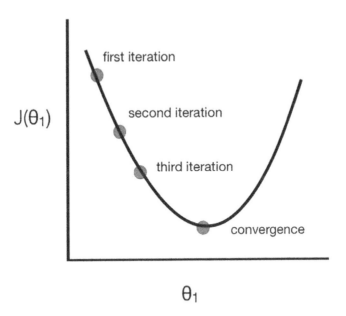

With every iteration the attempt is to reduce the error magnitude. The plot of the cost function forms a convex graph as the one above and the objective of error reduction is to find the point which has the minimum value along the plotted graph. The point marked as *convergence* is the one where the error is least and best fit for the regression line. This process of converging to the minima of the graph is called *Gradient descent*. The gradient descent algorithm, at each step does the following operation -

$$\theta_j \rightarrow \theta_j - \alpha \frac{\partial}{\partial \theta_j} J(\boldsymbol{\theta})$$

The magnitude of descent along the slope of the curve plot by the cost function, is calculated as the derivative of J(θ) multiplied by the learning rate α. The value for learning rate specifies the magnitude of the leap down on the slope at each iteration. The gradient descent algorithm starts with an arbitrary point on the convex graph and the result of the derivative of J(θ) at each point on the cost function curve, decides in which direction to move next. Suppose the gradient descent starts from the following arbitrary point -

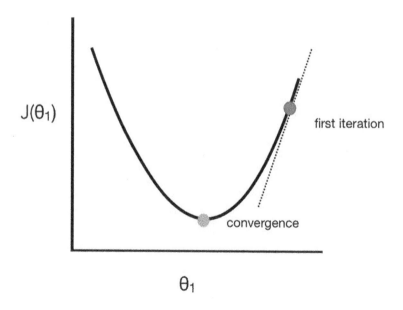

The tangent at the point marks the derivative that evaluates the direction in which the next leap is to be taken. The slope of the tangent in this case is a *positive slope* and so the derivative is positive. The value for $\theta_1$ will be updated accordingly -

$$\theta_j \rightarrow \theta_j - \alpha \frac{\partial}{\partial \theta_j} J(\boldsymbol{\theta})$$

and the next leap would be as the following -

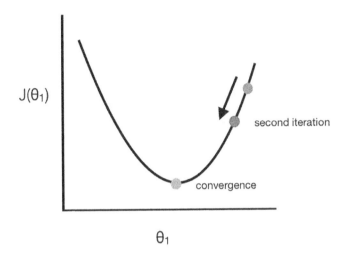

Again, if the arbitrary starting point is as the following -

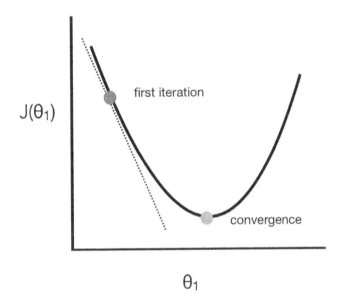

the slope of the tangent would yield a negative derivative and the next value for $\theta_1$ is calculated accordingly -

$$\theta_j \rightarrow \theta_j - (\text{-}\alpha \frac{\partial}{\partial \theta_j} J(\boldsymbol{\theta}))$$

The corresponding next step is -

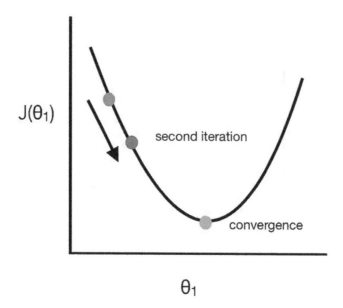

The magnitude of the step as we have mentioned earlier, is regulated by the value provided for $\alpha$ parameter, i.e. the learning rate. The value for $\alpha$ has to be set conservatively, as a large value may cause the leap to over shoot the convergence.

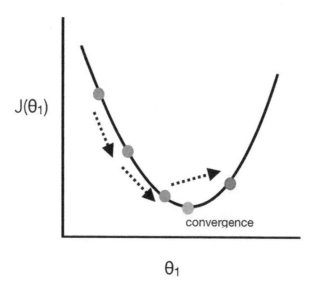

The above plot shows the overshooting problem for $\alpha$ set at a high value, but if the value for $\alpha$ is set to too small, the gradient descent will be slow.

The gradient descent algorithm takes this problem of learning rate adjustment and automatically regulates it with the change in steepness of the slope.

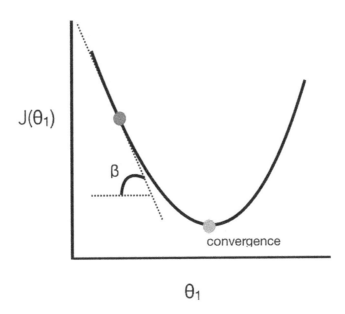

The above plot shows the angle β formed by the slope. With the descent down the gradient (slope), the angle β decreases as shown in the plot below.

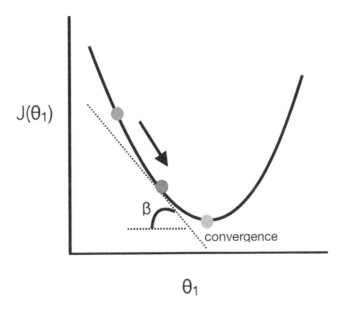

Therefore, the gradient descent algorithm adjusts the learning rate w.r.t. the change in the angle β.

Up till now, all the plots for cost function have been done for a single variable and the plot for cost function has been depicted just as a single convex curve. However, the cost function will consist of multiple crests for multiple variables.

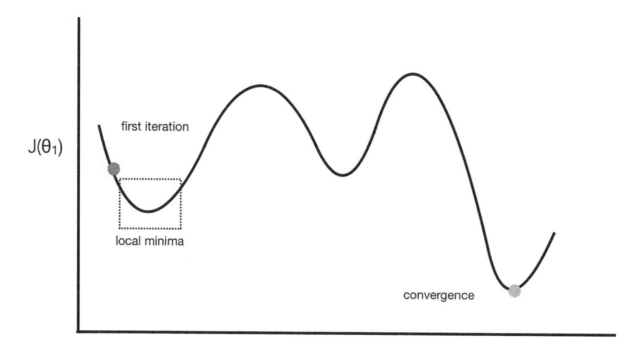

The above plot shows such a landscape for the cost function with multiple variables, which consists of local minima(s). The gradient descent function would execute in the same way irrespective of the cost function plot and it is susceptible to the problem of local minima.

The gradient descent function, in order to take a single step has to take all the $m$ tuples in the dataset and calculate the sum of residuals, as described in the formula below -

$$J(\theta) = \frac{1}{2m} \sum_{i}^{m} \left(h_\theta(x^{(i)}) - y^{(i)}\right)^2.$$

Now, this is a slow process when the value of $m$ is large. This method of gradient descent is also called batch gradient descent as it has to consider the entire dataset (batch) for every iteration.

A speed up to the batch gradient descent process can come from something called the *stochastic gradient descent (SDG)*. In SDG, the cost function does not need to consider the sum of squares over the entire dataset to take a single step of descent, instead, it considers only one data tuple for a step. This is the corresponding cost function definition -

$$J(\theta) = \frac{1}{2} \left(h_\theta(x^{(i)}) - y^{(i)}\right)^2$$

The term stochastic means randomness in a distribution of statistical dataset. The idea behind SDG is to randomly take one $_i{}^{th}$ training data tuple at a time and calculate the $J(\theta)$ for it. In order to visualise how stochastic gradient descent is different from batch gradient descent, we will use a contour plot. Here is the descent of a batch gradient function -

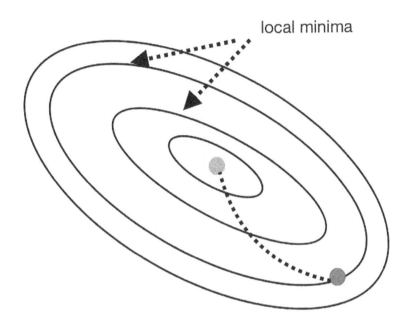

Starting from a point, the descent trajectory is made toward the global minima for the cost function.

The contour plot for SDG -

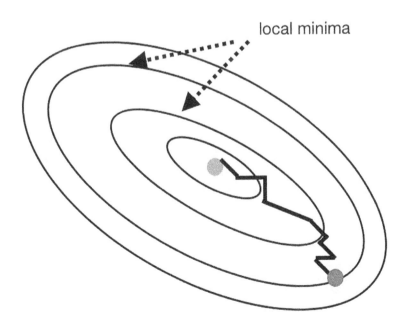

In comparison to the trajectory of batch gradient descent, SDG is uneven yet faster since it does not have to consider the sum of all the residuals to take a single step. The unevenness of the descent to a global minima is due to the random selection of training data. The derivative of the cost function states the direction in which the next step is to be taken and $\alpha$ specifies the length of the step. The below diagram shows how the randomly selected states specify the direction.

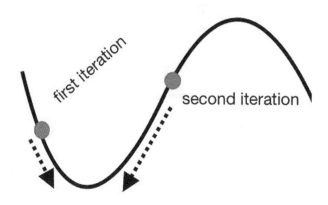

local minima

The above plot can be related to the following contour section -

Therefore, an SDG algorithm runs the cost reduction process of updating the descent path over the entire dataset. Here is a pseudocode for SDG -

a) Randomly shuffle dataset
b) for i=1,2,...,m

$$\theta_j \rightarrow \theta_j - \alpha \frac{\partial}{\partial \theta_j} J(\boldsymbol{\theta})$$

c) Goto step a) until n times.

The learning rate in SDG is typically held constant for a certain number of iterations until the locality of global minimum has arrived, unlike batch gradient descent where $\alpha$ is adjusted w.r.t. the steepness of the slope. Despite all of this, SDG can still take time to converge and can get stuck in a local minima, but the randomisation factor in SDG gives it the advantage of finding a better local minima than batch gradient descent. Keeping the learning rate constant for SDG, also introduces the problem of over shooting when a global minima has arrived.

The *mini-batch* gradient descent algorithm takes a different approach while updating the descent path by taking inspiration from both SDG and batch gradient descent. Instead of considering all the tuples in the training dataset, for updating a step, mini-batch gradient descent considers a preset batch of *k* tuples called mini-batch. The reason for such approach is to speed up the cumbersome process of evaluating all the training data for a step as in batch gradient descent and also bring some stability in the convergence process, as compared to SDG. For example, suppose there is 1 million training data tuples. Each mini-batch can be made of 1000 training data tuples such that the training algorithm is comprised of the following steps -

a) loop i from 1 to 1000, where each i is made of 1000 data tuples (hence 1 million).
b) calculate Y = wX + c for all of the 'i' training data tuples.
c) calculate the gradients for all the 'i' training data tuples.
d) compute and update the cost $\theta$ from $J(\theta)$.
e) update the weights and bias.

The above step constitute one pass through the entire dataset, and is called an *epoch*.

This type of gradient descent is useful in training neural networks which we will learn later in the book, but it is still not immune to the convergence problem at local minima. Choosing a proper learning rate is a difficult task. Learning rates could be scheduled through a process called *simulated annealing*, when a heuristic approach is taken to estimate the global optimum of a function.

We are going to go through the methods that are optimisations on the gradient descent algorithms and have use majorly in deep learning problems.

Moving forward, we are going to come across a lot a of mathematical expressions that briefly encapsulate the background calculations involved in each of the optimisation algorithms and are not required to be memorised for application purposes. We need to just focus on the intuition behind each of the optimisation methods.

## Gradient descent with momentum

In batch gradient descent, the leaps toward a minima is dependant on the steepness of the slope at that point.

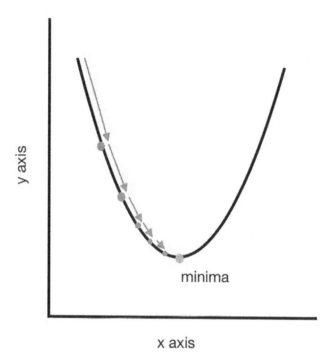

We can see how larger steps are taken in the direction of y axis and the steps become shortened along the x axis due to the automatic adjustment of the learning rate. We know that the change in learning rate affects the convergence by making it a slow process, the SDG method is a betterment by keeping the learning rate fixed. Again, the SDG method, although being faster, has its own problem of overshooting due to fixed learning rate.

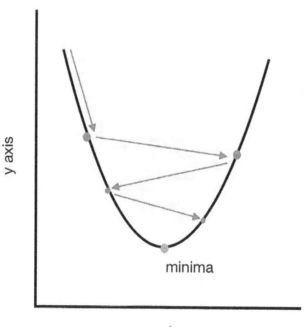

Momentum is a physics concept that is applied to the gradient descent process. The inspiration for momentum comes from the natural phenomenon that we will observe as a ball rolls down a ravine. A convex curve is compared to such a ravine, and a ball that starts from the top of the ridge gains speed as it approaches the bottom, which in our case is the minima. This change in speed in called momentum. The below diagram shows how such a phenomenon shall look like -

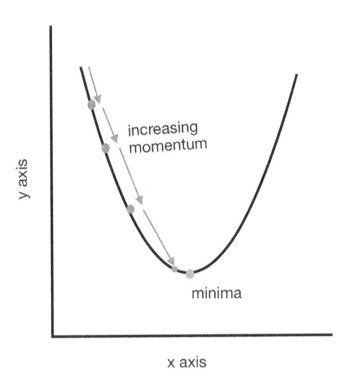

The SDG algorithm with momentum accelerates the convergence along the x axis, i.e. closer to the minima, greater is the travel along the x axis. A momentum hyper-parameter γ (gamma) is added to the update expression which is usually set to 0.9 and takes values from 0 to 10. Here is a simplified updation expression -

$$V_t = \gamma V_{t-1} + \alpha.\partial/\partial_\theta J(\theta)$$
$$\theta = \theta - V_t$$

The γ hyper-parameter is supposed to impact the magnitude of leaps toward a minima with increase in movement along x axis and thats why, Vt-1 takes the points till the last leap and accounts for significant increase in the result of the product γVt-1 when value for 'x' changes.

## Nesterov accelerated gradient descent

This is an upgrade to the SDG with momentum method. The SDG with momentum method reacted during the downward travel toward minima by increasing the leap magnitude, but during an ascent upward the minima region, its momentum did not re-adjust. Let us understand this from the diagrams below -

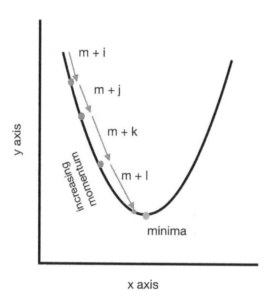

In the diagram, m is the value for momentum set to a certain value before starting the descent down the slope. As the descent increases m increases, since l > k > j > i. Reaching the local minima and climbing out of the 'ridge' region continues with the momentum γ which undergoes slight change.

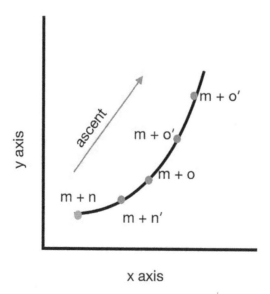

The values n, n', o and o' have negligible difference among themselves. During ascent most change occurs in the Y axis, and so the SDG with momentum method will have very little change of momentum. The above diagram shows that the momentum at minima is *m + n*. With change along x axis, the momentum undergoes a slight change and thus designated as *m +n'*. Similarly, as the ascent along the steepness increases the momentum settles at *m + o'* and continues to remain the same. The *Nesterov* method adds a smartness quotient to the momentum change, such that, the momentum decelerates during ascent.

$$V_t = \gamma V_{t-1} + \alpha.\partial/\partial_\theta J(\theta - \gamma V_{t-1})$$
$$\theta = \theta - V_t$$

What the $J(\theta - \gamma V_{t-1})$ component in the above expression does is, get rid of the previous gain in momentum and keep decelerating on the way up.

## *Adagrad*

This is a differential learning technique that has usage widely in training neural networks, where models with high number of features is common. The techniques discussed so far, all consider the same learning rate for updating the cost function, therefore, features and their corresponding coefficients do not have any effect on the learning rate. After dimension/feature reduction of a dataset, there can be features that are more important than others. More importantly, in case of a sparse dataset, significance of features should be varied based upon the feature values in a data tuple encountered during the training process. Suppose, a model is being trained to identify cats and the training set consists of cats photos that are more or less alike.

The above two photos from the dataset are representative of the kind of knowledge that the model will form about cats, i.e. they have whiskers, four legs, pointy ears, etc. Now the next picture shows a cat that is quite different from the the previous ones in terms of features.

Ideally the model should be trained for recording special edge cases such as in the above image. Adagrad takes this notion and applies into its process of cost reduction. In *Adagrad*, different learning rates are set for different features. Now since the first two cat images are fairly similar, the feature values remain similar and they should not significantly affect the cost function. Whereas, the above cat image has pixel values quite different from other ones and so this should account for significant change in the cost function. The learning rate in Adagrad are adjusted to a lower value for frequently occurring features, and to a higher value for infrequently ones. It is for this reason, Adagrad is well suited for sparse datasets. The cost function for Adagrad is in accordance to a time step $t_i$ during the training phase, as shown in the expression below -

$$g_{i,t} = \partial / \partial_\theta J(\theta_{i,t})$$

So now the SDG $\theta$ update at timestamp $t_i$ becomes,

$$\theta_{t+1} = \theta_{i,t} - \alpha.g_{i,t}$$

The learning rate $\alpha$ is changed at each time-step based on the past gradients that have been compute. Hence the updation expression takes the following state,

$$\eta = \alpha / \sqrt{(G_{t,i,i} + \varepsilon)}$$
$$\theta_{t+1} = \theta_{i,t} - \eta.g_{i,t}$$

Here G is a diagonal matrix where each diagonal element i,i is the sum of the square of the gradients.

$$\begin{bmatrix} G_t^{(1,1)} & 0 & \cdots & 0 \\ 0 & G_t^{(2,2)} & \cdots & 0 \\ \vdots & \vdots & \ddots & \vdots \\ 0 & 0 & \cdots & G_t^{(m,m)} \end{bmatrix}$$

A diagonal matrix is used because at higher number of features it would become very costly to compute the square root of the matrix.

The term $\eta$ does preforms an l2 norm of all previous gradients on a per-feature basis. As the training process progresses, the l2 normalization on the gradients continue to happen. We know that l2 does not completely reduce the value of a coefficient to 0 but to some value that approaches to 0. As the model keeps getting trained with cat images similar to one another, the G matrix approaches more and more toward 0. When a new image of cat comes up, that has significantly new features, it will have higher gradient value w.r.t. the continually reducing gradient values and ultimately learning rate $\alpha$, due to the l2 regularisation. This fluctuation in gradient is picked up by the algorithm and it updates the cost function accordingly. The *Adagrad* or *Adaptive subGradient* method although is smarter in updating the cost differentially, but has the eventual problem of decaying learning rate $\alpha$ due to the l2 regularisation.

The term $\varepsilon$ is added to G to avoid division of $\alpha$ by zero.

## Adadelta

Adadelta is an extension of the Adagrad method that focuses to reducing the consistently decreasing trend of the learning rate. Instead of considering all the past gradients, it just focuses on a fixed number of them. Instead of recording directly the k previous squared gradients like that of Adagrad, a running average of previous gradients is used instead of the matrix G, as previously seen in the case of Adagrad. Thus the running average at time step t, depends on the previous average and the current gradient. The expression for *Adadelta* takes the following updated form from *Adagrad*,

$$\eta = \alpha / \sqrt{(E[g^2]_t + \varepsilon)}$$
$$\theta_{t+1} = \theta_{i,t} - \eta . g_{i,t}$$

$$E[g^2]_t = \gamma E[g^2]_{t-1} + (1 - \gamma) g_t^2$$

$\gamma$ is our momentum term.

The diagonal matrix G is replaced with the decaying average over past gradients $E[g^2]_t$ where $gt^2$ is the square of each gradient. The denominator $\sqrt{(E[g^2]_t + \varepsilon)}$ is basically root mean squared, so it is replaced with the RMS expression shorthand -

$$\eta = \alpha/RMS[g_t]$$
$$\theta_{t+1} = \theta_{i,t} - \eta.g_{i,t}$$

The Adadelta method not only handles the problem of continually decaying learning rate by turning the denominator to RMS of gradients, but also gets rid of the learning rate hyper-parameter altogether. It does this by replacing the numerator with the RMS of previous cost updates. This RMS of cost updates removes the requirement of setting the $\alpha$ parameter at the beginning of the training process and will be calculated dynamically in the following way,

$$E[\partial/\partial_\theta\theta^2]_t = \gamma E[\partial/\partial_\theta\theta^2]_{t-1} + (1 - \gamma)\partial/\partial_\theta\theta_t{}^2$$

The RMS of the cost updates then becomes,

$$RMS[\partial/\partial_\theta\theta]_t = \sqrt{(E[\partial/\partial_\theta\theta^2]_t + \varepsilon)}$$

Finally, the update function becomes the following with the learning rate $\alpha$ removed,

$$\eta = RMS[\partial/\partial_\theta\theta]_{t-1}/RMS[g]_t$$
$$\theta_{t+1} = \theta_{i,t} - \eta.g_{i,t}$$

## RMSProp

This is an adaptive learning rate method that is available in machine learning libraries, but stemmed from an unpublished paper. RMSprop and Adadelta were both developed independently in order to tackle the problem of Adagrad's diminishing learning rate problem. The only difference of RMSProp from Adadelta is that, it has a preset learning rate,

$$\eta = \alpha/RMS[g]_t$$
$$\theta_{t+1} = \theta_{i,t} - \eta.g_{i,t}$$

## Adam

The Adaptive Moment Estimation (Adam) is another method that computes adaptive learning rates. In addition to keeping the decaying *average of past squared gradients* like Adadelta and RMSProp, Adam in addition to that, also keeps a decaying *average of past gradients*. The Adam algorithm brings together the intuition for RMSProp and momentum as was first seen in *gradient descent with momentum* algorithm. In order to understand the implementation of Adam in depth, we have to have some knowledge about *moment*, which is a concept used in statistics for a distribution of data. In our case, that distribution is represented in the form of all the gradients. As stated, we use both average of past gradients ($m_t$) and average of the square of the past gradients ($V_t$), their significance is based upon the statistical concept of order of moment. The first order of moment $m_t$ gives the *mean* of the distribution and the second order of moment $V_t$, gives the *variance* of the distribution. We will not go into further details on these statistical terms of mean and variance calculation based on degrees of moment, since they are beyond the scope of this book. The expression for $m_t$ and $V_t$ are as follows -

$$m_t = \beta_1 m_{t-1} + (1-\beta_1)g_t$$
$$V_t = \beta_2 V_{t-1} + (1-\beta_2)g_t^2$$

As $m_t$ and $V_t$ are initialized as vectors of 0's, it is found that they are biased towards zero during the initial steps and especially when the decay rates are small. To counteract these biases, the first and second moments are corrected the following way -

$$m_{\hat{t}} = m_t / (1 - \beta^t_1)$$
$$V_{\hat{t}} = V_t / (1 - \beta^t_2)$$

$\beta_1$ and $\beta_2$ are the decay rates set to 0.9 and 0.999 respectively for best results. Therefore, the update rule for the Adam optimization is,

$$\eta = \alpha / \sqrt{(V_{\hat{t}} + \epsilon)}$$
$$\theta_{t+1} = \theta_t - \eta.m_{\hat{t}}$$

Adam is a highly sought candidate for neural networks and deep learning problems as it involves easy computation, requiring less memory.

## Adamax

We have discussed in *Adagrad* algorithm, how the term $\eta = \alpha/\sqrt{(G_{t,i,i} + \varepsilon)}$ performed L2 normalization and in the similar way Adadelta, RMSProp and Adam also does this. Adamax focuses on this normalization at higher degrees and generalizes it. The $V_t$ parameter from Adam is rewritten as,

$$V_t = \beta_2{}^p V_{t-1} + (1-\beta_2{}^p)g_t{}^2$$

where p is the degree of L2 normalization. Normalization is possible at higher degrees than L2 but is unpopular because of its instability. However the p approaching $\infty$ becomes stable and converges. The remaining concept for Adamax remain similar to that of Adam, and it transforms the update expression into the following,

$$V_t = \beta_2{}^p V_{t-1} + (1-\beta_2{}^p)g_t{}^2$$
$$\Rightarrow V_t = \max(\beta_2.V_{t-1}, g_t)$$

This changed Vt can be used as is with the Adam method, and so conceptually we can call Adamax as the Adam optimisation for the infinity norm. Good values for $\alpha$ is 0.002, $\beta_1 = 0.9$, $\beta_2 = 0.999$.

## Nadam

This optimisation method is again based upon several other methods - Adam, Nesterov gradient descent with momentum, and RMSProp. RMSProp contributes the decaying average of past squared gradients Vt, while momentum accounts for decaying average of past gradients and we have also seen how Nesterov accelerated gradient descent makes the momentum effect smarter.
The Nesterov update expression is as follows -

$$V_t = \gamma V_{t-1} + \alpha.\partial/\partial_\theta J(\theta - \gamma V_{t-1})$$
$$\theta = \theta - V_t$$

and the Adam update expression is -

$$m_t = \beta_1 m_{t-1} + (1-\beta_1)g_t$$
$$V_t = \beta_2 V_{t-1} + (1-\beta_2)g_t{}^2$$

$$\eta = \alpha/\sqrt{(Vt + \varepsilon)}$$
$$\theta_{t+1} = \theta_{i,t} - \eta.m_t$$

Timothy Dozat proposed a modification to Nesterov, that rather than applying the momentum term twice, once during the updating the gradient $\alpha.\partial/\partial\theta_\theta\, J(\theta - \gamma Vt-1)$ and again during updating the cost parameter $\theta$. So, the following Nesterov update expression -

$$V_t = \theta - \gamma Vt-1 + \alpha.\partial/\partial\theta\, J(\theta)$$
$$\theta = \theta - V_t$$
$$\theta = \theta - \{\gamma Vt-1 + \alpha.\partial/\partial\theta\, J(\theta)\}$$

becomes,

$$\theta = \theta - \{\gamma V_t + \alpha.\partial/\partial\theta\, J(\theta)\}$$

Rather than using the previous momentum vector Vt-1 we are using the current momentum vector Vt.

Now in order to add Nesterov momentum to Adam, we can similarly replace the previous momentum with current momentum. Here is the Adam update expression for the first moment (mean) -

$$m_t = \beta_1 m_{t-1} + (1-\beta_1)g_t$$
$$m_{\hat{t}} = m_t / (1 - \beta^t{}_1)$$
$$\theta_{t+1} = \theta_t - \eta.m_{\hat{t}} /(\sqrt{V_{\hat{t}}} + \varepsilon)$$

Expanding the expression with the corrected bias $m_t$.

$$\theta_{t+1} = \theta_t - \frac{\eta}{\sqrt{\hat{v}_t} + \epsilon}\left(\frac{\beta_1 m_{t-1}}{1 - \beta_1^t} + \frac{(1 - \beta_1)g_t}{1 - \beta_1^t}\right)$$

The term $\frac{\beta_1 m_{t-1}}{1-\beta_1^t}$ is the bias-corrected estimate of the first moment and therefore it is replaced with $\hat{m}_{t-1}$, and the Nadam update expression becomes -

$$\theta_{t+1} = \theta_t - \frac{\eta}{\sqrt{\hat{v}_t} + \epsilon}\left(\beta_1 \hat{m}_{t-1} + \frac{(1-\beta_1)g_t}{1-\beta_1^t}\right)$$

# Classification

With classification we enter into the role of solving a new kind of problem, using machine learning techniques. Regression is the kind of problem where a function is trained to mimic an objective function and predict a single value based on the features from which it learns. In case of classification problems, we have to deal with prediction of more than one values.

The term classification as we know, is the act of separating objects, in this case data objects, based upon some distinguishable properties. The way humans do this is absolutely intuitive. But it is not that simple, as rather complex operation is the human brain are involved, yet they seem effortless to us. In order to understand the true nature of how humans accomplish the task of classification, we have to first recollect how the task of classification is based upon acquired knowledge about an object.

Suppose we are given an collection of alien objects, each one unknown and the task is to sort them in groups. The procedure a human brain uses is to first observe the various distinguishable features of the object and since we do not know what the objects actual name is, we create a new label for ourselves say U1 as in unknown - 1. With this label creation, we have created a class. Each class as we know has unique features and an object that match the kind of features portrayed by a class, belong to that class. A human performing the task of grouping the collection of alien objects is basically creating a new class every time an object comes along that has at least one property that is unique w.r.t. the other created classes, say U1, U2, etc.

This is the act of classification. Now, we have to emphasise on the knowledge quotient involved in this activity of classification. Any object that comes along, the human brain compares its features to the already established features that describe a particular class. This comparison is possible because of the knowledge-base created in our brain which got trained to identify an object belonging to an already created class. This knowledge-base in the brain is the machine learning model.

In the case of regression, a model's task was to predict a value that had a range distinguished by the regression line.

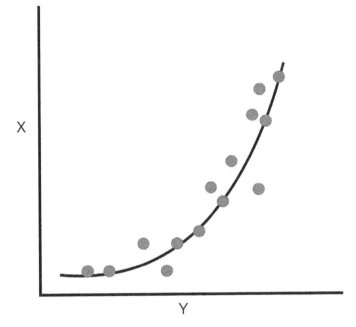

In the above plot, we see a model has a good fit on the training data, therefore, the model should be able to predict the value for Y based upon input X, and since its a good fit model, the value for Y shall belong to the desired range as the regression line (exponential function) progresses as shown in the below plot -

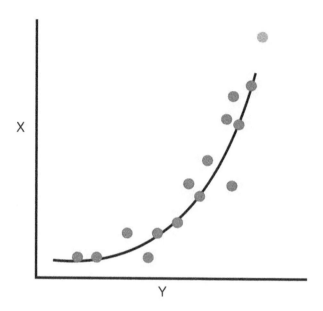

A regression line in the above plots show us how it is representative of the data points that is continually and evenly spread out. In other words, we can say that the motive of the regression line is to follow the trend of the function. *This prediction process is of an ability of a model to know where to place the data point Y on the XY 2D plane.*

Now let us take a look at a different kind of plot depicted here -

The above plot is also the result of an X value that is fed as input to a function which outputs the result Y in this manner.

Our idea from training linear regression models would suggest to fit a line that goes through the data points and the result shall look something like this among several possibilities -

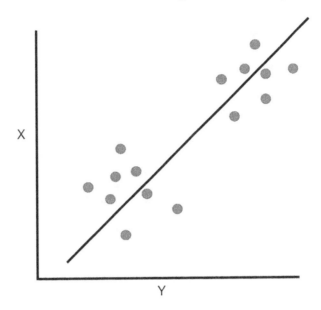

Although the regression line passes through the data points, it fails to capture the intent of the function. This is because, the objective function has been treated as a linear regression problem, where the job is to find a good fitting line that aligns with the data plot. All said, there is a catch, the model in the above plot *may still be able to plot a point* Y, but not a good one. That may seem contradictory to the way we are trying to describe a linear regression solution being unfit in this use case. We are going to take the example of yet another type of data plot to understand the implications further deeply.

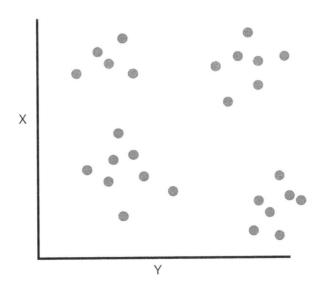

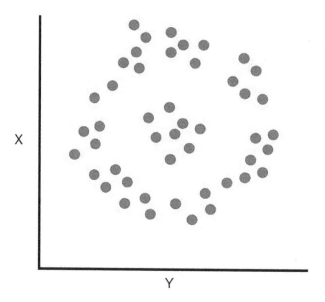

The above two plots showcase completely different kind of use cases for linear regression. If such functions are tried to be mapped as linear regression problems, they would fail miserably. This is because the data points are spread out based upon *some conditional criteria in the objective function*. In order to understand what that means we take another look at the following plot -

Here the nature of the objective function is such, that its results are discretely placed and is separated by a decision boundary. Each cluster of plotted points are representative of a particular class. We would see that because of the nature of the objective function being based upon a condition, any data sent as input to the function results in the output to belong in either of the two classes for the above plot. Since the function is decisive, it is therefore based upon propositional logic and internally performing these decisions using IF and ELSE queries.

Let us address two real world examples that such a function would represent -

a) Classification of demographic prone to a set of diseases based upon eating habits, sanitation, etc.
b) A bank receives applications for loans. Based upon the provided documents per application, the bank has to decide which applications are have good credit to avail a loan, which applications have bad credit and cannot avail a loan, and which have credit that are requires further background checking and validation.

These types of problem statements are quite different from linear regression problems. In Linear regression, we have to deal with problems that result in the objective function outputting a single value, such as predicting the amount of money to be spent on fuel given the distance to be travelled, prediction of sales growth given the spendings in advertisement of a product, or predicting the sea-level rise based upon global carbon emission rates.

In the case of linear regression problems, it is also valid to state that a linear regression's objective function also performs some form of propositional logical operations based upon the data fields known as features and is able to make predictions on things such as sales growth among many others. *Classification problems are always not of the type that result in binary outcomes.* Each class if viewed separately, will seem similar to a linear regression problem where a value Y is output for a certain input X. At this point, it may strike as a confusion between classification problems and linear regression problems as they both in fact seem similar.

For an input X, a classification objective function outputs a value for Y. This value as stated is not always binary. Let us expand on the example of classification of diseases. In order to train the model it has to be fed training dataset that comprises of bodily vitals as features. Here is such a sample -

| Time | RelativeTimeMilliseconds | HR | ST-II | Pulse | SpO2 | Perf | etCO2 | imCO2 | awRR | NBP (Sys) | NBP (Dia) | NBP (Mean) |
|---|---|---|---|---|---|---|---|---|---|---|---|---|
| 00:20:00_000 | 1200000 | 71 | | 72 | 100 | 4.5 | 32 | 1 | 12 | 108 | 64 | 74 |
| 00:20:00_010 | 1200010 | 71 | | 72 | 100 | 4.5 | 32 | 1 | 12 | 108 | 64 | 74 |
| 00:20:00_020 | 1200020 | 71 | | 72 | 100 | 4.5 | 32 | 1 | 12 | 108 | 64 | 74 |
| 00:20:00_030 | 1200030 | 71 | | 72 | 100 | 4.5 | 32 | 1 | 12 | 108 | 64 | 74 |
| 00:20:00_040 | 1200040 | 71 | | 72 | 100 | 4.5 | 32 | 1 | 12 | 108 | 64 | 74 |
| 00:20:00_050 | 1200050 | 71 | | 72 | 100 | 4.5 | 32 | 1 | 12 | 108 | 64 | 74 |
| 00:20:00_060 | 1200060 | 71 | | 72 | 100 | 4.5 | 32 | 1 | 12 | 108 | 64 | 74 |
| 00:20:00_070 | 1200070 | 71 | | 72 | 100 | 4.5 | 32 | 1 | 12 | 108 | 64 | 74 |

This concise sample is is representative of the X's features that would result in some Y value for WBC count (not shown in the dataset). Suppose the WBC count at different levels depicts different stages of a particular disease and so the various levels of WBCs can be labelled as different classes. This is a classic case of classification function but taking the case of just plotting the WBC level for only one type of disease given the vital stats, the problem becomes linear regression type. In the perspective of linear regression, a model's motive will be to predict the WBC count.

At this point, we may have gotten a little confused, but the reason for this comparative study on linear regression and classification problems is to have an in depth intuition about how to perceive data.

Machine learning algorithms provides those statistical tools that enable us to do data science, but they do not define the problem. Here is another example where a linear regression problem can be perceived as a classification problem. Imagine there is a function that outputs the pH level of a compound based upon the percentage of acid molecules provided as input.

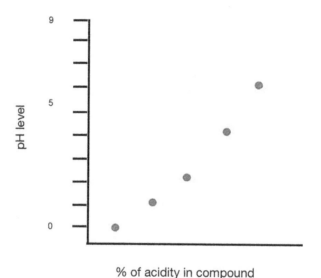

% of acidity in compound

The above plot is clearly a linear regression problem, but it can also be viewed as a classification job. The objective function is to approximate the logic which decides the pH level. So this same function can be used to classify a compound to be either alkaline if below and equal to pH 5 and acidic if above pH 5. Therefore, the intent of a machine learning problem statement, defines how a dataset will be perceived. A model trained with linear regression outputs the pH level Y and this result can be checked for the threshold value 5 for alkalinity or acidity using simple IF-ELSE comparators, or can be trained with classification algorithms such as *decision tree regression*, which we already have learnt or the ones we are going to learn next.

For classification type of problems, the motive of a machine learning algorithm is to learn the decision boundary among classes as shown with the dotted regression line below -

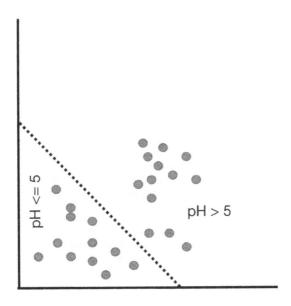

## Logistic regression

With logistic regression, we are going to address those classification problems that have binary outcome. For understanding this type of regression, we are going to use the following plot.

The problem at hand is to determine if a person will buy a car given the salary a person gets. The plot points as we can see are discretely placed either at Y = 0 or Y = 1. If we try to apply simple linear regression to model the logic behind the choice, we will get a regression line as shown above. Although the regression line touches the data points, it by nature is trying to estimate for a function that is continuous.

The section of the regression line marked with dotted square, represents the section that reflects the values ranging between 0 and 1. But since the outcome is binary, obviously there are no data points between 0 and 1.

Again, the most important section where the linear regression model fails to describe the objective function, is as illustrated below -

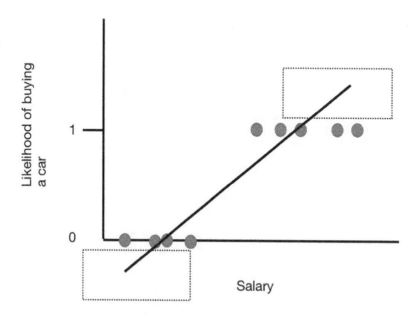

A linear regression trend line extends to infinity and in this case it is unable to define all the points at the values 0 and 1.

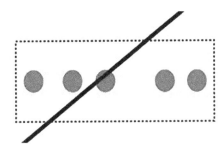

We are going to apply the *sigmoid* function on Y, that would change this regression line suited to the data points.

A *sigmoid* function is a mathematical function that has an "S" shaped curve.

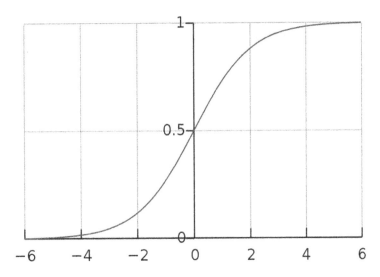

It has the formula -

$$S(Y) = 1 / ( 1 + e^{-Y} )$$

A sigmoid function is bounded and ranges between 0 and 1 or -1 to +1. The logistic and hyperbolic tangent sigmoid functions have wide usage in machine learning, as they are used as activation for artificial neurons and we will discuss about this in details later in this book. A sigmoid function takes any numeric value and converts it to a value between 0 and 1. This type of function is called a monotonic function, which means its outcome value is non-increasing or non-decreasing, and is always fixed within a subset of real numbers.

In our plot for likelihood of buying a car, the regression line takes the following form when it is passed through a sigmoid function.

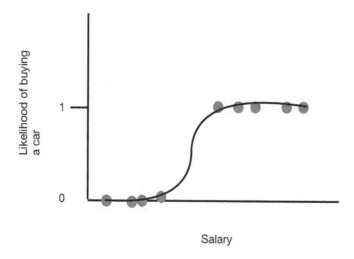

Now as we can see, the regression line has the best fit. The sigmoid function acts as a switch, and when a value for X is sent as input, the Y gets converted into either 0 or 1. The linear regression expression gets transformed in the following way -

$$1 / ( 1 + e^{-Y} ) = p$$
$$\Rightarrow \ln( p / 1 - p ) = Y$$

$$Y = mX + c$$
$$\Rightarrow \ln( p / 1 - p ) = mX + c$$

Our example objective function has binary outcome but the sigmoid function does just provide discrete result. The range from 0 to 1 can be interpreted as a probability distribution too.

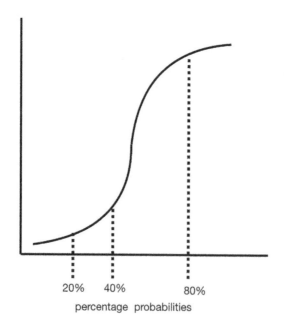

Therefore, a sigmoid function can be used to interpret probabilities of an event and this probability will be used as a score for classification purposes.

Next, we will go ahead an implement logistic regression on a dataset of users on a social media who purchased from ads. Here is a portion of the dataset -

| User ID | Gender | Age | EstimatedSalary | Purchased |
|---|---|---|---|---|
| 15624510 | Male | 19 | 19000 | 0 |
| 15810944 | Male | 35 | 20000 | 0 |
| 15668575 | Female | 26 | 43000 | 1 |
| 15603246 | Female | 27 | 57000 | 0 |
| 15804002 | Male | 19 | 76000 | 1 |

We discussed logistic regression with examples and comparison with linear regression and the effect of the sigmoid function on it to understand how the linear regression model can be used as a classifier. Here we are not going to do that, but use the LogisticRegression class.

```
import numpy as np
import matplotlib.pyplot as plt
import pandas as pd
```

```
ds = pd.read_csv('Social_Network_Ads.csv')
X = ds.iloc[:, [2,3]].values
Y = ds.iloc[:, 4].values
```

```
from sklearn.cross_validation import train_test_split
X_train, X_test, Y_train, Y_test = train_test_split(X,Y,test_size=0.25,random_state=0)
```

```
from sklearn.preprocessing import StandardScaler
scaler = StandardScaler()
X_train = scaler.fit_transform(X_train)
X_test = scaler.fit_transform(X_test)
```

```
from sklearn.linear_model import LogisticRegression
classifier = LogisticRegression(random_state=0)
classifier.fit(X_train,Y_train)
```

```
LogisticRegression(C=1.0, class_weight=None, dual=False, fit_intercept=True,
          intercept_scaling=1, max_iter=100, multi_class='ovr', n_jobs=1,
          penalty='l2', random_state=0, solver='liblinear', tol=0.0001,
          verbose=0, warm_start=False)
```

And now the prediction on test data.

```
Y_pred = classifier.predict(X_test)
```

```
# Checking the performance of the model
from sklearn.metrics import confusion_matrix
cm = confusion_matrix(Y_test, Y_pred)
```

```
cm
```

```
array([[63,  5],
       [ 7, 25]])
```

In linear regression we used $R^2$ and Adjusted-$R^2$ to measure the accuracy of the model. In this problem we will check the ratio of correct and incorrect predictions and so *confusion_matrix* is being used. A *confusion matrix* is a table also known as error matrix that lays out the performance of a classification job. There are four types of error it tries to measure - true positive (TP), true negative (TN), false positive (FP), false negative (FN). Here is a sample confusion matrix -

| n=165 | Predicted: NO | Predicted: YES | |
|---|---|---|---|
| Actual: NO | TN = 50 | FP = 10 | 60 |
| Actual: YES | FN = 5 | TP = 100 | 105 |
| | 55 | 110 | |

This is a matrix shown for a dataset of 165 tuples. The cell with FP=10 depicts the actual value for Y being false/no/0 but the model predicted it as true/yes/1, and there were 10 such occurrences of false positives. Similarly, in the cell FN=5, the expected value was true/yes/1, but 5 observations were wrongly predicted as false/no/0.

In our regression program, the confusion matrix flagged 5 FPs, and 7 FNs according to -

```
array([[63,  5],
       [ 7, 25]])
```

We will next visualise the training phase results.

```
# Visualising the Training set results
from matplotlib.colors import ListedColormap
X_age_range = np.arange(start = X_train[:, 0].min() - 1,
                        stop = X_train[:, 0].max() + 1, step = 0.01)
x_salary_range = np.arange(start = X_train[:, 1].min() - 1,
                           stop = X_train[:, 1].max() + 1, step = 0.01)

X1, X2 = np.meshgrid(X_age_range,x_salary_range)

X_plot = np.array([X1.ravel(), X2.ravel()]).T

plt.contourf(X1, X2, classifier.predict(X_plot).reshape(X1.shape),
             alpha = 0.75, cmap = ListedColormap(('gold', 'white')))
```

We may have noticed the relevant columns we selected for this regression were Age and Salary as X and the column Purchased is out Y. Our plot will be Age on the x axis and Salary on y axis.

The *arange* method returns a 1-D array from the *start* value to *stop* value with a difference (*step*) of 0.01. The arrays *X_age_range* and *X_salary_range* contain more granular values between the max and the min values compared to the dataset. This is required to make granular plotting scales.

The *meshgrid* method converts n-D vectors to n-D matrices. Suppose the size of *X_age_range* and *X_salary_range* is j and k correspondingly, the *meshgrid* method returns matrices each of dimension k x j. Now for X1, meshgrid returns a matrix where each row is a copy of *X_age_range* repeated k times. Similarly, for X2, it returns a matrix of where each column is a copy of *X_salary_range* repeated k times as columns.

The 1-D arrays *X_age_range* and *X_salary_range* cannot be directly used to map the axes for plotting because we are going to use the *contourf* method which takes a 2-D array as input. The *ravel* method takes all the elements in a n-D array and returns a 1-D array. This is required since we will be using the *predict* method of the classifier. The contourf method requires all the input arrays to be of the same dimensions and so the array returned by predict method is reshaped according to X1. The *T* method converts an array to its transpose to match with the dimension of X input array.

```
plt.xlim(X1.min(), X1.max())
plt.ylim(X2.min(), X2.max())
for i, j in enumerate(np.unique(Y_train)):
    choose_rows = (Y_train == j)
    plt.scatter(X_train[choose_rows, 0], X_train[choose_rows, 1],
                c = ListedColormap(('red', 'green'))(i), label = j)
plt.title('Logistic Regression (Training set)')
plt.xlabel('Age')
plt.ylabel('Estimated Salary')
plt.legend()
plt.show()
```

The *Y_train == j* expression returns an array of True and False values based upon the comparison with all elements of Y_train. Suppose the current value in j is 0, and if the value at Y_train[k] == 0 then True is retuned else False. The expression *X_set[choose_rows, 0]* returns only the value in column 0 of those rows that have corresponding value True in *choose_rows*. Suppose the first element of choose_rows is True, then the first row of X_set will be selected.

We get the following plot for the training data -

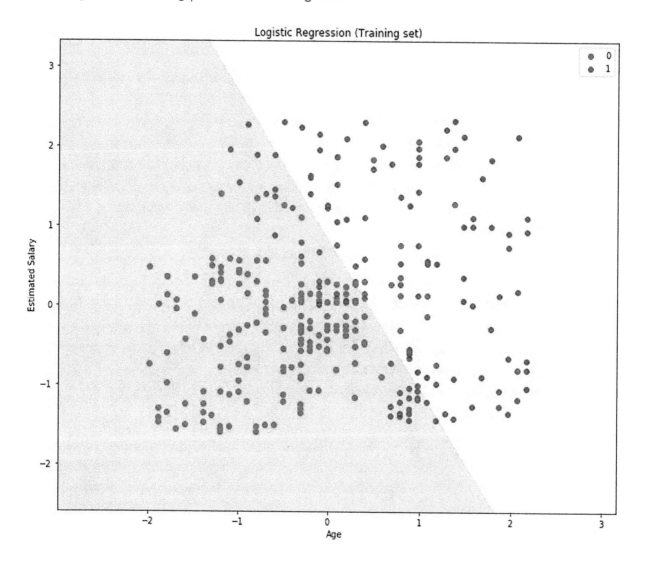

As we can see the split with 'yellow' coloured region marks the regression line.

Similarly, we plot for the test set and get the following result.

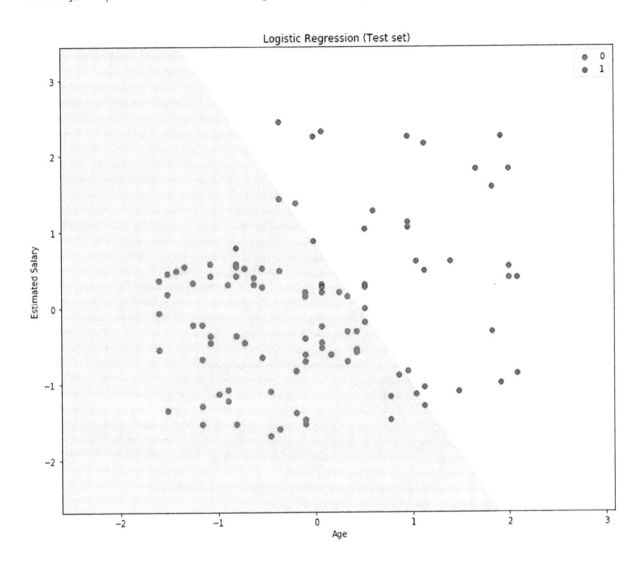

The LogisticRegression class can fit binary, one-vs-rest, or multinomial logistic regression with L2 or L1 regularisation. There are several types of optimisers that can be used - *liblinear* (default), *newton-cg*, *lbfgs*, *sag* and *saga*. The newton-cg, lbfgs and sag optimising algorithms only support L2 norm and converge faster for high dimensional dataset (high number of features).

## K-Nearest Neighbours

This classification algorithm classifies data points based on closest distance from neighbouring data points of a particular class. Here is a dataset consisting of data points belonging to tow classes -

Now a new data point in 'grey' is added to the plot. The task of the K-NN algorithm is to measure the euclidean or manhattan distance of the new data point with the nearest data points from both classes. The data points of the class closer to the new data will include it in the class.

We will perform K-NN on the same dataset used for logistic regression.

```
from sklearn.preprocessing import StandardScaler
scaler = StandardScaler()
X_train = scaler.fit_transform(X_train)
X_test = scaler.fit_transform(X_test)
```

```
from sklearn.neighbors import KNeighborsClassifier
classifier = KNeighborsClassifier(n_neighbors=5, metric='minkowski',p=2)
classifier.fit(X_train,Y_train)
```

```
KNeighborsClassifier(algorithm='auto', leaf_size=30, metric='minkowski',
        metric_params=None, n_jobs=1, n_neighbors=5, p=2,
        weights='uniform')
```

The *n_neighbors* parameter specifies the number of nearest data points to be compared. The default *metric* set to 'minkowski' with the power of the 'minkowski' metric, set to p = 2 is equivalent is the minkowski distance algorithm used for measuring distances between neighbours.

The plot for the test data is done the same way as that of logistic regression.

```python
# Visualising the Test set results
from matplotlib.colors import ListedColormap
X_age_range = np.arange(start = X_test[:, 0].min() - 1,
                        stop = X_test[:, 0].max() + 1, step = 0.01)
x_salary_range = np.arange(start = X_test[:, 1].min() - 1,
                           stop = X_test[:, 1].max() + 1, step = 0.01)

X1, X2 = np.meshgrid(X_age_range,x_salary_range)

X_plot = np.array([X1.ravel(), X2.ravel()]).T

plt.contourf(X1, X2, classifier.predict(X_plot).reshape(X1.shape),
             alpha = 0.75, cmap = ListedColormap(('gold', 'white')))


plt.xlim(X1.min(), X1.max())
plt.ylim(X2.min(), X2.max())
for i, j in enumerate(np.unique(Y_train)):
    choose_rows = (Y_test == j)
    plt.scatter(X_test[choose_rows, 0], X_test[choose_rows, 1],
                c = ListedColormap(('red', 'green'))(i), label = j)
plt.title('K-NN Regression (Test set)')
plt.xlabel('Age')
plt.ylabel('Estimated Salary')
plt.legend()
plt.show()
```

This is the generated plot -

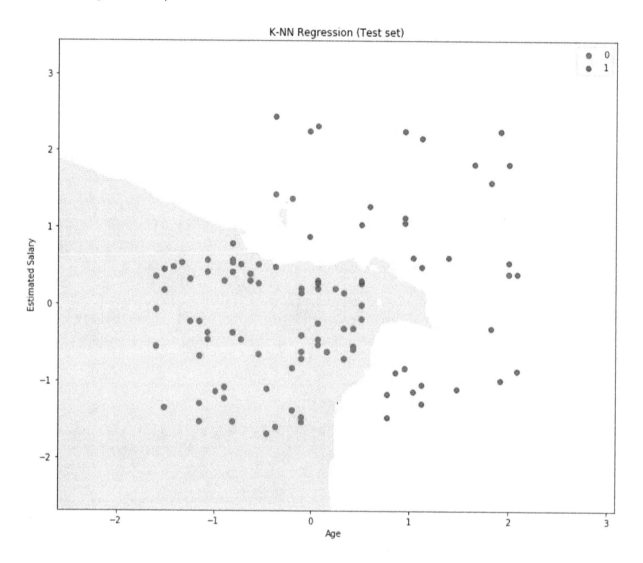

We can see the clear improvement over logistic regression as the decision boundary is not a straight line, thereby enabling it to create a distinct boundary for the classes.

There are three types of nearest neighbour algorithms - Brute force, K-D tree and Ball tree.

*Brute force algorithm* - This is a naive method where each pair of datapoint is compared for distances. For a point A, its distance is compared with all the n data points. This algorithm is competitive for small dataset, but becomes infeasible with the increase in dataset size.

*K-D tree* - This algorithm takes care of the redundant computations of brute force method, by applying efficiently efficiently storing the aggregate distance information in tree data structure. Suppose point A is at a distance x from point B and point C is closer to point A. Without having to calculate the distance between points B and C, it is known to the algorithm that point C is at around the same distance x from B. The K-D tree stores the distance values between points in a k-dimensional tree where each intermediate node has maximum k children. This algorithm is fast but it can get memory intensive with the increase in dimension of data.

*Ball tree* - To address the problems of K-D tree at higher dimensions, the ball tree was created. The ball tree partitions the data into a series of nesting hyper-spheres. The distance of each data point is measured and stored in the tree.

On the first iteration -

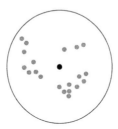

On the n-th iteration -

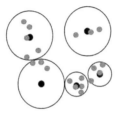

## Support Vector Machine (SVM)

We have already used SVM for regression problems, in support vector regression, and now we will understand its application in classification context. Let us refer to previously used plot -

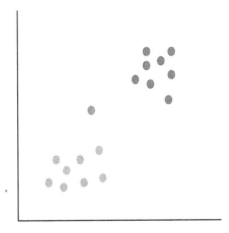

The general motive while classifying a data point is to compare it with properties of both classes and depending on the score of closeness to the properties of a class, the new data point (in grey) is assigned to a class. SVM takes a different perspective to this comparison. When a comparison is done in general, the idea is usually to compare with the best example of a class. Suppose, while finding if the image of an animal is either of the dogs class or cat class, it is compared with an image that is the best fitting example of each of the classes. SVM does this comparison with the least fitting example for each of the classes. It compares the differences between new data point and those data points belonging to a class, whose features are marginally differentiating them from the other classes. This gives the model trained with SVM, the knowledge about the extreme edge cases of a class. Therefore, it is known to the model, which cat looks more like a dog and vice-versa.

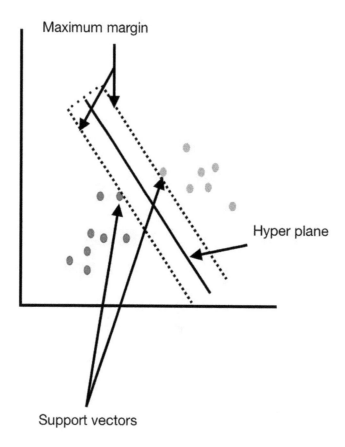

The data points at the extremities of either class are identified as the support vectors such that margin lines touching the vectors are equidistant from the decision boundary. These support vectors define the learning of the algorithm about the extreme edge cases. The reason these data points are referred to as vectors, because, each point is the representation of multiple dimensions i.e. features.

The decision boundary however is addressed with a special name called hyper-plane. A hyper-plane is a sub-space, whose dimension is one less than that of its ambient space (space in which it is existent). For a 2-D space, a hyper-plane is a 1-D line and for a 3-D space a hyper-plane is a 2-D plane. Here is an illustration of a 2-D hyper-plane (in green) -

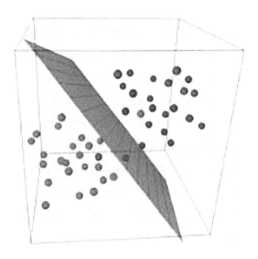

We will now implement SVM on the same dataset used before.

```
ds = pd.read_csv('Social_Network_Ads.csv')
X = ds.iloc[:, [2,3]].values
Y = ds.iloc[:, 4].values
```

```
from sklearn.cross_validation import train_test_split
X_train, X_test, Y_train, Y_test = train_test_split(X,Y,test_size=0.25,random_state=0)
```

```
from sklearn.preprocessing import StandardScaler
scaler = StandardScaler()
X_train = scaler.fit_transform(X_train)
X_test = scaler.fit_transform(X_test)
```

```
from sklearn.svm import SVC
classifier = SVC(kernel = 'linear', random_state = 0)
classifier.fit(X_train,Y_train)
```

```
SVC(C=1.0, cache_size=200, class_weight=None, coef0=0.0,
    decision_function_shape='ovr', degree=3, gamma='auto', kernel='linear',
    max_iter=-1, probability=False, random_state=0, shrinking=True,
    tol=0.001, verbose=False)
```

```
: Y_pred = classifier.predict(X_test)
```

We reuse the code used in previous classification examples, and get the following result -

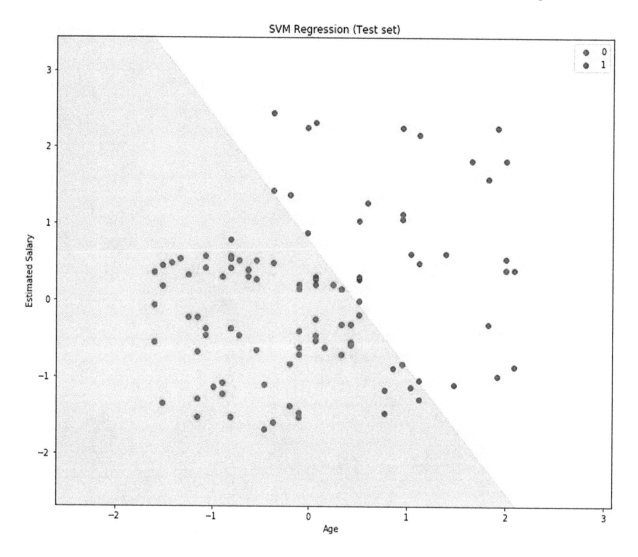

We have a linear decision boundary due to the *kernel* parameter of SVC constructor set to 'linear'.

The kernel method used in the above case was the default 'linear'. The other kernels available to the SVC class are *poly, rbf (radial basis function), sigmoid* and *precomputed*. A *kernel method* in machine learning, also referred to as the *kernel trick*, that enables a linear classifier to solve a problem that is linearly inseparable. Any linear model can be transformed into non-linear by applying a kernel trick. We came across the concept of kernel trick in support vector regression (SVR) and we will be discussing about it shortly.

When an *rbf* kernel is used, a non-linear decision boundary is created.

```
from sklearn.svm import SVC
classifier = SVC(kernel = 'rbf', random_state = 0)
classifier.fit(X_train,Y_train)
```

```
SVC(C=1.0, cache_size=200, class_weight=None, coef0=0.0,
    decision_function_shape='ovr', degree=3, gamma='auto', kernel='rbf',
    max_iter=-1, probability=False, random_state=0, shrinking=True,
    tol=0.001, verbose=False)
```

Here is the generated plot -

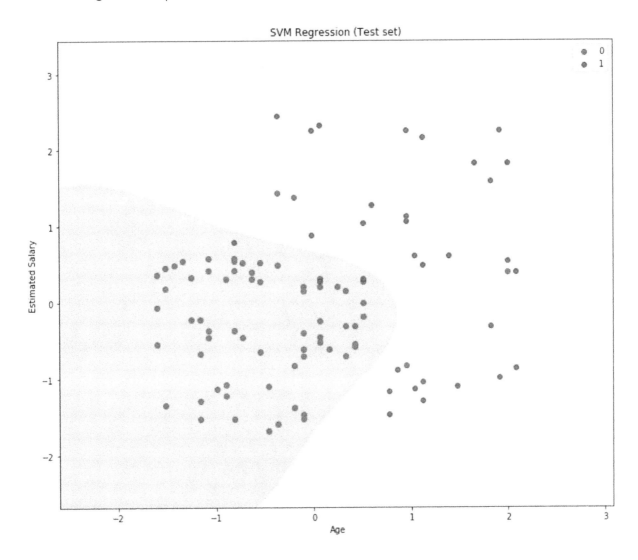

The model tells us about the number of support vectors that were used using the *n_support_* attribute. In this case it is 44 -

```
classifier.n_support_
```

```
array([44, 44], dtype=int32)
```

Similarly, on using the *poly* kernel, we get the following plot -

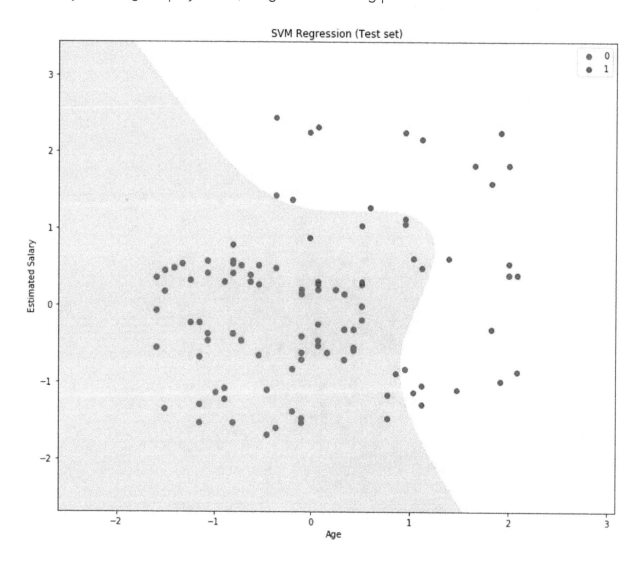

The *decision_function_shape* member variable of the SVC class defines how the comparison of classes are done using one of the two methods - one-versus-one (ovo) and one-versus-rest (ovr). In the ovo approach if there are n number of classes, then n * (n - 1) /2 classifiers are created and each one trains data from two classes.

SVMs can also be used to detect outliers using the OneClassSVM class. SVMs are effective in high dimensional spaces but do not directly provide probabilities like that of logistic regression and has to be calculated by setting the *probability* member variable to *True*.

## Kernel trick

In order to understand the kernel method or function and what is the kernel trick, we start with a few data plots that we have seen right at the beginning of the classification chapter of this book.

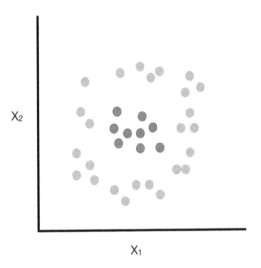

This is a linearly inseparable plot. A decision boundary for such a plot can be possible in the following way -

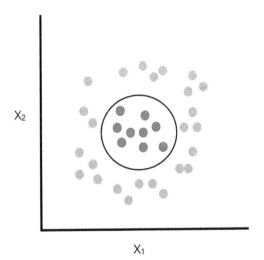

As we can see the decision boundary is not linear and obviously requires some non-linear classifier.

A kernel function would be able to utilise a linear classifier to separate this non-linearly separable data plot. In order to understand how it does so, we start with the simplest plot of data points on a 1-D plane i.e. a line.

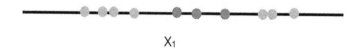

$X_1$

Such a plot is again non-linearly separable in its ambient space. The idea is to *look for separability in dimensions higher than the original* and so, this 1-D space is to be increased one more dimension and plotting the same points in 2-D.

Now in order to do that, the points on the 1-D space which only has one feature or dimension - $X_1$, has to have another dimension say $X_2$. Let the value for this extra dimension be calculated as $f(X_1) = X_1^2 = X_2$. The plot takes the following shape in 2-D -

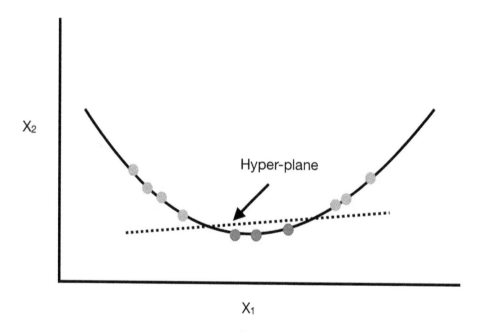

Surprisingly, now the 1-D hyper-plane is able to separate the classes. Now, let us introduce some more complexity to the plot points.

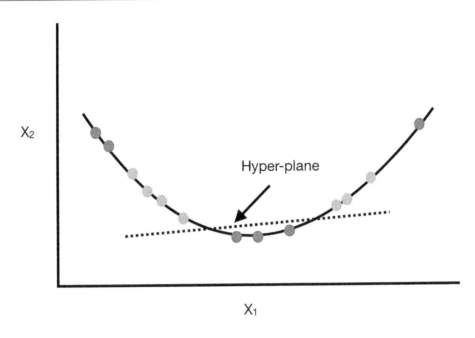

Again the points have become linearly inseparable as there is no way a single hyper-plane can separate the new red points. Therefore, we resort to looking up into a higher dimension and check if a separation is possible by adding $X_3$.

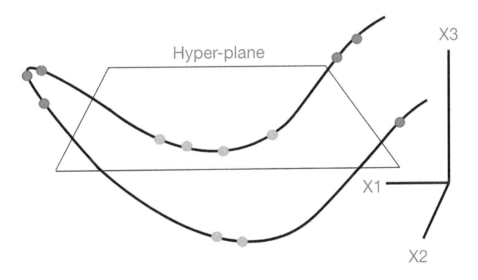

Now the data points are again separable with a 2-D hyper plane in a 3-D ambient space. We can see how the based on the arrangement of plotted points, the dimensions have to increased. This is the key inspiration behind the kernel trick.

Increasing the dimensions mean increasing the feature vector of $X = [X_1, X_2, X_3]$. Mapping to a new dimension means doing an inner product (dot product) of the existing dimensions with the new dimension. If we refer to our preliminary intuition about vectors in the first chapter, we know that a dot product between vectors a and b (a.b) implies how the vector a will be projected along the direction of the vector b. In our case when we are adding a new dimension $X_2$, there also has to be a dot product of X input vector to a vector in the direction of the target dimension. This dot product is basically matrix multiplication which can become computationally challenging. Therefore, in order to project a data point to higher dimensions there is some method required that bypasses the need for calculating the coordinates in higher dimension by performing inner products. It is this kernel trick that is performed by using kernel functions that calculates the new features $X_2$ and $X_3$ using a lower dimensional vector. The *kernel trick* is that mathematical shortcut that makes the effect of the required inner product implicit without requiring to actually perform it.

A kernel trick is performed by using any of the several kernel functions -

a) *Polynomial kernel*

$$k(x_i, x_j) = (x_i.x_j + 1)^d$$

Here d is the degree of the polynomial

b) *Gaussian kernel*

$$k(x_i, x_j) = e^{(- ||xi - xj||^2 / 2\sigma^2)}$$

c) *Gaussian radial basis kernel*

$$k(x_i, x_j) = e^{(- \gamma||xi - xj||^2)}$$

d) *Hyperbolic tangent kernel*

$$k(x_i, x_j) = \tanh(kx_i.x_j + c)$$

e) *Sigmoid kernel*

$$k(x_i, x_j) = \tanh(\alpha x_i^T.x_j + c)$$

These are among the most popular ones, and Gaussian RBF kernel is the most widely used. A kernel function therefore is in charge of performing the kernel trick and mapping a data point to a higher dimension.

Now, we will see the kernel function in action. A kernel function is basically a *similarity function* that finds the similarity between two points. As we know, the task of projecting a data point to another dimension is the vector inner product and therefore, the similarity test measures how much a vector is in the direction of the vector in the other dimension. A similarity test is conducted with a vector known as a land mark (L) and the result of the corresponding kernel function k(X, L) is closer to the value 1 if the data point given by vector x is closer to the land mark. For our example, we pick an arbitrary landmark from the plot -

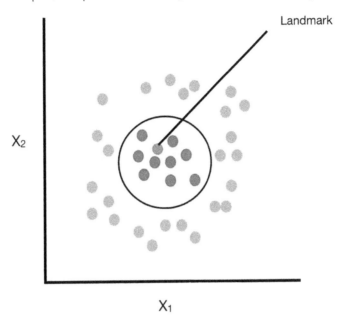

This is the effect of the RBF kernel at the landmark -

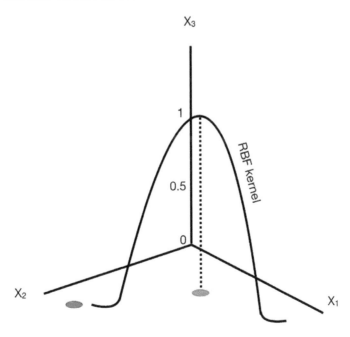

The closer/similar a data point (red) to the landmark (blue), the higher it climbs up the mound created by the Gaussian RBF. If a data point coincides with the landmark, the result of the kernel function is exactly 1. The kernel function measures the euclidean distance between the landmark and a data point as we can see from the expression -

$$K\left(\vec{x}, \vec{l^i}\right) = e^{-\frac{\left\|\vec{x}-\vec{l^i}\right\|^2}{2\sigma^2}}$$

The denominator $2\sigma^2$ controls the circumference of the base of the gaussian curve and is directly proportional to the value of $\sigma$.

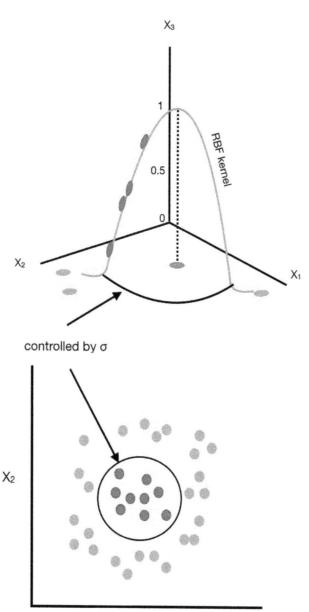

## Naive Bayes classifier

This is a classification method which from the name we can infer, that it is based upon the Bayes theorem and we will at first recap the theorem.

Bayes theorem measures the conditional probability of an event. Suppose there are two bags containing mangoes. The bag B1 has 30 mangoes and bag B2 has 20. Out of all the mangoes, only 1% are defective and 50% of the defective mangoes come from B1 and 50% from B2. The task now is to find the probability that a mango from bag B2 is defective.

The total number of mangoes = 30 + 20 = 50
The probability of a defective mango from bag B1 = 30/50 = 0.6
The probability of a defective mango from B2 = 20/50 = 0.4
The probability of a defective mango = P(Defect) = 1%
The conditional probability that a mango is defective, given that it is from B1 = P(B1 | Defect) = 50%
The conditional probability that a mango is defective, given that it is from B2 = P(B2 | Defect) = 50%
We have to find, the conditional probability that a mango from B2 is defective = P(Defect | B2)

The essence of the Bayes theorem lies in finding the probability of an event predicated upon a condition being satisfied. Here that predefined condition is the bag being B2 and the probability of a mango being defective has to be found. According to the formula for the Bayes theorem -

$$P(Defect \mid B2) = \frac{P(B2 \mid Defect) * P(Defect)}{P(B2)}$$

This formula can also be written as -

$$Posterior\ probability = \frac{Likelihood * Prior}{Marginal\ likelihood}$$

The *marginal likelihood* is the stated evidence, which in this case is the stated fact that the mango is from bag B2. The *prior* probability is the knowledge of an event before performing further tests, which in this case is the probability of defective mangoes. Likelihood states the probability of the event B2 happening given event Defect is already stated.

Now we take this brief introduction and apply to solving classification problem. We can refer to the same dataset which we have been using, but we will now approach the problem from a slightly different perspective. From the classification with SVM we got the following plot -

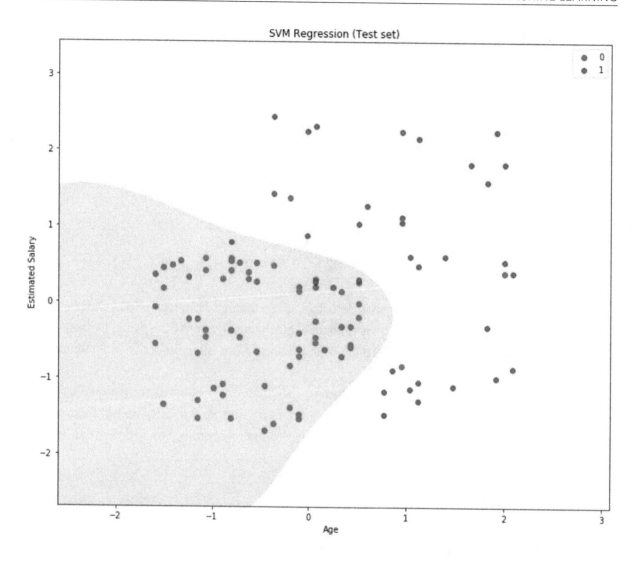

The members of the two classes distinguished as red who do not buy a social advertisement and green who buy an advertisement. From a Bayes theorem's perspective, the probability of belonging to a class is expressed as P(red | X) where X is the features age and salary, and similarly p(green | X) for the other class. The reason it is called *naive Bayes* because the classification simply depends on comparison of the probability values from each of the classes or events. For each data tuple, both a conditional probability is calculated for each of the classes and the one with the highest value wins.

Here is the code for this classification -

```
ds = pd.read_csv('Social_Network_Ads.csv')
X = ds.iloc[:, [2,3]].values
Y = ds.iloc[:, 4].values
```

```
from sklearn.cross_validation import train_test_split
X_train, X_test, Y_train, Y_test = train_test_split(X,Y,test_size=0.25,random_state=0)
```

```
from sklearn.preprocessing import StandardScaler
scaler = StandardScaler()
X_train = scaler.fit_transform(X_train)
X_test = scaler.fit_transform(X_test)
```

```
from sklearn.naive_bayes import GaussianNB
classifier = GaussianNB()
classifier.fit(X_train,Y_train)
```

```
GaussianNB(priors=None)
```

```
Y_pred = classifier.predict(X_test)
```

and the visualisation of the result -

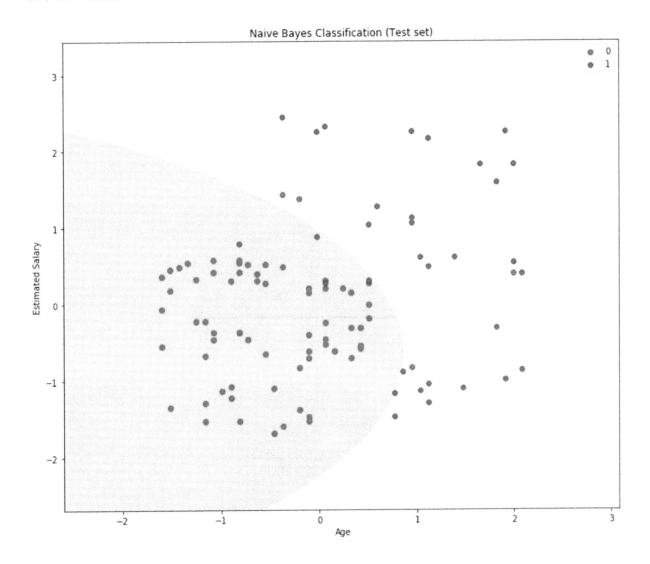

As we can see the naive Bayes method used here is the GaussianNB, which is a variant among the other two types -*multinomial naive Bayes* and *complement naive Bayes*. The se naive Bayes classifiers performs very well in text classification jobs such as spam filter. The multinomial naive Bayes classifier is suited for discrete features such as word counts for text classification, but complement naive Bayes which is an adaptation of multinomial method, outperforms this in text classification tasks. Multinomial method is also best suited for imbalanced datasets, i.e. datasets that do not account for all the edge cases alongside the regular cases for training a model.

## Decision Tree classification

We already had an introduction to decision trees during regression and now we will use decision trees for classification purposes.

Suppose we have a plot as the following, the classification would involve breaking up the data points into separate classes as leaves on a decision tree.

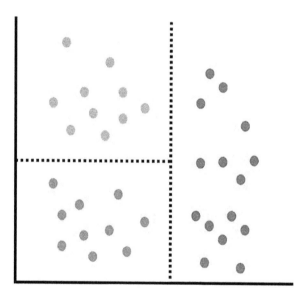

The code to implement this -

```
ds = pd.read_csv('Social_Network_Ads.csv')
X = ds.iloc[:, [2,3]].values
Y = ds.iloc[:, 4].values
```

```
from sklearn.cross_validation import train_test_split
X_train,X_test,Y_train,Y_test = train_test_split(X,Y,test_size=0.25,random_state=0)
```

```
from sklearn.preprocessing import StandardScaler
scaler = StandardScaler()
X_train = scaler.fit_transform(X_train)
X_test = scaler.fit_transform(X_test)
```

```
: from sklearn.tree import DecisionTreeClassifier
  classifier = DecisionTreeClassifier(criterion='entropy', random_state=0)
  classifier.fit(X_train,Y_train)

: DecisionTreeClassifier(class_weight=None, criterion='entropy', max_depth=None,
              max_features=None, max_leaf_nodes=None,
              min_impurity_decrease=0.0, min_impurity_split=None,
              min_samples_leaf=1, min_samples_split=2,
              min_weight_fraction_leaf=0.0, presort=False, random_state=0,
              splitter='best')

: Y_pred = classifier.predict(X_test)
```

The plot will look quite different from what we have seen so far -

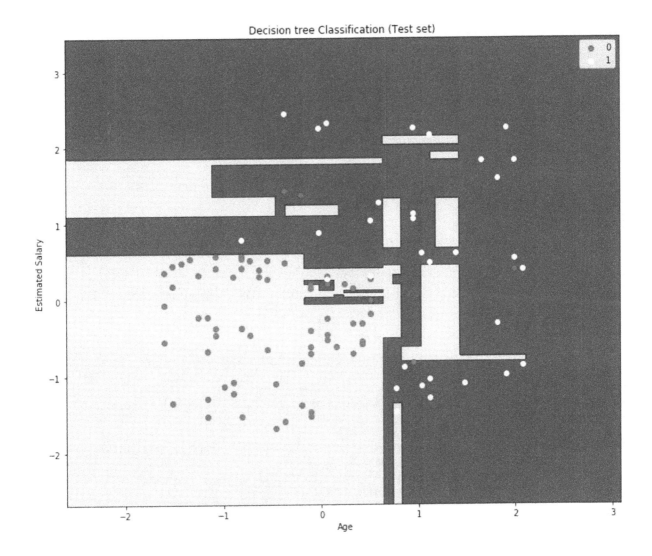

The sections marked with yellow represent the class of people who did not buy the advertisement i.e. data points in red and the sections marked by blue are the ones who did buy.

The model generated the above classification plot based upon *information gain entropy* as specified in the criterion parameter of *DecisionTreeClassifier*. The other option is *gini impurity/index*. In order to understand the significance of each of these, we have to understand the role of entropy in decision trees.

Given a dataset, the task of a decision tree classification is to be able segregate data items according specified labels or classes. The training phase begins with data tuples from all classes belonging to a single group. At this state the entropy is highest and the decision tree has comprises of just the root node. The motive of branching is to reduce the entropy at each step. Suppose root node contains 50% data tuples from class A and 50% from class B. Either of the nodes that split and originated from the root node, contains the some percentage of data tuples less from other other class. Say the node on left has data 70% data tuples from class A and 30% from class B, while the right child node has 60% from class B and 40% from class A. This is an improvement in ordered state and reduction of entropy. There are two major types of algorithms for building decision trees - a) ID3 (Interactive Dichotimizer 3) uses entropy function and information gain, b) CART (Classification And Regression Trees) uses gini impurity. A decision tree is built based on the choice of an attribute upon which a node will be split. A chosen attribute best splits the data into its cleanest possible children nodes and it is this purity (containing data items only from a single class) of the data items in each node which is called *information*. Entropy on the other hand is a measure of impurity and therefore, the *entropy function* reaches its maximum value when data items from both classes have 50% share in a node. The difference in entropy before and entropy after a split into child nodes is called the *information gain*.

The *gini* impurity/index is another metric used for measuring the goodness of a classification. *Gini* index does this by selecting items from a population of data elements in a node at random and calculating the probability that they belong to the same class. Higher the value of the index, the greater is the homogeneity of data tuples of a particular label/class.

For our dataset, when we use *gini* for the criterion parameter, we get the following plot -

```
classifier = DecisionTreeClassifier(criterion='gini', random_state=0)
classifier.fit(X_train,Y_train)
```

```
DecisionTreeClassifier(class_weight=None, criterion='gini', max_depth=None,
            max_features=None, max_leaf_nodes=None,
            min_impurity_decrease=0.0, min_impurity_split=None,
            min_samples_leaf=1, min_samples_split=2,
            min_weight_fraction_leaf=0.0, presort=False, random_state=0,
            splitter='best')
```

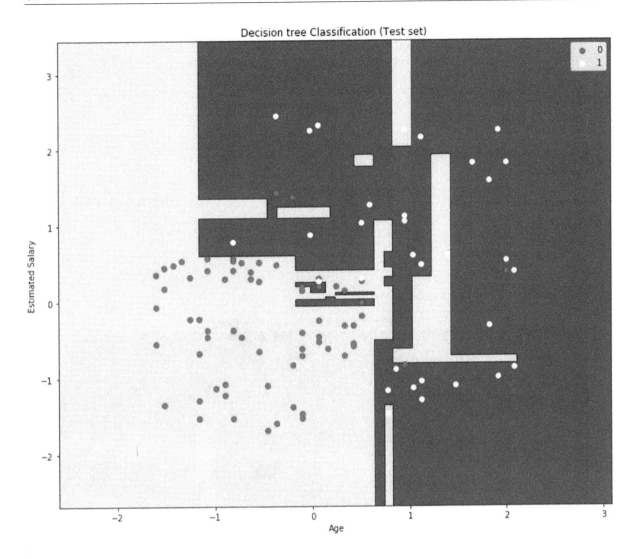

Decision tree Classification (Test set)

## *Random Forest classification*

We learnt about ensemble learning in regression with Random forest regression and here we will be using the same technique but for classification purposes. The intuition for Random forest classification being, rather than relying on the classification of one decision tree classifier, a collective decision from a forest of decision trees generates a better and more reliable result.

It works by pre-setting the desired number of trees in the forest, and then each tree is created by randomly selecting k data points. For making a prediction, each tree casts a vote and the majority of the predicted class wins.

Here is the code snippet for such classifier -

```
from sklearn.ensemble import RandomForestClassifier
classifier = RandomForestClassifier(n_estimators=10,criterion='entropy')
classifier.fit(X_train,Y_train)
```

```
RandomForestClassifier(bootstrap=True, class_weight=None, criterion='entropy',
            max_depth=None, max_features='auto', max_leaf_nodes=None,
            min_impurity_decrease=0.0, min_impurity_split=None,
            min_samples_leaf=1, min_samples_split=2,
            min_weight_fraction_leaf=0.0, n_estimators=10, n_jobs=1,
            oob_score=False, random_state=None, verbose=0,
            warm_start=False)
```

```
: Y_pred = classifier.predict(X_test)
```

```
: from sklearn.metrics import confusion_matrix
  cm = confusion_matrix(Y_test,Y_pred)
  cm
```

```
: array([[64,  4],
         [ 4, 28]])
```

The visualisation of the prediction -

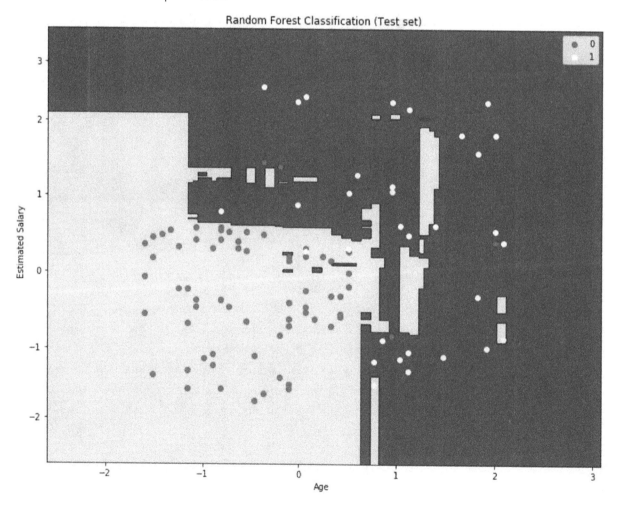

The random forest classifier is a fast method and the above plot, for which we have been using the same dataset so far, shows significant improvements.

# Model evaluation and selection

We have seen the usage of several classification techniques. The accuracy of the prediction made by a trained model, is dependant on the type of the classifier chosen based upon the target dataset. The example dataset used for classification tasks are same for all the types of classifiers used - Logistic, K-Nearest, SVC, Naive Bayes, etc. and the corresponding visualisation for the performance of the classifier gave us an idea about which classifier yields the best result. The *random forest classifier* stood out to be the best one in our case, but that should not misguide us into thinking the random forest method is best for all cases. Therefore, it becomes a very important exercise to have some mechanism for comparison among the prediction results generated by each of the type of classifier.

The confusion matrix gives an account of a model's performance in terms of the ratios of false positives, false negatives, true positives and true negatives. But the result of a confusion matrix isn't enough. Suppose we have following confusion matrix as produced from random forest classification -

```
array([[64,  4],
       [ 4, 28]])
```

| | Predicted | |
|---|---|---|
| Actual | 0 | 1 |
| 0 | 64 | 4 |
| 1 | 4 | 28 |

This matrix declares 64 true negatives and 28 true positives, and 4 false negative as well as false positive.

The accuracy percentage is of correct predictions = total number of correct predictions / total number of predictions.

$$(64+28) / (64+28+4+4) = 92/100 = 92\%.$$

Now suppose, we want to check if this accuracy holds true for all scenarios and so we mask one class in a binary classification considering that all the false positives will be considered true negative and the true positives are considered as false negatives.

| Actual | Predicted | |
|---|---|---|
| | **0** | **1** |
| **0** 64+4 | | 0 |
| **1** 28+4 | | 0 |

As we may have guessed that such a step should affect and reduce the accuracy and accordingly the accuracy reduces to (64+4) / 100 = 68%. We expect such an effect to be consistent for all volumes of dataset but the next example will show the contrary.

Say we have a confusion matrix from prediction on some dataset -

| Actual | Predicted | |
|---|---|---|
| | **0** | **1** |
| **0** | 9700 | 150 |
| **1** | 50 | 100 |

The accuracy percentage = (9,700 + 100) / (9,700+100+150+50) = 9,800 / 10,000 = 98%.

Now we do the same merging of actual and false data as before such that the matrix becomes the following -

| Actual | Predicted | |
|---|---|---|
| | **0** | **1** |
| **0** 9700+150 | | 0 |
| **1** 50+100 | | 0 |

The accuracy percentage = 9,850/10,000 = 98.5%

We can see the anomaly as the accuracy percentage has increased by 0.5%. This is suggestive that confusion matrix is not completely reliable and in order to have a consistent measurement that holds true for all cases, we will be using another method called the *Cumulative Accuracy Profile (CAP)* analysis.

The CAP analysis works by asking questions such as how accurate a model is in predicting the outcome between the ideal situation, when it can be determined for which data tuples the outcome will be positive and the random situation. To understand this, we have to take an example of our classification dataset of buying social advertisement. A model trained for that dataset, predicts whether a person buys an advertisement based on the factors age, gender and salary. The actual dataset of users, using which a model is trained, it is found always that say 10% of the users buy the advertisement. Therefore, a frequency plot is drawn from this 10% average rate of buying based on the population of users targeted with the advertisement.

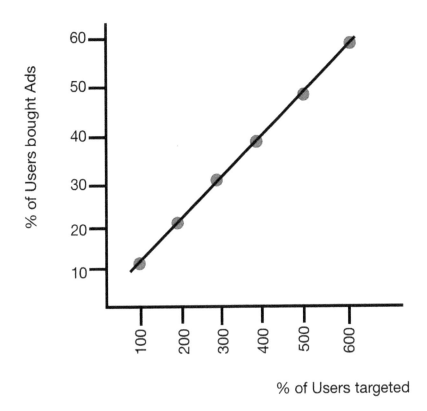

This case can be called the random state as the advertisement was targeted to users randomly without selecting based on some criteria. The purpose of the machine learning model is to be able to predict if a user would buy an advertisement and so the advertisement campaign can become for effective targeted at first toward those selected users who are most likely to buy the advertisement.

A perfect model's outcome would be to exactly predict which users would buy the advertisement and so only those users can be sent the advertisement for a 100% success rate. This shall look something like this -

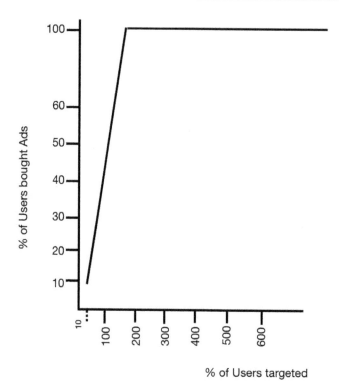

The choice of a model will be based upon the closeness of a prediction with the ideal case. Here is such a sample plot of user responses to the advertisement when the users are chosen based on the prediction of a model.

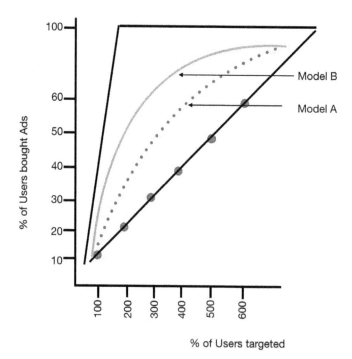

It is evident from the above plot that model B is better choice than model A. The accuracy is calculated as a ratio between the area under the ideal curve w.r.t. random curve and area under the model's curve w.r.t. random curve.

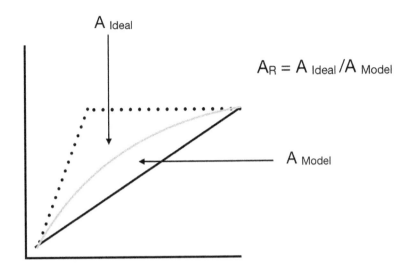

The closer the ratio is to 1, better is the model. We will do this analysis on the model fit with decision tree classifier.

```
from sklearn.tree import DecisionTreeClassifier
classifier = DecisionTreeClassifier(criterion='gini', random_state=0)
classifier.fit(X_train,Y_train)
```

```
from scipy import integrate
def capcurve(y_values, y_preds_proba):
    #Calculating the ideal curve datapoints for 'rate_pos_obs'
    # percent of users
    num_pos_obs = np.sum(y_values)
    num_count = len(y_values)
    rate_pos_obs = float(num_pos_obs) / float(num_count)
    ideal = pd.DataFrame({'x':[0,rate_pos_obs,1],'y':[0,1,1]})
    xx = np.arange(num_count) / float(num_count - 1)

    y_cap = np.c_[y_values,y_preds_proba]
    y_cap_df_s = pd.DataFrame(data=y_cap)
    y_cap_df_s = y_cap_df_s.sort_values([1], ascending=False)

    yy = np.cumsum(y_cap_df_s[0]) / float(num_pos_obs)
    yy = np.append([0], yy[0:num_count-1])

    percent = 0.5
    row_index = int(np.trunc(num_count * percent))
```

```python
        val_y1 = yy[row_index]
        val_y2 = yy[row_index+1]
        if val_y1 == val_y2:
            val = val_y1*1.0
        else:
            val_x1 = xx[row_index]
            val_x2 = xx[row_index+1]
            val = val_y1 + ((val_x2 - percent)/(val_x2 - val_x1))*(val_y2 - val_y1)


#Area under the ideal curve
sigma_ideal = 1 * xx[num_pos_obs - 1 ] / 2 + (xx[num_count - 1] - xx[num_pos_obs]) * 1
#Area under the selected model's curve
sigma_model = integrate.simps(yy,xx)
#Area under the random curve
sigma_random = integrate.simps(xx,xx)

#Accuracy ratio
ar_value = (sigma_model - sigma_random) / (sigma_ideal - sigma_random)


#Plotting the curves
fig, ax = plt.subplots(nrows = 1, ncols = 1)

ax.plot(ideal['x'],ideal['y'], color='grey', label='Ideal Model')

ax.plot(xx,yy, color='red', label='Random-Forest Model')

ax.plot(xx,xx, color='blue', label='Random Model')

ax.plot([percent, percent], [0.0, val], color='green', linestyle='--', linewidth=1)
ax.plot([0, percent], [val, val], color='green', linestyle='--',
        linewidth=1, label=str(val*100)+'% of positive obs at '+str(percent*100)+'%')

plt.xlim(0, 1.02)
plt.ylim(0, 1.25)
plt.title("CAP Curve - accuracy ratio ="+str(ar_value))
plt.xlabel('% of the users selected')
plt.ylabel('% of users bought ads')
plt.legend()
plt.show()
```

This is the function definition to calculate and plot the CAP curves. We are using Simpson's rule to calculate the are under the curve using the method *integrate.simps()*.

```
from matplotlib.pyplot import rcParams
rcParams['figure.figsize'] = 12,10
Y_pred_proba = classifier.predict_proba(X=X_test)
capcurve(y_values=Y_test, y_preds_proba=Y_pred_proba[:,1])
```

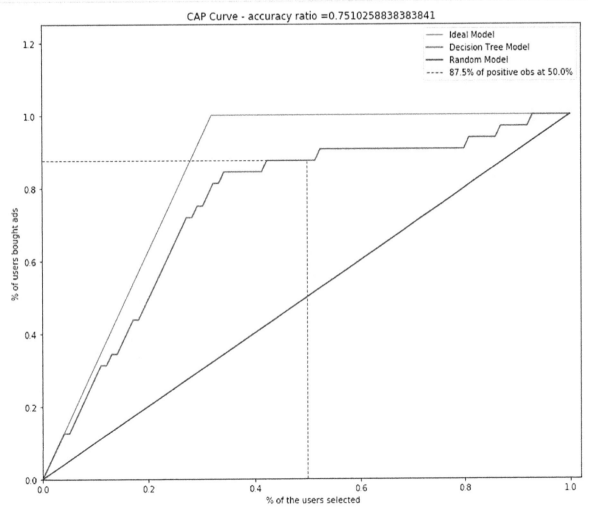

The green line shows that 87.5% of the users are likely to buy the ads when targeted to 50% of the users and this gives us a good estimation of the users to choose for an advertisement campaign. If we compare this accuracy with random forest classification model, we get the following CAP curve -

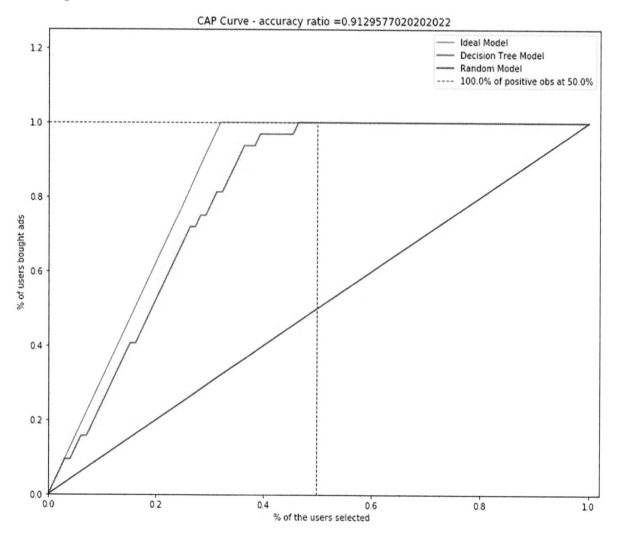

The random forest classifier as we can see, stands out to be a very good model for our dataset.

Although CAP analysis is a better metric to measure model goodness than confusion matrix, there still remains another problem that needs to be corrected in the process of select ing the best model. The dataset we have used is based upon actual data collected for user behaviour for buying advertisements and it is yet to ensure that our classification model is not overfit. We discussed methods to handle overfitting in regression problems, and similarly, for classification problems we are going to use *K-fold cross-validation* for checking the goodness of a model against overfitting.

The approach we take to verify prediction performance on the same dataset by reserving a portion of data for only testing purposes and rest is used for training. This does not completely ensure that the resulting model is generalized because the hyper-parameters could have been tuned to get an optimum result. We can think of partitioning the dataset into yet another group reserved for testing after tuning of hyper-parameters have been done conservatively (avoiding overfitting). But partitioning the dataset would lead to less amount of data for training. The solution to such a problem is to keep the splitting of dataset into just two groups, training and testing as before and, applying the procedure of *cross-validation*.

In K-fold cross-validation, the dataset is split into k smaller sets and for each such set the following steps are preformed -

a) A model is trained using k - 1 sets as training data.
b) The resulting model is then is tested with the remaining 1 set.

The final result of the cross validation process is the average of the prediction scores for all of the k sets. Based on such score, we can decide if the classification model is good for our use. Although such validation process is computationally expensive, it solves the problem of compensation of training data for comparatively smaller datasets.

The first function and the simplest way of finding cross-validation scores is by using the *cross_val_score* method.

```
import numpy as np
import pandas as pd
```

```
ds = pd.read_csv('Social_Network_Ads.csv')
X = ds.iloc[:, [2,3]].values
Y = ds.iloc[:, 4].values
```

```
from sklearn.cross_validation import train_test_split
X_train,X_test,Y_train,Y_test = train_test_split(X,Y,test_size=0.25,random_state=0)
```

```
from sklearn.preprocessing import StandardScaler
scaler = StandardScaler()
X_train = scaler.fit_transform(X_train)
X_test = scaler.fit_transform(X_test)
```

```
from sklearn.svm import SVC
from sklearn.model_selection import cross_val_score

classifier = SVC(kernel = 'rbf', random_state = 0)
scores = cross_val_score(classifier,X_train,Y_train,cv=10)
```

```
scores
```

```
array([0.80645161, 0.96666667, 0.8       , 0.93333333, 0.86666667,
       0.83333333, 0.93333333, 0.93333333, 0.96666667, 0.96551724])
```

```
: print("Accuracy: %0.2f (+/- %0.2f)" % (scores.mean(), scores.std() * 2))

  Accuracy: 0.90 (+/- 0.13)
```

The other function for calculating the cross-validation score is *cross_validate* which allows specifying separate metrics for evaluation such as accuracy and precision. It also returns more metrics than *cross_val_score*.

```
from sklearn.model_selection import cross_validate

scores = cross_validate(classifier,X_train,Y_train,scoring=['accuracy','precision'],cv=10)
```

```
pd.DataFrame.from_dict(scores)
```

|   | fit_time | score_time | test_accuracy | test_precision | train_accuracy | train_precision |
|---|----------|------------|---------------|----------------|----------------|-----------------|
| 0 | 0.004029 | 0.002914 | 0.806452 | 0.687500 | 0.921933 | 0.875000 |
| 1 | 0.003268 | 0.002330 | 0.966667 | 1.000000 | 0.907407 | 0.844037 |
| 2 | 0.003119 | 0.002010 | 0.800000 | 0.727273 | 0.918519 | 0.848214 |
| 3 | 0.002996 | 0.002540 | 0.933333 | 0.909091 | 0.903704 | 0.842593 |
| 4 | 0.003169 | 0.001918 | 0.866667 | 0.769231 | 0.918519 | 0.867925 |
| 5 | 0.003210 | 0.001886 | 0.833333 | 0.800000 | 0.907407 | 0.844037 |
| 6 | 0.003080 | 0.002131 | 0.933333 | 0.846154 | 0.907407 | 0.850467 |
| 7 | 0.002751 | 0.001945 | 0.933333 | 0.846154 | 0.907407 | 0.850467 |
| 8 | 0.002888 | 0.001735 | 0.966667 | 1.000000 | 0.907407 | 0.837838 |
| 9 | 0.002503 | 0.001573 | 0.965517 | 0.916667 | 0.904059 | 0.842593 |

A complete list of metrics is available here -

# Unsupervised learning

All the machine learning algorithms for regression and classification problems, that we have discussed so far in this book, were based on a common method of learning a model. The methodology involved a three step generic process of gathering data containing the input - output of a function, building a mathematic model with statistical tools through training on that data and reduction of the error in approximation by the model. The whole process of learning is predicated upon learning through training, with real examples of the objective function. A model learns the behaviour of a target function based solely upon the training dataset and therefore the corner stone of creating a good model, assuming a good choice of objective function (type of regressor or classifier) has been made, is to gather enough data for the training process such that it generally reflects the behaviour of the function to future inputs. This method of learning is called *supervised learning*.

*Supervised learning* has been rightly named, as the model that gets trained, is dependant on the volume and quality of the labelled training dataset. We can relate easily to such method of learning, as it is similar to the way a teacher trains a student. All the algorithms for supervised learning have their own strengths and weaknesses and there are broadly four types of issues that we have to consider while choosing a learning algorithm. We already know about these, yet here is a summary of for recapitulation -

## Bias-Variance trade-off

We have learnt how a model is able to make good predictions based upon the fine tuning of bias and variance with L1 & L2 regularisation. A model trained with dataset values representing high bias causes the model to *underfit* i.e. to miss a desired outcome by a consistent margin. On the other hand if a model is trained on a dataset that is high on variance, it will give rise to the *overfitting* problem, where the model accounts for not just the fluctuations but outliers as well. The resulting trained model will be trained specific to the training dataset and not be a generic model that performs consistently for all types of future inputs for prediction.

## Function complexity and amount of training data

This is an extension of the previous point as a model the complexity of a model increases with the increasing focus to account variance in a dataset. The more a model will try to change its weights to accommodate fluctuations, the more it would fixated on the training dataset. Even if the error gets reduced through overfitting, it would perform badly on new datasets. But there a trade-off between the amount of training data and overfitting. If the training dataset is carefully gathered in greater amount that accounts for all types of inputs and outputs, the resulting overfit model would be a good one as it has fit a model for majority of the possible reactions from the target function. In such as setting, the resulting model is not an overfit one, but rather a good fit. On the other hand if the training dataset is small in amount, it would not contain the variety of reactions from the target function and so, it becomes important for a model to not indulge in inclusion of fluctuations. Therefore, a simple model can provide good generalised outcome upon training with a small dataset.

## Dimensionality of predictors

A fairly good amount of dataset is desirable for training a good model, but not all signals from the input space is necessary. Imagine a scenario where, a human worker is trying to learn how a machine with a lot of switches and moving parts work. The machine has an input panel consisting of a number of switches that start the machine. The input switches have redundancies as fail safe, dependence upon the ON state of other switches, and also dummy switches that serve no purpose. Such a setup is more like a maze and would take an absolute knowledge able person who knows the exact combination of the switches to get the machine working. Although such an example is unfit in real world, but just for the sake of analogy, we can sufficiently state that it is an utter confusion for a learner to work the machine and the ideal solution would be to first get rid of the unnecessary input switches. Similarly, through dimensionality reduction we attempt reduce the input space of a dataset, keeping only the significant ones.

## Noise in output

In supervised learning there are situations when a model cannot be trained to account for all of the data values in the dataset resulting in error or noise in the output. One type of noise categorised as *stochastic noise* exists when there are fluctuations in the data and it is not modelled to avoid fitting outliers. There is another type of noise known as *deterministic noise*, when say a subset of the dataset contains complex features and would attribute to the complexity of the model. Here is a representation of stochastic noise -

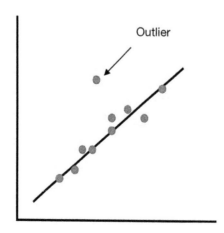

and deterministic noise would be introduced into model if the model was trained according to the dotted line as shown below -

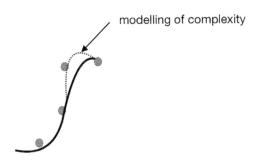

modelling of complexity

Attempting to fit data for both of the types of noises lead to overfitting.

In machine learning, a contrasting learning method exists in the form of *unsupervised learning*, in which, a model learns from data that is not labelled or classified. Before getting into details about how it works, let us take an example with the procedure of human learning in an unsupervised setting.

Suppose we are given a task of categorising the items in a mixed bag upon the pretext that none of the items are known to us. This is quite similar to the scenario of being taught about various fruits, vegetables, or things in general, when we were in schools. Our usual process of learning involves a teacher guiding on a subject matter. We are carefully taught about the subject matter not only with examples that describe and consolidate our understanding, but also, provided the knowledge of the error state or wrong answer. So if a teacher is teaching us about the items inside the bag, the identity of any particular item, which is also its label, will be provided by the teacher. It is based upon the description about each item and its corresponding label, we learn about an item. In order to teach about an apple, a good number of apple images as well as actual apples have to be shown. Our understanding of an apple becomes concrete when we have seen apples that have less apple like features but still are apples. Similar in the case of supervised learning, where it is upon the data scientist to choose the dataset carefully when training a model, to include both examples that represent the correct answer and also noisy data.

Now let us contemplate the scenario, when we have the task of learning about the items in a mixed by without the guidance of a teacher.

Each time an item is taken out of the bag, its features are to be registered visually in our mind without the knowledge of its label. The items in the bag are not all of unique types. We are in the process of categorizing the items and only when a new item is encountered, its features are recorded. For each unique item a label is assigned by our brain. This label is ofcourse not the original one but an arbitrary identifier for the object. When an item comes up that has been previously encountered and classified, it is kept in a group with its kind. The operation that our brain is performing is same as that of what classification algorithms do, which is to compare attributes between our acquired knowledge and the fetched item.

In an unsupervised setup, the knowledge is acquired about an item's attributes when it is first encountered and from then on, the learning comes from observed commonalities and dissimilarities. In grouping the items from the bag, whenever an item is fetched, its attributes are compared to the currently established distinct classes/groups. It is to be assumed that all the items of one group are not absolutely identical, and so when majority of the attributes match a group, our brain learns from the portion of dissimilarities in the item. Also, the very act of comparison with distinct groups accounts for knowledge from dissimilarities alongside partial similarities, for example, an item may have some attributes that are similar to that of multiple groups. In such a scenario, the presence and absence of similarities contributes to the knowledge.

In order for a machine to learn classification from an unsupervised scenario, it has to learn as a human does. In the example of bag and items, the items grouped together undergoes a *clustering* operation. It will easier for us to understand if we visualize the example not as a items inside a bag that is taken out one at a time, but, all the items scattered on the floor. Classification among items and grouping results in the items forming clusters. There are machine learning algorithms that perform such clustering and based on these clusters, perform prediction.

## K-means cluster

To understand the workings of this algorithm, let us first visualise a scatter plot.

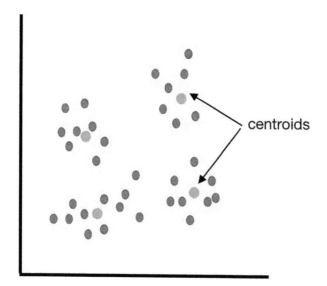

In the above plot, the centroids (green) are those points around which cluster of data points are formed. Although this is not the only configuration in which the clusters can be formed. The above plot is segregated into four clusters, and below are two more configurations.

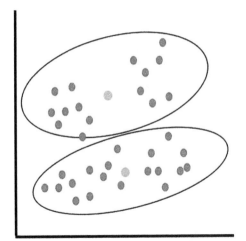 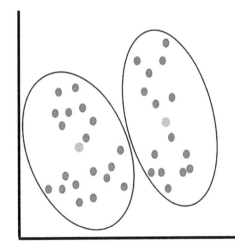

The choice of the number of classes or clusters are dependant on the number of centroids. The k-means clustering algorithm starts with pre-setting the *k* number of clusters that we want to form. Each cluster has a centroid and the intuition behind forming the clusters is adjustment of the centroid positions w.r.t. their euclidean distances from the points. Initially, the clustering process sets k random points as centroids. Each data point is assigned to a class depending on its distance from a particular centroid. Therefore, the data points are clustered in k groups based upon k centroids. This is an iterative process where in the first iteration the mean of the distances of the points around a centroid is calculated and then the position of the centroids are shifted in the direction that reduces the mean distance from the points. This sum of squared distances inside a cluster is also called *inertia*. The aim of the k-means algorithm is to reduce this *inertia* per cluster till a threshold is met. The centroids are placed randomly in the initial step, which it leads to a certain problem. Say we choose value for k=3. The data points can be clustered in a few different arrangements, such that the algorithm would generate different cluster configuration each time. This is due to the randomly chosen initial positions of the centroids, and here is an example of two such configurations -

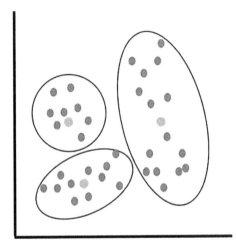 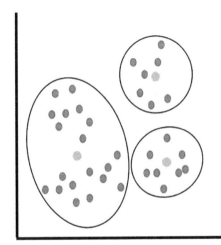

In order to tackle this problem of cluster initialization, the k-means algorithm is updated to use a weighted probability distribution to select a centroid and is called *k-means++*. In case of k-means clustering there is another uncertainty that we have to overcome, and which is, choosing the sufficient number of clusters or the value for *k*. The previous plots for the clusters have shown us how the example data points can be clustered with four, three and also two centroids. We are going to use something known as the *elbow* method to select the number of centroids.

The mean squared distance of a centroid from the points in its cluster decreases with the increase in the number of centroids. Here is cluster with one centroid -

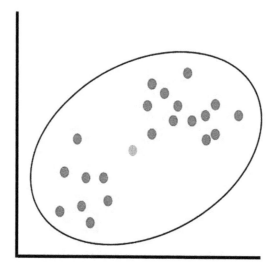

Now the mean squared distance will be reduced if this one cluster is broken into two.

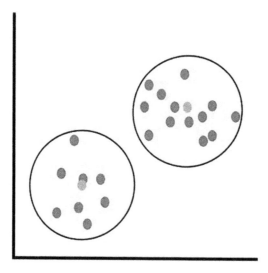

As the mean keeps decreasing, if plotted, it generates the following generic graph -

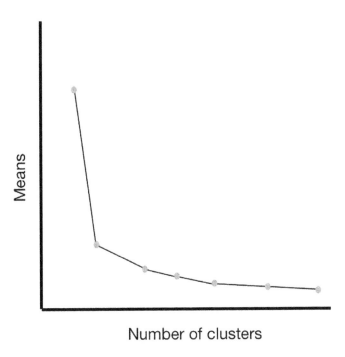

After the first three splits of the data points (increase in centroids), the within cluster square sum reduces at a gradual rate and flattens. The previously mentioned *elbow*, can be seen from the plot as follows -

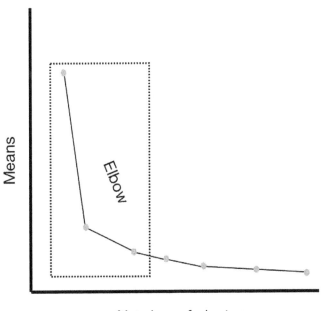

This elbow is the clue for choosing the right value for k, as the drastic change in the mean values can be observed. Therefore, the optimal value for k, as inferred from the above plot should be, k=3.

Now let us implement the k-means algorithm with a dataset representing people and their annual spending at malls. Here is a snippet -

| CustomerID | Gender | Age | Annual Income (k$) | Spending Score (1-100) |
|---|---|---|---|---|
| 1 | Male | 19 | 15 | 39 |
| 2 | Male | 21 | 15 | 81 |
| 4 | Female | 23 | 16 | 77 |

The objective with this dataset is different from other machine learning problems that we have come across so far. The traditional task has been about splitting the dataset into X containing the predictors, and Y containing the predictions in the training dataset, and then train a model. In clustering, a model is supposed to predict which cluster a data point shall belong, and so the above data tuples represented in the above snippet does not require to be split into X and Y. We will only select the relevant attributes as our X, which in this case is *Age* and *Annual Income*.

```
import numpy as np
import pandas as pd
import matplotlib.pyplot as plt
```

```
ds = pd.read_csv('Mall_Customers.csv')
```

```
X = ds.iloc[:, [3,4]].values
```

```
from sklearn.cluster import KMeans
wcss = []
for i in range(1,10):
    kmeans = KMeans(n_clusters=i,init = 'k-means++', random_state=0)
    kmeans.fit(X)
    wcss.append(kmeans.inertia_)
```

The *wcss* represents list of *within-cluster-sum-of-squares*. What we are trying to here, is to run the *KMeans* algorithm for cluster value *k* ranging from 1 through 10 and storing the corresponding sum of cluster in wcss.

*n_clusters* - This parameter specifies the number of centroids to use or clusters to form.

*init* - This parameter is set to 'k-means++ ' algorithm for picking the initial centroid positions.

*kmeans.inertia_* contains the mean of the sum of squares.

To choose the value of k suitable for our dataset, we will plot the *wcss* and trace the elbow pattern.

```
from matplotlib.pyplot import rcParams
rcParams['figure.figsize'] = 12,10

plt.plot(range(1,10), wcss)
plt.scatter(range(1,10), wcss, color = 'red')
plt.title('Elbow method')
plt.xlabel('Number of clusters')
plt.ylabel('WCSS')
plt.show()
```

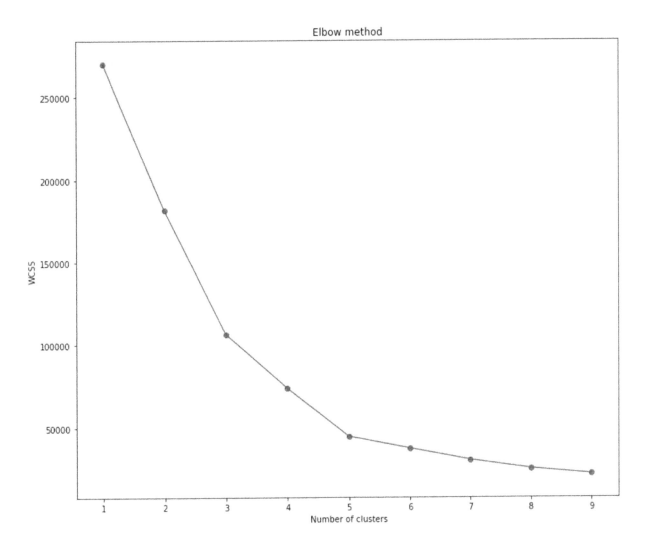

This plot shows the optimum value for *k* should be *k=5* as the elbow is significant till the value 5 along x axis. With this knowledge, we can now train the model with five centroids.

```
kmeans = KMeans(n_clusters=5, init = 'k-means++', random_state=0)
y_kmeans = kmeans.fit_predict(X)
```

```
y_kmeans
```

```
array([4, 3, 4, 3, 4, 3, 4, 3, 4, 3, 4, 3, 4, 3, 4, 3, 4, 3, 4, 3, 4, 3,
       4, 3, 4, 3, 4, 3, 4, 3, 4, 3, 4, 3, 4, 3, 4, 3, 4, 3, 4, 1,
       4, 3, 1, 1, 1, 1, 1, 1, 1, 1, 1, 1, 1, 1, 1, 1, 1, 1, 1, 1, 1, 1,
       1, 1, 1, 1, 1, 1, 1, 1, 1, 1, 1, 1, 1, 1, 1, 1, 1, 1, 1, 1, 1, 1,
       1, 1, 1, 1, 1, 1, 1, 1, 1, 1, 1, 1, 1, 1, 1, 1, 1, 1, 1, 1, 1, 1,
       1, 1, 1, 1, 1, 1, 1, 1, 1, 1, 1, 1, 2, 0, 2, 1, 2, 0, 2, 0, 2,
       1, 2, 0, 2, 0, 2, 0, 2, 0, 2, 1, 2, 0, 2, 0, 2, 0, 2, 0, 2, 0, 2,
       0, 2, 0, 2, 0, 2, 0, 2, 0, 2, 0, 2, 0, 2, 0, 2, 0, 2, 0, 2, 0, 2,
       0, 2, 0, 2, 0, 2, 0, 2, 0, 2, 0, 2, 0, 2, 0, 2, 0, 2, 0, 2, 0, 2,
       0, 2], dtype=int32)
```

*y_means* contains the predicted cluster among 0-4 for each corresponding value for X. The corresponding visualisation of the clusters is generated by the following code -

```
#Visualizing the clusters
plt.scatter(X[y_kmeans == 0, 0], X[y_kmeans == 0, 1], s = 100, c = 'red', label = 'Cluster 1')
plt.scatter(X[y_kmeans == 1, 0], X[y_kmeans == 1, 1], s = 100, c = 'blue', label = 'Cluster 2')
plt.scatter(X[y_kmeans == 2, 0], X[y_kmeans == 2, 1], s = 100, c = 'green', label = 'Cluster 3')
plt.scatter(X[y_kmeans == 3, 0], X[y_kmeans == 3, 1], s = 100, c = 'cyan', label = 'Cluster 4')
plt.scatter(X[y_kmeans == 4, 0], X[y_kmeans == 4, 1], s = 100, c = 'magenta', label = 'Cluster 5')
plt.scatter(kmeans.cluster_centers_[:, 0], kmeans.cluster_centers_[:, 1], s = 300,
            c = 'yellow', label = 'Centroids')
plt.title('Clusters of customers')
plt.xlabel('Age')
plt.ylabel('Annual Income (k$)')
plt.legend()
plt.show()
```

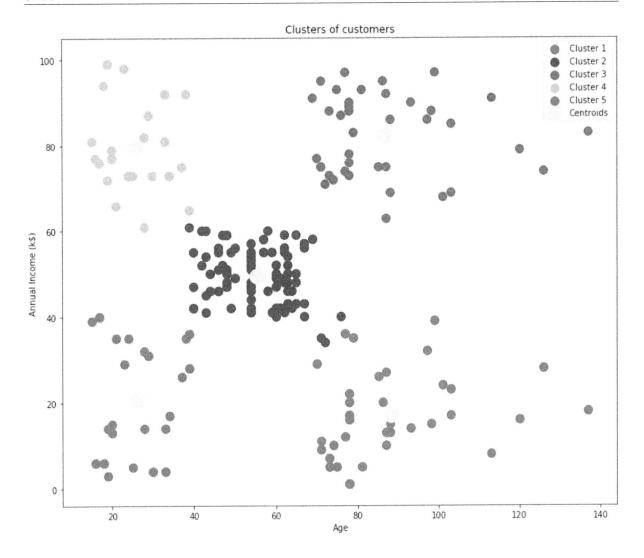

## Hierarchical clustering

This method involves creation of clusters with a memory component at each step to remember to which cluster a point belongs. It uses dendrons or tree data structure for this memory. The algorithm does not depend on centroids as in k-means, and starts with considering each datapoint as a single point cluster. Based on euclidean distance, it then joins to such single point clusters into a single cluster.

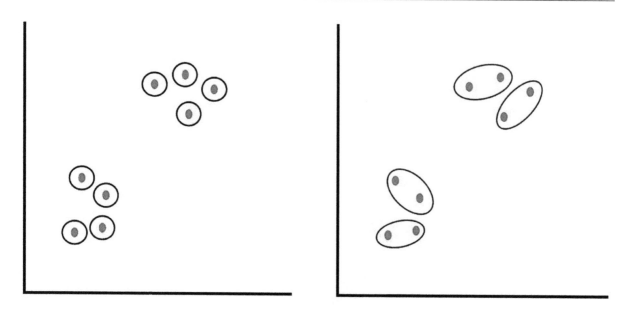

This inclusion of neighbouring clusters to form new clusters is represented with dendrons, such as the following -

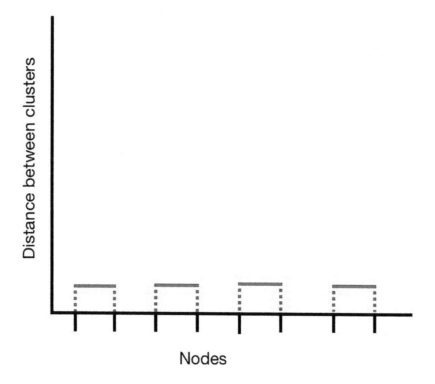

The distance between two (single point) clusters as shown by the dotted line -

is equal to the height of the dendron as depicted by the red dotted line -

The decision of not including a cluster or point in a cluster is based upon the preset threshold for this distance. We will write a program to visualise the dendron formation with our mall dataset used in the previous example.

```python
import numpy as np
import pandas as  pd
import matplotlib.pyplot as plt
```

```python
ds = pd.read_csv('Mall_Customers.csv')
X = ds.iloc[:,[3,4]].values
```

```python
from matplotlib.pyplot import rcParams
rcParams['figure.figsize'] = 12,10
```

```python
import scipy.cluster.hierarchy as dendro
dendrogram = dendro.dendrogram(dendro.linkage(X, method='ward'))
plt.title('Dendrogram')
plt.xlabel('customers')
plt.ylabel('euclidean distance')
plt.show()
```

The above code generates the following dendrogram -

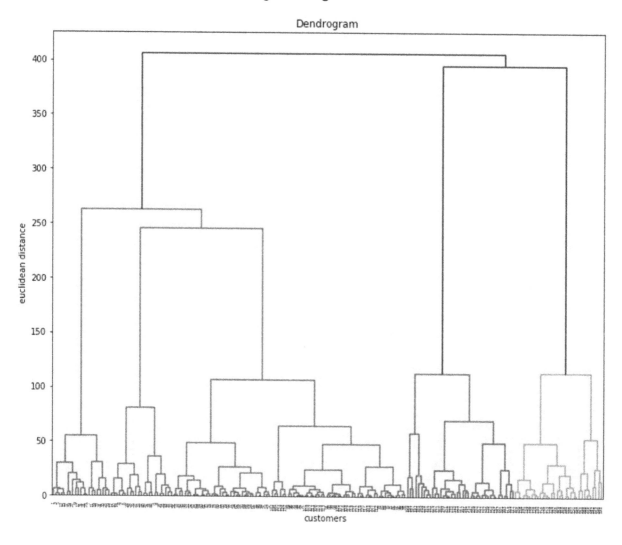

The formation of dendrons and creation of clusters is implemented by the *Agglomerative* clustering algorithm internally.

```
from sklearn.cluster import AgglomerativeClustering
clustering = AgglomerativeClustering(n_clusters=5, affinity='euclidean',linkage='ward')
Y_clusters = clustering.fit_predict(X)
```

```
#Visualizing the clusters
plt.scatter(X[Y_clusters == 0, 0], X[Y_clusters == 0, 1], s = 100, c = 'red', label = 'Cluster 1')
plt.scatter(X[Y_clusters == 1, 0], X[Y_clusters == 1, 1], s = 100, c = 'blue', label = 'Cluster 2')
plt.scatter(X[Y_clusters == 2, 0], X[Y_clusters == 2, 1], s = 100, c = 'green', label = 'Cluster 3')
plt.scatter(X[Y_clusters == 3, 0], X[Y_clusters == 3, 1], s = 100, c = 'cyan', label = 'Cluster 4')
plt.scatter(X[Y_clusters == 4, 0], X[Y_clusters == 4, 1], s = 100, c = 'magenta', label = 'Cluster 5')

plt.title('Clusters of customers')
plt.xlabel('Age')
plt.ylabel('Annual Income (k$)')
plt.legend()
plt.show()
```

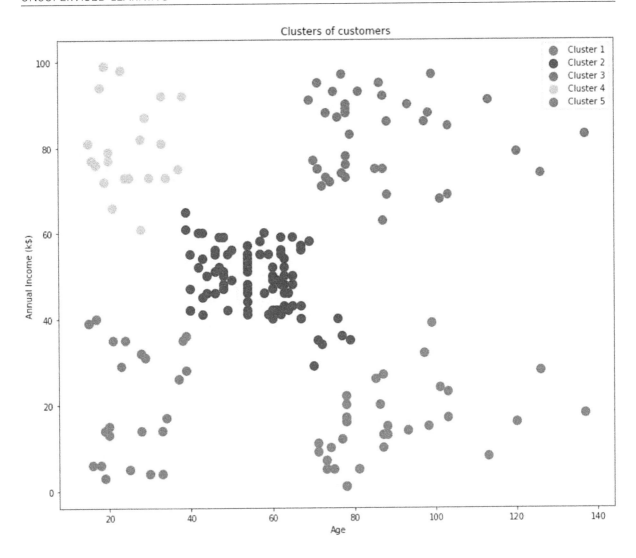

The clustering algorithms that we have used do not account for outliers, as the motive of the algorithms are to keep including data points into a particular cluster based on their closeness to clusters in a vector space. The next algorithm we are going to discuss has the capability to acknowledge outlier points.

## DBSCAN

This is a density based clustering method unlike k-means, which is a centroid based method. It views the vector space as areas of high density separated by areas of lower density. We will first understand what density means in a cluster.

Here is a cluster that comprises of 19 data points in its neighbourhood.

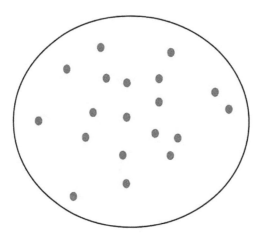

The density of the cluster is given by the area of the neighbourhood divided by the number of data points in it. The density as in some cases increases with decrease in the area of the neighbourhood.

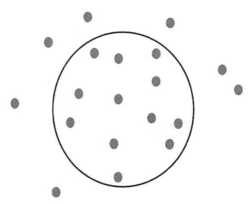

Now there are 12 points in a much smaller neighbourhood which makes it a higher density cluster, but the density again reduces for the following neighbourhood area.

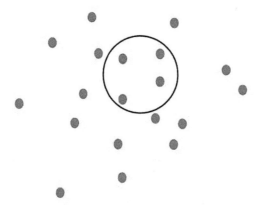

The *DBSCAN (Density Based Spatial Clustering of Applications with Noise)* algorithm takes inspiration from this concept of density and does local density approximations for all data points, i.e. each data point has an approximation of the surrounding density of the vector region. The points can be clustered to be in the same neighbourhood having similar local density approximations. Unlike K-Means or Hierarchical algorithm, DBSCAN does not require the number of clusters as a parameter, but it automatically computes this from the dataset.

The DBSCAN algorithm has two key parameters - $\varepsilon$ which is the maximum radius of the neighbourhood around a data point, and *minPts* is the minimum number of data points that are to be present in a neighbourhood. The data points are also categorized into three types, namely -

Core point - A data point $p$ belonging to a cluster's neighbourhood such that | neighbourhood($p$, $\varepsilon$) | >= minPts. Core points satisfy the minimum density requirement of clusters, as the value of $\varepsilon$ remains constant. A point $p$ is a core point if at least minPts points are within the distance $\varepsilon$ of including $p$. The other points in the cluster are said to be *directly reachable* from $p$. DBSCAN has another concept called density reachability according to which, two points $p$ and $q$ are density reachable if they lie in separate clusters and there is a point $o$ from which both points $p$ and $q$ are reachable.

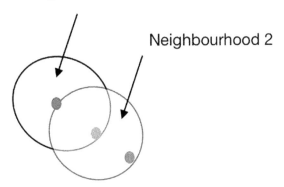

The red point's neighbourhood is 1 and green point's neighbourhood is 2. The blue point lies in neighbourhood 2, and as the red and the blue points are reachable from green point, we can say that point red is density reachable from blue point. This density based reachability of points with a hop from neighbourhood 2 to1, for going to red point from green, is used for clustering of points in DBSCAN.

Border point - A data point $q$ is a border point if the | neighbourhood($q$, $\varepsilon$)| contains less than minPts points, but the point $q$ is close from some point $p$ in the neighbourhood.

*Outlier* - A point that is neither a core or a border point is regarded as belonging to another class/cluster w.r.t. the cluster in focus. It is at the end of the clustering, the points that are unable to become part of any cluster, comes to be identified as the outlier points of the dataset.

The algorithm for DBSCAN can be defined as the following steps -

a)  Find the points in the neighbourhood of radius ε for each data point and identify the core points with more than minPts neighbours.

b)  For each core point, the cluster is expanded by including all the density reachable points to the cluster. In order to add a point, perform neighbourhood jumps.

Here is the code to implement DBSCAN -

```python
import numpy as np
import pandas as pd
import matplotlib.pyplot as plt
```

```python
ds = pd.read_csv('Mall_Customers.csv')
```

```python
X = ds.iloc[:, [3,4]].values
```

```python
dbscan = DBSCAN(eps=12, min_samples=10)
dbscan.fit(X)
```

```
DBSCAN(algorithm='auto', eps=12, leaf_size=30, metric='euclidean',
    metric_params=None, min_samples=10, n_jobs=1, p=None)
```

```python
core_samples_mask = np.zeros_like(dbscan.labels_, dtype=bool)
core_samples_mask[dbscan.core_sample_indices_] = True
labels = dbscan.labels_
```

```python
plt.rcParams['figure.figsize'] = 12,10

# Black removed and is used for noise instead.
unique_labels = set(labels)
colors = [plt.cm.Spectral(each) for each in np.linspace(0, 1, len(unique_labels))]

for k, col in zip(unique_labels, colors):
    if k == -1:
        # Black used for noise.
        col = [0, 0, 0, 1]

    class_member_mask = (labels == k)
    xy = X[class_member_mask & core_samples_mask]
    plt.plot(xy[:, 0], xy[:, 1], 'o', markerfacecolor=tuple(col),
            markeredgecolor='k', markersize=14)

    xy = X[class_member_mask & ~core_samples_mask]
    plt.plot(xy[:, 0], xy[:, 1], 'o', markerfacecolor=tuple(col),
            markeredgecolor='k', markersize=6)

plt.title('Clusters of customers')
plt.xlabel('Age')
plt.ylabel('Annual Income(k$)')
plt.show()
```

The *core_samples_mask* is an array containing the value True at indexes of data points which have been identified as core points. labels is an array containing the class labels for each data point. At each iteration *class_member_mask* is instantiated as an array containing only those members as True whose value matches the class label value in *k*. We wanted to plot the core data points with larger markers than other data points and thats why, *X[class_ member_mask & core_samples_mark]* performs a AND operation and returns True for those data points that are core. The core points are plotted with a *markersize* of 14. Again the non-core points are identified by performing an AND operation between *class_member_mask* and the complement of *core_samples_mask* with *~core_samples_mask*.

The plot generated for DBSCAN -

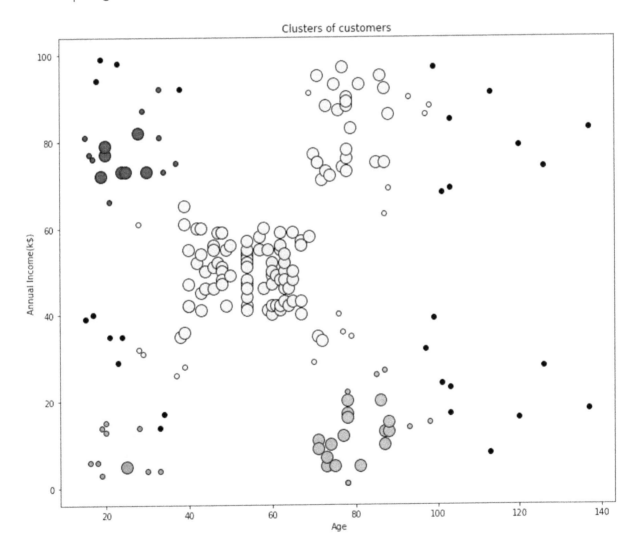

## Gaussian Mixture Model

This is a probabilistic model for predicting the cluster to which a data point shall belong. Having stated that, we must understand the requirements for a probabilistic approach in an unsupervised setup. In a supervised use-case of probabilistic prediction, which we have come across previously in the form of Bayesian models used for regression and classification problems, the main motive of the model was to probabilistically determine the outcome when the input attributes are known. In an unsupervised environment, that is still the case but we know, both the input and.

The training process involves estimating about the model parameters from the data points as provided by the training dataset and adjust the weights and biases accordingly. In contrast to supervised learning, where the model parameters - weights, and variance and means, are calculated with an initial estimation from the attribute values in the training dataset, in unsupervised learning as seen in K-Means and DBSCAN, these parameters are learnt through the inference gathered from forming clusters with the data points.

# Associative rule learning

With this form of learning we are going to learn about finding interesting patterns that may exist in the dataset. The machine learning techniques that we have learnt so far, would enable us to make statistically driven decisions on real world problems apart from the central idea of learning a trend or any function.

The main inspiration for association rule learning comes from the intent of finding patterns in large datasets which led the founders of the concept Rakesh Agrawal, Tomasz Imielinski and Arun Swami to introduce the association rules. They found regularities in products that appear in large scale transaction databases recorded at point of sale. For example, a rule such as { onions, potatoes } => {burger} can be derived if a customer buys onions and potatoes at a supermarket, implying the customer would also have to buy the ingredients for making burger. This relation or association among supermarket items which are otherwise unrelated to each other, can give huge strategic benefit to a store owner.

Association rule learning is an attempt toward approximating the function that governs the association among mutually unrelated events, but are relatable of course in a particular context. In another example of supermarket transaction, it is suppose seen, a trend of among people buying of buying beer when shopping for baby diapers. On the first instance what we can right away conclude that these two items are absolutely unrelated despite the buying pattern being consistent. This is a quite popular trend which makes sense on the following premise.

A working mother when at home after work with her baby, usually sends the father at the store to pick up diapers. When the father goes to buy diapers, he has plans to watch sports on television when back to home, while the mother is with the baby. The father usually drinks beer while watching the sports channel. Therefore, a non-working father buying diapers for the baby usually ends up buying beer.

We can now see how two unrelated events of buying diaper and buying beer can be bind with a context. Based on this a rule can be formed {game night, diaper, male buyer} => {beer}. Now based upon the inference from this rule, a store owner can position the beer racks closer to the check out counter and improve the sales.

It is not just that associations can be found only in the case of supermarket buying events but in other use cases as well like in a restaurant where people who order spicy food have the tendency to order salads.

Before getting into the implementation of this, we should clear our understanding whether it is a supervised or unsupervised form of learning.

The correct way to look at an associative learning problem is is to first grasp the motive of such an experiment and how it is subtly different from our usual supervised or unsupervised learning problems. A machine learning problem has had a common motive of training a model based to predict an outcome. In supervised learning, the algorithms learn the relations between an input data tuple and its corresponding output and in unsupervised learning, the algorithms learn from only the output, about the function, and not having the input dataset as a reference. But in the case of associative learning the focus is not on building a model that predicts the outcome of an input. A very usual mistaken way of approaching the supermarket buying use case, from the perspective that, as if we are interested in predicting the probability of a person buying beer given that diapers are bought. This is a classic problem for Bayes theorem which we already have encountered. The intent is not find whether a person would buy, but to find the association rules in a dataset from the hidden trends. In association learning, an input dataset is required to find out these rules and to assign strength values suggesting if a rule truly holds for the dataset. Therefore, association learning is about finding patterns based on statistics.

As we have stated that this form of learning requires an input dataset for finding patterns, it is considered in supervised learning category.

The *Apriori* algorithm can be used for mining the sets of frequently co-occurring events from a dataset and performing association rule learning on them. The association learning method is based upon four constraints that are used as a metric to elect a significant association rule.

## Support

This indicates the frequency of an item-set such as { beer, diapers } appearing in a dataset. The support of X with respect to T gives the proportion of transactions t in a dataset which contains the item-set X and is expressed as the following -

$$\text{supp}(X) = \frac{|\{t \in T; X \subseteq t\}|}{|T|}$$

Suppose in a dataset, the item-set is X = { beer, diapers } has a supp(X) = 0.2. It means that 20% of transactions among all of the transactions, has the items in X.

## Confidence

This metric states the frequency of a rule found true. The confidence of a rule X => Y for T transactions is the proportion of the transactions containing Y, given that X is contained. The confidence can be expressed as the following which is basically the probability of event X and Y occurring, given X -

$$\text{conf}(X \Rightarrow Y) = \text{supp}(X \cup Y)/\text{supp}(X)$$

The claim that people buying diapers also buy beer is a hypothesis in this context and the confidence is a metric whose job is find the strength of that condition. Suppose in an example dataset, a rule is { potato, onion } => { burger bread }. The confidence is the ratio =

$$\{ \text{potato, onion} \} \text{ and } \{ \text{burger bread} \} / \{ \text{potato, onion} \}$$

## Lift

The lift of a rule X => Y is the ratio of the confidence for event X and Y happening *conf(X=> Y)*, with the support for Y. This is basically the Bayes theorem in action and it is defined as -

$$\text{lift}(X \Rightarrow Y) = \frac{\text{supp}(X \cup Y)}{\text{supp}(X) \times \text{supp}(Y)}$$

## Conviction

It is the ratio of the frequency that X occurs without Y and the frequency of incorrect predictions. It is expressed in the following way -

$$\text{conv}(X \Rightarrow Y) = \frac{1 - \text{supp}(Y)}{1 - \text{conf}(X \Rightarrow Y)}.$$

Therefore, conviction provides the measure for wrongness or contradiction of the claim for X=>Y events.

Now we will get to the implementation of associative learning. The dataset we will be using are transactions in a supermarket.

```
import numpy as np
import pandas as pd
import matplotlib.pyplot as plt

ds = pd.read_csv('Market_Basket_Optimisation.csv', header=None)

ds.head()
```

|   | 0 | 1 | 2 | 3 | 4 | 5 | 6 | 7 | 8 | 9 | 10 | 11 | 12 | 13 | 14 | 15 | 16 | 17 |
|---|---|---|---|---|---|---|---|---|---|---|----|----|----|----|----|----|----|----|
| 0 | shrimp | almonds | avocado | vegetables mix | green grapes | whole weat flour | yams | cottage cheese | energy drink | tomato juice | low fat yogurt | green tea | honey | salad | mineral water | salmon | antioxydant juice | frozen smoothie | sp |
| 1 | burgers | meatballs | eggs | NaN | NaN | NaN | NaN | NaN | NaN | NaN | NaN | NaN | NaN | NaN | NaN | NaN | NaN | NaN |
| 2 | chutney | NaN | NaN | NaN | NaN | NaN | NaN | NaN | NaN | NaN | NaN | NaN | NaN | NaN | NaN | NaN | NaN | NaN |
| 3 | turkey | avocado | NaN | NaN | NaN | NaN | NaN | NaN | NaN | NaN | NaN | NaN | NaN | NaN | NaN | NaN | NaN | NaN |
| 4 | mineral water | milk | energy bar | whole wheat rice | green tea | NaN | NaN | NaN | NaN | NaN | NaN | NaN | NaN | NaN | NaN | NaN | NaN | NaN |

Each row corresponds to the items a particular customer bought and we can see all the column headers are represented as numeric values corresponding to each type of product available in the supermarket.

The apriori algorithm requires the input in a format of a list where each item in the list is a transaction containing only the list of items involved in a transaction.

```
transactions = []
for i in range(0, ds.__len__()):
    transactions.append([str(ds.values[i,j]) for j in range(20)])
```

```
: transactions[1]
```

```
: ['burgers',
  'meatballs',
  'eggs',
  'nan',
  'nan',
  'nan',
  'nan',
  'nan',
  'nan',
  'nan',
  'nan',
  'nan',
  'nan',
  'nan',
  'nan',
  'nan',
  'nan',
  'nan',
  'nan',
  'nan']
```

For performing the *apriori* algorithm of the dataset, we will have to install the *apyori* python package -

```
pip install apyori
```

```
from apyori import apriori
```

```
rules = apriori(transactions, min_support = 0.003,
                min_confidence = 0.2, min_lift = 3, min_length = 2)
```

The parameter min_support, min_confidence, and min_lift are set to minimum values for considering a rule valid. The *min_length* parameter specifies the minimum number of items to be present in a relation i.e. { potato, onion} => { burger bread } would hold with 3 items in the relation.

Next we execute and store the result of *apriori* algorithm on the dataset in a python list.

```
results = list(rules)
```

```
results[0]
```

```
RelationRecord(items=frozenset({'light cream', 'chicken'}), support=0.004532728969470737, ordered_statistics=[Ordered
Statistic(items_base=frozenset({'light cream'}), items_add=frozenset({'chicken'}), confidence=0.29059829059829057, li
ft=4.84395061728395)])
```

```
results.__len__()
```

```
154
```

As we can see there are 154 rules created for our dataset and these rules are enlisted in *results* in decreasing order of relevance. The confidence is 29% and the lift is 4.9 (rounded off) which is greater than the minimum lift 3 that we have specified. The least relevant rule has the least lift among all rules -

```
results[153].ordered_statistics
```

```
[OrderedStatistic(items_base=frozenset({'nan', 'milk', 'mineral water', 'spaghetti'}), items_add=frozenset({'tomatoe
s'}), confidence=0.211864406779661, lift=3.0978458387022165)]
```

If the confidence is high but the lift is not comparatively high, it will be regarded as less relevant. The *Apriori* algorithm uses a breadth first search strategy to count the item-sets whereas there is another algorithm for associative learning that uses a depth-first search approach and is called *Eclat*.

# SECTION 2

# Cloud with Openstack

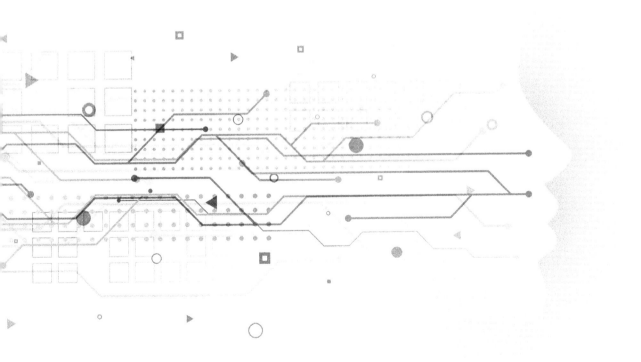

# Introduction

Cloud computing is a ubiquitous technology that is driving the growth of internet and stands out to be the most significant actors in building a secure world wide web. Before cloud computing, companies had to maintain servers at data centres for hosting web applications, which obviously is an extremely costly affair. Therefore, it was infeasible for solo developers or small companies to host their application on the web.

Rackspace and Amazon Web Services were the two most important actors in democratising cloud computing technology since their introduction in the early 2000's. Earlier if a solo developer had to host a web application, the scenario was to host it on a home computer or something that is equivalent to an ad-hoc web hosting. Such setup always had feeble resistance against looming cyber threats in the form of DDoS attacks. The cloud hosting platforms as provided by Amazon, and now Google and Microsoft as well, provides the needed enormity of infrastructure required for both defending against cyber threats as well as to serve high web traffic. With the democratisation of cloud infrastructure, a web based application irrespective of its size, can avail the benefits of hosting on sever grade machines at data centres.

The pay per use pricing structure of cloud services make it more convenient for application hosting for independent developers as well as small startups to big companies. Previously when a startup had to setup their infrastructure at a data centre, it included steps such as setting up the hardware network lines, large scale investment for buying server machines, and configuring the network, etc. Cloud providers eradicate these steps so that an application can directly be hosted right after the build process.

OpenStack is a cloud infrastructure and services management software that was initially developed by Rackspace and NASA to manage data centres. From there on, it went on to become one of the most promising open source project for cloud. Therefore, a company that has to provide cloud services such as Amazon or Google or Microsoft, it can use the Openstack software to provide all the same array of services that as provided by the contemporaries. There are certain uses cases where an application is hosted not on the internet by on a private network on data centre servers. Such are the examples in the form of financial institutions, governments, high end research facilities, etc. who usually build and manage their own on-premises data centres and use OpenStack.

From the perspective of a startup company, it is undoubtedly convenient to go for a cloud based solution. But as it turns out, as a startup steadily grows into a business, it is more economic over time to host their applications in a data centre as compared to the pay per use pricing structure. So, with sufficient amount of capital to spend on infrastructure, a mature startup company can transition from public cloud to on-premises, as it includes one time investment on hardware.

Again in some cases, companies maintain a mixed setup of partly public cloud and partly on-premises servers. Therefore, for all such use cases, OpenStack is the only candidate for server cluster management with the most advanced set of features.

# Understanding Cloud

The cloud computing technology became mainstream when in 2006 Amazon web services (AWS) was launched with the primary offering of Elastic cloud compute, alongside Rackspace (came before AWS), another company involved in building softwares for managing cloud. In the succeeding years a majority shift was observed towards using cloud technology for internet applications.

## *Our initial acquaintance with cloud computing*

The fundamental concept of cloud computing existed even before the term became popularised. Online storage of data files is the first form of applications of cloud computing. File storage solutions such as the one provided by MegaUpload.com is the inspiration behind present day cloud drives in the form of Google Drive, DropBox, etc. The term cloud is basically an allegorical one, which means data is not housed on a user's personal computer but stored in a different geographical location, on a different computer. This data is accessible by the user from anywhere, thus giving the feeling as if the data files are stored in the clouds in the skies. The data files stored in the cloud acted as the extension of a user's hard drive in a personal computer, but with the introduction of cloud computing, that experience extended beyond mere storage of data files to entire computing on the cloud.

## *Under the hood of cloud based applications*

To understand the schematics and build a cloud of our own with Openstack, we have to learn about the intuitions behind the abstraction that comes with the term cloud computing or cloud computer in general. Although we have mentioned about cloud based file storage as an example of cloud computing, it must be noted that file storage is only an application and the actual cloud is the infrastructure of server computers that hide behind the abstraction of as provided by the application. When we use any data storage application such as Google Drive, the application takes the data files of all users and stores it in such a seamless manner that gives us the perception that the data is on our hard drive itself. While we know this isn't the case. The file gets stored away in a hard disk whose location is unknown to the user. The storage details are hidden behind the abstraction created by the application. The most important and noticeable thing among all such cloud storage applications is that, they never seem run out of space unlike a personal computer. Obviously, there isn't a perpetual source of storage, but it is the abstraction of cloud services that gives a user this seamlessness. A user having selected for a particular storage pricing option can keep on storing files without caring about addition of new disk volumes when space runs out.

Now if we move past the abstraction layer as created by the application and delve into the underlying details about how the application is storing the data, the first thing that we have to remember is that, every computer system comes with a finite amount of storage. The cloud storage application being able to store data without any limit on the number of users that can use the service or total storage capacity, obviously hints toward an every growing pool of storage. The favourable candidate for such an application is an array of storage drives that can be appended to a computer, but the problem with such a solution, is that, it has a limit. The number of disk storage that can be added to a single computer is dependant on and limited by the filesystem used by the operating system, and hence it has an upper limit to it. Therefore, the way a cloud storage application can obtain unlimited storage capacity, is by adding computers to form a cluster. This is our key hint toward what is a cloud computer. *A cloud computer is not a single big computer but a clusters of computers.*

## A cluster of computers

A cluster among computers is formed using a LAN connection. There is a cluster of server grade computers that runs in the background of our referred cloud based storage application. Although a cloud computer is a group of computers forming a cluster, we will be forming our intuition about cloud not by visualising it as a group of computers, but by perceiving this cluster as a singleton computer, and we will draw comparisons of a cloud computer with that of a personal computer. Moving forward we will find out that a cloud computer behaves as a singleton computer despite being composed of a cluster. We will first take a note of the fundamentals of a computer. The various components that make up a computer system is a CPU, a storage unit and a fast memory unit. In a computer, all of these components are available as a collection of composite units interconnected through direct wires and circuitry on a motherboard. With a LAN connection, two or more such computer systems can be connected with each other such that they can exchange files between them and even one computer can execute a program on another computer. As an outcome of forming a LAN, resources across the cluster are accessible and of course a cloud storage solution takes this solution as mentioned earlier. Therefore, the initial step toward forming a singleton computer is achieved through a LAN network, such that every cloud service provider for example Google cloud, is perceived as a single computer.

## A cloud computer as a personal computer

For moving the experience of a personal computer, to the internet, such that the user receives a seamless computing experience, all the components and the interconnections between them have to remain hidden under layers of software abstractions. Imagine being able to have a computer with desired choice of operating system and also a hardware configuration as per requirement, without physically owning such a personal computer. Cloud service providers such as AWS, Google, etc. provide this capability, where the only thing required by a user to access such a computer is an internet connection and a browser application. We will understand this in detail as we compare how a personal computer has to undergo changes when moved to the cloud.

As stated earlier, behind every cloud computing services such as Google Cloud or AWS or Azure, remains clusters of large scale server computers housed in data-centres. The idea is to club together all these servers together such that all the CPUs, memory and storage in each machine come together to emulate a single computer system. Forming a simple LAN among computers will only be able to connect these computers together. In order for a seamless aggregation among the connected computers, there is a software required that would logically bind the otherwise separate systems. This is our software that will form the necessary logical layer on a simple cluster of computers.

In order to comprehend a cluster of computers as a singleton computer, where resources of all the participating computers are aggregated by a software we have to correlate the components of a personal computer to that of the cluster of computers.

Here is a generic diagram of a personal computer -

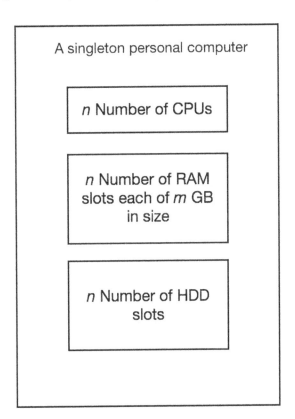

Recent generations of personal computers have multiple CPU cores and the above diagram outlines such a computer with multiple RAM and HDD slots.

Now if we resemble this kind of a setup with a cluster of server computers as in cloud computing, it would look something like the following generic diagram -

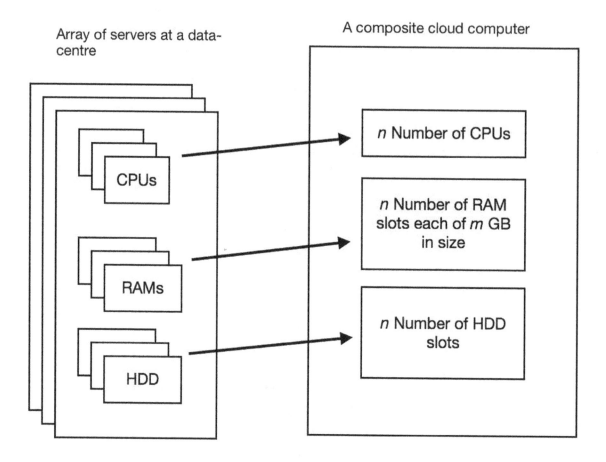

Unlike a personal computer, where all the components are present together in a single hardware housing, the cluster of servers of a cloud computing company such as Amazon or Google span data-centres geographically located throughout the world. Since a cloud computer is a LAN (or WAN) of server computers, there is required a software that manages these cluster of computers such that they together work in unison as as parts of a single system. To delve more into the resemblance of a cloud computer to a personal computer, here are diagrams that shows how the LAN interconnections among server computers are comparable to that of the interconnections of the various components in a personal computer.

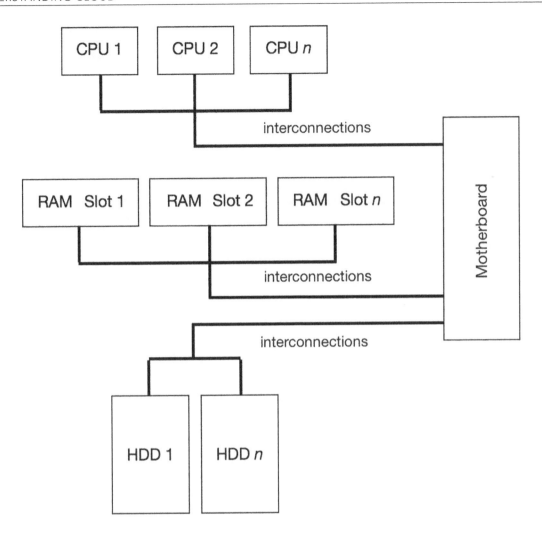

The above diagram shows the generic interconnections formed by the circuitry on a motherboard among the components. The CPUs in actual computer are present as multiple cores on a single chip, but here we are representing them the cores as an array of CPU units. Next, here is a diagram of computers connected over LAN.

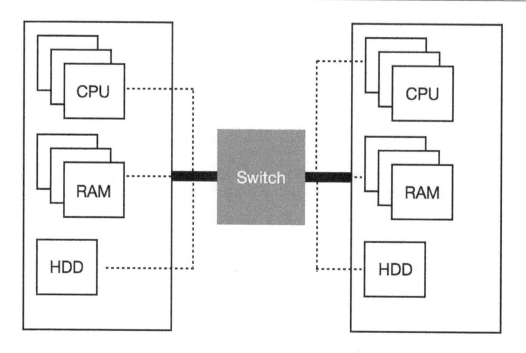

We have stated this earlier that computers connected through LAN enables one computer to execute a task on some other computer, and therefore, it uses the resources of the other computer. The dotted lines in the above diagram is representative of that fact by showing that the individual resources in each computer is connected to the interconnection hub between computers in the form of *Switch*. It must be clear that a LAN connection with cables and the interconnections on a motherboard are not the same things. The reason we are drawing this resemblance, is to establish the motto of treating each RAM unit, CPU or disk storage as independent computing resources irrespective of either they are on a separate computer systems or on a single motherboard.

A LAN enables a user to access resources of another computer, but it cannot convert the resources of the connected machines into a singleton computer, such that all CPUs or storage units are treated as part of the same setup. The motivation of creating a composite computer that keeps growing by adding of new server computers, is only made possible if a software layer aggregates the resources. The following diagram shows how OpenStack logically aggregates all resources spanning across cluster of servers, irrespective of their physical geographic locations.

Cloud computing software

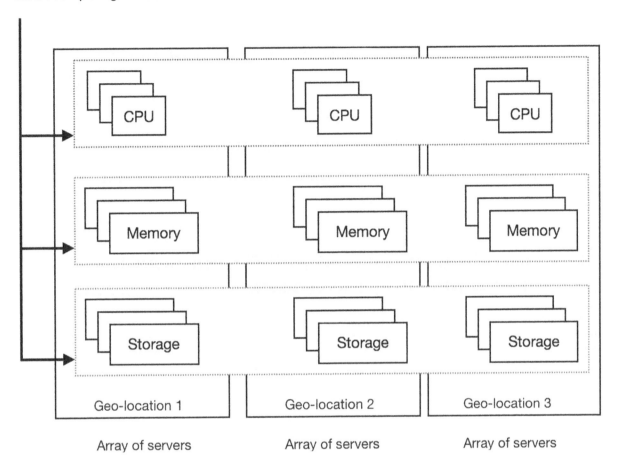

The above diagram is a generalised view of what a cloud computing software such as OpenStack does, but the key takeaway is the demonstration of how cloud computing is a software based solution.

The need for cloud computing originated from the convenience of being able to access any data file on a computer from anywhere. The location agnostic accessibility is made possible by internet, but the seamless connectivity is only be made possible by the cloud computing software - OpenStack. For example, a user when storing a big data file in a cloud computer, should not have to care about storage management issues and it is the system software that undertakes the task of placing portions of the big data file across hard drives spanning across multiple servers.

In this section of the book, we are going to learn about implementing such a software that manages a cloud computer. We must not confuse a cloud computing software such as Openstack, as some sort of an operating system is installed on a cluster of computers. All the server computers in a cloud cluster have a dedicated operating system installed on each server. The cloud computing software which is not a single but a collection of softwares are installed on each of such servers. These softwares communicate with each other to connect the resources on separate machines into a resource pool.

Although we used the example of a personal computer to draw reference to cloud computing, unlike a personal computer, the cloud computing service provided by companies such as Amazon, is not limited to a single person but open for all users who use and build applications in the cloud.

## Virtual machines in a cloud computer

The various components of Openstack are dedicated toward managing specific resources such as memory, storage, processing, network, etc. and this pool of resources together behave as a singleton massive server. Now we can refer to such a cluster a cloud computer and compare its usage to that of a personal computer. In a personal computer the operating system allows multiple users to create their respective users isolated from one another. Openstack although is not an operating system but for our generalised comparison with a personal computer we can of think of it as a software that operates the cloud computer.

Virtualisation enables a user to install guest operating systems on a virtual machine. We may have installed virtualisation softwares such as VMware or VirtualBox on our personal computers. These softwares enable users of a computer to have the virtual experience of own multiple computers, all running on a base computer. Here is a diagram depicting such a use case of computer usage -

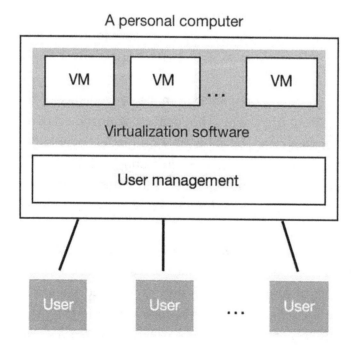

The user management as shown in the above diagram is done by the host operating system. The user get past the authentication process to access their virtual machines, but in this case of virtualisation, a user also has access to the host operating system. In the case of a cloud computer, the same concept of virtualisation is used, such that a user can own a virtual computer that is accessible over the internet. Here is a diagram depicting a generic cloud computer in comparison with a personal computer shown in the previous diagram.

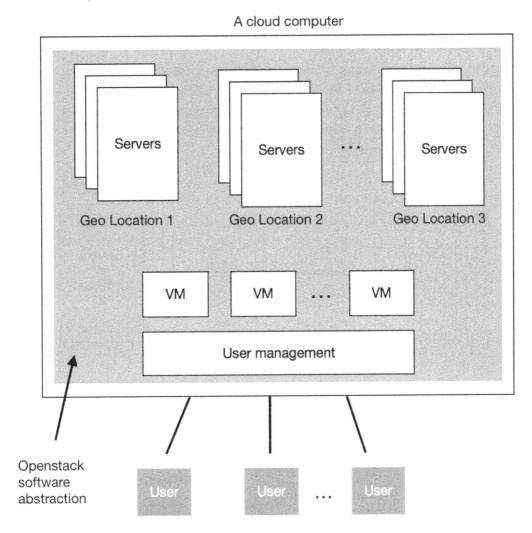

A cloud computer

Any user can then have a computer in the cloud by launching a virtual machine on this clustered computer network. The user management unlike in a personal computer is not done by the host OS but through an authentication service of Openstack. This is exactly similar to that of using VMware or VirtualBox to launch a virtual machine in a personal computer. The striking difference being, that unlike running a virtual machine in a personal computer, where all the hardware resources being used by the virtual machine is usually physically located on the hardware of a single computer, a cloud setup has its resources spanning across multiple machines. A user's virtual machine can be provisioned in a way that it uses the CPU on one server machine and uses the hard drive of another server for storage purposes. This is only made possible by the abstraction provided by the Openstack software layer.

The Openstack software is responsible for all types management and provisioning activities associated with virtual machines. A cloud computing platform can therefore be referred to as a collection of virtual machines and they run on shared hardware. The concept of machines forming networks as LAN or WAN isn't new, and in the case of cloud computing, the virtual machines can form subnets that can be isolated from others. Just like our cloud computer is a network of computers, the virtual machines in a cloud computer can form networking amongst themselves, isolated from others. A physical network connects machines with data communication cables. In the case of cloud, these networks are formed through a software based solution. As we know, how the servers of a cloud computing platform are connected through physical cables in a data-centre, the inter-connection among virtual machines are formed virtually through logical groupings and rules. Here is a generic diagram representation of a cloud computing platform -

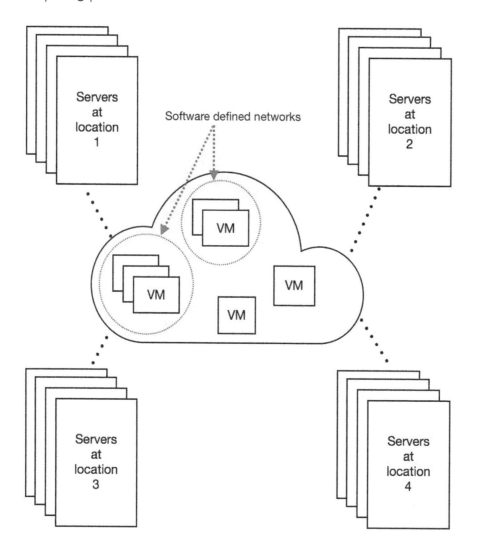

The circled group of VMs depict a network achieved through software based networking service as provided by Openstack and in the next section we will read in details about all of Openstack services.

## Applications in the cloud

We began our introduction to cloud computing with reference to cloud based storage applications such as Google Drive, or DropBox. These applications just like any other, are hosted on a cloud computer in a network of virtual machines where various components of an application are running. Google provides a ton of cloud based applications, and here is a simple representation of few of those cloud services.

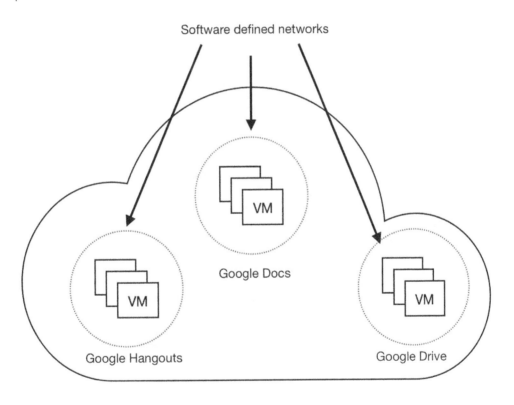

These cloud applications are deployed on virtual networks of VMs similar to that of applications installed on a personal computer.

# What is Openstack?

In the previous chapter we formed an intuition behind cloud computing. How servers and their resources are shared to form a resource pool, from which virtual machines are provisioned to a user. Openstack, is an open-source collection of softwares written in python to run and manage cloud computing services. Openstack provides these collection of tools that are built with the design philosophy of *infrastructure-as-a-service*. We will take a moment to understand why this form of computing is referred to *as-a-service*.

## Service and As-a-service

A software is categorised as a *service* when it is setup in the form of a client-server architecture and communication going on over TCP/IP socket. A cloud implementation of computing comprises of component software parts which collaborate together to provide one seamless service. Since Openstack aggregates and manages resource pools, we can take the example of all the storage units in each of the participating servers who are aggregated by a component software of Openstack called *Cinder*. The Cinder block storage software aggregates all the storage and provisions this storage through API requests to be used with a virtual machine. There is a software component responsible for handling each of the tasks, and so, the Compute component software of Openstack which is responsible for creating a virtual machine, sends an API request to Cinder for say a 50 GB block storage to be provisioned. The Cinder software provides the requested block storage from its pool. Similarly, each virtual machine that is to be created has to have an operating system of its own, provisioning of which is again managed by another software component, known as *Glance*. This *Glance* software maintains a list of all the various operating systems, from which a user can choose to install one in a virtual machine. While creating a virtual machine, the request for a particular operating system is intercepted by the *Compute* software which in turn communicates with the *Glance* software through API calls. All communications, either between a user and Openstack cloud or among the software components of Openstack, occur through HTTP(s) requests.

This is the reason that Openstack component softwares are referred to as services because all the components of required by a personal computer say storage unit, memory unit, compute power, etc., are accessible through sending HTTP(s) requests to a port. Each software is always listening to their designated ports and reply accordingly to HTTP(s) requests, thereby forming the client-server schema.

The whole cloud computing offering of Openstack is referred to as infrastructure-as-a-service because, a user does not have to own a physical computer. Instead, it is made available through sending requests to a service provider which in this case is Openstack. Openstack provides services for virtual machines, storage devices, network, etc. which all together is referred to as computing *infrastructure*.

## The component services of Openstack -

## Compute

This consists of a constellation of services for creating and managing virtual machines in the private/public cloud. This component service like any other, is not just a single service but a group of services each dedicated toward accomplishing a particular task associated with creating of a virtual machine. All these services can be referred to as agent services which together form the *Compute* infrastructure as service. When a request is made by a user for a virtual machine, the resource specifications selected by the user has to be provisioned in communication with other services. From the receipt of a request for provisioning of a virtual machine to the actual creation, there are a number of steps involved and each of the component services of Compute take part in a particular one. For example, a virtual machine consists of persistent storage which is managed by Cinder service, operating system image managed by *Glance*, CPU and memory managed by *Compute* service itself. Provisioning a virtual machine consists of executing of a sequence of steps with adequate amount of status reporting on the status of each intermediate step. The *Compute* collection of services is referenced by another name called *nova*, which we will see being used in naming of each of the compute services. Below is the list of cogs that make up the compute machinery work.

### nova-api

It is the api server that accepts requests and delegates them to the responsible compute or nova-* service and returns the response.

### nova-api-metadata

Metadata is required by Openstack instances/virtual machines to be informed about its configurations such as RAM, disk space, CPU, etc. which is periodically checked by this service for every virtual machine and recorded in the database. The configurations for every virtual instance is subject to change by a user, so the metadata is kept updated at all times both in the database as well as in the virtual machine itself. The use of metadata is not just limited to that. The virtual machines created with Openstack can be instructed to perform certain operations during or exactly after the build phase. These tasks post build phase is also handled by the metadata service. With metadata, an instance can be instructed to perform tasks for example, doing a yum update (for Centos) on startup, or install certain packages or execute a shell script. This metadata is configurable at anytime for a particular instance.

## nova-compute

This service is responsible for creation of virtual machine instances by making calls to hypervisor APIs such as libvirt for KVM or QEMU, VMwareAPI for VMware, XenAPI for XenServer/XCP.

## nova-scheduler

Determines on which Compute server an instance will be launched. Openstack has various architectural flavours on implementation which will be discussed later. The simplest deployment of Openstack has only one server configured for the Compute service, but it can have a swarm of Computes. In the case of an Openstack installation comprising of only one server, the virtual machine is created by default on that single server designated as a resource pool for the Compute service. As the *Compute* service is responsible for managing the virtual machines, it has to keep record of the total CPU and RAM available across all the servers where virtual machines are to be launched. The nova-scheduler service chooses the server from Openstack's resource pool where a virtual machine will be launched, when there is a cluster of servers in the Openstack setup.

## nova-conductor

Mediates interactions between the nova-compute and the database.

## nova-cert

It is responsible for generation of X509 certificates for instances. Each virtual instance is issued a certificate as it requires private key based login by default.

## nova-network-worker

Manages networking tasks such as creation of bridges or setting of IP table rules for instances.

## nova-consoleauth

Each virtual instance can be accessed from the web browser through a VNC client which is installed on each instance. Nova-consoleauth provides the authentication service for web based GUI access to instances as provided by console proxies.

## nova-novnproxy

Provides a web based GUI proxy for accessing instances thought VNC.

*nova-xvpvncproxy*

Provides a java based client for accessing instances.

*nova*

CUI client to access *Compute* services.

The *Compute* service therefore is a collection of services that are installed in those servers, that are configured to be used as compute nodes. The *Compute* services when installed and configured on a server, registers the server as a hypervisor for the virtual machines. A cloud setup in production usually would contain a cluster of physical servers.

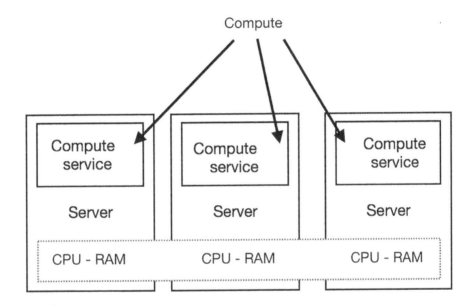

In the above diagram, *Compute* services that are installed on each of the servers, communicate among each other and register themselves to the Openstack cloud as a single Compute unit for the cloud computer. These component services of Compute work in unison to aggregate all the CPU, RAM (and also block storage) available across the nodes.

## Network

This service consists of the creation and managing of networks and subnets, communication among servers spanning through subnets in the Openstack cloud and the internet, and protocols for limitation of access to servers.

*network plugins and agents*

Consists of a number of plugins for purposes like plugging and unplugging of software defined ports creation of networks or subnets, creation and management of dhcp agents for provisioning of IP addresses.

*neutron-server*

Accepts and routes API requests to the appropriate OpenStack Networking plug-in for action.

## Image

This service handles the registering of virtual machine's operating system images in formats such as *.iso, *.qemu, *.vdi etc. such that virtual machines are launched with the registered images, images can be edited on the fly and plenty of other features.

### glance-api

Accepts Image API calls for image discovery, retrieval, and storage.

### glance-registry

Stores, processes, and retrieves metadata about images. Metadata includes items such as size and type.

### metadata definition service

As mentioned in the Compute service about metadata requirement and purpose, the metadata service is a common API for Openstack services and users to define custom metadata which can be used in images, artefacts, volumes, flavours, and aggregates.
repository for image files
   The glance image files in the registry are stored as normal filesystems, object storage, VMware datastore etc.

## Storage

This service provides block storage volumes for instances through various drivers such as NAS/SAN, NFS, iSCSI, Ceph etc. Although this service is not the recommended necessary service for a minimal setup of Openstack, but it is a very useful one. Using this service, one can attach or remove block storage disk volumes to any instance/VM.

## cinder-api

Accepts requests, delegates to relevant cinder service for action and returns response.

## cinder-scheduler

Similar to the purpose of nova-scheduler to decide on which cinder node a volume creation action to be delegated, in a clustered Storage setup for Openstack.

## cinder-volume

Interacts with cinder-scheduler and cinder-api and is involved in creating the volume upon request. It is capable of working with a variety of storage providers with its list of driver compatibility.

## cinder-backup

This service provides backing up volumes of any type to a backup storage. Supports all the major storage driver providers.

## *Identity*

It provides a single point of integration for managing authentication, authorization, and a catalog of all Openstack services. By creation of users and segregation into groups, Openstack provides the rules of accessibility to service(s). It works in a token generation based method through a RESTful interface. Identity is the first point of access for a user interacting with Openstack, and once authenticated, users can access the cloud services as provided by the service catalog. It can integrate with third party user management system such as LDAP.

## *The other dependant softwares used by Openstack services -*

## *Message Queue*

A message queue is at the heart of all of the communication that goes on among the sub-services/daemons for each of the Openstack components Identity, Compute, Network, Cinder, Image (and also the remaining of the components that aren't mentioned here). For example, cinder-api, cinder-volume, cinder-scheduler, cinder-backup are the parts that make up the Block Storage service and these services talk to each other through their assigned queues in the Message Queue.

## Database

At the heart of all the data flow among the components discussed briefly above, a database, of course is the data storage backbone for Openstack. Starting from user and service information for Identity, to the statuses of the Compute virtual machines, to the Network details about subnets, routers, IP allocations and ports, the Glance details of image metadata, and information about cinder Storage volume types and their associations with instances.

Openstack comprises of other more components/services. The above mentioned ones are the minimum requirement to deploy a public/private cloud (with the exception of cinder, which is optional). The robustness of Openstack comes from the decoupled nature of the components. The components are devoid of system affinity, i.e. the components may reside on different physical systems. This is achieved through the usage of a message queue for inter-intra process/ service communication and the Openstack components talk to each other through HTTP/HTTPS requests at service (Identity, Image, Network etc.) endpoints. The term service has interchangeably used for Openstack components such as Compute as well as nova-compute which is a sub-component of Compute. For our convenience we may call them service and sub-service.

When a new service is added, HTTP service endpoints are registered of three types - admin, internal or public for accessing API(s). In a production environment, different endpoint types might reside on separate networks exposed to different types of users for security reasons. For instance, the public API network might be visible from the Internet so customers can manage their clouds. The admin API network might be restricted to operators within the organization that manages cloud infrastructure. The internal API network might be restricted to the hosts that contain OpenStack services. For a cloud deployment that has data centers spanning across multiple geographical locations, Openstack supports multiple regions, the default being *RegionOne*.

## A quick round up on the types of installation

Designing an OpenStack cloud requires a n understanding of the cloud user's requirements and needs to determine the best possible configuration. Openstack can be deployed in two major ways -

### All-in-one

In this method of deployment, all the services are installed in a single physical hardware.

### Multi-node

In this method of deployment, the services are distributed across multiple nodes. For example, the Network service is installed on one node, the Compute on another, the database in a database cluster of nodes, and similarly, the remaining of the services in separate nodes.

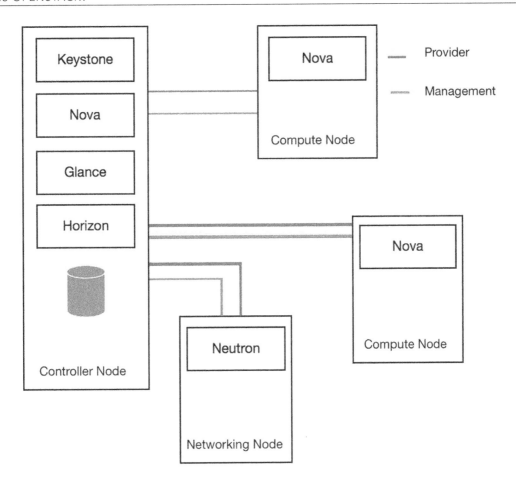

The above setup shows the true modular architecture of the Openstack software. The node that has the keystone service installed will be referred to as the *Controller* node. The servers that are to be joined to the Openstack cluster as the hardware where the virtual machines will be provisioned are designated as *Compute* nodes and will have the *Compute* (Nova) service installed.

These two methods of deployment are assumed to be having a single instance for each of the services and are not highly available. High availability means bringing about fault tolerance among the services. An actual production deployment is ideally highly available where there are redundant Identity, Compute, Network service processes running. The Openstack deployment although will always identify a particular service through a single endpoint URI.

Openstack provides a enough flexibility when it comes to bringing about redundancy in services. A deployment may choose to make only one service highly available. The diagram for multi-node setup shows three installations for the *Compute* (Nova) service. These three installations of the Compute service should not be mistaken for high availability. Whenever the CPU and RAM resources are exhausted, the cloud computer requires new servers for provisioning virtual machines and so, for adding new servers, the Compute service has to be installed which registers itself to the cloud setup.

## Architecture of an Openstack service

Every Openstack service is composed of multiple components. These components have to be present on the controller node, for registering themselves to the cloud. Now since, Openstack services can span across multiple nodes, these component packages can be sub-divided into two groups. One group consists of those packages that are required to be installed on the controller node, and the other to be installed on compute nodes. An Openstack installation in basically composed of two types of nodes - controller and compute. This may seem contradictory to the diagram shown in the *multi-node* section, where there is a separate node for the networking service and no packages are installed on the controller node. We will understand the configuration of Openstack services using the following diagram of a hypothetical Openstack service -

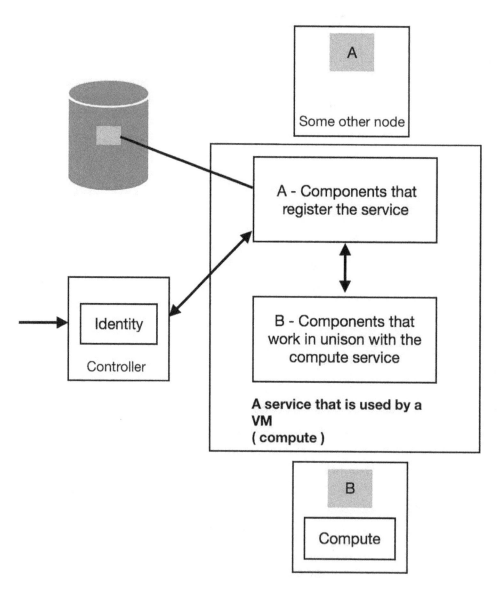

The above diagram depicts an Openstack service that is used throughout the lifetime of a virtual machine. Such services are the Compute service, Network service, and Block storage service and so, every node which is designated as a compute node for hosting virtual machines requires some components of these three services to be present. We may be able get the intuition behind such a requirement as these three resources are required by a computer in a network to run, which in this case is a virtual machine. The service is divided into two group of components A and B. Usually the components in B are basically a subset of the components in A, and so the service components register themselves in the Openstack database where they also store the API endpoints for the service. The name *Controller* node is used in the context of a node that hosts the components of a service that act as the first point of contact and participate in the controlling role for an incoming request. Now w.r.t. to our diagram, the group of component packages A, that control the fate of an incoming request are not placed in the Controller node where the Identity service is located. Rather it is placed in some arbitrary node. This scenario is same as the diagram we used to depict a multi-node setup, where the Neutron service components are not installed on the controller. It is a standard architectural design of an Openstack setup, to place the controller group of components of the Compute, Network and Block storage services, on the same node as that of Keystone and therefore, refer the node as a controller node. Therefore, Openstack services are identified by their API endpoints and the components can reside on any of the nodes in the cloud cluster. The components of a service communicate with each other through socket based communication, and so a certain service that has N number of components can talk to each other and carry out tasks even if all of the N components are installed on separate individual nodes.

The services other than Compute, Network and Block storage do not have group B of components and so the packages are traditionally installed on a controller node.

## Controller and Compute nodes

To summarise the distinction between two types of servers in an Openstack cloud, we can conclude that, servers that are solely responsible for hosting virtual machines are called *Compute* nodes, and the servers where those packages are installed that participate in management and provisioning tasks are referred to as *Controller* nodes. The freedom of deploying Openstack services enables us to install all the services in a single server as mentioned in an All-in-One setup. In such a case, both Controller and Compute nodes are one and is referred to as an AIO node.

## A High-availability setup

We have formed some idea about the role of controller nodes, and its these nodes that define the degree of fault tolerance of an Openstack setup. We are going to take inspiration from the

All-in-One setup and create an array of AIO nodes which will be placed behind a proxy server. Each Openstack cloud is identified by its database. An individual AIO node is an Openstack cloud on its own with its own database. For our high-availability setup, we are going to keep a single database for all of the AIO nodes. The Openstack service are loosely coupled and stateless, and so it order to take any action for an incoming request, the service does a database lookup to fetch information about the Openstack cloud (API endpoints). Therefore, multiple instances of an Openstack service are identical to each other when pointing to the same database. A diagram to show a highly available deployment.

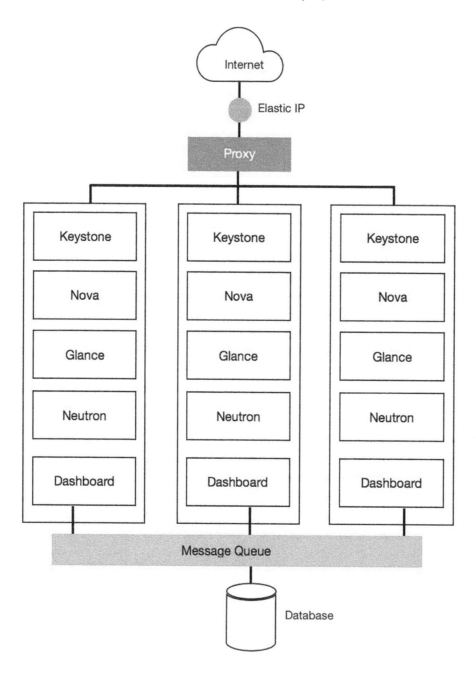

For our installation we are going to achieve high availability through a hybrid deployment where we will have five all-in-one Openstack nodes, sitting behind a proxy, storing data in a database cluster.

Officially openstack provides bare-metal deployment through Ansible and also containerised deployment called Kolla. For this book, we are going to go through manual installation understanding each step.

The minimal installation of a proof-of-concept cloud, in a multi-node setup, requires at least two nodes, one for controller and another as compute.

## Statelessness of Openstack services

The stateless nature of Openstack services stands out to be one of the most powerful aspects of it. Openstack keeps all of the information in the database, therefore service components can exist on any node. Suppose we have two Openstack installations for two different companies. Now the two setups are different from each other by databases and the IP configurations of the different components, assuming the default configurations are used for all the services. If the Openstack installations are interchanged and pointed to the other one's database, the cloud's behaviour for each company will be unchanged. Of course, it has to be ensured that the configurations have to be updated with the new IP addresses in the configuration files. Here is a generic diagram depicting this -

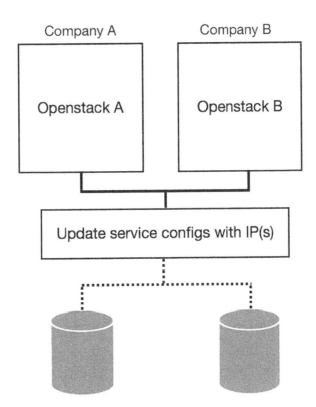

# Discussing some major terminologies

## Node

A physical hardware machine where the Openstack software packages are installed.

## Controller

The physical hardware node where Openstack services are installed and may or may not have virtual machines launched in them. The minimum hardware requirements for such a node - 1 processor, 4 GB memory, and 5 GB storage.

## Compute

The physical hardware node where Openstack instances/virtual machines are launched. Some of the compute component packages are installed on the Controller node, and some are configured on Compute node as well. The component packages on compute node participate in executing the API request received from the Controller node, launch an instance and report back the status to the API endpoint on the Compute service components running on the Controller node. The minimum hardware requirements for such a node - 1 processor, 2 GB memory, and 10 GB storage.

## Management and Provider Network

Openstack, as we have earlier discussed, works by responding to HTTP(S) requests made to service API(s). There are two types of data packets that flow through Openstack, the ones that communicate with the API endpoints upon user interaction with the cloud services and the data packets from the virtual machines. Here, the network is the physical network thats connecting the nodes and not to be confused with Openstack's Network service. It is recommended in a production environment, for segregation of the networks into Management and Provider for security as well as for scenarios where traffic from a rouge cloud instance shall not be able to affect the rest of the system.

Although, for proof-of-concept deployment, all communications can be set on the same network.

A diagram showing traffic flow through management and provider networks

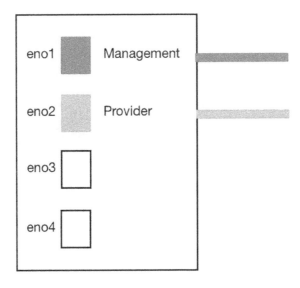

1) *Preparing the architecture*

The Openstack deployment that we are going to establish is a five node, highly available, all-in-one installation.

Here is a diagram of such an arrangement.

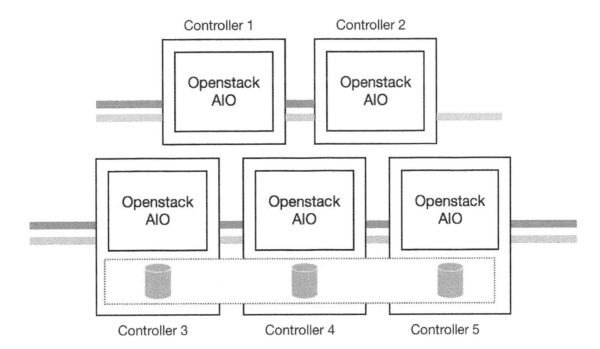

Each of the nodes require at least two NIC(s). One for the management network and other for provider.

The node hardware configuration used are server grade machines used in data-centres and have four NICs each eno1, eno2, eno3, eno4. The two network ranges are - 10.10.0.0/24 and 10.10.4.0/24.

10.10.0.0/24 - Management network
10.10.4.0/24 - Provider network

In all of the five Openstack nodes, eno1 is used for the management network and eno2 is used for provider network.

*To be executed on all five controller nodes.*

First we update all the packages after installing centos. The following version is being used for this setup -

```
centos-release-7-2.1511.el7.centos.2.10.x86_64
```

```
yum update -y
```

The speed and duplex values for each of the network interfaces are checked on all of the hosts -

```
[root@controller5 ~]# ethtool eno1
Settings for eno1:
        Supported ports: [ TP ]
        Supported link modes:   10baseT/Half 10baseT/Full
                                100baseT/Half 100baseT/Full
                                1000baseT/Half 1000baseT/Full
        Supported pause frame use: No
        Supports auto-negotiation: Yes
        Advertised link modes:  10baseT/Half 10baseT/Full
                                100baseT/Half 100baseT/Full
                                1000baseT/Half 1000baseT/Full
        Advertised pause frame use: Symmetric
        Advertised auto-negotiation: Yes
        Link partner advertised link modes:  10baseT/Half 10baseT/Full
                                             100baseT/Half 100baseT/Full
                                             1000baseT/Full
        Link partner advertised pause frame use: No
        Link partner advertised auto-negotiation: Yes
        Speed: 1000Mb/s
        Duplex: Full
```

```
[root@controller5 ~]# ethtool eno2
Settings for eno2:
        Supported ports: [ TP ]
        Supported link modes:   10baseT/Half 10baseT/Full
                                100baseT/Half 100baseT/Full
                                1000baseT/Half 1000baseT/Full
        Supported pause frame use: No
        Supports auto-negotiation: Yes
        Advertised link modes:  10baseT/Half 10baseT/Full
                                100baseT/Half 100baseT/Full
                                1000baseT/Half 1000baseT/Full
        Advertised pause frame use: Symmetric
        Advertised auto-negotiation: Yes
        Link partner advertised link modes:  10baseT/Half 10baseT/Full
                                             100baseT/Half 100baseT/Full
                                             1000baseT/Full
        Link partner advertised pause frame use: No
        Link partner advertised auto-negotiation: Yes
        Speed: 1000Mb/s
        Duplex: Full
```

Sometimes the values Speed and Duplex get set at different values and can be configured with -

```
ethtool -s eno1 speed 1000; ethtool -s eno1 duplex full
```

Next, the the network files have to be configured for both the network interfaces eno1 and eno2.
    For *eno1* -

```
[root@controller5 ~]# cat  /etc/sysconfig/network-scripts/ifcfg-eno1
TYPE="Ethernet"
BOOTPROTO="static"
DEFROUTE="yes"
PEERDNS="yes"
PEERROUTES="yes"
#IPV4_FAILURE_FATAL="no"


IPADDR=10.10.0.43
NETMASK=255.255.254.0
GATEWAY=10.10.0.1
DNS1=10.10.3.11
DNS2=10.10.3.21

NAME="eno1"
UUID="4dca255b-ffdb-4b52-abee-c58b7db72a2f"
DEVICE="eno1"
ONBOOT="yes"
NM_CONTROLLED="no"
```

For *eno2* -

```
[[root@controller5 ~]# cat /etc/sysconfig/network-scripts/ifcfg-eno2
NM_CONTROLLED="no"
DEVICE=eno2
TYPE=Ethernet
ONBOOT="yes"
BOOTPROTO="none"
UUID=19c506d1-5a42-4882-b757-443f69b1cd39
```

The same is done for all the other controller nodes, with their specified IPs. Here is the ones from controller3 for further reference -

```
[root@controller3 ~]# cat /etc/sysconfig/network-scripts/ifcfg-eno1
TYPE="Ethernet"
BOOTPROTO="static"
DEFROUTE="yes"
PEERDNS="yes"
PEERROUTES="yes"
#IPV4_FAILURE_FATAL="no"


IPADDR=10.10.0.34
NETMASK=255.255.254.0
GATEWAY=10.10.0.1
DNS1=10.10.3.11
DNS2=10.10.3.21



NAME="eno1"
#UUID="5c76c91a-ee66-4efa-b0fa-3ee547ee69d9"
DEVICE="eno1"
ONBOOT="yes"
NM_CONTROLLED="no"
```

```
[root@controller3 ~]# cat /etc/sysconfig/network-scripts/ifcfg-eno2
TYPE=Ethernet
BOOTPROTO=none
NAME=eno2
DEVICE=eno2
ONBOOT=yes
NM_CONTROLLED=no
UUID=67763f45-ef2d-47c2-b7ce-07abde4fab26
```

After, the configuration of network device files, NetworkManager has to be disabled. Initially after the base OS is installed, the network devices are set to dhcp by default and that is why the *NM_CONTROLLED* option is set to *"no"*. Change the device files with the static IP addresses, restart the the network service, and make sure the assigned IP addresses are able to communicate to the internet.

The next step is to disable all sort of firewalls on the system.

```
service firewalld disable
service firewalld stop

service iptables disable
service iptables stop
```

Disable selinux from config file -

```
[root@controller5 ~]# cat /etc/selinux/config

SELINUX=disabled
SELINUXTYPE=targeted
```

Openstack provides security to virtual machines through *security groups*. A security group is a logical layer of rule set that defines the ports and protocols with which a virtual machine can be accessed, for ingress or egress flow of traffic. Suppose an application running in a virtual machine requires the port 3306 (default port for mysql) to be open for ingress traffic. A security group can be added to that particular instance to for a custom TCP rule.

Now, as we have configured the network devices eno1 and eno2 for usage, we have to make sure traffic is flowing through both the NIC devices and for that we have to make the following changes in sysctl.conf.

```
[root@controller5 ~]# cat /etc/sysctl.conf
net.ipv4.conf.default.rp_filter = 0
net.ipv4.conf.all.rp_filter = 0


# For Openstack
net.ipv4.ip_forward=1
net.ipv4.ip_nonlocal_bind=1
net.core.netdev_budget=900
```

At this point we will *reboot all of the controller nodes* for the changes in selinux to permanently take effect.

*ip_nonlocal_bind* is used for VRRP usage in our setup and it allows binding to IP addresses that are not assigned to a network interface on the host.

Our high availability cloud setup contains three nodes and all the nodes and the corresponding Openstack services are identified by a single IP address. Such an IP address can be referred to as a virtual address as it will not be bound to any of the network interface on the nodes. We have discussed earlier that each service is identifiable to the rest of the cloud services and user s through an HTTP endpoint. For example, there are three backends for *Compute* service which has the following admin endpoint *http://<IP>:8774/v2.1/*.

## Floating IP for our cloud

Here, *<IP>* is the IP address for our cloud deployment, that is to be provided by the VRRP protocol and it is our virtual/Floating IP address.

In all of the nodes, the *Compute* service listens to requests from *<IP>* address. We are going to achieve our high availability with *keepalived* software. Keepalived after installed and configured on all our Openstack nodes, form the first point of contact when any traffic is sent to the cloud deployment through *management network.* A keepalived daemon has to be running on all controller nodes, and they are always in sync among each other. Whenever, a node becomes unavailable or goes into a problem state such that it is no longer healthy to service requests, the keepalived daemons re-sync among themselves and no longer route traffic to the unavailable node. We will register a virtual IP address with keepalived to access any of the controller nodes. Such an IP address will be attached to one of the nodes at a time on the designated management network interface - eno1. Here is a diagram representing the working of a virtual IP with just three controller nodes -

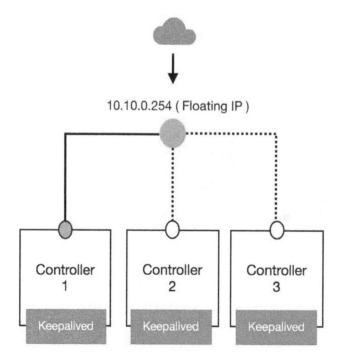

Before we install and configure keepalived, we need to ensure all nodes are able to access each other.

Now, our nodes have the following IP addresses for management network (eno1)-

Node 1 - 10.10.0.35

Node 2 - 10.10.0.33

Node 3 - 10.10.0.34

Node 4 - 10.10.0.31

Node 5 - 10.10.0.43

Node 6 - 10.10.0.138 (Compute node to be added later). We are currently going to focus on setting up our controller nodes 1 through 5.

From now onward, we are going to refer to the nodes as controller(s) interchangeably, and establish a host name for the aforesaid <IP> address.

We configure the host files on all the nodes/controllers as follows -

```
[root@controller5 ~]# cat /etc/hosts
127.0.0.1    localhost localhost.localdomain localhost4 localhost4.localdomain4
::1          localhost localhost.localdomain localhost6 localhost6.localdomain6


10.10.0.254 controller
10.10.0.35 controller1 controller1.infra.ts
10.10.0.33 controller2 controller2.infra.ts
10.10.0.34 controller3 controller3.infra.ts
10.10.0.31 controller4 controller4.infra.ts
10.10.0.43 controller5 controller5.infra.ts

10.10.0.138 compute01 compute01.infra.ts
```

As we can see, the nodes are now referred to as controller[1-5]. We go ahead and change the hostname on each node as well from localhost to controller[1-5].

```
[root@controller5 ~]# ssh controller1 hostname -a
controller1.infra.ts
[root@controller5 ~]# ssh controller2 hostname -a
controller2.infra.ts
[root@controller5 ~]# ssh controller3 hostname -a
controller3.infra.ts
[root@controller5 ~]# ssh controller4 hostname -a
controller4.infra.ts
[root@controller5 ~]# hostname -a
controller5.infra.ts
```

There is also another entry in the host file for - 10.10.0.254 controller, which is our virtual IP address and will be discussed shortly. We have previously discussed about the two types of nodes, *Controller* and *Compute* in a the proof-of-concept deployment where the node designated as *Compute* serves the purpose of launching and hosting the virtual machines. Since, our Openstack installation will be all-in-one, the virtual machines are going to be launched on the same node on which Controller is established. Therefore, we are collectively referencing each node as controller[1-5].

Next, we install epel-release (repository for RHEL extra packages) and keepalived on all controllers/nodes.

```
yum install epel-release keepalived -y
```

Configure the keepalived.conf file -

```
[root@controller5 ~]# cat /etc/keepalived/keepalived.conf
global_defs {
  router_id controller5
}
vrrp_script haproxy {
  script "killall -0 haproxy"
  interval 2
  weight 2
}
vrrp_instance 100 {
  virtual_router_id 100
  advert_int 1
  priority 100
  state MASTER
  interface eno1
  virtual_ipaddress {
    10.10.0.254 dev eno1
  }
  track_script {
    haproxy
  }
}
```

This file has to be configured on all of the controller nodes 1 through 5, and here is the one from controller1.

```
[root@controller1 ~]# cat /etc/keepalived/keepalived.conf
global_defs {
  router_id controller1
}
vrrp_script haproxy {
  script "killall -0 haproxy"
  interval 2
  weight 2
}
vrrp_instance 100 {
  virtual_router_id 100
  advert_int 1
  priority 105
  state MASTER
  interface eno1
  virtual_ipaddress {
    10.10.0.254 dev eno1
  }
  track_script {
    haproxy
  }
}
```

As we can see only the *global_defs* key in the keepalived.conf file has to be changed w.r.t. each node name, because we want to identify each of the *router_ids* with their corresponding node names for the ease of reference.

```
service enable keepalived

service start keepalived
```

The node where keepalived is started first, has the IP 10.10.0.254 attached to eno1 interface as specified in the config file in the *virtual_ipaddress* key.

```
[root@controller1 ~]# ip a|head -n 15
1: lo: <LOOPBACK,UP,LOWER_UP> mtu 65536 qdisc noqueue state UNKNOWN
    link/loopback 00:00:00:00:00:00 brd 00:00:00:00:00:00
    inet 127.0.0.1/8 scope host lo
       valid_lft forever preferred_lft forever
    inet6 ::1/128 scope host
       valid_lft forever preferred_lft forever
2: eno1: <BROADCAST,MULTICAST,UP,LOWER_UP> mtu 1500 qdisc mq state UP qlen 1000
    link/ether 1c:98:ec:1d:d1:ac brd ff:ff:ff:ff:ff:ff
    inet 10.10.0.35/23 brd 10.10.1.255 scope global eno1
       valid_lft forever preferred_lft forever
    inet 10.10.0.254/32 scope global eno1
       valid_lft forever preferred_lft forever
    inet6 fe80::1e98:ecff:fe1d:d1ac/64 scope link
       valid_lft forever preferred_lft forever
```

None of the other nodes will have the virtual IP attached to it initially. Here is the output of another node -

```
[root@controller5 ~]# ip a|head -n 10
1: lo: <LOOPBACK,UP,LOWER_UP> mtu 65536 qdisc noqueue state UNKNOWN
    link/loopback 00:00:00:00:00:00 brd 00:00:00:00:00:00
    inet 127.0.0.1/8 scope host lo
       valid_lft forever preferred_lft forever
    inet6 ::1/128 scope host
       valid_lft forever preferred_lft forever
2: eno1: <BROADCAST,MULTICAST,UP,LOWER_UP> mtu 1500 qdisc mq state UP qlen 1000
    link/ether 40:a8:f0:25:14:34 brd ff:ff:ff:ff:ff:ff
    inet 10.10.0.43/23 brd 10.10.1.255 scope global eno1
       valid_lft forever preferred_lft forever
```

If and when the keepalived service is stopped on controller1, where the IP is attached initially, the IP gets re-attached to any of the other nodes where keepalived daemon is running. There is no bias toward on which controller the virtual IP gets attached. A restart of keepalived reattaches the IP to a different controller and that way we can check how the virtual IP floats around the network interfaces of the controllers and it is this property which derives the terms *floating/elastic IP*, which we will come across again later in the book.

Since, our host files have been updated with virtual IP address as well, when we ssh to the hostname *controller*, an ssh session will be created with the node where the virtual IP is currently attached.

```
[root@controller5 ~]# ssh root@controller
The authenticity of host 'controller (10.10.0.254)' can't be established.
ECDSA key fingerprint is ce:06:9e:37:d4:25:78:7a:80:02:7d:e2:e4:e6:8d:db.
Are you sure you want to continue connecting (yes/no)? yes
Warning: Permanently added 'controller,10.10.0.254' (ECDSA) to the list of known hosts.
Last login: Mon Dec  3 17:46:50 2018 from controller5
############## WELCOME TO CONTROLLER 1 ###################
#        ~ PLEASE BE CAREFUL WITH WHAT YOU TYPE IN ~      #
#              ~ DO NOT DELETE ANY DATA ~                 #
#        ~ DO NOT KEEP PERSONAL DATA-FILES HERE ~         #
##########################################################
```

We have established communication and routing of traffic among the controller nodes and before moving forward we will refer to a diagram that state the current state of our deployment architecture. The highlighted portions of the diagram represent what we have completed and we would refer this diagram at the end of each service or component that we add to the cloud.

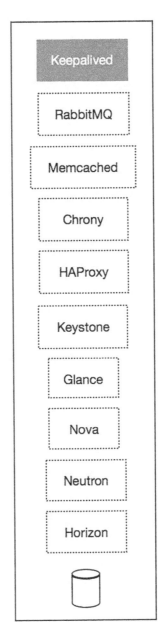

**Controllers 1 - 5**

## Database cluster

An Openstack cloud relies entirely upon the data it stores in a database and it constitutes the most important component of the cloud. Every service that is added to cloud installation creates a database for itself. Openstack services during installation, first register themselves with *Identity* service, which is when data for the service is stored into the service catalog of

*Identity* in the database. Three of the controllers will have a database that participate to form a single cluster. This database cluster acts as a single data store for all the five Openstack installations. Therefore, whichever controller node among the five, is servicing a request, it is communicating to the same data source provided by the database cluster.

*To be executed on controller3, controller4 and controller5.*

We will build a Galera cluster, by first adding the repository to the nodes.

```
[root@controller3 ~]# cat /etc/yum.repos.d/MariaDB.repo
[mariadb]
name = MariaDB
baseurl = http://yum.mariadb.org/10.1/centos7-amd64
gpgkey=https://yum.mariadb.org/RPM-GPG-KEY-MariaDB
keepcache=1
gpgcheck=1
```

The necessary packages are installed.

```
yum -y install MariaDB-server MariaDB-client MariaDB-common rsync lsof
```

Then MariaDB is configured on the controller nodes 3 through 5.

*For controller3,*

```
[root@controller3 ~]# cat /etc/my.cnf.d/server.cnf
[server]

[mysqld]
log_error=/var/log/mariadb.log
max_connections=4096
collation-server = utf8_general_ci
max_allowed_packet=64M
character-set-server = utf8

#
# * Galera-related settings
#
[galera]
binlog_format=ROW
default-storage-engine=innodb
innodb_autoinc_lock_mode=2
bind-address=10.10.0.34
wsrep_on=ON
wsrep_provider=/usr/lib64/galera/libgalera_smm.so
#wsrep_cluster_address="gcomm://"
wsrep_cluster_address="gcomm://10.10.0.34,10.10.0.31,10.10.0.43"
```

```
### Galera Cluster Configuration
wsrep_cluster_name="openstack-cluster"
### Galera Synchronization Configuration
wsrep_sst_method=rsync
wsrep_sst_auth=sstuser:SST_PASS
wsrep_sst_donor='10.10.0.34'

### Galera Node Configuration
wsrep_node_address="10.10.0.34"
wsrep_node_name="openstack-vm1"
wsrep_debug=1
```

For controller4,

```
[[root@controller4 ~]# cat /etc/my.cnf.d/server.cnf
[server]

[mysqld]
log_error=/var/log/mariadb.log
max_connections=4096
collation-server = utf8_general_ci
max_allowed_packet=64M
character-set-server = utf8

#
# * Galera-related settings
#
[galera]
binlog_format=ROW
default-storage-engine=innodb
innodb_autoinc_lock_mode=2
bind-address=10.10.0.31
wsrep_on=ON
wsrep_provider=/usr/lib64/galera/libgalera_smm.so
#wsrep_cluster_address="gcomm://"
wsrep_cluster_address="gcomm://10.10.0.34,10.10.0.31,10.10.0.43"

### Galera Cluster Configuration
wsrep_cluster_name="openstack-cluster"
### Galera Synchronization Configuration
wsrep_sst_method=rsync
wsrep_sst_auth=sstuser:SST_PASS

### Galera Node Configuration
wsrep_node_address="10.10.0.31"
wsrep_node_name="openstack-vm2"
wsrep_debug=1
```

For controller5,

```
[[root@controller5 ~]# cat /etc/my.cnf.d/server.cnf
[server]

[mysqld]
log_error=/var/log/mariadb.log
max_connections=4096
collation-server = utf8_general_ci
max_allowed_packet=64M
character-set-server = utf8
#bind-address = 10.10.0.43


#
# * Galera-related settings
#
[galera]
binlog_format=ROW
default-storage-engine=innodb
innodb_autoinc_lock_mode=2
bind-address=10.10.0.43
wsrep_on=ON
wsrep_provider=/usr/lib64/galera/libgalera_smm.so
#wsrep_cluster_address="gcomm://"
wsrep_cluster_address="gcomm://10.10.0.34,10.10.0.31,10.10.0.43"

### Galera Cluster Configuration
wsrep_cluster_name="openstack-cluster"
### Galera Synchronization Configuration
wsrep_sst_method=rsync
wsrep_sst_auth=sstuser:SST_PASS
#wsrep_sst_donor='10.10.0.34'

### Galera Node Configuration
wsrep_node_address="10.10.0.43"
wsrep_node_name="openstack-vm3"
wsrep_debug=1
```

Next we create the log file locations with proper permissions.

```
touch /var/log/mariadb.log
chown mysql:mysql /var/log/mariadb.log
```

Before, starting the cluster, we take a look at the - *gcomm://* parameter in the MariaDB configuration.

```
wsrep_cluster_address="gcomm://10.10.0.34,10.10.0.31,10.10.0.43"
```

This is the cluster builder or we can say, this parameter registers the cluster. So the node on which MariaDB is started first, needs to have this parameter on, since being the first node in the cluster it registers the identity of all the nodes in the cluster. The rest of the nodes would be started with *wsrep_cluster_address="gcomm://"* parameter.

When the cluster is stopped such that none of the databases are running, the *wsrep_cluster_address="gcomm://"* parameter is to be used to for starting the most updated node.

The following files output show which database is the most updated by comparing the value of *seqno* parameter.

```
[root@controller3 ~]# cat /var/lib/mysql/grastate.dat
# GALERA saved state
version: 2.1
uuid:    12214274-6d70-11e8-9e1d-477a9b32ceeb
seqno:   -1
safe_to_bootstrap: 0
```

Say, controller3 is stopped first, then controller4 and finally controller5. The last one to stop is the one which is most updated. To restart the cluster, controller5 has to be started first, followed by either of controller3 or controller4. When starting the controller5 database, *wsrep_cluster_address="gcomm://"* has to be uncommented and active, whereas *wsrep_cluster_address="gcomm://10.10.0.34,10.10.0.31,10.10.0.43"* has to be kept commented out and inactive because the cluster node addresses are already registered during the first run.

When a new database is added to the cluster, the database must start with including the IP address of the database node in the *gcomm* parameter. For example, the new database node has IP 10.10.0.100, the gcomm parameter should be -

wsrep_cluster_address="gcomm://10.10.0.34,10.10.0.31,10.10.0.43,**10.10.0.100**"

Now, first we start controller1's database with the command -

```
galera_new_cluster
```

After starting the database, we log into the database and check the status of the cluster with the following command -

```
MariaDB [(none)]> SHOW STATUS LIKE 'wsrep_cluster_size';
+--------------------+-------+
| Variable_name      | Value |
+--------------------+-------+
| wsrep_cluster_size | 1     |
+--------------------+-------+
1 row in set (0.00 sec)
```

The rest of the nodes are started with the following command, we recheck the cluster size which should be showing 3.

```
[MariaDB [(none)]> SHOW STATUS LIKE 'wsrep_cluster_size';
+--------------------+-------+
| Variable_name      | Value |
+--------------------+-------+
| wsrep_cluster_size | 3     |
+--------------------+-------+
1 row in set (0.00 sec)
```

We must then check if the cluster is functionally replicating data across all nodes by creating a test database from any one of the database nodes and have that database available to all the other database nodes.

As the database cluster is ready, we'll refer to our architecture diagram.

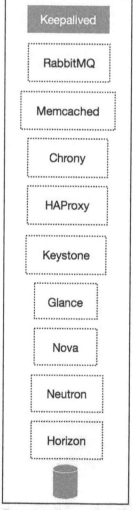

**Controllers 3 - 5**

## Proxy

By now, we have our virtual IP that would be the first point of contact for accessing any of the Openstack services. The VRRP routing with keepalived, gives any of the controllers [1-5] to service a request. All the five AIO nodes will have the same services installed and thus when suppose the *Compute* service in any of the controllers is receiving an API request and responding, the communications happen with the virtual IP address, 10.10.0.254. Our virtual IP address is the one with which all our API endpoints are registered - *http://<IP>:8774/v2.1/*. Here *<IP>* will be set to *controller* which is the hostname for our virtual IP as set in /etc/hosts.

With 10.10.0.254 as our API address, all the Openstack services will bind their ports to the virtual IP. Now, since keepalived will be listening to the designated API ports, the Openstack services cannot bind to that port with IP - 10.10.0.254.

For example, keepalived listens to the port 8774 and the corresponding socket is *10.10.0.254:8774*. Now when the *Compute* service (nova-compute sub-service) starts, it will not be able to create the socket *10.10.0.254:8774*, obviously. Therefore, we will configure the Openstack services to create a socket with the *Management* IP address for example in eno1 - *10.10.0.35:8774* in case of controller1.

We now require an actor that can forward the traffic from the socket *10.10.0.254:8774/ controller:8774* to *10.10.0.35:8774/controller1:8774*. This we will achieve with a reverse proxy software, *HAProxy*.

Installing the HAProxy package on all controllers.

```
yum install haproxy -y
```

We are configuring all the required bindings for our Openstack services before installing them on all the controllers in */etc/haproxy/haproxy.cfg*

```
global
    chroot /var/lib/haproxy
    user haproxy
    group haproxy
    daemon
    log 10.10.0.43 local0
    stats socket /var/lib/haproxy/stats
    maxconn 4000

defaults
  log  global
  maxconn  8000
  option  redispatch
  retries  3
  timeout  http-request 10s
  timeout  queue 1m
  timeout  connect 10s
  timeout  client 1m
  timeout  server 1m
  timeout  check 10s
```

```
listen stats 10.10.0.254:1936
        mode http
        stats enable
        stats uri /stats
        stats realm HAProxy\ Statistics
        stats auth admin:password

listen database 10.10.0.254:3306
        balance roundrobin
        mode tcp
        option tcpka
        option mysql-check user haproxy
        server MySQL1 10.10.0.34:3306 check weight 1
        server MySQL2 10.10.0.31:3306 check weight 1
        server MySQL3 10.10.0.43:3306 check weight 1

listen memcached 10.10.0.254:11211
        balance roundrobin
        mode tcp
        option tcpka
        maxconn 10000
        server controller1 10.10.0.35:11211 check inter 2000 rise 2 fall 5
        server controller2 10.10.0.33:11211 check inter 2000 rise 2 fall 5
        server controller3 10.10.0.34:11211 check inter 2000 rise 2 fall 5
        server controller4 10.10.0.31:11211 check inter 2000 rise 2 fall 5
        server controller5 10.10.0.43:11211 check inter 2000 rise 2 fall 5

listen keystone_admin 10.10.0.254:35357
        balance roundrobin
        option tcpka
        option httpchk
        maxconn 10000
        server controller1 10.10.0.35:35357 check inter 2000 rise 2 fall 5
        server controller2 10.10.0.33:35357 check inter 2000 rise 2 fall 5
        server controller3 10.10.0.34:35357 check inter 2000 rise 2 fall 5
        server controller4 10.10.0.31:35357 check inter 2000 rise 2 fall 5
        server controller5 10.10.0.43:35357 check inter 2000 rise 2 fall 5

listen keystone_api 10.10.0.254:5000
        balance roundrobin
        option tcpka
        option httpchk
        maxconn 10000
        server controller1 10.10.0.35:5000 check inter 2000 rise 2 fall 5
        server controller2 10.10.0.33:5000 check inter 2000 rise 2 fall 5
        server controller3 10.10.0.34:5000 check inter 2000 rise 2 fall 5
        server controller4 10.10.0.31:5000 check inter 2000 rise 2 fall 5
        server controller5 10.10.0.43:5000 check inter 2000 rise 2 fall 5
```

```
listen glance-api 10.10.0.254:9292
        balance roundrobin
        option tcpka
        option httpchk
        maxconn 10000
        server controller1 10.10.0.35:9292 check inter 2000 rise 2 fall 5
        server controller2 10.10.0.33:9292 check inter 2000 rise 2 fall 5
        server controller3 10.10.0.34:9292 check inter 2000 rise 2 fall 5
        server controller4 10.10.0.31:9292 check inter 2000 rise 2 fall 5
        server controller5 10.10.0.43:9292 check inter 2000 rise 2 fall 5

listen glance-registry 10.10.0.254:9191
        balance roundrobin
        option tcpka
        maxconn 10000
        server controller1 10.10.0.35:9191 check inter 2000 rise 2 fall 5
        server controller2 10.10.0.33:9191 check inter 2000 rise 2 fall 5
        server controller3 10.10.0.34:9191 check inter 2000 rise 2 fall 5
        server controller4 10.10.0.31:9191 check inter 2000 rise 2 fall 5
        server controller5 10.10.0.43:9191 check inter 2000 rise 2 fall 5

listen nova_osapi 10.10.0.254:8774
        balance roundrobin
        option tcpka
        option httpchk
        maxconn 10000
        server controller1 10.10.0.35:8774 check inter 2000 rise 2 fall 5
        server controller2 10.10.0.33:8774 check inter 2000 rise 2 fall 5
        server controller3 10.10.0.34:8774 check inter 2000 rise 2 fall 5
        server controller4 10.10.0.31:8774 check inter 2000 rise 2 fall 5
        server controller5 10.10.0.43:8774 check inter 2000 rise 2 fall 5

listen nova_metadata 10.10.0.254:8775
        balance roundrobin
        option tcpka
        option httpchk
        maxconn 10000
        server controller1 10.10.0.35:8775 check inter 2000 rise 2 fall 5
        server controller2 10.10.0.33:8775 check inter 2000 rise 2 fall 5
        server controller3 10.10.0.34:8775 check inter 2000 rise 2 fall 5
        server controller4 10.10.0.31:8775 check inter 2000 rise 2 fall 5
        server controller5 10.10.0.43:8775 check inter 2000 rise 2 fall 5
```

```
listen heat_api 10.10.0.254:8004
        balance roundrobin
        option tcpka
        option httpchk
        maxconn 10000
        server controller1 10.10.0.35:8004 check inter 2000 rise 2 fall 5
        server controller2 10.10.0.33:8004 check inter 2000 rise 2 fall 5
        server controller3 10.10.0.34:8004 check inter 2000 rise 2 fall 5
        server controller4 10.10.0.31:8004 check inter 2000 rise 2 fall 5
        server controller5 10.10.0.43:8004 check inter 2000 rise 2 fall 5

listen heat_api_cfn 10.10.0.254:8000
        balance roundrobin
        option tcpka
        option httpchk
        maxconn 10000
        server controller1 10.10.0.35:8000 check inter 2000 rise 2 fall 5
        server controller2 10.10.0.33:8000 check inter 2000 rise 2 fall 5
        server controller3 10.10.0.34:8000 check inter 2000 rise 2 fall 5
        server controller4 10.10.0.31:8000 check inter 2000 rise 2 fall 5
        server controller5 10.10.0.43:8000 check inter 2000 rise 2 fall 5

listen novnc 10.10.0.254:6080
        balance roundrobin
        option tcpka
        maxconn 10000
        server controller1 10.10.0.35:6080 check inter 2000 rise 2 fall 5
        server controller2 10.10.0.33:6080 check inter 2000 rise 2 fall 5
        server controller3 10.10.0.34:6080 check inter 2000 rise 2 fall 5
        server controller4 10.10.0.31:6080 check inter 2000 rise 2 fall 5
        server controller5 10.10.0.43:6080 check inter 2000 rise 2 fall 5

listen neutron 10.10.0.254:9696
        balance roundrobin
        option tcpka
        maxconn 10000
        server controller1 10.10.0.35:9696 check inter 2000 rise 2 fall 5
        server controller2 10.10.0.33:9696 check inter 2000 rise 2 fall 5
        server controller3 10.10.0.34:9696 check inter 2000 rise 2 fall 5
        server controller4 10.10.0.31:9696 check inter 2000 rise 2 fall 5
        server controller5 10.10.0.43:9696 check inter 2000 rise 2 fall 5


listen dashboard 10.10.0.254:80
        balance   roundrobin
        capture   cookie vgnvisitor= len 32
        cookie    SERVERID insert indirect nocache
        mode   http
        option   forwardfor
        option   httpchk
        option   httpclose
        rspidel   ^Set-cookie:\ IP=

        server controller3 10.10.0.34:80 cookie control03 check inter 2000 rise 2 fall 5
        server controller4 10.10.0.31:80 cookie control04 check inter 2000 rise 2 fall 5
        server controller5 10.10.0.43:80 cookie control05 check inter 2000 rise 2 fall 5
```

Start haproxy and goto the url -

`http://10.10.0.254:1936/stats`

with credentials - *User*: admin, *Password*: password, as configured in haproxy.conf.

```
systemctl start haproxy
```

The dashboard shows all services in red, for obvious reasons, except MYSQL1,MYSQL2 and MYSQL3 which should be in green. This is because we have to create an haproxy user in the database and give the user permission so that haproxy process can access mysql and report the status.

Log into mysql in any of the nodes controller[3-5] and execute the following commands.

```
MariaDB [(none)]> CREATE USER 'haproxy'@'controller';
MariaDB [(none)]> GRANT ALL PRIVILEGES ON *.* to 'haproxy'@'controller';
MariaDB [(none)]> GRANT ALL PRIVILEGES ON *.* to 'haproxy'@'%';
```

After creating the privileges, when we return to the haproxy dashboard, we will find the MYSQL service status turned into green.

← → C  ⊙ Not Secure | 10.10.0.254:1936/stats

# HAProxy version 1.5.18, released 2016/05/10

## Statistics Report for pid 12177

> General process information

**pid = 12177 (process #1, nbproc = 1)**
**uptime = 112d 7h30m07s**
**system limits:** memmax = unlimited; ulimit-n = 8102
**maxsock** = 8102; **maxconn** = 4000; **maxpipes** = 0
current conns = 721; current pipes = 0/0; conn rate = 4/sec
Running tasks: 1/795; idle = 98 %

| active UP | | backup UP |
|---|---|---|
| active UP, going down | | backup UP, going down |
| active DOWN, going up | | backup DOWN, going up |
| active or backup DOWN | | not checked |
| active or backup DOWN for maintenance (MAINT) | | |
| active or backup SOFT STOPPED for maintenance | | |

Note: "NOLB"/"DRAIN" = UP with load-balancing disabled.

**Display option:**
- Scope :
- Hide 'DOWN' servers
- Refresh now
- CSV export

**External resources:**
- Primary site
- Updates (v1.5)
- Online manual

### stats

| | Queue | | | Session rate | | | Sessions | | | | | Bytes | | Denied | | Errors | | | Warnings | | Server | | | | | | | | |
|---|---|---|---|---|---|---|---|---|---|---|---|---|---|---|---|---|---|---|---|---|---|---|---|---|---|---|---|---|---|---|
| | Cur | Max | Limit | Cur | Max | Limit | Cur | Max | Limit | Total | LbTot | Last | In | Out | Req | Resp | Req | Resp | Conn | Retr | Redis | Status | LastChk | Wght | Act | Bck | Chk | Dwn | Dwntme | Thrtle |
| Frontend | | | | 2 | 2 | - | 2 | 3 | 8 000 | 231 | | | 198 142 | 37 199 446 | 0 | 0 | 0 | 26 | | | | OPEN | | | | | | | | |
| Backend | 0 | 0 | | 0 | 1 | | 0 | 1 | 800 | 21 | 0 | 0s | 198 142 | 37 199 446 | 0 | 0 | 0 | 21 | 0 | 0 | 112d7h UP | | 0 | 0 | 0 | 0 | 0 | | | |

### database

| | Queue | | | Session rate | | | Sessions | | | | | Bytes | | Denied | | | Errors | | | Warnings | | Server | | | | | | | | |
|---|---|---|---|---|---|---|---|---|---|---|---|---|---|---|---|---|---|---|---|---|---|---|---|---|---|---|---|---|---|---|
| | Cur | Max | Limit | Cur | Max | Limit | Cur | Max | Limit | Total | LbTot | Last | In | Out | Req | Resp | Req | Resp | Conn | Retr | Redis | Status | LastChk | Wght | Act | Bck | Chk | Dwn | Dwntme | Thrtle |
| Frontend | | | | 1 | 109 | - | 684 | 923 | 8 000 | 8 837 039 | | | 685 451 947 724 | 1 652 865 128 530 | 0 | 0 | 0 | | | | | OPEN | | | | | | | | |
| MySQL3 | 0 | 0 | - | 1 | 109 | | 684 | 923 | - | 8 837 039 | 8 837 039 | 0s | 685 451 947 724 | 1 652 865 128 530 | | 0 | 0 | 0 | 0 | 0 | 0 | 112d7h UP | L7OK/0 in 0ms | 1 | Y | - | 1 | 0 | 0s | - |
| MySQL4 | 0 | 0 | - | 1 | 109 | | 684 | 923 | - | 8 837 039 | 8 837 039 | 0s | 685 451 947 724 | 1 652 865 128 530 | | 0 | 0 | 0 | 0 | 0 | 0 | 112d7h UP | L7OK/0 in 0ms | 1 | Y | - | 1 | 0 | 0s | - |
| MySQL4 | 0 | 0 | | 1 | 109 | | 684 | 923 | - | 8 837 039 | 8 837 039 | 0s | 685 451 947 724 | 1 652 865 128 530 | | 0 | 0 | 0 | 0 | 0 | 0 | 112d7h UP | L7OK/0 in 0ms | 1 | Y | - | 1 | 0 | 0s | - |

The diagram below shows entries for the rest of the services as green. This is only for referential purpose for how it should look in the future when the corresponding services are turned on. In real, all other entries other than MySQL will show red.

**memcached**

| | Queue Cur | Queue Max | Queue Limit | SessRate Cur | SessRate Max | SessRate Limit | Sess Cur | Sess Max | Sess Limit | Sess Total | Sess LbTot | Sess Last | Bytes In | Bytes Out | Denied Req | Denied Resp | Err Req | Err Conn | Err Resp | Warn Retr | Warn Redis | Status | LastChk | Wght | Act | Bck | Chk | Dwn | Dwntme | Thrtle |
|---|---|---|---|---|---|---|---|---|---|---|---|---|---|---|---|---|---|---|---|---|---|---|---|---|---|---|---|---|---|---|
| Frontend | | | | 1 | 27 | - | 14 | 161 | 10 000 | 713 402 | | | 3 395 170 795 | 44 135 916 876 | 0 | 0 | 0 | | | | | OPEN | | | | | | | | |
| controller1 | 0 | 0 | - | 0 | 6 | - | 3 | 35 | - | 142 681 | 142 681 | 2s | 682 801 392 | 8 941 427 760 | | 0 | | 0 | 0 | 0 | 0 | 112d7h UP | L4OK in 0ms | 1 | Y | - | 0 | 0 | 0s | - |
| controller2 | 0 | 0 | - | 1 | 6 | - | 4 | 37 | - | 142 681 | 142 681 | 1s | 627 711 143 | 7 101 810 430 | | 0 | | 0 | 0 | 0 | 0 | 112d7h UP | L4OK in 0ms | 1 | Y | - | 0 | 0 | 0s | - |
| controller3 | 0 | 0 | - | 1 | 5 | - | 1 | 35 | - | 142 680 | 142 680 | 8s | 584 781 952 | 5 714 871 224 | | 0 | | 0 | 0 | 0 | 0 | 112d7h UP | L4OK in 0ms | 1 | Y | - | 1 | 0 | 0s | - |
| controller4 | 0 | 0 | - | 0 | 5 | - | 3 | 34 | - | 142 680 | 142 680 | 5s | 638 935 053 | 7 391 994 528 | | 0 | | 0 | 0 | 0 | 0 | 112d7h UP | L4OK in 0ms | 1 | Y | - | 0 | 0 | 0s | - |
| controller5 | 0 | 0 | - | 0 | 5 | - | 3 | 33 | - | 142 680 | 142 680 | 5s | 860 941 255 | 14 985 812 934 | | 0 | | 0 | 0 | 0 | 0 | 112d7h UP | L4OK in 0ms | 1 | Y | - | 0 | 0 | 0s | - |
| Backend | 0 | 0 | | 1 | 27 | | 14 | 161 | 1 000 | 713 402 | 713 402 | 1s | 3 395 170 795 | 44 135 916 876 | 0 | 0 | | 0 | 0 | 0 | 0 | 112d7h UP | | 5 | 5 | 0 | | 0 | 0s | |

**keystone_admin**

| | Queue Cur | Queue Max | Queue Limit | SessRate Cur | SessRate Max | SessRate Limit | Sess Cur | Sess Max | Sess Limit | Sess Total | Sess LbTot | Sess Last | Bytes In | Bytes Out | Denied Req | Denied Resp | Err Req | Err Conn | Err Resp | Warn Retr | Warn Redis | Status | LastChk | Wght | Act | Bck | Chk | Dwn | Dwntme | Thrtle |
|---|---|---|---|---|---|---|---|---|---|---|---|---|---|---|---|---|---|---|---|---|---|---|---|---|---|---|---|---|---|---|
| Frontend | | | | 1 | 9 | - | 9 | 93 | 10 000 | 780 315 | | | 721 286 645 | 5 847 425 153 | 0 | 0 | 0 | | | | | OPEN | | | | | | | | |
| controller1 | 0 | 0 | - | 0 | 2 | - | 1 | 19 | - | 156 063 | 156 063 | 6s | 144 304 883 | 1 169 885 114 | | 0 | | 0 | 0 | 0 | 0 | 112d7h UP | L7OK/200 in 4ms | 1 | Y | - | 0 | 0 | 0s | - |
| controller2 | 0 | 0 | - | 0 | 2 | - | 2 | 20 | - | 156 063 | 156 063 | 5s | 144 395 192 | 1 170 405 228 | | 0 | | 0 | 0 | 0 | 0 | 112d7h UP | L7OK/200 in 4ms | 1 | Y | - | 0 | 0 | 0s | - |
| controller3 | 0 | 0 | - | 0 | 2 | - | 1 | 20 | - | 156 063 | 156 063 | 2s | 144 153 239 | 1 168 753 212 | | 0 | | 0 | 0 | 0 | 0 | 112d7h UP | L7OK/200 in 4ms | 1 | Y | - | 1 | 0 | 0s | - |
| controller4 | 0 | 0 | - | 0 | 2 | - | 2 | 20 | - | 156 063 | 156 063 | 2s | 144 323 647 | 1 170 222 119 | | 0 | | 0 | 0 | 0 | 0 | 112d7h UP | L7OK/200 in 6ms | 1 | Y | - | 0 | 0 | 0s | - |
| controller5 | 0 | 0 | - | 1 | 2 | - | 3 | 19 | - | 156 063 | 156 063 | 1s | 144 109 684 | 1 166 159 480 | | 0 | | 0 | 0 | 0 | 0 | 112d7h UP | L7OK/200 in 3ms | 1 | Y | - | 0 | 0 | 0s | - |
| Backend | 0 | 0 | | 1 | 9 | | 9 | 93 | 1 000 | 780 315 | 780 315 | 1s | 721 286 645 | 5 847 425 153 | 0 | 0 | | 0 | 0 | 0 | 0 | 112d7h UP | | 5 | 5 | 0 | | 0 | 0s | |

**keystone_api**

| | Queue Cur | Queue Max | Queue Limit | SessRate Cur | SessRate Max | SessRate Limit | Sess Cur | Sess Max | Sess Limit | Sess Total | Sess LbTot | Sess Last | Bytes In | Bytes Out | Denied Req | Denied Resp | Err Req | Err Conn | Err Resp | Warn Retr | Warn Redis | Status | LastChk | Wght | Act | Bck | Chk | Dwn | Dwntme | Thrtle |
|---|---|---|---|---|---|---|---|---|---|---|---|---|---|---|---|---|---|---|---|---|---|---|---|---|---|---|---|---|---|---|
| Frontend | | | | 0 | 19 | - | 0 | 14 | 10 000 | 13 372 | | | 7 039 166 | 34 276 300 | 0 | 0 | 0 | | | | | OPEN | | | | | | | | |
| controller1 | 0 | 0 | - | 0 | 4 | - | 0 | 4 | - | 2 675 | 2 675 | 3h12m | 1 424 128 | 6 877 250 | | 0 | | 0 | 0 | 0 | 0 | 112d7h UP | L7OK/200 in 8ms | 1 | Y | - | 0 | 0 | 0s | - |
| controller2 | 0 | 0 | - | 0 | 4 | - | 0 | 4 | - | 2 675 | 2 675 | 3h12m | 1 418 334 | 6 885 868 | | 0 | | 0 | 0 | 0 | 0 | 112d7h UP | L7OK/200 in 2ms | 1 | Y | - | 0 | 0 | 0s | - |
| controller3 | 0 | 0 | - | 0 | 4 | - | 0 | 4 | - | 2 674 | 2 674 | 4h38m | 1 402 747 | 6 913 051 | | 0 | | 0 | 0 | 0 | 0 | 112d7h UP | L7OK/200 in 3ms | 1 | Y | - | 1 | 0 | 0s | - |
| controller4 | 0 | 0 | - | 0 | 4 | - | 0 | 4 | - | 2 674 | 2 674 | 4h38m | 1 372 600 | 6 744 245 | | 0 | | 0 | 0 | 0 | 0 | 112d7h UP | L7OK/200 in 3ms | 1 | Y | - | 1 | 0 | 0s | - |
| controller5 | 0 | 0 | - | 0 | 4 | - | 0 | 4 | - | 2 674 | 2 674 | 4h37m | 1 421 357 | 6 855 886 | | 0 | | 0 | 0 | 0 | 0 | 112d7h UP | L7OK/200 in 7ms | 1 | Y | - | 0 | 0 | 0s | - |
| Backend | 0 | 0 | | 0 | 19 | | 0 | 14 | 1 000 | 13 372 | 13 372 | 3h12m | 7 039 166 | 34 276 300 | 0 | 0 | | 0 | 0 | 0 | 0 | 112d7h UP | | 5 | 5 | 0 | | 0 | 0s | |

Here is our architecture diagram after HAProxy has been setup.

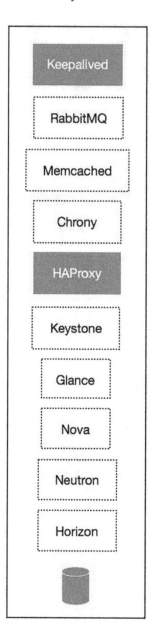

**Controllers 1 - 5**

## Message queue

We had an introduction with the Openstack services and their component packages who work together to accomplish a task earlier in the book. The Openstack sub-services like nova-compute, nova-scheduler etc. of the *Compute* service talk to each other through message passing. Since, the communication is asynchronous, the messages are published in a message queue. We are going to use *RabbitMQ* software to establish such message queueing. As we have redundancy for all of the Openstack services in the controller nodes, we will be forming a *RabbitMQ* cluster on all the controllers. Doing so makes all the messages for all the sub-services available in a common pool. This is necessary for the Openstack deployment to the truly highly available, since a message published into the queue by a sub-service, say, nova-scheduler from controller1, can be picked up by controller2 or controller3 and be serviced. Such a configuration ensures messages are not bound to Openstack nodes, and that, if and when any of the services/sub-services become unavailable or a complete node becomes unhealthy, the task can be still completed by the node where the virtual IP has reattached or where the HAProxy is pointing to as a healthy backend.

The required version for rabbitmq-server (rabbitmq-server-3.6.1-1.noarch) for our Openstack installation and the erlang packages for rabbitmq, are all hosted in at this repository - https://bitbucket.org/bhoson/rabbit_3.6.1-1_and_erlang_19.1-1.el7/src/master

The rabbitmq-server version provided with *epel-release* that is installed on the nodes, would collide with the packages downloaded. Hence, we will disable the yum repo(s), install the packages and re-enable the yum repo(s). Execute the same command given below with toggled values for *enabled* for re-enabling the repo(s).

```
sed -i 's/enabled=1/enabled=0/g' /etc/yum.repos.d/epel.repo
```

*To be installed on all controller nodes.*

Install *rabbitmq-server* and *erlang* packages from the downloaded git repo directory. Trying to install a single package at a time gives rise to cyclic dependency. *yum* handles that when all packages are named at once for installation.

```
yum install -y *
```

After installation, rabbitmq-server has to be started for the first time and immediately stopped. When rabbitmq-server starts, it creates an erlang cookie which has to be copied across all controller[1-5] nodes. This cookie identifies each rabbitmq-server installed on controller[1-5] nodes as a part of the same cluster.

```
[root@controller1 ~]# systemctl start rabbitmq-server
[root@controller2 ~]# systemctl enable rabbitmq-server
[root@controller3 ~]# systemctl stop rabbitmq-server
```

Copying the erlang cookie to controller2, controller3, controller4 and controller5 from controller1.

```
[root@controller1 ~]# scp /var/lib/rabbitmq/.erlang.cookie root@controller2:/var/lib/rabbitmq/.erlang.cookie
[root@controller1 ~]# scp /var/lib/rabbitmq/.erlang.cookie root@controller3:/var/lib/rabbitmq/.erlang.cookie
[root@controller1 ~]# scp /var/lib/rabbitmq/.erlang.cookie root@controller4:/var/lib/rabbitmq/.erlang.cookie
[root@controller1 ~]# scp /var/lib/rabbitmq/.erlang.cookie root@controller5:/var/lib/rabbitmq/.erlang.cookie
```

We have to start rabbitmq-server on all nodes and execute the following commands only on controller2, controller3, controller4 and controller5. The cluster builder will be controller1 and so all other nodes will have to join themselves with the cluster.

```
[root@controller1 ~]# rabbitmqctl stop_app
[root@controller1 ~]# rabbitmqctl join_cluster rabbit@controller1
[root@controller1 ~]# rabbitmqctl start_app
```

For Openstack services to use the message queue, we have to create a user for Openstack and provide permissions. Here, RABBIT_PASS is the password for user *openstack* and these credentials will be added to Openstack service configuration files for accessing the queues.

```
[root@controller1 ~]# rabbitmqctl add_user openstack RABBIT_PASS
[root@controller1 ~]# rabbitmqctl set_permissions openstack ".*" ".*" ".*"
```

Here is our architecture diagram after rabbitmq has been setup.

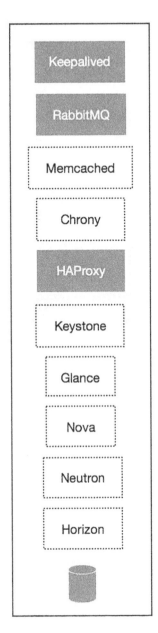

**Controllers 1 - 5**

## Memory caching and system time service

Openstack keeps all its data in a database, and so all API request is followed by a database query. Since, reading from and writing to magnetic storage is slower, we need to be able to speed up the response time for a request. We will establish a caching mechanism in the RAM that optimises the backed database performance by storing recently or frequently requested database records in the RAM, thereby reducing the number of direct requests to database. For installing the next packages, we will download a tarball from the following google drive that contains all the remaining rpm packages that will be required throughout our installation - https://drive.google.com/open?id=1cNYVQ0AXl8VRrft8Q5jVkxtKal5hWMBF (https://bit.ly/2Jz84XQ).

*To be installed on all controller nodes.*
  We will install *memcached*,

```
[root@controller1 ~]# yum install memcached  python-memcached -y
```

and configure -

```
[root@controller1 ~]# cat /etc/sysconfig/memcached
PORT="11211"
USER="memcached"
MAXCONN="1024"
CACHESIZE="64"
OPTIONS="-l 10.10.0.35"
```

For controller2 through controller5, the IP addresses will be 10.10.0.33, 10.10.0.34, 10.10.0.31 and 10.10.0.43 respectively.
  In the Openstack service(s) configuration files for example *Compute* or *Network*, we will refer to memcached servers such that the memcached cache present in individual controller nodes can together behave as a single cache.
  Next, we setup the system time service with chrony such that all the controller nodes aligned with the same network time-server. This would be especially required for nodes where

only *Compute* service is installed to receive time from controller node. But in our cloud setup, all the nodes are All-In-One and so we will keep the default network time-server for centos.

```
[root@controller1 ~]# yum install chrony -y
```

Configuring the chrony.conf file with the hostname *controller* set as the clock time provider.

```
server 0.centos.pool.ntp.org iburst
server 1.centos.pool.ntp.org iburst
server 2.centos.pool.ntp.org iburst
server 3.centos.pool.ntp.org iburst

driftfile /var/lib/chrony/drift

makestep 1.0 3

rtcsync

allow 10.10.0.0/20

server controller iburst
keyfile /etc/chrony.keys

logdir /var/log/chrony
```

We have to configure top allow our management network range for NTP access - 10.10.0.0/20.
    This is how our architecture looks after we have installed the third party packages that enable Openstack to function in our desired architecture.

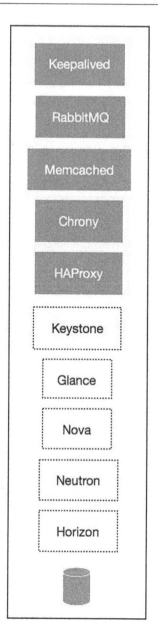

**Controllers 1 - 5**

The Openstack packages for version Newton are no longer hosted officially by Openstack foundation, so we are going to install the packages from our downloaded collection of rpms. In the upcoming chapters we are going to install all the openstack services and for that, we will be requiring an openstack-client application. This client will be used to interact with the openstack cloud through the command line. Here is its installation from our downloaded collection of rpms -

```
yum install python-openstackclient-3.2.1-1.el7.noarch.rpm
```

# Identity/Keystone

We will first, create a database for keystone and provide permissions to keystone user in the database.

*This is to be executed only on any one of the nodes as databases are clustered across the nodes.*

```
MariaDB [(none)]> CREATE DATABASE keystone;

MariaDB [(none)]> GRANT ALL PRIVILEGES ON keystone.* TO 'keystone'@'controller' \
IDENTIFIED BY 'KEYSTONE_DBPASS';

MariaDB [(none)]> GRANT ALL PRIVILEGES ON keystone.* TO 'keystone'@'%' \
IDENTIFIED BY 'KEYSTONE_DBPASS';
```

The configuration files will be set with *KEYSTONE_DBPASS* as the password to access keystone database.

Keystone service is the first point of contact when accessing any of the Openstack service APIs, and that's why, an http web server has to be installed which will serve as our HTTP interface for access Openstack API endpoints.

```
yum install openstack-keystone httpd mod_wsgi -y
```

The configuration for keystone.

```
[root@controller5 ~]# cat /etc/keystone/keystone.conf
[database]
connection = mysql+pymysql://keystone:KEYSTONE_DBPASS@controller/keystone

[token]
provider = fernet
```

Populating the database for *Identity* service. We execute this command on any one of the controller nodes as it performs database write operation.

```
[root@controller3 ~]# su -s /bin/sh -c "keystone-manage db_sync" keystone
```

The Identity/Keystone service authenticates a user with Fernet symmetric encryption method and so for encrypted token generation, keystone requires keys with which encryption is to be done. The fernet key repositories are created as follows and execute them on all nodes.

```
[root@controller3 ~]# keystone-manage fernet_setup --keystone-user keystone --keystone-group keystone
[root@controller3 ~]# keystone-manage credential_setup --keystone-user keystone --keystone-group keystone
```

After this you will find two files named *0* and *1* created at */etc/keystone/fernet-keys/*
    Copy both those keys to the other controllers.

```
[root@controller3 ~]# scp -p /etc/keystone/fernet-keys/* root@controller1:/etc/keystone/fernet-keys/
[root@controller3 ~]# scp -p /etc/keystone/fernet-keys/* root@controller2:/etc/keystone/fernet-keys/
[root@controller3 ~]# scp -p /etc/keystone/fernet-keys/* root@controller4:/etc/keystone/fernet-keys/
[root@controller3 ~]# scp -p /etc/keystone/fernet-keys/* root@controller5:/etc/keystone/fernet-keys/
```

We then bootstrap the keystone with creation of API service endpoints and other internal configurations.

```
[root@controller3 ~]# keystone-manage bootstrap --bootstrap-password ADMIN_PASS \
  --bootstrap-admin-url http://controller:35357/v3/ \
  --bootstrap-internal-url http://controller:35357/v3/ \
  --bootstrap-public-url http://controller:5000/v3/ \
```

Here ADMIN_PASS is the password for the administrator user (admin) of *Identity* service.
    Next we configure the http web-server in */etc/httpd/conf/httpd.conf* and add/change the values of the *ServerName* and *Listen* to the following -

```
Listen 10.10.0.43:80

Include conf.modules.d/*.conf
User apache
Group apache

ServerAdmin root@localhost
ServerName controller
```

Finally, start hosting the keystone API gateway by creating a soft link of the *wsgi* (web server gateway interface) file to the httpd configuration directory for being server by the http web-server.

```
[root@controller1 ~]# ln -s /usr/share/keystone/wsgi-keystone.conf /etc/httpd/conf.d/
[root@controller2 ~]# ln -s /usr/share/keystone/wsgi-keystone.conf /etc/httpd/conf.d/
[root@controller3 ~]# ln -s /usr/share/keystone/wsgi-keystone.conf /etc/httpd/conf.d/
[root@controller4 ~]# ln -s /usr/share/keystone/wsgi-keystone.conf /etc/httpd/conf.d/
[root@controller5 ~]# ln -s /usr/share/keystone/wsgi-keystone.conf /etc/httpd/conf.d/
```

This marks the end of deploying the first and most crucial service of an Openstack deployment. All openstack services can be accessed from CLI with *openstack* command. The *openstack* CLI client required environment variables to be set for authenticating a user and so we are going to create an 'rc' file that instantiates the variables. This would be our admin-rc file.

```
export OS_USERNAME=admin
export OS_PASSWORD=ADMIN_PASS
export OS_PROJECT_NAME=admin
export OS_USER_DOMAIN_NAME=Default
export OS_PROJECT_DOMAIN_NAME=Default
export OS_AUTH_URL=http://controller:35357/v3
export OS_IDENTITY_API_VERSION=3
```

The authentication process requires a combination of PROJECT, DOMAIN, USER and ROLES.

A *domain* is the topmost logical segregation unit for Openstack. It is a container for projects, users, and groups.

A *project* represents the base unit of ownership in Openstack. A project is a container for resources such as subnets, virtual machines, etc.

A *role* is represents a set of rights and privileges for a user. It's a personality that a user assumes to perform a specific set of operations.

A *user* is always created/registered under a domain. A user always has to be associated with a project bearing role(s).

Suppose an organisation has three teams who would be using the cloud such that each team's resources are separated from other. We would create there separate projects for those respective teams, say, project alpha, beta and gamma.

Openstack services (*Compute, Network* etc.) are resources as well and therefore the cloud service resources would be contained in a project named - service. Identity not only provides authentication to user(s) such as ourselves, but also to its deployed services. When a new service is added to the cloud, say Compute, a corresponding user *nova* is created and the Compute service resource is contained in the service project. Similarly, all the services that are added to the Openstack deployment are contained in the service project bearing a unique user for each service.

When a request for launching a virtual machine is made from the project alpha by alpha user, first the request is authenticated by *Identity/Keystone* service. The keystone user then delegates the requests to nova user for launching the virtual machine. The capabilities of *users*, *keystone* and *nova* is determined by their role(s).

We are yet to create the service project that we discussed and the following commands have to be executed. Since, this is an administrative operation, the 'rc' file for admin user has to be instantiated.

```
[root@controller1 ~]# source admin-rc
```

```
[root@controller1 ~]# openstack project create \
--domain default --description "Service Project" service
```

Lets us also create the projects, users and roles for alpha, beta and gamma.

```
[root@controller1 ~]# openstack project create \
--domain default --description "Alpha Project" alpha
[root@controller1 ~]# openstack user create \
--domain default —password ALPHA_PASS alpha
[root@controller1 ~]# openstack role create user
[root@controller1 ~]# openstack role add --project alpha --user alpha user
```

Here we showed only for alpha user, and now we add the role - *user* to alpha project and user.

Finally, we verify the alpha project and user that we just created by generating a token. Since we want to issue a token for exclusively the alpha user, the 'rc' file has to be instantiated for alpha user - alpha-rc.

```
export OS_USERNAME=alpha
export OS_PASSWORD=ALPHA_PASS
export OS_PROJECT_NAME=alpha
export OS_USER_DOMAIN_NAME=Default
export OS_PROJECT_DOMAIN_NAME=Default
export OS_AUTH_URL=http://controller:35357/v3
export OS_IDENTITY_API_VERSION=3
```

A quick look at the process so far after adding the *Identity* service.

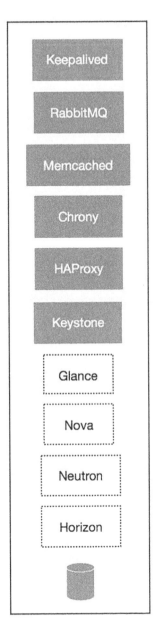

**Controllers 1 - 5**

# Image/Glance

We will start with the similar step as the previous service, of creating the database user and permissions for the *Image* service. The following commands that are with the command *openstack* make changes to the database and so shall be executed on any one of the controller nodes.

```
MariaDB [(none)]> CREATE DATABASE glance;

MariaDB [(none)]> GRANT ALL PRIVILEGES ON glance.* TO 'glance'@'controller' \
  IDENTIFIED BY 'GLANCE_DBPASS';
MariaDB [(none)]> GRANT ALL PRIVILEGES ON glance.* TO 'glance'@'%' \
  IDENTIFIED BY 'GLANCE_DBPASS';
```

Source the admin-rc file and create the *glance* user

```
[root@controller1 ~]# source admin-rc
[root@controller1 ~]# openstack user create
--domain default —password GLANCE_PASS glance
```

Add the *admin* role to the *glance* user and *service* project.

```
[root@controller1 ~]# openstack role add \
--project service --user glance admin
```

Then register the glance service in the cloud service catalogue.

```
[root@controller1 ~]# openstack service create \
--name glance --description "OpenStack Image" image
```

Now creating the API endpoints for glance.

```
[root@controller1 ~]# openstack endpoint create --region RegionOne \
    image public http://controller:9292
[root@controller1 ~]# openstack endpoint create --region RegionOne \
    image internal http://controller:9292
[root@controller1 ~]# openstack endpoint create --region RegionOne \
    image admin http://controller:9292
```

Populating the database.

```
[root@controller3 ~]# su -s /bin/sh -c "glance-manage db_sync" glance
```

Next we install the glance packages on all controller nodes.

```
yum install openstack-glance -y
```

Then we configure */etc/glance/glance-api.conf*. This is for controller1, replace the IP for rabbit_ hosts, bind_host, registry_host for the other controller nodes.

** correction — showing for controller1 and not controller5 as shown in the shell prompt

```
[root@controller5 ~]# cat /etc/glance/glance-api.conf
[DEFAULT]
rabbit_hosts = 10.10.0.35
bind_host = 10.10.0.35
verbose = False
debug = False
registry_host = 10.10.0.35
rpc_backend = rabbit

[keystone_authtoken]
auth_uri = http://controller:5000
auth_url = http://controller:35357
memcached_servers = controller:11211
auth_type = password
project_domain_name = Default
user_domain_name = Default
project_name = service
username = glance
password = GLANCE_PASS

[paste_deploy]
flavor = keystone

[database]
connection = mysql+pymysql://glance:GLANCE_DBPASS@controller/glance

[glance_store]
stores = file,http
default_store = file
filesystem_store_datadir = /var/lib/glance/images/

[oslo_messaging_notifications]
driver = messagingv2

[oslo_messaging_rabbit]
rabbit_host = controller
rabbit_userid = openstack
rabbit_password = RABBIT_PASS
```

Finally start the service.

```
[root@controller1 ~]# systemctl enable openstack-glance-api openstack-glance-registry
[root@controller1 ~]# systemctl start openstack-glance-api openstack-glance-registry
```

The HAProxy stats will show *green* for glance-api and glance-registry.

**glance-api**

| | Queue Cur | Queue Max | Queue Limit | Sess rate Cur | Sess rate Max | Sess rate Limit | Sessions Cur | Sessions Max | Sessions Limit | Sessions Total | Sessions LbTot | Sessions Last | Bytes In | Bytes Out | Denied Req | Denied Resp | Errors Req | Errors Conn | Errors Resp | Warn Retr | Warn Redis | Status | LastChk | Wght | Act | Bck | Chk | Dwn | Dwntime | Thrtle |
|---|---|---|---|---|---|---|---|---|---|---|---|---|---|---|---|---|---|---|---|---|---|---|---|---|---|---|---|---|---|---|
| Frontend | 0 | 0 | - | 0 | 6 | - | 0 | 12 | 10 000 | 7 531 | | | 462 844 072 935 | 586 122 921 866 | 0 | 0 | 0 | | | | | OPEN | | | | | | | | |
| controller1 | 0 | 0 | - | 0 | 2 | - | 0 | 3 | - | 1 507 | 1 507 | 5h13m | 109 313 002 066 | 120 634 126 716 | | 0 | | 0 | 0 | 0 | 0 | 112d19h UP | L7OK/200 in 2ms | 1 | Y | - | 5 | 0 | 0s | - |
| controller2 | 0 | 0 | - | 0 | 2 | - | 0 | 4 | - | 1 506 | 1 506 | 5h14m | 3 470 246 | 88 292 371 502 | | 0 | | 0 | 0 | 0 | 0 | 112d19h UP | L7OK/200 in 3ms | 1 | Y | - | 3 | 0 | 0s | - |
| controller3 | 0 | 0 | - | 0 | 2 | - | 0 | 4 | - | 1 506 | 1 506 | 5h14m | 116 161 272 544 | 120 869 323 396 | | 0 | | 0 | 0 | 0 | 0 | 112d19h UP | L7OK/200 in 3ms | 1 | Y | - | 4 | 0 | 0s | - |
| controller4 | 0 | 0 | - | 0 | 2 | - | 0 | 3 | - | 1 506 | 1 506 | 5h14m | 165 649 984 761 | 140 531 754 017 | | 0 | | 0 | 0 | 0 | 0 | 112d19h UP | L7OK/200 in 3ms | 1 | Y | - | 4 | 0 | 0s | - |
| controller5 | 0 | 0 | - | 0 | 2 | - | 0 | 3 | - | 1 506 | 1 506 | 5h13m | 71 716 343 318 | 115 795 346 235 | | 0 | | 0 | 0 | 0 | 0 | 112d19h UP | L7OK/200 in 4ms | 1 | Y | - | 4 | 0 | 0s | - |
| Backend | 0 | 0 | | 0 | 6 | | 0 | 12 | 1 000 | 7 531 | 7 531 | 5h13m | 462 844 072 935 | 586 122 921 866 | 0 | 0 | 0 | 0 | 0 | 0 | 0 | 112d19h UP | | 5 | 5 | 0 | | 0 | 0s | |

**glance-registry**

| | Queue Cur | Queue Max | Queue Limit | Sess rate Cur | Sess rate Max | Sess rate Limit | Sessions Cur | Sessions Max | Sessions Limit | Sessions Total | Sessions LbTot | Sessions Last | Bytes In | Bytes Out | Denied Req | Denied Resp | Errors Req | Errors Conn | Errors Resp | Warn Retr | Warn Redis | Status | LastChk | Wght | Act | Bck | Chk | Dwn | Dwntime | Thrtle |
|---|---|---|---|---|---|---|---|---|---|---|---|---|---|---|---|---|---|---|---|---|---|---|---|---|---|---|---|---|---|---|
| Frontend | 0 | 0 | - | 0 | 0 | - | 0 | 0 | 10 000 | 0 | 0 | 0 | 0 | 0 | 0 | 0 | 0 | | | | | OPEN | | | | | | | | |
| controller1 | 0 | 0 | - | 0 | 0 | - | 0 | 0 | - | 0 | 0 | ? | 0 | 0 | | 0 | | 0 | 0 | 0 | 0 | 112d19h UP | L4OK in 0ms | 1 | Y | - | 4 | 0 | 0s | - |
| controller2 | 0 | 0 | - | 0 | 0 | - | 0 | 0 | - | 0 | 0 | ? | 0 | 0 | | 0 | | 0 | 0 | 0 | 0 | 112d19h UP | L4OK in 0ms | 1 | Y | - | 4 | 0 | 0s | - |
| controller3 | 0 | 0 | - | 0 | 0 | - | 0 | 0 | - | 0 | 0 | ? | 0 | 0 | | 0 | | 0 | 0 | 0 | 0 | 112d19h UP | L4OK in 0ms | 1 | Y | - | 4 | 0 | 0s | - |
| controller4 | 0 | 0 | - | 0 | 0 | - | 0 | 0 | - | 0 | 0 | ? | 0 | 0 | | 0 | | 0 | 0 | 0 | 0 | 112d19h UP | L4OK in 0ms | 1 | Y | - | 4 | 0 | 0s | - |
| controller5 | 0 | 0 | - | 0 | 0 | - | 0 | 0 | - | 0 | 0 | ? | 0 | 0 | | 0 | | 0 | 0 | 0 | 0 | 112d19h UP | L4OK in 0ms | 1 | Y | - | 3 | 0 | 0s | - |
| Backend | 0 | 0 | | 0 | 0 | | 0 | 0 | 1 000 | 0 | | | 0 | 0 | 0 | 0 | 0 | 0 | 0 | 0 | 0 | 112d19h UP | | 5 | 5 | 0 | | 0 | 0s | |

We will then verify our installation by downloading and uploading a cirros *.iso image.

```
[root@controller1 ~]# wget http://download.cirros-cloud.net/0.3.4/cirros-0.3.4-x86_64-disk.img
[root@controller1 ~]# source admin-rc
[root@controller1 ~]# openstack image create "cirros" \
  --file cirros-0.3.4-x86_64-disk.img \
  --disk-format qcow2 --container-format bare \
  --public
```

Lastly, confirm the registration of the image.

```
[root@controller1 ~]# openstack image list
+--------------------------------------+--------+--------+
| ID                                   | Name   | Status |
+--------------------------------------+--------+--------+
| 38047887-61a7-41ea-9b49-27987d5e8bb9 | cirros | active |
+--------------------------------------+--------+--------+
```

Here is the status of the installation -

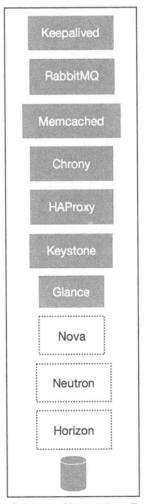

**Controllers 1 - 5**

The uploaded images will be stored in the location */var/lib/glance/images/* in the node controller1 since the Virtual IP is pointing to that node. All of our controller nodes have this location and so we will setup an *rsync* among them. All the image files inside this directory should have file's user and group set to *glance* as shown below -

```
[root@controller1 ~]# ll /var/lib/glance/images/
total 356110620
-rw-r----- 1 glance glance  1240866816 Aug  8 18:55 01ada3ae-e1a0-480b-bcf7-17eaa2a5b4bb
-rw-r----- 1 glance glance   800784384 May 28  2018 c5479c4b-7504-46f7-956c-09286e24886a
-rw-r----- 1 glance glance 51324911616 Sep 24 01:18 d41267f0-948c-436f-ba28-d02700e7ffa1
-rw-r----- 1 glance glance    13287936 May 23  2018 e05ba222-82fe-4a08-a51d-8e901406101c
-rw-r----- 1 glance glance 25489309696 Sep 24 00:23 e2d87ec7-d18c-4e8c-89ac-3389d852cfee
-rw-r----- 1 glance glance 17685872640 Nov 12 14:35 fbf8b12f-19eb-4b8a-8fa6-1e6f93942890
-rw-r----- 1 glance glance 34597306368 Sep 14 12:59 ff7528c2-8c47-4599-9b41-16534a44391b
```

# Compute/Nova

We create the databases for nova service and user permissions.

```
MariaDB [(none)]> CREATE DATABASE nova_api;
MariaDB [(none)]>CREATE DATABASE nova;
MariaDB [(none)]>GRANT ALL PRIVILEGES ON nova_api.* TO 'nova'@'controller' \
   IDENTIFIED BY 'NOVA_DBPASS';
MariaDB [(none)]>GRANT ALL PRIVILEGES ON nova_api.* TO 'nova'@'%' \
   IDENTIFIED BY 'NOVA_DBPASS';
MariaDB [(none)]>GRANT ALL PRIVILEGES ON nova.* TO 'nova'@'controller' \
   IDENTIFIED BY 'NOVA_DBPASS';
MariaDB [(none)]>GRANT ALL PRIVILEGES ON nova.* TO 'nova'@'%' \
   IDENTIFIED BY 'NOVA_DBPASS';
```

Then we register the nova service, apply role to the nova user.

```
[root@controller1 ~]# source admin-rc

[root@controller1 ~]# openstack user create --domain default —password NOVA_PASS nova
[root@controller1 ~]# openstack role add --project service --user nova admin
[root@controller1 ~]# openstack service create --name nova --description "OpenStack Compute" compute
```

Creating the API endpoints.

```
[root@controller1 ~]# openstack endpoint create --region RegionOne \
    compute public http://controller:8774/v2.1/%\(tenant_id\)s
[root@controller1 ~]# openstack endpoint create --region RegionOne \
    compute internal http://controller:8774/v2.1/%\(tenant_id\)s
[root@controller1 ~]# openstack endpoint create --region RegionOne \
    compute admin http://controller:8774/v2.1/%\(tenant_id\)s
```

Populating the database.

```
[root@controller3 ~]# su -s /bin/sh -c "nova-manage api_db sync" nova
[root@controller3 ~]# su -s /bin/sh -c "nova-manage db sync" nova
```

Installing the nova packages on all controller nodes.

```
yum install openstack-nova-api openstack-nova-conductor \
   openstack-nova-console openstack-nova-novncproxy \
   openstack-nova-scheduler openstack-nova-compute
```

Configuring */etc/nova/nova.conf* on all controller nodes.

```
[vnc]
enabled = True
novncproxy_base_url = http://$my_ip:6080/vnc_auto.html
vncserver_listen = $my_ip
vncserver_proxyclient_address = $my_ip

[keystone_authtoken]
auth_uri = http://controller:5000
auth_url = http://controller:35357
memcached_servers = controller1:11211,controller2:11211,controller3:11211,controller4:11211,controller5:11211
auth_type = password
project_domain_name = Default
user_domain_name = Default
project_name = service
username = nova
password = NOVA_PASS

[api_database]
connection = mysql+pymysql://nova:NOVA_DBPASS@controller/nova_api

[database]
connection = mysql+pymysql://nova:NOVA_DBPASS@controller/nova
```

Based on the hardware where the cloud is being deployed, we will have to configure the virtualisation type for our virtual machines to be either - qemu or kvm.

If the out of the following command return a value 1 or greater, it supports hardware acceleration and we will configure virt_type = kvm, else it will be virt_type = qemu.

```
egrep -c '(vmx|svm)' /proc/cpuinfo
```

For the installation in this book, we are using server grade hardware which has hardware acceleration and hence our configuration is -

```
[libvirt]
virt_type = kvm
```

Finally starting the services.

```
[root@controller1 ~]# systemctl enable openstack-nova-api.service \
    openstack-nova-consoleauth.service openstack-nova-scheduler.service \
    openstack-nova-conductor.service openstack-nova-novncproxy.service \
    libvirtd openstack-nova-compute

[root@controller1 ~]# systemctl start openstack-nova-api.service \
    openstack-nova-consoleauth.service openstack-nova-scheduler.service \
    openstack-nova-conductor.service openstack-nova-novncproxy.service \
    libvirtd openstack-nova-compute
```

We now verify our installation by checking the status of the *Compute* service components.

```
[root@controller1 ~]# source admin-rc
[root@controller1 ~]# openstack compute service list

+------+------------------+-------------+----------+----------+-------+
| ID   | Binary           | Host        | Zone     | Status   | State |
+------+------------------+-------------+----------+----------+-------+
| 85   | nova-compute     | controller5 | nova     | enabled  | up    |
| 84   | nova-conductor   | controller5 | internal | enabled  | up    |
| 83   | nova-scheduler   | controller5 | internal | enabled  | up    |
| 82   | nova-consoleauth | controller5 | internal | enabled  | up    |
| 10   | nova-compute     | controller3 | nova     | enabled  | up    |
| 21   | nova-conductor   | controller3 | internal | enabled  | up    |
| 22   | nova-scheduler   | controller3 | internal | enabled  | up    |
| 25   | nova-consoleauth | controller3 | internal | enabled  | up    |
| 30   | nova-compute     | controller2 | nova     | enabled  | up    |
| 36   | nova-conductor   | controller2 | internal | enabled  | up    |
| 48   | nova-consoleauth | controller2 | internal | enabled  | up    |
| 66   | nova-scheduler   | controller2 | internal | enabled  | up    |
| 69   | nova-conductor   | controller1 | internal | enabled  | up    |
| 78   | nova-consoleauth | controller1 | internal | enabled  | up    |
| 81   | nova-scheduler   | controller1 | internal | enabled  | up    |
| 93   | nova-compute     | controller1 | nova     | enabled  | up    |
| 57   | nova-compute     | controller4 | nova     | enabled  | up    |
| 56   | nova-conductor   | controller4 | internal | enabled  | up    |
| 55   | nova-scheduler   | controller4 | internal | enabled  | up    |
| 54   | nova-consoleauth | controller4 | internal | enabled  | up    |
+------+------------------+-------------+----------+----------+-------+
```

** Sections of the output has been omitted.

The output indicates four components for each controller node for the *Compute* service - nova-compute, nova-conductor, nova-scheduler, nova-consoleauth.

Here is our installation status -

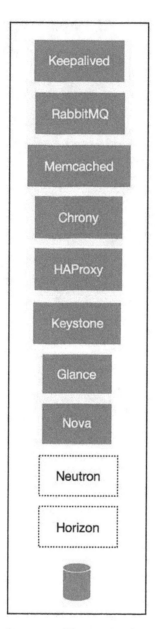

**Controllers 1 - 5**

# Network/Neutron

Executing the commands for database user creation and permissions.

```
MariaDB [(none)]> CREATE DATABASE neutron;
MariaDB [(none)]> GRANT ALL PRIVILEGES ON neutron.* TO 'neutron'@'controller' \
  IDENTIFIED BY 'NEUTRON_DBPASS';
MariaDB [(none)]> GRANT ALL PRIVILEGES ON neutron.* TO 'neutron'@'%' \
  IDENTIFIED BY 'NEUTRON_DBPASS';
```

Registering the service, role and the API endpoints.

```
[root@controller1 ~]# source admin-rc
[root@controller1 ~]# openstack user create --domain default —password NEUTRON_PASS neutron
[root@controller1 ~]# openstack role add --project service --user neutron admin

[root@controller1 ~]# openstack service create --name neutron \
  --description "OpenStack Networking" network
[root@controller1 ~]# openstack endpoint create --region RegionOne \
  network public http://controller:9696
[root@controller1 ~]# openstack endpoint create --region RegionOne \
  network internal http://controller:9696
[root@controller1 ~]# openstack endpoint create --region RegionOne \
  network admin http://controller:9696
```

Populating the database.

```
[root@controller3 ~]# su -s /bin/sh -c "neutron-db-manage --config-file /etc/neutron/neutron.conf \
  —config-file /etc/neutron/plugins/ml2/ml2_conf.ini upgrade head" neutron
```

Now before, we go ahead and configure the *Network* service, we will discuss the two networking options that Openstack provides for our virtual machines.

We have configured our controller nodes to use two network devices, namely eno1 and eno2. This is for the recommended segregation of network traffic, one for management of Openstack traffic and the other for the traffic that traverse to and from our virtual machines. In our installation the network device eno2 is called *Provider* and it is to be used for our virtual machines' traffic flow. Openstack provides another kind of networking for our virtual machines called Self-service, which is an SDN (software defined network).

*For Networking option 1: Provider*

The Provider network is our physical network device which is used by virtual machines. This network device is kept unnumbered because it would host a bridge with which virtual machines from our Openstack projects (alpha, beta, gamma) would be connected through TAP devices. The TAP devices connect virtual machines to the bridge, which then sends the traffic via eno2, our *Provider* network interface, and vice-versa. A TAP is a layer 2 device that operates with Ethernet frames. After configuration of Network service, we would define our Provider IP pool range, which will be between 10.10.4.x - 10.10.4.y (since an ethernet cable connects eno2 to the 10.10.4.0/24 IP range from our network switch device).

*For Networking option 2: Self-service*

Openstack gives the capability to create private subnets through creation of SDNs. Using TUN devices, which route layer 3 packets, multiple subnets are managed. For a virtual machine in a private subnet to be accessed from the public range of our organisation, i.e. 10.10.4.0/24, a *Floating IP* address has to be attached to the virtual machine. The *Floating IP* is from the Provider IP pool range that we are going to declare later. It's called Floating or Elastic IP because of its nature of being detachable from virtual machines. A virtual machine can have more than one Floating IP attached to it. This network has its DHCP server that provides the (private) IPs to the virtual machines which connect to physical network via NAT. For self-service networks, bridges are also created but unlike *Provider* bridge on eno2, they are created in eno1. Each Self-service network has a *qrouter* (software defined), which has a connection with the *Provider* bridge and the *Self-service* bridge.

Installing packages.

```
yum install openstack-neutron openstack-neutron-ml2 \
    openstack-neutron-linuxbridge ebtables
```

Configuring */etc/neutron/neutron.conf.*

```
[root@controller5 ~]# cat /etc/neutron/neutron.conf
[DEFAULT]
bind_host = 10.10.0.43
core_plugin = ml2
service_plugins = router
transport_url = rabbit://openstack:RABBIT_PASS@controller
auth_strategy = keystone
notify_nova_on_port_status_changes = True
notify_nova_on_port_data_changes = True
allow_overlapping_ips = True

[oslo_concurrency]
lock_path = /var/lib/neutron/tmp
```

```
[nova]
auth_url = http://controller:35357
auth_type = password
project_domain_name = Default
user_domain_name = Default
region_name = RegionOne
project_name = service
username = nova
password = NOVA_PASS

[database]
connection = mysql+pymysql://neutron:NEUTRON_DBPASS@controller/neutron

[keystone_authtoken]
auth_uri = http://controller:5000
auth_url = http://controller:35357
memcached_servers = controller:11211
auth_type = password
project_domain_name = Default
user_domain_name = Default
project_name = service
username = neutron
password = NEUTRON_PASS
```

```
[oslo_messaging_notifications]
driver = messagingv2
```

Configuring */etc/neutron/plugins/ml2/ml2_conf.ini.*

```
[root@controller5 ~]# cat /etc/neutron/plugins/ml2/ml2_conf.ini
[ml2]
type_drivers = flat,vlan,vxlan
tenant_network_types = vxlan
mechanism_drivers = linuxbridge,l2population
extension_drivers = port_security

[ml2_type_flat]
flat_networks = provider

[ml2_type_geneve]
[ml2_type_gre]
[ml2_type_vlan]
[ml2_type_vxlan]
vni_ranges = 1:1000
[linux_bridge]
physical_interface_mappings = provider:eno2

[securitygroup]
enable_ipset = True
```

Configuring */etc/neutron/plugins/ml2/linuxbridge_agent.ini*.

```
[root@controller5 ~]# cat /etc/neutron/plugins/ml2/linuxbridge_agent.ini
[DEFAULT]
[agent]
[linux_bridge]
physical_interface_mappings = provider:eno2

[vxlan]
enable_vxlan = True
local_ip = 10.10.0.43
l2_population = True

[securitygroup]
enable_security_group = True
firewall_driver = neutron.agent.linux.iptables_firewall.IptablesFirewallDriver
```

For Networking option 1, enable_vxlan has to be set to **False**.

Configuring */etc/neutron/dhcp_agent.ini*.

```
[root@controller5 ~]# cat /etc/neutron/dhcp_agent.ini
[DEFAULT]
interface_driver = neutron.agent.linux.interface.BridgeInterfaceDriver
dhcp_driver = neutron.agent.linux.dhcp.Dnsmasq
enable_isolated_metadata = True
dhcp_domain = dev.ts
dnsmasq_dns_servers = 10.10.3.11, 8.8.8.8
```

Configuring */etc/neutron/l3_agent.ini*. This configuration is only for Networking option 2.

```
[root@controller5 ~]# cat /etc/neutron/l3_agent.ini
[DEFAULT]
interface_driver = neutron.agent.linux.interface.BridgeInterfaceDriver
```

Configuring /etc/neutron/metadata_agent.ini.

```
[root@controller5 ~]# /etc/neutron/metadata_agent.ini
[DEFAULT]
nova_metadata_ip = controller
metadata_proxy_shared_secret = METADATA_SECRET
```

Next we need to configure */etc/nova/nova.conf* with information about *Network/Neutron* service, such that the virtual machines created with the *Compute/Nova* service have a network allocated to them. The following configuration snippet has already been added in *nova.conf* when we configured the service.

```
[neutron]
url = http://controller:9696
auth_url = http://controller:35357
auth_type = password
project_domain_name = Default
user_domain_name = Default
region_name = RegionOne
project_name = service
username = neutron
password = NEUTRON_PASS
service_metadata_proxy = True
metadata_proxy_shared_secret = METADATA_SECRET
```

For bridging and switching purposes in the layer 2 networking, ML2 plugin is used. The *Network* service initialisation scripts expects a symbolic link */etc/neutron/plugin.ini* pointing to */etc/neutron/plugins/ml2/ml2_conf.ini* (ML2 plugin initialisation file).

```
[root@controller1 ~]# ln -s /etc/neutron/plugins/ml2/ml2_conf.ini /etc/neutron/plugin.ini
[root@controller2 ~]# ln -s /etc/neutron/plugins/ml2/ml2_conf.ini /etc/neutron/plugin.ini
[root@controller3 ~]# ln -s /etc/neutron/plugins/ml2/ml2_conf.ini /etc/neutron/plugin.ini
[root@controller4 ~]# ln -s /etc/neutron/plugins/ml2/ml2_conf.ini /etc/neutron/plugin.ini
[root@controller5 ~]# ln -s /etc/neutron/plugins/ml2/ml2_conf.ini /etc/neutron/plugin.ini
```

Finally we, start the services.

```
[root@controller1 ~]# systemctl enable neutron-server.service \
    neutron-linuxbridge-agent.service neutron-dhcp-agent.service \
    neutron-metadata-agent.service
[root@controller1 ~]# systemctl start neutron-server.service \
    neutron-linuxbridge-agent.service neutron-dhcp-agent.service \
    neutron-metadata-agent.service
```

For Networking option 2, start the layer-3 service.

```
[root@controller1 ~]# systemctl enable neutron-l3-agent.service
[root@controller1 ~]# systemctl start neutron-l3-agent.service
```

Verify the installation.

```
+----------------------------------+----------------------------------------------------------+
| alias                            | name                                                     |
+----------------------------------+----------------------------------------------------------+
| default-subnetpools              | Default Subnetpools                                       |
| network-ip-availability          | Network IP Availability                                  |
| network_availability_zone        | Network Availability Zone                                |
| auto-allocated-topology          | Auto Allocated Topology Services                         |
| ext-gw-mode                      | Neutron L3 Configurable external gateway mode            |
| binding                          | Port Binding                                             |
| agent                            | agent                                                    |
| subnet_allocation                | Subnet Allocation                                        |
| l3_agent_scheduler               | L3 Agent Scheduler                                       |
| tag                              | Tag support                                              |
| external-net                     | Neutron external network                                 |
| net-mtu                          | Network MTU                                              |
| availability_zone                | Availability Zone                                        |
| quotas                           | Quota management support                                 |
| l3-ha                            | HA Router extension                                      |
| flavors                          | Neutron Service Flavors                                  |
| provider                         | Provider Network                                         |
| multi-provider                   | Multi Provider Network                                   |
| address-scope                    | Address scope                                            |
| extraroute                       | Neutron Extra Route                                      |
| timestamp_core                   | Time Stamp Fields addition for core resources            |
| router                           | Neutron L3 Router                                        |
| extra_dhcp_opt                   | Neutron Extra DHCP opts                                  |
| dns-integration                  | DNS Integration                                          |
| security-group                   | security-group                                           |
| dhcp_agent_scheduler             | DHCP Agent Scheduler                                     |
| router_availability_zone         | Router Availability Zone                                 |
| rbac-policies                    | RBAC Policies                                            |
| standard-attr-description        | standard-attr-description                                |
| port-security                    | Port Security                                            |
| allowed-address-pairs            | Allowed Address Pairs                                    |
| dvr                              | Distributed Virtual Router                               |
+----------------------------------+----------------------------------------------------------+
```

- *The output may vary a little.* Above is the list of extensions.

Here is a list of the *Network* agents.

```
[root@controller5 ~]# openstack network agent list
+--------------------------------------+--------------------+-------------+-------------------+-------+-------+--------------------------+
| ID                                   | Agent Type         | Host        | Availability Zone | Alive | State | Binary                   |
+--------------------------------------+--------------------+-------------+-------------------+-------+-------+--------------------------+
| 00156c62-0b83-4d55-98a4              | Metadata agent     | controller3 | None              | True  | UP    | neutron-metadata-agent   |
| -6a534e47336d                        |                    |             |                   |       |       |                          |
| 3e5e6910-16c7-421c-                  | Linux bridge agent | controller4 | None              | True  | UP    | neutron-linuxbridge-     |
| 8cff-cd6b15283bd4                    |                    |             |                   |       |       | agent                    |
| 47845a86-3021-4287                   | Metadata agent     | controller5 | None              | True  | UP    | neutron-metadata-agent   |
| -a31c-0075c4c2726                    |                    |             |                   |       |       |                          |
| 52fcff03-5d74-4b78-b2d3              | Metadata agent     | controller4 | None              | True  | UP    | neutron-metadata-agent   |
| -81e60b2379c7                        |                    |             |                   |       |       |                          |
| 576d6d1c-e217-4cfb-                  | DHCP agent         | controller4 | nova              | True  | UP    | neutron-dhcp-agent       |
| 9a97-edc265cea80f                    |                    |             |                   |       |       |                          |
| 58efbfc2-c112-4aa9-aad3              | DHCP agent         | controller3 | nova              | True  | UP    | neutron-dhcp-agent       |
| -cd5729f1d837                        |                    |             |                   |       |       |                          |
| 9fad5053-66d4-47b7                   | Linux bridge agent | controller5 | None              | True  | UP    | neutron-linuxbridge-     |
| -a76a-bb9ada64a172                   |                    |             |                   |       |       | agent                    |
| a9a33220-5ffb-4260-ac16              | DHCP agent         | controller2 | nova              | True  | UP    | neutron-dhcp-agent       |
| -3ce9aa6f31f8                        |                    |             |                   |       |       |                          |
| cd0626d0-5d63-4c2f-                  | Linux bridge agent | controller1 | None              | True  | UP    | neutron-linuxbridge-     |
| 983d-61cf860d968                     |                    |             |                   |       |       | agent                    |
| d67e7afc-8dd7-4e7b-                  | Metadata agent     | controller1 | None              | True  | UP    | neutron-metadata-agent   |
| 8c7f-137528fec5a8                    |                    |             |                   |       |       |                          |
| e43d1de0-9b33-44e5-8cf6              | L3 agent           | controller3 | nova              | True  | UP    | neutron-l3-agent         |
| -f43b61c834a0                        |                    |             |                   |       |       |                          |
| e9da848f-4e77-4f9a-                  | Metadata agent     | controller2 | None              | True  | UP    | neutron-metadata-agent   |
| a5ab-a9c2a111c1e4                    |                    |             |                   |       |       |                          |
| ea72030c-5ffa-4b69                   | Linux bridge agent | controller2 | None              | True  | UP    | neutron-linuxbridge-     |
| -a4ac-6fb19e8831b7                   |                    |             |                   |       |       | agent                    |
| eeeb5243-bf77-492d-9485              | Linux bridge agent | controller3 | None              | True  | UP    | neutron-linuxbridge-     |
| -2273474cbe4c                        |                    |             |                   |       |       | agent                    |
| f7e4291e-34b3-4ea9                   | DHCP agent         | controller1 | nova              | True  | UP    | neutron-dhcp-agent       |
| -8e1b-82a5e1facca0                   |                    |             |                   |       |       |                          |
| fae92060-7111-48b8                   | DHCP agent         | controller5 | nova              | True  | UP    | neutron-dhcp-agent       |
| -9ebd-68bfb38dd488                   |                    |             |                   |       |       |                          |
+--------------------------------------+--------------------+-------------+-------------------+-------+-------+--------------------------+
```

Till here we have the Network service agents running, but we are yet to define our network ranges for Provider and Self-service networks.

The Provider network and subnet creation is mandatory.

```
[root@controller3 ~]# admin-rc

[root@controller3 ~]# openstack network create  --share --external \
    --provider-physical-network provider \
    --provider-network-type flat provider

[root@controller3 ~]# openstack subnet create --network provider \
    --allocation-pool start=10.10.4.10,end=10.10.4.250 \
    --dns-nameserver 8.8.8.8 --gateway 10.10.4.1 \
    --subnet-range 10.10.4.0/24 provider
```

Choosing the Networking option 2 requires creation of the Self-service network and subnet. notice how the 'rc' file for alpha project is used here. This is because unlike the *Provider* network, which is shared by all projects and users, we want to create the *Self-service* private network for alpha project.

```
[root@controller3 ~]# source alpha-rc

[root@controller3 ~]# openstack network create selfservice

[root@controller3 ~]# openstack subnet create --network selfservice \
   --dns-nameserver 8.8.4.4 --gateway 172.16.1.1 \
   --subnet-range 172.16.1.0/24 alpha-selfservice
```

Now creating the software defined router for connecting the private subnet with the Provider network gateway.

```
[root@controller3 ~]# openstack router create router
[root@controller3 ~]# neutron router-interface-add router selfservice
[root@controller3 ~]# neutron router-gateway-set router provider
```

We can check our network namespace and find one qrouter and two qdhcp.

```
[root@controller3 ~]# ip netns
qrouter-89dd2083-a160-4d75-ab3a-14239f01ea0b
qdhcp-7c6f9b37-76b4-463e-98d8-27e5686ed083
qdhcp-0e62efcd-8cee-46c7-b163-d8df05c3c5ad
```

We will refer to the progress we made so far with our architecture diagram.

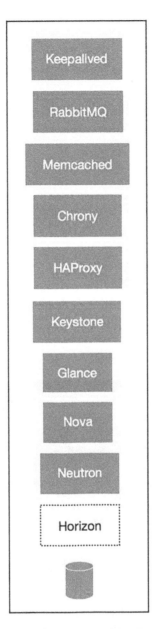

**Controllers 1 - 5**

# Dashboard/Horizon

Up till now, we have only interacted with Openstack with the *openstack* CLI client. The client is functionally complete with all features that Openstack provides. There are few other CLI client tools that we have used such as *nova*, *neutron* etc. which will be deprecated in the future as stated by the Openstack development community and *openstack* CLI client is going to be the standard.

In this section we are going to install the GUI dashboard.

Start with installing the package on all nodes.

```
yum install openstack-dashboard
```

The dashboard is built with python-django, and the configuration */etc/openstack-dashboard/local_settings* is as follows -

```
ALLOWED_HOSTS = ['*',]
#SESSION_ENGINE = 'django.contrib.sessions.backends.cache'

CACHES = {
    'default': {
        ##'BACKEND': 'django.core.cache.backends.memcached.MemcachedCache',
        'BACKEND': 'django.core.cache.backends.locmem.LocMemCache',
    'LOCATION': 'controller:11211',
    },
}
EMAIL_BACKEND = 'django.core.mail.backends.console.EmailBackend'
OPENSTACK_HOST = "controller"
OPENSTACK_KEYSTONE_URL = "http://%s:5000/v2.0" % OPENSTACK_HOST
OPENSTACK_KEYSTONE_DEFAULT_DOMAIN = "default"
OPENSTACK_KEYSTONE_DEFAULT_ROLE = "user"
OPENSTACK_API_VERSIONS = {
    "identity": 3,
    "image": 2,
    "volume": 2,
}
OPENSTACK_KEYSTONE_MULTIDOMAIN_SUPPORT = True
```

The above configuration is a snippet highlighting the major sections of the config. The highlighted section has to be sent to all *False* values it Networking option 1 is being used.

```
OPENSTACK_NEUTRON_NETWORK = {
    'enable_router': True,
    'enable_quotas': True,
    'enable_ipv6': True,
    'enable_distributed_router': False,
    'enable_ha_router': False,
    'enable_lb': True,
    'enable_firewall': True,
    'enable_vpn': True,
    'enable_fip_topology_check': True,
    'profile_support': None,
    'supported_vnic_types': ['*'],
}

TIME_ZONE = "Asia/Kolkata"
```

The CACHES configuration for BACKEND may not work with MemcachedCache, and so LocMemCache is used as a replacement. The SESSION_ENGINE parameter can be left commented out if not using MemcachedCache for BACKEND.

We finalize the installation with restarting the httpd and memcached services.

```
[root@controller1 ~]# systemctl restart httpd memcached
[root@controller2 ~]# systemctl restart httpd memcached
[root@controller3 ~]# systemctl restart httpd memcached
[root@controller4 ~]# systemctl restart httpd memcached
[root@controller5 ~]# systemctl restart httpd memcached
```

The url for dashboard - *http://controller/dashboard*

In our case, controller would be 10.10.0.254

With the final service installed here is the state of our installation -

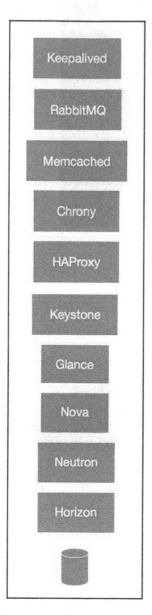

**Controllers 1 - 5**

# Creating a virtual machine

Now that we have set-up our necessary cloud services, we can go launch the first virtual machine/instance in the cloud. We will use the cirros *.iso image that we uploaded to the *Image* service, after a comparable disk image *flavour* is created.

A *flavour* is Openstack's way of defining the properties of an instance, such as RAM, disk, CPU. When an instance is launched, the selected disk image and flavour has to be compatible with each other. For example, unlike cirros image which has an optimum requirement of 64MB RAM, a Centos image has a minimum requirement of 1 GB RAM and 10 GB disk space. Therefore, a flavour that is created with the minimal requirements of cirros is incompatible with Centos.

For launching our first cloud instance, we first create a flavour suited to the requirements of cirros called m1.nano.

```
[root@controller1 ~]# source admin-rc
[root@controller1 ~]# openstack flavor create --id 0 --vcpus 1 --ram 64 --disk 1 m1.nano
```

Say we want to launch the virtual machine from alpha project, we will create a key pair for our virtual machines. Most could based images support public key based authentication rather than password.

```
[root@controller1 ~]# source alpha-rc
[root@controller1 ~]# ssh-keygen -q -N ""
[root@controller1 ~]# openstack keypair create --public-key ~/.ssh/id_rsa.pub mykey
```

Openstack does not rely by default on iptables/firewalld based port access for virtual machines. Rather, it provides a pluggable logical configuration for virtual machines' access & security in the form of *security groups*.

A *security group* is a named definition for the ingress and egress capabilities of an instance. We require a ping access to our instance, so we create an icmp security group.

```
[root@controller1 ~]# openstack security group rule create --proto icmp mysg
```

We will SSH to the instance, so we create a TCP port for ingress access to 22 port.

```
[root@controller1 ~]# openstack security group rule create --proto tcp --dst-port 22 mysg
```

*mysg* is the name of the security group to which both above rules are added.

Now we are ready to launch an instance in the Provider network.

```
[root@controller1 ~]# source alpha-rc
[root@controller1 ~]# openstack server create --flavor m1.nano --image cirros \
   --nic net-id=provider --security-group mysg \
   --key-name mykey provider-instance
```

*provider-instance* is the name of our virtual machine.

Here is the status of the instance.

```
[root@controller1 ~]# openstack server list

+-------------------------------------+------------------+--------+-------------------+------------+
| ID                                  | Name             | Status | Networks          | Image Name |
+-------------------------------------+------------------+--------+-------------------+------------+
| 181c52ba-aebc-4c32-a97d-2e8e82e4eaaf | provider-instance | ACTIVE | provider=10.10.4.50 | cirros   |
+-------------------------------------+------------------+--------+-------------------+------------+
```

The virtual machines can be accessed through SSH shell access, also we have *nova-nonvncproxy* component of Compute service which provides browser based access to instances through VNC.

The url for VNC access.

```
[root@controller1 ~]# openstack console url show provider-instance

+-------+-----------------------------------------------------------------------------+
| Field | Value                                                                       |
+-------+-----------------------------------------------------------------------------+
| type  | novnc                                                                       |
| url   | http://controller:6080/vnc_auto.html?token=5eeccb47-525c-4918-ac2a-3ad1e9f1f493 |
+-------+-----------------------------------------------------------------------------+
```

We launch another instance in the self-service network.

```
[root@controller1 ~]# source alpha-rc
[root@controller1 ~]# openstack server create --flavor m1.nano --image cirros \
   --nic net-id=self-service --security-group mysg \
   --key-name mykey selfservice-instance
```

# Orchestration/Heat

Openstack gives us the sheer taste of convenience of cloud computing, when we introduce yet another service that we haven't mentioned earlier. This service is called *Orchestration*. Evolving from the early ways of server infrastructure and machine cluster maintenance, Openstack gives us a software driven approach. As we have seen, how we are able to do all tasks through the openstack CLI client, automation becomes a possibility and cloud infrastructure maintenance/management activities can be done through code. This *Orchestration* service introduces to us, the concept of infrastructure-on-code, with what Openstack calls as Heat scripts or Cloud-formation scripts. These scripts are written in simple YAML format and with them we can describe virtual machine clusters and more. *Heat* is the main project in the Openstack Orchestration program. It implements an orchestration engine to launch multiple composite cloud applications based on templates in the form of text files that can be treated like code.

We will delve deep into the scripts and their capabilities after we install the service. First of, we create the database and user permissions.

```
MariaDB [(none)]> CREATE DATABASE heat;
MariaDB [(none)]> GRANT ALL PRIVILEGES ON heat.* TO 'heat'@'controller' \
   IDENTIFIED BY 'HEAT_DBPASS';
MariaDB [(none)]> GRANT ALL PRIVILEGES ON heat.* TO 'heat'@'%' \
   IDENTIFIED BY 'HEAT_DBPASS';
```

Registering the service and its endpoints.

```
[root@controller1 ~]# source admin-rc
[root@controller1 ~]# openstack user create --domain default --password HEAT_PASS heat
[root@controller1 ~]# openstack role add --project service --user heat admin
[root@controller1 ~]# openstack service create --name heat \
   --description "Orchestration" orchestration
[root@controller1 ~]# openstack service create --name heat-cfn \
   --description "Orchestration" cloudformation
```

The Orchestration service requires registration of not just *heat* service entity but also *heat-cfn* (cloud formation). This is because Openstack heat API is compatible with AWS CloudFormation API.

Heat consists of four sub services namely -

*heat* - The heat tool is a CLI which communicates with the heat-api to execute AWS CloudFormation APIs. Of course this is not required—developers could also use the Heat APIs directly.

*heat-api* - Its the RESTful API thats sends requests heat-engine.

*heat-api-cfn* - It provides an AWS-style query API that is compatible with AWS CloudFormation.

*heat-engine* - It does the work of orchestrating the launch of templates.

The API endpoints.

```
[root@controller1 ~]# openstack endpoint create --region RegionOne \
   orchestration public http://controller:8004/v1/%\(tenant_id\)s
[root@controller1 ~]# openstack endpoint create --region RegionOne \
   orchestration internal http://controller:8004/v1/%\(tenant_id\)s
[root@controller1 ~]# openstack endpoint create --region RegionOne \
   orchestration admin http://controller:8004/v1/%\(tenant_id\)s

[root@controller1 ~]# openstack endpoint create --region RegionOne \
   cloudformation public http://controller:8000/v1
[root@controller1 ~]# openstack endpoint create --region RegionOne \
   cloudformation internal http://controller:8000/v1
[root@controller1 ~]# openstack endpoint create --region RegionOne \
   cloudformation admin http://controller:8000/v1
```

*heat* and *heat-cfn* service entities have their respective endpoints.

Orchestration requires additional information in the Identity service to manage cluster/stack, following are the steps. Previously, when we discussed about Openstack *domains*, we had only one created during the *Keystone* service installation, which is *default* and the projects alpha, beta and gamma were all contained inside the *default* domain. The *Orchestration* service will be installed under a separate domain. This domain separation is done for segregating projects and users that have permission to launch Stack/Cluster with Heat scripts. From our *admin* project, we can select which projects and users will have such privileges.

```
[root@controller1 ~]# openstack domain create --description "Stack projects and users" heat
[root@controller1 ~]# openstack user create --domain heat --password-prompt heat_domain_admin
[root@controller1 ~]# openstack role add --domain heat --user-domain heat --user heat_domain_admin admin
[root@controller1 ~]# openstack role create heat_stack_owner
[root@controller1 ~]# openstack role add --project demo --user demo heat_stack_owner
[root@controller1 ~]# openstack role create heat_stack_user
```

Populating the database.

```
[root@controller3 ~]# su -s /bin/sh -c "heat-manage db_sync" heat
```

Installing the packages.

```
yum install openstack-heat-api openstack-heat-api-cfn \
   openstack-heat-engine -y
```

## Configuring /etc/heat/heat.conf

```
[DEFAULT]
heat_metadata_server_url = http://controller:8000
heat_waitcondition_server_url = http://controller:8000/v2/waitcondition
stack_user_domain_name = heat
stack_domain_admin=heat_domain_admin
stack_domain_admin_password=HEAT_PASS
rpc_backend = rabbit
rabbit_hosts=10.10.0.35:5672,10.10.0.34:5672,10.10.0.33:5672,10.10.0.31:5672,10.10.0.43:5672

[clients_keystone]
auth_uri = http://controller:35357

[database]
connection = mysql+pymysql://heat:HEAT_DBPASS@controller/heat

[ec2authtoken]
auth_uri = http://controller:5000

[heat_api]
bind_host = 10.10.0.35
bind_port = 8004

[heat_api_cfn]
bind_host = 10.10.0.35
bind_port = 8000

[oslo_messaging_notifications]
driver = messagingv2

[oslo_messaging_rabbit]
rabbit_host = controller
rabbit_userid = openstack
rabbit_password = RABBIT_PASS
```

```
[trustee]
auth_type = password
auth_url = http://controller:35357
username = heat
password = HEAT_PASS
user_domain_name = default

[keystone_authtoken]
auth_uri = http://controller:5000
auth_url = http://controller:35357
memcached_servers = controller:11211
auth_type = password
project_domain_name = default
user_domain_name = default
project_name = service
username = heat
password = HEAT_PASS
admin_tenant_name = service
admin_user = heat
admin_password = HEAT_PASS
```

Verify the service.

```
[root@controller1 ~]# source admin-rc
[root@controller1 ~]# openstack orchestration service list
+-------------+-------------+--------------------------------------+-------------+--------+---------------------------+--------+
| hostname    | binary      | engine_id                            | host        | topic  | updated_at                | status |
+-------------+-------------+--------------------------------------+-------------+--------+---------------------------+--------+
| controller1 | heat-engine | 3e85d1ab-a543-41aa-aa97-378c381fb958 | controller1 | engine | 2018-10-13T14:16:06.000000 | up     |
| controller1 | heat-engine | 45dbdcf6-5660-4d5f-973a-c4fc819da678 | controller1 | engine | 2018-10-13T14:16:06.000000 | up     |
| controller1 | heat-engine | 51162b63-ecb8-4c6c-98c6-993af899c4f7 | controller1 | engine | 2018-10-13T14:16:06.000000 | up     |
| controller1 | heat-engine | 8d7edc6d-77a6-460d-bd2a-984d76954646 | controller1 | engine | 2018-10-13T14:16:06.000000 | up     |
+-------------+-------------+--------------------------------------+-------------+--------+---------------------------+--------+
```

The output here shows only heat-engines for controller1, the heat-engines for other controllers has been omitted. These engines partake in the task of compiling a heat scripts and delegate tasks to other services to launch a Stack/Cluster.

A HOT (Heat Orchestration Template) has the following structure.

```
heat_template_version: 2016-10-14

description:
  # a description of the template

parameter_groups:
  # a declaration of input parameter groups and order

parameters:
  # declaration of input parameters

resources:
  # declaration of template resources

outputs:
  # declaration of output parameters

conditions:
  # declaration of conditions
```

*heat_template_version* - This key value 2016-10-14 indicates the YAML document is a template of a specific version. HOT uses a date base versioning system.

*description* - This is an optional section where the metadata about the script can be declared.

*parameter_groups* - This specifies the grouping of the input parameters.

*parameters* - This section is for specifying put parameters that have to be provided while instantiating the template.

*resources* - This section declares the resources that are to be present in the stack such as virtual machine, floating IPs, network specifications etc.

*outputs* - This section specifies the desired the output we want for the template, such as information about the stack or URLs for application running in the stack's virtual machines or some other data.

*conditions* - This section includes statements that is used to restrict when a resource is created. They can be associated with resource attributes in the *resources* section as well as the *outputs* section.

This is a sample heat script.

```yaml
heat_template_version: 2013-05-23
description: >
  This template provisions an httpd App on port 80

outputs:
  VM_IP:
    description: IP address of VM accessible through provider network
    value:
      get_attr: [app-vm, first_address]
  Monitoring(if enabled):
    description: Graphical view of System Resource Utilization
    value:
      str_replace:
        template: http://host:80/
        params:
          host: { get_attr: [app-vm, first_address] }

parameters:
  key_name:
    type: string
    description: Key to use for servers
    default: mykey
  flavor:
    default: m1.large
    description: The desiered configuration of the VM (C for vCPU,M for RAM & D for Disk)
    type: string
    constraints:
      - allowed_values: [ m1.nano,m1.medium,m1.large ]
  image:
    default: centos-v7
    description: The desiered OS to be used
    type: string
    constraints:
      - allowed_values: [ centos-v6.9,centos-v7,centos-v7.5 ]
  enable_monitoring:
    default: disable
    description: Enabling System Monitoring on VM
    type: string
    constraints:
      - allowed_values: [ enable,disable ]

resources:
  app-vm:
    type: "OS::Nova::Server"
    properties:
      flavor: {get_param: flavor}
      image: {get_param: image}
      key_name: {get_param: key_name}
      name: MY_APP_VM
      user_data:
        str_replace:
          params:
            __GALEILI__: { get_param: enable_monitoring }
          template: |
            #!/bin/bash
            service iptables stop
            chkconfig iptables off
            echo "Monitoring has been __GALEILI__" >> /var/log/VM_Logs.html

            if [[ __GALEILI__ == "enable" ]];then
                echo "\n\n Cloning GALEILI for monitoring vm metrics \n\n" >> /var/log/VM_Logs.html
                git clone https://github.com/seamless-distribution-systems/galilei.git >> /var/log/VM_Logs.html
                yum install zlib-devel -y
                chmod +x ~/galeili/galieli-netdata-installer/linux-netdata_installer.bash
                cd ~/galeili/galieli-netdata-installer/
                bash ~/galeili/galieli-netdata-installer/linux-netdata_installer.bash --libs-are-really-here
                >> /var/log/VM_Logs.html
            fi
      networks:
        - port: { get_resource: vm_port }
  vm_port:
    type: OS::Neutron::Port
    properties:
      admin_state_up: true
      network_id: provider
      security_groups:
        - default
```

# SECTION 3

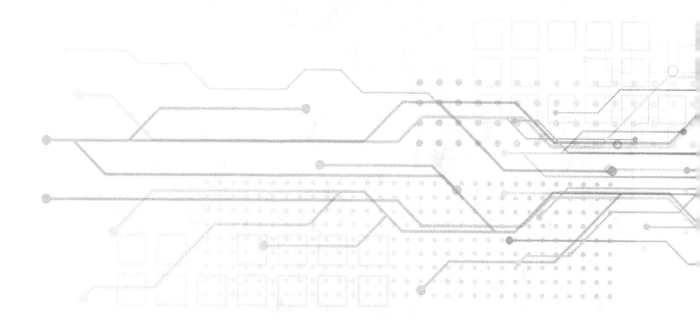

# Logging with
# Elastic Stack

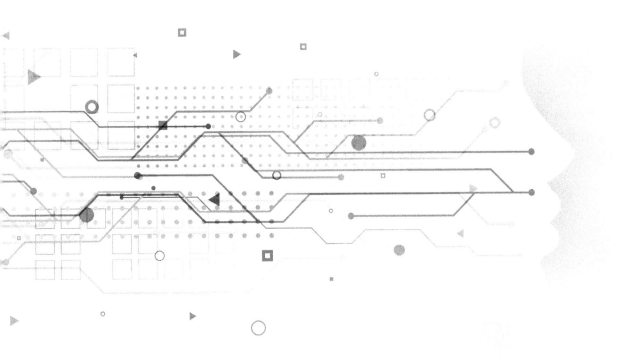

# Introduction

Any application development phase, big or small, has an inevitable occurrence in the form of errors, and so, it becomes most important to find a good way to tackle events through logging, that halt development.

As much as it is a good practice to build a robust logging functionality before beginning a relatively big software project, the utility of logging do not end at just the development phase. An informative logging mechanism, for all events in a production application is necessary, for quick resolution of error events. Openstack is one such example of good logging mechanism for a software, and as it is made of several other software components working together, having a good logging system makes possible to trace the origin of an error among the haystack of logs of all components.

Even with good and informative logging, tracing the origin of an error by searching through log files can still get cumbersome. In some scenarios, it may require to have to investigate archived log files, and each such file may be of several gigabytes in size. Previously, the usual method of investigation of log files involved manually searching through files, which is not scalable for large applications producing lots of log. In pursuit of a better log handling mechanism, we will be learning about Elastic Stack, a collection of tools that help in setting up an interactive way of accessing and searching log files. Log files are made of plain textual data, and the only way to search for messages is to do linear search. Elastic stack enables the creation of compound search queries. The requirement of an intelligent logging system is the ability to set alarms informing error events and Elastic stack does exactly that by parsing plain textual data into interactive data objects and storing in a database. The usual approach toward log investigation is reactive as log investigation is done post an event. Elastic stack takes a proactive approach by reading logs from log files, parsing and forming meaning from them, and storing the log data for efficient searching.

# What is Elastic stack?

Elastic Stack is a a collection of four application softwares namely Elasticsearch, Logstash, Kibana, Beats which was previously called ELK stack, but through the addition of Beats has come to be called as the Elastic Stack.

*Elasticsearch* - It is an open source highly scalable textual search engine based on Lucene (a search engine library written in Java). It has rank based search indexing like that of PageRank algorithm that sits at the heart of Google's search engine.

*Logstash* - It is an open source data processing pipeline that ingests logging data from multiple sources, converts them into a json format and sends it to Elasticsearch in an Elastic Stack setup.

*Kibana* - It is an open source data visualisation and analytics platform that acts as a plugin to work with Elasticsearch. It provides capabilities to search through the indexed content of Elasticsearch and also provides statistical metrics for the same.

*Beats* - This is a collection of agents - Audiobeat, Filebeat, Heartbeat, Metricbeat, Packetbeat and Winlogbeat. The one we are going to use is Filebeat, that collects the logging data from configured locations and ships them to Logstash and/or Elasticsearch. Filebeat can be configured to either send data directly to Elasticsearch, or to Logstash for some preprocessing which is then sent to Elasticsearch.

# Deploying the Elastic stack

Updating the all packages

```
yum update -y
```

Installing the vim text editor and wget for downloading from the internet

```
yum install vim wget -y
```

We are going to use the dockerized implementation of Elastic Stack. We will be discussing vividly about Dockers or LXC in general in the section dedicated to it. For the moment, lets us adhere to the abstraction that our dockerized implementation contains Elasticsearch (E), Logstash (L) and Kibana (K), all pre-configured and ready to deploy.

Downloading and installing from the docker installer script online

```
curl -fsSL https://get.docker.com/ | sh
```

Starting and enabling docker service

```
systemctl start docker
systemctl enable docker
```

Download the docker image for ELK

```
docker pull sebp/elk
```

Before starting the ELK docker container, we have to change the virtual memory usage parameter of our machine or virtual machine which is set to 65536 by default.

```
echo "vm.max_map_count=262144" >> /etc/sysctl.conf
sysctl -p
```

For our ELK, we do not need Logstash and all Filebeat instances will send data directly to Elasticsearch. We are referring our docker image as ELK because it consists of E, L and K and not Filebeat. Filebeat has to be installed on machines or virtual machines where from we want to collect logs.

docker run -p 5601:5601 -p 9200:9200 -p 5044:5044 -e TZ=Asia/Kolkata -e LOGSTASH_START=0 —name elk sebp/elk &

The *LOGSTASH_START*, *KIBANA_START* and *ELASTICSEARCH_START* are the variables used to control which services are to be started. The default is 1 which means 'Yes'. The TZ variable is used to set the timezone to be used inside the docker container to timestamp the logs.

There is complete documentation present at the following url for the various parameters for dockerized ELK.

https://elk-docker.readthedocs.io/

Next up, we will setup Filebeat. Lets download the rpm.

curl -L -O https://artifacts.elastic.com/downloads/beats/filebeat/filebeat-6.4.0-x86_54.rpm

The latest version for Filebeat can be found at -

https://bit.ly/2Al6zYX

Installing from Filebeat rpm

rpm -vi filebeat-6.4.0-x86_64.rpm

Say we wish to monitor the logs of Openstack services for each Openstack cluster node. We will configure Filebeat /etc/filebeat/filebeat.yml.

```
filebeat.inputs:
- type: log
  enabled: true
  paths:
    - /var/log/keystone/*.log
    - /var/log/nova/*.log
    - /var/log/neutron/*.log
    - /var/log/heat/*.log
    - /var/log/glance/*.log

  #exclude_lines: ['^DBG']

  include_lines: ['ERROR','WARN']

  #exclude_files: ['.gz$']


filebeat.config.modules:
  path: ${path.config}/modules.d/*.yml

  reload.enabled: false

setup.template.settings:
  index.number_of_shards: 3


setup.kibana:
  host: "10.10.0.208:5601"

output.elasticsearch:
  hosts: ["10.10.0.208:9200"]
```

The ip addresses are to be replaced by the ip address of the host machine where ELK is deployed.

The filebeat.yml has been configured to ingest only log file lines that contain the keywords - *ERROR* and *WARN* and thus the configuration *include_lines*.

Starting and enabling Filebeat

```
systemctl start filebeat
systemctl enable filebeat
```

Once setup, the Kibana dashboard for our deployment will be at - http://10.10.0.208:5601/. This is how the dashboard looks like -

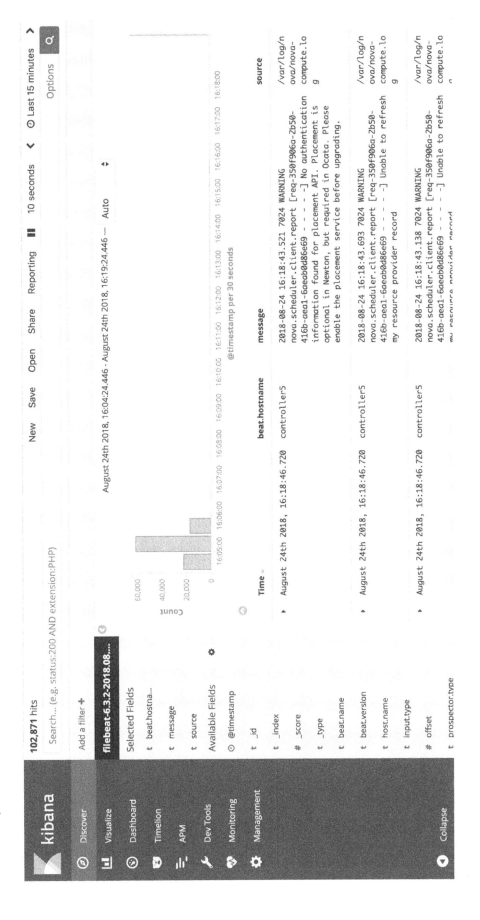

On the initial run, there would be no data visible right away as shown above. Elasticsearch creates indexes for our logs with the default name of type - filebeat-<version>-<year>.<month>.<day-of-month>. A new index is created each day by Elasticsearch and for viewing the indexed logs, we have to create index patterns for viewing in Kibana dashboard. It has to be first created from *Management* menu on the left panel. This would open to the following -

Selecting *Kibana* Index patterns, opens the dashboard for creating patterns by which we want to filter the indexes available in Elasticsearch for viewing in Kibana. We would create an index pattern *filebeat-\**.

Choose the @timestamp field from the drop-down menu and finally create the pattern.

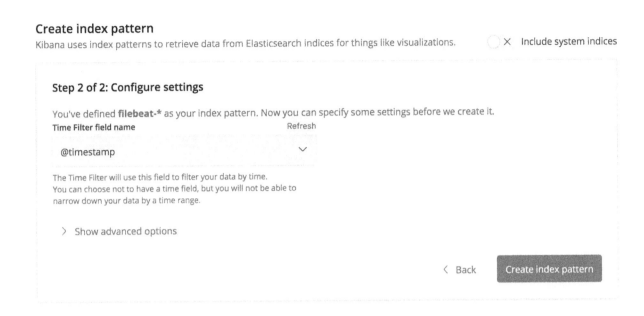

As the index is created, it will be visible as follows.

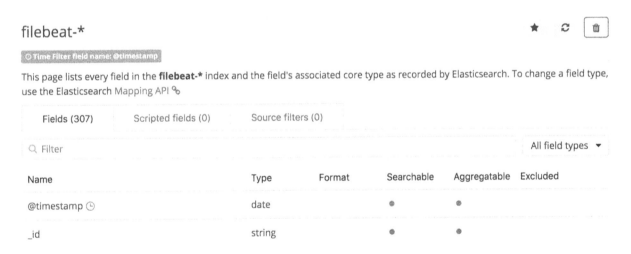

Now in the *Discover* menu, our index pattern shall be visible and Kibana will be showing data in all the Elasticsearch indexes that match the index pattern that we just created.

If Logstash has to be enabled, a server certificate has to be placed at the Filebeat host. The docker image comes with a certificate *logstash-beats.crt*. The certificate can be found at - https://bit.ly/2MR5duC

Copy this certificate content and place it at the location - */etc/pki/tls/rts/logstash-beats. crt*, on Filebeat host(s). Since Logstash is to be enabled, logs from Filebeat will no longer be sent directly to Elasticsearch. The configuration for Elasticsearch endpoint will be closed and Logstash has to be setup in filebeat.yml. Both Elasticsearch and Logstash sections in the configuration cannot be turned on at the same time.

```
logstash:
  hosts:
    - elk:5044
  enabled: true
  ssl:
    certificate_authorities: ["/etc/pki/tls/certs/logstash-beats.crt"]
  timeout: 15
```

The final step before starting the services is to add an entry to */etc/hosts* file identifying *elk* with the ip of the ELK host, which is 10.10.0.208 in our case.

Filebeat comes pre-packaged with indexing templates. Filebeat is capable of handing almost all major logging formats say for Apache, Nginx etc. These indexing templates are format description for, how the contents from a log file line is going to be indexed as an Elasticsearch tuple and these templates are configurable too.

When Logstash is not being used, Filebeat is in direct communication with Elasticsearch and the templates are loaded automatically. However, in this case when we are using Logstash we will have to load them manually in the Filebeat host(s).

```
filebeat setup --template -E output.logstash.enabled=false -E 'output.
elasticsearch.hosts=["10.10.0.208:9200"]'
```

# SECTION 4

# Search with
# Elasticsearch

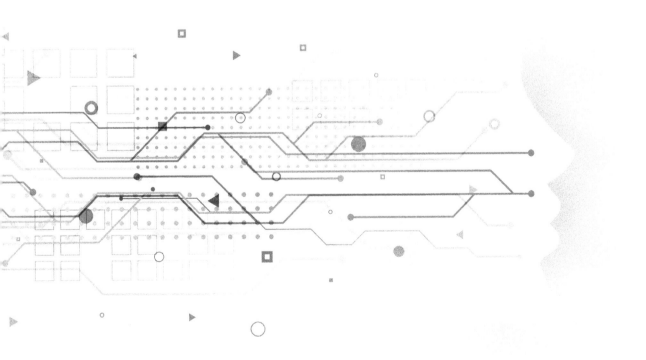

# Introduction

All category of applications be it e-commerce, social networking, service based applications, etc., have some sort of search feature. The best search engine we know as Google search, is obviously the ideal one for usage and Google search also provides a feature that enables embedding its search into a web application. This is although limited only to the web pages and the various web resources of an application, that are publicly accessible on the world wide web. A search bar powered by Google search is integrated with the web application and the various web resources are indexed exclusively, as the contents of the web application can be searched with complex search queries.

Embedding of Google's search into an application is only limited to the static web content of an application, and for adding a search feature into a dynamic application, developers are required to either build a search tool ground up, or use one of the open source engines such as Apache Lucene, Solr, Sphinx, etc. Using any of the available open source search engines requires mapping of the application data with the engine indexes, and these open source search engines provide enough customisability to configure w.r.t. the data schema.

Elasticsearch is one such search engine built on top of Apache Lucene and implements Google like keyword based indexing and search. Elasticsearch provides a rich search API that makes forming complex search queries possible.

With the competence of Elasticsearch to be used in large scale applications, it completely removes the requirement of developing a search feature ground up and the JSON interface makes it programming language agnostic.

# What is Elasticsearch?

Elasticsearch is a full textual search engine written in java. It is open source and based on the Apache Lucene search engine which is also completely written in java. The power of Elasticsearch comes from its highly scalable architecture and the ability to form complex searches through a RESTful API.

Elasticsearch provides almost realtime search performance and this is made possible by the way data is stored and *indexed* in the data store. Unlike other search engines such as Solr, that use a relational database to store data, elasticsearch is a combination of a NoSQL database for data storage on top of which is a search API.

These are the few components that make up the data storage for elasticsearch -

Cluster - It is a collection of servers that or *nodes* where data is stored. The high scalability of elasticsearch comes from the ease of adding a new node to the data storage cluster.

Document - This is a concept found in NoSQL databases and represents a unit of information that can be stored in the database. Elasticsearch uses JSON format to represent a document.

Index - This is a collection of documents that have been grouped together based on some similar characteristics.

Shards - Elasticsearch stores data in logical units called indexes and these indexes grow in sizes such that can span across nodes. For this reason, a particular index can be broken into shards that divide the index data into pieces. Each shard is independent of the other and function if other shards are not available. The concept of shards is also fruitful in bringing parallelisation to search operations and increasing throughput. Suppose, a search query is made up of parts, that perform operations that are non blocking and independent w.r.t. the index, elasticsearch splits the query parts to work in parallel on the shards and then aggregates the results. Shards are also used for data replication purposes, increasing the reliability.

# Deploy and setup

Elasticsearch is based on java and so we are going to install java 8.

```
yum install java-1.8.0-openjdk java-1.8.0-openjdk-devel
```

```
[[root@elasticsearch ~]# java -version
openjdk version "1.8.0_181"
OpenJDK Runtime Environment (build 1.8.0_181-b13)
OpenJDK 64-Bit Server VM (build 25.181-b13, mixed mode)
```

We will download and install from the tar archive.

```
curl -L -O https://artifacts.elastic.co/downloads/elasticsearch/elasticsearch-6.4.0.tar.gz
```

```
tar -xvf elasticsearch-6.4.0.tar.gz
```

Elasticsearch cannot be run as root and so changing the directory permission to centos user, the java application is run by executing the elasticsearch bash script.

```
[[centos@elasticsearch ~]$ cd elasticsearch-6.4.0/bin/
[[centos@elasticsearch bin]$ ll
total 17932
-rwxr-xr-x. 1 centos centos     1777 Aug 17 23:11 elasticsearch
```

```
[[centos@elasticsearch bin]$ ./elasticsearch &
[1] 19680
```

On starting the application, it echoes the loading status of various modules, templates and index patterns.

   Alongwith all the echoed information, there are two warning messages -

```
max file descriptors [4096] for elasticsearch process is too low, increase to at least [65536]
max virtual memory areas vm.max_map_count [65530] is too low, increase to at least [262144]
```

It says that the file descriptor limit set at 4096 by default is too low for elasticsearch and the virtual memory size also needs to be set at 262144, from 65530, which is set by default in Centos 7.

   From the root user, the virtual memory in increased -

```
echo "vm.max_map_count=262144" >> /etc/sysctl.conf
```

```
[root@elasticsearch ~]# sysctl -p
vm.max_map_count = 262144
```

and then the file descriptor count -

```
echo "centos  -  nofile  65536" >> /etc/security/limits.conf
```

Since we will be running elasticsearch with the centos user, the file count for centos is changed and for the change to take effect, a new session has to be established.

Elasticsearch by default binds to 127.0.0.1 and so this has to be changed to the public IP address of the node. For this, change the *network.host* key in *elasticsearch-6.4.0/config/elasticsearch.yml*.

```
network.host: 10.10.0.225
```

Now finally elasticsearch is started without warnings. The output echoed on startup such as this and more -

```
[czjKWY0] loaded module [aggs-matrix-stats]
[czjKWY0] loaded module [analysis-common]
[czjKWY0] loaded module [ingest-common]
[czjKWY0] loaded module [lang-expression]
[czjKWY0] loaded module [lang-mustache]
```

has the name of the node *czjKWY0* as provided by default by elasticsearch, which can be changed too.

A successful elasticsearch deployment should show the following message -

```
←  →  C    ⓘ Not Secure | 10.10.0.225:9200
```

```
{
  "name" : "czjKWY0",
  "cluster_name" : "elasticsearch",
  "cluster_uuid" : "okDsAkgLQ6yR6ze4Sfzd7Q",
  "version" : {
    "number" : "6.4.0",
    "build_flavor" : "default",
    "build_type" : "tar",
    "build_hash" : "595516e",
    "build_date" : "2018-08-17T23:18:47.308994Z",
    "build_snapshot" : false,
    "lucene_version" : "7.4.0",
    "minimum_wire_compatibility_version" : "5.6.0",
    "minimum_index_compatibility_version" : "5.0.0"
  },
  "tagline" : "You Know, for Search"
}
```

Port 9200 is for API access and port 9300 is for communication between elasticsearch nodes in a cluster.

Since we have only one node, the query about node info shows the following details -

```
← → C     ⓘ Not Secure | 10.10.0.225:9200/_cat/nodes?v
```

```
ip             heap.percent ram.percent cpu load_1m load_5m load_15m node.role master name
10.10.0.225             9          49   2    0.00    0.04     0.09 mdi          *     czjKWYO
```

The indexes will be shown at the following URL, but since we are yet to create the first index, it shows empty -

```
← → C     ⓘ Not Secure | 10.10.0.225:9200/_cat/indices?v
```

```
health status index uuid pri rep docs.count docs.deleted store.size pri.store.size
```

In order to communicate with the REST API, we will use another application called postman, which is available as a browser extension in Chrome web store.

We create our first index named *sample* using the PUT HTTP request.

Checking the index details now shows -

```
← → C     ⓘ Not Secure | 10.10.0.225:9200/_cat/indices?v
```

```
health status index  uuid                        pri rep docs.count docs.deleted store.size pri.store.size
yellow open   sample YotIIaWxTci-1gmSSOJk4w        5   1          0            0      1.2kb          1.2kb
```

It says there are 5 primary shards and 1 replica.

For interacting with the elasticsearch API we will use both the curl based requests as well as the python library Elasticsearch DSL. Elasticsearch DSL is built upon the elasticsearch-py client.

# Working with Elasticsearch

## *Creating a document*

We would start with creation of a simple document. The document consists of the following key/value pairs -

name = milky way
description = average sized galaxy
star count = 25,000 crores

The curl form -

```
[centos@elasticsearch ~]$ curl -X POST http://10.10.0.225:9200/sample/_doc/1 -H 'Content-Type: application/json' -d '{
    "name":"Milky Way", "description":"Average sized galaxy", "star count":"25,000 Crores"
}'
```

Here /sample/ is the name of the index, using _doc since we are populating a single document, and /1 is the id of the document. The id is optional.

The output received -

```
{"_index":"sample","_type":"_doc","_id":"1","_version":1,"result":"created","_shards":{"total":2,"successful":1,"failed":0},"_seq_no":0,"_primary_term":1}
```

We execute the same request now from postman application and this is the output we get -

```
{
    "_index": "sample",
    "_type": "_doc",
    "_id": "1",
    "_version": 2,
    "result": "updated",
    "_shards": {
        "total": 2,
        "successful": 1,
        "failed": 0
    },
    "_seq_no": 4,
    "_primary_term": 2
}
```

The noteworthy item here is the key *_version* which is 2 unlike in the curl output where *_version* is set to 1. This is because elasticsearch provides versioning for data in a particular document.

Here we have executed the write operation on the document with the same data. We now update the data in name key and again write to the same document.

```
POST  ∨          http://10.10.0.225:9200/sample/_doc/1
```

```
1 ▾ {
2        "name":"Milky way galaxy",
3        "description":"Average sized galaxy",
4        "star count":"25,000 Crores"
5   }
```

The response -

```
{
    "_index": "sample",
    "_type": "_doc",
    "_id": "1",
    "_version": 3,
    "result": "updated",
```

As expected, a new version is created.

## Deleting a document

The deletion operation is straightforward.

```
DELETE  ∨      http://10.10.0.225:9200/sample/_doc/1
```

The response for deleting the document at id 1 -

```
{
    "_index": "sample",
    "_type": "_doc",
    "_id": "1",
    "_version": 4,
    "result": "deleted",
    "_shards": {
        "total": 2,
        "successful": 1,
        "failed": 0
    },
    "_seq_no": 6,
    "_primary_term": 2
}
```

The version is again incremented by 1 even though the document at the index is no longer present. This is because elasticsearch is recording and updating the changes at the id 1 for the index *sample* and deletion also being an operation that updates the data content w.r.t. the document created initially. If now a new document is created the version will be reset to 1.

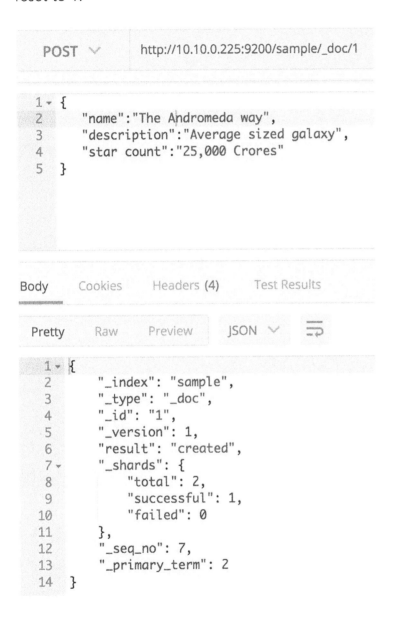

## Updating a document

The updation of a document is done with POST operation, but elasticsearch provides an update API as well, where updation is done not by just sending the new value for the fields but through performing function on the key(s)/value(s).

| POST ⌄ | http://10.10.0.225:9200/sample/_doc/1/_update |
|---|---|

Authorization    Headers (1)    **Body ●**    Pre-request Script    Tests

○ form-data    ○ x-www-form-urlencoded    ● raw    ○ binary    JSON (application/json)

```
1 ▾ {
2 ▾     "script" : {
3           "source": "ctx._source.star_count = params.stars",
4 ▾         "params" : {
5               "stars" : "More than 25,000 crores"
6           }
7       }
8 }
```

The ctx variable gives access to the fields of a document as shown above - *ctx._source.start_count.* There is a vivid description on the usage of script at the following url -

## Deleting a document

We are going to delete the sample index and created two new index each of which will have same content. One will be inserted with values with curl based requests and the other with python.

After deletion the new indexes are -

```
←  →  C   ⓘ Not Secure | 10.10.0.225:9200/_cat/indices?v

health status index         uuid                     pri rep docs.count docs.deleted store.size pri.store.size
yellow open   python_index _Zm2ZqXaROOiFmiIJh8P9A      5   1          0            0      1.1kb          1.1kb
yellow open   curl_index   RvqNN2RhRAyNoSxkajYn1A      5   1          0            0      1.1kb          1.1kb
```

## Search with elasticsearch

Elasticsearch comes with a rich Search API that is accessible from both a URI and a Query DSL to perform request body search. Query DSL is a JSON based search query definition language and to be described in details in the next section.

The storage data structure for elasticsearch isn't like the that of relational databases where a tuple with all its field values are taken into account when a query is run. In elasticsearch, a _doc i.e. document, is equivalent to that of a relational database tuple in terms of the purpose of acting as an encapsulation of related data items. Indexing is done for all the fields in a _doc such that each individual field is searchable and is not codependent on the other fields in the _doc item as compared to tuple fields in relational databases. This is what gives elasticsearch's data storage mechanism the advantage of speed compared to traditional databases.

Search with elasticsearch can be broadly categorised into three types -

a) A query that compares values in specific fields such as date, age, etc. and returns documents sorted upon particular fields.
b) A full text search query that looks up all relevant documents matching the search keywords and returns documents sorted according to relevance.
c) A combination of both.

There are no documents currently in the created indexes, and an empty search query returns the following output -

This is the most basic form of search accessing the search API with a URL *10.10.0.225:9200/_search*. The same output will be returned from accessing elasticsearch with the Query DSL.

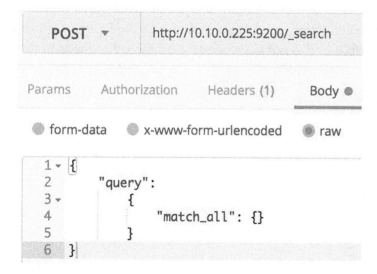

Although both the methods - a) URI based method, b) request body method (DSL), access the same URI endpoint 10.10.0.255:9200/_search, the Query DSL method specifically has a JSON request body sent as a POST.

Here various components of the search response and their meanings -

## hits

a)  *hits* - This key represents the total number of documents that matched the query and contains a *hits* array as a child key, that contains the first 10 matching documents. When documents are returned, the hits array shows the following attributes -

b)
```
"hits": [
    {
        "_index": "curl_index",
        "_type": "_doc",
        "_id": "1",
        "_score": 1,
        "_source": {
            "user": "tesla",
            "post_date": "2009-11-15T14:12:12",
            "message": "trying out Elasticsearch"
        }
    }
]
```

c)  _source - Contains the actual document.
d)  _index - The name of the index where from the document was matched.
e)  _score - The score of a single document.
f)  *total* - Number of documents matched.
j)  *max_score* - The highest _score value recieved by any document.

## took

Tells about the execution time of a query.

## _shards

This tells about the total number of shards that participated in the search query for document look up.

a)  *total* - Total number of shards that were searched.
b)  *successful* - The number of shards that responded successfully to a query.

The remaining field *skipped* tells us the number of shards that were skipped in cases where a query is aimed at a subset of the shards and the *failed* field represents the number of shards that failed. In case of a primary shard failure, the replica shard participates. The *timeout* field tells us if the query has timed out waiting for a query execution to finish.

## Paginating the search results

The search results can be paginated using the *size* and *from* parameters of the elasticsearch's URI based API. We will entry a number of documents as a bulk using the _bulk parameter -

```
[centos@elasticsearch ~]$ curl -X POST http://10.10.0.225:9200/curl_index/_doc/_bulk -H 'Content-Type: application/json' -d '
> { "index":{} }
> { "user" : "newton", "post_date" : "2009-12-01T14:09:11", "message" : "trying out Elasticsearch" }
> { "index":{} }
> { "user" : "einstein", "post_date" : "2010-10-03T14:02:40", "message" : "trying out Elasticsearch" }
> { "index":{} }
> { "user" : "hawking", "post_date" : "2018-05-06T14:04:40", "message" : "trying out Elasticsearch" }
> '
```

The empty search query is executed and the response is limited with the *size* and *from* parameters. The *from* parameter states the number of items to skip from the beginning and *size* represents the number of items to show, defaults to 0.

| POST ▼ | http://10.10.0.225:9200/_search?size=2&from=2 |
|---|---|

retty    Raw    Preview    JSON ▼    ⇥

```
11              "total": 4,
12              "max_score": 1,
13 ▾            "hits": [
14 ▾                {
15                      "_index": "curl_index",
16                      "_type": "_doc",
17                      "_id": "MxohcWYBDKW5lplsG9ub",
18                      "_score": 1,
19 ▾                    "_source": {
20                          "user": "newton",
21                          "post_date": "2009-12-01T14:09:11",
22                          "message": "trying out Elasticsearch"
23                      }
24                  },
25 ▾                {
26                      "_index": "curl_index",
27                      "_type": "_doc",
28                      "_id": "1",
29                      "_score": 1,
30 ▾                    "_source": {
31                          "user": "tesla",
32                          "post_date": "2009-11-15T14:12:12",
33                          "message": "trying out Elasticsearch"
34                      }
35                  }
36              ]
```

## Auto-generation of _id

A noticeable thing from the above output is the _id fields of both the documents are different in style. The _id for user tesla is 1 whereas the _id for newton is an alpha-numeric string. This is because while creating the document for user tesla, the _id was explicitly mentioned in the URI - 10.10.0.225:9200/curl_index/_doc/1, but the rest of documents were created as a bulk request without mentioning the _id explicitly and so elasticsearch auto-generates IDs. The _id format can be changed by updating the *action.auto_create_index* setting in elasticsearch.yml config file on all nodes. The _id field can be mentioned in a _bulk request in the following way -

```
[centos@elasticsearch ~]$ curl -X POST http://10.10.0.225:9200/curl_index/_doc/_bulk -H 'Content-Type: application/json' -d
> { "index":{"_id": 2} }
> { "user" : "n.tyson", "post_date" : "2018-05-06T14:04:40", "message" : "trying out Elasticsearch" }
> '
```

Now that we have documents in the index curl_index, we can execute a simple query to find the documents that have the value *"newton"* in user field. The query DSL for such a query is as follows -

The same query when written as URI, takes the following form -

```
GET ▼    http://10.10.0.225:9200/curl_index/_search?q=user:newton
```

In both the queries, it has been specified that the *"user"* field in a document has to be compared for the searched string. Elasticsearch has provision for cases where the field(s) are not specified, yet document(s) that match a strings would be returned.

## The _all field

A simple query to search for the *"user"* *newton* can be formed without mentioning the details about where to look up.

| GET ▼ | http://10.10.0.225:9200/curl_index/_search?q=newton |
|---|---|

The query successfully returns the correct document, similar to that of the previous queries where the field name was mentioned.

```
"hits": {
    "total": 1,
    "max_score": 0.6931472,
    "hits": [
        {
            "_index": "curl_index",
            "_type": "_doc",
            "_id": "MxohcWYBDKW5lplsG9ub",
            "_score": 0.6931472,
            "_source": {
                "user": "newton",
                "post_date": "2009-12-01T14:09:11",
                "message": "trying out Elasticsearch"
            }
        }
    ]
}
```

This is made possible by the special field, _all. For each document, a special field is reserved as the _all field, which is a concatenation of all the values in the fields of a document using space as a delimiter. However, the _all field has been deprecated from version 6.0.0 due to space saving purpose but the functionality remains available when no fields are mentioned in a search query. If it is required to create a document that explicitly has an extra field as the string concatenation of all values, a *copy_to* field can be explicitly defined in the index with the mappings API.

## Mappings

In example of creating an index, there was no formal definition required for the document schema. A PUT/POST query with its fields and data for a document was all that was required to create a document for a particular index.

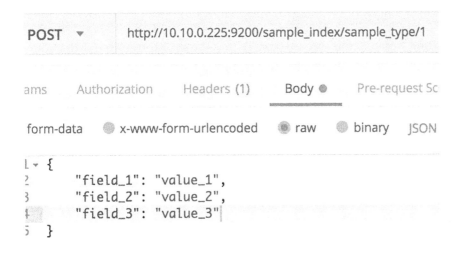

POST ▾    http://10.10.0.225:9200/sample_index/sample_type/1

ams    Authorization    Headers (1)    Body ●    Pre-request Sc

form-data    ● x-www-form-urlencoded    ● raw    ● binary    JSON

```
1 ▾ {
2       "field_1": "value_1",
3       "field_2": "value_2",
4       "field_3": "value_3"
5   }
```

Here the document schema which in elasticsearch is called *mapping*, is evaluated from the data fields dynamically at creation time. Mapping can be explicitly specified for an index using the mapping API. Here is the mapping definition for the index *sample_index* shown above.

PUT ▾    http://10.10.0.225:9200/sample_index/

ams    Authorization    Headers (1)    Body ●    Pre-re

form-data    ● x-www-form-urlencoded    ● raw    ● binary

```
1 ▾ {
2 ▾   "mappings": {
3 ▾     "sample_type_1": {
4 ▾       "properties": {
5             "field_1":    { "type": "text"  },
6             "field_2":    { "type": "text"  },
7             "field_3":    { "type": "text"  }
8         }
9       }
10    }
11  }
```

In order to accommodate the copy_to field to this index, the same mapping has to be defined the following way -

| PUT ▼ | http://10.10.0.225:9200/sample_index/ |
|---|---|

Params    Authorization    Headers (1)    **Body ●**    Pre-request Script    Tests

● form-data    ● x-www-form-urlencoded    ● raw    ● binary    JSON (application/json)

```
1 ▾ {
2 ▾     "mappings": {
3 ▾         "sample_type_1": {
4 ▾             "properties": {
5                   "field_1":    { "type": "text", "copy_to": "all_fields" },
6                   "field_2":    { "type": "text", "copy_to": "all_fields" },
7                   "field_3":    { "type": "text", "copy_to": "all_fields" },
8                   "all_fields": { "type": "text" }
9             }
10        }
11    }
12 }
```

The mapping of an index can be found with the mapping parameter in URI.

| GET ▼ | http://10.10.0.225:9200/sample_index/_mapping |
|---|---|

The key *sample_type_1* represents the type of the mapping similar to that of *_doc* as seen earlier. The concept of mapping types has been drawn from relational databases where an index is compared to a database and a mapping type is compared to a table. In versions previous to 6.0.0 a single index could have multiple mapping types, but it has been deprecated and reduced to an index having just one mapping type.

## Types of searches

There are two broad categories of search in elasticsearch - a) *exact values search* and *full text search*.

Exact value searches are those that are commonly done with SQL over data fields such as matching username, email address or filtering search results based on a date range, or sorting of results. Exact value searches are all field centric and greatly depend on how the various fields are mapped. The *copy_to* parameter is a good candidate for usage when there are a number of small string fields and a query to search on concatenated field shall be convenient.

Full text searches are performed on textual data written in some human language such as the body of an email or a tweet. Such a type of search is fundamentally different from that of exact value search, since the data to be searched has to go through an analysis phase. Full text search consists of unstructured data that is subject to typos in spelling as well as grammar and require preprocessing before performing any comparison tasks. As a contrast from *exact value queries* which result in binary decision, a *full text search* relies on ranking of matched documents based on their relevance with the search query. For example there can be a number of documents containing dialogues from various movies and a query has to find the document that is the closest to the phrase - "Live long and prosper". There can be documents containing the words in our searched query, but in different order or containing derivatives of the words in the phrase such as - "And they lived long in prosperity". Therefore, a full text query has to examine the documents on properties much more than simple comparison and return search results based on how well the search matches the documents.

In full text searches, it is not always that we want to search for an entire phrase but for specific words and its derivations that imply the intent of the search operation. A search for the term "game" shall return documents containing the terms - games, gamer, gaming and even related to the term "sport" which is a synonym for game. In order to facilitate these types of searches on full text fields, elasticsearch analyses the text and creates an *inverted index*.

## Inverted index

Elasticsearch creates this data structure to enable fast full text searches. An inverted index consists of a list of all the unique words in a document. In this list, each word points to a list of documents that contain the word. Here is the example of such an index -

| Term | Document 1 | Document 2 |
|---|---|---|
| quick | yes | |
| brown | yes | |
| fox | yes | |
| brownish | | yes |
| quicker | | yes |
| lazyness | | yes |
| jump | yes | |
| jumping | | yes |

To create such as index, the text content in a field is split into separate words called *tokens*. Then the list of tokens are sorted and placed in a list. Now if a query is searching for the words *quick* and *jump*, both the documents will be returned. Since the search type is full text search, the returned documents will be ranked in terms of relevance, such as the document with most count of the words *quick* and *jump* will be ranked higher. In our example, Document 1 has the exact terms *quick* and *jump*, but Document 2 will also be returned because of the word *jumping* in it. It might be the case, that although Document 1 has exact matches with the searched terms, Document 2 is more relevant to our purpose. It is for such cases and others that the token terms are normalised and placed in the inverted index such that, the derivatives of a word is stripped down to its origin.

| Term | Document 1 | Document 2 |
|---|---|---|
| quick | yes | yes |
| brown | yes | yes |
| fox | yes | |
| lazyness | | yes |
| jump | yes | yes |

This process of tokenisation and normalisation is called *analysis*.

## Analysis

In this process the unstructured textual data in a field is first tokenised and then normalised to a standard form to increase their search-ability. This is done by analysers that performs three specific functions - a) Character filtration to clean up the text by removing unwanted items such as HTML, b) Tokenisation to split the text into terms, c) Token filtration that converts words to lowercase, removes stop words such as *a* and *the*, adds synonyms of words. Elasticsearch comes with a collection of built-in analysers and we are going to take a look at few of them.

Standard analyser - This is the default analyser and provides grammar based tokenisation. We will configure the standard analyser such that it tokenises words with maximum length of 5 and uses the set of english stop-words to eliminate.

| PUT ▼ | http://10.10.0.225:9200/sample_index/ |
|---|---|

ams    Authorization    Headers (1)    Body ●    Pre-r

form-data   ○ x-www-form-urlencoded   ● raw   ○ binar

```
1 ▾ {
2 ▾     "settings":{
3 ▾         "analysis":{
4 ▾             "analyzer":{
5 ▾                 "a_sample_analyzer":{
6                       "type":"standard",
7                       "max_token_length": 5,
8                       "stopwords": "_english_"
9                   }
10              }
11          }
12      }
13  }
```

The following text when analyzed -

```
POST  ▼        http://10.10.0.225:9200/sample_index/_analyze


ams    Authorization    Headers (1)    Body ●    Pre-requ

form-data    ● x-www-form-urlencoded    ● raw    ● binary

1 ▼ {
2     "analyzer": "a_sample_analyzer",
3     "text": "THE Brown-Foxes jumped"
4   }
```

produces the following tokens -

```
{
    "token": "brown",
    "start_offset": 4,
    "end_offset": 9,
    "type": "<ALPHANUM>",
    "position": 1
},
{
    "token": "foxes",
    "start_offset": 10,
    "end_offset": 15,
    "type": "<ALPHANUM>",
    "position": 2
},
{
    "token": "jumpe",
    "start_offset": 16,
    "end_offset": 21,
    "type": "<ALPHANUM>",
    "position": 3
},
{
    "token": "d",
    "start_offset": 21,
    "end_offset": 22,
    "type": "<ALPHANUM>",
    "position": 4
}
```

The word jumped was broken into *jumpe* and *d* because of the size limit of 5.

Simple analyser - This analyser breaks text into terms upon encountering a character other than a letter and it is not a configurable analyser.

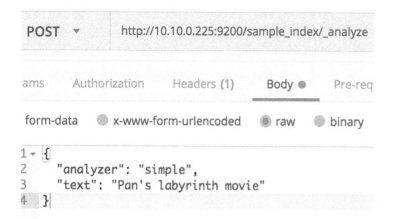

```
1 ▾ {
2       "analyzer": "simple",
3       "text": "Pan's labyrinth movie"
4   }
```

The tokens produced is -

```
{
    "token": "pan",
    "start_offset": 0,
    "end_offset": 3,
    "type": "word",
    "position": 0
},
{
    "token": "s",
    "start_offset": 4,
    "end_offset": 5,
    "type": "word",
    "position": 1
},
{
    "token": "labyrinth",
    "start_offset": 6,
    "end_offset": 15,
    "type": "word",
    "position": 2
},
{
    "token": "movie",
    "start_offset": 16,
    "end_offset": 21,
    "type": "word",
    "position": 3
}
```

*pan* and *s* are broken into separate terms because the have an apostrophe in between.

Pattern analyser - This analyser uses regular expressions to to split text into terms. The default for this analyser is \W+ i.e. all non-word characters.

| POST ▾ | http://10.10.0.225:9200/sample_index/_analyze |
|---|---|

ams    Authorization    Headers (1)    **Body** ●    Pre-req

form-data  ◉ x-www-form-urlencoded  ◉ raw  ◉ binary

```
1 ▾ {
2     "analyzer": "pattern",
3     "text": "%%bhoson@milky-way.comm*"
4   }
```

Produces the following tokens -

```
{
    "token": "bhoson",
    "start_offset": 2,
    "end_offset": 8,
    "type": "word",
    "position": 0
},
{
    "token": "milky",
    "start_offset": 9,
    "end_offset": 14,
    "type": "word",
    "position": 1
},
{
    "token": "way",
    "start_offset": 15,
    "end_offset": 18,
    "type": "word",
    "position": 2
},
{
    "token": "comm",
    "start_offset": 19,
    "end_offset": 23,
    "type": "word",
    "position": 3
}
```

Custom analyser - With the choice of required character filters, tokeniser and token filters, an analyser can be created suited to a special case.

| PUT ▼ | http://10.10.0.225:9200/sample_index |
|-------|--------------------------------------|

ıms      Authorization      Headers (1)      **Body** ●      I

form-data    ● x-www-form-urlencoded    ● raw    ● b

```
1 ▾ {
2 ▾   "settings": {
3 ▾     "analysis": {
4 ▾       "analyzer": {
5 ▾         "custom_analyzer": {
6             "type":      "custom",
7             "tokenizer": "standard",
8 ▾           "char_filter": [
9               "html_strip"
0             ],
1 ▾           "filter": [
2               "lowercase",
3               "asciifolding"
4             ]
5           }
6         }
7       }
8     }
9 }
```

The tokeniser chosen is standard, the character filter is html_strip that identifies html tags in a text, and the token filters are lowercase - to convert all terms to lowercase and asciifolding - to convert unicode and alpha-numeric characters into 127 bit ASCII if such a corresponding conversion is available.

On analysing the following string -

| POST ▼ | http://10.10.0.225:9200/sample_index/_analyze |
|--------|-----------------------------------------------|

ams      Authorization      Headers (1)      **Body** ●      Pre-req

form-data    ● x-www-form-urlencoded    ● raw    ● binary

```
1 ▾ {
2     "analyzer": "custom_analyzer",
3     "text": "Is this <b>déjà vu</b>?"
4 }
```

the following tokens are returned -

```
{
    "token": "is",
    "start_offset": 0,
    "end_offset": 2,
    "type": "<ALPHANUM>",
    "position": 0
},
{
    "token": "this",
    "start_offset": 3,
    "end_offset": 7,
    "type": "<ALPHANUM>",
    "position": 1
},
{
    "token": "deja",
    "start_offset": 11,
    "end_offset": 15,
    "type": "<ALPHANUM>",
    "position": 2
},
{
    "token": "vu",
    "start_offset": 16,
    "end_offset": 22,
    "type": "<ALPHANUM>",
    "position": 3
}
```

These were the few among many other types of analyzers in elasticsearch.

A complete list of analyzers can be found at -

List of tokenizers -

List of token filters -

List of character filters -

## Summerizing elasticsearch

Elasticsearch facilitates searching of two types - a) Exact value search, b) Full text search.

The exact value search is similar to that of traditional search based on comparison of values in fields and the search response is binary, resulting in either match or no-match upon the search criteria.

A full text search is the kind found in search engines such as google or bing, which comprises of searching through documents of unstructured data and returning documents based on the relevance w.r.t. search query. This type of search involves ordering of results upon a rank/score.

The search API can be accessed either through an URI request or a request body search with a query DSL. A limited set of actions can be performed with a URI request, whereas query DSL is expressive.

In order to provide useful results, each document is fed to an analyser that parses the content and prepares an index.

# Query DSL

Query DSL is a JSON based structured language for defining a search query. When a query is parsed by the elasticsearch engine, it forms a tree data structure containing primarily a *leaf query clause* whose task is to compare the exact value in a certain field and a compound query clause that joins other leaf or compound query clauses.

## Query and Filter context

All the types of queries that can be formed with query DSL, have two major context - a) Query context, b) Filter context. A query can be entirely composed of *Filter* context, or it can be composed of *Query* context or a mixture of both.

The *Query* context is determines how well a document matches to the search request. Suppose there is a search requirement - find all the documents that summarises the concepts of artificial intelligence. This kind of full text search involves examining documents from an index that comprises of unstructured text on the topic of "artificial intelligence". Let the index have the following mapping -

```
{
  "mappings": {
    "_doc": {
      "properties": {
        "document_title":    { "type": "text"  },
        "document_body":     { "type": "text"  }
      }
    }
  }
}
```

The intent of such a query is not to just look for documents that have the value string "artificial intelligence" in either of the fields, like comparing exact values in fields such as age or gender, but to find out which documents suit the best according our search criteria and ranking then results. The documents will be ranked on various properties such as documents that have higher number of keywords match with the search string, documents that have more synonymous words to the search string and many more.

On the other hand the Filter context is another fundamental ingredient of search in general and it is used in cases where a search is about finding an exact value in a field or filtering those documents that lie within a range or criterion based on the exact value in one or more fields. Therefore, the logical outcome of a Filter query always results in either true or false for a comparison on the field value.

Each of the two contexts are established by dedicated functions.

A filter context has the following functions -

term - The *term* filter is used to compare exact values such as date, boolean, integers/long and text/keyword types. The following are examples of the basic usage -

```
{
    "query":{
        "term":{"age": 6}
    }
}
 OR
{
    "query":{
        "term": {"public": true}
    }
}
OR
{
    "query":{
        "term": {"date": "2018-10-17"}
    }
}
OR
{
    "query":{
        "term": {"tag": "h8374fh83"}
    }
}
```

The term query can be used to compare strings without spaces.

range - The range filter is used when selecting documents based on a range of integer/long type values or date type values.

```
{
    "query":{
        "range":{
            "age":{ "gt": 15, "lt": 25 }
        }
    }
}
```

The operators accepts by range filter are - lt (less than), gt (greater than), lte (less than equal to), gte (greater than equal to).

bool - The bool filter is used to combine multiple filter clauses with boolean logic. The operators accepted by bool filter are - must (like logical AND), must_not (like logical NOT) and should(like logical OR).

```
{
    "query":{
        "bool":{
            "must":{ "term": { "age": 6 } },
            "must_not":{ "term": {"tag": "S56H6NEW8ff" } },
            "should": { "term": {"public": true }}
        }
    }
}
```

In case of binding multiple criterion with an operator, the query would be of the form -

```
{
    "query":{
        "bool":{
            "must":[ {"term": { "age": 6 }}, {"term": { "age": 9 }} ],
            "must_not":{ "term": {"tag": "S56H6NEW8ff" } },
            "should": { "term": {"public": true }}
        }
    }
}
```

exists - This filter is used to check and return documents if it has a specified field.

```
{
    "query":{
        "exists":{
            "field": "age"
        }
    }
}
```

The functions in query context are -

match - The *match* query is used for full text searches, therefore ideal for comparing strings separated by spaces.

```
{
    "query":{
        "match": {
            "description": "Learning about match query"
        }
    }
}
```

The *match* query does not look for exact matches for the words in the same order, but analyses the searched field's content in documents and returns the closest match if found. There are other variations of the *match* query - *match_phrase, match_phrase_prefix, multi_match*.

bool - The *bool* query is used to combine multiple query clauses. Like the *bool filter* it also accepts *must, must_not* and *should* operators.

```
{
    "query":{
        "bool": {
            "must": { "match": { "age": 6 }},
            "must_not": { "match": { "tag": "S56H6NEW8ff" } },
            "should": {"match": { "public": true } }
        }
    }
}
```

## Disambiguation between query and filter context

We had a brief description on the various functions that act in each of the contexts, and there are similarities between the functionalities. That is why Queries and Filters have been merged in the recent elasticsearch releases. There used to be separate conceptual grouping of functions under Filter and Query contexts such as the *bool* function. Similarly, the *match* query can perform the same function as that of *term* filter, not vice versa, and the below examples return the same documents -

Using match -

```
{
    "query":{
        "bool": {
            "must": { "match": { "age": 6 }},
            "must_not": { "match": { "tag": "S56H6NEW8ff" } },
            "should": {"match": { "public": true } }
        }
    }
}
```

The bool function here, is a bool query.

Using term -

```
{
    "query":{
        "bool":{
            "must":{ "term": { "age": 6 } },
            "must_not":{ "term": {"tag": "S56H6NEW8ff" } },
            "should": { "term": {"public": true }}
        }
    }
}
```

The bool function here, is a bool filter.

The usage of the terminologies filter and query creates an impression of them being separate entities when in fact both are queries. Therefore, the paradigm of filter and query contexts have been simplified by merging the bool query and bool filter into bool query. The term filter has been changed to term query. The range and exists filters have been converted to queries as well.

With the merging of Query and Filter functions, the significance of a filter context is usually required in uses cases where the task is to find the documents that contain a certain string in one or multiple fields (full text query or exact value query) and only those documents are to be included in the result, that contain a certain exact value in a field and/or fall within a range (filtering). A filter context in a query does not contribute to the rank/_score of the documents received in the query context. A filter context is activated by using the *filter operator* in a *bool* query or *constant_score* query or *filter aggregation*.

Here is an example usage with the bool query -

```
{
    "query":{
        "bool": {
            "must": [{ "match":{ "description": "Change the world" } },{ "match":{ "title": "A.I." } }],
            "filter": [{"term":{ "published": true}},{"range":{ "date":{"gte":"2018-10-10"}}}]
        }
    }
}
```

In this query the documents are ranked based on the search criterion defined with must operator and then selecting only those documents that meet the filtering criterion given by the operator *filter*.

A query request such as the following -

```
{
    "query":{
        "term": {"age":6}
    }
}
```

which was previously shown as an example for the *term* filter, is now a query similar to that of match, and no longer hold a separate classification as a function of Filter context. The notable difference between using the term query as shown above and when used inside the filter operator of *bool* query, is that, the later case does not evaluate any _score.

```
{
    "query":{
        "bool":{
            "filter":{
                "term":{
                    "num_field":1
                }
            }
        }
    }
}
```

Here the document returned have 0 for _score.

```
"hits": {
    "total": 1,
    "max_score": 0,
    "hits": [
        {
            "_index": "sample_index",
            "_type": "_doc",
            "_id": "NhqvgGYBDKW5lplspttJ",
            "_score": 0,
            "_source": {
                "num_field": 1,
                "text_field": "Halo"
            }
        }
    ]
}
```

Now compared to the usage of *term* query such as this -

```
{
    "query":{
        "term": {"num_field":1}
    }
}
```

The returned document has 1 for _score.

```
"hits": {
    "total": 1,
    "max_score": 1,
    "hits": [
        {
            "_index": "sample_index",
            "_type": "_doc",
            "_id": "NhqvgGYBDKW5lplspttJ",
            "_score": 1,
            "_source": {
                "num_field": 1,
                "text_field": "Halo"
            }
        }
    ]
}
```

The _score value for *term* query is provided 1 as in the logical *true* value for being found after analysing and normalising. Here we can see for multiple matches, all the documents are provided the _score 1.

```
"hits": {
    "total": 2,
    "max_score": 1,
    "hits": [
        {
            "_index": "sample_index",
            "_type": "_doc",
            "_id": "PBoZhmYBDKW5lplsU9vH",
            "_score": 1,
            "_source": {
                "num_field": 1,
                "text_field": "Halo 2"
            }
        },
        {
            "_index": "sample_index",
            "_type": "_doc",
            "_id": "NhqvgGYBDKW5lplspttJ",
            "_score": 1,
            "_source": {
                "num_field": 1,
                "text_field": "Halo"
            }
        }
    ]
}
```

The match query although should ideally always be used for comparing space separated text with _score and not for exact value comparison, but it can still function for the later purpose. Using match query for exact value comparison within the filter context yields no _score.

```
{
    "query":{
        "bool": {
            "filter": {
                "match":{
                    "num_field":1
                }
            }
        }
    }
}
```

Produces the following result with _score set to 0.

```
"hits": [
    {
        "_index": "sample_index",
        "_type": "_doc",
        "_id": "PBoZhmYBDKW5lplsU9vH",
        "_score": 0,
        "_source": {
            "num_field": 1,
            "text_field": "Halo 2"
        }
    },
    {
        "_index": "sample_index",
        "_type": "_doc",
        "_id": "NhqvgGYBDKW5lplspttJ",
        "_score": 0,
        "_source": {
            "num_field": 1,
            "text_field": "Halo"
        }
    }
]
```

## Full text queries

Match query - The match query treats the search string as a boolean expression with each word joined by either OR or AND logic. The search text is analysed, compared and a _score with each matched document is returned. The _score parameter gives the measure of how well the searched string matches the documents found.

For example, a field in an index contains the text "Lorem Ipsum", and below are the results of search on the field value -

```
{
    "query":{
        "match":{
            "str_val":"Lorem Ipsum"
        }
    }
}
```

```
    "_score": 0.5753642,
    "_source": {
        "bool_val": true,
        "char_val": "a",
        "date_val": "2018-10-18",
        "int_val": 99,
        "str_val": "Lorem Ipsum"
}
```

By default, the match query is set to OR logic so the presence of any of the two words shall be considered a success. The operator for match query can be explicitly set in the following way -

```
{
    "query":{
        "match":{
            "str_val":{
                "query":"Lorem Dolor",
                "operator":"and"
            }
        }
    }
}
```

Match phrase query - This query function analyses the text and searches for phrases. The default analyser expects the search string to start with the same word as that of the actual phrase and so to be able to query with just a subset of the words in the phrase in any order, the analyser has to be set with the analyser parameter.

```
{
    "query":{
        "match_phrase":{
            "str_val": {
                "query":"hello",
                "analyzer": "keyword"
            }
        }
    }
}
```

Match phrase prefix query - This is similar to that of match phrase query with the addition of prefix match on the last term in the search text. This query serves as a rudimentary implementation of text autocompletion.

Suppose there are three documents containing the phrases - "This is a hello to the world", "This is a humid day" and "This is a hell of a ride". A search operation with the following text returns documents containing all these phrases.

```
{
    "query":{
        "match_phrase_prefix":{
            "str_val": "This is a h"
        }
    }
}
```

Multi-match query - This query functions the same way as match query but on multiple fields.

```
{
    "query":{
        "multi_match":{
            "query":"artificial",
            "fields": ["title","description"]
        }
    }
}
```

This query has a type parameter which can be set to the following values -

best_fields - This is set as the default type and it gives more bias to the _score parameter for documents that have the search terms all in a single field. Here a search for the text "Lorem Ipsum" returns the following documents -

```
"hits": {
    "total": 2,
    "max_score": 0.5753642,
    "hits": [
        {
            "_index": "sample_index_2",
            "_type": "_doc",
            "_id": "QRqIi2YBDKW5lplsTdvV",
            "_score": 0.5753642,
            "_source": {
                "fisrt_field": "Lorem Ipsum",
                "second_field": "Dolor Sit"
            }
        },
        {
            "_index": "sample_index_2",
            "_type": "_doc",
            "_id": "QhqIi2YBDKW5lplsidt0",
            "_score": 0.2876821,
            "_source": {
                "fisrt_field": "Lorem Dolor",
                "second_field": "Ipsum Sit"
            }
        }
    ]
}
```

most_fields - This type of multi-match search addresses the query situation when the documents that match the search text are returned, but also the documents that feature detivations of the terms in the search. The search text is analyzed with multiple analyzers to account for derivations. Suppose we want to get documents for the search "artificial intelligence". As much as the desired result is to _score documents higher that have the exact terms in searched fields, it is also important to return documents that have derivations of the search terms say - artificially or intelligent as they may have necessary content w.r.t. the search. It is for such reason, documents with derivations of the search terms as well as *best matches* are provided _score that is a combined _score from each of the fields. The fundamental idea behind most_fields is to give importance to those documents that have the search terms and its derivations spread across more fields.

Suppose there are three documents in an index -

a)

```
"_source" : {
  "field_one" : "Artificial intelligence will change the world",
  "field_two" : "Artificial intelligence will change the world",
  "field_three" : "Artificial intelligence will change the world"
}
```

b)

```
"_source" : {
  "field_one" : "Artificial intelligence will change the world",
  "field_two" : "The future is for artificially intelligent systems",
  "field_three" : "Its artificial and intelligent"
}
```

c)

```
"_source" : {
  "field_one" : "Artificial intelligence will change the world",
  "field_two" : "The systems will be super smart",
  "field_three" : "Computers will be like humans"
}
```

Document "a" has the same data in all the fields making the terms *artificial* and *intelligent* available in most of the fields. Document "b" has the terms artificial and intelligent present on one field and derivations of the terms in the other fields. Document "c" has the terms in only one field and no derivations in the other fields. A search on the text "artificial intelligence", yields the following ranking of the results.

```
"_score": 1.7260926,
"_source": {
    "field_one": "Artificial intelligence will change the world",
    "field_two": "Artificial intelligence will change the world",
    "field_three": "Artificial intelligence will change the world"


"_score": 1.0907973,
"_source": {
    "field_one": "Artificial intelligence will change the world",
    "field_two": "The future is for artificially intelligent systems",
    "field_three": "Its artificial and intelligent"


"_score": 0.36464313,
"_source": {
    "field_one": "Artificial intelligence will change the world",
    "field_two": "The systems will be super smart",
    "field_three": "Computers will be like humans"
```

The document with the least mentions of the search text in all of its fields has the least _score.

cross_fields - This type of multi-field search is used to handle situations where we search for documents that have the searched text distributed across multiple fields such as name -

```
{
    "first_name": "Neil",
    "last_name": "Tyson"
}
```

Or, a address -

```
{
    "street": "Second street",
    "city": "Sim city",
    "country": "la la land",
    "postcode":"42"
}
```

Here the requirement is to rank those documents higher, that have the search terms spreads across multiple fields but unlike most_fields, it does not _score documents higher based on the existence of the search terms on majority of the fields.

It may seem like that most_fields can accomplish the search task for the above mentioned types of document fields, but the method by which the _score of a document is calculated, there will be erroneous results in certain cases. The problem with most_fields is that it is designed to find the most number of fields matching the searched terms rather than finding the most matching words across all fields.

With most_fields type, the document -

```
{
    "street": "Second street Sim city",
    "city": "Sim city, la la land",
    "country": "la la land",
    "postcode":"42"
}
```

will be ranked higher than -

```
{
    "street": "Second street",
    "city": "Sim city",
    "country": "la la land",
    "postcode":"42"
}
```

because, it is field centric and therefore rewards those documents to be ranked higher where the search terms are present in majority of the fields. The following document will be ranked higher than the other two despite being a low quality document that the other two.

```
{
    "street": "Second street, Sim city, la la land, 42",
    "city": "Second street, Sim city, la la land, 42",
    "country": "Second street, Sim city, la la land, 42",
    "postcode":"Second street, Sim city, la la land, 42"
}
```

The search terms frequency in each field gives an undue bias to the above document in most_fields search.

*cross_fields* search tackles this problem with most_fields by treating all the fields as a combined single field because documents with more matching words will trump documents with repeated words. Therefore a document that has the full name as the content of both the first_name field and last_name field will be ranked lower -

```
"hits": [
    {
        "_index": "sample_index_2",
        "_type": "_doc",
        "_id": "ThpVkWYBDKW5lpls4Nsw",
        "_score": 0.5753642,
        "_source": {
            "first_name": "Will",
            "last_name": "Smith"
        }
    },
    {
        "_index": "sample_index_2",
        "_type": "_doc",
        "_id": "URpgkWYBDKW5lplsIdtv",
        "_score": 0.5753642,
        "_source": {
            "first_name": "Will Smith",
            "last_name": "Will Smith"
        }
    },
```

Here we see, all the searched terms are available in the fields and so the documents have the same _score, yet the one with "Will" in first_name field and "Smith" in last_field is at the first of the result.

Common terms query - This query deals with handling of stop-words and ranks documents such that, the presence of commonly used terms should not be able to give undue importance to documents that may have low quality content. The common terms query divides the terms in a search text into two groups - one with uncommon terms which is of a high priority and another with common terms such as "a","an" or "the","this", etc. which is of lower priority. It then performs a search operation for only the high priority group of terms followed by another search with the low priority terms. The documents that appear on both the searches are then returned as the final results.

Query string query - This type of full text search gives has the ability to convert a search string's terms into a boolean expression separated by AND and/or OR logic.

```
{
    "query":{
        "query_string":{
            "default_field" : "content",
            "query":"(Starman lands on Mars) OR (We go to Moon)"


        }
    }
}
```

The parameter *default_field* is represents the field that is to be searched and if it is omitted, then all the fields are searched. Query string search parses the search string and splits the terms with operators. The default_operator field can be mentioned in a query to either split all the terms by AND or OR logic and is set to OR by default. If the query is of the following form -

```
{
    "query":{
        "query_string":{
            "default_field" : "content",
            "query":"Starman lands on Mars. We go to Moon",
            "default_operator": "and"
        }
    }
}
```

the query string would be parsed as "Starman AND lands AND on AND Mars. We AND go AND to AND Moon".

Although when the query string is of this form -

```
"query":"(Starman lands on Mars) OR (We go to Moon)"
```

it does not mean the parsed string will be converted to "(Starman OR lands OR on OR Mars.) OR (We OR go OR to OR Moon)". The text "Starman lands on Mars" will be a normal string separated by spaces.

Simple query string search - Like the *Query string* query, the search string with this type can also be converted to a boolean expression, but also the ability to discard unnecessary parts of the search string. Here is an example -

```
{
    "query":{
        "simple_query_string":{
            "fields": ["title^5", "body"],
            "query": "\"spam ham\" +(eggplant | potato) -lasagna",
            "default_operator": "and"
        }
    }
}
```

The \ is used as an escape sequence for the double quotes in the string, the + signifies the mandatory requirement of the next term to be either of the two - *eggplant* OR (|) *potato* and those documents are to be excluded that have the word *lasagna* in them. The document is to be boosted by 5 points in ranking if it the search string is found in the field *title*. If the default_operator parameter was not mentioned, it would have been set to OR logic by default and the documents would be looked up for the following strings -

a) *"spam ham" eggplant,* without having the word *lasagna.*
b) *"spam ham" potato,* without having the word *lasagna.*
c) All documents that do not have the word *lasagna* in it.

It is the option c which is an undesired consequence and therefore the use of AND as *default_operator* converts the string into -

a) *"spam AND ham" AND +(eggplant | potato) AND - lasagna*

## Compound queries

Such queries are those that combine multiple compound or leaf queries, change the behaviour of a constituent query or use to the filter context to affect the the result when multiple sub-queries are joined.

Constant score query - This query wraps another query in a filter context and returns the filtered results with a constant _score given by the *boost* parameter.

```
{
    "query": {
        "constant_score" : {
            "filter" : {
                "term" : { "age" : "18"}
            },
            "boost" : 1.2
        }
    }
}
```

Dis max query - It does a union of the documents returned by each constituent sub-query and the documents returned by each sub-query is set to the _score which is the maximum _score achieved by any document returned in the sub-query. This query can union results that are produced by two or more unrelated or disjoint query strings with each document having the _score of the highest scored document in a sub-query, hence it draws the name Dis (joint) Max (imum).

```
{
    "query": {
        "dis_max" : {
            "queries" : [
                {"term": {"age":"18"}},
                {"match": {"last_name":"Johnson"}}
            ]
        }
    }
}
```

Function score query - This query is used not to combine multiple sub-queries like the previous ones, but to score independently the subsets of all the documents returned by a main query.

```
{
    "query": {
        "function_score": {
            "query": { "match_all": {} },
            "boost": "5",
            "functions": [
                {
                    "filter": { "match": { "test": "bar" } },
                    "random_score": {},
                    "weight": 23
                },
                {
                    "filter": { "match": { "test": "cat" } },
                    "weight": 42
                }
            ],
            "max_boost": 42,
            "score_mode": "max",
            "boost_mode": "multiply",
            "min_score" : 42
        }
    }
}
```

Here the main query used is *match_all* that fetches the documents. The *boost* parameter is used for boosting all the documents returned by the *match_all* query. The new score that is to be provided by the functions parameter is given an upper bound with the *max_boost* parameter. The documents that have *_score* less than the score defined by the *min_score* parameter are to be discarded. The documents are to be independently scored by the defined functions and the parameter *score_mode* specifies how the scores are combined to form the value of *max_score* parameter. In the above example, there are two functions - one that filters those documents that *match* the value "bar" and the other "cat".

The *weight* parameter is a score function and in each of the functions, its value is multiplied with the _score computed for the documents. The *random_score* parameter generates scored that are uniformly distributed between [0,1]. For the first function both types of score functions are used.

The *boost_mode* parameter specifies how the score computed with a function is combined with the score of the query, here given by *match_all*.

Boosting query - This query is used to demote the score of those documents that match a given query.

```
{
    "query": {
        "boosting" : {
            "positive" : {
                "term" : {
                    "field1" : "value1"
                }
            },
            "negative" : {
                "term" : {
                    "field2" : "value2"
                }
            },
            "negative_boost" : 0.2
        }
    }
}
```

Bool query - A bool query returns the documents of multiple sub-queries joined together by boolean logic.

```
{
    "query":{
        "bool":{
            "must":{"term":{ "field1":"value1" }},
            "must_not":{ "term":{ "field2":"value2" }},
            "should":{"term":{"field3":"value3"}},
            "filter":{"range":{"field4": { "gte":10, "lte":20 }}}
        }
    }
}
```

## Query DSL with python *(elasticsearch-py)*

Elasticsearch-py provides a low level library to access elasticsearch endpoint. The reason it is called low-level because the methods to form various queries ahve less python abstraction and more closer to the syntax used in Query DSL.

The library is installed with -

```
pip install elasticsearch
```

Code to create a document -

```python
#!/bin/python
from elasticsearch import Elasticsearch
from datetime import datetime

es = Elasticsearch(hosts=['10.10.0.225'])
doc = {'user':'Alice','text':'Elasticsearch will find me','date':datetime.now()}

result = es.index(index='python_index',doc_type='_doc',id=1,body=doc)


print result['result']
```

Code to retrieve a document -

```python
#!/bin/python
import pprint
from elasticsearch import Elasticsearch
from datetime import datetime

es = Elasticsearch(hosts=['10.10.0.225'])

result = es.get(index='python_index',doc_type='_doc',id=1,_source=True)

# For pretty printing the JSON
pp = pprint.PrettyPrinter()
pp.pprint(result)
```

Code to execute a query -

```python
#!/bin/python
import pprint
from elasticsearch import Elasticsearch
from datetime import datetime

es = Elasticsearch(hosts=['10.10.0.225'])

query = {"query":{"bool":{"must":{},"must_not":{},"should":{},"filter":{}}}}

result = es.search(index='python_index',body=query)

# For pretty printing the JSON
pp = pprint.PrettyPrinter()
pp.pprint(result)
```

Here the search clauses are deliberately left empty as the purpose is to demonstrate the usage of the *search* function.

# Aggregations

The aggregation framework performs analytical functions such as calculating the average value or minimum value, on the data field(s) of all documents in an index and returns the result.

The various aggregations functions can be segregated into four categories based on their purpose -

Bucketing - This is the family of aggregations that create a named bucket which is just a logical group, and those documents are to be put into a bucket that fulfil the criteria of set by the bucket. Each bucket is associated with a key.

Date range aggregation - This is a type of aggregation belonging to the bucketing family and it works by creating buckets based on the *to* and *from* criteria set upon a date field.

```
{
    "aggs": {
        "range": {
            "date_range": {
                "field": "date",
                "format": "MM-yyy",
                "ranges": [
                    { "key":"Older_than_10_months_from_now", "to": "now-10M/M" },
                    { "key":"After_10_months_from_now", "from": "now-10M/M", "to":"now-8M/M" },
                    { "key":"Now_onwards", "from": "now/d"}
                ]
            }
        }
    }
}
```

Here *range* is not the range query, but a name given to the aggregation. *aggs* is the keyword for aggregation. The *ranges* parameter set the respective buckets based on the criteria set by *to* and *from*. There are three buckets created in the above example with names - Older_than_10_months_from_now, After_10_months_from_now, Now_onwards. The notation "now-10M/M" states a date that is 10 months behind the current date-time and the trailing /M specifies the start of the date from the beginning of the month. The various other date formats can be found here -

Metric - This type of aggregation computes metrics based on the value in data field such as average calculation.

```
{
    "aggs" : {
        "avg_age" : { "avg" : { "field" : "age" } }
    }
}
```

Matrix - This type aggregation works with multiple fields and produce a matrix result w.r.t. the parameters - count, mean, variance, skewness, kurtosis, covariance, correlation.

```
{
    "aggs": {
        "statistics": {
            "matrix_stats": {
                "fields": ["salary", "investment"]
            }
        }
    }
}
```

Pipeline - This type of aggregation enables the use of the result from another aggregation.

```
{
    "aggs" : {
        "sales_per_month" : {
            "date_histogram" : { "field" : "date", "interval" : "month"},
            "aggs":{"sales":{"sum":{"field":"price"}}}
        },
        "sum_monthly_sales": {
            "sum_bucket": {"buckets_path": "sales_per_month>sales" }
        }
    }
}
```

There are two sibling aggregations by the name *sales_per_month* and *sum_monthly_sales*. The *sales_per_month* aggregation also has a nested aggregation named *sales*. The *sales_per_month* aggregation alone produces the following result -

```
"aggregations": {
    "sales_per_month": {
        "buckets": [
            {
                "key_as_string": "2018-01-01T00:00:00.000Z",
                "key": 1514764800000,
                "doc_count": 2,
                "sales": {
                    "value": 220
                }
            },
            {
                "key_as_string": "2018-02-01T00:00:00.000Z",
                "key": 1517443200000,
                "doc_count": 2,
                "sales": {
                    "value": 260
                }
            },
            {
                "key_as_string": "2018-03-01T00:00:00.000Z",
                "key": 1519862400000,
                "doc_count": 2,
                "sales": {
                    "value": 285
                }
            }
        ]
```

The *sum_monthly_sales* sibling aggregation calculates the sum with the values in a field of the sibling aggregation specified by the parameter *buckets_path*. Therefore, the sum of the *sales* field given by "sales_per_month>sales" is produced as follows -

```
"sum_monthly_sales": {
    "value": 765
}
```

A complete documentation on the aggregators can be found at -

# Suggesters

Among one of the most advanced and useful features of elasticsearch, the suggester feature, augments the search experience by introducing capabilities such as suggesting corrections to searched text or phrase, providing suggestions for autocompletion of search text and even suggesting documents that are related to the context of a particular search.

Here is a brief walkthrough of the different suggesters provided by elasticsearch.

Term suggester - It takes in the entire search text, tokenises and analyses each term in the search text and returns suggestions upon incorrect spelling based on the data value already present in the field of an index.

The documents in our index are -

```
"hits" : [
  {
    "_index" : "curl_index",
    "_type" : "_doc",
    "_id" : "XhrYnGYBDKW5lpls9tsy",
    "_score" : 1.0,
    "_source" : {
      "title" : "Learning elasticsearch",
      "description" : "trying elasticsearch"
    }
  },
  {
    "_index" : "curl_index",
    "_type" : "_doc",
    "_id" : "XxoQnWYBDKW5lplsgdtP",
    "_score" : 1.0,
    "_source" : {
      "title" : "Learning python",
      "description" : "trying python"
    }
  }
]
```

Here is the request body of a *term* suggester -

```
POST  ▼          http://10.10.0.225:9200/curl_index/_search

rams    Authorization     Headers (1)      Body ●     Pre-

 form-data    ● x-www-form-urlencoded    ● raw    ● binar

 1 ▾ {
 2 ▾     "suggest":{
 3           "text" : "I am ting easticsearch",
 4 ▾         "simple-suggestion":{
 5 ▾             "term":{
 6                   "field": "description"
 7               }
 8           }
 9       }
10   }
```

The parameter *text* contains the search text. The text comprises of incomplete words - "ting" which corresponds to the term "trying" and "elasticsearch" corresponds to the term "elasticsearch". *simple-suggestion* is the name given to the suggest request. The term suggester is supposed to compare the terms provided in the search text with the content of the *description* field of all documents. The suggest request returns the following result -

```
"suggest": {
    "simple-suggestion": [
        {
            "text": "i",
            "offset": 0,
            "length": 1,
            "options": []
        },
        {
            "text": "am",
            "offset": 2,
            "length": 2,
            "options": []
        },
        {
            "text": "ting",
            "offset": 5,
            "length": 4,
            "options": [
                {
                    "text": "trying",
                    "score": 0.5,
                    "freq": 2
                }
            ]
        },
```

```
    {
        "text": "easticsearch",
        "offset": 10,
        "length": 12,
        "options": [
            {
                "text": "elasticsearch",
                "score": 0.9166667,
                "freq": 1
            }
        ]
    }
]
```

The result consists of all the terms in the search text and their corresponding suggestions given by the *options* parameter.

Phrase suggester - This type of suggester adds further logic upon the term suggester and suggests possible corrected phrases instead of just terms. The index has the following document -

```
"_source": {
    "tagline": "Sailing in starships"
}
```

Upon querying with typos in the search text such as -

```
{
    "suggest":{
        "text" : "Sailng in starsihp",
        "phrase-suggestion":{
            "phrase":{
                "field": "tagline",
                "confidence": 0
            }
        }
    }
}
```

the following suggestions are returned -

```
"text": "Sailng in starsihp",
"offset": 0,
"length": 18,
"options": [
    {
        "text": "sailing in starships",
        "score": 0.19056533
    },
    {
        "text": "sailing in starsihp",
        "score": 0.1562766
    },
    {
        "text": "sailng in starships",
        "score": 0.14928691
    },
    {
        "text": "sailng in starsihp",
        "score": 0.12242546
    },
    {
        "text": "sail in starships",
        "score": 0.037456717
    }
]
```

Although the term and phrase suggester's may seem similar, but unlike *term* suggester which does a spell correction term-wise and suggests corrections or alternatives, *phrase* suggester returns entire phrases with possible corrections without breaking down the terms as we see above. Just for comparison's sake if the same query is applied with the *term* suggester, we get the following result (output shown for one term) -

```
"text": "sailng",
"offset": 0,
"length": 6,
"options": [
    {
        "text": "sailing",
        "score": 0.8333333,
        "freq": 1
    },
    {
        "text": "sail",
        "score": 0.5,
        "freq": 1
    }
```

Completion suggester - This type of suggester provides the search-as-you-type functionality found in contemporary search engines. Unlike term or phrase suggesters which act as the did-you-mean feature found in Google search for spell check, the completion suggester hints a user with the probable search terms that lead to correct documents. For this, a special mapping is required and so we will create an index with the following mapping -

```
{
    "mappings": {
        "_doc" : {
            "properties" : {
                "suggest" : {
                    "type" : "completion"
                },
                "title" : {
                    "type": "keyword"
                }
            }
        }
    }
}
```

It has two fields, named *suggest* and *title* and the type of the field - suggest is set to *completion* as we will be doing suggestion operations based on the searches on this field. Next we will add a list of terms from which we want to suggest when the searched term contains a partial portion of any of the terms enlisted. Since we will query only the *suggest* field for our example, document will be created only with values in that field.

| POST ▼ | http://10.10.0.225:9200/curl_index/_doc |
|---|---|

ams    Authorization    Headers (1)    **Body** ●    Pre-request Script    Test

form-data    ○ x-www-form-urlencoded    ● raw    ○ binary    JSON (application/

```
1
2 ▾ {
3       "suggest" :[ "Cloverfield", "Cloverfield lane", "Alien" ]
4   }
5
```

A query on the suggest field yields the following result -

```
{
    "suggest": {
        "movie-suggest" : {
            "prefix" : "ali",
            "completion" : {
                "field" : "suggest"
            }
        }
    }
}
```

```
"text": "ali",
"offset": 0,
"length": 3,
"options": [
    {
        "text": "Alien",
        "_index": "curl_index",
        "_type": "_doc",
        "_id": "ZBokwWYBDKW5lplsZdsq",
        "_score": 1,
        "_source": {
            "suggest": [
                "Cloverfield",
                "Cloverfield lane",
                "Alien"
            ]
        }
    }
]
```

As we can see, the *suggest* query of completion type returns a value in the field suggest as the search term "ali" partially matches the term Alien.

Context suggester - It provides suggestions based on the context of the search query. In an index where there are multiple documents with the same values listed in fields, but they are different in category, a suggest query with the context specified filters out the required documents. The index for this purpose has to be special mapping catered to context based suggestion -

```
{
    "mappings": {
        "_doc" : {
            "properties" : {
                "suggest" : {
                    "type" : "completion",
                    "contexts": [
                        {
                            "name": "place_type",
                            "type": "category"
                        }
                    ]
                }
            }
        }
    }
}
```

The context suggester filters out the relevant document after searching all the documents that match a particular context. In the above mapping we see the suggestion query would perform a *completion* type of suggestion on the field named *suggest*. The parameter *contexts* is used to define the kind of context values are to be present in the documents for the mapping. There are two kinds of contexts *category* and *geo*, and *geo* is used in cases for dealing with gps co-ordinates. Two documents are created -

```
{
    "suggest": {
        "input": ["timmy's", "starbucks", "dunkin donuts"],
        "contexts": {
            "place_type": ["warehouse", "storage"]
        }
    }
}
```

and

```
{
    "suggest": {
        "input": ["timmy's", "starbucks", "dunkin donuts"],
        "contexts": {
            "place_type": ["cafe", "food"]
        }
    }
}
```

A completion suggestion type field can have three parameters - *input* for setting the value(s) of the field, *context* for setting the context value(s) and *weight* for boosting the field.

A search on the context specified as "cafe" -

```
{
    "suggest": {
        "place_suggestion" : {
            "prefix" : "tim",
            "completion" : {
                "field" : "suggest",
                "contexts": {
                    "place_type": [ "cafe"]
                }
            }
        }
    }
}
```

produces the following result -

```
"suggest": {
    "place_suggestion": [
        {
            "text": "tim",
            "offset": 0,
            "length": 3,
            "options": [
                {
                    "text": "timmy's",
                    "_index": "curl_index",
                    "_type": "_doc",
                    "_id": "ZRpRwWYBDKW5lpls89tj",
                    "_score": 1,
                    "_source": {},
                    "contexts": {
                        "place_type": [
                            "cafe"
                        ]
                    }
                }
            ]
        }
    ]
}
```

Again when the query is made with context of say "warehouse" -

```json
{
    "_source": "false",
    "suggest": {
        "place_suggestion" : {
            "prefix" : "dun",
            "completion" : {
                "field" : "suggest",
                "contexts": {
                    "place_type": [ "warehouse"]
                }
            }
        }
    }
}
```

returns the respective document -

```json
"suggest": {
    "place_suggestion": [
        {
            "text": "dun",
            "offset": 0,
            "length": 3,
            "options": [
                {
                    "text": "dunkin donuts",
                    "_index": "curl_index",
                    "_type": "_doc",
                    "_id": "ZhpgwWYBDKW5lpls-tsM",
                    "_score": 1,
                    "_source": {},
                    "contexts": {
                        "place_type": [
                            "warehouse"
                        ]
                    }
                }
            ]
        }
    ]
}
```

# SECTION 5

# Automating
# with Ansible

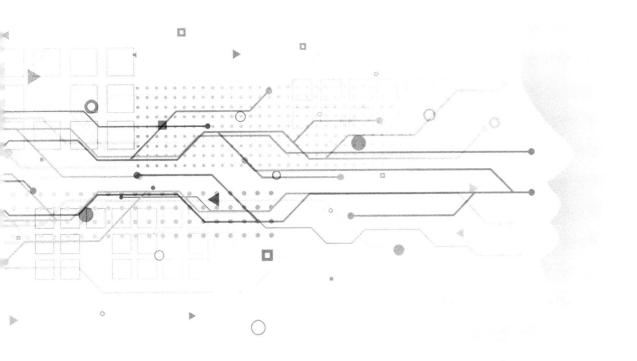

# Introduction

The whole of internet and all of the applications that are available on the web are running on clusters of servers. Any dynamic web application be it a social networking site or an e-commerce site, has its application portions such as database, backend, middleware, transcoding and frontend, spanning across array of servers. The maintenance of these servers and the enabling infrastructure is undertaken by system engineers, whose job is to make sure that an application has all its system requirements met and also keeping servers healthy with security updates.

A web application usually has three environments, namely - development, staging and production, where tests are run with varying volume in traffic. Thus for each of these environments there are server clusters that have to be managed. When a particular version of the application is moved from the development environment to staging, the servers have to be first prepared with all the required packages in their particular versions. The same is true when the application is deployed in the production environment. This involves performing same tasks repeatedly in managing the configuration of each server. As the array of servers keep growing, the tasks tend to become unmanageable and prone to human errors.

The inspiration behind bringing automation in configuration management stems from the ability of programs to accomplish a task with accuracy, in a pre-estimated time, and producing the desired result in parallel. Previously, a system engineer had to login into each of the servers and manually perform tasks. With configuration management, the state of a server's software configuration can be written and stored as source code files, which when executed, performs the defined tasks on the targeted servers. Unlike in the case of a human engineer, the configuration source files can be run in parallel thereby drastically reducing the required time. Also, a human is prone to errors which in the case of a program is unlikely and any change when required in configuration, it needs to be done only once in the source files, which then can be reflected back to the servers, and thereby further reducing the scope for errors.

# What is Ansible?

Ansible is an open source automation software primarily written in python, that is used for tasks such as provisioning, configuration management and application deployment all defined in the form of code.

*Provisioning* - From the perspective of a machine virtual/physical, ansible is a provider for all sort of applications, changes in files, and other activities than interact with the host OS.

*Configuration management* - In a clustered server environment, ansible handles versioning and maintaining of application configuration as well as host OS or virtual machine configurations in groups and sub-groups.

*Application deployment* - Ansible takes an object oriented perspective toward server groups and sub-groups and does application deployment for appointed namespaces such as dev, staging, preproduction, production, etc.

Ansible scripts are written in yaml or yml format and are interpreted at runtime. What makes ansible such a lean yet powerful configuration management tool is its least dependant architecture. The architecture involves two types of servers: a controlling machine and a node. A node is the target machine where the ansible scripts take action. A node does not require any agents running to whom the controlling machine delegates the tasks in a script, unlike other automation softwares such as Chef, Puppet and CFEngine. A managed node requires only SSH and python for the controller machine to delegate tasks to it. A controlling machine on the other hand just requires *ansible* installed along with SSH. Ansible has a family of over 750 modules, each for a type of task and also application specific such as MySQL, MongoDB, etc. An ansible module can be written with any scripting language. On interpreting a script, ansible modules are sent to the managed nodes through SSH, where the modules are temporarily stored and execute tasks, send response to the controlling machine in JSON format.

*Playbook* - It is a yaml script inside an ansible project. Ansible uses the analogy of theatrical plays and therefore each playbook defines activities of an ansible project organised through roles. A managed node is an actor in terms of the analogy of plays. The ideal directory structure of an ansible project is as follows -

```
├── appservers.yml
├── dbservers.yml
├── group_vars
│   ├── appservers
│   └── webservers
├── host_vars
│   ├── ww-z1.server.com
│   └── ww-z2.server.com
├── production
├── roles
│   ├── apptier
│   ├── common
│   │   ├── defaults
│   │   │   └── main.yml
│   │   ├── files
│   │   │   ├── bar.txt
│   │   │   └── foo.txt
│   │   ├── handlers
│   │   │   └── main.yml
│   │   ├── library
│   │   ├── lookup_plugins
│   │   ├── meta
│   │   │   └── main.yml
│   │   ├── module_utils
│   │   ├── tasks
│   │   │   └── main.yml
│   │   ├── templates
│   │   │   └── something.conf.j2
│   │   └── vars
│   │       └── main.yml
│   └── webtier
├── site.yml
├── staging
└── webservers.yml
```

Filename extension *.yml are optional but it is a good design principle to not end inventory files such as *staging* and *production* with *.yml extension, so that, a directory organisation such as the one above, is self explanatory about the purpose of each file.

## Inventory files

*staging* and *production* are the files that contain hostnames or IP information about servers that can be grouped. The following is for *production* -

```
[zone1-servers]
ww-z1.server.com
ww-z2.server.com

[zone2-servers]
ww-z3.servers.com
ww-z4.servers.com


[intel-xeon-servers:children]
zone2-servers

[quantum-servers:children]
zone1-servers

[appservers:children]
zone1-servers

[webservers:children]
zone2-servers
```

Here servers for example, *ww-z1.server.com* and *ww-z2.server.com*, are the first level of grouped servers, under *zone1-servers* namespace. *quantum-servers* and *appservers* are groups that have contain other groups as its children.

## Group and Host variables

The variables declared in the *.yml files under *group_vars* directory are accessible to the servers included in the groups *webservers* and *appservers*.

```
appversion: 9.9.0
maxbuffer: 2000
```

The variables *appversion* and *maxbuffer* declared in *appservers* file will be available to ansible during executing tasks on the servers in the group *appservers*.

Likewise, variables declared in the *.yml files under *host_vars* directory will be available to the ansible session on those specific hosts.

The filenames under *host_vars* and *group_vars* have to be same as declared in the inventory files such as *production* and *staging*.

## Roles

From the perspective of a managed node (eg. *ww-z1.server.com*), when a role is assigned to that node or the group that contains the node (eg. zone1-servers), the tasks defined in yaml files under *tasks* directory, inside each named role sub-directory (eg. apptier, common), will be executed on that node.

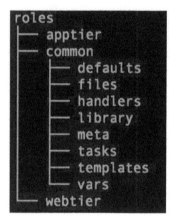

The remaining of the directories in a particular role such as *common* are the peripherals of the tasks defined in a role and the relevance is as follows -

*handlers* - They contain tasks that are executed when accessed from *tasks* through the *notify* keyword.
*defaults* - They declare the default variables of a role.
*vars* - Contains other variables for the a role.
*files* - Contains files that are deployed by a role on a node.
*meta* - If a role requires any metadata, they are to be declared here.
*templates* - Ansible uses jinja2 templating format, and files with jinja2 templates used in them are placed in this directory.
*library* - Contains custom modules.

## site.yml

Following along the theatrical play analogy, this file can be identified as a theatre house and therefore, it is defined in this file about the plays that are to be run. A particular play is defined in a playbook, and it looks like the following in the *webservers.yml* file.

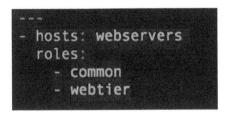

```
---
- hosts: webservers
  roles:
    - common
    - webtier
```

In the site.yml file, those playbooks are to be included which are to be performed. The site.yml file is as follows -

```
---
- import_playbook: webservers.yml
- import_playbook: dbservers.yml
```

# Installation and setup

We start off with installing ansible with yum.

#yum install -y ansible

The version we are using is -

```
[[root@ansiblebox ~]# ansible --version
ansible 2.4.2.0
  config file = /etc/ansible/ansible.cf
  configured module search path = [u'/r
  ansible python module location = /usr
  executable location = /bin/ansible
  python version = 2.7.5 (default, Jul
```

As ansible uses SSH for communication with the managed nodes, therefore we will first have to identify our ansible controlling node to the managed node. Ansible projects most of the times require root privileges on a managed node to execute administrative tasks. We will create an public-private key pair (using a passphrase is optional) for the root user on the controlling node -

#ssh-keygen

and copy the /root/.ssh/id_rsa.pub file's content to the managed node's /etc/.ssh/authorized_ keys file for root user.

   To test if our controlling node is able to communicate with the managed node, we will first place the IP of the managed node into /etc/ansible/hosts file and then invoke *ping* with ansible.

```
[[root@ansiblebox ansible_project]# ansible all -m ping
 The authenticity of host '10.10.0.150 (10.10.0.150)' can't be established.
 ECDSA key fingerprint is SHA256:KTLAsphpb1tqZgG/Hoou/Skauw1hqu03/Lz4PU6VYUE.
 ECDSA key fingerprint is MD5:6c:d8:84:94:67:31:60:37:7e:f6:1e:93:92:34:8e:72.
[Are you sure you want to continue connecting (yes/no)? yes
 10.10.0.150 | SUCCESS => {
     "changed": false,
     "ping": "pong"
 }
```

Above, a successful communication has been ensured.

# A sample project

We will create a sample project that addresses most of the common activities. Our appserver, webserver and dbserver, all will be a single node for the walkthrough. The source code for this is available at the following location -

First the inventory file has to be updated with the hostname of the managed node which we consider to be in production.

The hostname ww-z1.server.com is fictional and its IP is 10.10.0.150, which will be identified in the /etc/hosts file since there is no actual DNS entry for such a hostname.

```
127.0.0.1      localhost localhost.localdomain localhost4 localhost4.localdomain4
::1            localhost localhost.localdomain localhost6 localhost6.localdomain6


10.10.0.150 ww-z1.server.com
```

Also, we will include the hostname in /etc/ansible/hosts

```
[dbservers]
ww-z1.server.com
```

Since the theatre (site.yml) will host all the plays (dbserver, appserver, webserver), we will be importing them.

In site.yml -

```
---
- import_playbook: dbservers.yml
- import_playbook: webservers.yml
- import_playbook: appservers.yml
```

When ansible connects to a managed node, it collects necessary information about the node and stores as session variables. The variables can be accessed through setup module. Say we want to check the processor details of the managed node, we will use ansible client to fetch the details with setup module.

```
[[root@ansiblebox ansible_project]# ansible -m setup ww-z1.server.com -a 'filter=ansible_processor*'
ww-z1.server.com | SUCCESS => {
    "ansible_facts": {
        "ansible_processor": [
            "0",
            "GenuineIntel",
            "Intel Core Processor (Skylake)"
        ],
        "ansible_processor_cores": 1,
        "ansible_processor_count": 1,
        "ansible_processor_threads_per_core": 1,
        "ansible_processor_vcpus": 1
    },
    "changed": false
}
```

The filter keyword is used to limit output only for ansible_processor* keys in the JSON response.

We want all the plays dbservsers.yml, appservers.yml and webservers.yml to print information about the hostname and IP address of the managed node before carrying out of the tasks that are to be defined in the roles. The following snippet will be placed in each of the playbooks. Showing for dbservers.yml -

```
- hosts: dbservers
  become: True
  become_user: root
  gather_facts: True
  pre_tasks:
    - debug:
        msg: " IP {{ ansible_default_ipv4.gateway }} for managed node {{ inventory_hostname }}"
    - debug:
        msg: "{{ ansible_hostname }}"
```

Fig. 1

*become* - This module is used to activate escalation of privilege, similar to the effects of sudo command.

*become_user* - For switching to a particular user for executing a task. Since we have configured ansible to communicate with managed nodes through root user, this is not necessary and can be omitted along with become keyword.

*gather_facts* - By default ansible collects facts about the managed node, which can be disabled by setting it to False.

*pre_tasks* - As the name suggests, the tasks defined under this module executes them before executing any roles on a managed node.

*debug* - This ansible module is used to echo any message, along with value of any variable during the execution of a play.

For now the plays appservers.yml and webservers.yml will be kept commented out in site.yml and executing the play for only dbservers.yml would produce the following output -

```
[[root@ansiblebox ansible_project]# ansible-playbook site.yml -i production

PLAY [dbservers] ************************************************************

TASK [Gathering Facts] *****************************************************
ok: [ww-z1.server.com]

TASK [debug] ***************************************************************
ok: [ww-z1.server.com] => {
    "msg": " IP 10.10.0.1 for managed node ww-z1.server.com"
}

TASK [debug] ***************************************************************
ok: [ww-z1.server.com] => {
    "msg": "ww-z1"
}

PLAY RECAP *****************************************************************
ww-z1.server.com           : ok=3    changed=0    unreachable=0    failed=0
```

The noteworthy points are with reference to Fig. 1, there are two different keywords used for hostname resolution: inventory_hostname and ansible_hostname. ansible_hostname is the hostname gathered as facts from the managed node during the execution session and inventory_hostname is the one defined in the inventory file production.

{{ ansible_hostname }} is in the jinja2 templating format and when placed inside quotes "", return the string value of the variable.

Tasks to be done by common role -

1. Updating yum package manager
2. Synching system clock with ntp servers

Updating package manager - First the epel repository will be added in roles/common/asks/main.yml.

```
---
- name: Add the epel repository
  yum_repository:
    name: epel
    description: EPEL YUM repo
    baseurl: https://download.fedoraproject.org/pub/epel/$releasever/$basearch/
    gpgcheck: no
    state: present
  notify: yum-clean-metadata
```

*baseurl* - This attribute of yum_repository module fixes the url where the repository exists.

*notify* - After adding a repository we want to clean the yum meta-data, hence we call a handler named yum-clean-metadata with this module.

The corresponding handler can be found at roles/common/handlers/main.yml and is as the following -

```
---
- name: yum-clean-metadata
  command: yum clean metadata
```

Now before executing the common role, it has to be declared in dbservers.yml, in the following way -

```
pre_tasks:
  - debug:
      msg: " IP {{ ansible_default_ipv4.gateway }} for managed node {{ inv
  - debug:
      msg: "{{ ansible_hostname }}"
roles:
  - common
```

And make sure the remaining of the playbooks other than dbservers.yml are commented out, since they are empty.

```
---
- import_playbook: dbservers.yml
#- import_playbook: webservers.yml
#- import_playbook: appservers.yml
```

The output we get -

```
[[root@ansiblebox ansible_project]# ansible-playbook site.yml -i production

PLAY [dbservers] ****************************************************

TASK [Gathering Facts] *********************************************
ok: [ww-z1.server.com]

TASK [debug] *******************************************************
ok: [ww-z1.server.com] => {
    "msg": " IP 10.10.0.1 for managed node ww-z1.server.com"
}

TASK [debug] *******************************************************
ok: [ww-z1.server.com] => {
    "msg": "ww-z1"
}

TASK [common : Add the epel repository] ****************************
changed: [ww-z1.server.com]

RUNNING HANDLER [common : yum-clean-metadata] *********************
 [WARNING]: Consider using yum module rather than running yum

changed: [ww-z1.server.com]

PLAY RECAP ********************************************************
ww-z1.server.com            : ok=5    changed=2    unreachable=0    failed=0
```

Now we add the task for updating packages.

```
- name: Updating yum for all the latest packages
  yum:
    name: '*'
    state: latest
```

name - Refers to the name of the package which has to be updated. Since our requirement is for all packages, we use '*'.

1. *Synching system clock with ntp servers*

We want to install ntp if not present, copy our own configured configuration file for ntp and start ntp if not running.

```
- name: Install ntp
  yum:
    name: ntp
    state: present

- name: Copy the ntp configuration
  template:
    src: ntp.conf.j2
    dest: /etc/ntp.conf
  notify:
    - restart-ntpd

- name: Ensure ntp is started and enabled
  systemd:
    name: ntpd
    enabled: yes
```

The configuration file for ntp is at roles/common/templates/ntp.conf.j2

```
fudge 127.127.1.0 stratum 10

server {{ ntp_server }}

driftfile /var/lib/ntp/drift




# By default, exchange time with everybody, but don't allow configuration.
restrict -4 default kod notrap nomodify nopeer noquery limited
restrict -6 default kod notrap nomodify nopeer noquery limited

# Local users may interrogate the ntp server more closely.
restrict 127.0.0.1
restrict ::1
```

{{ ntp_server }} is defined in group_vars/dbservers.

```
ntp_server: pool.ntp.org
```

Tasks to be done in dbtier role -

## 1. *Setup a mysql database*

We are going use mysql community version 5.7, where on installation a temporary password for root user is created and is stored in /var/log/mysqld.log. Our strategy would be to change the the temporary password and issue a new password.

For mysql installation, a repo file will be transferred to the managed node and mysql along with other supporting packages are installed.

```
- name: Copy repo file
  template: src=../templates/mysql.repo dest=/etc/yum.repos.d/mysql.repo

- name: Install mysql(5.7)-community version
  yum: name={{ item }}
  with_items:
    - mysql-community-server
    - mysql-community-client
    - mysql-community-common
    - mysql-community-libs
    - mysql-community-libs-compat
    - MySQL-python

- name: Start database
  systemd: state=started name=mysqld
```

Just for informational purposes, the temporary password is shown.

```
- name: Fetch temporary password for mysql
  shell: "grep 'temporary password' /var/log/mysqld.log | awk '{print $11}'"
  register: tmp_mysql_pass
  ignore_errors: True

- debug:
    msg: "The temporary password as declared in /var/log/mysqld.log is {{ tmp_mysql_pass.stdout}}"
```

We will change the temporary password by executing a bash script on the node. The script is to be kept in roles/dbtier/files/mysql_change_temp_pass.bash.

```
- name: Execute shell script to change temp mysql password
  script: ../files/mysql_change_temp_pass.bash "{{ mysql_root_password }}"
  run_once: true
  ignore_errors: yes
```

The script module works by transferring a script to the managed node and then execute it. The script is referenced as ../files/mysql_change_temp_pass.bash through its relative path in project directory and its content is as follows -

```
#!/bin/bash
NEW_ROOT_PASS=$1
temp_pass=$(grep 'temporary password' /var/log/mysqld.log | awk '{print $11}')
mysql -p$temp_pass --connect-expired-password -e "ALTER USER 'root'@'localhost' IDENTIFIED BY '$NEW_ROOT_PASS';"
```

As the script accepts the new password as a command line argument, it is provided as "{{ mysql_root_password }}" in the script module.

*run_once* - This parameter ensures that the script is run only once on the managed node. A notable thing here is, the boolean values supported by ansible are True, true and yes for affirmative.

"{{ mysql_root_password }}" variable is declared in roles/dbtier/vars/main.yml -

```
mysql_root_password: root@DB112358
mysql_application_user: appuser
mysql_application_password: appuser@DB112358
application_db: appdb
```

The final task would be to create an application database with mysql_db module and provide privileges to the database with mysql_user module.

```
- name: Create application database
  mysql_db:
    name: "{{ application_db }}"
    login_user: root
    login_password: "{{ mysql_root_password }}"
    state: present

- mysql_user:
    name: "{{ mysql_application_user }}"
    password: "{{ mysql_application_password }}"
    priv: '{{ application_db }}.*:ALL'
    login_user: root
    login_password: "{{ mysql_root_password }}"
    state: present
```

The mysql_user modules usage here is equivalent to the command used in mysql to change the privileges.

```
GRANT ALL on appdb.* TO 'appuser'@'localhost';
```

Now that the database has been established, we will prepare the apptier role to install and configure a python-Django web framework sample project.

Tasks to be done in apptier role -

1. Installing python if required
2. Installing other dependant packages for Django web framework development
3. Installing Django
4. Create a sample project in Django

## Installing python if required

Ansible provides the when parameter to be used with any tasks for performing conditional activities such as installing python only if the required version is not present. The tasks for apptier role is to be declared in roles/apptier/tasks/django.yml which will be imported into roles/apptier/tasks/main.yml.

```
- name: Check python version (required 2.7.5)
  yum:
    list: python
  register: python_version


- debug:
    var: python_version

- name: Install python if required
  yum:
    name: python
  when: python_version.results[0]["version"] != "2.7.5"
```

register - It is used to hold the output returned by a task. Here python_version is the name of the variable that stores the output.

The var attribute used with debug prints the content of the variable python_version. The value of the variable is as follows -

```
TASK [apptier : debug] ****************************************
ok: [ww-z1.server.com] => {
    "python_version": {
        "changed": false,
        "failed": false,
        "results": [
            {
                "arch": "x86_64",
                "envra": "0:python-2.7.5-68.el7.x86_64",
                "epoch": "0",
                "name": "python",
                "release": "68.el7",
                "repo": "base",
                "version": "2.7.5",
                "yumstate": "available"
            },
```

```
    {
            "arch": "x86_64",
            "envra": "0:python-2.7.5-69.el7_5.x86_64",
            "epoch": "0",
            "name": "python",
            "release": "69.el7_5",
            "repo": "installed",
            "version": "2.7.5",
            "yumstate": "installed"
    },
    {
            "arch": "x86_64",
            "envra": "0:python-2.7.5-69.el7_5.x86_64",
            "epoch": "0",
            "name": "python",
            "release": "69.el7_5",
            "repo": "updates",
            "version": "2.7.5",
            "yumstate": "available"
    }
    ]
}
```

Since the output returned consists of a JSON array (due to checking w.r.t to different repos on the node), we need to fetch only the version key. It is done with when by referencing the version key from the 0th index of the results array.

```
when: python_version.results[0]["version"] != "2.7.5"
```

The installation of python will not be done since its already present.

```
TASK [apptier : Install python if required]
skipping: [ww-z1.server.com]
```

If python had to be installed by ansible, it would have been shown *changed* instead of *skipping*.

### Installing other dependant packages for Django web framework development

We will install a few more packages with yum.

```
- name: Install required packages with yum
  yum: name={{ item }}
  with_items:
    - python2-pip
    - python-devel
    - mysql-community-devel
    - openssl-devel
    - gcc
```

*python-pip* is package manager for python, *python-devel* is for extending the python interpreter with dynamically loaded extension, and also same for *mysql-community-devel* and *openssl-devel*.

with_items - This is used to iterate over a list of values. In this case, yum will be fed values from the list through the variable *{{ item }}*.

1. *Installing Django*

Next up, we are going to install django with python package manager pip. We have already installed pip on the node which like yum, can be used to install all python packages indexed in PyPI (Python package index), but here we are going to use the ansible module for pip.

```
- name: Install django (required 1.11.x)
  pip:
    name: django
    version: 1.11.13
```

There are a few more packages that we'll install which will be required later in the book for creating a sample web application with Django web framework.

```
- name: Install other required packages with pip I
  pip: name={{ item }}
  with_items:
    - django-redis
    - mysqlclient
    - django-mysql
    - Pillow
    - six
    - pycrypto
    - boto
    - boto3
    - awscli
    - elasticsearch
    - googlemaps

- name: Install other required pip packages with pip II
  pip: name=cryptography version=2.2.2

- name: Install other required pip packages with pip III
  pip: name=pyasn1 version=0.4.3
```

For execution of the apptier role on our managed node, the playbook has to be imported to site.yml.

1. *Create a sample project in Django*

```
- name: Start sample a Django project
  command: django-admin.py startproject {{ sample_project_name }} {{ sample_django_proj_dir }}
  run_once: yes
  ignore_errors: yes
```

The name of the sample project *sample_project_name* and project directory *sample_django_proj_dir* are as usual variables declared in *roles/apptier/vars/main.yml* which is as follows -

```
sample_django_proj_dir: /var/www/http/
sample_user_name: sample
sample_user_pass: sampass
sample_user_email: sample@email.com
sample_project_name: sample_project
```

The django project on creation requires configurations in the project's *settings.py* file, which in our case would be at */var/www/html/sample_project/settings.py*.

Django provides the module lineinfile, with which the contents of a line in a file can be changed with a regular expression comparisn using *regexp* parameter.

```
- name: Change settings.py of Django project to be accessed from any IP
  lineinfile:
    path: "{{ sample_django_proj_dir }}/{{ sample_project_name }}/settings.py"
    regexp: '^ALLOWED_HOSTS ='
    line: 'ALLOWED_HOSTS = ["*",]'

- name: Configure the location for static files in settings.py
  lineinfile:
    path: "{{ sample_django_proj_dir }}/{{ sample_project_name }}/settings.py"
    insertafter: '^STATIC_URL '
    line: 'STATIC_ROOT = os.path.join(BASE_DIR, "static/")'
```

insertafter - Specifies if the line is to be inserted after the line containing the string (regular expression).

Django comes in with default settings for database using SQLite, but as we are using mysql, the settings have to be configured by adding a block of configuration text into the settings.py file.

```
- name: Configure settings.py  to use mysql
  blockinfile:
    path: "{{ sample_django_proj_dir }}/{{ sample_project_name }}/settings.py"
    block: |
      DATABASES = {
        'default': {
        'ENGINE': 'django.db.backends.mysql',
        'NAME': 'appdb',
        'USER': 'appuser',
        'PASSWORD': 'appuser@DB112358',
        'HOST': '{{ ansible_default_ipv4.address }}',
        'PORT': '3306',
        'OPTIONS': {
            'init_command': "SET sql_mode='STRICT_TRANS_TABLES',innodb_strict_mode=1",
            'charset': 'utf8mb4',
                },
        }
      }
    insertafter: '^STATIC_ROOT'
```

The *blockinfile* module adds the *block* after the text mentioned in *insertafter*.

The remaing section is the post configuration task set.

```
- name: Initial setup of project with DB
  command: python {{ sample_django_proj_dir }}/manage.py {{ item }}
  with_items:
    - makemigrations
    - migrate
  run_once: yes


- name: Create super user for sample project
  command: python {{ sample_django_proj_dir }}/manage.py shell -c "from django.contr
er_email }}', '{{ sample_user_pass }}')"
  run_once: yes
  ignore_errors: yes


- name: Collect static files for django project
  command: python {{ sample_django_proj_dir }}/manage.py collectstatic --no-input
  run_once: yes
```

At this point, if the test server for django is run, it will be serving the sample project, but we will setup Apache HTTP web server and server the sample app.

Our Django project has the following directory structure inside /var/www/http/ -

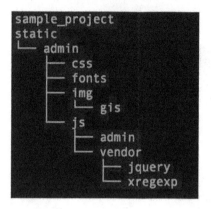

```
sample_project
static
└── admin
    ├── css
    ├── fonts
    ├── img
    │   └── gis
    └── js
        ├── admin
        └── vendor
            ├── jquery
            └── xregexp
```

When the test server is run, it would serve pages, but Django in production with Apache httpd requires the parent directory of a project to be nested inside another directory with the same name as the project, something of the manner, /var/www/html/sample_project/sample_project. This requires relocation of the files in the project directory and we are going to take up this task in the webtier role. We will be able to explore the usage of a few ansible modules in the excercise.

Finally, the remaining role *webtier* for our play.

Tasks to be done *webtier* role -

1. Re-arrange the project directory structure
2. Install httpd and mod_wsgi
3. Configure apache to server Django pages

## Re-arrange the project directory structure

This task involves creation of a temporary directory where the contents of in the present project directory will be transferred. Then the project directory contents are to be relocated from the temporary location after, first deletion of the project directory contents and recreation of the parent directory for the project.

The temporay directory is created. The directory name will be of the format ansible. <0-9><aA-zZ>django.

```
- name: create temporary build directory
  tempfile:
    path: /tmp/
    state: directory
    suffix: django
```

*suffix* - The directory name ends with the string passed in this parameter.

Since the exact name of the temporary directory is not known, the *find* module is used to get the name of the directory.

```
- name: Find the name of the temporary directory
  find:
    paths: /tmp/
    patterns: "ansible*"
    recurse: no
    file_type: directory
  register: temp_dir_name

- debug:
    var: temp_dir_name.files[0]["path"]
```

*patterns* - Directory names matching th regex pattern passed with this parameter will be returned.

Next the contents inside the project directory are moved to the temporary location. The *synchronize* module does *rsync* netween the source and destination.

The sync is happening within the same node, so, this step requires a ensuring two things - a) The hostname of the managed node is present in its /etc/hosts file, b) The public key (id_rsa. pub) of the managed node is present in the authorized_keys file.

```
- name: Sync contents from current project directory to temporary directory
  synchronize:
    src: "{{ sample_django_proj_dir }}"
    dest: "{{ temp_dir_name.files[0]['path'] }}"
  delegate_to: "{{ ansible_hostname }}"
```

*delegate_to* - This parameter specifically dictates that the task is executed on the specified host such that both source and destination for rsync are on the same node.

The contents of the project directory is deleted and recreated. Initially the contents in /var/www/http/ were manage.py, sample_project, static and it is re-instantiated as -

```
sample_project
├── manage.py
├── sample_project
│   ├── __init__.py
│   ├── __init__.pyc
│   ├── settings.py
│   ├── settings.pyc
│   ├── urls.py
│   ├── urls.pyc
│   ├── wsgi.py
│   └── wsgi.pyc
└── static
```

```
- name: Re-create project directory
  file:
    path: "{{ sample_django_proj_dir }}{{ sample_project_name }}"
    state: directory
    mode: 0755

- name: Re-sync back the data from temp directory
  synchronize:
    src: "{{ temp_dir_name.files[0]['path'] }}/"
    dest: "{{ sample_django_proj_dir }}{{ sample_project_name }}/"
  delegate_to: "{{ ansible_hostname }}"
```

1.  *Install httpd and mod_wsgi*

```
---
- name: Install apache http webserver
  yum: name={{ item }}
  with_items:
    - httpd
    - mod_wsgi
```

*httpd* is the HTTP webserver and *mod_wsgi* is the HTTP module for hosting a webserver written in python and supports the python WSGI specification.

The remaining of the tasks consist of configuring of Django WSGI script to work with httpd.

```
- name: Create the configuration file for django WSGI
  template:
    src: ../templates/django.conf
    dest: /etc/httpd/conf.d/django.conf
    mode: 0755

- name: Configure httpd.conf
  lineinfile:
    path: /etc/httpd/conf/httpd.conf
    regexp: '^Listen 80$'
    line: 'Listen {{ ansible_default_ipv4.address }}:80'
```

Finally, the directory permissions and ownership will be set to *apache* user.

```
- name: Change apache directory permission
  file:
    path: "{{ item }}"
    owner: apache
    group: apache
    recurse: yes
    mode: 0755
  with_items:
    - "/etc/httpd/"
    - "/var/www/http/"
```

Now, the Apache HTTP webserver is ready to server pages, and test page is at http://10.10.0.150 and the admin console is at http://10.10.0.150/admin.

# Ad-hoc

The directory structure followed in the sample project is a standard defined by ansible, but ansible is also open toward use cases that require robust scripting without such organisational requirement for the scripts.

Ansible provides the *ansible* client with which commands and modules can be executed on the managed nodes from the command-line. When using *ansible-playbook* command, it required an inventory file that defines the managed host groupings. For using the *ansible* command, the host groups have to be declared in /etc/ansible/hosts in the same way as the inventory file (production) in our sample project.

The ansible modules are referenced with -m flag and the arguments for the module with -a.

```
[[root@ansiblebox ansible_project]# ansible dbservers -m shell -a "echo 'Hello'"
ww-z1.server.com | SUCCESS | rc=0 >>
Hello
```

All modules are referenced by the same name as in the playbooks, for example here, the *service* module is used to restart a service on the managed node.

```
[[root@ansiblebox ansible_project]# ansible dbservers -m service -a "name=httpd state=restarted"
ww-z1.server.com | SUCCESS => {
    "changed": true,
    "name": "httpd",
    "state": "started",
    "status": {
        "ActiveEnterTimestamp": "Tue 2018-09-04 17:51:08 UTC",
        "ActiveEnterTimestampMonotonic": "294651722264",
        "ActiveExitTimestamp": "Tue 2018-09-04 17:51:07 UTC",
        "ActiveExitTimestampMonotonic": "294650492577",
        "ActiveState": "active",
```

# SECTION 6

# Blockchain with Ethereum

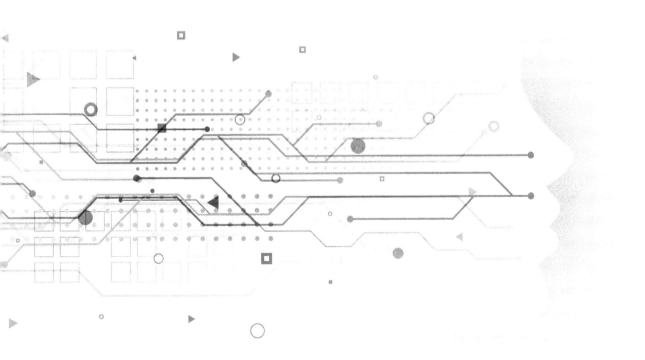

# Introduction

The birth of the world wide web has been the most engaging and fast growing technology that has affected the greatest collective population than any other of its predecessors such as newspaper, radio and television. All of these technologies have been a medium for bringing people closer such that ideas and options can be exchanged, thereby conversations can get going. From print media to internet today, what has changed is the exponential growth in the number of people who can communicate with each other.

During the time there was only print media available, it was onto the press houses to put out the written word out in the form of news, stories, advertisements, job listings, etc., pretty much all of the things that we do still today. The only difference being, it was only possible for a journalist to publish and the conversation used to be unidirectional. It was no way possible for a reader to directly be able to publish an opinion.

An upgrade to that came in the form of radio along with the telephone, as news, advertisements and other types of information exchange started happening in a bi-directional way for the first time. Any person owning a telephone was able to call the radio station and engage in a conversation with a radio host on any topic. No longer a person required to become either a journalist or own a printing press.

The next milestone as we know was in the form of television, as unlike radio, television had its reachability to a global audience. The ability to being heard and seen from any part of the world expanded for a lot of people through television, but still it required a person to have a career in television media to be featured. The desire of people to be able to express themselves globally without any such pre-conditions as required by the previous technologies, was fulfilled by the invention of the internet.

With the introduction of each form of communication medium, and the consequent set of technologies that established around them, the cost of communication has been reduced. Therefore, technology has been the medium for democratisation of communication.

All the modes of communication that we discussed, have been made possible by investment in technology and infrastructure from a central source in the form of a company, who own the proprietorship. In our trajectory towards a future, where any person would be able to communicate or engage in exchange of information with the rest of the world, with having complete control over the process and without requiring any middle man, requires total democratisation of the communication enabling technology. Which means, centralised companies who provide internet and companies who provide applications over the internet that act as enablers of communication have to be decentralised.

Blockchain technology is enabled in the current world by internet provider companies, but its fundamental concept is about distributed computing and consensus through direct participation. Blockchain technology gives any person the capability to engage in information exchange with any person over the internet, without requiring a middle man to act as a host or validator, depending upon the context it is used. The blockchain does this is discussed in detail in the forthcoming sections of this chapter, but to summarise, we can think of blockchain technology as a solution to the requirement of a third party for any sort of transaction, whether it is data of an enterprise or internet traffic. In comparison to today's scheme of things, in order to send a money transaction over the internet to an e-commerce company's account, the transaction has to be validated by a middle man such as any financial institution. The blockchain technology removes this requirement, such that, a consensus can be formed through decentralised computing. Again, in case of how internet is provided to us today, true decentralisation is not yet available as the money transfer through blockchain will be hosted on an internet built by centralised companies. Therefore, a truly decentralised system of the future will have the internet built with infrastructure owned by individuals, with the blockchain technology at the heart of it.

Blockchain can be considered as the first step toward complete decentralisation. It is the enabling technology to bring about decentralisation in the software layer that runs the internet. But in order to truly convert the software layer of internet to a structure, where it is no longer required for a social networking company or a e-commerce company to exist as a centralised entity, the blockchain technology has to be programmable such that applications can be built for all types of uses. Again, it is not just the software part that requires changes. The current schema of internet involves centrally managed entities who invest in building the infrastructure and therefore, as stated before, true decentralisation would give the ability to any person to build an infrastructure for creating an inter-network with which communication can be made on a global scale.

The growth of computer technology has taken an exponential rate and as a consequence more people now have access to compute power for lower prices with every passing year. Computing devices such as mobile phones, desktops or laptops, are becoming powerful enough to be able to function as servers that can participate in hosting internet services. Such a future in internet technology requires a completely different types of enabling softwares and security protocols. Ethereum not just extends the distributed computing technology, but also introduces new concepts as programmable blockchain, that paves the way to a truly decentralised internet of the future.

# What is blockchain?

A blockchain is a distributed data-structure where, unlike conventional case of storing records in a central database, the entire data store has a copy with all the participants of an enterprise. A blockchain uses to *Merkel tree* data-structure and in the case of blockchain, it forms a list (chain).

In *Merkel tree* data-structure, each node is identified through a hash value that is evaluated from the hash value of its contents and the hash of parent nodes.

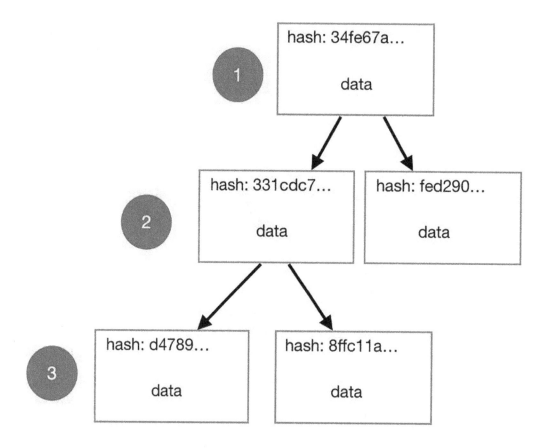

The hash for the node 1 is calculated based upon its data. Subsequently, the hash of node 3 is calculated from its own data along with the hash of node 2 and node 1.

A blockchain applies it to form a 'linked' list data-structure where the hash for node $k$ is calculated from its own data and the hashes of previous nodes. In blockchain, a *block* is basically a node in the daisy chaining.

The node 1 being the first is called a *Genesis* block.

As it has been stated at the start of this chapter that blockchain is a distributed data-structure, it should not be confused with nodes themselves being distributed. A blockchain is not just this data-structure but a software implementation of the fundamental logic that, there would be participants in a enterprise where each one of them must have a copy of the entire blockchain i.e. the entire list of nodes.

In decentralisation, accomplishing a task requires every participant or the majority to agree with one another. In order to truly understand the root of the blockchain technology, we have to understand the intent and intuition behind its inception. We take the example of any task that is done via a centrally managed entity, which is practically everything in this present world. Banking, voting, governance, economy exchanges, etc. all these entities work in a model where all peers or workers are arranged in a hierarchy and they report to one central decision forming body. The below diagram briefly outlines the central system execution -

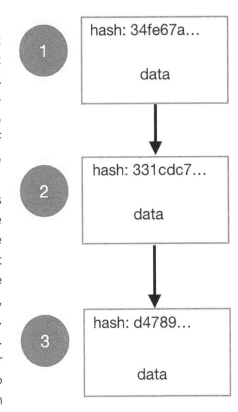

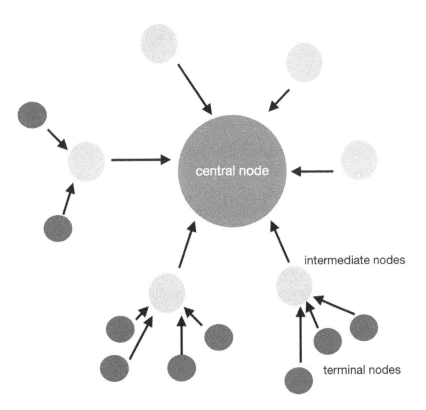

A centralised system works through delegation of decision forming rights from the terminal nodes up till the central node. Here the term node does not mean a cell or node in the blockchain data structure, but a functional entity. Therefore, the central node is responsible for the state of the entire system and acts as a mediator in case of any discrepancy. For example, in a banking system, a bank sanctions a transaction between two parties because the notary power has been provided to the bank by the people using its services.

In order for a decentralised system to be able to incorporate such services and remove a third party mediator, all the participants have to be peers without any hierarchy and collectively validate all actions. It is this requirement for a consensus from which stems the idea of using a Merkel tree and the philosophy of blockchain to keep a copy of the entire data-structure's state with all the peers.

Any enterprise is basically a changing and ever-growing list of validated actions and each action can be represented as a data tuple. For any enterprise, a task involves an exchange between two parties and here is such a list of such actions represented as tuples -

a)  *Dr. X prescribes a medicine to patient P.*
    Here this transaction is validated by either the hospital or clinic as local bodies and ultimately by the medical association. Any dispute for this transaction will be settled by the local bodies and in case of escalation, by the medical association.

b)  *Person K of the logistics department checks and certifies a document to be forwarded to the sales department.*
    In such a transaction the immediate parties involved are bonded into a mutual agreement. This agreement is transitively done behalf on the higher authorities in the hierarchy leading upto the central control.

In case of a discord among parties, the higher authorities will be responsible for validation and settlement for establishing the correct agreement. A centralised system therefore, is an agreement among participating entities to vest trust into a single appointed entity and the central entity in turn is responsible for maintaining transparency to all the participants.

To establish transparency in a decentralised setup, information has to be made available to all entities and not only to just a single body. With that stated, it must be cleared that, availability does not entail open access privilege. Let us take the example of traditional banking system, which if exercised in a decentralised manner, would require all the paper works, all details of account holders, all transaction information to be available to all participants of the service. It is absolutely impossible to function with such a system using analog technology such as *paper*. Imagine subscribing to a banking system where a new customer has to store an ever-updating copy of all the paperworks of that bank.

Digitisation of all the information of an enterprise, is the first step toward establishing a decentralised order. Taking the example of banking system where all the transactions are recorded in a database, a decentralised approach would require a software that constantly updates this database not at a central location but the copy that is present with all the peers.

The intuition behind keeping a copy with everyone and updating all copies upon each transaction, is that, every peer is acknowledging the transaction.

The database to be used to maintain all the transaction history cannot be done with a conventional B+ tree (the data structure for all database management softwares). The database used should be additive in nature which means no deletion or edit operation should be supported. For example, in a decentralised banking system if a peer tries to change any value in a tuple say - account XYZ has INR 99 to account has INR 999, it can only do so by issuing a new transaction of INR 900 and not by editing the value the tuple. Moreover, even if a data tuple somehow gets changed in any record, it should affect other records. A database that can ensure such rigidity is a good candidate for decentralised application.

## Ensuring safety and security

The merkel tree data-structure of blockchain, is an excellent candidate for decentralised data storage because it ensures the rigidity against data corruption. This is possible because each node's hash identifier is dependant upon the hashes of all the previous nodes. Suppose a bad actor tries to change the data in a node for one copy of the database, it corrupts the entire copy as it would not match with other copies to form consensus. Each node or block, that stores transaction records are themselves not simple data-structures that can be produced with ease like any other data-structure. There should be a certain degree of difficulty attached to the creation of block because, otherwise a chained hash identifier will not be sufficient in ensuring the sanctity of the blockchain. The blockchain technology was created keeping in mind that it should not demand ASICs (Application Specific Integrated Circuits) and that's why it is created as a *memory-hard* technology, meaning, it requires a certain amount of memory to execute a task not some specialised hardware. If hashing is the only way to ensure the validity of a blockchain, then a peer with relatively larger compute power can change the data in a block and also re-hash and re-generate all the other blocks in the blockchain. In order to make the generation of a block computationally challenging, a special process is introduced called *mining*.

## Keeper of consensus

In a centralised system, people delegate the authority of maintaining the fairness and neutrality among all its users to a third party and constraints are set up to maintain the proper functioning of the system. A decentralised system however, due to its very design philosophy, should not ideally have any form of central dependency. A decentralised system's purpose is to establish consensus through mutual agreement without an external non-benifitor.

For comparison, a bank being the manager of all users accounts, charges a portion as interest, for holding our accounts. They are a centralised system, which means its user and the bank have agreed on a contact, and as a part of that contract, the bank will be charging an amount for its service.

A truly decentralised system has to achieve this mutual agreement among its users without involving an agent. The tasks that an external agent such as the bank performs, are generally a set of rules which ensure its users that the bank cannot mishandle the money in accounts, and, the limitations and penalties are established same for all users. A blockchain achieves neutrality through keeping the latest copy of the database with all its users. Imagine the way a bank keeps a database of all user details in a secure central location, and in order to remove the bank as an external actor, a decentralised system has to make sure it keeps trust among its users without storing all data in a central location. The copy maintaining property of blockchain, originated as a solution to the otherwise central storage architecture. It can also be imagined, that the users could have chosen to establish mutual trust by storing the data at a central location through automation, without any actual agent behind managing it. This could have been a rather more convenient approach as all users would not have to maintain a copy of the data. Such an architecture if applied in the context of a bank, it would mean, the bank is run through complete automation and the server of all data. The end user will establish consensus through a client application software to transfer funds and avail banking facilities. But such a banking system cannot be called a truly decentralised system. The example of banking system in explaining centralised architecture of a system can create a wrong perspective about decentralisation. Decentralisation in the case of a banking system does not mean removing a human controller at the centre and delegating the task to computer programs to function with established guidelines without error. Having a single storage location creates a single point of failure. A central storage facility, although automated in functioning, would require an enabler of infrastructure maintenance. The central storage of a bank involves storing data in huge servers running in data centres and the cost for running the infrastructure is included in the subscription fees paid to the bank by a user.

True decentralisation in the banking system can therefore be achieved only if all of the data is kept with all users. That way, no individual entity is responsible. A copy of data with all users, establishes the mutual trust and consensus by being accountable for own data as well as others, bringing a sense of ownership. This design philosophy of blockchain technology of maintaining distributed copies, is applicable to all types of applications and not just banking. Suppose in another form of application of blockchain, the traditional e-commerce system has been decentralised. In such a scenario, instead of keeping the inventory data, transaction data, etc. with a single company like Amazon or Flipkart, it is kept as copies with all users.

As we are contemplating the possibilities of blockchain technology to be used in various fields, the nodes of the network have to be able to not just maintain a copy of data but also be able to perform constituent computer functions of the relevant service. For instance, a banking application that runs in data centres as we traditionally know, require powerful servers. In order for a decentralised banking service, the hardware capability of a node in the blockchain network has to be able to meet such hardware standards. But again it is not a feasible approach to form a decentralised network with server grade machines owned by individuals. We have already stated that blockchain technology is built keeping in mind that it should not require specialised hardware, and using of server grade computers come with the maintenance costs associated with such hardware. Current generation of compute power in average personal computers may not be sufficient in hosting all kind of applications implemented on blockchain, but the future holds possibility.

Blockchain is an emerging technology whose application capabilities are only going to increase with the increase in small scale integration in computer technology. The cellular phones in 2018 have orders of magnitude more compute power than in 80's large scale business computers. Therefore, in the coming years, personal computing devices will become more capable of handling critical computing problems. The blockchains of this generation are built with a design principle against using of ASICs (Application Specific Integrated Circuits) as nodes. This makes the operations in the blockchain software to be memory-hard without requiring special computing capabilities, although there is no barring for ASICs if chosen to be used as a blockchain node.

## Trustlessness

As a blockchain network's goal is to be connected with people, without a external agent, the key focus is to have some mechanism that ensures the sanctity of the network is preserved. Keeping copies of the entire data with all its users is one of the steps toward establishing fairness and mutual agreement among its users, and the same powers are bestowed with all participants of the network. The most important entity in this entire decentralised enterprise is a blockchain's merkel tree data structure. Each block as we know holds some data of the network and as data keeps growing, new blocks will be created. Block generation is the foundation of a blockchain network and it has to ensure that the network is not compromised when a bad block is added to the network.

A blockchain network has the central idea of not requiring to bestow privileged capabilities to selected entities on the network and so all nodes be treated as peers. A blockchain network is therefore called a *trust-less* system. In a trust-less environment, a peer does not have to reserve trust for a neutral entity to ensure fair transactions, unlike the traditional banking system where a bank holds and ensures to maintain the trust in the system. In a trust-less environment, like our blockchain network, each node keeps a copy of the entire blockchain, and that way, no user has to trust the validity of a transaction on a peer. The perspective that a node should have toward a blockchain network, that it wants to join, is that, it does not have to trust an insider who ensures the legitimacy of the network. *The blockchain network is built around certain constraints, which has to be full filled by all participating nodes to ensure the trust in the system.* The network itself is an embodiment of trust and each joining node keeps the trust as a quantifiable unit in the form of the copy of the entire blockchain. This gives us a perspective on the network as itself being a trust-keeper.

Now as the network itself is the agent of trust, the block generation task has to be based upon constraints set by the network, that makes the validity of a block measurable. We already have established the fact that there will be no entities in the network that have exclusive privileged capabilities, and so it is out of the question that blocks will be generated by some specific node(s) in the network. This brings us to the next feature of blockchain that enables any node to perform the block generation operation.

## Block generation

*Mining* is the process of generation of a blockchain block. Any peer node is given the capability of mining a block, and when a block is included in the network, it defines the state of truthfulness of the network at that point in time. If a rogue node generates a bad block (malformed or duplicate), the entire network's truthful state will be compromised if added to the network. Therefore, there must be some form of metric to measure the validity of a block which can be checked by all the other peer nodes before making a copy of the newly added node.

Each block requires to perform a *Proof-of-Work* to be considered a valid block. A Proof-of-Work (PoW) involves performing difficult mathematical calculations with the computer that is time and compute power demanding. A blockchain network when first setup, establishes certain configurations among others, that specifies thresholds which have to maintained by the nodes when mining a block. In order to understand the inner workings of the PoW operation, we will briefly discuss the mining process.

A hash function is the single most important enabler of the blockchain technology. Previously in the book, we discussed how each block is identified by a hash value, that is generated from the content of the last block in the chain. A hash function basically maps data of an arbitrary size into a fixed size. That way no matter how many blocks have been added to a chain, the data size of each new block's hash remains constant and the hash value of a new block is representation of the entire blockchain at that time. The PoW operation can be thought of as the following example mathematical problem -

Suppose there is data X representative of some transactions contained in the latest block '*i*'. The hash value of block '*i*' is generated with data X and a *Nonce* value as inputs to the hash function. The output of the hash function is compared against a threshold value known as *difficulty*. A hash function reads the input data as a stream of hexadecimal bytes and returns a 32 bit hexadecimal string. If the hash value is less than the difficulty set by the network, the block is deemed valid. The difficulty is a target hash value which is of the aforesaid constraints set by the network. Due to the nature of the SHA-256 algorithm, which is used to generate all hash values, any change in the payload data X, will result in a completely different hash value. If the hash is to be generated using only the data X, the resulting value almost always results in a value greater than the threshold. This is a problem because the data input X cannot be changed to re-calculate until the hash is less than or equal to the difficulty threshold. The *Nonce* is an incremental number whose value is adjusted and appended with the input data X. It is this combination of DATA + NONCE for which the hash is calculated. Nonce should be thought of as a regulator that is adjusted (usually incremented by 1) to make the output hash match the difficulty standard set. Therefore, it is an iterative process of incrementing the nonce value and re-calculating the hash. Now when a new block $j$ containing data Y, is to be added to the chain, the previous block's hash (block $i$) + the current data Y + a nonce, is sent as an input to the hash function. The hash function is composed of mathematical steps that is by design computation intensive. The PoW is designed to be deliberately a difficult task and this difficulty increases with the growth of network. On a successful mining of a block, the miner is awarded with a *coin* relevant to that particular blockchain network.

The difficulty in mining a block is a mechanism that ensures an attempt in cheating the blockchain network results in compensation from the bad actor and also, the possibility of creating a bad block or tampering a block becomes exponentially difficult, in terms of compute power requirement, as the network grows. A blockchain network is additive and there is no way to delete any record from a block. Suppose a bad actor is trying to tamper a transaction in the blockchain. Due to the underlying merkel tree data structure of blockchain, all the blocks from the tampered block till the block at the end of the chain has to be regenerated. We are going to see how this happens with a great online tool that can be found at the following address (http://anders.com/blockchain/blockchain.html) -

In this demo blockchain, we have a blockchain of four blocks -

| Block: | # 1 | Block: | # 2 |
|---|---|---|---|
| Nonce: | 40546 | Nonce: | 16473 |
| Data: | Hello | Data: | blockchain |
| Prev: | 0000000000000000000000000000000000000000000000000000000000000000 | Prev: | 0000b3db41cb3918560115ce7300a08e78f9ae044496ea462c454 |
| Hash: | 0000b3db41cb3918560115ce7300a08e78f9ae044496ea462c454 | Hash: | 00009df9ea6c0b57389cfc3fc456256d642b1e5bb659eee93f683 |
| Mine | | Mine | |

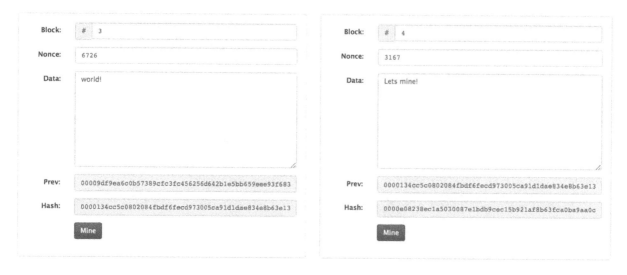

We will change the data in block #2 from 'blockchain' to 'Amazing blockchain'. All the blocks till the end will be rendered corrupted.

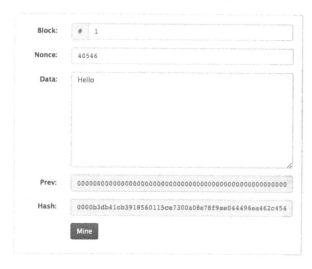

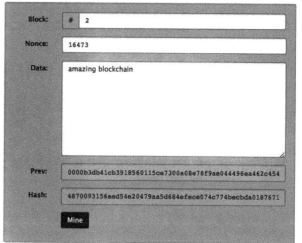

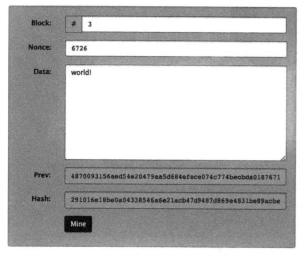

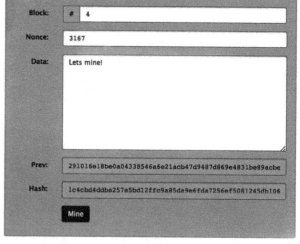

Each block has a hash value as its unique identifier and as we have already learnt, this hash value is used to generate the hash value for the next block in the chain. A blockchain network is not mutable. Therefore, making any change in any data in a particular block, is equal to mining a new block to store that data. But since succeeding hashes get changed, they all have to be re-mined as well.

The hash function has the speciality such that generating a hash value involves difficulty but checking the validity of the hash function is easy. Therefore, when a miner generates a new block, the hash has to be verified by all other or majority of the miners in the network. A consensus is reached when a block's hash is valid and only then the new block is added to the chain.

The mining operation becomes exponentially difficult with growth of the network. We will take the approach of a bad actor to understand how the computation demanding requirement PoW would make it almost impossible to cheat the network. Like everyone else, the bad actor also has a copy of the entire blockchain and the changes made to the copy of blockchain will be copied by all other peers if the changed state is truthful (hashes and other metrics are correct).

In the first scenario, the PoW algorithm is designed in a way that is not computation intensive and requires only a constant magnitude of difficulty to generate a new block. Under such circumstances, if an attacker wants to change the block $k$ in the blockchain containing $n$ blocks, the amount of computation time required to regenerate the $k$ to $n$ blocks is calculate-able. The attacker knows the rate of new block creation, so the time required to regenerate all the $k$ to $n$ new blocks should be less than the average block creation rate. It is extremely difficult to regenerate the blocks as it would require a great amount of compute power to beat the average block creation time.

In this next scenario, the difficulty of PoW algorithm increases over time as the difficulty setting of the network changes periodically, and as a result mining of new blocks takes longer times. With a periodically changing difficulty, more iterations are required to find the correct nonce value that produces a valid block. The compute power required for an attacker to re-mine all the blocks becomes exponentially high than before.

All public blockchain networks like Bitcoin, Ethereum, etc. have a consistent rate of new block creation and it is not that only new blocks are created when new data is available. Under such circumstances it becomes impossible to re-mine the blocks within the block-time (average time required to create new block).

Therefore, the strength and security of a blockchain network increases with the growth of the network and volume of transactions. A blockchain network is different from a traditional computer network that we have known as LANs or WANs. A user with malicious intent finds a way to harm other peers on the network or the network itself through several phishing techniques. The reason blockchain technology is most times referred to as - *crypto*, because it is guarded with cryptography at every step and it is bounded by rigid constraints unlike a LAN network. It is this rigid constraints that ensure every peer node is able to perform only a well defined set of operations on the network. The ingenious design philosophy of deliberately introducing difficulty, imposes a compensation on a malicious intent toward the network. A peers node which is attempting to tamper the blockchain, will have to undertake an enormous cost in terms of electricity spending, for running powerful server computers and cooling system for those servers.

## Mining

The term *mining* resembles the difficulty involved in the actual process of mining minerals from earth. The way honest labour is emulated in mining a block compared to mining gold, is through spending on electrical energy. Every node on a blockchain network has the capability to mine blocks. But since mining is costly, it raises the question as how would be the responsibility of mining allocated to a node. We will discuss about what is the driving force or intent in general, for building a de-centralised network and thereby, the responsibility of mining. Before that, we will learn what happens on a successful mining operation.

Since generation of a block is inspired by the process of mineral mining, a blockchain network has a reward associated with it in the form of a virtual *coin*. A virtual coin is the currency relevant in a blockchain network and has a value attached to it like any other currency such as rupee or dollar. The price of a coin and other intricacies are decided and configured during the creation of the network and is out of the scope of this book. But the idea and capabilities of a virtual coin is exactly same as that of the ones that we have in our physical wallets.

Now that we have got quite a generalised idea about the key elements of blockchain network, we will next take a look at the generic schema of a block.

A block has the following structure -

| Field |
|---|
| Magic no |
| Blocksize |
| Blockheader |
| Transaction counter |
| transactions |

Magic no - This is a constant value that identifies the blockchain network.
Blocksize - It tells the maximum size of a block for hte entire network.
Blockheader - It consists of a few identifiers such as nonce, difficulty target, previous block's hash, version, timstamp, etc.
Transaction counter - This value represents the number of transactions stored in a block.
Transactions - As the name suggests, it consists the linear list of transactions.

## Hash and nonce

For any blockchain network, the *Proof-of-Work* yields a hash which is used to create a block. Every network has a threshold hash value as preset such that, a unique hash value will be considered valid for the network, if it is less than the threshold. This is because of the nature of hash generating function, which in the use case of blockchain takes the value of previous block hash and generates a new hash value. This new hash value may be greater than the threshold value and so a *nonce* value that is present in a block is re-adjusted to re-hash and keep this process going until a valid hash is produced. The threshold value is represented as *difficulty target* in a block header and this target is set during the creation of the network with the genesis block.

## What true decentralisation means

There is enough mystery surrounding the founding of blockchain technology. In the year 2008, the paper Bitcoin: A peer to peer electronic cash system was introduced under the alias name Satoshi Nakamoto that laid the foundation of a decentralised currency. Bitcoin went on to become an actual publicly traded company and ushered in the age of blockchain technology. The popularity of crypto from then on took off such that countries such as Sweden, United States, Brazil, Uzbekistan, etc. have accepted this as a currency in parallel with the national currency. A trader and buyer who has a Bitcoin wallet, can buy and sell goods with *bit-coins*, the virtual currency of Bitcoin. Bitcoin on the front-end is basically an exchange and its actions are similar to that of a foreign exchange embassy, which converts the local currency and converts it to the currency. Therefore, a person wanting to buy some bit-coins, buys a wallet on the Bitcoin blockchain and receives coins corresponding to the exchange rate.

Until the introduction of Bitcoin and the corresponding blockchain technology, the perspective to every service or commodity has been centralised. A government is a collective of public servants who provides public service in exchange for public currency in the form of taxes and delegated vote and, it is so because of people's choice of being managed from a central body. Similarly, any private or public sector company is a collection of people that work under the supervision of a central head. The reason centralised approach has been the natural one since the dawn of civilisation, is because there has been no such commendable automation or computing power accessible to majority of the world population, as it has been in the recent decade, with the advent of smartphones. The place we are at as human civilisation and the direction we are headed, the handheld devices that we have today are going to evolve into server grade devices as powerful as today's servers. We are in the transition period when starting with small services, all things will someday become decentralised.

In order to understand what would be the motivation behind transitioning to decentralised services, we have to briefly identify the problems with centralised approach. A central system such as a publicly traded company or a private one, is basically a group of people who manufacture tangible or non-tangible (software) objects and are controlled from a single source. The users are dependant on a company, and they cast a vote of confidence for the company, by buying into the products they make or services they provide. A company on the other hand is dependant on the customers too, because the profits and sales enable a company to function. The primary problem in this form of exchange is the lack of transparency. The consumers delegate the their trust to a company to be lawful or trustful in their practices. But the world history of business and commerce has plenty of examples where companies have consorted to censorship or practices that are not supported by its customers. There are several examples of banking scams from banks which have attained a stature of trust with its customers.

The inspiration for Bitcoin or crypto-currency originated from the desire to remove the requirement and involvement of a banking institution for transferring money and establish a direct democratic form of currency reserve. But what Bitcoin brought with itself is the blockchain technology that has the capability to extend into all sectors and decentralise them. Taking the example of a blockchain based banking institution, all the information, all activities, as a default have to be accessible as a copy to all its users and in order for the banking institution to introduce any scheme or change, it has to have a direct vote from its users. In another example, imagine a social media platform to be built on a blockchain. In such a scenario, no one company will have the rights on user data, and it is the collective decision of the peers that will direct programmers (who are also users of the network) to built new features.

We know that virtual coins are not like our usual currency which is tangible, so it might be little difficult for us to grasp the idea of money that is available only in the form of some numeric value digitally. In reality, the money that exists in the form of notes and coins are basically value assigned to a tangible entity. For example, when we are transferring money between accounts through a bank cheque, it is not that actual notes and coins are transferred, but the account balance value in the involved accounts reflect the transaction. Since the institution of currency reserve is hosted by governments, the issued notes and coins are the testimonial of trust that people have vested upon the government to be the only authority involved in such an exercise. Traditional money minting process has shortcomings and as a result counterfeit currencies come into existence. Counterfeit currency is always distinguishable from real money because the exact same steps were not executed. It therefore depends on the accuracy of a forger, about how difficult it is to distinguish a fake from real. Blockchain on the other hand is devoid of the shortcomings of traditional currency. In a blockchain network, the difficulty of generating a coin is same for everyone and its intelligent design philosophy enables it to be practically impossible for a bad actor to cheat the system and produce counterfeit currency in the network.

Now coming to the natural concern regarding allocation of responsibility for mining blocks, the benefits of decentralised systems as discussed up till now, along with the reward for virtual coin are the most powerful motivators to embrace blockchain.

## Scope and future

With having discussed about the primary concepts of blockchain, we will now address the scope of this technology. A statement that gets used widely in order to describe blockchain is - blockchain is a distributed ledger which is not an appropriate description of the technology. A ledger means a collection of financial records. Blockchain technology only when used in the use case of financial sector such as Bitcoin, Litecoin, and many others, can be referred to as a ledger. Blockchain in general is an immutable distributed data-structure. This also poses the obvious question that what range of sectors and services can be built upon blockchain. The answer lies in the state of compute power available in the consumer market and the generation of data speed. Currently we have 4G data speeds available for public use and smartphones CPU(s) have billions of transistors in them which makes it possible to have a blockchain network with phones. But right now only textual data is possible to be stored in a block. The most popular blockchain applications of this generation have a block size limit of 1 MB, and the blockchains such as Bitcoin or Ethereum are primarily made of desktop and server grade computers. With the advent of 5G data speeds, there shall be more applications that embrace decentralisation as larger block sizes will be possible to maintain without choking the network. In coming years even a new completely decentralised internet may be created which is powered by blockchain technology.

Let us take a simple trading example how a transition to a blockchain network shall happen for a regular person when there are multiple blockchain networks coexisting. In should not be difficult to imagine how crypto-currency can co-exist alongside all other national currencies. Each country has its own currency issued by the government and so, we can think of a country as a network where, the government is the only node responsible for generating currency. Similarly, a blockchain network can be thought of a territory (open to all) where only a specific type of currency is valid. Therefore, a person owning accounts in multiple blockchain networks is same as owning currency from various countries.

# What is Ethereum?

In the last chapter, we discussed how applications of blockchain technology is limited to the data rate and only 1 MB of block sizes can be smoothly handled. The widespread adoption of blockchain technology came since the historic paper - Bitcoin: A peer-to-peer electronic cash system, published under the author name - Satoshi Nakamoto, which laid out the use of blockchain technology as a distributed ledger for digital currency.

The way peer to peer payments work is, person A having an account at a bank and person B also having an account at the same or different bank and if a transaction has to be sent between the two, it has to be via the bank since its holds the accounts. Bitcoin decentralises the whole approach by removing the requirement of a central controller that maintains the ledger for all transactions and puts it on a blockchain. Therefore, a transaction between two parties is basically just textual data about how much funds will be transferred from person A's account to person B's account -

```
("100", "AC0001F", "AC0002F")
```

Every user of the blockchain has digital wallet identified by a hash string which is the endpoint for any transaction of crypto-currency.

The actual currency - Bitcoin, is produced during the mining process. The electrical energy used in running servers to mine coins converts dollars of electricity bills into Bitcoins. The Bitcoin crypto-currency also has an exchange like any other currency. Bitcoin is the first generation of blockchain technology used in crypto-currency and took around 10 minutes to complete a transaction i.e. updating all the copies of the blockchain.

*Ethereum* is an open source blockchain platform that extends the traits and capabilities of Bitcoin and its predecessors. Ethereum makes the crypto-currency more flexible according to use cases and most importantly it is the blockchain that is programmable. Like Bitcoin, each user on the blockchain will have one account and a wallet linked to it which is called *Externally Owned Accounts (EOA)*. Ethereum introduces another form of account called *Contract Accounts* which is controlled by contract code. It is this concept of *Contract Accounts* that brings programmability on the blockchain.

## *Differentiating from Bitcoin and the others*

The crypto-currency space consists of around 400 publicly traded currencies starting with of course the predecessor to all, Bitcoin. Majority of other crypto-currencies are just distributed ledgers using the blockchain technology. The introduction of Bitcoin, was the application of blockchain to banking and peer-to-peer money transfer. We have discussed in the earlier section, that blockchain technology's applications are extensive and at the current moment just limited by the bandwidth limitations.

In the previous chapter, while discussing the way blockchain technology is the rightful candidate for decentralised connections among people for any sort of service or interaction, we may be mislead into thinking that the fundamental requirement for a person to join a decentralised network is to own a computer that is an active node in the network. Although the trust factor in a trust-less system comes from the ownership of the copy of the entire chain, the contemporary public crypto-currencies do not necessarily require for a user to own a node themselves. Therefore, it is important to understand how current crypto-currencies are different than the idea about decentralisation that we got in the previous chapter.

Bitcoin, Litecoin, Ripple, etc. are currency exchanges that convert an accepted currency into the corresponding currency of that particular chain network. Bitcoin, Litecoin - these are separate companies with their separate coin offerings. The currency from one network is not directly interchangeable with other, but is subject to exchange rates like any other form of currency systems - physical or digital. For a person to join any of these crypto-currency networks, he/she has to own a crypto-wallet (account) in that network and this wallet will contain crypto-currency. These crypto-currency exchanges are private companies that host their own coins. These crypto networks are started with servers from a primary company and is referred to as *main-net* where users can join their own nodes to the network. Each crypto-wallet has a corresponding wallet address which is used to send and receive money. Each such crypto network as Bitcoin, although is started and managed by a company, the blockchain is not owned by any single entity.

## Need for programmability

Every software requires three components - programs that accomplish particular tasks, data which servers as input to those programs and a computer system to execute the code. Blockchain is like any other data structure - arrays or linked lists, but with features that make it a suitable candidate for secure decentralised data storage. We are headed toward a future where the current bandwidth limitations associated with blockchain will no longer be a roadblock and full fledged decentralised applications could be built using blockchain. We will discuss what kind of architecture would be required by an application to exist on blockchain and how ethereum addresses those requirements.

The current and past architecture of application softwares have been about a collection of software packages that are deployed in a server(s) and a generic request to the application over the network results in look up into a database from the software and returning the result after processing. Now for a software that has to be hosted on a blockchain network has to be functionally capable of doing those things. Here is a diagram of a typical blockchain network -

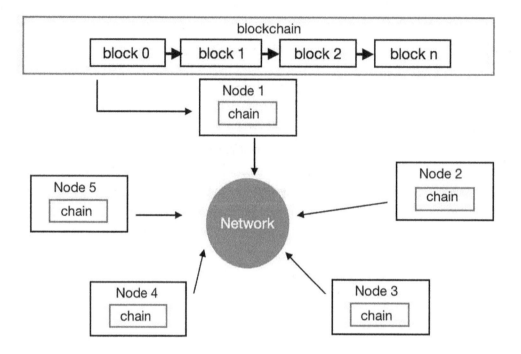

Here each node keeps a copy of the chain and the blocks are maximum of 1MB to ~ 2MB in size storing data. Now here is the diagram depicting a traditional application components -

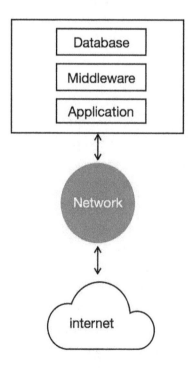

A traditional software consists of application code (middleware code and application frontend code) and database. In order to host an application on blockchain, programmability has to be brought to it. The contemporary application of blockchain in the form of a distributed ledger - Bitcoin, is a currency exchange software that runs on each node of the network. Each of such distributed ledger applications have a specific software running and therefore, such a blockchain network is not equipped to host any user created application. The Bitcoin ledger runs on each of the nodes of its network as an application and it does not have the generic three-tiered architecture as in a traditional application.

In order for an application to be hosted on a blockchain, suppose an e-commerce application or a messenger application, the various components such as database or middleware, all have to be using the blockchain data structure. We can imagine a true blockchain based implementation of our known traditional apps to use the blockchain data structure for serving the purpose of database as well as storing the application program executables. This is because, a blockchain based implementation of our regular applications will be built because of the benefits of decentralisation and so, having separate node(s) for storing suppose a relational database or application binaries will not server the ideal architecture. The ideal decentralised application requires keeping copies with all participant nodes and so all components of the application should be replicable for a newly added node.

Ethereum is aimed at making user created applications possible on the blockchain technology. The ethereum network is an open network that any node can connect by running the ethereum client application. As we are discussing the possibility of using blockchain beyond storing money transaction details, ethereum provides the entire platform upon which applications can be created. The public ethereum network can be thought of as a cloud platform where applications can be deployed and thus introducing the concept of *Dapp (decentralised app)*. Unlike Bitcoin and its contemporary ledgers that use blockchain technology for a specific application, an ethereum network is supposed to be application agnostic. Therefore, for anyone to be able to create dapps on blockchain, there needs to be programmability available. The numerous programming languages that we have such as Python or Java is well suited for traditional applications, but since decentralisation comes with a number a strict constraints, ethereum provides its own programming language *Solidity*, that is of course specifically compliant of those constraints.

## Code on blockchain

The identity of a user on ethereum is in the form of an address associated with an account. Ethereum like Bitcoin and other contemporaries, can be used as a ledger and therefore, the ethereum accounts and wallets associated with them, enable users to transfer money. A user can join the ethereum network by creating a wallet with *Metamask* - a Google Chrome browser extension or *Mist* - a standalone application. The currency or coin used in ethereum is called *Ether*, and similar as Bitcoin, a user's currency is converted to ether. The smallest unit of ether is called *Wei* and 1 ether is corresponding to 1,000,000,000,000,000,000 wei.

In order to understand how code is deployed on blockchain, we must have a generic perspective on the type of user interactions possible with ethereum. When it comes to application programming on blockchain, we have to change our perspective of traditional applications deployed in the cloud. Here is a diagram briefly depicting a cloud based application deployment platform such as *Heroku* -

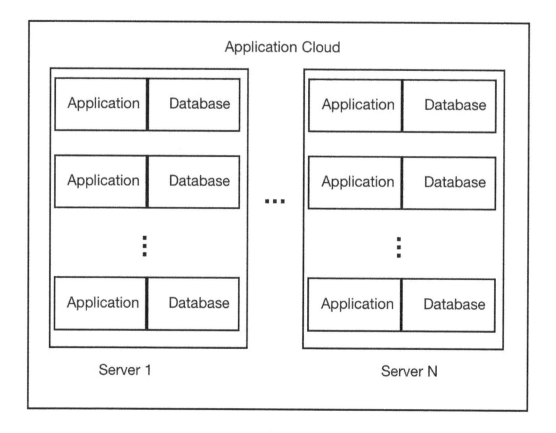

All the applications are deployed into servers that make up the cloud. A developer creates an account with the application cloud platform provider to deploys applications, but such a account is radically different from that of the ones we create with ethereum. The ethereum cloud consists of nodes (servers), user accounts and the blockchain containing all the account details and transaction details among those accounts. Now to introduce application deployability to the chain, the primary concern is to store the application code on the blockchain. The ethereum blockchain contains account details (Externally Owned Account), transaction details, and along with these, application code is stored in a new type of account called *Contract account*.

A *Contract account* also has a wallet linked to it and is a special type of account, because unlike EOA(s) that it managed by a human, a *Contract account* is managed by programming code. In comparison to Bitcoin, which only provides users with a limited set of operations (e.g. Bitcoin transactions), a Contract account makes it possible to transfer crypto-currency based upon a programmed logic with the *Solidity* programming language. Contract accounts have contract code written in the *Solidity* language and are called *Smart contracts*.

Each ethereum node runs an EVM (Ethereum Virtual Machine) that compiles the high-level code written in Solidity, and returns the EVM bytecode similar to how JVM returns bytecode for programs written in Java language. It is within a *Smart contract*, the logic for performing *Turing* complete operations are defined. A contract consists of not just the bytecode, but also the data associated with it that resides at a specific address. This data is referred to as the state of the contract account. Like every application code requires data from some persistent storage, each contract has a key value store that can store 32 bytes sized values per key. The static data in a contract is stored as key value pairs called *state variables* and when the code in a particular contract makes changes to the values, it causes a state change. A hash of this changed state is stored in the contract. When the bytecode inside a contract account has to be executed, it has to be loaded into a high speed memory and that volatile memory is used for runtime variables created by the program.

## Why store code in contract accounts

Ethereum has two types of accounts - Externally owned Accounts that are managed by human users, and Contract accounts that are managed by code, but let us understand why the creators of ethereum choose to use an account for storing application code.

A contract account is no different in structure than that of EOA containing balance, nonce, bytecode, previous hash and root hash of a storage tree as its various components. In EOA's the bytecode field is left blank. A contract account has ether associated with it, same as an EOA.

A blockchain network due to decentralisation consists of server nodes from different sources or users. All the accounts of both types are stored in servers from different enterprises and the code in contract accounts also have to be run on these resources. Whenever a program makes changes in the state variables' values or makes a transaction, the blockchain copy has to be updated at all the nodes. The ether that is allocated for a contract, is spent as an execution fee when it is run on a node. Therefore, it only makes sense to treat a program unit in the form of an account, because like any other Externally Owned Account which makes changes to the blockchain by transferring ether, a contract account containing code is also capable of making changes to the blockchain and needs to transfer ether when executing the code.

## Ethereum: A world computer

The knowledge that we have gathered till now about this new form of peer to peer decentralised networking and application deployment on such a network, it can be summarised in the following diagram -

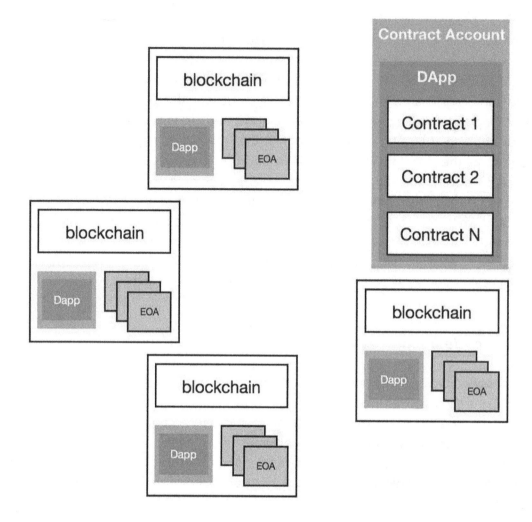

All the nodes in an ethereum network has a copy of the entire blockchain, the contracts, the contract accounts, and the Externally Owned Accounts. Since ethereum brings programmability to the blockchain, it brings about the concept of decentralised applications called *Dapps*. Each contract contains the bytecode for the solidity code and therefore a Dapp is basically one contract or a collection of contracts.

When a user deploys the collection of contract that make up the Dapp, it gets created at a contract account address and it gets replicated across all the nodes. This happens for all the Dapps or just contracts that are deployed on the ethereum cloud. In comparison to app deployment in cloud this is completely different as we have discussed earlier and now we try to understand the reason behind such a trait.

Let us imagine a cloud platform like Heroku, for app deployment. When a developer deploys an app on a centralised app hosting platform, a hosting fees has to be payed to the cloud provider. The ethereum network belongs to no one provider, so there has to be a mechanism that incorporates a hosting fees for the publisher of a Dapp. A developer with an EOA deploys a contract, which in turn makes changes to the blockchain in one node and this change will also made on remaining nodes. Updating a change to the blockchain requires spending of CPU cycles and usage of other resources such as RAM and persistent storage. Therefore, any transaction added to the blockchain, which in this the creation of a contract, should be met with spending some ether as a cost for resource usage. This brings us to the concept of *gas*.

*Gas* is a concept inspired from the fuel that is spent for running a vehicle. In this case, we can refer to gas as our crypto-fuel. Gas is the unit of spending for each transaction on ethereum. A particular transaction that takes up N units of gas to execute, is equal to *units of gas used* times the *gas price*. The ethereum blockchain requires gas for every execution. Although the total spending in the form gas is equivalent to some amount of ether, the spending on a transaction is deliberately not referred to as ether spent. This is due to the same reason a car is said to spend fuel and not money. Ethereum gas is the incentive system that serves as the lifeblood of the network. Gas is the used to calculate the amount of fees that needs to be paid to the network to in order to execute an operation.

Now for deploying a contract, the user first buys some gas from a miner in exchange for some ether. This is analogous to buying natural gas for our car at the gas station. A transaction on the chain has two address, a *from* address representing the user who initiated the transaction, and a *to* address representing the recipient of the transaction. In this case of deploying a contract, a transaction will be created but it is not a peer to peer payment between accounts and so, the to address section of a transaction is set to '0' or left blank. The gas bought is spent as fees to the network.

In the case of sending a transaction of ether from one account to another, gas is also used in the similar fashion.

Next, with all the contracts deployed for a Dapp, it is available for any account on the network to be used. An application publisher yields earnings from users for using the app in two ways - either through displaying advertisements or through charging a premium for the usage. In ethereum a user when executes a contract, the contract bytecode is executed in EVM and ether is spent from the user's account for the gas required for this execution. Every contract has to be specified with a gas limit, which is the maximum amount of gas that can should be spent on a executing the contract. Say a contract performs three tasks - a) initialising two variables with integer values and requires 4 units of gas, b) adding the two values requires

3 units of gas, and c) storing the result in another variable which requires 2 units of gas. The execution of the contract therefore requires 4 + 3 + 2 = 9 units of gas. Say the gas price is 21,000 wei and so the total cost of executing the contract is gas price x gas units used = 21,000 x 9 = 1,81,000 wei. The gas units we used here is imaginary and so in order to know the exact amount of gas spending on a contract enables the publisher of a contract to set the correct gas limit. The estimateGas API of ethereum can be used to estimate the amount of gas that may be required for a contract execution and based on it the gas limit can be set. Therefore, a user who is using the contract, must have the at least 1,81,000 wei in account to be spent on gas. The execution of a contract is a transaction and so this has will be recorded in the chain. A miner or just a node who is ahead in ranking though polling (out of the scope of this book) and chooses to undertake the task of executing the contract bytecode in EVM, gets paid for the gas used.

Our example ethereum diagram represents a single *Dapp* that is made up of N contracts. A contract when deployed, is created in a contract account and the concept of gas usage makes it obvious to treat each program unit as an account. The diagram of ethereum network that we used earlier consisted of four nodes, where each node performs the same set of operations. On the other hand, a traditional app that is hosted in a server farm usually consists of multiple nodes where each node has a separate set of functionalities. For example, there is a database server, an application server, a middleware server, etc.

The ethereum world computer is a host to all Dapps, similar to that of a personal computer system, which hosts all the applications of a user. Let us do a comparison between a personal computer system, a cloud based app hosting platform and an ethereum network to better understand the reason behind ethereum to be called a world computer.

A personal computer is a closed system owned by a single individual. Such a system is host to multiple applications that run on multiple CPU hardware (present generation of computers).

A app hosting platform such as Heroku, is home to multiple such applications that run on a cluster of servers. Each server consists of multiple CPUs which together can be thought of as a single computer consisting of multiple CPUs. A user interacting any application hosted in such a cloud gets the feeling of interacting with a single computer due to the layers of abstraction that hides the clustered backend. Unlike a personal computer which belongs to a single user, the cloud based system is owned by a central entity in a form of a company.

A public ethereum network is a cluster of computers that form a cloud based app hosting platform that is not owned by a single company but belongs to all its users who join the network bringing in their own hardware. An ethereum network is an open world for computers to join the network, and as we have drawn the similarity of all nodes serving as a collective behind layers of abstraction, the ethereum network exactly that description.

An ethereum network is no different than a cloud computing platform when it comes to cluster formation with servers, with one major fundamental difference. In a network such as Heroku, each node is not a host to all the applications that are present in the cloud. As we have discussed several times, it is due to the necessity of establishing consensus and trust, each of the servers in an ethereum network maintains a copy of all transactions and also Dapps.

## What types of apps are meant for ethereum?

In the final section of discussing the capabilities, we will have a brief overview of the capabilities of the current generation of ethereum and what kinds of Dapps are suitable. With the continued increase in compute power and VLSI (very large scale integration), a smartphone of recent years is orders of magnitude more powerful than past generations of server computers. A trust-less decentralised system is made possible by layers of encryption which require intense compute power. Ethereum lays the foundation of the concepts that would make decentralisation possible and paves the way for a completely decentralised internet in near future.

*Ethereum is suited specifically for applications that engage in direct interaction with peers.* With that said, it must be understood that ethereum is a new technology that is paving the way toward a truly decentralised web application hosting platform without having any sort of centralised facets. The current generation of ethereum does not make it possible for hosting all types of applications that are present on the web. A very common type of application with blockchain based technologies is its use in the financial sector. This is purely based upon the fact that every type of blockchain comes with its designated coins. Ethereum similarly has its coin as ether, but it is not just the financial applications that it can be used. We will take the example of building an e-commerce web application with the current generation of ethereum's programmable blockchain technology.

As we have already discussed that current generation of ethereum and the mobile computing technology is not yet completely able to host a truly decentralised application and thats why, the ethereum blockchain will not be able to store all the information such as database and application code as would be ideally required by a truly decentralised application. Solidity, the programming language has its capabilities limited to just programming the logic for executing transactions that essentially affect the ether values among accounts. An e-commerce web application needs a data creation and manipulation medium through a programming language on the data stored in a database. Below is a simple diagram depicting the database of such a hypothetical e-commerce application -

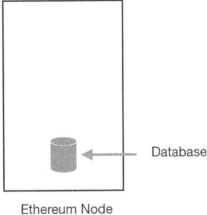

Ethereum Node

The e-commerce application joins the public ethereum network by adding node(s) to it. The database for the application is suppose to be stored in this node as shown in the above diagram. It must be understood that this isn't a recommended setup. Next, the application will generally have three distinct sections as frontend, middleware and backend which are usually distributed among servers. The next diagram will showcase such a generic setup -

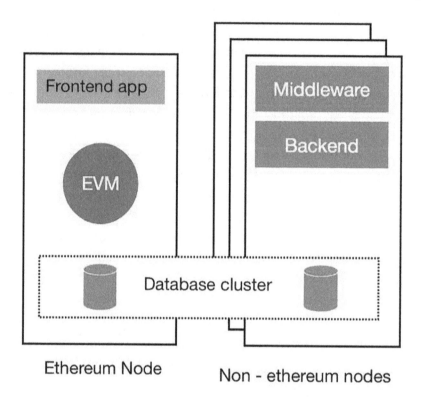

Here we can see that the application architecture is not so different from that of a traditional web application. There is a cluster of servers where the different components of the application are hosted. The major difference therefore, is the presence of at least one node dedicated as an ethereum node running the EVM. Again, it must be made clear that it is not required for the application to have a dedicated EVM node at all. The application can use an ethereum client to connect to an ethereum network and may choose not to participate in the ethereum cluster.

Now coming to the application itself, we can imagine a situation where for every user of the e-commerce platform, an ethereum wallet will be created, or a user already possessing an ethereum wallet, has to connect it to the application by submitting the wallet address during signup. This ethereum wallet is applicable for both sellers and buyers and every transaction will happen with ether exchange among these wallets. Therefore, an e-commerce application like this is not completely decentralised, but participating in the ethereum cluster with own nodes qualifies itself to be regarded as a Dapp where most control may remain with its users. We have to imagine a scenario where there is a motivation for a company (a group of application developers), to create a decentralised application. A perfectly logical question that arises from the concept of Dapps, is that, since the purpose of a company is to provide a service or a product and make profit in return, how would that concept fit in a decentralised setup where the true intent is to replace the requirement of a central controller.

In order to understand this, we will re-evaluate how a company earns through an application or service it provides to its customers, and compare the context with that of a ethereum based scenario. First of all, a company such as an e-commerce, it does not charge its customers for the web application or mobile app, it is for the service of delivery and pickup that the customers pay. From the context of the company, the cost of building an application, hiring a pool of employees, still remains the same on either types of setup. So we can guess, that it is the sheer need of people to discard usage of centralised systems and embrace the revolutionary idea, that is blockchain. It is only through blockchain based solutions that users can maintain complete control over the changes a company makes to its policies or product. Assuming the company participates in the public network with its own nodes, it has to maintain the infrastructure on its portion, same as in traditional situations that we have today.

# Interacting with Ethereum

We will build our own private ethereum network by compiling it from source. The gcc and golang compilers have to to first installed. The client which we are going to use *geth* is built with golang. All the source files are available at the following location -

Adding the golang repository to yum -

```
[root@ethereum-primary ~]# rpm --import https://mirror.go-repo.io/centos/RPM-GPG-KEY-GO-REPO
[root@ethereum-primary ~]# curl -s https://mirror.go-repo.io/centos/go-repo.repo | tee /etc/yum.repos.d/go-repo.repo
[go-repo]
name=go-repo - CentOS
baseurl=https://mirror.go-repo.io/centos/$releasever/$basearch/
enabled=1
gpgcheck=1
gpgkey=https://mirror.go-repo.io/centos/RPM-GPG-KEY-GO-REPO
```

and now installing the packages -

```
[root@ethereum-primary ~]# yum install golang gcc -y -q -e 0
[root@ethereum-primary ~]# which go
/bin/go
```

The go-ethereum repository is cloned -

```
[root@ethereum-primary ~]# git clone https://github.com/ethereum/go-ethereum
Cloning into 'go-ethereum'...
remote: Enumerating objects: 4, done.
remote: Counting objects: 100% (4/4), done.
remote: Compressing objects: 100% (2/2), done.
remote: Total 75898 (delta 2), reused 2 (delta 2), pack-reused 75894
Receiving objects: 100% (75898/75898), 104.96 MiB | 1.96 MiB/s, done.
Resolving deltas: 100% (50607/50607), done.
```

Building the geth client -

```
[root@ethereum-primary ~]# cd go-ethereum/
[root@ethereum-primary go-ethereum]# make geth
build/env.sh go run build/ci.go install ./cmd/geth
```

Setting the path for the geth client -

```
[root@ethereum-primary ~]# export PATH=$PATH:"/root/go-ethereum/build/bin"
```

The *geth* client is not just a gateway to the public ethereum but itself is capable of building a full fledged private network. Since we will be building our own private network, we have to mention special attributes to notify the geth client to form a local network and not connect to the main network.

The geth client requires a data directory which we created at the location -

```
/root/eth_data_dir
```

For every blockchain created, a genesis block is created which marks the first block on the network. A genesis block does not have a predecessor block and ensures that no other block on this blockchain will agree with other blockchains if they do not have the same genesis block. Therefore, no two different nodes belonging to two separate ethereum networks can become the part of the same network. We will create a JSON genesis file which will be used to initialise the network. This genesis file is basically the settings for our blockchain and the network starts with configs set during the initialisation process.

The current generation of ethereum supports only four parameter which can be set in the genesis file - config, difficulty, gasLimit and alloc.

Here is a sample config file -

```
{
"config": {
"chainId": 15,
"homesteadBlock": 0,
"eip155Block": 0,
"eip158Block": 0
},
"difficulty": "20",
"gasLimit": "2100000",
"alloc": {
"7df9a875a174b3bc565e6424a0050ebc1b2d1d82":
    { "balance": "300000" },
"f41c74c9ae680c1aa78f42e5647a62f353b7bdde":
    { "balance": "400000" }
}
}
```

config - This contains all the configurations for our genesis block and thresholds that control basis network operations.

chainID - As key in the config parameter, this represents a random value that is set by the creator of the network to protect against replay attacks. A *replay attack* is a form of network attack where a valid data packet is fraudulently delayed and repeated with malformed contents. This is done either by the originator of a transaction (data packet) or a bad actor who intercepts the data packet and re-transmits it, hence the term replay is used to describe it. A replay attack is basically a man-in-the-middle attack.

homesteadBlock - This represents the version of ethereum to use. Homestead is the first major release of ethereum in public domain and the value 0 specifies the use of this version.

eip155Block & eip158Block - This parameter is to be assigned the value 0 since we are not going to do any hard forks with our ethereum private network. EIP stands for Ethereum Improvement Proposal and on incorporating a hard fork, a custom value is to be provided. eip155 was introduced to help prevent replay attacks and eip158 was introduced to change how ethereum clients deal with empty accounts, treating them non-existent and saving space for the network.

difficulty - It defines the level of difficulty in mining a block and should be set to low values for private test networks.

gasLimit - This is the limit of gas that all the transactions contained in a single block can use.

alloc - Allows defining a list of pre-filled wallets. Each entry is a wallet address with its corresponding ether amount as *balance*.

There are few other parameters -

coinbase - This is a 160 bit address to which the rewards (in ether) is collected for mining the genesis block. This is a beneficiary account where refunds for contract transactions are accumulated.

nonce - This is a 64 bit hash value which combined with another value *mixhash* must satisfy a mathematical condition to justify the Proof-of-Work for a mined block.

timestamp - This contains the output of the Unix time function when a block is created. A smaller time period between the last two blocks results in an increase in the difficulty level and thus additional computation is required to validate the next block. Similarly, the difficulty is adjusted when the time gap between last two created blocks increase.

parentHash - This is a 256 bit hash of the entire parent block header including the nonce and mixhash acting as a pointer to the identity of the parent block. In case of genesis block its 0.

extraData - Contains additional data to be packed while creation of the block.

The genesis file we are going to use for building our own private test network is the following -

```json
{
    "config": {
        "chainId": 15,
        "homesteadBlock": 0,
        "eip155Block": 0,
        "eip158Block": 0
    },
    "difficulty": "0x400",
    "coinbase": "0x3333333333333333333333333333333333333333",
    "gasLimit": "5000000",
    "alloc": {
    }
}
```

We can see we have to pre-allocated any funds to any accounts because our private network has not been initialised yet and there are no accounts that are created in the network.

We have to first initialise the network. At this step, a database is created as per the specifications in the genesis file.

```
[root@ethereum-primary ethereum]# geth --identity "ETH_node_1" --nodiscover --maxpeers 2 \
> --rpc --rpcapi "admin,db,eth,net,web3" \
> --rpcaddr "10.10.0.215" \
> --rpcport "8080" \
> --datadir "/root/ethereum/test_net_data_dir" \
> --port "30303" \
> --networkid 666 \
> init genesis.json
```

identity - This is the name of our node in the private network.

nodiscover - This is to make sure our node is not discoverable by other nodes on a different network who has the exact same genesis file and network id.

maxpeers - Sets the number of nodes that can join the network.

rpc - This enables the RPC (Remote Procedure Call) interface on the node and its is enabled by default.

rpcapi - It enlists the APIs that are accessible with the RPC interface.

rpcaddr - It is the IP address to which the RPC interface shall bind.

rpcport - The port number for the RPC socket.

datadir - This is the data directory to be used by the node.

port - This is the port which will be used to connect to other peer nodes in the network.

networkid - This value is a numeric identifier of the network and advised to be set at a big enough value in production environment.

On successful initialisation, the following output is produced -

```
INFO [12-06|06:56:06.238] Maximum peer count                       ETH=2 LES=0 total=2
INFO [12-06|06:56:06.241] Allocated cache and file handles         database=/root/ethereum/test_net_data_dir/geth/chaindata cache=16 handles=
16
INFO [12-06|06:56:06.259] Writing custom genesis block
INFO [12-06|06:56:06.260] Persisted trie from memory database      nodes=0 size=0.00B time=36.431µs gcnodes=0 gcsize=0.00B gctime=0s livenode
s=1 livesize=0.00B
INFO [12-06|06:56:06.260] Successfully wrote genesis state         database=chaindata                                       hash=643f87…93c7a
9
INFO [12-06|06:56:06.260] Allocated cache and file handles         database=/root/ethereum/test_net_data_dir/geth/lightchaindata cache=16 han
dles=16
INFO [12-06|06:56:06.275] Writing custom genesis block
INFO [12-06|06:56:06.275] Persisted trie from memory database      nodes=0 size=0.00B time=6.935µs  gcnodes=0 gcsize=0.00B gctime=0s livenode
s=1 livesize=0.00B
INFO [12-06|06:56:06.276] Successfully wrote genesis state         database=lightchaindata                                  hash=643f87…
93c7a9
```

After this we can find the following contents in the data directory -

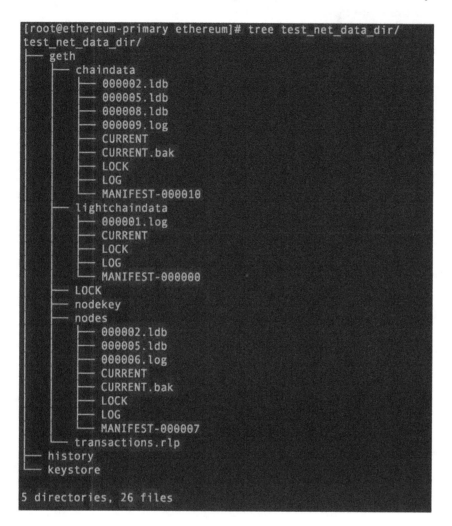

```
[root@ethereum-primary ethereum]# tree test_net_data_dir/
test_net_data_dir/
├── geth
│   ├── chaindata
│   │   ├── 000002.ldb
│   │   ├── 000005.ldb
│   │   ├── 000008.ldb
│   │   ├── 000009.log
│   │   ├── CURRENT
│   │   ├── CURRENT.bak
│   │   ├── LOCK
│   │   ├── LOG
│   │   └── MANIFEST-000010
│   ├── lightchaindata
│   │   ├── 000001.log
│   │   ├── CURRENT
│   │   ├── LOCK
│   │   ├── LOG
│   │   └── MANIFEST-000000
│   ├── LOCK
│   ├── nodekey
│   ├── nodes
│   │   ├── 000002.ldb
│   │   ├── 000005.ldb
│   │   ├── 000006.log
│   │   ├── CURRENT
│   │   ├── CURRENT.bak
│   │   ├── LOCK
│   │   ├── LOG
│   │   └── MANIFEST-000007
│   └── transactions.rlp
├── history
└── keystore

5 directories, 26 files
```

The chaindata directory contains the database files representing our private network in *.ldb files.

The lightchaindata directory also contains information about our network but it for use by light clients which is still under development. The purpose of the light client is to allow users in low-resource environments such as embedded systems, browser extensions, smartphones, etc. to maintain a high security state and verify transactions.

Next, we create our first account in the network.

```
[root@ethereum-primary ethereum]# geth account new
INFO [12-06|06:57:02.218] Maximum peer count                       ETH=25 LES=0 total=25
Your new account is locked with a password. Please give a password. Do not forget this password.
Passphrase:
Repeat passphrase:
Address: {3ca0ea28c9dc92926ca49deb725cecb18db5db7d}
```

We want to pre-allocate funds to this account and so we will re-initialise the blockchain with the updated genesis file. But before that, we will log into the console check details about the newly created account and wallet.

By default the location of the keyfile is /root/.ethereum/keystore. To bring an account created with *geth account new* command under the scope of our private network, the keyfile has to be copied in the keystore of our node's data directory.

```
[root@ethereum-primary ethereum]# cp \
> /root/.ethereum/keystore/UTC--2018-12-06T06-57-16.463184289Z--3ca0ea28c9dc92926ca49deb725cecb18db5db7d \
> test_net_data_dir/keystore/
```

Starting the geth console -

```
[root@ethereum-primary ethereum]# geth --identity "ETH_node_1" \
> --nodiscover \
> --maxpeers 2 \
> --rpc \
> --rpcapi "admin,db,eth,net,web3" \
> --rpcaddr "10.10.0.239" \
> --rpcport "8080" \
> --datadir "/root/ethereum/test_net_data_dir" \
> --port "30303" \
> --networkid 666 \
> console
```

The presonal.listWallets command from the personal API gives us details about the wallets associated with accounts.

```
> personal.listWallets
[{
    accounts: [{
        address: "0x3ca0ea28c9dc92926ca49deb725cecb18db5db7d",
        url: "keystore:///root/ethereum/test_net_data_dir/keystore/UTC--2018-12-06T06-57-16.463184289Z--3ca0ea28c9dc92926ca49deb725cecb18db5db7d"
    }],
    status: "Locked",
    url: "keystore:///root/ethereum/test_net_data_dir/keystore/UTC--2018-12-06T06-57-16.463184289Z--3ca0ea28c9dc92926ca49deb725cecb18db5db7d"
}]
```

We will now exit from the console session by typing *exit*. The address of our account is added to the genesis.json file and some funds are allocated.

```
{
    "config": {
        "chainId": 15,
        "homesteadBlock": 0,
        "eip155Block": 0,
        "eip158Block": 0
    },
    "difficulty": "0x400",
    "coinbase": "0x3333333333333333333333333333333333333333",
    "gasLimit": "5000000",
    "alloc": {
        "0x3ca0ea28c9dc92926ca49deb725cecb18db5db7d":{"balance":"1000"}
    }
}
```

Since the initialisation phase has already been executed, the genesis block has already been created for our network. In order to re-initialise we will empty the contents of chaindata and lightchaindata. After a successful initialisation, we can go back to check the balance in the account.

```
> personal.listAccounts
["0x3ca0ea28c9dc92926ca49deb725cecb18db5db7d"]
>
> eth.getBalance('0x3ca0ea28c9dc92926ca49deb725cecb18db5db7d')
1000
```

As we can see the account has been credited with 1000 ethers. We have used two different APIs - *personal* for querying the list of accounts and *eth* for checking the balance in an account. The list of management commands are available here -

The geth console exposes to the web3 API namespace by default. Here is a list of web3 functions and objects which are visible one pressing tab for text completion at the console prompt -

```
> web3
Array           Number          _setInterval       encodeURIComponent   loadScript            toLocaleString
BigNumber       Object          _setTimeout        escape               miner                 toString
Boolean         RangeError      admin              eth                  net                   txpool
Date            ReferenceError  clearInterval      ethash               parseFloat            undefined
Error           RegExp          clearTimeout       eval                 parseInt              unescape
EvalError       String          console            hasOwnProperty       personal              valueOf
Function        SyntaxError     constructor        inspect              propertyIsEnumerable  web3
Infinity        TypeError       debug              isFinite             require
JSON            URIError        decodeURI          isNaN                rpc
Math            Web3            decodeURIComponent  isPrototypeOf        setInterval
NaN             XMLHttpRequest  encodeURI          jeth                 setTimeout
```

The web3 object is the gateway to an ethereum network and on hitting enter after typing web3, we get a complete listing of the available functions. Here are some concise portions of the output -

```
eth: {
  accounts: ["0x3ca0ea28c9dc92926ca49deb725cecb18db5db7d"],
  blockNumber: 0,
  coinbase: "0x3ca0ea28c9dc92926ca49deb725cecb18db5db7d",
```

```
  compile: {
    lll: function(),
    serpent: function(),
    solidity: function()
  },
  defaultAccount: undefined,
  defaultBlock: "latest",
  gasPrice: 1000000000,
  hashrate: 0,
  mining: false,
  pendingTransactions: [],
  protocolVersion: "0x3f",
  syncing: false,
  call: function(),
  chainId: function(),
  contract: function(abi),
  estimateGas: function(),
  filter: function(options, callback, filterCreationErrorCallback),
  getAccounts: function(callback),
  getBalance: function(),
  getBlock: function(),
  getBlockNumber: function(callback),
  getBlockTransactionCount: function(),
  getBlockUncleCount: function(),
  getCode: function(),
  getCoinbase: function(callback),
  getCompilers: function(),
  getGasPrice: function(callback),
  getHashrate: function(callback),
  getMining: function(callback),
```

```
ethash: {
  getHashrate: function(),
  getWork: function(),
  submitHashRate: function(),
  submitWork: function()
},
isIBAN: undefined,
miner: {
  getHashrate: function(),
  setEtherbase: function(),
  setExtra: function(),
  setGasPrice: function(),
  setRecommitInterval: function(),
  start: function(),
  stop: function()
},
```

The objects such as eth, admin, personal, etc. namespaces, are all by default accessible without requiring to explicitly refer to the web3 object.

We will now mine some blocks for our network using the miner management API.

```
> miner.start()
INFO [12-06|13:32:06.585] Updated mining threads                    threads=1
INFO [12-06|13:32:06.585] Transaction pool price threshold updated  price=1000000000
null
> INFO [12-06|13:32:06.586] Commit new mining work                  number=1 sealhash=1a4d9d…ea0138 uncles=0 txs=0
55µs
INFO [12-06|13:32:15.518] Generating DAG in progress                epoch=0 percentage=0 elapsed=7.719s
INFO [12-06|13:32:23.125] Generating DAG in progress                epoch=0 percentage=1 elapsed=15.327s
INFO [12-06|13:32:30.395] Generating DAG in progress                epoch=0 percentage=2 elapsed=22.596s

> miner.INFO [12-06|13:32:37.906] Generating DAG in progress         epoch=0 percentage=3 elapsed=30.107s
> miner.stop()
null
> INFO [12-06|13:32:45.735] Generating DAG in progress               epoch=0 percentage=4 elapsed=37.936s
INFO [12-06|13:32:53.748] Generating DAG in progress                epoch=0 percentage=5 elapsed=45.949s
INFO [12-06|13:33:01.353] Generating DAG in progress                epoch=0 percentage=6 elapsed=53.554s
INFO [12-06|13:33:08.203] Generating DAG in progress                epoch=0 percentage=7 elapsed=1m0.405s
```

The *miner.stop()* function when entered stops the mining process after the current mining session is completed till percentage=100 is reached.

A complete reference of the web3.eth API for javascript can be found here -

We will write a simple javascript function to print the balance in all accounts converted Wei to ether.

```
function checkAllBalances() {
  web3.eth.getAccounts(function(err, accounts) {
    accounts.forEach(function(id) {
      web3.eth.getBalance(id, function(err, balance) {
        console.log("" + id + ":\tbalance: " + web3.fromWei(balance, "ether") + " ether");
      });
    });
  });
  return true;
};
```

The script is loaded and run in the console -

```
> loadScript('/root/ether_scripts/check_balance.js')
true
> checkAllBalances()
0x3ca0ea28c9dc92926ca49deb725cecb18db5db7d:       balance: 1e-15 ether
true
```

During the startup of the ethereum node and console, we specified the APIs we want to be accessible through the RPC (HTTP) protocol. The other protocols supported by ethereum are

IPC (Inter Process Communication) and ws (WebSocket). It can be chosen to selectively make APIs available over each type of protocol.

We will create an account by sending a curl request to the RPC endpoint.

```
[root@ethereum-primary ~]# curl -X POST -H "Content-Type: application/json" \
> --data '{"jsonrpc":"2.0","method":"personal_newAccount","params":["account_three_pass"],"id":99}' \
> 10.10.0.239:8080
{"jsonrpc":"2.0","id":99,"result":"0xcbc84695527cff8830bda43a24ad0b947b0b9df2"}
```

The *method* key of the data section specifies the API method that is being invoked, which in this case is personal_newAccount. The *result* returned is the account address. The *id* key in data represents an arbitrary id value.

Now that the account has been created, we will send some ether between accounts.

```
> personal.listAccounts
["0x3ca0ea28c9dc92926ca49deb725cecb18db5db7d",
"0x91cc2687bbae33f7d859ba7278644a7ca9232adf",
"0xcbc84695527cff8830bda43a24ad0b947b0b9df2"]
>
```

The account from which we will send a transaction has to be first unlocked.

```
> personal.unlockAccount('0x3ca0ea28c9dc92926ca49deb725cecb18db5db7d')
Unlock account 0x3ca0ea28c9dc92926ca49deb725cecb18db5db7d
Passphrase:
true
```

A transaction is sent -

```
> eth.sendTransaction({
...... from: '0x3ca0ea28c9dc92926ca49deb725cecb18db5db7d',
...... to: '0x91cc2687bbae33f7d859ba7278644a7ca9232adf',
...... value: web3.toWei(1.0, 'ether')
...... })
INFO [12-06|19:09:05.293] Submitted transaction
fullhash=0x9f1e871bf9679e51856c10f9d739d1924673c08c659825448e45d957099ab0c3
recipient=0x91Cc2687BBAE33f7D859ba7278644a7Ca9232ADF
"0x9f1e871bf9679e51856c10f9d739d1924673c08c659825448e45d957099ab0c3"
>
```

The *web3.toWei* method converts the value *1.0 ether* into its equivalent wei units. The transaction details can be fetched using the *fullhash* value.

```
> eth.getTransaction('0x9f1e871bf9679e51856c10f9d739d1924673c08c659825448e45d957099ab0c3')
{
  blockHash: "0x0000000000000000000000000000000000000000000000000000000000000000",
  blockNumber: null,
```

```
  from: "0x3ca0ea28c9dc92926ca49deb725cecb18db5db7d",
  gas: 90000,
  gasPrice: 1000000000,
  hash: "0x9f1e871bf9679e51856c10f9d739d1924673c08c659825448e45d957099ab0c3",
  input: "0x",
  nonce: 5,
  r: "0x23c8d7c7dc9a6a22a572c923114d8c4077c0dc5df342004a2b1c372cc5548fb9",
  s: "0x41219aa8823e7b9a8ed49df7406e3f665c703e875b990785bdc77df91936ff01",
  to: "0x91cc2687bbae33f7d859ba7278644a7ca9232adf",
  transactionIndex: 0,
  v: "0x41",
  value: 1000000000000000000
}
```

If there are no new mined blocks available to hold the transactions, the account balances will wait to be updated until new blocks are mined as transactions will once again be able to execute.

We wrote a small function bal() to display the account balances.

```
> function bal(){
...   console.log(web3.eth.accounts[0].toString()+": "+web3.fromWei(web3.eth.getBalance(web3.eth.accounts[0])).toString());
...   console.log(web3.eth.accounts[1].toString()+": "+web3.fromWei(web3.eth.getBalance(web3.eth.accounts[1])).toString());
...   console.log(web3.eth.accounts[2].toString()+": "+web3.fromWei(web3.eth.getBalance(web3.eth.accounts[2])).toString());
... }
undefined
```

The state of the balances in the three accounts are as follows (after some transactions already made) -

```
> bal()
0x3ca0ea28c9dc92926ca49deb725cecb18db5db7d:  2930.000000000000001
0x91cc2687bbae33f7d859ba7278644a7ca9232adf:  2
0xcbc84695527cff8830bda43a24ad0b947b0b9df2:  13
undefined
```

In order for the transaction to take place we again mine some blocks by invoking the *miner. start* method.

```
INFO [12-06|19:31:44.283] Successfully sealed new block           number=590
INFO [12-06|19:31:44.283] ⏀block reached canonical chain          number=583
INFO [12-06|19:31:44.283] ⌃mined potential block                  number=590
INFO [12-06|19:31:44.283] Commit new mining work                  number=591
```

Now we can find the updated value in account.

```
> bal()
0x3ca0ea28c9dc92926ca49deb725cecb18db5db7d:  2959.000000000000001
0x91cc2687bbae33f7d859ba7278644a7ca9232adf:  3
0xcbc84695527cff8830bda43a24ad0b947b0b9df2:  13
undefined
```

Comparing the transaction details with after a successful transaction shows the changes. Here is the output of *eth.getTransaction* method right after creation of the transaction -

```
> eth.getTransaction('0x9f1e871bf9679e51856c10f9d739d1924673c08c659825448e45d957099ab0c3')
{
  blockHash: "0x0000000000000000000000000000000000000000000000000000000000000000",
  blockNumber: null,
  from: "0x3ca0ea28c9dc92926ca49deb725cecb18db5db7d",
  gas: 90000,
  gasPrice: 1000000000,
  hash: "0x9f1e871bf9679e51856c10f9d739d1924673c08c659825448e45d957099ab0c3",
  input: "0x",
  nonce: 5,
  r: "0x23c8d7c7dc9a6a22a572c923114d8c4077c0dc5df342004a2b1c372cc5548fb9",
  s: "0x41219aa8823e7b9a8ed49df7406e3f665c703e875b990785bdc77df91936ff01",
  to: "0x91cc2687bbae33f7d859ba7278644a7ca9232adf",
  transactionIndex: 0,
  v: "0x41",
  value: 1000000000000000000
}
```

As we can see no block has been allocated for this transaction as its specified as *null* in the *blockNumber* field.

Now after mining when the transaction details are checked again, the blockNumber field is changed from null to the block number which holds this transaction.

```
> eth.getTransaction('0x72ff90b8c8041698850cfbb98c6c638620d8a8eee0f5283621f546665b1a6cc3')
{
  blockHash: "0x4863971eb8e9ebc577f5baac91d6ca87c67ec79dc3e1b84fb4c51ea6443fcac9",
  blockNumber: 590,
  from: "0x3ca0ea28c9dc92926ca49deb725cecb18db5db7d",
  gas: 90000,
  gasPrice: 1000000000,
  hash: "0x72ff90b8c8041698850cfbb98c6c638620d8a8eee0f5283621f546665b1a6cc3",
  input: "0x",
  nonce: 6,
  r: "0x6aec7716d001b4112f86355a39c20f6e830ceb43e5a811b7f129ecc0c48f21ce",
  s: "0x36420dde481116e1c976b8a7bc87a027a48289c00d4ecd01da5c626551ee193b",
  to: "0x91cc2687bbae33f7d859ba7278644a7ca9232adf",
  transactionIndex: 0,
  v: "0x42",
  value: 1000000000000000000
}
```

The blockNumber *590* has been mined recently as we will find it in the snippet of the miner. start method's output.

# Solidity and contracts

We have learnt about Solidity, the language used popularly to program smart contracts and the compilation of that code is done by the Ethereum Virtual Machine (EVM). We will touch on some of the concepts that we have already discussed in the previous section and relate to them w.r.t. their connection with EVM and programmability of blockchain in general.

Every node in ethereum network runs the EVM as a part of *geth* client. Like most VMs, it runs in a sandboxed environment without access to filesystem or other processes.

We have already discussed in plenty how the two types of actors in ethereum are Externally Owned Accounts managed by human users and Contract Accounts that are managed by code written in Solidity and stored in a contract account. The two types of accounts are treated same by EVM as the fields in each account are the same. In case of a EOA, the bytecode field will remain empty as compared to a contract account and, both of the accounts contain balance as Wei (Ether).

## More about transactions

A transaction is the fingerprint of every such events in a blockchain network that change the state of the blockchain and are recorded in mined blocks. Since the only two types of actors in the network are the two types of accounts, the only times there occurs a change in blockchain state are when there is a transfer of ether between EOAs and another when a contract inside a contract account is used by an EOA or another contract such that the contract is involved in changing some data on the chain or transferring funds among accounts. Here we have just broadly generalised the use cases when accounts are involved in changing the chain data, without mentioning the obvious use cases of chain data change during creation of a contract or user, etc.

For creating a contract, a transaction has to be made and all transactions have the default structure of containing sender and receiver fields. For normal transfer of funds these fields would contain the addresses of the corresponding sender and recipient. But a transaction that creates a contract is addressed to the '0' zero address in the recipient field. The sender address of the contract is derived from the address of the EOA that issued the contract creation transaction, and the nonce. When a transaction for a contract creation is submitted it is compiled by the EVM and the output of EVM is permanently stored as code of the contract.

## Use of gas

We have discussed in the previous chapter about the concept of gas and how this is metaphor used in context with vehicles using fuel as a resource. Each transaction is charged with a certain amount of gas. Gas can be perceived as a limiting agent whose purpose is to limit the amount of work, in terms of execution of CPU cycles, usage of system resources, etc., that needs to be done to execute a transaction and in return pay for it. We have to understand why such a limiting factor is necessary in a blockchain based network. Since the network and its component nodes are not managed by a single company, there may be a bad actor who creates a rouge contract that suppose deliberately runs a loop for running for a long time and block the resources. A user when uses this rogue contract, the EVM will get stuck in this loop and therefore a limiting factor is required as processing power is the resource that has been democratised by a public blockchain. Not just during the use of the contract but also during the creation process of the contract. During creation the contract code is executed by the EVM and this process is repeated for every node on the network. Every node will have to verify the result of a transaction that invokes smart contract. The gas price is set by the creator of the the the contract, who will be paying wei according to gas price multiplied by gas allotted for the contract. This gas quantity can be set based on an estimate as returned by the estimateGas API method. The gas cost is collected up front before execution from the sender account of the contract and any remaining gas from after execution is returned to the account of the sender. If all the allotted gas is exhausted during the execution, an out of gas exception will be triggered which in turn will revert all the changes that were made to the state of data during execution of the steps of a contract.

## Storage, memory and stack

Every contract is associated with its own contract account, but if we refer to a diagram is the previous chapter, we may run into a confusion.

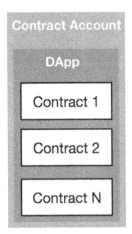

Here we see there are N number of contracts that are contained in a single contract account. We will get understand more about contracts in more detail in the succeeding section but to make a sense of the diagram with our definition, we take a reference to a generic structure of a solidity program script.

```
pragma solidity ^0.4.22;

contract One
{
    ...
}


contract Two
{
    One contract_object;
    ...
}
```

The above pseudo-snippet consists of two contract definitions that inside a solidity script. The contract keyword can be thought similar to that of classes as in object oriented programs. This script is representative of an example Dapp and upon compilation produces a single contract bytecode. Therefore, this contract although has definition for multiple contracts, will be bound to one contract account on creation. Now we know, like any program requires storage space for persistent data, each contract account is allotted a *storage* in the form of a key value store and each such store has a limit of 256 keys where the corresponding value is of size 256 bit words each. A contract has restricted access and cannot read/write to the storage space of other contracts.

Apart from persistent storage a program requires temporary volatile memory which is allocated to each contract. The memory space is not limited by EVM but obviously limited to the amount of RAM available to the executing node like any other program. A fresh instance of memory is allocated for every message or function call, and the reads are limited to words of size 256 bits. Writing to storage as well as memory, both are paid with gas, but the gas units for a single memory write is higher than storage and also the incentive paid in the form of gas increases with the increase in the size of used memory by a contract. That way, a a rogue contract cannot block available RAM with unnecessary data as a trickery to defer the availability of other RAM for other executions by a node.

For the computations the EVM uses a stack data structure in storing an expression. It has the maximum size of 1024 elements each of size 256 bits.

## EVM's instruction set

Solidity is a Turing complete language, but the instruction set is kept minimal and restricted. Such a design principle is important for a language that is running on a blockchain based system. A language such as C or Python are common choices for building applications that we traditionally have known. With the introduction of programmability to blockchain technology, it became very important to provide the programmer a constrained environment. Bugs are an unavoidable facet of programming that many times lead to catastrophic consequences. A public blockchain network is one where any such an event will have a widespread effect as it is by design a replicative system. A bug ridden Dapp will be copied to all the nodes and the consequence of any such bug will not be limited to a company as with centralised setup. Some modern day programming languages such as Python have a design philosophy of keeping the syntax and other programming constructs clean so that the chances of writing buggy code reduces. With a complex programming language it is easy for a programmer to make mistakes. Solidity has a fairly simple and relatable syntax, but the most importantly the instruction set is kept precise. The current generation of solidity should not be compared to other programming languages that we know. Programming on blockchain is a new concept and technology and so, it is unrealistic to think about creating full fledged applications. The usual types of problems that are faced by most applications such as memory leaking, null pointers, buffer overflows, etc. are due to the limitless capabilities that the instruction set provides and it becomes the responsibility of a programmer to avoid such bug events. With solidity's list of keywords, it is made sure that memory management and other such facets of programming are removed from the scope of the programmer.

## Calling library functions

Messages are the fundamental mode of communication on a blockchain such that a transaction call is wrapped inside a message call. There is a special variant of message calls in the form of *delegatecall*. With a message call, a contract can call another contract and on doing so the control and scope of the program transfers to the scope of the called function. *Delegatecall* gives the ability to dynamically load contract code from a different address into the scope of the current contract code. This constitutes the library function-call like feature of solidity.

## Deletion on blockchain

The blockchain is an additive system, where transaction data on the chain cannot be deleted, but this capability is available to contracts in the form of the *selfdestruct* keyword's usage. The code at the contract address is deleted and any remaining ether in the contract account is returned to the creator account of the contract.

Now that we have gained some prior idea about the schematics of the EVM and solidity, we will jump right into creating contracts with installation of solidity at first. According to the official documentation of solidity, it is a contract-oriented high level language inspired by C++, Python and JavaScript. The compiler for solidity is called *solcjs* and is written in JavaScript and so it is available as a NodeJS package.

We will install node and other required packages to write solidity from the CLI, but not right now.

```
yum install -y nodejs

npm i solc mocha ganache-cli web3@1.0.0-beta.26
```

The name for the current version of solidity compiler is *solcjs* but the name with which it is indexed in npm is *solc*. This is because perviously the used to be a solc compiler written in C++ with which code can be compiled and directly executed in the geth console, which is now deprecated.

*mocha* is a testing suite for solidity contracts. *ganache-cli* is a blockchain emulator on which the solidity contracts can be tested. *web3* is a JavaScript API using which we will interact with the ethereum network.

We will now write our first solidity script and for this we will use the online Remix browser (remix.ethereum.org) which provides a demo blockchain network right in the browser.

https://**remix.ethereum.org**/#optimize=false&version=soljson-v0.5.2+commit.1df8f40c.js

**browser/Dummy.sol** ✕

```
1   pragma solidity ^0.5.1;
2 ▾ contract Dummy{
3        string public message;
4
5 ▾     function setMessage(string memory initialMessage) public {
6            message = initialMessage;
7        }
8
9 ▾     function getMessage() public view returns (string memory) {
10           return  message;
11       }
12  }
13
14  |
```

We will get into the details of the contract code but first we will work our way through the remix browser. On the left of the browser, the various actions are available as the following -

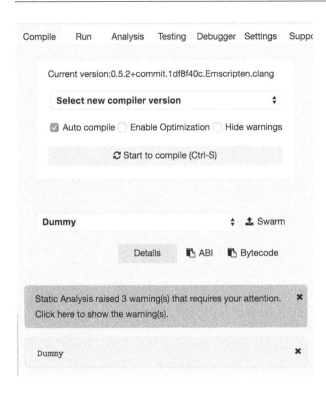

A successful compilation would show the created contract in the light green box, as shown at the bottom of the above image. The name of our contract is Dummy and it will be deployed into the built-in sample blockchain with the remix browser. The *Run* tab when clicked shows the following contents -

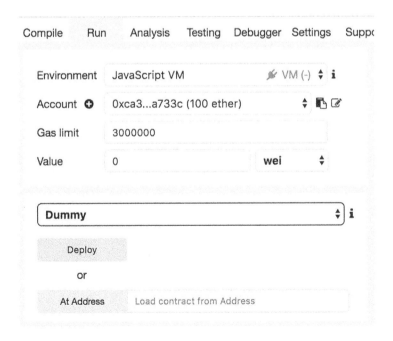

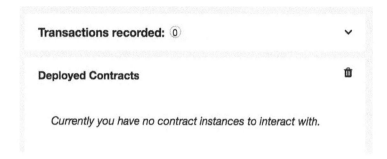

Here we can see that remix browser has created a sample account with 100 ether in it. On clicking the deploy button, the contract is deployed in the sample network inside the browser, as shown below -

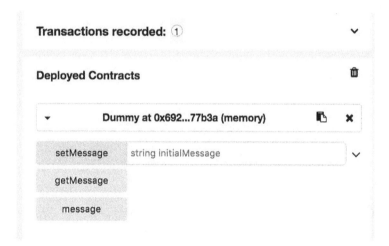

Our sample contract Dummy consists of two methods, *setMessage* which sets a string value to the contract variable message and the method *getMessage* which outputs the value set into the message variable. The following diagram shows the usage of this contract -

The remix browser is a good tool to check the behaviour of a contract before deploying it to the actual network.

We are going to walkthrough some example contracts as provided in the official documentation of solidity. The following example contract is for creating a voting contract that emulates an actual electronic voting process.

```solidity
pragma solidity ^0.5.1;


contract Ballot
{

    struct Voter {
        uint weight;
        bool voted;
        address delegate;
        uint vote;
    }


    struct Proposal {
        bytes32 name;
        uint voteCount;
    }

    address public chairperson;


    mapping(address => Voter) public voters;


    Proposal[] public proposals;

}
```

The first line tells the EVM about the version of the compiler to be used, which in this case is compiler versions greater than 0.5.1.

The name of the contract is *Ballot* and the contract keywords should be thought similar to that of a class.

The Voter is a struct definition that defines a complex datatype that will represent a single voter.

A voter may cast his or her vote, or choose to delegate the vote to another person who would vote on behalf. When a certain person who also is a voter, is delegated to vote on someone's behalf, the *weight* field of *Voter* struct is set with unsigned integer type of data (uint).

The *voted* field stores boolean type of data and contains true if a person voted.

The *delegate* field contains the account address of the person who has been delegated to vote on behalf of another person and so it has a datatype of *address*.

The vote field contains the index of the proposal or candidate who has been nominated.

The *Proposal* struct is another complex datatype used to define a candidate proposal for voting. Instances of this type will be the nominated candidates for whom votes will be cast. Each such proposal has a name field and the voteCount field would contain the count of the votes the candidate receives.

The *chairperson* variable would contain the address of the chairperson for the hosting of vote and it is only a chairperson who has the privilege of creating a ballot.

The mapping datatype is used for declaring a hash table and in this case the *voters* variable contains the addresses of accounts of all voters. In the statement *mapping(address => Voter) public voters*, the address keyword specifies the datatype of each key in the hash table and *Voter* represents the type of the value corresponding to a key.

*proposals* variable is a list of the nominated candidate proposals of the type *Proposal*.

```
constructor(bytes32[] memory proposalNames, address cperson) public {
    chairperson = cperson;
    voters[chairperson].weight = 1;

    /// logging the address of chairperson
    log1(bytes32("Chairperson: "),bytes32(uint256(chairperson) << 96));

    for (uint i = 0; i < proposalNames.length; i++)
    {

        proposals.push(Proposal({
            name: proposalNames[i],
            voteCount: 0
        }));
    }
    /// logging the address
    log1(bytes32("Proposal Count: "),bytes32(proposalNames.length));
}
```

Like in the case of a class, the constructor function gets called during creation of its instance, same in the case of a contract. The constructor takes as input a list of proposed candidate names and the address of the person invoking the contract. The *memory* keyword is used to tell the EVM to load the input data into RAM. The *public* keyword is used for variables that we wish to access from outside the contract. In the above snippet, during creation of a Ballot contract, first the name of the chairperson is stored in the *voters* mapping (hash table) with weight set to

1, as delegation has been provided to host the voting. As we have mentioned how every call in ethereum is wrapped inside a message call, therefore, the call to create a contract by invoking the constructor function is a message object which can be accessed from inside a contract with the identifier *msg*. Our Ballot contract will be invoked from another contract and so the input parameter *cperson* would contain the account address of chairperson. We will shortly, learn how the control will flow through the life-cycle of the voting exercise. We have introduced logging throughout the contract with *logN()* method. Here the value for N in logN is 1, which means it will have two input parameters. The parameter *bytes32(uint265(chairperson) << 96)* converts the hexadecimal address of the chairperson to bytes32 format.

Next, the entire list of proposed candidate names are stored into the *proposals* list instance variable.

```
function giveRightToVote(address voter, address sender) public
{
    require(
        sender == chairperson,
        "Only chairperson can give right to vote."
    );
    require(
        !voters[voter].voted,
        "The voter already voted."
    );
    /// logging the address
    log1(bytes32("Giving rights to: "),bytes32(uint256(voter) << 96));

    require(voters[voter].weight == 0,"Already rights given!");
    voters[voter].weight = 1;
    voters[voter].voted = false;
}
```

In this member function, a voter is given the right to vote, based upon the conditions that, only the chairperson can give the right to vote to a person. The *require()* function checks if the function was invoked by the account of the chairperson and if it is false, the quoted texted is displayed and exited from the function. The second condition checks if a voter has already cast a vote. The last condition checks if the weight field of a voter is set to 0, and then the right to vote is awarded with the weight field set to 1.

```
function delegate(address delegator, address to) public
{
    Voter memory sender = voters[delegator];
    require(!sender.voted, "You already voted.");

    require(to != delegator, "Self-delegation is disallowed.");
```

```
    voters[delegator].voted = true;
    voters[delegator].delegate = to;

    Voter storage delegate_ = voters[to];
    if (delegate_.voted) {

        proposals[delegate_.vote].voteCount += sender.weight;
    } else {

        delegate_.weight += sender.weight;
    }
}
```

As from the name of the function we may guess, that this member function is called when a voter does not want to directly cast the vote, and instead delegates someone else from the list of voters to vote on the person's behalf. The input to the function is the address of the person to who is being delegated on the sender's behalf and the address of the delegator. The *storage* keyword specifies the usage of the persistent storage provided with each contract. Since the sender of the function invocation message has delegated the vote, the *voter[delegator].voted* field is set to true. The person who has been delegated to cast a vote on someone's behalf, the choice of proposed candidate for that person will be considered the choice of the delegator. That is why, *proposals[delegate_.vote].voteCount* is incremented.

```
function vote(uint proposal, address voter) payable public
{
    /// logging the voter
    log1(bytes32("Voter Addr: "),bytes32(uint256(voter) << 96));

    require(voters[voter].weight == 1,"No voting right!");
    require(!voters[voter].voted, "Already voted.");

    Voter memory sender = voters[voter];


    voters[voter].voted = true;
    voters[voter].vote = proposal;
    proposals[proposal].voteCount += sender.weight;
}
```

This function is called to cast a vote. The function of payable type because casting a vote would require certain amount of ether to be spent.

```
function winningProposal() public view
        returns (uint winningProposal_)
{
    uint winningVoteCount = 0;
    for (uint p = 0; p < proposals.length; p++) {
        if (proposals[p].voteCount > winningVoteCount) {
            winningVoteCount = proposals[p].voteCount;
            winningProposal_ = p;
        }
    }
}
```

The *view* keyword is used in case of this member function because it returns a value which will be displayed, which in this case is the index of the winning candidate in the list *proposals*.

```
function winnerName() public view
        returns (bytes32 winnerName_)
{
    winnerName_ = proposals[winningProposal()].name;
}
```

This function displays the name of the winning candidate from the index returned by *winningProposal* member function.

This was our entire contract definition, but to invoke this contract, we will create another contract where this contract will be instantiated.

```
pragma solidity >=0.4.22 <0.6.0;
import "./Ballot.sol";

contract HostBallot {

    Ballot ballotToTest;
    bytes32[] candidateProposals;


    function beforeAll () public
    {
        candidateProposals.push("Person A");
```

```
        candidateProposals.push("Person B");
        candidateProposals.push("Person C");
        ballotToTest = new Ballot(candidateProposals, msg.sender);
        ballotToTest.giveRightToVote(0x14723A09ACff6D2A60DcdF7aA4AFf308FDDC160C,msg.sender);
        ballotToTest.giveRightToVote(0x4B0897b0513fdC7C541B6d9D7E929C4e5364D2dB,msg.sender);
        ballotToTest.giveRightToVote(0x583031D1113aD414F02576BD6afaBfb302140225,msg.sender);
        ballotToTest.giveRightToVote(0xdD870fA1b7C4700F2BD7f44238821C26f7392148,msg.sender);

    }


        function delegatetion(address delegateTo) public
        {
            ballotToTest.delegate(msg.sender, delegateTo);
        }

        function castVote(uint proposal) public
        {
            ballotToTest.vote(proposal,msg.sender);
        }

        function winner() public view
            returns (bytes32 winner)
        {
            winner = ballotToTest.winnerName();
        }
    }
```

First the ballot.sol contract is imported and a instance ballotToTest is created. The addresses that are granted the rights to vote are ethereum address checksum converted. The remix browser loads with some sample accounts as we can see here -

These addresses are initially not checksum compliant, so we are going to select and copy an address at a time and use an online tool - ethsum.netlify.com to convert the address to checksum version.

# Ethereum Address Checksum

◆  0x4B0897b0513fdC7C541B6d9D7E929C4e5364D2dB

Address has been checksummed

**SUBMIT**

We will now understand the flow of control w.r.t. every action. Remix browser initially provides five accounts. We select one of the accounts to create the contract *HostBallot* defined in *test_ballot.solc*. The contract *Ballot* will be instantiated inside the contract *HostBallot* and we want to designate the creator of the contract *HostBallot* as the chairperson. With the *HostBallot* selected under the Run tab, the contract is deployed with the *Deploy* button.

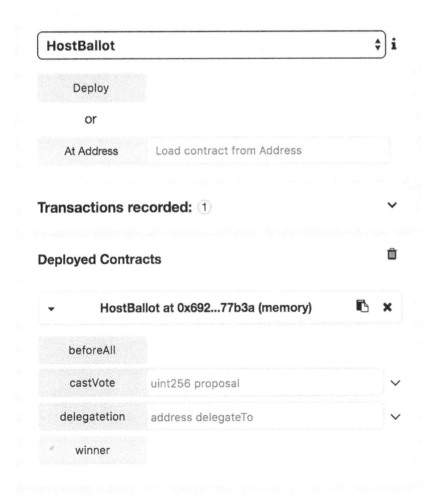

| HostBallot | ⬍ | i |

Deploy

or

At Address    Load contract from Address

**Transactions recorded:** ① ⌄

**Deployed Contracts** 🗑

▼     **HostBallot at 0x692...77b3a (memory)**    📋  ✕

beforeAll

castVote    uint256 proposal    ⌄

delegatetion    address delegateTo    ⌄

winner

The deployed contract has three methods that change some data on the chain and so the buttons depicting each of the methods are differently coloured than that of the method winner, which is of *view* type. The creation of the contract will be notified in the console output as the following -

```
creation of HostBallot pending...

[vm]  from:0xca3...a733c to:HostBallot.(constructor) value:0 wei
      data:0x608...50029 logs:0 hash:0xf59...f7759                          Debug   ∨
```

Now we have to create the *Ballot* contract by calling the *beforeAll* method with that account selected, which we want to be made the chairperson. The *Ballot* contract will not be visible as a deployed contract in the right panel of remix browser, but it will be deployed at a particular address. The console output of the transaction will provide a lot of information and so we are going to investigate the details to see if the actions were desired.

> [vm]  **from:**0xca3...a733c **to:**HostBallot.beforeAll() 0x692...77b3a **value:**0 wei
> **data:**0x7fe...a0d4b **logs:6 hash:**0x7c4...30c4e

| status | 0x1 Transaction mined and execution succeed |
|---|---|
| transaction hash | 0x7c451158ef3d34b3c393e54edab50a6712b08b9d7d41cfca1886b8d465730c4e 📋 |
| from | 0xca35b7d915458ef540ade6068dfe2f44e8fa733c 📋 |
| to | HostBallot.beforeAll() 0x692a70d2e424a56d2c6c27aa97d1a86395877b3a 📋 |
| gas | 3000000 gas 📋 |
| transaction cost | 1236332 gas 📋 |
| execution cost | 1215060 gas 📋 |
| hash | 0x7c451158ef3d34b3c393e54edab50a6712b08b9d7d41cfca1886b8d465730c4e 📋 |
| input | 0x7fe...a0d4b 📋 |

The *from* key represents the address of the account that generated the message to call the *beforeAll* method. The *To* key tells about the method name which is stored in the contract at the address -

0x692a70d2e424a56d2c6c27aa97d1a86395877b3a

We will skip over the logging done inside the constructor and straightaway checkout logging inside the *giveRightToVote* method as called from inside *beforeAll*.

Here we are showing just two of the four calls to the *giveRightToVote* method -

```
ballotToTest.giveRightToVote(0x14723A09ACff6D2A60DcdF7aA4AFf308FDDC160C,msg.sender);
ballotToTest.giveRightToVote(0x4B0897b0513fdC7C541B6d9D7E929C4e5364D2dB,msg.sender);
ballotToTest.giveRightToVote(0x583031D1113aD414F02576BD6afaBfb302140225,msg.sender);
ballotToTest.giveRightToVote(0xdD870fA1b7C4700F2BD7f44238821C26f7392148,msg.sender);
```

```
        {
                "from": "0x755014da263fc47d238078bb47d217f743e5b6a
5",
                "data": "0x476976696e67207269676768747320746f3a20000
00000000000000000000000000",
                "topics": [
                        "0x14723a09acff6d2a60dcdf7aa4aff308fddc160
c00000000000000000000000000"
                ]
        },
        {
                "from": "0x755014da263fc47d238078bb47d217f743e5b6a
5",
                "data": "0x476976696e67207269676768747320746f3a20000
00000000000000000000000000",
                "topics": [
                        "0x4b0897b0513fdc7c541b6d9d7e929c4e5364d2d
b00000000000000000000000000"
                ]
        },
```

The output of logN functions contains three fields - *from*, *data* and *topics*. Here is the logging statement corresponding to the output -

```
/// logging the address
log1(bytes32("Giving rights to: "),bytes32(uint256(voter) << 96));
```

The *data* key in the log output represents the first parameter to *log1()*. Since the contents are in hexadecimal, we will use an online hexadecimal to string converter. We although could have written a helper method inside our contract to convert the same, but it is better to keep a contract as lean as possible due to the limited storage capability in current generation blockchain, and also for the fact, that it is always a good idea to keep only the code that is closely relevant to the task at hand. We are using codebutify.org/hex-string-converter -

**Enter the hexadecimal text to decode**　　　　　　🗑 get

0x476976696e6720726967687473206f3a200000000000000000000000000000000

**Convert**　　　　**Load**　　　　**Browse**

**The decoded string:**

Giving rights to:

As we can see the *data* key's content represents the text - "Giving rights to".

The next parameter in log1() is the address of the voter and it is represented in the console output in the *topics* key.

```
                    "topics": [
                        "0x14723a09acff6d2a60dcdf7aa4aff308fddc160
c0000000000000000000000000"
                    ]
```

This address is corresponding to the address -

```
ballotToTest.giveRightToVote(0x14723A09ACff6D2A60DcdF7aA4AFf308FDDC160C,msg.sender);
```

We have three candidates and the first vote will be cast by the chairperson by invoking the method *castVote* -

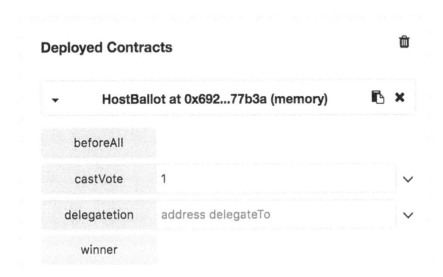

When the castVote method is called, a message is generated and the sender address of this message is sent to the vote method of Ballot contract.

```
function castVote(uint proposal) public
{
    ballotToTest.vote(proposal,msg.sender);
}
```

Since a person or more accurately an account can vote only once, a castVote method call with the account unchanged will result in a error situation as the following -

```
[vm] from:0xca3...a733c to:HostBallot.castVote(uint256) 0x692...77b3a        Debug   ⌄
value:0 wei data:0x3eb...00001 logs:0 hash:0x845...2659e

transact to HostBallot.castVote errored: VM error: revert.
revert  The transaction has been reverted to the initial state.
Reason provided by the contract: "Already voted.".     Debug the transaction to get more informa
tion.
```

Each action that changes or adds data to the chain costs ether and so after each of these transaction we will notice a decrease in the total amount of sample ether provided in each account by remix. We select other accounts and cast the votes. One of the accounts delegated the chairperson to vote and the following snip shows the invocation -

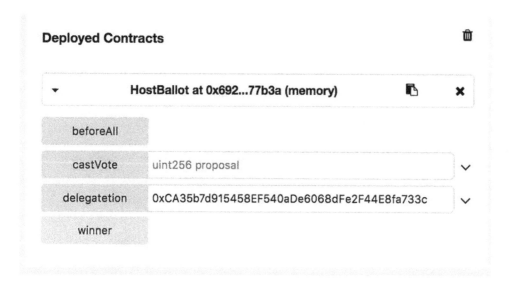

Finally, after all the accounts have cast their votes, the winner will be returned on invoking the winner method.

The result of the winner method is returned as a hexadecimal value, so we will use our online convertor to check out the winner -

**Enter the hexadecimal text to decode**                    🗑 get :

0x506572736f6e20420000000000000000000000000000000000000000000000000000

| Convert | Load | Browse |

**The decoded string:**

Person B

We have a general idea about handling solidity code, and so we will move to the next chapter where we see how JavaScript is related to solidity code and the use of other JavaScript packages that we have installed.

# Web3 in Python and JS

Web3 is a library to connect to an ethereum network, written in JavaScript and available as *web3.js*. It is also implemented in other languages and we are going to use the Python implementation which is *Web3.py*. With the knowledge we have accumulated about decentralised networks from the previous chapters, we can conclude that ethereum is no different than a new internet. Our current version of the internet which we call web2.0 is an inter-connection among servers from various companies and individuals that all work on the established web standards. The web2.0 is governed by the w3 consortium, which regularises the security and other web standards, but still the web protocols are not able to make the entire web trustful and secure. This is because unlike ethereum, where each node has to run the ethereum client application to participate in the inter-network, the world wide web has no such controlled and constrained environment that would qualify a server to join the internet. In such a constrained environment with ethereum, the fundamental thing that can be ensured, is that, every node on the network will have the same set of capabilities and limits. For example, the current web2.0 has a large portion of hosted websites that use an unencrypted HTTP channel for communication, and as a result privacy and security is hampered. The ethereum network as we have learnt is heavy on security at each step through the use of encryptions and therefore is rightfully called the web 3.0. Web3 is an implementation of the necessary service DNS, for identification and discovery of other entities on the network.

We will first prepare our host machine to have Python3.6 installed and the web3 Python Pip package. We will setup a separate host from where we will connect to our private ethereum network.

```
yum install -y https://centos7.iuscommunity.org/ius-release.rpm
yum install -y python36u python36u-libs python36u-devel python36u-pip
```

```
pip install web3
```

On this host we will create a simple solidity script and compile it with NodeJS as we have stated earlier that the *solcjs* compiler is implemented in JavaScript.

We will start with creating a project directory with the name simple_inbox -

```
[root@ethereum eth_scripts]# cd simple_inbox/
[root@ethereum simple_inbox]# ll
total 0
```

Before writing any code, we will setup our directory for NodeJS as the following -

```
[root@ethereum simple_inbox]# npm init .
This utility will walk you through creating a package.json file.
It only covers the most common items, and tries to guess sensible defaults.

See `npm help json` for definitive documentation on these fields
and exactly what they do.

Use `npm install <pkg> --save` afterwards to install a package and
save it as a dependency in the package.json file.

Press ^C at any time to quit.
name: (simple_inbox)
version: (1.0.0)
description:
entry point: (index.js)
test command:
git repository:
keywords:
author:
license: (ISC)
About to write to /root/eth_scripts/simple_inbox/package.json:

{
  "name": "simple_inbox",
  "version": "1.0.0",
  "description": "",
  "main": "index.js",
  "scripts": {
    "test": "echo \"Error: no test specified\" && exit 1"
  },
  "author": "",
  "license": "ISC"
}

Is this ok? (yes) yes
```

This will create a *package.json* file. The *npm init* command prompts for user inputs which we have left our to defaults by just clicking enter for all entries for this sample project.

Next we create our source file in a directory we choose to name contracts.

```
[root@ethereum simple_inbox]# tree .
.
├── contracts
│   └── SimpleInbox.sol
└── package.json
```

And here is our source solidity script -

```
[root@ethereum simple_inbox]# cat contracts/SimpleInbox.sol
pragma solidity ^0.4.25;
contract SimpleInbox{
    string public message;

    function setMessage(string memory initialMessage) public {
        message = initialMessage;
    }

    function getMessage() public view returns (string memory) {
        return  message;
    }
}
```

In order to compiler our solidity script, we will create a index.js file -

```
[root@ethereum simple_inbox]# ll
total 4
drwxr-xr-x. 2 root root  28 Jan  8 05:21 contracts
-rw-r--r--. 1 root root   0 Jan  8 05:24 index.js
-rw-r--r--. 1 root root 208 Jan  8 04:54 package.json
```

After this we npm install the *solcjs* compiler specific to our application directory in the following way -

```
[root@ethereum simple_inbox]# npm install --save solc@0.4.25
simple_inbox@1.0.0 /root/eth_scripts/simple_inbox
└─┬ solc@0.4.25
  ├─┬ fs-extra@0.30.0
  │ ├── graceful-fs@4.1.15
  │ ├── jsonfile@2.4.0
  │ ├── klaw@1.3.1
  │ ├── path-is-absolute@1.0.1
```

Here portion of the output has been truncated, and the installation creates the following node_modules directory -

```
[root@ethereum simple_inbox]# ll
total 12
drwxr-xr-x.  2 root root   28 Jan  8 05:21 contracts
-rw-r--r--.  1 root root  312 Jan  8 05:36 index.js
drwxr-xr-x. 69 root root 4096 Jan  8 05:43 node_modules
-rw-r--r--.  1 root root  255 Jan  8 05:43 package.json
```

We install the other packages as well -

```
[root@ethereum simple_inbox]# npm install npm i web3@1.0.0-beta.26 mocha ganache-cli
```

and finally compile our index.js file.

Here is the contents of the index.js file -

```
[root@ethereum simple_inbox]# cat  index.js
const path = require('path');
const fs = require ('fs');
const solc = require('solc');



const projectPath = path.resolve(__dirname,'contracts','SimpleInbox.sol');
const src = fs.readFileSync(projectPath,'utf8');

console.log(solc.compile(src,1));
```

As we can see we will be displaying the output of the compilation with console.log, the following snippet is a portion of the output -

```
[root@ethereum simple_inbox]# node index.js
{ contracts:
   { ':SimpleInbox':
     { assembly: [Object],
       bytecode: '608060405234801561001057600080fd5b5061035580610020600039600 0f30060806040526004361061005657
00000000000000000000000000000000000000006000350416633668b8772811461005b578063ce6d41de146100b6578063e21f37ce14610
00080fd5b5060408051602060048035808201356 01f810184900484028501840190955528484526100b49436949293602493928401919 0
559650505050505050565b005b3480156100c257600080fd5b506100cb61016c565b6040805160208082528351818301528351919283 9
015610101055781810151838201526020001610 0ed565b5050505090509081019060011680156101013257808203805160018360020036101001 00
5060405180910390f35b34801561014c57600080fd5b506100cb610203565b80516101016890600090602084019061029156 5b5050565b6
961010060018816150201909516949094049 38401819004810282018101909252828152606009390929091830182820156101f8578060
9160200191610191600052620060002090 5b815481529060001019060200188 3116101db57829003601f168201915b5505
0516020600260018516156101000 26000190190941693909304601 f810184900484028201840190925281815292918301828280156102
0402835291602001916102895565b8 20191906006002520200600020905b8154815290600010190602001 80831161026c57829003601f16820
160011615610100020316600029 00490600052620060002090601f0160 20900481019282601f10610 2d257805160ff191683800117855 5
02ff579182015b828111156102ff578251825591601 6020019190600010190610 2e4565b5061030b9291 5061030f565b5090565b61020 0919
16103155600a165627a7a72305820730 3775d19a1af9426c8ea5063ad9a19 027f6539de993904b5da2f6e415ab8e70029',
       functionHashes: [Object],
       gasEstimates: [Object],
       interface: '[{"constant":false,"inputs":[{"name":"initialMessage","type":"string"}],"name":"setMessag
"stateMutability":"nonpayable","type":"function"},{"constant":true,"inputs":[],"name":"getMessage","outputs":
ayable":false,"stateMutability":"view","type":"function"},{"constant":true,"inputs":[],"name":"message","outp
}],"payable":false,"stateMutability":"view","type":"function"}]',
       metadata: '{"compiler":{"version":"0.4.25+commit.59dbf8f1"},"language":"Solidity","output":{"abi":[{"
":"initialMessage","type":"string"}],"name":"setMessage","outputs":[],"payable":false,"stateMutability":"nonp
stant":true,"inputs":[],"name":"getMessage","outputs":[{"name":"","type":"string"}],"payable":false,"stateMut
"},{"constant":true,"inputs":[],"name":"message","outputs":[{"name":"","type":"string"}],"payable":false,"sta
ction"}],"devdoc":{"methods":{}},"userdoc":{"methods":{}}},"settings":{"compilationTarget":{"":"SimpleInbox"}
```

The solidity compiler produces two things - a) an ABI (Application Binary Interface) and b) solidity bytecode. The ABI is the interface which will is used as a communication layer between solidity bytecode and any programming language like JavaScript or Python. As to the concept of API, where a system allows accessing of its features through predefined function calls to the system, that can be made from an external program. The ABI is such an interface to the compiled binary. The binary in this case is the bytecode which will be deployed in the blockchain. Here is a diagram depicting the usage of both ABI and bytecode in a test network which we are going to create with ganache -

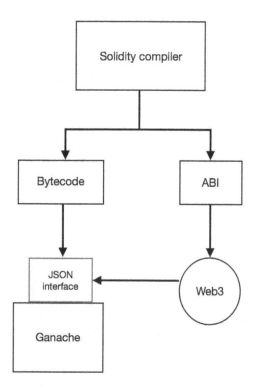

As stated, the solidity compiler produces two artefacts, the ABI and the bytecode. The bytecode is the binary Dapp corresponding to our solidity code. This bytecode is no longer human readable code, so when it is placed in the ethereum network, there must be some way for an application program to interact with it. The snippet we saw earlier as produced by the compilation was crammed all together, so here is a clean formatted portion of the ABI -

```
[
    {
            "constant": false,
            "inputs": [
                    {
                            "name": "initialMessage",
                            "type": "string"
                    }
            ],
            "name": "setMessage",
            "outputs": [],
```

```
        "payable": false,
        "stateMutability": "nonpayable",
        "type": "function"
    },
    {

        "constant": true,
        "inputs": [],
        "name": "getMessage",
        "outputs": [
            {
                        "name": "",
                        "type": "string"
            }
        ],
        "payable": false,
        "stateMutability": "view",
        "type": "function"
    },
```

The ABI as we can see is human readable JSON formatted compared to the bytecode, which is ready to be run in the EVM, exactly like how Java bytecode runs in JVM -

```
bytecode: '6060604052341561000f57600080fd5
00000000000000000000000006000350416633681
c6004602481358181019083013580602060601f82018
156100b957600080fd5b6100c1610162565b60405
5020016100e5565b5050505090509081019060601f168
4357600080fd5b6100c161020b565b60008180516
16020809104026020016040519081016040528092
835291602001916161020200565b820191906000526020
0018160011615610100020316600290004800601f010
6102a15780601f10610276576101008083540402833
68201915b5050505050508156b828054600181600011
8555610317565b8280016001018555821561031757
6040519081016040526000815290565b61020891905
```

The bytecode gets deployed in a contract account and when the contract has to be interacted, it can be do with the web3 interface which serves as a gateway to the ethereum network. The ABI is basically JSON definition which means it is not dependant on any language. We are going to see how this ABI is bind with the web3 instance to connect to the contract on the chain. The remix browser that we used in the previous chapter also emulates a demo network in the browser, but we are going to also learn the use of ganache demo test network from CLI.

Our contract has compiled successfully so we are going to use the mocha testing framework to test our *simple_inbox* Dapp.

We start with creating a test directory where we will put our testing script *simple_inbox. test.js* -

```
[[root@ethereum simple_inbox]# ll
total 28
drwxr-xr-x.   2 root root    28 Jan  8 08:30 contracts
-rw-r--r--.   1 root root   312 Jan  8 05:36 index.js
drwxr-xr-x. 351 root root 12288 Jan  8 05:52 node_modules
-rw-r--r--.   1 root root  2693 Jan  8 11:37 npm-debug.log
-rw-r--r--.   1 root root   299 Jan  8 11:32 package.json
drwxr-xr-x.   2 root root    33 Jan  8 11:42 test
[[root@ethereum simple_inbox]# tree test
test
└── simple_inbox.test.js
```

Mocha has a very limited set of functions in the form of *it*, *describe* and *beforeEach*, that will be used for writing our tests. Testing involves a lot of assertions where we check if a variable or the returned value of a function during the execution phase, contains the desired value. The *it* function does exactly that, by echoing assertions. The *describe* function is used to group it statements together under a namespace. The *beforeEach* function from the name itself gives us the idea that, it will be used whenever certain steps have to be executed before each testing statement.

The dependant packages we will be using are ganache-cli@6.0.3, mocha@4.0.1, solc@0.4.19, asyncawait@1.0.7 and web3@1.0.0-beta.26 specific for our project -

```
[root@ethereum simple_inbox]# npm install --save solc@0.4.19
[root@ethereum simple_inbox]# npm install --save ganache-cli@6.0.3
[root@ethereum simple_inbox]# npm install --save mocha@4.0.1
[root@ethereum simple_inbox]# npm install --save web3@1.0.0-beta.26
[root@ethereum simple_inbox]# npm install --save asyncawait@1.0.7
```

Our project contains the package.json file where we will define the packages as following -

```
{
  "name": "simple_inbox",
  "version": "1.0.0",
  "description": "",
  "main": "index.js",
  "scripts": {
    "test": "mocha"
  },
  "author": "",
  "license": "ISC",
  "dependencies": {
    "asyncawait": "^1.0.7",
    "ganache-cli": "^6.0.3",
    "mocha": "^4.0.1",
```

```
    "solc": "^0.4.19",
    "web3": "^1.0.0-beta.26",
    "asyncawait": "1.0.7"
  }
}
```

Since we are using the mocha testing framework, the scripts key is given the value *mocha* for *test*.

Here is the content of our test script where we first check if the contract is being successfully deployed -

```
const assert = require('assert');
const ganache = require('ganache-cli');
const Web3 = require('web3');
const { interface, bytecode } = require('../index');
const async = require('asyncawait/async');
const await = require('asyncawait/await');

const w3 = new Web3(ganache.provider());


let accounts;
let simpleInbox;



const doThis = async(function () {

  // Fetch accounts from ganache
  accounts = await (w3.eth.getAccounts());

  // Use one of the accounts to deploy the contract
  simpleInbox = await (new w3.eth.Contract(JSON.parse(interface))
  .deploy({ data: bytecode, arguments: ['dotdash'] })
  .send({ from: accounts[0], gas: '1000000', gasPrice: '3000'}));

});

beforeEach(doThis);
```

The *beforeEach* function invokes *doThis*, in which, first all accounts are fetched. The *w3* variable contains an instance of *Web3* using the provider the ganache demo network. A provider in the context of Web3 is a connection builder with an ethereum network. In a very simple analogy, a Web3 provider can be though of a browser for the ethereum inter-network as corresponding to the web browsers that we use for surfing the web2.0.

```
describe('Testing for SimpleInbox Contract',() => {

  it('deploys a contract',() => {
    console.log(simpleInbox);
  });

});
```

In the *beforeEach* function call, the first parameter is just a description of the testing block. Right now we are only interested in testing if the contract is being successfully deployed and so, there is only one *it* statement in the *beforeEach* block which simply asserts the value returned on of deploying the contract. After creation of the contract, we print the contract object as contained as returned by *eth.Contract()*. Here is the output of running the test -

```
[root@ethereum simple_inbox]# npm run test

> simple_inbox@1.0.0 test /root/eth_scripts/simple_inbox
> mocha



  Testing for SimpleInbox Contract
Contract {
  currentProvider: [Getter/Setter],
  _requestManager:
   RequestManager {
     provider: Provider { options: [Object], engine: [Object], manager: [Object] },
     providers:
      { WebsocketProvider: [Function: WebsocketProvider],
        HttpProvider: [Function: HttpProvider],
        IpcProvider: [Function: IpcProvider] },
     subscriptions: {} },
  givenProvider: null,
  providers:
   { WebsocketProvider: [Function: WebsocketProvider],
     HttpProvider: [Function: HttpProvider],
     IpcProvider: [Function: IpcProvider] },
  _provider:
```

Some portion of the output has been omitted. The trailing section of the output is as follows -

```
  _jsonInterface:
   [ { constant: false,
       inputs: [Object],
       name: 'setMessage',
       outputs: [],
       payable: false,
       stateMutability: 'nonpayable',
       type: 'function',
       signature: '0x368b8772' },
     { constant: true,
       inputs: [],
       name: 'getMessage',
       outputs: [Object],
       payable: false,
       stateMutability: 'view',
       type: 'function',
       signature: '0xce6d41de' },
     { constant: true,
       inputs: [],
       name: 'message',
       outputs: [Object],
       payable: false,
       stateMutability: 'view',
       type: 'function',
       signature: '0xe21f37ce' } ] }
  ✓ deploys a contract


1 passing (271ms)
```

Now for the next test, we will use the setMessage and getMessage methods in our contact. The corresponding definition of the *describe* block after adding our new test is as the following -

```
describe('Testing for SimpleInbox Contract',() => {

  it('deploys a contract',() => {
   console.log("The contract address is: "+simpleInbox._address);
   assert.ok(simpleInbox._address);
  });


  it('set and display a  message', async( function() {
    await( simpleInbox.methods.setMessage('dotdash').send({from: accounts[0] })
    .then(function(result){  }));
    const message = await (simpleInbox.methods.getMessage().call());
    console.log("The message is: "+message);
    assert.equal(message,'dotdash')
  }));
```

The output of executing the test is as follows -

```
[root@ethereum simple_inbox]# npm run test

> simple_inbox@1.0.0 test /root/eth_scripts/simple_inbox
> mocha



  Testing for SimpleInbox Contract
The contract address is: 0xC290C59294aF9F6A798e14345ede2f85D2acC61E
    ✓ deploys a contract
The message is: dotdash
    ✓ contains default message (192ms)


  2 passing (562ms)
```

With the testing phase over, the last thing we will be doing is to deploy our contract on our private ethereum test network using Python. Our aim is to have a way with web3 in both languages Python and JavaScript.

We need to install the required packages for the Python implementation -

```
[root@ethereum simple_inbox]# pip install py-solc
[root@ethereum simple_inbox]# pip install web3
```

```
[root@ethereum simple_inbox]# python -m solc.install v0.4.19
[root@ethereum simple_inbox]# npm install -g solc-cli
```

The py-solc library is a wrapper around the solc binary which gets installed at the location *$HOME/. py-solc/solc-v0.4.25/bin/solc* from the list of locations where we can see solc made changes -

```
[root@eth-test ~]# find / -name solc
/root/.py-solc/solc-v0.4.25/bin/solc
/root/.npm/registry.npmjs.org/solc
/root/.npm/solc
/tmp/npm-18708-49ee9c8a/registry.npmjs.org/solc
/usr/lib/python3.6/site-packages/solc
/usr/lib/node_modules/solc
```

Next thing we have to do is, to set the environment variable for the installation location of the solc binary for use by py-solc -

```
export SOLC_BINARY=/root/.py-solc/solc-v0.4.25/bin/solc
```

We will now compile the same SimpleInbox.sol file in python from the python shell -

```
[root@eth-test ~]# python
Python 3.6.7 (default, Dec  5 2018, 15:02:05)
[GCC 4.8.5 20150623 (Red Hat 4.8.5-36)] on linux
Type "help", "copyright", "credits" or "license" for more information.
>>>
>>> from solc import compile_files
>>> compiled_sol=compile_files(["/root/contracts/SimpleInbox.sol"])
>>> import json
>>>
```

The pretty printed compiled contract can be seen in the following way -

```
print(json.dumps(compiled_sol, indent=4,sort_keys=True))
```

This will show us the entire contents, a snippet of which is shown as the following -

```
>>> print(json.dumps(compiled_sol, indent=4,sort_keys=True))
{
    "/root/contracts/SimpleInbox.sol:SimpleInbox": {
        "abi": [
            {
                "constant": false,
                "inputs": [
                    {
                        "name": "initialMessage",
                        "type": "string"
                    }
                ],
                "name": "setMessage",
                "outputs": [],
                "payable": false,
                "stateMutability": "nonpayable",
                "type": "function"
            },
```

```
{
    "constant": true,
    "inputs": [],
    "name": "getMessage",
    "outputs": [
        {
            "name": "",
            "type": "string"
        }
    ],
    "payable": false,
    "stateMutability": "view",
    "type": "function"
},
{
    "constant": true,
    "inputs": [],
    "name": "message",
    "outputs": [
        {
            "name": "",
            "type": "string"
```

We have our primary ethereum network running 10.10.0.239 -

```
[root@ethereum-primary ~]# geth --identity "ETH_node_1" --maxpeers 2 \
> --rpc --rpcapi "admin,personal,db,eth,net,web3" \
> --rpcaddr "10.10.0.239" --rpcport "8080" \
> --ipcdisable --datadir "/root/ethereum/test_net_data_dir" \
> --nat extip:10.10.0.239 --port "30303" \
> --networkid 666  console
```

We will connect to this private node from python shell on a different node -

```
[root@eth-test ~]# python
Python 3.6.7 (default, Dec  5 2018, 15:02:05)
[GCC 4.8.5 20150623 (Red Hat 4.8.5-36)] on linux
Type "help", "copyright", "credits" or "license" for more information.
>>>
>>> from web3 import Web3
>>> web3 = Web3(Web3.HTTPProvider("http://10.10.0.239:8080"))
>>>
>>> web3.isConnected()
True
```

For deploying a contract we need the *abi* (application binary interface) and the bytecode, as fetched from the compiled solidity shown below -

```
>>> compiled_sol['/root/contracts/SimpleInbox.sol:SimpleInbox']['abi']
[{'constant': False, 'inputs': [{'name': 'initialMessage', 'type': 'string'}], 'nam
tion'}, {'constant': True, 'inputs': [], 'name': 'getMessage', 'outputs': [{'name':
tant': True, 'inputs': [], 'name': 'message', 'outputs': [{'name': '', 'type': 'str
>>>
```

```
>>> compiled_sol['/root/contracts/SimpleInbox.sol:SimpleInbox']['bin']
'60806040523480156100105760008fd5b5061041080610020600396000f30060806040526004361061005757600
b87721461005c578063ce6d41de146100c5578063e21f37ce14610155575b600080fd5b3480156100685760008fd
160405190810160405280939291908181526020018383808284378201915050505050919291929050505060101e5
26020019150805190602001908083836000905b8381101561011a57808201518184015260208101905060600ff565b50
b5092505050604051800910390f35b348015610161615760008fd5b5061016a6102a1565b60405180806020018281030
081019050610018f565b5050505090509081019060011f680156101d7578082038051600183602003610100a031910
b5050565b606060008054600181600116156101000203166002900480601f016020809104026020016040519081010
1026c57610100808354040283529160200191610297565b820191906000526020600020905b81548152906001019
```

There will be some wei used for deploying the contract and so we will set the first account out of the three as our default account from where wei shall be deducted -

```
>>> web3.eth.accounts
['0x9E3bA41B3CfC741F10f22A920741fE29D332a2e8', '0x709f9490BCd189e8f176BCb9960c59101f264779', '0xb43daE6421D52FD73B9c9B097Aaf288Ae17023f7']
>>> web3.eth.defaultAccount = web3.eth.accounts[0]
>>>
```

Also, the account designated as the default account has to be unlocked -

```
>>> web3.personal.unlockAccount('0x9E3bA41B3CfC741F10f22A920741fE29D332a2e8','account_one_pass')
True
```

Finally, we go ahead and deploy the contract on our private network -

```
>>> deployed_contract=web3.eth.contract(\
... abi=compiled_sol['/root/contracts/SimpleInbox.sol:SimpleInbox']['abi'], \
... bytecode=compiled_sol['/root/contracts/SimpleInbox.sol:SimpleInbox']['bin'])
>>>
```

Here is the transaction hash returned on a successful contract deployment -

```
>>> deployed_contract.constructor().transact()
HexBytes('0xcf7117b2a92dcaef94041e8136fb7e6ff14b6cdf9bf5e7f8c31b83d4f9eb6592')
>>>
```

The transaction will be completed when a block is ready to be used and on a successful contract deployment, it would return the transaction receipt -

```
tx_receipt = \
 web3.eth.waitForTransactionReceipt(\
 '0xcf7117b2a92dcaef94041e8136fb7e6ff14b6cdf9bf5e7f8c31b83d4f9eb6592'\
 )
```

Here is the contents of the transaction receipt -

```
>>> tx_receipt
AttributeDict({'blockHash': HexBytes('0x441e573d6c3340c6f43b1a18530a01edd11525ae7d66fb1503a052255419fdd1'), 'blockNumber': 144, 'contractAddr
ess': '0x714256f0653B10B44103EcE1697DBB682908A4f2', 'cumulativeGasUsed': 329539, 'from': '0x9e3ba41b3cfc741f10f22a920741fe29d332a2e8', 'gasUs
ed': 329539, 'logs': [], 'logsBloom': HexBytes('0x0000000000000000000000000000000000000000000000000000000000000000000000000000000000000000000
0000000000000000000000000000000000000000000000000000000000000000000000000000000000000000000000000000000000000000000000000000000000000000000
000000000000000000000000000000000000000000000000000000000000000000000000000000000000000000000000000000000000000000000000000000000000000000'
), 'root': '0xecfac09b135916bedb533688da651da7818248e5960e8b885778c77a9031e188', 'to': None, 'transactionHash': HexBytes('0xcf7117b2a92dcaef94
041e8136fb7e6ff14b6cdf9bf5e7f8c31b83d4f9eb6592'), 'transactionIndex': 0})
>>>
```

The transaction receipt contains all the required information for identifying a contract, such as the contract address -

```
>>> tx_receipt['contractAddress']
'0x714256f0653B10B44103EcE1697DBB682908A4f2'
```

Since we have deployed a contract and not sent a transaction of ether to another account, the 'to' and 'from' addresses will be as follows -

```
>>> tx_receipt['from']
'0x9e3ba41b3cfc741f10f22a920741fe29d332a2e8'
>>> tx_receipt['to']
>>>
```

As we can see, the 'to' address is blank and does not have a target address.

We have deployed our contract to the private network, but to use it, we have to create an instance of it

```
>>> contract_instance=web3.eth.contract(\
... address=tx_receipt.contractAddress,\
... abi=compiled_sol['/root/contracts/SimpleInbox.sol:SimpleInbox']['abi'],\
... )
>>>
```

We will set a message to the contract by using setMessage() function as defined in our contract -

```
tx_hash = contract_instance.functions.setMessage("Ahoy!").transact()
```

Here is the transaction hash and receipt -

```
>>> tx_hash
HexBytes('0x3bb672d43c309820fd0342b03ded7f17014ddebc0d3056a4ce42c7eef8ae67cf')
>>> web3.eth.waitForTransactionReceipt(tx_hash)
AttributeDict({'blockHash': HexBytes('0xd930def8ca0b014ccb820a0b4dfec7b6136c6f04fad50e2
'from': '0x9e3ba41b3cfc741f10f22a920741fe29d332a2e8', 'gasUsed': 43011, 'logs': [], 'lo
0000000000000000000000000000000000000000000000000000000000000000000000000000000000000000
0000000000000000000000000000000000000000000000000000000000000000000000000000000000000000
000000000000000000000000000000000000000000000000000000000000000000'), 'root
10b44103ece1697dbb682908a4f2', 'transactionHash': HexBytes('0x3bb672d43c309820fd0342b03
>>>
>>>
```

The successful setting of the message can be checked by calling the *getMessage()* function -

```
>>> contract_instance.functions.getMessage().call()
'Ahoy!'
>>>
```

# SECTION 7

# Building server-side app with Django

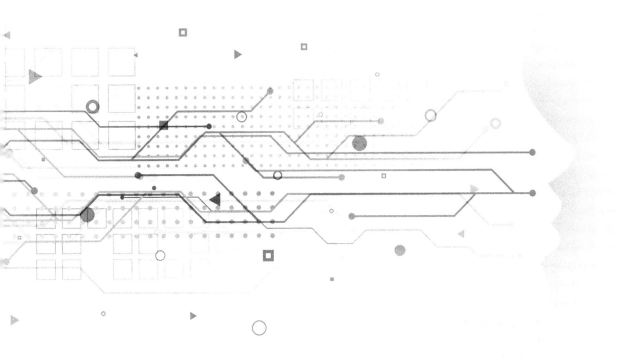

# Introduction

In the midst of numerous programming languages to choose from, it is very important to pick the one that has the most extended benefits. The language python has been a candidate of choice for this book and undoubtedly, we are going to use it for writing the server side application. But the choice of Django framework for building on server side did not stem from the adherence to a python based stack for this book.

Not just in a startup environment or in a time constrained use case where the developed items are customer facing products, being able to build and test things quickly is a prime attraction for all developers. Python since its inception has addressed this philosophy and so has become one of the most widely adopted programming languages among others. The clean and succinct syntax along with a rich library set is a great attractor but, python's ability to be used as a scripting language, the support for both procedural as well as object oriented programming and of course, web programming, gives it a Swiss knife like capability.

The Django web framework's power comes from the clean organisational structuring of application code that creates an intuitive mental model for the various artefacts of a project and thus encourages rapid development. The framework ships a collection of tools that handles most of the secondary and tertiary tasks of web application development so that, the prime focus remains on writing code. Django can be used to build web applications of all types without any limitations in terms of scalability.

# What is Django?

In a world with a constellation of web frameworks, it becomes a critical matter of choice when it comes to development of web applications using a web framework. Since we are heavily inclined toward pythonic solutions and tools throughout this book, our choice of the language for development will be python as well.

What makes python such a great language to write code, is its cleanliness, simplicity and conciseness. For rapid web development it is very important that the server side code is scalable such that new features for a web application can be introduced with least amount of coding and is easy in maintaining. There are already close to 15 web frameworks for python as of 2018. The most compelling, powerful and popular of all, is the Django web framework, at least according to the most number of stars on github compared to others.

From a python programmer's perspective, writing application (web) in Django isn't so different from writing scripts in python. Django supports the MVC architecture and takes an object oriented approach towards it. Django comes prepackaged with tons of functionality for each of them Model, View and Controller that are ready to be deployed out of the box.

The Model with Django uses ORM which makes defining database and performing CRUD operations on it possible, through python code. The Controller can be described both through traditional pythonic functional programming as well as classes. The requests and responses follow a neatly definable and maintainable URL mapping system. The View in Django is defined through a rich templating system in jinja2 format.

# Understanding the framework

The interaction with Django framework should begin with creating a sample project using the command-line tools provided with it and understanding their usage. We are going to take an approach where we would first list down and figure out the common activities that may arise during the development phase and create possible quick solutions in the form of scripts that will come in handy.

On installation of django, it provides the command-line tool django-admin or django-admin.py for performing administrative tasks.

Creating a new project.

```
django-admin startproject sample_project
```

This creates a directory with the project name and has the following directory structure -

```
sample_project/
├── manage.py
└── sample_project
    ├── __init__.py
    ├── settings.py
    ├── urls.py
    └── wsgi.py

1 directory, 5 files
```

The root project directory contains another directory of the same name as the project directory and contains project specific artefacts.

*settings.py* - Contains project specific settings and environment variables.
*urls.py* - Contains url mappings of the project. This is the root namespace for the defined the url(s) in a project.
*wsgi.py* - WSGI (Web Server Gateway Interface) is a python standard for web server applications. It can be thought of as the python directive for CGI (a program designed to accept requests and respond based on established web protocols). This file contains a simple default WSGI configuration for a project created with the management utility sub-command *startproject*. Therefore this is the file that contains information about our application and will be used by a HTTP web server to host the application.

The project/application written in django is referenced as an application object by the web servers that are capable of serving django projects such as *Apache HTTP server with mod_wsgi module, Gunicorn server, uWSGI (a fast web server written purely in C)*. The *startproject* utility creates the wsgi.py file which contains the application as a callable object.

```
os.environ.setdefault("DJANGO_SETTINGS_MODULE", "sample_project.settings")

application = get_wsgi_application()
```

A web server's access point to a django project is through this *application* object. When a web server hosts a django project it needs to load the settings for the project and it is set as an environment variable by the name DJANGO_SETTINGS_MODULE that points to the root settings file of a project, which in this case is *sample_project/settings.py (sample_project. settings)*. Django makes everything highly pluggable and so its possible for maintaining separate settings file for say, production and development environments.

The other notable file created by *createproject* sub-command is *manage.py* which has the same set of capabilities as the django-admin command, plus a few extra functionalities w.r.t. a project.

With *manage.py*, super users for a project can be created with *createsuperuser* sub-command, expired sessions for a project can be cleared with *clearsessions*, the static files for a project can be managed with *collectstatic* and *findstatic,* and other tasks such as removing stale content-types in a project with *remove_stale_contenttypes* sub-command and running the development server that comes with django framework with the *runserver* sub-command.

Now that a vanilla setup of our sample project has been created, we will run the test server with *manage.py*. It would produce the following output -

```
[root@vv-z1 sample_project]# python manage.py runserver 9200
Performing system checks...

System check identified no issues (0 silenced).

You have 13 unapplied migration(s). Your project may not work properly until you apply the migrations for app(s): admin, auth, contenttypes, sessions.
Run 'python manage.py migrate' to apply them.

September 07, 2018 - 12:05:08
Django version 1.11.13, using settings 'sample_project.settings'
Starting development server at http://127.0.0.1:9200/
Quit the server with CONTROL-C.
```

It says, that its running at http://127.0.0.1:9200/, but also points out to run

```
python manage.py migrate
```

When we stop the development server after running it for the first time, a new file appears - *db.sqlite3*. This is because the vanilla setup of django runs with SQLite as its database and the database file gets instantiated as it is configured in the *settings.py* file.

This brings us to the *migrate* sub-command whose job is to perform create, update, alter and delete operations on the database schema defined in a django project. After any changes made to the database definition the *migrate* command needs to be run for the changes to be reflected to the actual database tables.

Let us go ahead and execute the command -

```
[root@ww-z1 sample_project]# python manage.py migrate
Operations to perform:
  Apply all migrations: admin, auth, contenttypes, sessions
Running migrations:
  Applying contenttypes.0001_initial... OK
  Applying auth.0001_initial... OK
  Applying admin.0001_initial... OK
  Applying admin.0002_logentry_remove_auto_add... OK
  Applying contenttypes.0002_remove_content_type_name... OK
  Applying auth.0002_alter_permission_name_max_length... OK
  Applying auth.0003_alter_user_email_max_length... OK
  Applying auth.0004_alter_user_username_opts... OK
  Applying auth.0005_alter_user_last_login_null... OK
  Applying auth.0006_require_contenttypes_0002... OK
  Applying auth.0007_alter_validators_add_error_messages... OK
  Applying auth.0008_alter_user_username_max_length... OK
  Applying sessions.0001_initial... OK
```

With our vanilla setup, migration operations are performed for - *admin, auth, contenttypes, sessions*, which are pre-built applications that come with the default configuration in *settings. py*. Each of these applications have database schemas defined, which take effect in the SQLite database. Django gives a way to have a shell access to the database that is configured in setting.py through the *dbshell* sub-command for both manage.py and django-admin. Here are the tables that are created from the migration operation -

```
[[root@ww-z1 sample_project]# python manage.py dbshell
SQLite version 3.7.17 2013-05-20 00:56:22
Enter ".help" for instructions
Enter SQL statements terminated with a ";"
[sqlite>
[sqlite> .tables
auth_group                      auth_user_user_permissions
auth_group_permissions          django_admin_log
auth_permission                 django_content_type
auth_user                       django_migrations
auth_user_groups                django_session
[sqlite>
```

These apps - auth, sessions etc., come in a plugin ready state for project(s) to use them.

Until now, we have referenced our sample django project as django application interchangeably. But django framework has a separate reservation to the term *app* (short for application) itself and it should not be mistaken with the *application* object as defined in the wsgi.py file that we discussed earlier.

The design philosophy of django enables distinction among various features and functionalities of a project into separate *apps*.

Suppose, our *sample_project* has a user login feature and a blog feature. These two features define our project and they can be built as separate apps which have their own namespace, database schema definition, url mappings and business logic. It is this design that makes *apps* in a django project highly pluggable and capable of being used by other projects. We will create three sample apps in our project namely - app1, app2 and app3.

```
[[root@ww-z1 sample_project]# python manage.py startapp app1
[[root@ww-z1 sample_project]# python manage.py startapp app2
[[root@ww-z1 sample_project]# python manage.py startapp app3
[[root@ww-z1 sample_project]# ll
total 60
drwxr-xr-x. 3 root root  4096 Sep  7 15:25 app1
drwxr-xr-x. 3 root root  4096 Sep  7 15:25 app2
drwxr-xr-x. 3 root root  4096 Sep  7 15:25 app3
-rw-r--r--. 1 root root 37888 Sep  7 14:16 db.sqlite3
-rwxr-xr-x. 1 root root   812 Sep  7 08:59 manage.py
drwxr-xr-x. 2 root root  4096 Sep  7 13:18 sample_project
```

The contents inside an app directory is as follows -

```
— app1
    ├── admin.py
    ├── apps.py
    ├── __init__.py
    ├── migrations
    │   └── __init__.py
    ├── models.py
    ├── tests.py
    └── views.py
```

*views.py* - The request and responses bound to the URLs for this app, and their business logic is defined in this file.

*models.py* - All the database tables, relations and schema related definitions w.r.t. the app is defined here.

*tests.py* - All unit tests for the app is present here.

*admin.py* - Django provides an admin console website with which database tables can be accessed. This file has to be configured for the tables defined in this app, to be accessible from the admin console.

*apps.py* - This is the namespace of an app and from here various app specific attributes can be configured.

*migrations* - This directory contains the code generated by *migrate* command w.r.t. the tables and relations defined in models.py for an app. All the changes in the schema are recorded in files that are logically dependant such that it is easy to track the changes in schema. The main purpose of the files in this directory is to provide a versioning for the changes in database schema. Suppose a new field is added to a certain database table defined in models.py. Upon executing the *migrate* command, the change is recorded in the form of a separate file in this directory. For instance a table is defined in models.py containing one field str_value. On executing migrate command, the database table is created and at the same time a file named *0001_initial.py* is created in this directory. This *0001_initial.py* marks the first version of the database table. Next, another field is added to the schema definition and when the migrate command is executed again, results in the following state of the migrations directory -

```
-rw-r--r--. 1 root root 572 Sep  7 18:25 0001_initial.py
-rw-r--r--. 1 root root 456 Sep  7 18:30 0002_samplemodel_str_value2.py
```

The naming of the files also define the sequential relationship among the changes, and in this case *0002_samplemodel_str_value2.py* defines, *samplemodel* which is the name of the table and *str_value2* is the name of the new field added.

The three sample apps - app1, app2 and app3, with their schema definitions will not be ready for reflecting changes to the database and migrations just by executing the *migrate* command. Right after creation of the app with *startapp* command and defining of the schema in model.py, when *makemigrations* is run, it shows the following output -

```
[root@ww-z1 sample_project]# python manage.py makemigrations app1
App 'app1' could not be found. Is it in INSTALLED_APPS?
```

The *makemigrations* command creates only the migration files in the *migrations* directory, while the *migrate* command makes the actual changes in the database. The *migrate* command internally does the task of *makemigrations* command before reflecting to the database.

According to the above snippet, the *makemigrations* command was unsuccessful because the app - app1, is not yet plugged into our project. This brings us to the file which holds all the apps and the entire project together, the setting.py file at *sample_project/sample_project/ settings.py*.

## The settings file

In the *settings.py* file, all the apps that are going to be used for a project will have to mentioned in the *INSTALLED_APPS* list.

```
INSTALLED_APPS = [
    'django.contrib.admin',
    'django.contrib.auth',
    'django.contrib.contenttypes',
    'django.contrib.sessions',
    'django.contrib.messages',
    'django.contrib.staticfiles',
    'app1.apps.App1Config',
]
```

Here app1.apps.App1Config is the reference to the App1Config class defined in the file at app1/apps.py. After listing the app's namespace, *migrate* and *makemigrations* command take action.

The *dbshell* shows the table created by app1 as *app1_samplemodel*.

```
[sqlite> .tables
app1_samplemodel            auth_user_user_permissio
auth_group                  django_admin_log
auth_group_permissions      django_content_type
```

A project may have apps that use multiple types of databases, such as relational along with NoSQL. The DATABASES configuration in *settings.py* describes their identities. The default settings use SQLite -

```
DATABASES = {
    'default': {
        'ENGINE': 'django.db.backends.sqlite3',
        'NAME': os.path.join(BASE_DIR, 'db.sqlite3'),
    }
}
```

The other initial settings consist of the following keys.

```
SECRET_KEY = 'w#=*x64%_2vvhq!9n*i6lrqc+t-iv75qc5m_(5dr)$d=r_i!8q'

DEBUG = True

ALLOWED_HOSTS = []
```

*SECRET_KEY* - Each project has a unique key. Django framework issues a lot of hashes and this key is used as a salt for those hashes.

*DEBUG* - When set to True, the django application is run in the debug mode and in case of an error, the entire stack trace is shown on the webpage along with all the environment variables partaking in the application. It should without a doubt be set to False in production.

*ALLOWED_HOSTS* - A comma separated list of host IPs can be mentioned here, and the application would respond only to request from those hosts. For global accessibility, it is set to

$$ALLOWED\_HOSTS = [\text{"}*\text{"},]$$

```
MIDDLEWARE = [
    'django.middleware.security.SecurityMiddleware',
    'django.contrib.sessions.middleware.SessionMiddleware',
    'django.middleware.common.CommonMiddleware',
    'django.middleware.csrf.CsrfViewMiddleware',
    'django.contrib.auth.middleware.AuthenticationMiddleware',
    'django.contrib.messages.middleware.MessageMiddleware',
    'django.middleware.clickjacking.XFrameOptionsMiddleware',
]
```

A list of packages that come bundled with django, that provide middleware functionalities such as security, session maintenance, authentication, etc. For example, django provides built-in protection against cross site forgery through CsrfViewMiddleware.

```
ROOT_URLCONF = 'sample_project.urls'
```

This key specifies the reference to sample_project/sample_project/urls.py, which is where URLs are declared and mapped to functions that respond to requests and carry out the business logic.

```
WSGI_APPLICATION = 'sample_project.wsgi.application'
```

This key refers to the application object for our project in *sample_project/sample_project/wsgi.py file*.

```
TEMPLATES = [
    {
        'BACKEND': 'django.template.backends.django.DjangoTemplates',
        'DIRS': [],
        'APP_DIRS': True,
        'OPTIONS': {
            'context_processors': [
                'django.template.context_processors.debug',
                'django.template.context_processors.request',
                'django.contrib.auth.context_processors.auth',
                'django.contrib.messages.context_processors.messages',
            ],
        },
    },
]
```

For a web server, it is required to generate HTML responses dynamically. Django comes with a rich templating library, that contains the static HTML parts for the corresponding template used. The *BACKEND* key is a reference to the python path of the template class, implementing the template backend API in jinja2 format. *DIRS* defines the list of directories the templating engine should look up for template source files. *APP_DIRS* when set to True tells django to look up for templates, in the directories of the apps listed in *INSTALLED_APPS* key. *context_processors* are a list of dotted python paths to objects that populate the template (HTML) relevant to the context.

```
AUTH_PASSWORD_VALIDATORS = [
    {
        'NAME': 'django.contrib.auth.password_validation.UserAttributeSimilarityValidat
    },
    {
        'NAME': 'django.contrib.auth.password_validation.MinimumLengthValidator',
    },
    {
        'NAME': 'django.contrib.auth.password_validation.CommonPasswordValidator',
    },
    {
        'NAME': 'django.contrib.auth.password_validation.NumericPasswordValidator',
    },
]
```

Django comes with a whole library of input validators for common tasks such as user password validation. The list *AUTH_PASSWORD_VALIDATORS* enlists the validators relevant to an application project and like all other configuration keys, can be extended with custom created validators.

The timezone to be used by the application project are set using the following keys.

```
LANGUAGE_CODE = 'en-us'
TIME_ZONE = 'UTC'
USE_I18N = True
USE_L10N = True
USE_TZ = True
```

The final key in the settings.py file is for the root url namespace for static files. Django looks into directory named *static,* inside each apps' directory to collect and deliver the static content such as images, javascript files or CSS, relevant to the app.

```
STATIC_URL = '/static/'
```

Both *django-admin* and *manage.py* provide another utility command called *collectstatic*, that is very frequently used and whose function is tied to the *STATIC_URL* key's value. Django already provides the *django.contrib.staticfiles* app that takes care of all the management issues that arise when a project has lots of static files distributed amongst various apps' directories. The *django.contrib.staticfiles* app has to be enlisted in INSTALLED_APPS and the static files specific to an app have to be placed in the following way -

```
├── app1
│   ├── admin.py
│   ├── admin.pyc
│   ├── apps.py
│   ├── apps.pyc
│   ├── __init__.py
│   ├── __init__.pyc
│   ├── migrations
│   │   ├── 0001_initial.py
│   │   ├── 0001_initial.pyc
│   │   ├── 0002_samplemodel_str_value2.py
│   │   ├── 0002_samplemodel_str_value2.pyc
│   │   ├── __init__.py
│   │   └── __init__.pyc
│   ├── models.py
│   ├── models.pyc
│   ├── static
│   │   ├── example.jpg
│   │   └── sample.js
│   ├── tests.py
│   └── views.py
```

Here the files, example.jpg and sample.js are the static files, which will get accumulated by the *collectstatic* command on setting of the *STATIC_ROOT* key in settings.py, which do not get created in the default setup and will be discussed in later sections.

Another distinguished command provided by both django-admin and manage.py, is *shell*, which is the python interactive shell. The entire of django framework with its object orientation of web forms, views, urls, models, etc. is accessible through the shell.

# Hello world with django

For our first 'hello world' project with django, we will create a simple JSON based user login on our own as well as using the existing authentication system provided by django. All the source files are available at the following location -

We create a new project *hello_world* and the first app *login*.

```
hello_world/
├── hello_world
│       ├── __init__.py
│       ├── __init__.pyc
│       ├── settings.py
│       ├── settings.pyc
│       ├── urls.py
│       └── wsgi.py
├── login
│       ├── admin.py
│       ├── apps.py
│       ├── __init__.py
│       ├── migrations
│       │       └── __init__.py
│       ├── models.py
│       ├── tests.py
│       └── views.py
└── manage.py
```

We are going to use mysql-community version 5.7 and therefore configure settings.py accordingly.

```
DATABASES = {
  'default': {
  'ENGINE': 'django.db.backends.mysql',
  'NAME': 'hellowdb',
  'USER': 'appuser',
  'PASSWORD': 'appuser@DB112358',
  'HOST': '10.10.0.150',
  'PORT': '3306',
```

```
'OPTIONS': {
    'init_command': "SET sql_mode='STRICT_TRANS_TABLES',innodb_strict_mode=1",
    'charset': 'utf8mb4',
        },
    }
  }
```

After including *login.apps.LoginConfig*, the dotted python path notation for our login app's namespace, into the INSTALLED_APPS list, *migrate* is run. The other apps in INSTALLED_APPS are -

*django.contrib.admin* - This the admin site that enables performing administrative operations on a project w.r.t. the type of user privilege.

*django.contrib.auth* - This is the in built authentication system we are going to user later in the hello world application.

*django.contrib.contenttypes* - A framework for the various content types.

*django.contrib.sessions* - A session management framework.

*django.contrib.messages* - A messaging framework.

*django.contrib.staticfiles* - A static file management framework.

We will create the database schema for the AppUser table in the file *login/models.py*. Django provides an object oriented approach to the schema definition, where each table/relation or model is defined as a python class and fields or attributes of the model as class member variables. The object of such a class represents a tuple in the actual database table.

```python
from django.db import models
from cryptography.fernet import Fernet
# Create your models here.

class AppUser(models.Model):
    first_name = models.CharField(max_length = 150,null=True)
    middle_name = models.CharField(max_length = 150,null=True)
    last_name = models.CharField(max_length = 150,null=True)
    email = models.EmailField(max_length=50, null=False,unique=True)
    phone = models.CharField(max_length=15, null=False,unique=True)
    created = models.DateTimeField(auto_now=True)
    password = models.CharField(max_length=120,null=False)
    key = models.CharField(max_length=44,null=True)
```

Each model in django such as AppUser has to be the subclass of *django.db.models.Model*. The Meta inner class is optional, and it is used to override the default naming convention of table name used by *migrate*. Each of the fields are instantiated with a specific field type's class - CharField, EmailField. The shell provided by manage.py is an extremely handy tool to learn about the various other parameters and functions of these classes.

```
[root@vw-z1 hello_world]# python manage.py shell
Python 2.7.5 (default, Jul 13 2018, 13:06:57)
[GCC 4.8.5 20150623 (Red Hat 4.8.5-28)] on linux2
Type "help", "copyright", "credits" or "license" for more information.
(InteractiveConsole)
>>>
>>> from django.db import models
>>> dir(models.CharField())
['_class_', '_copy_', '_deepcopy_', '_delattr_', '_dict_', '_doc_', '_eq_', '_format_', '_ge_', '_getattribute_', '_gt_', '_hash_', '_init_', '_le_',
'_module_', '_new_', '_reduce_', '_reduce_ex_', '_repr_', '_setattr_', '_sizeof_', '_str_', '_subclasshook_', '_unicode_', '_weakref_', 'check_backend_
specific_checks', 'check_choices', 'check_db_index', 'check_deprecation_details', 'check_field_name', 'check_max_length_attribute', 'check_null_allowed_for_primary_keys', 'c
ear_cached_lookups', 'description', 'error_messages', 'get_default', 'get_flatchoices', 'get_lookup', 'unique', 'unregister_lookup', 'validators', 'ver
bose_name', 'auto_created', 'auto_creation_counter', 'blank', 'cached_col', 'check', 'choices', 'class_lookups', 'clean', 'contribute_to_class', 'creation_counter', 'db_che
ck', 'db_column', 'db_index', 'db_parameters', 'db_tablespace', 'db_type', 'db_type_suffix', 'deconstruct', 'default', 'default_error_messages', 'default_validators', 'description',
'editable', 'empty_strings_allowed', 'empty_values', 'error_messages', 'flatchoices', 'formfield', 'get_attname', 'get_attname_column', 'get_cache_name', 'get_choices', 'get_col
'get_db_converters', 'get_db_prep_save', 'get_db_prep_value', 'get_default', 'get_filter_kwargs_for_object', 'get_internal_type', 'get_lookup', 'get_lookups', 'get_pk_value_on_save',
'get_prep_value', 'get_transform', 'has_default', 'help_text', 'hidden', 'is_relation', 'many_to_many', 'many_to_one', 'max_length', 'merge_dicts', 'name', 'null', 'one_to_many',
'one_to_one', 'pre_save', 'primary_key', 'register_lookup', 'rel', 'rel_db_type', 'related_model', 'remote_field', 'run_validators', 'save_form_data', 'select_format', 'serialize',
'set_attributes_from_name', 'system_check_deprecated_details', 'system_check_removed_details', 'to_python', 'unique', 'unique_for_date', 'unique_for_month', 'unique_for_year', 'vali
date', 'validators', 'value_from_object', 'value_to_string', 'verbose_name']
```

Since models are represented as class, the behaviour of the data stored in the member variables can be controlled through defining functions. Here in this case, the password field stores data in plain text and so an encryption and decryption function is to be defined. We will use Fernet library to generate a key string that is stored in *key = models.CharField(...)* field, and this key is to be used to encrypt and decrypt the plain text password.

```python
class AppUser(models.Model):
  first_name = models.CharField(max_length = 150,null=True)
  middle_name = models.CharField(max_length = 150,null=True)
  last_name = models.CharField(max_length = 150,null=True)
  email = models.EmailField(max_length=50, null=False,unique=True)
  phone = models.CharField(max_length=15, null=False,unique=True)
  created = models.DateTimeField(auto_now=True)
  password = models.CharField(max_length=120,null=False)
  key = models.CharField(max_length=44,null=True)

  def __str__(self):
    return self.email + " " + self.phone
  def generate_key(self):
    self.key = Fernet.generate_key()
  def encrypt_password(self):
    f = Fernet(str(self.key))
    self.password = f.encrypt(str(self.password))
  def decrypt_password(self):
    f = Fernet(str(self.key))
    return f.decrypt(str(self.password))
  def save(self,*args,**kwargs):
    self.generate_key()
    self.encrypt_password()
    models.Model.save(self, *args, **kwargs)
  class Meta:
    db_table = "app_user"
```

After migrating the model, the *shell* can be used to interact with the table(s).

Each of the directories in a django project is made as a python module and here the AppUser class is imported from login/models.py.

```
[>>> from login.models import AppUser
```

The __str__ function is just the string representation of the object and it echoes the default values that are set for an instance of AppUser.

```
[>>> AppUser()
<AppUser: mail@address.com 9000000000>
```

An object of AppUser is created with fictional values.

```
>>> user = AppUser(first_name="Stephen",middle_name="William",last_name="Hawking",email="mail@galaxy.com",phone="3141592653",password="black@holes@suck")
>>> user.first_name
'Stephen'
>>> user.password
'black@holes@suck'
```

We will use the member functions of the AppUser to generate a key, encrypt and decrypt the password.

```
>>> user.generate_key()
>>> user.key
'KdXJF5cJN1I_KDi5DvTNc8NLQ5j4gnMaWmy441BM07Y='
>>> user.password
'black@holes@suck'
>>> user.encrypt_password()
>>> user.password
'gAAAAABblOwQYTaHswSCjweeAQ6GNoBcrbpkzsF3HIbuqELF7_NxUv7-rPgZ_fWGK-jLN29RU8cWsGb5sslGZ4TAZIu63oxFpl2ej8xxtNM5wrW--_Ynv9I='
>>> user.decrypt_password()
'black@holes@suck'
```

The django framework provides a rich Model API and among others, the *save* function is used to write back the data in an object to database table.

```
>>> user.save()
```

Now, we want the keys to be generated and encrypted automatically during the *save* operation and so we will override the *save* function.

```
def save(self,*args,**kwargs):
    self.generate_key()
    self.encrypt_password()
    models.Model.save(self, *args, **kwargs)
```

A tuple can be deleted from the database with the *delete* function invoked on the tuple object, in this case the instance of AppUser class - user.

```
>>> user.delete()
(1L, {u'login.AppUser': 1L})
```

The delete function returns the class name of the object (AppUser) and the *primary key value - 1L*. Although we did not create a field for primary key in the class definition, the Model super class adds a primary key field named *id* as default.

```
mysql> desc app_user;
+-------------+--------------+------+-----+---------+----------------+
| Field       | Type         | Null | Key | Default | Extra          |
+-------------+--------------+------+-----+---------+----------------+
| id          | int(11)      | NO   | PRI | NULL    | auto_increment |
| first_name  | varchar(150) | YES  |     | NULL    |                |
| middle_name | varchar(150) | YES  |     | NULL    |                |
| last_name   | varchar(150) | YES  |     | NULL    |                |
| email       | varchar(50)  | NO   | UNI | NULL    |                |
| phone       | varchar(15)  | NO   | UNI | NULL    |                |
| created     | datetime(6)  | NO   |     | NULL    |                |
| password    | varchar(120) | NO   |     | NULL    |                |
| key         | varchar(44)  | YES  |     | NULL    |                |
+-------------+--------------+------+-----+---------+----------------+
```

Now that our data model is prepared, we have to create a view in *login/views.py* that will accept an HTTP request, perform the business logic and send back a JSON response.

```python
from django.shortcuts import render
from django.db import IntegrityError
from django.http import JsonResponse
from .models import *
# Create your views here.

def signup(request):
  if request.method == 'POST':
    first_name = request.POST.get("first_name")
    middle_name = request.POST.get("middle_name")
    last_name = request.POST.get("last_name")
    email = request.POST.get("email")
    phone = request.POST.get("phone")
    password = request.POST.get("password")

    new_user = AppUser(first_name=first_name,middle_name=middle_name,
        last_name=last_name,email=email,phone=phone,password=password)
    try:
      new_user.save()
      return JsonResponse({'success':True,'msg':'User created successfully'})
    except IntegrityError, e:
      return JsonResponse({'success':False,'msg':e[1]})
    except Exception, e:
      return JsonResponse({'success':False,'msg':'Something went wrong! User could not be created.'})
  else:
    return JsonResponse({'success':False,'msg':'Hello there! Use POST request to create a user.'})
```

The view *signup* will service the request on POST method and send back a JsonResponse object. Since the *email* and *phone* fields have a unique clause, an exception of duplicate entry is handled by *IntegrityError* class. A list of all the exceptions can be found at -

The model defined in models.py is accessible in views.py for the import -

```python
from .models import *
```

and, remaining is declaring the URL that maps to this view. For this, we will register a url say http://<ip>:<port>/signup/ to the URL configuration (informally called URLconf) for our project, in hello_world/hello_world/urls.py. The URLconf is basically a python module that does mapping between url expressions and their corresponding views. Therefore, every view must return an object of some subclass of Response class, such as HTTPResponse, JsonResponse, StreamingHttpResponse.

In urls.py, we start by importing the signup view from login/views.py.

```
from login.views import signup
```

The url is enlisted in the list *urlpatterns,* which is the root location where the web server sends an incoming request for a url pattern lookup.

```
urlpatterns = [
    url(r'^admin/', admin.site.urls),
    url(r'^signup/', signup),
]
```

The entry for "admin/" is for the in-built admin dashboard, that is by default added on project creation. Django uses of course regular expression for declaring a url pattern and so each url expression is preceded by an - *r*. The url function returns an instance of RegexURLPattern class and the view associated with the regex is a callback as demonstrated below -

```
>>> def foo():
...     print "foo"
...
>>> u = url(r'^admin/$', foo)
>>> u.callback()
foo
```

With our database model prepared, and view mapped to a desired url, we are almost ready to test the signup functionality. The residual is to configure ALLOWED_HOSTS in settings.py to accept our web request.

```
ALLOWED_HOSTS = ["*",]
```

Lastly, the development server that comes with django framework is run on the public IP at port 9200. We must ensure that there is no *selinux, iptables* or *firewalld* blocking access to the port.

The signup view as expected returns the following json response when accessed over a GET request.

← → C ⓘ Not Secure | **10.10.0.150**:9200/signup/

```
{"msg": "Hello there! Use POST request to create a user.", "success": false}
```

A POST request is required with proper data for the fields to create a new user and we use the following data for our new user signup.

```
curl -d '{"first_name":"Nikola","middle_name":"","last_name":"Tesla",
         "email":"nikola@mail.com","phone":"9292929292","password":"electric@dream"}'
         -H "Content-Type: application/json" -X POST http://10.10.0.150:9200/signup/
```

On submitting the request we will get the following response -

```
<p>Reason given for failure:</p>
<pre>
CSRF cookie not set.
</pre>


<p>In general, this can occur when there is a genuine Cross Site Request Forger
<a
href="https://docs.djangoproject.com/en/1.11/ref/csrf/">Django's
CSRF mechanism</a> has not been used correctly.  For POST forms, you need to
ensure:</p>

<ul>
  <li>Your browser is accepting cookies.</li>

  <li>The view function passes a <code>request</code> to the template's <a
  href="https://docs.djangoproject.com/en/dev/topics/templates/#django.template
  method.</li>

  <li>In the template, there is a <code>{% csrf_token
  %}</code> template tag inside each POST form that
  targets an internal URL.</li>

  <li>If you are not using <code>CsrfViewMiddleware</code>, then you must use
  <code>csrf_protect</code> on any views that use the <code>csrf_token</code>
  template tag, as well as those that accept the POST data.</li>

  <li>The form has a valid CSRF token. After logging in in another browser
  tab or hitting the back button after a login, you may need to reload the
  page with the form, because the token is rotated after a login.</li>
</ul>

<p>You're seeing the help section of this page because you have <code>DEBUG =
True</code> in your Django settings file. Change that to <code>False</code>,
and only the initial error message will be displayed.  </p>

<p>You can customize this page using the CSRF_FAILURE_VIEW setting.</p>
```

This is because our list of INSTALLED_APPS contain *django.middleware.csrf.CsrfViewMiddleware* app which expects a *csrf token* to be present with each incoming request containing form data. Since our signup view is not using POST data from a form, we will use the *csrf_exempt* python decorator on our view.

```
from django.views.decorators.csrf import csrf_exempt

@csrf_exempt
def signup(request):
  if request.method == 'POST':
```

Django has extensive usage of decorators which contribute to the clean and less code requirement. Csrf is a security feature that will be discussed broadly later.

When the request is again sent, it results in false.

```
{"msg": "Column 'email' cannot be null", "success": false}
```

Although we sent data for email field, the *request.POST.get()* function did not find any POST data because the data sent from the curl request is present in the *body* member variable of the request object.

Debugging the body and POST member variables -

```
if request.method == 'POST':

    print ("Body section: %s"%request.body)
    print ("POST section: %s"%request.POST)
```

shows the following contents -

```
Body section: {"first_name":"Nikola","middle_name":" ","last_name":"Tesla","email":"nikola@mail.com","phone":"9292929292","password":"electric@dream"}
POST section: <QueryDict: {}>
```

We will create our own decorator that copies the data present in the *body* member variable and casts into QueryDict class object to store in POST member variable of a request object.

We will create a lib module for use by apps in our project.

```
lib
├── decorators.py
└── __init__.py
```

The decorators.py file is where our decorator request_intercept is defined.

```
from functools import wraps
import json
import urllib
from django.http import QueryDict



def request_intercept(fn):
  @wraps(fn)
  def wrapper(request):
    try:
      if request.method == 'POST':
        q = QueryDict(urllib.urlencode(json.loads(request.body)))
        request.POST = q
      return fn(request)
```

```
    except Exception, e:
        print ("\n\n")
        print ("Exception while processing function: "+fn.__name__)
        print ("\nException info: ")
        print (e)
        return False
    return wrapper
```

The *@wraps* decorator maintains the identity of the function by preserving the function name, docstring, argument list, etc. when *fn* passed to it while calling the *@request_intercept* decorator.

The decorator is introduced to the signup view -

```
from lib.decorators import *

@csrf_exempt
@request_intercept
def signup(request):
    if request.method == 'POST':
```

and now when the curl request is sent, it results in success.

```
{"msg": "User created successfully", "success": true}
```

The debugging of body and POST member values of request object now have the following data -

```
Body section: {"first_name":"Nikola","middle_name":" ","last_name":"Tesla","email":"nikola@mail.com","p
POST section: <QueryDict: {u'first_name': [u'Nikola'], u'last_name': [u'Tesla'], u'middle_name': [u' ']
kola@mail.com']}>
```

Therefore, we have built the signup process of our *hello_world* application as JSON based POST.

Next we will create a form based user login feature. Django takes the object oriented approach toward forms as well and our will be defined as a class in *login/forms.py*, but first we will create an html file that is going to be serviced on access request to a url. Django's templating library dynamically expands the templates used in html files and so we will keep all the html files for a particular app in a directory - *app/templates/app/somefile.html*. This directory structure is recommended and used by the django framework and for our login app its as this -

```
[root@ww-z1 hello_world]# tree login/templates/
login/templates/
└── login
    └── login.html
```

Our html file will be using stylesheets and javascripts that will be common for other apps as well, and so a *base.html* file will be kept at a *templates* directory outside and separate from all apps.

```
drwxr-xr-x. 2 root root 4096 Sep 10 11:56 hello_world
drwxr-xr-x. 2 root root   84 Sep 10 11:51 lib
drwxr-xr-x. 5 root root 4096 Sep 10 11:53 login
-rwxr-xr-x. 1 root root  809 Sep  9 05:00 manage.py
drwxr-xr-x. 3 root root   18 Sep  9 21:07 static
drwxr-xr-x. 2 root root   22 Sep 10 12:47 templates
```

The content of the base.html is -

```html
{% load staticfiles %}

<!DOCTYPE html>

<html>
    <head>
        <meta charset="utf-8">
            <meta name="viewport" content="width=device-width, initial-scale=1.0">
                <title> Login - Hello World</title>

<!-- CSS -->
<link rel="stylesheet" href="{% static "custom.css" %}" screen="media">
<!-- JS -->
<script src="https://code.jquery.com/jquery-3.2.1.min.js"></script>
<script src="https://cdnjs.cloudflare.com/ajax/libs/popper.js/1.12.3/umd/popper.min.js"
 integrity="sha384-vFJXuSJphROIrBnz7yo7oB41mKfc8JzQZiCq4NCceLEaO4IHwicKwpJf9c9IpFgh" crossorigin="anonymous"></script>
<script src="https://maxcdn.bootstrapcdn.com/bootstrap/4.0.0-beta.2/js/bootstrap.min.js"
 integrity="sha384-alpBpkh1PFOepccYVYDB4do5UnbKysX5WZXm3XxPqe5iKTfUKjNkCk9SaVuEZflJ" crossorigin="anonymous"></script>

    </head>

<body>
{% block content %}

{% endblock %}
</body>

</html>
```

{% static 'custom.css' %} is the template tag that prepends the file path to the location of custom.css. The *static* template tag dynamically looks up at the locations mentioned in *STATICFILES_DIR* and *STATIC_URL* and returns the path.

```python
# Static files (CSS, JavaScript, Images)
STATIC_URL = '/static/'
STATICFILES_DIRS = [
    os.path.join(BASE_DIR, "templates/scripts/css"),
    os.path.join(BASE_DIR, "templates/scripts/js"),
]
```

The *STATICFILES_DIR* key, unlike *STATIC_URL* is not created in settings.py by default, and we have added the location *hello_world/templates/scripts*. For our project the location *hello_world/templates/scripts* will contain stylesheets and scripts that are common to all the apps in our project. The directory structure inside *templates* is as follows -

```
templates/
├── base.html
└── scripts
    ├── css
    │   └── custom.css
    └── js
```

In order to use the {% static '…' %} template tag, the tag library has to be loaded, {% load static %}, before using the *static* template. Think of *load* keyword equivalent to the function of *import* keyword and it is loading the template tag *static* provided by *django.contrib. staticfiles*. {% load static %} has to be added before every access to the {% static '…' %} template tag, and to avoid this tedium, {% load staticfiles %} is added at the beginning of base.html. The base.html is the file whose contents comprise of HTML sections outside the <body/> tag, such as <html/>,<head/>,<meta/>,<title/>, etc. All other HTML files who use base.html as a substrate will *extend* the base.html file in their HTML definition. Django evokes the style of code reusability as seen in programming languages such as python with the *import* keyword.

We will create login.html for our login app, which is going to *extend* base.html.

```
{% extends 'base.html' %}

{% block content %}

<h4>Login</h4>

{% endblock %}
```

We will first test the page with just a heading in <h4/>. The entire HTML content of login.html has to be put between the {% block content %} … {% endblock %} tags. When a request for servicing the login.html page is in process, the content inside the {% block content %} … {% endblock %} tags in login.html is placed inside the section designated by {% block content %} … {% endblock %} in base.html file.

```
<body>
{% block content %}

{% endblock %}
</body>
```

Next, we will define a view that services the template login.html.

```
def user_login(request):
    if request.method == 'POST':
        pass
    else:
        return render(request, 'login/login.html')
```

*render* - This is the function that expands the several template tags in login.hml file and returns the response HttpResponse object. Django's templating engine *django.template.backends. django.DjangoTemplates* as set for *TEMPLATES* in settings.py looks up for html files in each apps' *templates* directory. The *template_name* argument value 'login/login.html' instructs the templating engine to fetch the login.html file from login app's *templates* directory. This is because the templating engine learns about the relative location of login.html as provided to render function - login/login.html and that is why, django follows the following directory structure for keeping the *.html files for any app -

```
[root@ww-z1 hello_world]# tree login/templates/
login/templates/
└── login
    └── login.html
```

We declare a new url for *user_login* view in hello_world/urls.py.

```
urlpatterns = [
    url(r'^admin/', admin.site.urls),
    url(r'^signup/', signup),
    url(r'^login/', user_login),
]
```

If the server is now run, we will get the following error.

The Template loader postmortem section would show the locations where the template engine has performed look ups for base.html -

**Template-loader postmortem**

Django tried loading these templates, in this order:

Using engine django:

- django.template.loaders.app_directories.Loader: /usr/lib64/python2.7/site-packages/django/contrib/admin/templates/base.html (Source does not exist)
- django.template.loaders.app_directories.Loader: /usr/lib64/python2.7/site-packages/django/contrib/auth/templates/base.html (Source does not exist)
- django.template.loaders.app_directories.Loader: /root/hello_world/login/templates/base.html (Source does not exist)

As we can see, the render function does look-up for base.html in the *login/templates/* directory as well, when not found in *login/templates/login/* where from it has fetched login.html. Since base.html has been placed in hello_world/templates/ directory outside of all apps, this location has to the identified to the templating engine, which by default does look ups in each app's *templates* directory. For this, *TEMPLATES* key in settings.py has to be changed from -

```
TEMPLATES = [
    {
        'BACKEND': 'django.template.backends.django.DjangoTemplates',
        'DIRS': [],
```

to

```
TEMPLATES = [
    {
        'BACKEND': 'django.template.backends.django.DjangoTemplates',
        'DIRS': [os.path.join(BASE_DIR, 'templates'),],
```

Now on running the server and requesting the url http://10.10.0.150:9200/login/, the webpage is shown. Since new static files and templates (html files) have been introduced, we must run *collectstatic* before running the development server.

```
[[root@ww-z1 hello_world]# python manage.py collectstatic

You have requested to collect static files at the destination
location as specified in your settings:

    /root/hello_world/static

This will overwrite existing files!
Are you sure you want to do this?

[Type 'yes' to continue, or 'no' to cancel: yes
Copying '/root/hello_world/templates/scripts/css/custom.css'

1 static file copied to '/root/hello_world/static', 61 unmodified.
```

## Login

Now getting back to creating the login form in login/forms.py, we create three fields, for email, phone and password.

```python
from django import forms

class LoginForm(forms.Form):
    email = forms.CharField(label="Email",required=True,max_length=30,
                        widget=forms.TextInput(attrs={'class': 'form-control', 'name': 'email','placeholder':'eg. you@mailserver.com'}))
    phone = forms.CharField(label="Phone",required=True,max_length=30,
                        widget=forms.TextInput(attrs={'class': 'form-control', 'name': 'phone','placeholder':'eg. 9000000000'}))
    password = forms.CharField(label="Password",required=True,max_length=30,
                        widget=forms.PasswordInput(attrs={'class': 'form-control', 'name': 'password'}))
```

A widget is django's representation of an HTML <input/> element. The widget handles rendering of HTML and extraction of data for GET or POST requests. All the fields in our form is of character datatype and so a form field instantiated with *forms.CharField(…)* represents the data in that field, whereas widget=forms.TextInput(…) represents how the HTML for that field is to be rendered - <input type="text" …>. The email field for example, gets rendered into the following with all the attributes attrs={'class': form-control, 'name': 'email', 'placeholder': 'eg. you@mailserver.com'} -

<input class="form-control" name="email" placeholder="eg. you@mailserver.com"/>

We are using Bootstrap 4 and so class="form-control" is one of its CSS class. The final rendered HTML with the *label="Email"* and *required=True* set, is as -

email: <input class="form-control" name="email" placeholder="eg. you@mailserver.com" required/>

The benefits of this object oriented approach to forms along side models is that, instance of LoginForm can be accessed directly in html templates. This is our login.html with the form placed in -

```html
{% extends 'base.html' %}


{% block content %}
<div class="jumbotron text-center">
<h4>Login</h4>
```

```html
</div>
<div class="container">
<div class="col-sm-4">
<form  method="post">
    <div class="form-group">
        {% csrf_token %}
        {{ form.as_p }}
    <div class="text-right">
        <input class="btn btn-primary" type="submit" value="Login" />
    </div>
</form>
</div>
</div>
{% endblock %}
```

This is the view for our login page -

```python
def user_login(request):
  form = LoginForm()
  if request.method == 'POST':
    form = LoginForm(request.POST)
    if form.is_valid():
      email = form.cleaned_data["email"]
      phone = form.cleaned_data["phone"]
      password = form.cleaned_data["password"]
      user = AppUser.objects.get(email=email,phone=phone)
      if password == user.decrypt_password():
        request.session["user_id"] = user.id
        return HttpResponseRedirect(reverse('login:home'))
      else:
        content = "<p> You fed wrong data mate! </p>"
        return HttpResponse(content)
    else:
      form = LoginForm()
      return render(request, 'login/login.html',{'form':form})
  else:
    return render(request, 'login/login.html',{'form':form})
```

When a request method is POST, the *form* object is instantiated with *LoginForm(request. POST)*, which is POST data submitted by the form.

Django's django.db library provides functions to query the database and *AppUser. objects.get(...)* function return a object of the AppUser class here which corresponds to a tuple in the databse matching the values provided as parameters - email and phone. The *reverse(...)* function provided by *django.urls* is useful for referencing urls by short names. Here *reverse('login:home')* looks up the url with the short name *"home"* in the scope of the app *login*. In order to leverage the use to reverse(...) function the urls in *hello_world/urls.py* have to be reconfigured in the following way -

```
urlpatterns = [
    url(r'^admin/', admin.site.urls),
    url(r'', include('login.urls')),
]
```

With the *include(...)* function the urls in login/url.py are supposed to be included when a request is made to http://10.10.0.150:9200/ as the regex for *'login.urls'* is set to empty *r''*. The file login/urls.py is not created by default by the *startapp* command and is as follows -

```
from django.conf.urls import url
from .views import *

app_name = 'login'

urlpatterns = [
    url(r'^signup/$', signup, name='signup'),
    url(r'^login/$', user_login, name='login'),
    url(r'^home/$', home, name="home"),
    url(r'^logout/$', logout, name="logout"),
]
```

app_name declares the namespace for the app to django templating engine. This is the namespace the function reverse('login:home') uses to address the url named *"home"* i.e. url(r'^home/$', home, name="home"). We have moved all the urls for the login app inside the login app's directory, thus utilising the cleanliness and maintainability philosophy of django framework.

Now as reverse('login:home') requests for the url named *home* in the *login* namespace, it corresponds to http://10.10.0.150:9200/home/. The form object is sent to login.html for rendering the LoginForm and is referenced as *{{ form.as_p }}*. The "{{ }}" is the templating format supported by jinja2. If *{{ form }}* was used instead of *{{ form.as_p }}* the different fields in the form would have been rendered side by side contrary to *as_p* which means *as-paragraph*.

Email:

eg. you@mailserver.com

Phone:

eg. 9000000000

Password:

Login

Unlike signup where csrf_exempt was used since the POST transaction did not involve any form data, the login activity does POST form submission and uses csrf token attached with the form data.

```
<form  method="post">
    <div class="form-group">
        {% csrf_token %}
        {{ form.as_p }}
    <div class="text-right">
        <input class="btn btn-primary"
    </div>
</form>
```

The {% csrf_token %} tag is render and expanded as -

```
<input type='hidden' name='csrfmiddlewaretoken'
    value='uqBzqoFUMVh7DYhxvgid7vmAbzDIW8KmusANuwMNI93egcIJv17WMzwxvfXGuGwV'/>
```

where value is produced by CsrfViewMiddleware and is a certain alpha-numeric string for every new request. On a successful user login the user is redirected to the home page *login/ templates/login/home.html* after saving a session cookie with *request.session["user_id"]*.

```
{% extends 'base.html' %}

{% block content %}

<h4>You are home!</h4>

<a class="btn" href="{% url 'login:logout' %}">Log out</a>

{% endblock %}
```

The {% url 'login:home' %} tag gets expanded into <a class="btn" href="/logout/">Log out</a>. The views for *home* and *logout* are -

```
def home(request):
    if request.method == 'GET':
        if request.session.has_key("user_id"):
            return render(request, 'login/home.html')
        else:
            content = "<p>First login, mate! </p>"
            return HttpResponse(content)
```

```
def logout(request):
  if request.method == 'GET':
    if request.session.has_key("user_id"):
      del request.session["user_id"]
    return HttpResponseRedirect(reverse('login:login'))
    else:
      content = "<p>First login, mate! </p>"
      return HttpResponse(content)
```

From user creation to authentication to logging out a user, all are functional, but we do not have a mechanism to intimate the user about a successful user creation other than the output of curl request. So we are going to send en email to a user with the credentials. Django is ahead of us even here and already has the *django.core.mail* library built to minimise the task accomplishment steps. The following keys need to be set in settings.py for using the *mail* library -

```
#Email settings
EMAIL_BACKEND = 'django.core.mail.backends.smtp.EmailBackend'
EMAIL_HOST= 'smtp.gmail.com'
EMAIL_HOST_USER= 'some.mail.address@gmail.com'
EMAIL_HOST_PASSWORD= 'imaginary@@paas'
EMAIL_PORT= '587'
EMAIL_USE_TLS = True
```

The actual function call is pretty straight forward -

*send_mail('subject','message body','from@mail.com',['to@mail.com'],fail_silently=False).* fail_silently if set True, the failure to send mail will not be logged. We will put a wrapper around the *send_mail(...)* function with exception handling -

```
from django.core.mail import send_mail
from django.conf import settings

def send_email(password,email_to,subject=None,message=None):
  if subject == None and message == None:
    subject = "Confidential: Hello World"
    message = "Your password is : " + password
  status_msg = None
  try:
    status_msg = send_mail(subject,message,
        settings.EMAIL_HOST_USER,[email_to],fail_silently=False)
  except Exception, e:
    print ("\n\n")
    print ("Exception in function: "+"send_email")
    print ("\nException info: ")
    print (e)
    return False
  return status_msg
```

The keys set in settings.py are accessible by importing *settings* from *django.conf* module and from there we are utilizing the *EMAIL_HOST_USER* key as the sender's email address in the call to send_mail. Lastly, the signup view has been updated to send email on successful user creation -

```
new_user.save()
sent = send_email(new_user.decrypt_password(),new_user.email)
if not sent:
  return JsonResponse({'success':True,'msg':'User created successfully,
          but mail could not be sent!'})
else:
  return JsonResponse({'success':True,'msg':'User created successfully'})
```

Although we have created a user authentication system, django itself comes with a authentication framework of its own which is provided by the app - *django.contrib.auth*. The database table to store a user for *django.contrib.auth* is *auth_user* -

```
mysql> desc auth_user;
+---------------+--------------+------+-----+---------+----------------+
| Field         | Type         | Null | Key | Default | Extra          |
+---------------+--------------+------+-----+---------+----------------+
| id            | int(11)      | NO   | PRI | NULL    | auto_increment |
| password      | varchar(128) | NO   |     | NULL    |                |
| last_login    | datetime(6)  | YES  |     | NULL    |                |
| is_superuser  | tinyint(1)   | NO   |     | NULL    |                |
| username      | varchar(150) | NO   | UNI | NULL    |                |
| first_name    | varchar(30)  | NO   |     | NULL    |                |
| last_name     | varchar(30)  | NO   |     | NULL    |                |
| email         | varchar(254) | NO   |     | NULL    |                |
| is_staff      | tinyint(1)   | NO   |     | NULL    |                |
| is_active     | tinyint(1)   | NO   |     | NULL    |                |
| date_joined   | datetime(6)  | NO   |     | NULL    |                |
+---------------+--------------+------+-----+---------+----------------+
```

The model corresponding to this table is *User* and so we'll go ahead in creating a user from the *shell* given by *manage.py*.

```
>>> from django.contrib.auth.models import User
>>> user = User.objects.create_user(username='rocketman',
... first_name='Abul',
... last_name='Kalam',
... email='abkalam@mail.com',
... password='i@am@rocket@man')
```

The password is encrypted by producing a hash for the plaintext password using the pbkdf2 and sha256 hashing algorithms and stored in the database -

```
mysql> select email,password from auth_user;
+-------------------+-----------------------------------------------------------------------------+
| email             | password                                                                    |
+-------------------+-----------------------------------------------------------------------------+
| abkalam@mail.com  | pbkdf2_sha256$36000$UdSsuFd6OAyo$kF0FvMcMZvwklD/5oe6qetzEF+nbC5q1odDSTmU+xl8= |
+-------------------+-----------------------------------------------------------------------------+
```

This newly created user has a dashboard provided by the app *django.contrib.admin* and its url in *hello_world/urls.py* -

```
url(r'^admin/', admin.site.urls),
```

Here is the admin dashboard at http://10.10.0.150:9200/admin -

ⓘ Not Secure | **10.10.0.150**:9200/admin/login/?next=/admin/

Django administration

Username:

Password:

Log in

This dashboard is for access to only staff and super users. The user created with *create_user(...)* function is neither of those and so we will first elevate the privilege of user *'rocketman'*.

```
>>> user = User.objects.get(pk=6)
>>>
>>>
>>>
>>>
>>> user.is_staff
False
>>> user.is_staff = True
>>> user.save()
```

Logging in for the user gives us the following dashboard.

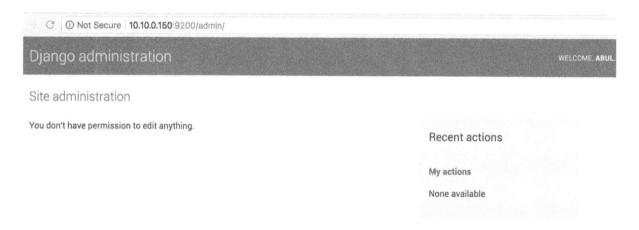

A staff type user will have no permissions by default where as a super user will be able to do all sort of operations of the database tables. The privileges of user 'rocketman' can be elevated to super user by re-settings the privilege from shell -

```
>>> user.is_staff
True
>>> user.is_superuser
False
>>> user.is_superuser = True
>>> user.save()
```

Now the dashboard's administrative sections are open.

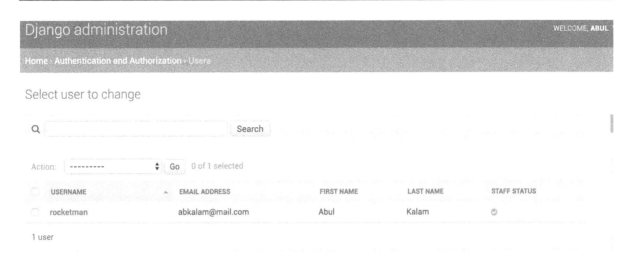

A super user can also be created using the *createsuperuser* sub-command provided by manage.py.

```
[root@ww-z1 hello_world]# python manage.py createsuperuser --email sg@mail.com --username superguy
Password:
Password (again):
Superuser created successfully.
```

Until now we have been in the development phase and have been using the development server provided by Django framework to test our application. We are now going to prepare our project for the production environment deployment.

First we will create separate settings.py files for development and production environments. The directory hello_world/hello_world had settings.py file which will be replaced by a directory named settings of the following structure -

```
hello_world/
├── __init__.py
├── __init__.pyc
├── settings
│   ├── base.py
│   ├── development.py
│   ├── __init__.py
│   └── production.py
├── urls.py
├── urls.pyc
├── wsgi.py
└── wsgi.pyc
```

The file base.py as the name suggests contain all the keys that we want to be common for all environments. Since *settings.py* no longer exists the key *BASE_DIR* in base.py has moved down one directory level and so it needs to be changed to -

```
# Build paths inside the project like this: os.path.join(BASE_DIR, ...)
BASE_DIR = os.path.dirname(os.path.dirname(os.path.dirname(os.path.abspath(__file__))))
```

The files production.py and development.py import base.py and declare the rest of the keys. The database settings on production.py are defined different than that of development.py and the DEBUG key is set to False as recommended in production.

```python
from .base import *

DEBUG = False


DATABASES = {
  'default': {
  'ENGINE': 'django.db.backends.mysql',
  'NAME': 'prod_appdb',
  'USER': 'prod_appuser',
  'PASSWORD': 'prod_appuser@DB112358',
  'HOST': '10.10.0.150',
  'PORT': '3306',
  'OPTIONS': {
      'init_command': "SET sql_mode='STRICT_TRANS_TABLES',innodb_strict_mode=1",
      'charset': 'utf8mb4',
          },
  }
  }



#Email settings
EMAIL_BACKEND = 'django.core.mail.backends.smtp.EmailBackend'
EMAIL_HOST= 'smtp.gmail.com'
EMAIL_HOST_USER= 'some.mail.address@gmail.com'
EMAIL_HOST_PASSWORD= 'imaginary@@paas'
EMAIL_PORT= '587'
EMAIL_USE_TLS = True
```

The development server can be run choosing any of the settings -

```
python manage.py runserver 10.10.0.150:9200 --settings=hello_world.settings.development
```

In the production environment we will be using Apache httpd web server and our working directory location will be shifted from /root/hello_world to /var/www/hello_world and so we have to relocate the static files in our development environment from /root/hello_world/static to /var/www/hello_world/static. The collectstatic command is going to be used to relocate the files after changing the value for STATIC_ROOT in hello_world/settings/base.py.

```
STATIC_ROOT = "/var/www/hello_world/static/"
```

```
python manage.py collectstatic --settings=hello_world.settings.production
```

The other contents in our project directory will be moved to /var/www/hello_world/ such that the directory structure looks the following -

```
[[root@ww-z1 www]# pwd
/var/www
[[root@ww-z1 www]# ll hello_world/
total 12
drwxr-xr-x. 3 root root 4096 Sep 12 14:05 hello_world
drwxr-xr-x. 2 root root   84 Sep 12 13:54 lib
drwxr-xr-x. 5 root root 4096 Sep 12 13:55 login
-rwxr-xr-x. 1 root root  809 Sep 12 13:55 manage.py
drwxr-xr-x. 3 root root   35 Sep 12 12:38 static
drwxr-xr-x. 3 root root   36 Sep 12 13:55 templates
```

The default settings file set by DJANGO_SETTINGS_MODULE in hello_world/hello_world/wsgi.py has to be set to production.py.

```
os.environ.setdefault("DJANGO_SETTINGS_MODULE", "hello_world.settings.production")
```

Finally, we will create a hello_world.conf in /etc/httpd/conf.d/ for Apache httpd web server,

```
Alias /static /var/www/hello_world/static
<Directory /var/www/hello_world/static>
    Require all granted
</Directory>

<Directory /var/www/hello_world/hello_world>
    <Files wsgi.py>
        Require all granted
    </Files>
</Directory>

WSGIDaemonProcess hello_world python-path=/var/www/hello_world:/usr/lib/python2.7/site-packages
WSGIProcessGroup hello_world
WSGIScriptAlias / /var/www//hello_world/hello_world/wsgi.py
```

And configure httpd.conf to listen to 10.10.0.150:80.

# Databases

Django has simplified the process of defining the database tables and relationships by taking an object oriented approach which we already had a glimpse in the earlier section. *Model* is the super class from which each defined database model inherits. Each model class is the representation of a table in a relational database, and a document in a NoSQL database. The latter although has a slightly different subclassing than relational which we will discuss later. The Django ORM (Object-Relational Mapping) enables the declaration of database schema through python classes and performing CRUD (Create - Retrieve - Update - Delete) operations in python syntax instead of SQL syntax.

In our hello_world project we already have a model AppUser and we will add another model AppService.

```python
class AppService(models.Model):
    service_name = models.CharField(max_length = 150)
    service_price = models.DecimalField(max_digits=5,decimal_places=2)
```

On applying the migrations the SQL equivalent statement for the model can be retrieved using the *sqlmigrate* command.

```
[root@ww-z1 hello_world]# python manage.py sqlmigrate login 0004 --settings=hello_world.settings.development
BEGIN;
--
-- Create model AppService
--
CREATE TABLE `login_appservice` (`id` integer AUTO_INCREMENT NOT NULL PRIMARY KEY, `service_name` varchar(150) NOT NULL, `service_price` numeric(5, 2) NOT NULL);
COMMIT;
```

For tables that do not have a field explicitly specified as the primary key field, django creates one automatically bearing the name *id* as shown in the output -

```
`id` integer AUTO_INCREMENT NOT NULL PRIMARY KEY
```

The *sqlmigrate* subcommand of *manage.py* has the following syntax -

```
python manage.py sqlmigrate <app-name> <migration-number>
```

Each change to the database schema whether adding a model or modifying a model, the changes are recorded in a sequential numbering format in the migrations directory of an app.

After applying the migrations for the newly added model AppService in login app, the changes are defined in the file *login/migrations/0004_appservice.py*. Therefore, sqlmigrate requires the name of the app and the sequence number of the migrations to display the SQL.

```
python manage.py sqlmigrate login 0004
```

Now coming back to the models, each member variable of a model class, which represents an attribute of a table, is defined using any of the desired Field class types such as - CharField, IntegerField, DecimalField, etc. Django uses these Field class types not just for models but also for defining Forms which we will be discussing later.

A Field class usually has the following parameters common to all of the Field types -

*null* - Django stores NULL value in database if set to True and it is set to False as default.
*blank* - This is different from *null* as it is related to form validation. When it is set to True, the respective form Field can be left empty.

Django's Field classes are used in defining both models and forms and they come together when *ModelForm* class is used to create a form from a model definition, which will be discussed later.

*choices* - This parameter also has its application in both models and forms and consists of a list of options. Each option is a tuple of two elements, one to be stored in the database and the other to be displayed in the web form. Here is such a list -

```
TITLES = (('Mr.','Mister'),
          ('Ms','Miss'))
```

Let us update the AppUser model to use this choices list by adding a new field *title*.

```
class AppUser(models.Model):
    title = models.CharField(choices=TITLES,max_length=2)
    first_name = models.CharField(max_length = 150,null=True)
    middle_name = models.CharField(max_length = 150,null=True)
    last_name = models.CharField(max_length = 150,null=True)
    email = models.EmailField(max_length=50, null=False,unique=True)
    phone = models.CharField(max_length=15, null=False,unique=True)
    created = models.DateTimeField(auto_now=True)
    password = models.CharField(max_length=120,null=False)
    key = models.CharField(max_length=44,null=True)
```

The first value in the tuple, say "Mr" is going to be inserted in the database corresponding to "Mister" being shown on the form.

Now when the migration task is executed once again, the changes are going to be affecting already existing tuples too. The title field will be added to the existing tuple and requires values for those fields. The following two options are provided on running migrations -

```
Please select a fix:
 1) Provide a one-off default now (will be set on all existing rows with a null value for this column)
 2) Quit, and let me add a default in models.py
```

We go ahead with the first option and enter "Mr" as our one-off default value.

```
Please select a fix:
 1) Provide a one-off default now (will be set on all
 2) Quit, and let me add a default in models.py
[Select an option: 1
Please enter the default value now, as valid Python
The datetime and django.utils.timezone modules are av
Type 'exit' to exit this prompt
[>>> "Mr"
Migrations for 'login':
  login/migrations/0005_appuser_title.py
    - Add field title to appuser
```

*default* - For the default value of a field.
*help_text* - Help test to be shown in a form field.
*primary_key* - To declare any field as the primary key by setting the value to True.
*unique* - It is to set a constraint on a field to contain only unique values.

There is a whole list of Field classes that ship with Django and can be found here -

The extensibility of Django allows creation of custom Fields if required and is discussed here -

The most significant purpose of relational database to form relationships with other tables and django makes definition of relations extremely easy. As we know that there are three types of relationships namely - One-to-One, One-to-Many and Many-to-One.

The One-to-One relationship means the use of ForeignKey with unique clause on the field and conceptually the association between tables is as follows -

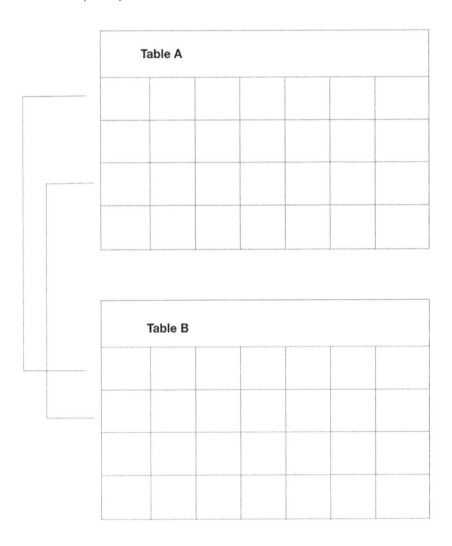

From the above diagram we can see how the values from Table A only appear once in Table B for a particular field. This One-to-One mapping is achieved in Django through the use of OneToOneField.

To demonstrate the relation we created a new ExecUser table that represents those app users who are also the executives of the app product.

```
class ExecUser(models.Model):
    user = models.OneToOneField(AppUser,on_delete=models.CASCADE)
```

The models.CASADE is a function which removes those tuples from ExecUser table for which the corresponding AppUser tuples have been deleted.

The table ExecUser has one one field - user, which is the Django ORM way to define a relation. In the background, django creates the table with two fields -

```
[mysql> desc login_execuser;
+----------+---------+------+-----+---------+----------------+
| Field    | Type    | Null | Key | Default | Extra          |
+----------+---------+------+-----+---------+----------------+
| id       | int(11) | NO   | PRI | NULL    | auto_increment |
| user_id  | int(11) | NO   | UNI | NULL    |                |
+----------+---------+------+-----+---------+----------------+
2 rows in set (0.00 sec)
```

The *id* field is a default primary key that is created by Django and *user_id* is the field that contains the value of primary key field of the related table similar to that of foreign key.

We create an entry in ExecUser -

```
>>> user = AppUser.objects.get(id=2)
>>> user
<AppUser: mail@galaxy.com 3141592653>
>>> euser = ExecUser(user=user)
>>> euser.save()
```

With relations such as this, Django ORM makes both forward and reverse lookup possible. Here we show the *euser* instance can be access from *user* and vice- versa -

```
>>> user.execuser.user_id
2L
>>> euser.user.id
2L
```

The One-to-Many relation conceptually is of the following form -

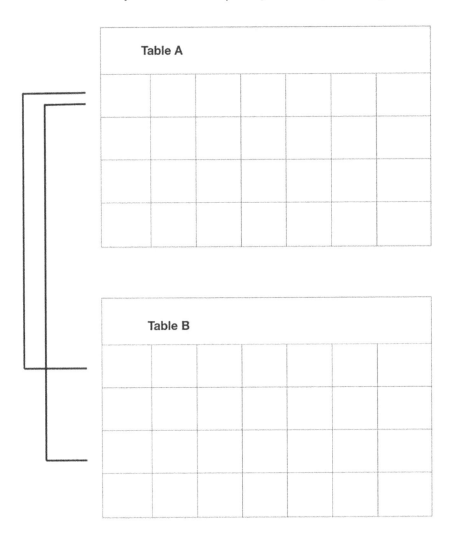

The Many-to-One relationship is established using the ForeignKey field -

```
class AppServiceManager(models.Model):
    manager = models.ForeignKey('ExecUser',on_delete=models.CASCADE)
    service = models.ForeignKey('AppService',on_delete=models.CASCADE)
```

The field *manager* forms a chain relation of AppServiceManager, from ExecUser to AppUser and this entire relation can be traversed just with an object of the AppServiceManager class.

Here we see how with an instance of the AppServiceManager class, we access the *manager* member of the ExecUser class and from the *user* member of ExecUser we are able to access the *first_name* member of AppUser Class.

```
>>> app_manager = AppServiceManager.objects.all()[0]
>>> app_manager.manager.user.first_name
u'Stephen'
```

The Many-To-Many relationship is required in cases where multiple tuples from one table are related to multiple tuples in another and is conceptually represented as the following -

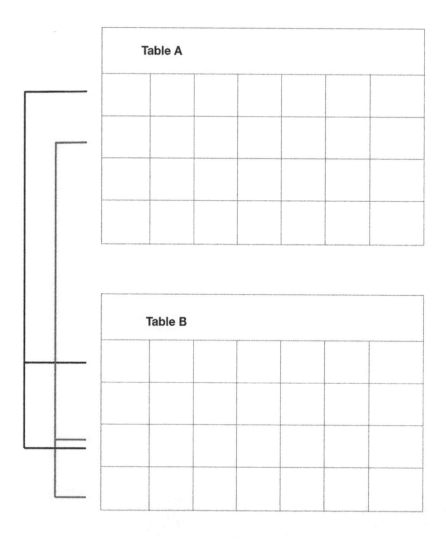

We will create such a relation between AppUser and AppService classes as a single AppUser can be subscribed to multiple AppService(s). A Many-to-Many relationship requires a single field to have multiple references, for example, AppUser needs to record all the primary key values of the subscribed services in its *subscriptions* field.

## AppUser Table

| id | title | first_name | ... | subscriptions |
|----|-------|------------|-----|---------------|
| 1  | Mr    | Stephen    |     | 1,3,4         |
|    |       |            |     |               |
|    |       |            |     |               |
|    |       |            |     |               |

But as we may know that it is against the guidelines of relational database management and so such a relationship requires a dedicated table in the following way -

## AppUser Table

| id | title | first_name |
|----|-------|------------|
| 1  | Mr    | Stephen    |

## AppService Table

| id | service_name     | service_price |
|----|------------------|---------------|
| 1  | Media Streaming  | 599.00        |
| 2  | Picture Upload   | 199.00        |

## Subscriptions Table

| appuser_id | appservice_id |
|------------|---------------|
| 1          | 1             |
| 1          | 2             |

Django removes the necessity of defining such a *Subscription* table for the relationship and creates an intermediate table internally.

A *subscriptions* field is added to the AppUser class.

```
class AppUser(models.Model):
    title = models.CharField(choices=TITLES,max_length=2)
    first_name = models.CharField(max_length = 150,null=True)
    middle_name = models.CharField(max_length = 150,null=True)
    last_name = models.CharField(max_length = 150,null=True)
    email = models.EmailField(max_length=50, null=False,unique=True)
    phone = models.CharField(max_length=15, null=False,unique=True)
    created = models.DateTimeField(auto_now=True)
    password = models.CharField(max_length=120,null=False)
    key = models.CharField(max_length=44,null=True)
    subscriptions = models.ManyToManyField(AppService)
```

Then multiple objects of the AppService class are added to the *subscriptions* field in the following way -

```
>>> from login.models import *
>>>
>>> user = AppUser.objects.all()[0]
>>> services = (AppService.objects.get(pk=1),AppService.objects.get(pk=2))
>>>
>>> user.subscriptions.add(*services)
>>> user.save()
```

and list of values can be viewed without knowing the reference to intermediate table -

```
>>> user.subscriptions.values_list()
<QuerySet [(1L, u'Media Streaming', Decimal('599.00')), (2L, u'Photo Upload', Decimal('199.00'))]>
>>>
```

The remaining of the pool of capabilities with the Model class in Django is described elaborately at -

Almost most of the modern day applications use both relational as well as NoSQL database and so we are going to use mongoDB. We are going to use *mongoengine*, which is an object oriented mapper for implementing mongoDB.

A NoSQL database is schema-less which means there is no such requirement to perform migrations. In RDBMS a schema was represented through a class definition in *models.py*, but in non-RDBMS a class represents a document whose fields can be added and/or removed without requiring migrations.

In our project, we will add another application *social* which will contain the social comments from the users. We have installed both mongoDB and mongoengine from their official installation documentation and created a database named *social*.

```
[> show dbs
admin   0.000GB
local   0.000GB
social  0.000GB
```

As usual we define the document class in social/models.py in the following way -

```python
from mongoengine import *
connect('social')


class Testimonial(Document):
    service_name = StringField(required=True,max_length=150)
    user_first_name = StringField(required=True,max_length=150)
    hash_tags = ListField(StringField(max_length=30))
```

The glaring difference from previous models we see here, is, the use of connect() function from mongoenigne to connect to the database. We can invoke the connect() function in hello_world/settings.py as well.

The insertion of documents into the database is pretty straightforward -

```
>>> from social.models import *
>>> from login.models import *
>>>
>>>
>>> user = AppUser.objects.get(pk=1)
>>> service = AppService.objects.get(pk=1)
>>>
>>> Testimonial(service_name=service.service_name,user_first_name=user.first_name,hash_tags=["#wow","#stream"]).save()
<Testimonial: Testimonial object>
```

A collection is created in the database social by the name *testimonial* corresponding to the name of our document class name *Testimonial*.

```
> use social
switched to db social
> show collections
testimonial
```

Here is an example for the retrieval of documents based on a criteria -

```
[>>> Testimonial.objects(user_first_name__startswith="nik")
[<Testimonial: Testimonial object>, <Testimonial: Testimonial object>]
```

Further details about querying the database can be found at -

When working with multiple databases in mongoDB, the class definitions need to use the *db_alias* meta variable. We have created another database *esocial* in mongoDB and re-write the connection function call with alias names for each connection -

```
from mongoengine import *
connect(db='social',alias='user-db')
connect(db='esocial',alias='exec-db')
```

Now these aliases are going to be specified in each of the model classes as required such as the following -

```
class Testimonial(Document):
    service_name = StringField(required=True,max_length=150)
    user_first_name = StringField(required=True,max_length=150)
    hash_tags = ListField(StringField(max_length=30))

    meta = {'db_alias':'user-db'}

class ExecTestimonial(Document):
    service_name = StringField(required=True,max_length=150)
    user_first_name = StringField(required=True,max_length=150)
    hash_tags = ListField(StringField(max_length=30))

    meta = {'db_alias':'exec-db'}
```

Documents will be written in the respective databases as specified through the meta member variable. The documents will always be written to the specified databases, but if there is a requirement to perform an operation on a different database, it can be done by temporarily switching using the switch_db() function.

```
>>> from mongoengine.context_managers import switch_db
>>> with switch_db(Testimonial,'exec-db') as Testimonial:
...     Testimonial(service_name=service.service_name,user_first_name=user.first_name,hash_tags=["#exec_switch","#switched"]).save()
...
<Testimonial: Testimonial object>
```

In the above snippet, a new *collection* was created in the *esocial* database with the name *testimonial* corresponding to the class Testimonial and the document of Testimonial type was created. Here we see there are now two collections are present in the database esocial - exec_testimonial for ExecTestimonial and testimonial -

```
> use esocial
switched to db esocial
> show collections
exec_testimonial
testimonial
```

As we have seen the use of NoSQL database along with an RDBMS in a project, it is also a common use case where multiple RDBMS are used in applications. Django has official support and drivers for most of the widely used RDBMS(s) such as MySQL, PostgreSQL, Oracle, SQLite and several others. Django provides database routers to apps in a project to switch between different databases.

Before using database routers, we will prepare a PostgreSQL setup for our project and below are the set of steps. We will setup the database on a different host (ww-z2) than the host where our Django project is running.

First we install, initialise and start the server -

```
[[root@ww-z2 ~]# yum install postgresql-server postgresql-contrib postgresql-devel -y -q -e 0
[[root@ww-z2 ~]# postgresql-setup initdb
 Initializing database ... Full path required for exclude: net:[4026532201].
 Full path required for exclude: net:[4026532290].
 Full path required for exclude: net:[4026532201].
 Full path required for exclude: net:[4026532290].
 Full path required for exclude: net:[4026532201].
 Full path required for exclude: net:[4026532290].
 OK

[[root@ww-z2 ~]# systemctl start postgresql;systemctl enable postgresql
```

The default port for the database server is 5432 and it binds to the localhost. We will change the bind IP to the public IP of the host which is 10.10.0.198.

The *listen_address* parameter's value will be set to 10.10.0.198 in */var/lib/pgsql/data/postgresql.conf -*

```
#--------------------------------------------
# CONNECTIONS AND AUTHENTICATION
#--------------------------------------------

# - Connection Settings -

listen_addresses = '10.10.0.198'
```

In order for our application to be able to connect to the database, it has to be allowed to accept connections with password based authentication. The */var/lib/pgsql/data/pg_hba.conf* file is responsible for managing the authentication methods and we add an entry to the end of the file allowing connections from 10.10.0.150.

```
# TYPE  DATABASE        USER            ADDRESS                 METHOD

# "local" is for Unix domain socket connections only
local   all             all                                     peer
# IPv4 local connections:
host    all             all             127.0.0.1/32            ident
# IPv6 local connections:
host    all             all             ::1/128                 ident
# Application host
host    all             all             10.10.0.150/32          md5
```

Next the postgresql service will be restarted for the changes to take action.

The installation of PostgreSQL creates a system user with the name *postgres* which has all the administrative privileges on the database. For our application we will create a database user by the name *socialuser*, create a database *socialdb*, but first we will have to switch to the postgres system user in order to perform these operations.

```
[root@ww-z2 ~]# sudo su - postgres
-bash-4.2$ createuser socialuser
-bash-4.2$ createdb socialdb
-bash-4.2$ psql
psql (9.2.24)
Type "help" for help.

postgres=# \l
                                  List of databases
   Name    |  Owner   | Encoding |   Collate   |    Ctype    |   Access privileges
-----------+----------+----------+-------------+-------------+-----------------------
 postgres  | postgres | UTF8     | en_US.UTF-8 | en_US.UTF-8 |
 socialdb  | postgres | UTF8     | en_US.UTF-8 | en_US.UTF-8 |
 template0 | postgres | UTF8     | en_US.UTF-8 | en_US.UTF-8 | =c/postgres          +
           |          |          |             |             | postgres=CTc/postgres
 template1 | postgres | UTF8     | en_US.UTF-8 | en_US.UTF-8 | =c/postgres          +
           |          |          |             |             | postgres=CTc/postgres
(4 rows)
```

The *createuser* and *createdb* commands are available from the installation. The database shell is connected with *psql* command and we can see in the above output, our database is successfully created. Next, a password has to be created for the *socialuser* user and granted access to the *socialdb* database.

```
[postgres=# alter user socialuser with encrypted password 'socialuser@DB112358';
ALTER ROLE
[postgres=# grant all privileges on database socialdb to socialuser;
GRANT
```

With that our PostgreSQL is ready to function with our application.

Now again getting back to the application project host (ww-z1), we install the *psycopg2* package for python to work with PostgreSQL -

```
pip install psycopg2
```

For Django to connect to the PostgreSQL database, the project's settings.py file has to be reconfigured for DATABASES parameter. The following is the updated settings in hello_world/settings/development.py -

```
DATABASES = {
    'default' : {},
    'app_db': {
    'ENGINE': 'django.db.backends.mysql',
    'NAME': 'appdb',
    'USER': 'appuser',
    'PASSWORD': 'appuser@DB112358',
    'HOST': '10.10.0.150',
    'PORT': '3306',
    'OPTIONS': {
        'init_command': "SET sql_mode='STRICT_TRANS_TABLES',innodb_strict_mode=1",
        'charset': 'utf8mb4',
            },
    },
    'social_db' : {
    'ENGINE': 'django.db.backends.postgresql',
    'NAME': 'socialdb',
    'USER': 'socialuser',
    'PASSWORD': 'socialuser@DB112358',
    'HOST': '10.10.0.198',
    'PORT': '5432',
    }
    }
```

Previously we had just MySQL database as the default and so to work with PostgreSQL alongside, both of the database connection configurations have to be scoped with separate namespaces. The *default* key of DATABASES parameter is left empty and the new keys *app_db* and *social_db* are the new namespaces for MySQL and PostgreSQL respectively.

Next we will define a new table which will store data in PostgresSQL database. Here is the model created in social/models.py -

```python
class PrimeAppUser(models.Model):
    title = models.CharField(choices=TITLES,max_length=2)
    first_name = models.CharField(max_length = 150,null=True)
    middle_name = models.CharField(max_length = 150,null=True)
    last_name = models.CharField(max_length = 150,null=True)
    email = models.EmailField(max_length=50, null=False,unique=True)
    phone = models.CharField(max_length=15, null=False,unique=True)

    def __str__(self):
        return self.email + " " + self.phone

    class Meta:
        app_label = "social"
```

Since we are working with multiple databases we are going to set the *app_label* Meta class member to the name of the app, here *social* and also in the data models defined in *login* app.

Now we run migrations -

```
[root@ww-z1 hello_world]# python manage.py makemigrations  --settings=hello_world.settings.development social
/usr/lib64/python2.7/site-packages/psycopg2/__init__.py:144: UserWarning: The psycopg2 wheel package will be re
 use "pip install psycopg2-binary" instead. For details see: <http://initd.org/psycopg/docs/install.html#binary
 """)
Migrations for 'social':
  social/migrations/0001_initial.py
    - Create model PrimeAppUser
```

```
[root@ww-z1 hello_world]# python manage.py migrate --database=social_db  --settings=hello_world.settings.development social
/usr/lib64/python2.7/site-packages/psycopg2/__init__.py:144: UserWarning: The psycopg2 wheel package will be renamed from relea
 use "pip install psycopg2-binary" instead. For details see: <http://initd.org/psycopg/docs/install.html#binary-install-from-py
 """)
Operations to perform:
  Apply all migrations: social
Running migrations:
  Applying social.0001_initial... OK
```

At this point the table has been created in the PostgreSQL database *socialdb*.

Database requests initially went to the default database as set in DATABASES parameter in setting, but now with multiple databases there has to be a routing mechanism that intercepts the incoming database requests and forwards to the correct endpoints. This routing mechanism is handled by the module *django.db.router* which is the first point of interception of a request. We have to define router classes specific to our project outlining the usage capabilities of each separate database. A router class needs to define four methods - *db_for_read*, *db_for_write*, *allow_relation* and *allow_migrate*. Each of these functions represent a fundamental database activity and it is defined in these functions, that which model classes are allowed to perform the operations and on which database.

We will create two routers one for the login app and the other for social app. The router for social app is defined in *social/social_router.py* -

```python
class SocialRouter:
    """
    A router to control all database operations on models in the
    social application.
    """
    def db_for_read(self, model, **hints):
        if model._meta.app_label == 'social':
            return 'social_db'
        return None


    def db_for_write(self, model, **hints):
        if model._meta.app_label == 'social':
            return 'social_db'
        return None

    def allow_relation(self, obj1, obj2, **hints):
        if obj1._meta.app_label == 'social' or obj2._meta.app_label == 'social':
            return True
        return None

    def allow_migrate(self, db, app_label, model_name=None, **hints):
        if app_label == 'social':
            return db == 'social_db'
        return None
```

In each of the functions it is being checked for the value of the *app_label* which has been defined in each of the model class' Meta inner class.

```python
if model._meta.app_label == 'social':
    return 'social_db'
```

In the above snippet, we provide the directive to master router *django.db.router* that a model that has the *app_label* set to *social* will be directed to the database that has the namespace set to *social_db* in DATABASES parameter of project setting.

We will define another router for the login app at login/login_router.py -

```python
class LoginRouter:
    """
    A router to control all database operations on models in the
    login application.
    """

    def db_for_read(self, model, **hints):
        if model._meta.app_label == 'login':
            return 'app_db'
        return None
```

```python
def db_for_write(self, model, **hints):
  if model._meta.app_label == 'login':
    return 'app_db'
  return None

def allow_relation(self, obj1, obj2, **hints):
  if obj1._meta.app_label == 'login' or obj2._meta.app_label == 'login':
    return True
  return None

def allow_migrate(self, db, app_label, model_name=None, **hints):
  if app_label == 'login':
    return db == 'app_db'
  return None
```

Now these two routers have to be identified by the mater router and so we will enlist the routers in project settings with the parameter DATABASE_ROUTERS.

```python
DATABASE_ROUTERS = ['social.social_router.SocialRouter','login.login_router.LoginRouter']
```

This is the flow of control for database routing -

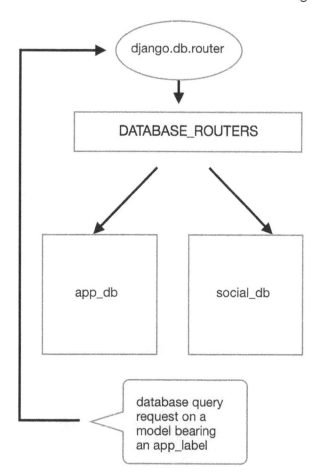

Therefore, now when we perform a query request to insert a tuple into PrimeAppUser, the request is intercepted by the master router (django.db.router), looked up for a matching directive among the list of routers in DATABASE_ROUTERS and forwarded to the correct database endpoint.

```
PrimeAppUser(title="Mr",first_name="Elon",last_name="Musk",email="em@galaxy.com",phone="9191919191").save()
```

The above query creates an entry in the PostgreSQL database - *socialdb*.

```
[root@ww-z2 ~]# sudo su - postgres
Last login: Fri Nov  2 09:03:45 UTC 2018 on pts/1
-bash-4.2$ psql -d socialdb
psql (9.2.24)
Type "help" for help.

socialdb=# \d
                    List of relations
 Schema |           Name            |   Type   |   Owner
--------+---------------------------+----------+------------
 public | django_migrations         | table    | socialuser
 public | django_migrations_id_seq  | sequence | socialuser
 public | social_primeappuser       | table    | socialuser
 public | social_primeappuser_id_seq | sequence | socialuser
(4 rows)

socialdb=# select * from social_primeappuser;
 id | title | first_name | middle_name | last_name |      email      |   phone
----+-------+------------+-------------+-----------+-----------------+------------
  1 | Mr    | Elon       |             | Musk      | em@galaxy.com   | 9191919191
(1 row)
```

The rest of the capabilities in working with database routers have been detailed here -

With the various types of databases setup in our project and having performed basic insert and deletion operations of data, we will now take a walkthrough of the ways Django lets us form database queries. All data retrieval queries return tuples as objects in a *QuerySet*. Querying the database involves performing comparisons on data fields of table or relation and Django has *filter()* and *exclude()* functions for this purpose.

Here is an example query to fetch tuples using filter() -

```
>>> AppUser.objects.filter(created__lt=datetime.now())
<QuerySet [<AppUser: nikola@galaxy.com 9292929292>]>
```

The arguments sent to filter(...) always has to be an operator on some field of the model being queried. In the above example, AppUser model is queried on the *created* field, such that those model objects i.e. tuples are to be fetched whose value is less than (lt) the current date-time. There are a whole list of operators such as lt, lte, gt, gte, eq, etc. and the argument sent to a filter function is always on the format - <field_name>__<operator>. The exclude(...) function is daisy chained with filter(...) function -

```
[>>> AppUser.objects.filter(created__lt=datetime.now()).exclude(first_name__startswith="nik")
<QuerySet []>
```

The tuples ordered using the order_by(...) function -

```
>>> AppUser.objects.filter(created__lt=datetime.now()).order_by('-created')
<QuerySet [<AppUser: sh@galaxy.com 93939393939>, <AppUser: nikola@galaxy.com 9292929292>]>
>>>
>>>
>>>
>>>
>>> AppUser.objects.filter(created__lt=datetime.now()).order_by('created')
<QuerySet [<AppUser: nikola@galaxy.com 9292929292>, <AppUser: sh@galaxy.com 93939393939>]>
```

The order_by(...) function argument is specified with a ' - ' (minus) character to order in descending order.

Django ORM makes database lookups that span relationships (SQL Join operations) extremely easy. In the below example, the ExecUser model which has a One-to-One mapping with the AppUser model on the *user* field, is being used to query the AppUser model objects.

```
[>>> ExecUser.objects.filter(user__first_name__exact="nikola")
<QuerySet [<ExecUser: ExecUser object>]>
```

Those ExecUser objects are returned that have an AppUser with the exact match with the value "nikola" in the first_name field.

These were few examples of relatively simple queries. Django provides Q objects to form complex queries involving multiple constraints for database lookup.

Suppose we have a SQL query such as the following -

SELECT * FROM appuser WHERE first_name LIKE "nik%" AND (created > '2018-10-01 01:00:00' OR created < '2018-11-30 23:00:00')

This query consisting of multiple criteria is constructed with Q objects in the following way by describing each selection criteria as parameter to Q -

```
>>> AppUser.objects.filter(Q(first_name__startswith='nik'),
... Q(created__gt='2018-10-01 01:00:00')|Q(created__lt='2018-11-30 23:00:00'))
<QuerySet [<AppUser: nikola@galaxy.com 9292929292>]>
```

Further details about making queries are here -

# Forms

The django web framework has takes an object oriented approach towards forms similar to the way it treats database models. Just as the way each field in the *Model* class represents a field in the database table, a field in the *Form* class represents an <input/> tag in the corresponding <form/>. The form fields are created using a similar set of sub-classes of Field class such as DateField, IntegerField, etc.

HTML forms can be created without defining them as Form classes which we have already seen in our project in the login form in login app, and here is such a snippet depicting a form that accepts a string value and has been rendered manually -

```
<form method="post">
  <label for="username"> User name: </label>
  <input id="username" type="text" name="username" value="{{ user_name }}">
  <input type="submit" value="OK">
</form>
```

In the above form, the textual data inserted in the *username* field is stored in the *user_name* variable defined in the corresponding *view* that renders the HTML. This same form when defined as a Form class in forms.py looks like the following -

```
from django import forms

class Username(forms.Form):
  user_name = forms.CharField(label="User name:", max_length=20)
```

The class Username defines a form whose instance will be used to render the HTML equivalent <form/> as well as extract the value inserted in the form, by views defined in views.py. This is a generic structuring of a view -

```
def some_view(request):
  user_form = Username()
  if request.method == 'POST':
    user_form = Username(request.POST)
    if user_form.is_valid():
      """
      Extract data from the form and do stuff.
      """
      pass
    else:
      user_form = Username()
      return render(request, 'sample/sample.html',{'form':user_form})
  else:
    return render(request, 'sample/sample.html',{'form':user_form})
```

The form object user_form when used in sample.html as *form*, takes the following form -

```
<form action="/some-url/" method="post">
    {% csrf_token %}
    {{ form }}
    <input type="submit" value="OK">
</form>
```

The Form class fields corresponds all <input/> tags except the *submit* type. The *form* variable can be represented in three more formats -

{{ *form.as_table* }} - The form fields are rendered as table cells wrapped in <tr/> tags.

{{ *form.as_p* }} - It rendered the fields wrapped in <p/> tags.

{{ *form.as_ul* }} - It renders the fields wrapped in <li/> tags.

The pythonic approach to things makes handling forms as well as models, a similar and sometimes a homogeneous experience in django. In fact as mentioned earlier in this section of the book, the Field class makes it possible to create *forms* from *model* definitions.

In a database driven application, there are use cases where the data submitted through a form requires to be stored in a database. A common example is of a user details form -

```
class User(forms.Form):
    first_name = forms.CharField(label="First name:",required=True,max_length=30)
    middle_name = forms.CharField(label="Middle name:",required=True,max_length=30)
    last_name = forms.CharField(label="Last name:",required=True,max_length=30)
    email = forms.EmailField(label="Email",requied=True)
```

A corresponding database model would be as this -

```
class UserModel(models.Model):
    first_name = models.CharField(max_length=30)
    middle_name = models.CharField(max_length=30)
    last_name = models.CharField(max_length=30)
    email = models.EmailField()
```

Django has classes and functions take care of data validation for form data and alongside the common Field class for usage in both forms and models, it becomes possible to build the forms from models using ModelForm class. The same User form when built using ModelForm, takes the following structure -

```
class User(ModelForm):
    class Meta:
        model = UserModel
        fields = ['first_name','middle_name','last_name','email']
```

Since the *User* form is using the fields defined in UserModel, the model definition has to be updated to account for the constraints such as - *required=True*, previously set for the form.

```
class UserModel(models.Model):
  first_name = models.CharField(max_length=30,null=False,blank=False)
  middle_name = models.CharField(max_length=30,null=False,blank=False)
  last_name = models.CharField(max_length=30,null=False,blank=False)
  email = models.EmailField(null=False,blank=False)
```

The *blank* parameter is in the context of a form, stating that a value is *required* in the field. Here is the official documentation for working with forms -

All the various Form fields are described here -

The final topic we will discuss about Django forms is the *Widget* class. As we know that each field is a Form class definition represents a corresponding HTML <input/> tag, but the form fields are not responsible for rendering the <input/> tags. Rather, they are responsible for the logic behind input validation of the data input in a form field. For example the *EmailField* class uses the *EmailValidator* class as it driver for input validation. In order to render the HTML corresponding to the Field instance, the *EmailInput* widget class is used which actually does the rendering of the proper <input/> tag. Each Field class comes with a default widget and it is customisable such as the following snippet -

```
class CommentForm(forms.Form):
  name = forms.CharField(widget=forms.TextInput(attrs={'class': 'form-control',
        'name': 'email','placeholder':'John Apppleseed'}))
  url = forms.URLField()
  comment = forms.CharField(widget=forms.Textarea)
```

The default widget for CharField is TextInput but the widget argument set to Textarea renders a <textarea/> HTML in the form. The base class of TextInput is *Widget* class which accepts the parameter attrs that is a dictionary of all the attributes of an HTML element as we can see in the below snippet -

```
>>> from django import forms
>>> name = forms.TextInput(attrs={'size': 10, 'title': 'Your name'})
>>> name.render('name', 'A name')
u'<input type="text" name="name" value="A name" size="10" title="Your name" />'
```

Widgets have been discussed in detail here -

# Logging

Django provides a great library to process and curate logs using the builtin *logging* module. For any application, generating and taking care of the logs serves as one of the most important factor in rapid development of any project. With good logging setup for an application right from the beginning of the development phase, the debugging cycles becomes less time consuming and the application as a whole is more descriptive of its activities.

The django logging framework consists of four constituents -

*Loggers* - They are named buckets and form the entry point into the logging system to which logs are sent. A logger can have one of the five log levels - DEBUG, INFO, WARNING, ERROR, CRITICAL. Log messages when sent to the logging system, it is compared against its log level to be sent to the designated bucket.

*Handler* - After a log message is directed to a bucket, the next task is to form the logic what to do with a certain log message. The term bucket is being used here simply in terms of a logical namespace, and so it is the handler that decides whether a log message should be written to a file or console terminal or to a network socket. A logger can have multiple handlers, one for each log level as well as multiple handlers that treat one log level (say CRITICAL) in multiple ways.

*Filter* - A filter as the name suggest performs the task of selection of logs that are then going to be handled by a handler. Filters can also be active even before the handling process such as, a filter that intercepts all incoming CRITICAL messages and changes the priority level to WARNING before even getting collected in a logger bucket. Therefore, filters can be applied on both loggers as well as handlers.

*Formatters* - Any log information is basically textual data and with formatters, a log string message is formatted w.r.t. python string formatting tools.

The logging system declaration is done through a dictionary LOGGING in settings -

```python
LOGGING = {
    'version': 1,
    'disable_existing_loggers': False,
    'formatters' : {},
    'filters': {},
    'handlers': {},
    'loggers': {}
}
```

The *version* key specifies the dictionary configuration format (dictConfig). The *disable_existing_loggers* is set to False, suggesting that the loggers that come by default with Django framework to be used.

We are going to setup a logging system for our project with a filter applied on handlers and so the filter will be declared first.

```
'filters': {
    'require_debug_true': {
        '()': 'django.utils.log.RequireDebugTrue',
        },
    },
```

The filter is named *require_debug_true*. The '()' is representative of calling the constructor function of the *RequireDebugTrue* class. The *RequireDebugTrue* class like all of the other filter classes have a *filter(...)* member function which gets called to perform the filter operation and here in case of *RequireDebugTrue* class it returns a boolean value for the state of the DEBUG mode of our project. Therefore, the filter will only pass on records if the DEBUG parameter in our project settings is set to True.

The filter to be applied on a handler is created and so we declare the handlers next.

```
'handlers': {
    'console': {
        'level': 'INFO',
        'filters': ['require_debug_true'],
        'class': 'logging.StreamHandler',
        'formatter': 'simple',
        },
    'mail_failure': {
        'level': 'ERROR',
        'class': 'django.utils.log.AdminEmailHandler',
        }
    },
```

We have two handlers - *console* and *mail_failure*. The *level* key sets the aforesaid level of a log message. Django already comes with a collection of pre-created handler classes and *StreamHandler* is one of them. The *StreamHandler* class handles the standard I/O stream. The *console* handler accepts all INFO level logs if it satisfies the *filters*. The formatter named *simple* is yet to be defined and it will format a log record accordingly and send it of the designated logger. The *mail_failure* handler gets active when a mail sending operation has failed and the error level is ERROR.

We will add another handler that handles to which log file the log messages will be directed.

```
'logfile': {
    'class':'logging.handlers.RotatingFileHandler',
    'filename': os.path.join(BASE_DIR, 'alllogs.log'),
    'maxBytes': 1024*1024*15,
    'backupCount': 2,
    },
```

The RotatingFileHandler takes care of log rotation for us and the keys maxBytes state the maz size of a log file and backupCount states how many old log files are to be maintained.

The formatter is defined as the following -

```
'formatters' : {
    'simple': {
            'format': '{levelname} {message}',
            'style': '{',
        },
},
```

The style key represents the literal separator in a log record. Python's str.format(...) methos is used to perform the string formatting operation and so the character '{' signifies the delimiter for registering keywords in the log record, like {levelname} in the following way -

```
>>> "{levelname}: is the level of log and {msg}: is the message".format(levelname="ERROR",msg="divide by zero")
'ERROR: is the level of log and divide by zero: is the message'
```

Lastly the loggers are defined -

```
'loggers': {
    'django': {
        'handlers': ['console','logfile'],
        'propagate': True,
        },
    'django.request': {
        'handlers': ['mail_failure','logfile'],
        'level': 'ERROR',
        'propagate': False,
        },
    }
```

The naming convention of loggers has a dotted naming format such as *django.request* as in the above snippet. This is a heirarchy and setting the propagate key to False, states that the handler should not pass on the log record to the parent handler which is *django (django <-request)*. The handler key as we can guess lists the handlers operating on a logger.

Further details about working with loggers can be found here -

The logging system has been set up and now in order to produce logs, first an instance of a logger has to be created -

```
[>>> import logging
[>>> logger = logging.getLogger('django.request')
[>>> logger.error("mail not sent")
[>>>
```

On generating a log message by calling the *error()* function, the message should be available in the *alllogs.log* file.

```
[root@ww-z1 hello_world]# cat alllogs.log
mail not sent
```

# Writing tests

For any application it is important to test each component after they are developed. Django comes with a robust testing framework that makes writing unit tests easy with the module *unittest*.

Each app in our project gets created with a tests.py file by default. For our case we are going to write a simple test for the *login* app. We will insert a tuple into the AppService table and check the field values in the tuple.

Here is the code for our test in login/tests.py -

```python
from __future__ import unicode_literals

from django.test import TestCase
from login.models import AppService
from decimal import *
# Create your tests here.


class AppServiceTestCase(TestCase):
  def setUp(self):
    AppService.objects.create(service_name='Test service',service_price=99.9)

  def test_app_service_creation(self):
    """ To check if tuples are getting created """
    service = AppService.objects.get(service_name='Test service')

    self.assertEqual(service.service_name,'The service name is "Test service"')
    self.assertEqual(service.service_price,Decimal('99.90'))
```

We have imported the subclass *TestCase* from the unittest framework and the model AppService. With the *setUP* method of AppServiceTestCase class, the tuple is created and test_app_service_creation method is used to test the field values.

The django test framework creates a temporary database and once the tests are finished, the database is removed. Before running the tests, we have to configure the DATABASES key in settings. For our project we are using multiple databases and database routers, but for for our testing purpose, we only need to ensure the desired data is available. We are going to comment out the DATABASE_ROUTERS key in *hello_world/settings/development.py* and only the default database available. The following snippet from development.py shows the required changes -

```python
DATABASES = {
  'default': {
    'ENGINE': 'django.db.backends.mysql',
    'NAME': 'appdb',
```

```
    'USER': 'appuser',
    'PASSWORD': 'appuser@DB112358',
    'HOST': '10.10.0.150',
    'PORT': '3306',
    'OPTIONS': {
        'init_command': "SET sql_mode='STRICT_TRANS_TABLES',innodb_strict_mode=1",
        'charset': 'utf8mb4',
                },
    'TEST':{'NAME':'test_appdb'},
    },
    }
```

```
#DATABASES = {
#    'default' : {},
#    'app_db' : {
#    'ENGINE': 'django.db.backends.mysql',
#    'NAME': 'appdb',
#    'USER': 'appuser',
#    'PASSWORD': 'appuser@DB112358',
#    'HOST': '10.10.0.150',
#    'PORT': '3306',
#    'OPTIONS': {
#        'init_command': "SET sql_mode='STRICT_TRANS_TABLES',innodb_strict_mode=1",
#        'charset': 'utf8mb4',
#                },
#    'TEST':{},
#    },
#    'social_db' : {
#    'ENGINE': 'django.db.backends.postgresql',
#    'NAME': 'socialdb',
#    'USER': 'socialuser',
#    'PASSWORD': 'socialuser@DB112358',
#    'HOST': '10.10.0.198',
#    'PORT': '5432',
#    }
#    }
```

```
#DATABASE_ROUTERS = ['social.social_router.SocialRouter','login.login_router.LoginRouter']
```

We are going to start the test with an intentional failed case. The field value for *service_name* is 'Test service', but we are testing assertion with the value 'The service name is "Test service"'.

```
service = AppService.objects.get(service_name='Test service')

self.assertEqual(service.service_name,'The service name is "Test service"')
```

On running the test, we should be expecting a failure. Here is the output of the test -

```
[root@ww-z1 hello_world]# ./manage.py test login.tests --settings=hello_world.settings.development
Creating test database for alias 'default'...
System check identified no issues (0 silenced).
F
======================================================================
FAIL: test_app_service_creation (login.tests.AppServiceTestCase)
To check if tuples are getting created
----------------------------------------------------------------------
Traceback (most recent call last):
  File "/root/django_hello_world_login/hello_world/login/tests.py", line 18, in test_app_service_creation
    self.assertEqual(service.service_name,'The service name is "Test service"')
AssertionError: u'Test service' != u'The service name is "Test service"'
- Test service
+ The service name is "Test service"


----------------------------------------------------------------------
Ran 1 test in 0.007s

FAILED (failures=1)
Destroying test database for alias 'default'...
```

As we can see, an AssertionError has been prompted. The last line shows how the framework gets rid of the temporary database. We will now check for the expected values after making the following change -

```
self.assertEqual(service.service_name,'Test service')
self.assertEqual(service.service_price,Decimal('99.90'))
```

Since the tuple field service_price is of type *DecimalField* in model definition, we are comparing the excepted value with the *Decimal* object from the decimal library of python. We will now get a successful run for the test cases -

```
[root@ww-z1 hello_world]# ./manage.py test login.tests --settings=hello_world.settings.development
Creating test database for alias 'default'...
System check identified no issues (0 silenced).
.
----------------------------------------------------------------------
Ran 1 test in 0.007s

OK
Destroying test database for alias 'default'...
```

# Security with Django

Django provides security against Cross-Site scripting, Cross-Site Request Forgery, SQL injection etc, right out of the box which we have discussed and used in hello_world application, but here we will secure our web application *hello_world* with an SSL/HTTPS connection. An SSL certificate for a web host requires to be signed by a globally accepted certificate authority (CA) such as GoDaddy, Symmantec, Digicert and many more. Getting a certificate from such a CA requires subscription fees. Although there is another alternative free of cost certificate provider Let's Encrypt, but it is only for domain names that are globally visible. In our case, we need to host our demo web application inside a private network and so we will issue a self-signed certificate for our application and set up apache web server for it.

First we need to install the ssl module for apache -

```
[root@ww-z1 ~]# yum install mod_ssl -y -q -e 0
```

The certificate and key will be stored in the following directories -

```
[root@ww-z1 ~]# mkdir /etc/ssl/private
[root@ww-z1 ~]# chmod 700 /etc/ssl/private
```

This next command creates the certificate -

```
[root@ww-z1 ~]# openssl req -x509 -nodes -days 365 -newkey rsa:2048 \
> -keyout /etc/ssl/private/apache-selfsigned.key \
> -out /etc/ssl/certs/apache-selfsigned.crt
Generating a 2048 bit RSA private key
.............................................................
..............+++
writing new private key to '/etc/ssl/private/apache-selfsigned.key'
-----
You are about to be asked to enter information that will be incorporated
into your certificate request.
What you are about to enter is what is called a Distinguished Name or a DN.
There are quite a few fields but you can leave some blank
For some fields there will be a default value,
If you enter '.', the field will be left blank.
-----
Country Name (2 letter code) [XX]:IN
State or Province Name (full name) []:West Bengal
```

```
Locality Name (eg, city) [Default City]:Kolkata
Organization Name (eg, company) [Default Company Ltd]:.
Organizational Unit Name (eg, section) []:.
Common Name (eg, your name or your server's hostname) []:helloworld.dev.ts
Email Address []:.
```

In the *Common Name* parameter we have specified *helloworld.dev.ts* as our domain name. We will setup apache ServerName with this domain name but before that we will ensure the SSL certificate preserves Perfect Forward Secrecy. This is required to ensure that the session keys will not be compromised even if the private key of the server is compromised. Here is the command and it takes a little time to complete -

```
[root@ww-z1 ~]# openssl dhparam -out /etc/ssl/certs/dhparam.pem 2048
Generating DH parameters, 2048 bit long safe prime, generator 2
This is going to take a long time
```

After this step, the content of the dhparam.pem file will be appended to the apache-selfigned. crt file which was generated in the previous step.

```
[root@ww-z1 ~]# cat /etc/ssl/certs/dhparam.pem >> \
> /etc/ssl/certs/apache-selfsigned.crt
```

Next we configure the /etc/httpd/conf.d/ssl.onf file to address the SSL connection and use the generated certificate and key. Since our project is hosted at /var/www/hello_world and the domain name we chose helloworld.dev.ts, the VirtualHost has to be setup accordingly -

```
<VirtualHost _default_:443>
DocumentRoot "/var/www/hello_world/"
ServerName helloworld.dev.ts:443
```

We will comment out two directives of the file -

```
# SSLProtocol all -SSLv2 -SSLv3
# SSLCipherSuite HIGH:3DES:!aNULL:!MD5:!SEED:!IDEA
```

The file paths to the certificate and the private key is configured -

```
SSLCertificateFile /etc/ssl/certs/apache-selfsigned.crt
SSLCertificateKeyFile /etc/ssl/private/apache-selfsigned.key
```

Lastly, the following block of configurations are added at the end of the </VirtualHost> tag -

```
</VirtualHost>


# Begin copied text
# from https://cipherli.st/
# and https://raymii.org/s/tutorials/Strong_SSL_Security_On_Apache2.html

SSLCipherSuite EECDH+AESGCM:EDH+AESGCM:AES256+EECDH:AES256+EDH
SSLProtocol All -SSLv2 -SSLv3
SSLHonorCipherOrder On
# Disable preloading HSTS for now.  You can use the commented out header line that includes
# the "preload" directive if you understand the implications.
#Header always set Strict-Transport-Security "max-age=63072000; includeSubdomains; preload"
Header always set Strict-Transport-Security "max-age=63072000; includeSubdomains"
Header always set X-Frame-Options DENY
Header always set X-Content-Type-Options nosniff
# Requires Apache >= 2.4
SSLCompression off
SSLUseStapling on
SSLStaplingCache "shmcb:logs/stapling-cache(150000)"
# Requires Apache >= 2.4.11
# SSLSessionTickets Off
```

We now set the ServerName to helloworld.dev.ts in /etc/httpd/conf/httpd.conf -

```
ServerName helloworld.dev.ts:80
```

We want to redirect all HTTP requests to HTTPS and so the following VirtualHost is created -

```
[root@ww-z1 ~]# cat /etc/httpd/conf.d/helloworld.conf
<VirtualHost *:80>
        ServerName helloworld.dev.ts
        Redirect "/" "https://helloworld.dev.ts/"
</VirtualHost>
```

Now a restart to httpd should server over HTTPS.

```
 🗋  Login - Hello World          ×    +

 C    ⚠ Not Secure │ https://helloworld.dev.ts/login/
```

The url shows "Not secure" because the certificate is a self signed one and the browser accepts certificates only from trusted certificate providers.

# SECTION 8

# Containerizing
# with Docker

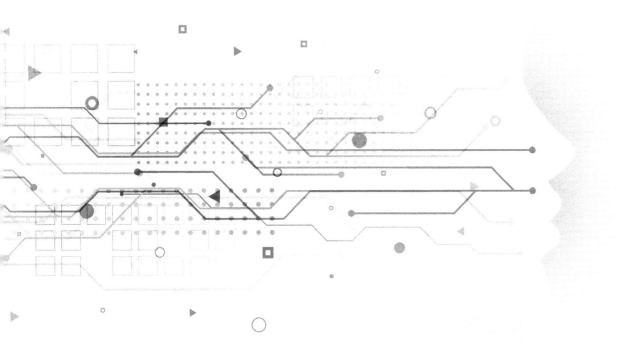

# Introduction

Program portability is not a new concept and just-in-time compilation as introduced by Java Virtual Machine, stood out to be one of the most widely adopted programming paradigm, as dependability on a physical or virtual machine for a program was lifted. Applications written in Java hence required only the JVM to be present on a machine.

Although the program portability through running application in a VM ensures an application to be architecture agnostic, the true necessity of application portability can be understood from the perspective of an application developer. An application development lifecycle that involves multiple programmers, require the same application development environment to be available to all developers. Not only that, an application development lifecycle involves developers working on separate versions of the same application, each of which require having the version specific development environment. A development environment is the availability of the various other files or programs as required by the application in development, with their specific permissions.

Now from the perspective of a developer, the development of an application involves installing of dependant software packages, thereby causing changes in the filesystem of the host operating system. Say application A has versions 5, 6, & 7 active, and receives updates. A developer who works on all of these versions has to maintain three environments, as it is obvious for packages to have varying dependancies. Every time a developer commits changes to the source files of a particular version or, starts working on a version, the environment has to be updated to the latest changes. Now, development involves changes that sometimes make an application unstable and breaking of a application build is one of the most common issues faced. In the midst of constant applying and reverting of changes, it becomes very difficult for a developer to manage the various environments in the host OS. Suppose a developer pulls the latest changes in the source code from version control and installs the required packages for further development. The new code added requires some more new dependant packages, which turns out to be incompatible with some existing packages in the current build. In this scenario, a developer has to revert the changes done to the filesystem by installing those incompatible packages. It may so be the case that a developer has to go through a series of trial and errors before getting to the dependant package that actually works. Under such circumstances where changes to filesystems is expected and regular, it becomes necessary to have some sort of mechanism that does not cause such frequent changes to affect other applications in a development environment.

Linux containers (LXC) address this problem and provides a method of containment for applications and their dependancies, so that they are isolated. The inspiration behind LXC is to be able to make as many changes in filesystem as required and be able to share the state of a development environment with ease. Therefore, in comparison with program portability brought about by JVM, LXC makes not just the application, but also its running environment portable. LXC does this by building an image of an application along with its required filesystem changes and dependancies, and it is this image that is required for running the application. Now, a developer does not have to make changes to the host operating system's filesystem in order to work on a particular version. Each of the supported versions of an application can exist in an LXC image and if any subsequent change breaks an application's build, the change stays confined in the image. The developer can discard the broken build in the image and start afresh with a new image before the changes.

Therefore, we can see how useful LXC container technology is, for any development environment, as it drastically reduces the hassle of managing environments.

# LXC and Docker

LXC (Linux Containers) is a virtualisation method that can run multiple isolated linux (unix based) systems on a single kernel. Each of the systems that share the kernel provided by a host operating system is called a *container*.

The primary virtualisation method prior to 2008 was through virtual machines, and then LXC came along and changed the landscape of virtualisation with the sheer increase in speed. Contrary to the way virtual machines work, where each virtual machine that is running on a physical machine need an operating system of its own, LXCs removed this requirement of a dedicated operating system for a virtualised environment. Here are two diagrams to show how an LXC and virtual machine is architecturally different from one another.

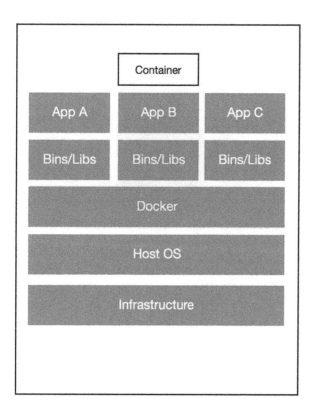
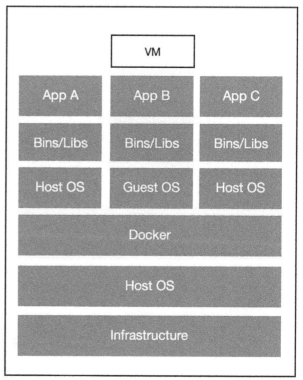

A virtual machine is installed on a physical machine that has an operating system of its own called a host OS and the unix based OS running inside a virtual machine is called a guest OS or Hypervisor. Each of these OS(s) have separate networking, memory, storage and process management mechanisms such that none affect the other, thereby establishing an isolated environment. But since a virtual machine shares the same hardware as the host OS, a system call that is invoked in the guest OS ultimately gets converted and mapped to the system call from the host OS. It is this propagation of system call through logical layers that makes a virtual machine slower than LXC.

An LXC take a radically different approach and address the concept of virtualisation with different perspective. Lets take the perspective of two different freshly launched linux virtual machines (say CentOs) on the same host OS, and a user interacting with them. When a user installs a program package, it usually comes with a number of dependencies in the from of library files and/or other packages. What these dependencies are doing is actually making configuration changes in the environment of either the guest OS system space or the user space. The remaining of the operations include execution of the installed package along with its configurations specific to each virtual machine environment. The core tasks in any computer system is to read, write and compute and so operating systems have system calls that execute these collection fundamental tasks. Both the virtual machines' system calls correspond to the same system calls of the substrate on which they run, i.e. the host OS. But for the case of virtual machines, they have the same algorithms for memory, process, storage and network management as that of the host OS. This is where the inspiration for LXC comes, to remove this redundancy. Each LXContainer corresponds to an isolated environment that mimics the entire filesystem of an OS, say CentOs. The only difference it has from a virtual machine is that it does not have dedicated OS kernel. When a package is installed in a *container* the changes that are made to the filesystem and the environment variables are only recorded in the *container's* internals. Now when the package installed is in its execution state, the underlying system calls are directly delegated to the host OS's kernel.

The very reason that makes containers lightweight compared to virtual machines is that, for a virtual machine, the memory of the host OS is laden with an entire separate guest OS along with the applications running in it. But with LXC, there is no such reservation of memory required and from the perspective of an application container, the only memory reservation is for just the application in a guest OS.

Docker is an implementation of LXContainers to develop, deploy and execute applications with containers. There are two fundamental elements of Docker/LXC technology - images and containers.

A Docker image is a substrate that contains all the program files, libraries, environment variables and configuration files that are required by a application.

A Docker container is just an instance of a particular docker image that is ultimately run on a machine.

# Into docker images

All the source files can be found in the following location -

We will install docker community edition (CE) with the script provided by docker.

```
curl -fsSL https://get.docker.com/ | sh
```

The version -

```
[root@ww-z1 ~]# docker --version
Docker version 18.06.1-ce, build e68fc7a
```

The docker daemon has to be started with

```
systemctl start docker
```

For our use case, we have installed *docker* in a Centos 7 virtual machine.
    The *docker* command is the client that communicates with the runtime provided by the docker daemon for maintaining the containers and the set of operations that can be performed by the various sub-commands of *docker* are as follows -

```
Management Commands:
  config      Manage Docker configs
  container   Manage containers
  image       Manage images
  network     Manage networks
  node        Manage Swarm nodes
  plugin      Manage plugins
  secret      Manage Docker secrets
  service     Manage services
  stack       Manage Docker stacks
  swarm       Manage Swarm
  system      Manage Docker
  trust       Manage trust on Docker images
  volume      Manage volumes
```

```
Commands:
  attach      Attach local standard input, output, and error streams to a running container
  build       Build an image from a Dockerfile
  commit      Create a new image from a container's changes
  cp          Copy files/folders between a container and the local filesystem
  create      Create a new container
  diff        Inspect changes to files or directories on a container's filesystem
  events      Get real time events from the server
  exec        Run a command in a running container
  export      Export a container's filesystem as a tar archive
  history     Show the history of an image
  images      List images
  import      Import the contents from a tarball to create a filesystem image
  info        Display system-wide information
  inspect     Return low-level information on Docker objects
  kill        Kill one or more running containers
  load        Load an image from a tar archive or STDIN
  login       Log in to a Docker registry
  logout      Log out from a Docker registry
  logs        Fetch the logs of a container
  pause       Pause all processes within one or more containers
  port        List port mappings or a specific mapping for the container
  ps          List containers
  pull        Pull an image or a repository from a registry
  push        Push an image or a repository to a registry
  rename      Rename a container
  restart     Restart one or more containers
  rm          Remove one or more containers
  rmi         Remove one or more images
  run         Run a command in a new container
  save        Save one or more images to a tar archive (streamed to STDOUT by default)
  search      Search the Docker Hub for images
  start       Start one or more stopped containers
  stats       Display a live stream of container(s) resource usage statistics
  stop        Stop one or more running containers
  tag         Create a tag TARGET_IMAGE that refers to SOURCE_IMAGE
  top         Display the running processes of a container
  unpause     Unpause all processes within one or more containers
  update      Update configuration of one or more containers
  version     Show the Docker version information
  wait        Block until one or more containers stop, then print their exit codes
```

Docker containers are run from Docker images. The docker command is used to pull/download images from the Docker Hub. The Docker Hub is the repository of ready made images provided by the parent company. The Docker Hub allows anyone to build and host their images and contains images almost for all linux distributions.

In order to check the docker command is able to download images, we can run -

```
[root@ww-z1 ~]# docker run hello-world
Unable to find image 'hello-world:latest' locally
latest: Pulling from library/hello-world
d1725b59e92d: Pull complete
Digest: sha256:0add3ace90ecb4adbf7777e9aacf18357296e799f81cabc9fde470971e499788
Status: Downloaded newer image for hello-world:latest

Hello from Docker!
This message shows that your installation appears to be working correctly.
```

```
To generate this message, Docker took the following steps:
 1. The Docker client contacted the Docker daemon.
 2. The Docker daemon pulled the "hello-world" image from the Docker Hub.
    (amd64)
 3. The Docker daemon created a new container from that image which runs the
    executable that produces the output you are currently reading.
 4. The Docker daemon streamed that output to the Docker client, which sent it
    to your terminal.
```

We can search for images, the Docker Hub's repository is queried and any image name that bears the "centos" string is returned in the search result -

```
[root@ww-z1 ~]# docker search centos
NAME                           DESCRIPTION                                      STARS
centos                         The official build of CentOS.                    4685
ansible/centos7-ansible        Ansible on Centos7                               117
jdeathe/centos-ssh             CentOS-6 6.10 x86_64 / CentOS-7 7.5.1804 x86…    99
consol/centos-xfce-vnc         Centos container with "headless" VNC session…   63
imagine10255/centos6-lnmp-php56  centos6-lnmp-php56                             45
tutum/centos                   Simple CentOS docker image with SSH access       43
centos/mysql-57-centos7        MySQL 5.7 SQL database server                    39
gluster/gluster-centos         Official GlusterFS Image [ CentOS-7 +  Glust…   34
openshift/base-centos7         A Centos7 derived base image for Source-To-I…   33
centos/python-35-centos7       Platform for building and running Python 3.5…   30
centos/postgresql-96-centos7   PostgreSQL is an advanced Object-Relational …   29
kinogmt/centos-ssh             CentOS with SSH                                  22
openshift/jenkins-2-centos7    A Centos7 based Jenkins v2.x image for use w…   15
pivotaldata/centos-gpdb-dev    CentOS image for GPDB development. Tag names…    7
openshift/wildfly-101-centos7  A Centos7 based WildFly v10.1 image for use …    5
openshift/jenkins-1-centos7    DEPRECATED: A Centos7 based Jenkins v1.x ima…    4
darksheer/centos               Base Centos Image -- Updated hourly              3
pivotaldata/centos-mingw       Using the mingw toolchain to cross-compile t…    2
pivotaldata/centos             Base centos, freshened up a little with a Do…    2
blacklabelops/centos           CentOS Base Image! Built and Updates Daily!      1
pivotaldata/centos-gcc-toolchain  CentOS with a toolchain, but unaffiliated wi…  0
pivotaldata/centos7-test       CentosOS 7 image for GPDB testing                0
smartentry/centos              centos with smartentry                           0
pivotaldata/centos7-build      CentosOS 7 image for GPDB compilation            0
jameseckersall/sonarr-centos   Sonarr on CentOS 7                               0
```

STARS is just vote of popularity by users who have a docker account and can upload images to the Hub.

To begin with, we will pull and run a a Centos container on a virtual machine running Centos 7.

```
[root@ww-z1 ~]# docker pull centos
Using default tag: latest
latest: Pulling from library/centos
256b176beaff: Pull complete
Digest: sha256:6f6d986d425aeabdc3a02cb61c02abb2e78e57357e92417d6d58332856024faf
Status: Downloaded newer image for centos:latest
```

The list of images we have -

```
[root@ww-z1 ~]# docker images
REPOSITORY              TAG               IMAGE ID          CREATED           SIZE
hello-world             latest            4ab4c602aa5e      5 days ago        1.84kB
centos                  latest            5182e96772bf      5 weeks ago       200MB
```

Before we go ahead to perform any operation on the centos image, we check if we have any running containers.

```
[root@ww-z1 ~]# docker container ls --all
CONTAINER ID      IMAGE         COMMAND      CREATED          STATUS                    PORTS        NAMES
e035f116dc61      hello-world   "/hello"     21 minutes ago   Exited (0) 21 minutes ago              amazing_poincare
```

The *hello-world* that we performed with the docker client actually looked locally for a image with that name and downloaded one from the Hub. The greetings message that we got from running hello-world was the container in execution. Each container is provided a unique NAME with which it can be referenced.

We will run a container with the Centos image that we pulled and launch ourselves into an interactive terminal inside the container.

```
[root@ww-z1 ~]# docker run -it centos
[root@d95a48bf94b3 /]#
[root@d95a48bf94b3 /]#
[root@d95a48bf94b3 /]#
[root@d95a48bf94b3 /]# ll
total 32
-rw-r--r--.   1 root root 12005 Aug  4 22:05 anaconda-post.log
lrwxrwxrwx.   1 root root     7 Aug  4 22:04 bin -> usr/bin
drwxr-xr-x.   5 root root   360 Sep 13 12:58 dev
drwxr-xr-x.   1 root root    62 Sep 13 12:58 etc
drwxr-xr-x.   2 root root     6 Apr 11 04:59 home
lrwxrwxrwx.   1 root root     7 Aug  4 22:04 lib -> usr/lib
lrwxrwxrwx.   1 root root     9 Aug  4 22:04 lib64 -> usr/lib64
drwxr-xr-x.   2 root root     6 Apr 11 04:59 media
drwxr-xr-x.   2 root root     6 Apr 11 04:59 mnt
drwxr-xr-x.   2 root root     6 Apr 11 04:59 opt
dr-xr-xr-x. 104 root root     0 Sep 13 12:58 proc
dr-xr-x---.   2 root root  4096 Aug  4 22:05 root
drwxr-xr-x.  10 root root  4096 Aug  4 22:05 run
lrwxrwxrwx.   1 root root     8 Aug  4 22:04 sbin -> usr/sbin
drwxr-xr-x.   2 root root     6 Apr 11 04:59 srv
dr-xr-xr-x.  13 root root     0 Apr 11 04:59 sys
drwxrwxrwt.   7 root root  4096 Aug  4 22:05 tmp
drwxr-xr-x.  13 root root  4096 Aug  4 22:04 usr
drwxr-xr-x.  18 root root  4096 Aug  4 22:04 var
```

The switch -i and -t provides an interactive terminal access. The hostname *d95a48bf94b3* is the container's ID.

```
[[root@ww-z1 ~]# docker container ls --all
CONTAINER ID            IMAGE                COMMAND
d95a48bf94b3            centos               "/bin/bash"
e035f116dc61            hello-world          "/hello"
```

The container created with the *centos* image has its own filesystem.

To start a stopped container -

```
[root@ww-z1 ~]# docker start  d95a48bf94b3
d95a48bf94b3
[root@ww-z1 ~]# docker container ls
CONTAINER ID        IMAGE            COMMAND            CREATED            STATUS
d95a48bf94b3        centos           "/bin/bash"        30 minutes ago     Up About a minute
```

The memory consumption when running the container *d95a48bf94b3* or *confident_tesla* (a random name generated by docker) -

```
[root@ww-z1 ~]# free -m
              total        used        free      shared  buff/cache   available
Mem:           3791         400         204          24        3186        3069
Swap:          4095           0        4095
```

And when the container is stopped -

```
[[root@ww-z1 ~]# docker stop d95a48bf94b3
d95a48bf94b3
[[root@ww-z1 ~]# free -m
              total        used        free      shared  buff/cache   available
Mem:           3791         397         207          24        3186        3073
Swap:          4095           0        4095
```

The efficiency in memory usage is visible as there is only 3 MB of usage on running a centos *container*. This is because unlike in the case of virtual machine, we were not running an entire operating system with all its runtime memory consumption. Our container is based upon a Centos 7 image and the only memory usage was for the *program that was running inside the container*.

We may have arrived at a confusing juncture where we do not recall consciously running any program inside the container when the container was run. Well, actually we did run a program, in the form of *bash*. When the container was created the **-it** switches spawned an interactive terminal as bash for us to interact with the container's environment. This is shown as COMMAND field in the list of containers -

```
[[root@ww-z1 ~]# docker container ls
CONTAINER ID          IMAGE              COMMAND
d95a48bf94b3          centos             "/bin/bash"
```

The memory usage during running this container was actually the memory usage of /bin/bash.

Similarly, when we ran *hello-world* image, a binary file written in C was executed. The hello-world image is a special one, and we are going to discuss about it a little later. But first, we will try to mimic what happened while running a container with the hello-world image with our container based on Centos 7.

Now before doing anything with the container confident_tesla, which has centos as its base, we are going to create another with the *centos* image that has a more familiar name and move forward with the changes in that.

```
[root@ww-z1 ~]# docker run -i -t --name=centos_container --hostname=centos_container centos
[root@centos_container /]# exit
exit
[root@ww-z1 ~]# docker container ls --all
CONTAINER ID     IMAGE        COMMAND        CREATED          STATUS                   PORTS        NAMES
dfbc89d30923     centos       "/bin/bash"    25 seconds ago   Exited (0) 15 seconds ago             centos_container
```

We have applied the name *centos_container* as the container's name as well as set it as the hostname for the container. We are going to start the container *centos_container*, which will be running /bin/bash command and bind to the COMMAND.

```
[root@ww-z1 ~]# docker attach centos_container
[root@centos_container /]#
```

The attach command binds our host OS's input/output stream to that of the running container. In other words, it basically launches us in the /bin/bash terminal that is running as a *COMMAND* in the container. The *attach* command although lands us in the bash program's session that the container is running, exiting from it exits the the container itself because we would be exiting the currently running session. Therefore, it would be better it we use the *exec* command to execute another *bash* session in *centos_container*.

```
[root@ww-z1 ~]# docker exec -it centos_container /bin/bash
[root@centos_container /]# cd home/
[root@centos_container home]# ll
total 0
```

We create a C file that would simply print a greetings to the terminal.

```
#include <sys/syscall.h>

const char message[] = "\nHello from Centos 7! \n";

void main()
{
  syscall(SYS_write, 1, message, sizeof(message) - 1);
  syscall(SYS_exit, 0);
}
```

After compiling the file and exiting the bash session, the program can be run from outside the running container.

```
[[root@ww-z1 ~]# docker exec -it centos_container /_hello

Hello from Centos 7!
```

We created a new image from the changes made inside *centos_container*. We will get into further details in later sections, but for now, our intent is to make the image behave the same way, the image *hello-world* did, when it was run. The new image has the name *centos_hello-world* and it is listed in the *docker images*.

On running the docker image, we are successful in echoing a greeting message as that of *hello-world*.

```
[root@ww-z1 ~]# docker commit --change='CMD ["/_hello"]' centos_container centos_hello-world
sha256:8c63502996981894bfc985f91f92371c45b64afafe100747176f01f7dda81685
[root@ww-z1 ~]# docker images
REPOSITORY            TAG          IMAGE ID           CREATED          SIZE
centos_hello-world    latest       8c6350299698       4 seconds ago    339MB
hello-world           latest       4ab4c602aa5e       6 days ago       1.84kB
centos                latest       5182e96772bf       5 weeks ago      200MB
[root@ww-z1 ~]# docker run centos_hello-world

Hello from Centos 7!
```

Here is the list of containers and shows the container created with the new image *centos_hello-world*.

```
[[root@ww-z1 ~]# docker container ls --all
CONTAINER ID          IMAGE                  COMMAND
59f1406c8cdb          centos_hello-world     "/_hello"
dfbc89d30923          centos                 "/bin/bash"
e035f116dc61          hello-world            "/hello"
```

Now that, we are able to perform the same job as that done while creating a container with the *hello-world* image, we are going to discuss the speciality of the *hello-world* image. Comparably the difference in size between *centos_hello-world* and *hello-world* is huge.

The small size of *hello-world* is due to the nature of the image used as a substrate, which is a *scratch* image.

A *scratch* image is the most minimal image in docker and servers as the base image for all images. And therefore, the scratch image is also the base for *centos_hello-world* and *centos*. *A scratch image is essentially an empty image.*

In order to make sense of the behaviour of *scratch* image, let us again indulge in creating an image based from *scratch* and then add an empty file in it.

```
[root@ww-z1 ~]# touch empty_file
[root@ww-z1 ~]# ll
total 4
-rw-r--r--. 1 root root    0 Sep 14 08:34 empty_file
drwxr-xr-x. 7 root root   91 Sep 12 14:01 hello_world
drwxr-xr-x. 3 root root   64 Sep  5 12:52 pay
-rw-r--r--. 1 root root 3875 Sep 12 10:58 settings.py
[root@ww-z1 ~]# vim Dockerfile
[root@ww-z1 ~]# docker build -t another_scratch .
Sending build context to Docker daemon  12.65MB
Step 1/2 : FROM scratch
 --->
Step 2/2 : COPY empty_file .
 ---> ba49f5152986
Successfully built ba49f5152986
Successfully tagged another_scratch:latest
[root@ww-z1 ~]# docker images
REPOSITORY          TAG           IMAGE ID         CREATED          SIZE
another_scratch     latest        ba49f5152986     7 seconds ago    0B
```

We will get into the details of a *Dockerfile* and the intricacies of building an image later, but for now we will emphasise on the empty file name empty_file that is of 0 Bytes that is put into the image *another_scratch*.

The noticeable thing, is the size of the image *another_scratch*, which is 0 Bytes, essentially making the image an empty one.

We will save the *another_scratch* docker image in a tar file and then traverse the contents of the image.

```
[[root@ww-z1 ~]# docker save -o another_scratch.tar another_scratch
[[root@ww-z1 ~]# ll
total 20
-rw-------. 1 root root 10240 Sep 14 09:03 another_scratch.tar
```

Extracting the file we get a directory with alpha-numeric string name which is essentially an ID for the image, such as this -

```
[root@ww-z1 ~]# tar -xvf another_scratch.tar
21076ef34b4522982c5c13ea1ef52bf9063fffa5d079dd81b948d3ed2c7a684b/
21076ef34b4522982c5c13ea1ef52bf9063fffa5d079dd81b948d3ed2c7a684b/VERSION
21076ef34b4522982c5c13ea1ef52bf9063fffa5d079dd81b948d3ed2c7a684b/json
21076ef34b4522982c5c13ea1ef52bf9063fffa5d079dd81b948d3ed2c7a684b/layer.tar
ba49f51529867bc1f78ca98bed89524e96d85f6721f31512eedc6363cc44f816.json
manifest.json
tar: manifest.json: implausibly old time stamp 1970-01-01 00:00:00
repositories
tar: repositories: implausibly old time stamp 1970-01-01 00:00:00
[root@ww-z1 ~]# ll
total 32
drwxr-xr-x. 2 root root    47 Sep 14 08:36 21076ef34b4522982c5c13ea1ef52bf9063fffa5d079dd81b948d3ed2c7a684b
```

The inside of the directory contains the following -

```
[root@ww-z1 ~]# cd 21076ef34b4522982c5c13ea1ef52bf9063fffa5d079dd81b948d3ed2c7a684b/
[root@ww-z1 21076ef34b4522982c5c13ea1ef52bf9063fffa5d079dd81b948d3ed2c7a684b]# ll
total 12
-rw-r--r--. 1 root root  968 Sep 14 08:36 json
-rw-r--r--. 1 root root 1536 Sep 14 08:36 layer.tar
-rw-r--r--. 1 root root    3 Sep 14 08:36 VERSION
```

And inside this layer.tar file, that we find our *empty_file*.

```
[root@ww-z1 21076ef34b4522982c5c13ea1ef52bf9063fffa5d079dd81b948d3ed2c7a684b]# tar xvf layer.tar
empty_file
```

We have arrived at a discord where the image *another_scratch* containing an empty file is 0 Bytes in size but when extracted contains extra files.

Actually if we notice carefully, all the other files *json*, *layer.tar* and *VERSION* are just meta information about the image. But again, if these files are a part of the *scratch* image, the size of the scratch image could not have been 0 Bytes. Therefore, there must be something special about the *scratch* image.

We have referenced *scratch* as a image so far, but it is not our usual image as *centos_hello-world*. If we try to pull the scratch image from Docker Hub, it results in failure.

```
[[root@ww-z1 ~]# docker pull scratch
Using default tag: latest
Error response from daemon: 'scratch' is a reserved name
```

Although we have referenced *scratch* as an image but it says that *scratch* is a reserved name for docker. It is not unreasonable to call *scratch* an image, but its speciality lies with the docker runtime.

Docker brings the LXC technology for deploying applications. A docker container's purpose is not be treated as a linux box but a containment for running an application along with its required dependencies. In the image *centos_hello-world*, the container created with it only has the purpose of executing a C object file. The container had the entire filesystem on Centos 7, which is necessarily not required in its entirety for running the C object file to print a statement. Therefore, we could have chosen to exclude the unnecessary portions of the filesystem that do not participate in the execution of the application and this basically is the core inspiration behind LXC.

For the image *another_scratch*, the only content was a file of 0 Bytes and therefore it can be thought of as a simple containment. It failed to form a container with the image because of course there was no process declared to be preformed with the file.

Since, it already has been stated that *scratch* forms the base of all images, we are going to see how the docker runtime interprets an image build from *scratch*. A *scratch* image although shows empty, but the docker runtime provides a *bootfs* (boot filesystem) as a substrate, which is never accessible to a user, and on which the *rootfs* is mounted and so on followed by other filesystem layers, as required by the application to be run. The tar archive file created for the *another_scratch* image did not reveal any such filesystem.

The hello-world image definitely requires a filesystem, especially *dev* because it is it is using the standard output stream. The tar archive of *hello-world* image would show us just the executable file name *hello* present in the image.

```
docker save -o hello_scratch.tar hello-world
```

```
[root@ww-z1 ~]# tar xvf hello_scratch.tar
4ab4c602aa5eed5528a6620ff18a1dc4faef0e1ab3a5eddeddb410714478c67f.json
f22789aafb439644ab76948424a0c1b64f328cecde82c95edad3813aaadbe077/
f22789aafb439644ab76948424a0c1b64f328cecde82c95edad3813aaadbe077/VERSION
f22789aafb439644ab76948424a0c1b64f328cecde82c95edad3813aaadbe077/json
f22789aafb439644ab76948424a0c1b64f328cecde82c95edad3813aaadbe077/layer.tar
```

We will therefore create a statically linked C executable file from *scratch* similar to the *hello-world* image and see the contents in the filesystem. The C executable file will have a wait of two minutes and we would check the /proc filesystem in our host OS to reveal the filesystem.

The Dockerfile for the new image -

```
FROM scratch
COPY sleeper /
CMD ["/sleeper"]
```

Here *sleeper* is our C executable. The contents of the C file -

```
#include<sys/syscall.h>
const char message[] = "\n\n Sleep for 2 minutes ... \n\n";
void main()
{
  syscall(SYS_write, 1, message, sizeof(message) - 1);
  sleep(120);
  syscall(SYS_exit,0);
}
```

The glibc-static package creates a statically linked executable.

```
gcc -static a_c_file.c -o sleeper
```

The image created is named yet_another_scratch.

```
[root@ww-z1 ~]# docker images
REPOSITORY            TAG        IMAGE ID        CREATED          SIZE
yet_another_scratch   latest     8213f719cda7    45 minutes ago   861kB
```

We will run a container with the image, extract the process id and look into the /proc directory.

```
[[root@ww-z1 ~]# docker run --name sleeper yet_another_scratch


  Sleep for 2 minutes ...
```

Here is the PID -

```
[root@ww-z1 ~]# PID=$(docker inspect -f '{{.State.Pid}}' sleeper)
[root@ww-z1 ~]# echo $PID
32741
```

And finally, this is what we find in /proc for the PID -

```
[root@ww-z1 ~]# cd /proc/32741/root
[root@ww-z1 root]# ll
total 844
drwxr-xr-x.    5 root root    340 Sep 14 11:41 dev
drwxr-xr-x.    2 root root     62 Sep 14 11:41 etc
dr-xr-xr-x. 112 root root      0 Sep 14 11:41 proc
-rwxr-xr-x.    1 root root 861216 Sep 14 11:34 sleeper
dr-xr-xr-x.   13 root root      0 Apr 11 04:59 sys
```

We can see the filesystems that are used by the container *sleeper*.

In conclusion the *scratch* image contains the *bootfs* which is not accessible to users and as per the requirement of an application, the required layers are provided by the docker runtime when a container is run. A docker container usually has layers of filesystems and when a substrate of Centos 7 is used to build an image, it forms yet another layer. Starting with the bootfs in scratch, the minimal rootfs layer is added when the file *sleeper* is copied into the location "/" inside the image.

```
COPY sleeper /
```

At this point, we have primer on how to perceive a container. In contrast to virtual machines, where it has all the required artefacts for resource management and to run applications, a docker image is essentially a tar archive of filesystem say for Centos, Ubuntu, etc. which we pull from the repository. When a container is run from the image, the runtime environment and its behaviour is provided by the docker engine.

In a very loosely constructed analogy, a container from the perspective of a host OS can be thought of as a device that has been mounted and has its own filesystem. The host OS would run the application residing in the mounted device just as any other applications. The application will have its own filesystem to incorporate changes without affecting the host OS's filesystem and environment settings. But obviously this is not how containers work, being treated as mounted devices. It is the use of *cgroups*, *namespaces*, *chroots*, etc. that creates the isolation of containers.

We will indulge in a simple experiment of seeing how an image is stacked layers of filesystem that can run applications inside it in isolation from the host OS but sharing its kernel. For this, we will use the rootfs of a Debian distro. The rootfs is extracted from the saved tar ball of an ubuntu OS's docker image pulled from the hub.

In order to understand the concept of how layers of filesystems are stack on each other inside an image, we will pull an ubuntu image and make changes upon it.

```
[root@ww-z1 ~]# docker images ubuntu
REPOSITORY          TAG             IMAGE ID          CREATED           SIZE
ubuntu              latest          cd6d8154f1e1      9 days ago        84.1MB
```

The ubuntu image does not have python installed so we are going to install.

```
[root@ww-z1 ~]# docker run -it ubuntu /bin/bash
root@88d16adbada0:/#
root@88d16adbada0:/#
root@88d16adbada0:/# apt-get -qq update
root@88d16adbada0:/# which python
root@88d16adbada0:/# apt-get -qq install python
```

```
root@88d16adbada0:/# which python
/usr/bin/python
```

The base ubuntu image when archived and extracted, shows the following directories -

```
[[root@ww-z1 ubuntu-base]# ll
total 84620
-rw-------. 1 root root 86647808 Sep 15 12:57 ubuntu-base.tar
[[root@ww-z1 ubuntu-base]# tar xf ubuntu-base.tar
tar: manifest.json: implausibly old time stamp 1970-01-01 00:00:00
tar: repositories: implausibly old time stamp 1970-01-01 00:00:00
[[root@ww-z1 ubuntu-base]# ll
total 84632
drwxr-xr-x. 2 root root       47 Sep  5 22:20 1053541ae4c67d0daa87babb7fe26bf2f5a3b29d03f4af94e9c3cb96128116f5
drwxr-xr-x. 2 root root       47 Sep  5 22:20 2652f5844803bcf8615bec64abd20959c023d34644104245b905bb9b08667c8d
drwxr-xr-x. 2 root root       47 Sep  5 22:20 386aac21291d1f58297bc7951ce00b4ff7485414d6a8e146d9fedb73e0ebfa5b
drwxr-xr-x. 2 root root       47 Sep  5 22:20 5ab4b0ea789686f75716c8b340c5e463bc7b4952ceccaf65e2d237339926bcaa
-rw-r--r--. 1 root root     3615 Sep  5 22:20 cd6d8154f1e16e38493c3c2798977c5e142be5e5d41403ca89883840c6d51762.json
drwxr-xr-x. 2 root root       47 Sep  5 22:20 fb1542f1963e61a22f9416077bf5f999753cbf363234bf8c9c5c1992d9a0b97d
-rw-r--r--. 1 root root      510 Jan  1  1970 manifest.json
-rw-r--r--. 1 root root       89 Jan  1  1970 repositories
```

Each of the directories contain the files *layers.tar*, *json* and *VERSION*. The layers.tar contains a certain layer of the filesystem. In this case, the first directory contains the rootfs for ubuntu -

```
[[root@ww-z1 1053541ae4c67d0daa87babb7fe26bf2f5a3b29d03f4af94e9c3cb96128116f5]# ll
total 28
drwxr-xr-x.  2 root root 4096 Aug 21 21:14 bin
drwxr-xr-x.  2 root root    6 Apr 24 08:34 boot
drwxr-xr-x.  4 root root 4096 Aug 21 21:12 dev
drwxr-xr-x. 29 root root 4096 Aug 21 21:14 etc
drwxr-xr-x.  2 root root    6 Apr 24 08:34 home
-rw-r--r--.  1 root root  401 Sep  5 22:20 json
drwxr-xr-x.  8 root root   90 Aug 21 21:12 lib
drwxr-xr-x.  2 root root   33 Aug 21 21:13 lib64
drwxr-xr-x.  2 root root    6 Aug 21 21:12 media
drwxr-xr-x.  2 root root    6 Aug 21 21:12 mnt
drwxr-xr-x.  2 root root    6 Aug 21 21:12 opt
drwxr-xr-x.  2 root root    6 Apr 24 08:34 proc
drwx------.  2 root root   35 Aug 21 21:14 root
drwxr-xr-x.  4 root root   40 Aug 21 21:12 run
drwxr-xr-x.  2 root root 4096 Aug 21 21:14 sbin
drwxr-xr-x.  2 root root    6 Aug 21 21:12 srv
drwxr-xr-x.  2 root root    6 Apr 24 08:34 sys
drwxrwxrwt.  2 root root    6 Aug 21 21:14 tmp
drwxr-xr-x. 10 root root   97 Aug 21 21:12 usr
drwxr-xr-x. 11 root root 4096 Aug 21 21:14 var
```

whereas the remaining of the directories contain subsets of the rootfs, for example -

```
[[root@ww-z1 fb1542f1963e61a22f9416077bf5f999753cbf363234bf8c9c5c1992d9a0b97d]# ll
total 8
drwxr-xr-x. 4 root root  27 Sep  5 22:20 etc
-rw-r--r--. 1 root root 477 Sep  5 22:20 json
drwxr-xr-x. 2 root root  20 Sep  5 22:20 sbin
drwxr-xr-x. 3 root root  17 Aug 21 21:12 usr
drwxr-xr-x. 3 root root  16 Aug 21 21:14 var
```

This distribution of filesystems among the extracted directories is the representation of the layers of filesystem that is used by docker engine. The above image shows a layer of filesystem, containing the directories that were the recipient of the changes made to the rootfs upon installing /sbin/*initctl* program.

```
sbin/
└── initctl

0 directories, 1 file
```

A tar archive of the image is created after installing python and extracted to reveal the directories of filesystem layers.

```
[[root@ww-z1 ubuntu-with-python]# ll
total 160168
drwxr-xr-x. 2 root root        47 Sep 16 06:57 1053541ae4c67d0daa87babb7fe26bf2f5a3b29d03f4af94e9c3cb96128116f5
drwxr-xr-x. 2 root root        47 Sep 16 06:57 10d19fb34e1db6a5abf4a3c138dc21f67ef94c272cf359349da18ffa973b7246
drwxr-xr-x. 2 root root        47 Sep 16 06:57 2652f5844803bcf8615bec64abd20959c023d34644104245b905bb9b08667c8d
drwxr-xr-x. 2 root root        47 Sep 16 06:57 386aac21291d1f58297bc7951ce00b4ff74854414d6a8e146d9fedb73e0ebfa5b
-rw-r--r--. 1 root root      3554 Sep 16 06:57 793c03e89e7af3325e816ba6dab0a85d470d19d6bd3cf22bce40b087261b76de.json
drwxr-xr-x. 7 root root        98 Sep 16 07:02 9ba5174c0985c387202b10c7115cf49dee20407058188478a89756666e366549
drwxr-xr-x. 2 root root        47 Sep 16 06:57 fb1542f1963e61a22f9416077bf5f999753cbf363234bf8c9c5c1992d9a0b97d
-rw-r--r--. 1 root root       599 Jan  1  1970 manifest.json
-rw-r--r--. 1 root root       101 Jan  1  1970 repositories
```

A new directory 9ba517… has been created and this directory contains the subset of the rootfs that underwent changes upon addition of python.

```
[[root@ww-z1 9ba5174c0985c387202b10c7115cf49dee20407058188478a89756666e366549]# ll
total 12
drwxr-xr-x. 5 root root 4096 Sep 15 12:36 etc
-rw-r--r--. 1 root root 1059 Sep 16 06:57 json
drwxr-xr-x. 3 root root   29 Aug 21 21:12 lib
drwx------. 2 root root   26 Sep 15 12:44 root
drwxr-xr-x. 7 root root   61 Aug 21 21:12 usr
drwxr-xr-x. 5 root root   38 Aug 21 21:14 var
-rw-r--r--. 1 root root    3 Sep 16 06:57 VERSION
[[root@ww-z1 9ba5174c0985c387202b10c7115cf49dee20407058188478a89756666e366549]# find . -name python
./etc/python
./usr/bin/python
./usr/share/doc/python
./usr/share/lintian/overrides/python
./usr/share/python
```

The above snippet shows the python files added to the filesystem.

# Containers

In the previous section, our attempt was to understand how a docker image is constructed and perceived by the docker engine as layers of filesystems w.r.t. changes in them. Although we already seen the use of docker commands to create and manage containers, it is in this section we will discuss them in detail.

A container is a snapshot/object of an image. When an application is implemented through docker container and it is in running state, a container can be referred to as a docker image in execution. In order to create a container for an application, first a docker image has to be created, and so a *docker image is just a definition of a container at the initial state*. Such a definition of a container is done with in a *Dockerfile*.

We will create our first Dockerfile that accomplishes the following tasks and then understand the syntax and the uses of each of the keywords -

1. Create a centos image from scratch by adding the rootfs for Centos 7.
2. Run an update for all packages
3. Install python 3.6, pip for python3.6 (python package manager) and remaining of the packages for development with python.
4. Expose ports 80 and 443

```
FROM scratch
ADD centos-7-docker.tar.xz /
LABEL org.label-schema.schema-version="1.0" \
    org.label-schema.name="CentOS Python 3.6 baked Image" \
    org.label-schema.vendor="bhoson" \
    org.label-schema.license="GPLv2" \
    org.label-schema.build-date="20180917"
RUN ["/bin/yum","--nogpgcheck","-y","-q","-e","0","update"]
RUN /bin/yum --nogpgcheck -y install python36u-pip;exit 0
RUN /bin/yum --nogpgcheck -y -q -e 0 install https://centos7.iuscommunity.org/ius-release.rpm;exit 0
RUN /bin/yum --nogpgcheck -y -q -e 0 install python36u;exit 0
RUN /bin/yum --nogpgcheck -y -q -e 0 install python36u-devel;exit 0

ENV PYTHON3_PATH /bin/python3.6

RUN echo "alias py3='${PYTHON3_PATH}'" >> /etc/bashrc
EXPOSE 80 443
CMD ["/bin/bash"]
```

*FROM* - For naming the base image from which a new image will be built. A Dockerfile must start with FROM instruction. If no specific *tag (<image name>:<tag name>)* or *digest (<image name>@<digest name>)* values are provided, the image builder assumes a *latest* tag by default.

*ADD* - To copy files, directories from a location on host machine or remote file URLs from source to the destination path in a docker image/container. It is used in two forms - a) *ADD*

—chown=<user>:<group> <src1> <src2>,... <dest> b) ADD —chown=<user>:<group> ["<src1>","<src2>",..., "<dest>"]. All files in the image are created with 'root' as a default user and group if not mentioned. All the files and directories are referenced relative to the Dockerfile's location and should be inside the same directory or a subdirectory of the location of the Dockerfile. For recognised archive format files (tar, xz, bz, gz, zip, etc.) as source, it is automatically extracted and copied to the destination.

*LABEL* - To set meta information about the author and the image. It is written as *key=value pairs*.

*RUN* - Execute commands during the build process of the docker image. IT will execute commands in a new layer on top of the current state of the image and commit the results. The resulted committed image is used to perform the next command in the Dockerfile. It is used in two forms - a) RUN <command with parameters>, b) RUN ["executable","param1","param2", ...]. Docker has a caching mechanism, and for commands such as *yum install update*, *apt-get dist-upgrade* the files are cached.

*ENV* - Set an environment variable that is accessible in the Dockerfile throughout the build phase of an image and also as the environment of the container created from the image.

*EXPOSE* - Informs docker that a container created with the image listens to the listed ports. This command does not publish the ports but acts as a setting for the image and the container, such that when the container is run with the switch *-P*, all the listed ports are published for both TCP and UDP. By default docker assumes a port number to be TCP and has to be mentioned explicitly otherwise - *EXPOSE 80/udp*. To publish ports *-p* has to be used as - *docker run -p 80/udp ...*

*CMD* - To execute a command when a container is being created. Its main purpose is to provide a default program to run in a container when started. This command can be used only once in a Dockerfile. This can be written in three formats - a) *CMD ["executable","param1","param2",...]*, b) *CMD command <param1> <param2> ...*, c) *CMD ["param1","param2"]* where <command> if not specified, is default for */bin/sh -c*.

In the previous section we created minimalist image possible for running a C executable that prints to the screen and also learnt about the various layers of the filesystems that are created for changes in containers. Although we had pulled a ready made Centos 7 image from the Docker Hub and created the image *centos_hello-world* based on it, here we are going to create a Centos 7 image from *scratch*.

Our current directory has the Dockerfile and the archive of the root filesystem of Centos 7 downloaded from the official Centos repository for docker at -

```
├── centos-7-docker.tar.xz
├── Dockerfile
```

We need not extract the *centos-7-docker.tar.xz* file as the docker runtime automatically takes care of that in the ADD command. The CMD instructions end with exit 0 so that when a command fails and returns a non-zero exit code, the build process is not stopped. A container must have a process to run and so we state "/bin/bash" as the default process for a container created with this image which we are about to build.

Here is an excerpt from the output during build phase, where the python36u-pip package was not found.

```
Step 5/12 : RUN /bin/yum --nogpgcheck -y install python36u-pip;exit 0
 ---> Running in bc724351bd4c
Loaded plugins: fastestmirror, ovl
Loading mirror speeds from cached hostfile
 * base: mirror.vbctv.in
 * extras: mirror.vbctv.in
 * updates: mirror.vbctv.in
No package python36u-pip available.
Error: Nothing to do
Removing intermediate container bc724351bd4c
 ---> cbe1cf73fa8d
```

Each of the commands that make changes to the filesystem are executed by creating an intermediate container from the state of the image from the previous command, and removing the command after commiting the changes to the image. This is shown in the output as -

```
 ---> Running in 4ccfec10b4fc
Removing intermediate container 4ccfec10b4fc
 ---> fb978a067328
```

The build process is started by executing the command from the directory where Dockerfile is located -

```
docker build -t centos_from_scratch .
```

On creation of the image *centos_from_scratch*, a container is spawned -

```
[root@ww-z1 ~]# docker run -it centos_from_scratch
[root@7b6ac2d753fb /]#
```

Here we are instructing the container to run with an interactive terminal (-it). The -i switch keeps the *STDIN* (standard input) open, i.e. the container will accept user interaction as inputs. The -t switch provides a pseudo terminal TTY / shell to interact with container. Since the default program is set with CMD to be /bin/bash and the switches (-it) has been used, we are taken right into the container after spawning one. If the -d switch for detached mode is used, then then the user will not be taken to then TTY right away and the /bin/bash program keeps running in the background in th container. To exit from the TTY, use *ctrl + pq*. To attach the local TTY to the container's TTY, use -

```
[[root@ww-z1 ~]# docker attach 7b6ac2d753fb
[[root@7b6ac2d753fb /]#
```

The *attach* command views the lands you in the scope of a container's process executed by CMD or ENTRYPOINT command in a Dockerfile.

Inside the container python package manager for python 3.6 is installed -

```
[root@7b6ac2d753fb /]# yum install python36u-pip
```

We will next create a Dockerfile using a new image created from the container (*7b6ac2d753fb*) running *centos_from_scratch*, to launch a simple webserver. For this, first the new image centos_from_scratch/py36 is created -

```
[[root@ww-z1 docker_files]# docker commit --author "bhoson" 7b6ac2d753fb centos_from_scratch/py36
sha256:3e97fe29b8020ee7e9ae4983ebcf7b14484717b29304d828d2726dfd8e9b4e68
[[root@ww-z1 docker_files]# docker images
REPOSITORY                TAG         IMAGE ID        CREATED         SIZE
centos_from_scratch/py36  latest      3e97fe29b802    8 seconds ago   699MB
```

The python script for running a simple HTTP server -

```
#!/usr/bin/python3.6
from http.server import BaseHTTPRequestHandler, HTTPServer

class SimpleHTTPServer_RequestHandler(BaseHTTPRequestHandler):
  def do_GET(self):
      self.send_response(200)

      self.send_header('Content-type','text/html')
      self.end_headers()

      message = "Hello world!\n"
      self.wfile.write(bytes(message, "utf8"))
      return

def run():
  print('starting server...')

  server_address = ('0.0.0.0', 80)
```

```
httpd = HTTPServer(server_address, SimpleHTTPServer_RequestHandler)
print('running server...')
httpd.serve_forever()


run()
```

This is the Dockerfile that creates a new image from centos_from_scratch/py36, to be named py3_simplehttp and runs the python script for an HTTP server.

```
FROM centos_from_scratch/py36

WORKDIR /app

ADD . /app

CMD ["/app/simple_HTTP_app.py"]
```

*WORKDIR* - Creates a directory at the path if does not exist.
   The image is built -

```
docker build -t py3_simplehttp .
```

and a container is created -

```
[root@ww-z1 py3_flash_from_centos]# docker run -d --hostname=simple_server --name=simple_server py3_simplehttp
152d95666ab845a122402973af54713f1f6eede22290e845b10d7671cf80204b
```

The container is created with -d switch for detached mode, because as we want the container to be running in the background. When run in detach mode, the container ID is returned and only the starting few characters of the ID is shown when running containers are listed.

```
[root@ww-z1 py3_flash_from_centos]# docker ps -a
CONTAINER ID    IMAGE           COMMAND              CREATED         STATUS          PORTS            NAMES
152d95666ab8    py3_simplehttp  "/app/simple_HTTP_ap…"  24 minutes ago  Up 24 minutes   80/tcp, 443/tcp  simple_server
```

The container *simple_server* listens to the ports 80 and 443 although it was not mentioned in Dockerfile to EXPOSE those ports. This is because the image *centos_from_scratch's* Dockerfile already had those ports exposed, and so the rest of the images build from *centos_from_scratch* also listen to those ports without explicitly mentioning in Dockerfile.
   As the container *simple_server* created from *py_simplehttp* image runs in background, we will execute the /bin/bash program in interactive mode to land up in the container.

```
[root@ww-z1 py3_flash_from_centos]# docker exec -it simple_server /bin/bash
[root@simple_server app]#
```

The IP address of the container - 172.17.0.3.

```
[[root@simple_server app]# ip a
1: lo: <LOOPBACK,UP,LOWER_UP> mtu 65536 qdisc noqueue state
    link/loopback 00:00:00:00:00:00 brd 00:00:00:00:00:00
    inet 127.0.0.1/8 scope host lo
       valid_lft forever preferred_lft forever
186: eth0@if187: <BROADCAST,MULTICAST,UP,LOWER_UP> mtu 1500
    link/ether 02:42:ac:11:00:03 brd ff:ff:ff:ff:ff:ff link-
    inet 172.17.0.3/16 brd 172.17.255.255 scope global eth0
       valid_lft forever preferred_lft forever
```

We will deal with network in detail in the next section.

Now from our host machine we should be able to curl the IP 172.17.0.3 and get response from the simple HTTP server.

```
[[root@ww-z1 py3_flash_from_centos]# curl 172.17.0.3
Hello world!
```

If we want to access the web page serverd by the simple HTTP server from the IP address of our host machine, the ports have to be bound to a desired port of the host machine using the **-p** switch with *docker run*. The **-p** switch *publishes* the addressed ports such that a port from the container is mapped to a port on the host machine.

The container is recreated with published ports -

```
docker run -d -p 9200:80 --name=simple_server --hostname=simple_server py3_simplehttp
```

The port 80 of the container (172.17.0.3:80) to the port 9200 of the host machine (10.10.0.150:9200). The web page is now accessible at the host IP -

Hello world!

Docker gives the ability for containers to be treated as an executable with the use of ENTRYPOINT command in Dockerfile. Here is such a Dockerfile -

```
FROM centos_from_scratch/py36

WORKDIR /app

ADD . /app

ENTRYPOINT ["/app/http_server_as_app.py"]
```

In comparisn to CMD command, which defines the default program to run during creation of a container, with the ENTRYPOINT command, parameters can be sent to the program set as ENTRYPOINT while creating a container. The program *http_server_as_app.py* accepts one commandline argument - *--greet* or *--info*. The image created from this Dockerfile is named *server_app* and a container can now be created the following ways -

```
docker run -d --name=greet_server_app -p 9200:80 server_app --greet
```

producing the output webpage -

← → C  ⓘ Not Secure | **10.10.0.150**:9200

Hello world!

and

```
docker run -d --name=info_server_app -p 9200:80 server_app --info
```

producing the output webpage -

← → C  ⓘ Not Secure | **10.10.0.150**:9200

b'processor\t: 0\nvendor_id\t: GenuineIntel\ncpu family\t: 6\nmodel\t\t: 94\nmodel
16384 KB\nphysical id\t: 0\nsiblings\t: 1\ncore id\t\t: 0\ncpu cores\t: 1\napicid\t: (
msr pae mce cx8 apic sep mtrr pge mca cmov pat pse36 clflush mmx fxsr sse sse2 s
pcid sse4_1 sse4_2 x2apic movbe popcnt tsc_deadline_timer aes xsave avx f16c rd
rdseed adx smap xsaveopt\nbogomips\t: 4195.14\nclflush size\t: 64\ncache_alignm(

All arguments passed after docker run <arguments> <image name> like in our case - --greet ot --info, are appended to ENTRYPOINT ["/app/http_server_as_app.py"] such that it becomes ENTRYPOINT ["/app/http_server_as_app.py","--greet"].

Another important command is VOLUME. It is used to create a directory that is mounted in the container. Inside a Dockerfile it is defined as -

```
VOLUME ["/data"]
```

and can be defined as parameters during creation of a container -

```
docker run -d -v /data server_app_with_volume
```

As the volume is created during container creation, all such volumes can be listed with -

```
[root@ww-z1 with_volume]# docker volume ls
DRIVER                  VOLUME NAME
local                   a89d3201c2d8fee7ddd0c35a769c026aacaa0b7e91c98bd10f99da28924d85d6
```

The name is produced as an alpha-numeric string as shown above. The volume is a directory created at the path /var/lib/docker/volumes/ and can be found with -

```
[root@ww-z1 with_volume]# docker inspect a89d3201c2d8fee7ddd0c35a769c026aacaa0b7e91c98bd10f99da28924d85d6
[
    {
        "CreatedAt": "2018-09-18T20:31:02Z",
        "Driver": "local",
        "Labels": null,
        "Mountpoint": "/var/lib/docker/volumes/a89d3201c2d8fee7ddd0c35a769c026aacaa0b7e91c98bd10f99da28924d85d6/_data",
        "Name": "a89d3201c2d8fee7ddd0c35a769c026aacaa0b7e91c98bd10f99da28924d85d6",
        "Options": null,
        "Scope": "local"
    }
]
```

Such a volume is unaffected by the existence of the container that created it and persists even after removal of the container. A volume can be independently created and attached to containers.

```
[root@ww-z1 ~]# docker volume create --name mydatavol
mydatavol
[root@ww-z1 ~]# docker volume ls
DRIVER                  VOLUME NAME
local                   a89d3201c2d8fee7ddd0c35a769c026aacaa0b7e91c98bd10f99da28924d85d6
local                   mydatavol
```

The newly created volume *mydatavol* is mounted at */d_vol* in a new container -

```
[root@ww-z1 ~]# docker run -it -v mydatavol:/d_vol centos_from_scratch /bin/bash
[root@2b83ef804cf7 /]# cd /d_vol/
[root@2b83ef804cf7 d_vol]# []
```

The volume *mydatavol* can be shared among containers, and so a file created in the volume by one container is accessible from another. Another container is created mounting the volume -

```
[root@ww-z1 ~]# docker run -it -v mydatavol:/d_vol2 centos_from_scratch /bin/bash
[root@44b50eb3d366 /]#
[root@44b50eb3d366 /]#
[root@44b50eb3d366 /]#
[root@44b50eb3d366 /]# cd /d_vol2/
[root@44b50eb3d366 d_vol2]# ll
total 0
-rw-r--r--. 1 root root 0 Sep 19 03:58 foo
```

The file *foo* is accessible from the other container as well -

```
[root@ww-z1 ~]# docker exec -it 2b83ef804cf7 /bin/bash
[root@2b83ef804cf7 /]#
[root@2b83ef804cf7 /]#
[root@2b83ef804cf7 /]# cd /d_vol/
[root@2b83ef804cf7 d_vol]# ll
total 0
-rw-r--r--. 1 root root 0 Sep 19 03:58 foo
```

When a container requires to have the same mounts for same volumes as in another container, it can be done by simply referring to the container while creation -

```
[root@ww-z1 ~]# docker run -it --volumes-from 2b83ef804cf7 centos
[root@15a89b89f423 /]# cd /d_vol/
[root@15a89b89f423 d_vol]# ll
total 0
-rw-r--r--. 1 root root 0 Sep 19 03:58 foo
```

The volumes from another container can be mounted in read-only mode as well -

```
[root@ww-z1 ~]# docker run -it --volumes-from 2b83ef804cf7:ro centos
[root@50c2e8a9a890 /]# cd /d_vol/
[root@50c2e8a9a890 d_vol]# touch bar
touch: cannot touch 'bar': Read-only file system
```

A volume can be mounted at a path inside the image of a container and in that case, the data at the path is copied into the mounted volume.

```
[root@ww-z1 ~]# docker volume inspect mydatavol
[
    {
        "CreatedAt": "2018-09-19T05:26:50Z",
        "Driver": "local",
        "Labels": {},
        "Mountpoint": "/var/lib/docker/volumes/mydatavol/_data",
        "Name": "mydatavol",
        "Options": {},
        "Scope": "local"
    }
]
[root@ww-z1 ~]# ll /var/lib/docker/volumes/mydatavol/_data
total 0
[root@ww-z1 ~]# docker run -d -v mydatavol:/etc centos
12618a56bb8bd2184494509ceac11cef568a6f4bddbeb706d564c2ca76ca3cc4
[root@ww-z1 ~]#
[root@ww-z1 ~]#
[root@ww-z1 ~]#
[root@ww-z1 ~]# ll /var/lib/docker/volumes/mydatavol/_data
total 896
-rw-r--r--. 1 root root   16 Aug  4 22:05 adjtime.rpmsave
-rw-r--r--. 1 root root 1518 Jun  7  2013 aliases
drwxr-xr-x. 2 root root   42 Sep 19 05:32 alternatives
drwxr-xr-x. 2 root root   27 Sep 19 05:32 bash_completion.d
-rw-r--r--. 1 root root 2853 Apr 11 04:18 bashrc
```

This copies the contents of the directory /etc of the container to *mydatavol* volume.

The removal of a volume is simple, but any container using it has to be first removed -

```
[root@ww-z1 ~]# docker volume ls
DRIVER              VOLUME NAME
local               a89d3201c2d8fee7ddd0c35a769c026aacaa0b7e91c
local               mydatavol
[root@ww-z1 ~]# docker volume rm mydatavol
Error response from daemon: remove mydatavol: volume is in use
```

Now after removal of the containers using the volume -

```
[root@ww-z1 ~]# docker rm 12618a56bb8b 44b50eb3d366 2b83ef804cf7
12618a56bb8b
44b50eb3d366
2b83ef804cf7
[root@ww-z1 ~]# docker volume rm mydatavol
mydatavol
```

It is also possible to send arguments to the the docker image builder process by using the ARG command. It is used in the form ARG <variable name>[=<default value>] in Dockerfile. This value can be provided from the coomandline while building an image by using the *--build-arg* *<variable name>=<value>* switch. The scope of an argument in a Dockerfile is from the line number of declaration till the end of Dockerfile. Say, ARG SHELL=bash is declared on line 2 of Dockerfile, the variable is accessible from line 3 to EOF.

# Containers in production

As we containerise applications during the build phase, it becomes extremely easy for developers to build up on the codebase without the hassle of preparing the environment for a project.

We are now going to learn about how containers can be used to deploy an application in production phase. An application almost all times are a collective of parts. In a distributed application, parts of the app, called *services*, communicate synchronous or asynchronously and these parts can be load balanced and dockerised. For example, a video streaming application consists of several parts - a front end app, a database cluster, a video transcoding middleware, a search engine, etc. The legacy way of building an infrastructure for hosting such an application is by deploying clusters of virtual machines for each of the services - database, search, middleware, etc. On top of having dedicated clusters for say, database also requires load balancing. The scaling capabilities of an architecture with virtual machines is slower because of sheer startup times of virtual machines.

This is where the solution provided by docker is extremely efficient and to top it all the load balancing is automatically configured.

Here we will build service stacks by creating *docker-compose.yaml* scripts to define, run and scale containers.

Our docker-compose.yml file -

```yaml
version: "3"
services:
  app:
    image: server_app
    deploy:
      replicas: 3
      resources:
        limits:
          cpus: "0.1"
          memory: 50M
      restart_policy:
        condition: on-failure
    ports:
      - "9200:80"
    networks:
      - webnet
networks:
  webnet:
```

*version* - The version of docker compose to be used.

*services* - Definition of all of the services in the application architecture.

*app* - Description of the cluster for the app service.

*image* - The name of the image to use for a single app container.

*deploy* - Schema for the cluster.

*replicas* - Number of containers in a service cluster.

*resources* - Definition of the resource limitations for a container cluster.

*restart_policy* - The condition upon which the cluster is to be restarted.

*ports* - The port mapping with of the container with the host machine.

*networks* - A load balanced overlay network for the container cluster.

In our use case we will be creating a cluster of three containers which constitute the app service. For a full fledged production application, there will be other services such as for database, middleware, etc. which can be defined in the same docker-compose.yml file if we wish to run those containers on the same host machine. In the previous section, we created an image *server_app* that runs a simple HTTP python webserver which will be used to launch a three node cluster.

This is the resultant architecture generated by docker compose -

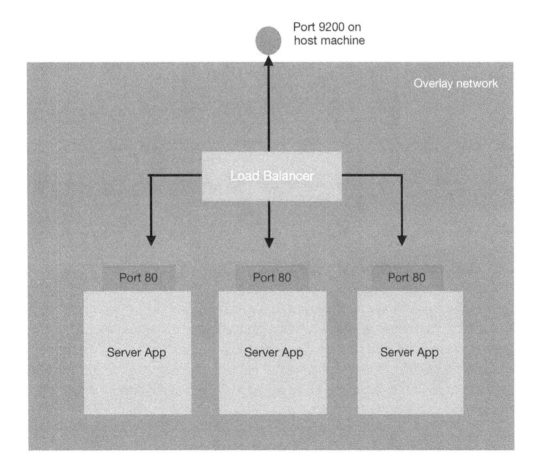

The overlay network named *webnet* is created by docker with load balancing. The network is created with default settings and can be configured with the *networks* key -

```
networks:
    webnet:
```

The other place where networks key is used is while defining the network to be used by the *app* service.

```
networks:
   - webnet
```

Each of the three *replicas* are limited to use only 0.1 i.e. 10% of CPU across all cores and 50 MB of RAM. The restart policy set for app service declares restarting of the app service (even the running containers along with the failed ones) upon single container failure.

To deploy this cluster, first we have to execute *docker swarm init* command.

```
[root@ww-z1 docker_files]# docker swarm init
Swarm initialized: current node (da51kw3synkb7pgolbfkxqpem) is now a manager.

To add a worker to this swarm, run the following command:

    docker swarm join --token SWMTKN-1-2p5iuk48f7hfij4a2uqr3x778ulnj4p0ap252ftel3vwizzz9e-eh3i8vsvobj8s4e1lfdeitj3d 10.10.0.150:2377

To add a manager to this swarm, run 'docker swarm join-token manager' and follow the instructions.
```

The purpose of initialising a swarm will be addressed in detail in the next section.

Next the cluster corresponding to the docker-compose.yml file is spawned.

```
[root@ww-z1 docker_files]# docker stack deploy -c docker-compose.yml server_app_prod
Creating network server_app_prod_webnet
Creating service server_app_prod_app
```

The *docker stack deploy* command creates a cluster of containers w.r.t. the defined services in *docker-compose.yml*. Therefore, in the context of this example, the *stack* comprises of only a cluster of three containers for the *app* service. In the case of an actual production setup, the *stack* could comprise of app service, middleware service and database service, all on the same host machine. The stack is named *server_app_prod* and the deploy command outputs the messages showing the creation of the network *webnet* bearing the name *server_app_prod_webnet* and a service for *app* bearing the name *server_app_prod_app* as described in *docker-compose.yml*. All the deployed services can be listed as follows -

```
[root@ww-z1 docker_files]# docker service ls
ID                NAME                 MODE        REPLICAS    IMAGE               PORTS
zp4ffnahuvn6      server_app_prod_app  replicated  3/3         server_app:latest   *:9200->80/tcp
```

The application is live -

Hello world!

Each of the containers in a service is called a *task*. The service - app consists of three of those and can be listed for details by -

```
[root@ww-z1 ~]# docker service ps server_app_prod_app
ID                  NAME                  IMAGE              NODE              DESIRED STATE
p07le1pdc4iv        server_app_prod_app.1 server_app:latest  ww-z1.server.com  Running
lq5bvaijwhw4        server_app_prod_app.2 server_app:latest  ww-z1.server.com  Running
q2zovk2b51zy        server_app_prod_app.3 server_app:latest  ww-z1.server.com  Running
```

The NODE field represents the name of the host machine.

Scaling of the app *server_app_prod_app* to increase or decrease the number of *tasks* can be done in runtime without requiring the other *tasks* to be affected or stopping of the stack. To scale up, the *replicas* in *docker-compose.yml* is changed from 3 to 5.

```
deploy:
  replicas: 5
```

The stack deploy command is run again in the updated docker-compose.yml -

```
[root@ww-z1 docker_files]# docker stack deploy -c docker-compose.yml server_app_prod
Updating service server_app_prod_app (id: zp4ffnahuvn6dgu9rrr9pm31e)
```

Listing the tasks in the service reflects the updation -

```
[root@ww-z1 docker_files]# docker service ps server_app_prod_app
ID                  NAME                  IMAGE              NODE              DESIRED STATE
p07le1pdc4iv        server_app_prod_app.1 server_app:latest  ww-z1.server.com  Running
lq5bvaijwhw4        server_app_prod_app.2 server_app:latest  ww-z1.server.com  Running
q2zovk2b51zy        server_app_prod_app.3 server_app:latest  ww-z1.server.com  Running
um35ezh4391z        server_app_prod_app.4 server_app:latest  ww-z1.server.com  Running
2h9963p98m3y        server_app_prod_app.5 server_app:latest  ww-z1.server.com  Running
```

The removal of the stack is straight forward and similar to removing a container -

```
[[root@ww-z1 docker_files]# docker stack rm server_app_prod
Removing service server_app_prod_app
Removing network server_app_prod_webnet
[[root@ww-z1 docker_files]# docker service ps server_app_prod_app
no such service: server_app_prod_app
```

The service and the network is removed and the listing of the service shows no registered services.

The swarm that was initialised at the beginning can be tore down by -

```
[[root@ww-z1 docker_files]# docker swarm leave --force
Node left the swarm.
```

*Node* is being referred to the host machine and --force option is required as the host machine is the only *master* in the *swarm*.

# Swarms

The previous section dealt with the concept of services and stacks. Our sample application consists of only a simple HTTP python webserver without the use of database or middleware or any other such functional parts that are usually present in an actual production application. Therefore, our *docker-compose.yml* file defined only a single service named - *app*, that contained *containers* or *tasks* hosting the HTTP webserver application.

In an actual production setup services are not confined to a single host machine but spreads across multiple machines. Here is the example of a sample production application -

Each host has *k* number of containers or tasks *(replicas)* running for each of the services - app, web and database. This type of architectural configuration is called *swarm*. A *swarm* is a group of machines that are running Docker and joined into a cluster. Each host here is called a *node* and one of them is the *swarm manager*. There can be multiple swarm managers and all the docker commands that either make changes to containers or query the containers in a cluster, are to be executed on the hosts that are swarm managers. Therefore, swarm managers are the only machines in a swarm that can execute commands and authorise other machines to join the swarm as *workers*.

We are going to setup a two node architecture to host a sample swarm. The image we used for the service - *app*, the *server_app* image, is not uploaded to the official Docker Hub repository and so the image has to be transported to the new node. For this we take the archive of the image *server_app* -

```
docker save -o server_app.tar server_app:latest
```

Move the tar archive from node ww-z1 to the new node (ww-z2) and load it into docker -

```
[root@ww-z2 ~]# ll
total 698272
-rw-------. 1 centos centos 715027456 Sep 20 12:26 server_app.tar
[root@ww-z2 ~]# docker load -i server_app.tar
dd91cbdbe659: Loading layer [===================================>]  207.9MB/207.9MB
8fc7aec1e350: Loading layer [===================================>]  130.8MB/130.8MB
ff8d806e632c: Loading layer [===================================>]  1.774MB/1.774MB
b86a61336592: Loading layer [===================================>]  21.85MB/21.85MB
150f8869e9b7: Loading layer [===================================>]  133.2MB/133.2MB
44cd2e7f6598: Loading layer [===================================>]  24.62MB/24.62MB
55fa9bf7db78: Loading layer [===================================>]  5.12kB/5.12kB
88e0a2b5a748: Loading layer [===================================>]  194.9MB/194.9MB
be70eb99c65a: Loading layer [===================================>]  1.536kB/1.536kB
fa86b426944e: Loading layer [===================================>]  4.608kB/4.608kB
Loaded image: server_app:latest
[root@ww-z2 ~]# docker images
REPOSITORY          TAG          IMAGE ID          CREATED          SIZE
server_app          latest       5cfe30b38bbb      2 days ago       699MB
```

Unlike an actual production setup as illustrated before, we will have only the service named *app* as our entire application stack. The docker-compose.yml file need not be present on the new node ww-z2, as the creation of the swarm and all other swarm related actions are to be done from the manager node.

   The machine ww-z1 is will be our swarm manager and so it is initialised there.

```
[root@ww-z1 docker_files]# docker swarm init --advertise-addr 10.10.0.150
Swarm initialized: current node (r1z2e99ff7irmv9qddy9vr4sh) is now a manager.
```

Previously, while creating a *service stack*, we did not need the requirement of the switch *--advertise-addr <manager ip>*. This is because the stack was deployed only on one node and it obviously did not require any communication with other nodes as it does when creating a *swarm*. The communication between swarm nodes are done through the ports 2376 (for docker daemon) and 2377 (for docker management) and so, both nodes have to be open. The swarm initialisation designates the node ww-z1 as manager and assigns a separate ID to it. Now, the the other machine, node ww-z2, will be joined as a *worker*. The following command has to be executed on the node -

```
docker swarm join --token SWMTKN-1-3qkzn06gy905u6zfb5yk5rk5sqg45m5hslkwkq971y0ygpk97n-5s9m9dd1fxqzn5pclo0j3zvl7 10.10.0.150:2377
```

which produces the following output -

```
[root@ww-z2 ~]# docker swarm join --toke
This node joined a swarm as a worker.
```

The entire of *swarm join* command with the token value will be provided as output for the *docker swarm init* command and this is the command that has to be executed on all such *nodes* that desire to be a part of the swarm.

Now that, a swarm of two nodes have been created, the nodes in a swarm can be listed by -

```
[root@ww-z1 docker_files]# docker node ls
ID                            HOSTNAME           STATUS    AVAILABILITY    MANAGER STATUS    ENGINE VERSION
r1z2e99ff7irmv9qddy9vr4sh *   ww-z1.server.com   Ready     Active          Leader            18.06.1-ce
oy9oxq6uwm9ral653vef3p0pa     ww-z2              Ready     Active                            18.06.1-ce
```

This command can be run only by the swarm manager.

We name our app stack as SAMPLE_APP and deploy the stack on ww-z1, the manger node -

```
[root@ww-z1 docker_files]# docker stack deploy -c docker-compose.yml SAMPLE_APP
Creating network SAMPLE_APP_webnet
Creating service SAMPLE_APP_app
```

The listing of the stack show all the five replicas as set in docker-compose.yml, are spread across the two nodes -

```
[root@ww-z1 docker_files]# docker stack ps SAMPLE_APP
ID              NAME               IMAGE                NODE               DESIRED STATE    CURRENT STATE
otfi2e83dn6f    SAMPLE_APP_app.1   server_app:latest    ww-z1.server.com   Running          Running 3 minutes ago
m3arkrmhoxln    SAMPLE_APP_app.2   server_app:latest    ww-z1.server.com   Running          Running 3 minutes ago
3ibrm24bfkat    SAMPLE_APP_app.3   server_app:latest    ww-z2              Running          Running 3 minutes ago
nenlv2sg3qqq    SAMPLE_APP_app.4   server_app:latest    ww-z1.server.com   Running          Running 3 minutes ago
v2738fcw9y1w    SAMPLE_APP_app.5   server_app:latest    ww-z2              Running          Running 3 minutes ago
```

The app can be accessed with the IP addresses of both the nodes.

We are going to add a visualization dashboard for our swarm and for this a new service will be added to the SAMPLE_APP stack. The service description for the dashboard is as follows in docker-compose.yml -

```
visualizer:
  image: dockersamples/visualizer:stable
  ports:
    - "8080:8080"
  volumes:
    - "/var/run/docker.sock:/var/run/docker.sock"
  deploy:
    placement:
      constraints: [node.role == manager]
  networks:
    - webnet
```

The service is named *visualizer* and has no replicas. The constraint parameter explicitly suggests that the container for this service should only be spawned in a *manager* node. This is required because docker does the arbitration decision of launching a container on a swarm's node on its own and the *visualizer* can only fetch data from a manager node. The volumes key mounts (in this case copies) the socket file on host machine to the container.

Now the updation of the stack -

```
[root@ww-z1 docker_files]# docker stack deploy -c docker-compose.yml SAMPLE_APP
Updating service SAMPLE_APP_app (id: sdcmk0cut7rwafac97k5ao21a)
image server_app:latest could not be accessed on a registry to record
its digest. Each node will access server_app:latest independently,
possibly leading to different nodes running different
versions of the image.

Creating service SAMPLE_APP_visualizer
```

The following message can be ignored, and it is shown because Docker looks up to the Hub for the *digest* of the image *server_app* and does not find one. The *digest* is a summary of the updated state of an image and if the docker daemon had found an updated version with the tag *latest* in Hub, it would have first updated the local image and then scaled the stack.

The *visualizer* applications dashboard shows the swarm health and state -

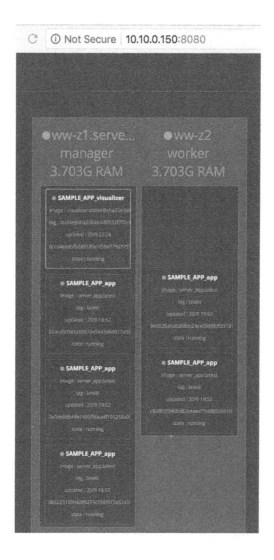

# Networking

As the sample application stack has been deployed in a swarm, this is how the network on each of the nodes look like,

on the manager node -

```
[[root@ww-z1 ~]# docker network ls
NETWORK ID      NAME                  DRIVER    SCOPE
ht1ieg51q9qz    SAMPLE_APP_webnet     overlay   swarm
2252f3f3b33e    bridge                bridge    local
6a95f6b02334    docker_gwbridge       bridge    local
a949ab021f57    host                  host      local
oustw58wx4ke    ingress               overlay   swarm
99d0c9ad07d7    none                  null      local
```

and on worker node -

```
[[root@ww-z2 ~]# docker network ls
NETWORK ID      NAME                  DRIVER    SCOPE
ht1ieg51q9qz    SAMPLE_APP_webnet     overlay   swarm
70a72c3ebe2e    bridge                bridge    local
0243e0778ad4    docker_gwbridge       bridge    local
73fc26ea0e11    host                  host      local
oustw58wx4ke    ingress               overlay   swarm
227f76728f48    none                  null      local
```

Each of the nodes have an *overlay network* named *ingress* and a bridge network named *docker_gwbridge* in common. The ingress overlay network is created by Docker swarm and this network is used to expose services external networks and provide a routing mesh. The *docker_gwbridge* connects the overlay network to that of the hosts machine's. The SAMPLE_APP_webnet is created due to the definition in docker-compose.yml. This is a service level overlay network that is used for communication among containers in the services of our stack.

Each of the containers are connected to the *ingress*, *SAMPLE_APP_webnet* and *docker_gwbridge* networks. The container running the *visualizer* dashbaord's IP allocation reveals three net ranges -

```
[root@ww-z1 docker_files]# docker exec SAMPLE_APP_visualizer.1.s20jmklid72d5betdd36645g7 ip a
1: lo: <LOOPBACK,UP,LOWER_UP> mtu 65536 qdisc noqueue state UNKNOWN
    link/loopback 00:00:00:00:00:00 brd 00:00:00:00:00:00
    inet 127.0.0.1/8 scope host lo
       valid_lft forever preferred_lft forever
298: eth1@if299: <BROADCAST,MULTICAST,UP,LOWER_UP,M-DOWN> mtu 1450 qdisc noqueue state UP
    link/ether 02:42:0a:ff:00:0b brd ff:ff:ff:ff:ff:ff
    inet 10.255.0.11/16 brd 10.255.255.255 scope global eth1
       valid_lft forever preferred_lft forever
```

```
300: eth2@if301: <BROADCAST,MULTICAST,UP,LOWER_UP,M-DOWN> mtu 1500 qdisc noqueue state UP
    link/ether 02:42:ac:12:00:06 brd ff:ff:ff:ff:ff:ff
    inet 172.18.0.6/16 brd 172.18.255.255 scope global eth2
        valid_lft forever preferred_lft forever
302: eth0@if303: <BROADCAST,MULTICAST,UP,LOWER_UP,M-DOWN> mtu 1450 qdisc noqueue state UP
    link/ether 02:42:0a:00:00:0b brd ff:ff:ff:ff:ff:ff
    inet 10.0.0.11/24 brd 10.0.0.255 scope global eth0
        valid_lft forever preferred_lft forever
```

The 10.255.0.0/16 range is for ingress -

```
[[root@ww-z1 docker_files]# docker network  inspect ingress
[
    {
        "Name": "ingress",
        "Id": "oustw58wx4ke6hwx4l1lu2214",
        "Created": "2018-09-20T13:35:22.68164192Z",
        "Scope": "swarm",
        "Driver": "overlay",
        "EnableIPv6": false,
        "IPAM": {
            "Driver": "default",
            "Options": null,
            "Config": [
                {
                    "Subnet": "10.255.0.0/16",
                    "Gateway": "10.255.0.1"
                }
```

and the 10.0.0.0./24 and 172.18.0.0/16 are for SAMPLE_APP_webnet and *docker_gwbridge* respectively.

The network diagram for our stack -

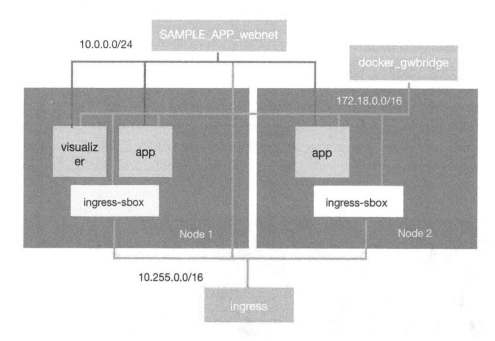

As earlier stated, *docker_gwbridge* connects all the containers but isn't used to connect to the external networks. The *ingress-sbox* provides a mesh routing for containers and connects the host network with the *ingress* network.

Another powerful and interesting aspect of Docker, is that, the containers can communicate seamlessly to non-docker and making Docker really platform agnostic. Docker's networking system supports various types of networks and does so by using pluggable drivers -

a) Bridge - This is the default driver and usually used for standalone containers.
b) Host - For container's to use the host machine's network, this type of driver is used.
c) Overlay - Multiple host machines running Docker to form either a swarm or standalone containers managed by different Docker daemons, can form a network using this driver.
d) Macvlan - This type of driver assigns mac address to individual containers, making them appear as a physical machine on a network.
e) None - Disables the networking for standalone containers and is not applicable to swarm services.

# SECTION 9

# UI/UX prototyping with InVision Studio

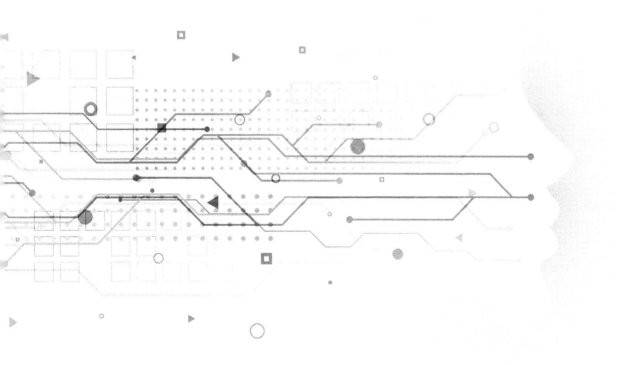

# Introduction

Application building has gone through a journey from desktop computers to now on phones, watches, virtual reality, and an array of other smart devices. The more computing technology extends and integrates with electronics devices around or with us, it would become more important to focus on the ergonomics of the interface that a device offers.

In this chapter of the book, we will take a comparative study on the good and bad design choices for software and discuss in the upcoming sections. The most common trait found among good programmers is the concentration of focus on the functionality and features of an application, and almost none on the look and feel of it. Such a reluctance is understandable from the point of view of a developer, but users are no longer are confined to just using applications on a desktop or laptop computer and also not just limited to using specialised applications where a user would not mind on just getting the work done.

Another common practice found among most developers, is thinking just about the functionality and internals of an application and getting started with them, with having only some sort of rough wireframe of the application's user interface (UI) on paper. The subsequent addition of interface elements naturally occur in a bottom up approach with first building the backend functionality and then introducing the activation object. There is although nothing wrong with this approach as it appears to be the only logical way and surely does not hamper the accomplishment of a function. This book explores the scope of full stack development which means, it would come down to the only developer who has to also work on the user interface for the application being built. A full stack developer set out to build a mobile app will be applying most of the development time for the first build on getting the functionalities for the app working. The focus of a full stack developer will be shifted to the look and feel on an app based in the demographic of the app, for example in case of a game app or an app targeted to an age group of less than 15. In any of the cases, if a proper UI design is not done keeping the list of features in consideration, what usually comes forth, is a development cycle where there may be incremental changes in the UI throughout, and most importantly an unnecessary amount of time being spent on making nifty changes to make all elements fit together.

In this chapter of the book we are going to learn about the virtues of having a well defined UI before the actual build phase of application features. In the current generation of application development there is a very good amount of requirement for a well designed UI and so the tool discussed in this chapter, not just makes creating intelligent design for an application easy with wire-framing features, but also provides interactivity among the various UI elements through custom built animations. Therefore, from the perspective of a full stack developer, all the UI elements spanning across all the pages or views of an app are possible to be created in a way that, the whole of the interactions and flow of control can be visualised before even writing any code for the actual app UI.

# UI/UX

The most common terms that we come across when indulging in application design are user interface (UI) and user experience (UX). We will first discuss what each of them mean as a lot of times they are confused with one another and used interchangeably.

The *user interface (UI)* is the space where an interaction between a human user and a machine occurs, also referred to as the human-machine interface (HMI). In this book we will be referring to UI only in the context of a user and a computer display for an application, but the concept in general is much broader and applies to describing any type of machinery. Let us take the example of a generic qwerty keyboard which has at least 104 keys. A keyboard in an interface device for a computer and for a user who does a lot of input from a keyboard, the positioning, key travel and shape and size of the keys are very important. The productivity of a user is to some extent dependant on this and that is the reason we can find so many different types of keyboard designs in the market. A very common attribute found among users who have to do a lot of typing, is the affinity toward the keyboard they use on a regular basis. The muscle memory gets accustomed to a particular keyboard and switching to a new keyboard, that is alike the previous with minor changes is an unpleasant experience. This effect can be observed even when switching between two identical keyboards, the new one feels a little different. Here is a sample of a keyboard used in gaming -

This is a very good starting point in understanding how a use case defines the appropriate interface design. In case of a gamer, the use of input devices are a combination of mostly keyboard and mouse. The keyboard contains only the keys that are required by most game controls and is devoid of the non-required ones. A noteworthy feature of this keyboard is the presence of a palm rest at the bottom. It is this feature that sets gaming keyboards apart from other general ones. Such palm rests are also available in gaming keyboards that contain the complete set of keys. The inclusion of such an element in the keyboard is not just from the intent of adding a sort of appeal toward the product as in the case for the colourful backlight for the keys. The palm rest is purposeful as for a gamer, it involves a lot of strain on the fingers and palm due to rapid reflexes and so, the palm rest provides a plane that matches to the table from the height of the keyboard. Some palm rests also have cushions that provide more comfort for the hands of a gamer and also prevents the palm from getting slippery due to sweat.

Another common practice among keyboard manufactures, in to include hot-keys. A hot-key is a key that has a dedicated purpose and is usually presented as a short cut to some common type of action.

The above keyboard is such a one, as we can see there are extra keys at the top of the traditional 104 keys. The lesson here for a company manufacturing keyboards with hot-keys is that, the positioning and utility of these keys must fit the use case of a user. For instance, these keys are almost always fixed to their designated features and cannot be customised according to the application. A good solution to this requirement came in the new generation of MacBook pro laptops from Apple, where the entire first row of the keyboard has been replaced by a customisable touch screen panel, which used to be previously dedicated to the function keys. Importance of a good design for user interface does not only end there and extends even to the details such as the texture on the keys, the elevation and the amount of sound a key press makes. Although these features, subtle or prominent, may seem unnecessary when it comes to comparison between a normal keyboard and a carefully designed keyboard with every importance to details, but from the perspective of a seller-buyer relationship, they provide a sense of implied importance given by the manufacturer to a customer. It is the attention to details that establishes a 'feel good factor'. This sense of thoughtfulness can be found in keyboards made by Apple, that come with an extra pair of usb ports at the bottom, for a user to discover like an 'easter egg'.

We have used the examples of keyboards to showcase the extent of the application of UI concepts and discussing about the perception that a customer forms about a company, brings us to the next topic which is the User eXperience (UX).

*User eXperience (UX)* goes hand in hand with the idea established about UI, as it can be considered as the effect of an UI. A feature makes sense in the right context, and UX is all about how the placement of a feature enhances the experience of a user, such that the feature is purposeful and somehow extend the list of features promised by the manufacturer. It is the satisfaction of a customer that ultimately decides the merit of a product. User experience is something that cannot be quantified and enlisted among the features promised by a product, but can only be experienced. In order to understand the significance of discoverability of features that extend the experience of a user, we have to look no further but the example of Apple keyboards. The presence of an added pair of usb ports are no where mentioned on the box. The idea is to give the user a pleasant surprise only after unboxing the product and discovering it. But again, user experience is not about putting in additional unsaid features in a product. A good user experience comes from intelligent assembly of a product. We take the example of a mobile phone and the placement of the speaker in it. There can be only two places where the speaker grill can be found on mobile phones, either at the bottom surface or on any of the four side edges. Among two phones that have equal sound quality, the one that will be regarded as better design choice over the other, is the one that will have the speakers on the side edge. This is because, when the speaker is in use and the phone is placed on a surface, the sound from the speaker will be blocked by the surface unless the phone is placed face down.

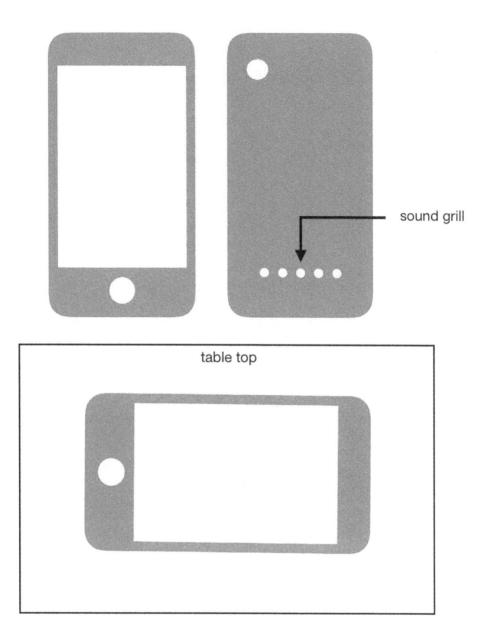

The above picture shows a phone with sound grill on its back surface obstructing the sound when placed face upward.

Even for the phone that has its speakers on the side edge, it is important for a manufacturer to decide where among the four sides the speaker should be placed. There have been few phones in the past that had speakers on the left and right sides but traditionally the two positions of choice are the top and the bottom edges. The bottom edge is though a better choice for the placing the sound grill, as the ideal orientation of putting a phone in a pocket is in the following way -

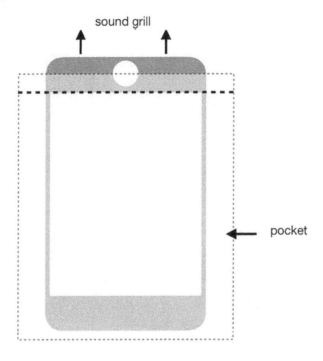

The reason this is an ideal orientation because, picking the phone out of the pocket, the thumb finger can be used right away to access the phone. It is from the sound grill that the ringing tone plays for an incoming call, and so, the sound is able to spread without obstruction. The contrary case is shown in the below picture where sound from the sound grill is obstructed by the closing end of the pocket -

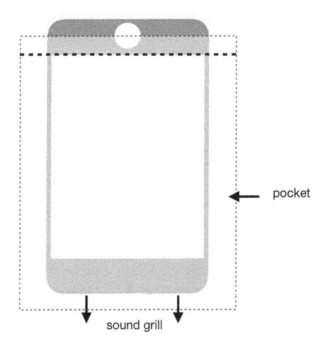

In the examples we used to describe the signs of a good user experience, it should be emergent as a concept that, it is only through a thorough study of all the situations that arise during the usage of a product, an appropriate user interface can be designed. It is this knowledge about a product that paves the way for a good design and ultimately leading to a rich user experience.

Now coming to the concepts of UI/UX in the context of application development, we will be dealing with buttons, animations, menu systems, fonts and colours. A good UX of an application is therefore dependant on its UI.

## UI - the first point of contact

The continued growth in adoption of the various mobile computing platforms has landed us in a competitive environment of application development where there are multiple apps for the same type of task. A developer building upon a fresh idea about an app will undoubtedly be faced with competition from other apps that provides the same set of features soon after the launch of the application. Therefore, in order to maintain a lead among competitors, it is very important to provide the user with an experience that is intuitive. This does not just means creating a UI thats is visually rich with vibrant colours, as if an app is desperate in grabbing the attention of a user.

The user interface of an app is the first point of interaction between a user and the creator(s). Be it a desktop, web or mobile device app, it should aim toward a particular style right from the beginning and should strive to leave its identity. It starts right from the signup process of the app. The behaviour found in most users is the reluctance in setting up the app with signup details. We know that most applications require setting up a user profile for accessing most features in an app, and so, the signup process should be as precise as possible.

It is the process of signing up a user, that may define the backend design of the user data handling. For example, most iOS/Android apps are now accessed on mobile phones and so it only makes sense to signup the user using the mobile number. There are APIs available on both types of mobile operating systems that can retrieve the active phone number of a device. The usual process during signup is to ask the user for either an email address or phone number to send an OTP, which then has to be input in the app to complete the remaining portion of the signup process. The current generation of API(s) support the capability of retrieving the mobile number, sending an SMS to that number, and collecting the sent OTP from inbox. Utilising such capabilities of the API gives a hassle free setup process to the user. It is also important to keep the email based signup option available, and in case of the app being installed on a non-cellular device, it should check with the API during startup and ask the user for an email address.

Another intelligent choice of presentation by app developers, is the allowing of user to go directly to using the app without having to signup. It is not possible for any app to showcase the richness of the app's content right on the signup screen after the splash screen and so, this is a very good practice. The signup process is reserved until the user takes any action that requires profile creation.

It is also a very important step to add a walkthrough section in the app right before landing into the home view or page of an app. Such a walkthrough should be precise and should capture the essential points in describing the purpose of the app and its working. For apps that have a lot of features, it is always a good practice to include a help section that briefly answers all the possible questions that a user may have about the app. The help menu must be put in a place that is easily discoverable.

## A friendly EULA

A lot of apps require a user to sign their consent on an End User License Agreement (EULA). A EULA usually consists of lines of text describing the contract, and almost hundred percent of the times, this document is skipped and agreed by a user without reading the details. A better approach would be to offer a summary about the EULA document in the form of a short video, which would play right before the actual agreement is to be signed. Importance to details being the key, it is important to not play the video with the sound turned on right away, and should the user ask for permission on turning on the volume. This is to show a user, the respect for privacy. It is always good to ask for permission than asking for forgiveness.

## Manage your Ads

There are only two ways that an app can make money, either through a premium subscription which involves an advertisement free experience, or through showing pop-up or banner ads in the app.

A good app respects its user, and so even if a user is not using a paid subscription of the app, the user should not be treated with an experience that appears to be an adverse consequence of not choosing a subscription. This is a common problem found in apps that provide news articles from the web, directly by scraping website contents. This leads to a situation where a user is shown two kinds of apps, those that belong to the app itself and the others are the ones that are originally present in a website where from a content is being showed.

When an app has to show ads to the user, it is a rather pleasant experience if ads are not shown right from the first use of the app. The goal is to reward the user with comfort in the usage of a product, and when it comes to something intangible as an application software, being a little conservative about intrusive ads has long term benefits. It is also a good gesture to politely let the user know about showing ads. The violation of one of the prime rules of a good UX comes from the act of applications trying to mislead a user into clicking ads. This is a problem plaguing most of the internet websites and when put inside an app, the user almost always ends up clicking and taken away from the app to elsewhere.

Therefore, the decision regarding the location of putting ads inside an app is very important and it should be avoided to put ads close to sections of an app where there is most finger movement. Some applications choose to put ads right at the bottommost panel of an app's viewport isolated from all the controls or menus in an app. This is although a comparatively less intrusive location, but the behaviour of such ad banners still remain the same. A user who unwillingly clicks an ad will almost always come out of the redirected location with an unpleasant experience. A better approach will be to prompt the user before redirecting to the ad content.

Not all applications have a subscription based model and so in those cases monetising with ads is a perfectly reasonable choice, but with that comes a lot of responsibility in the part of an app maker. The kind of ads to be displayed should be relevant to the context of the app. For example, a health and well being app showing ads for fast food is a contrast, and such ads fail at capturing effective future customers who would not buy into those ads.

In an unsubscribed use case of an app, it is also not pleasant to repetitively remind the user about the paid subscription based model as many apps do every time the app is launched.

## Golden ratio

Any lesson is design is incomplete without the mention of the golden ratio. Two quantities are said to be in golden ratio if their ratio is same as the ratio of the sum of the quantities, to the larger of the two quantities. The following mathematical expression represents the golden ratio -

$$\frac{a + b}{a}$$

$$= 1.6180339887\ldots.$$

The two values a and b can represent anything from area, length, colour code, etc., and the values are in golden ratio if their ratio is equal to the irrational number 1.618033…

The significance of the golden ratio can be understood from its presence spread throughout all of nature. Anything beautiful in nature is based upon this ratio and so, designing any user interface that is aesthetically pleasing must adhere to this ratio. The proportions of all the UI elements in an app when done by maintaining the ratio, what emerges is a UX that is comfortable for the eyes and ultimately pleasant for the brain. The question now arises that what are the numeric values that produce such golden ratios. As it turns out, that the well known Fibonacci sequence among computer programmers represents the golden ratio. Every two adjacent numbers in a fibonacci sequence produces the golden ratio. Here is an example where the elements are sized according to the golden ratio -

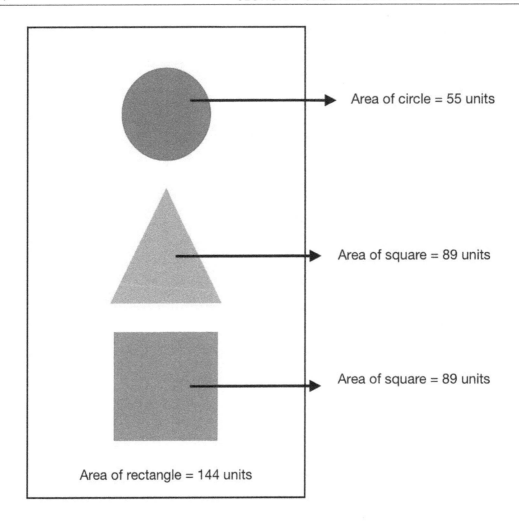

The three corresponding numbers in the Fibonacci sequence are 55,89 and 144, and so the area of both square and the triangle are in golden ratio with the area of the enclosing rectangle. The circle is in ratio with the square and triangle.

## Understanding the user

The success of a UI design comes from the proper identification of the target user base, age group and how these two correlate with the intent of an app. Apps developed for kids tend to be rich in animations and sport vibrant colours. Apps made for health and wellness need to evoke a soothing experience and so, usage of CYMK colours is a very good choice as they are softer on the eyes compared to the RGB palette.

The demographic of an app is very important to be determined because only then the arrangement and placement of menus can be suited accordingly. The most number of menu systems and buttons can be found in multiplayer games. The demographic for these games are the agile ones, mostly teens and youth, who are capable to navigate through the various menus and options. The next type of apps that have a lot of UI elements are social networking apps that provide a feature filled environment. Unlike games, a social network has its demographic spread through all types of age groups and so, it is a crafty task of arranging the features in an intuitive way. In order to find the right balance between options that are to be shown as direct access menus and options that are to be included in sub menus, constant walkthroughs are required with the full list of features and ranking these features w.r.t. to their frequency in usage.

Today most handheld devices have the average screen size of five inches. The natural way to hold phones is with a single hand, but the increasing screen sizes end up compensating the mobility of a single hand usage with using of two. As a UI developer, the key focus must remain on introducing gestures and placing buttons or menus in places that are most accessible with the fingers when a device is held in the palm. It is only then a good UX can be experienced on the user's part.

## Changes in UI

The simple reason a user using a product, continues to use it, because of the timely availability of all required features and the way a user grows accustomed to the usability of a product. As mentioned earlier, the competitive market of apps give the user a range of options to choose from, and so a loyal user who keeps up with the continued updates of an app. As much as it is important to keep updating the features of an app, it is also necessary to keep working on improvements in the UI. In a usual case, it is not possible for an app maker to perfect the UI of an app on the first version, and naturally we can find nifty changes in the UI along the evolution of any popular app. With that said, it has to be remembered that each change in design should be aimed at the improvement of the UX. A UI change that is purposeful and not just a gimmick always concedes to the value to users.

There can be use cases where the UI created in the first version is in itself sufficient and may not require further changes along the growth of trusted user base. But in those, cases too, updation of UI becomes due, as users may grow weary of the same look and feel, and a new competitor app with the same set of functionality may become able to attract a lot of users just due to the freshness in design.

Again, as much as changes are necessary with time, like the use of a new colour palette or theme, it must also be remembered that such changes should not come in between consecutive app releases. A fresh overhaul of any design is worthy only when there is a loyal user base, who would appreciate the design change. Brand redesign and design refreshes are common, and so an intelligent way for an app maker to know what the user wants, is to directly listen from the users. In some cases, hosting a poll in-app can be a good way of knowing how much a user is comfortable with the changes.

## *User specialization*

The intent of this chapter has been about understanding the necessity of an application's user interface design, and including this as one of the primary tasks in the development lifecycle of a customer facing application. Most iOS or Android applications are aimed at non-specialised users and so making an application whose features are intuitively accessible becomes important. Now, as we are emphasising upon the design of an app, it definitely should not be interpreted as a focus on just the look and feel.

We used the example of a keyboard to showcase how a product undergoes derivatives in design, based upon user requirements. Therefore, the choice of design ideas should undoubtedly originate from creating a list of user requirements and its target demographic. A user belonging to the age bracket of below 40, has a higher probability of being a gamer during the teenage years. MMORPGs are the types of games that sport a lot of options and a vivid menu system, and so, a user of such gaming apps is accustomed to traversing a diverse menu system. Such a user will be fluent in accessing other types of applications as well, compared to say a person who has had a limited exposure to computers or applications in general. Given that the modern era of smartphones began in 2007 with the release of the first iPhone, it has only been a decade and there exists a great number of users who are above 40 and can be identified as non-specialised users. A category of apps that are mostly used by these non-specialised users are banking and commodity services apps.

# What is InVision Studio?

InVision Studio is a rapid UI prototyping tool that not just enables designing mock ups, but also provides interactions among all the UI elements. InVision comes preloaded with animations and the interaction among elements are automatically animated without having to define each state of the animation of an element. InVision studio comes with a mobile app where a live design can be tested.

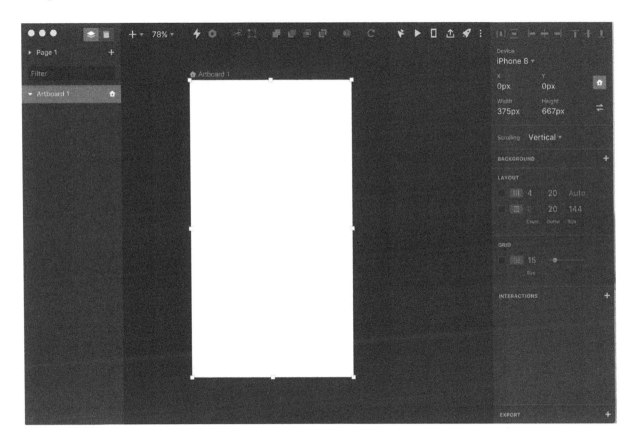

When the application is launched with a choice of the type of device for which the prototype is being made, we are taken into the work area with a blank view having the dimensions of the selected device called *Artboard*. An *Artboard* is the canvas representing the state a single view in the actual app UI and it is where all the visual elements are to be added.

Here are the contents on the left panel -

The highlighted menu in blue, represents the *Layers* in the UI mockup. A particular project can have multiple pages and so on launching the application, the default page created is *Page 1*. Suppose a project consists of more than one mockup design, and so each *Page* represents an instance of one of such mockups. Inside each *Page*, we will have Artboards corresponding to a particular design.

The other menu option at the top right corner beside *Layers* is, *Library*.

The purpose of *Library* is similar to that of the concept of library files as found in computer programming. In the context of InVision, *Library* is used to store and access the design components for the purpose of design reusability. From buttons, menus, icons, etc., everything can be exported as Library resources to be reused in other projects. InVision Studio is built with the philosophy of multiple UI designers working together in collaboration, and so, this Library feature gives designers quick access to design resources in a drag and drop environment.

InVision provides a basic collective of design elements using which all types of compound UI design elements can be created. With the Artboard selected, the top menu bar sports the following menu options -

Starting from the left, the first menu option '+' contains the design elements -

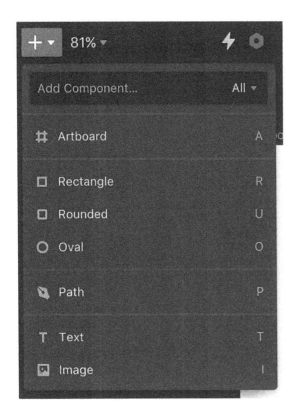

*Artboard* option is used to add a new *Artboard*, Rectangle and Oval represents those respective shapes, Rounded is for a rectangle with rounded corners, Path is used to draw a custom shape, Text and Image are obvious for adding the respective elements.

The next icons to be discussed are the following -

The first icon from left represents the option *Freehand*. Freehand enables users to collaborate live on designs. The next option is *Preview*, used to run the preview of the design interactions in an emulator. The next option *Mirror to device* is used to run the mockup on the phone app that comes with InVision. The next option is *Publish to InVision*, and it is used to upload projects and design elements to the InVision cloud. The last icon is an option yet to be introduced and named *App store*. It is a marketplace for all InVision designs.

The remaining of the options are the following on the top menu bar -

The first option from the left is to create a connection between two UI elements through interaction and is named *Add interaction*. The next option *Create component* is highlighted when a UI element is selected and using this option a design can be converted into a Library item as a component. The next icon from left is the *Cut path* option which is used to cut a UI element in a custom shape. The next option *Edit path* is used to make changes to a created custom shape with the Path tool. The next set of options are used to build UI elements with compound layers of shapes using various additive and subtractive layer manipulation.

Finally the options panel on the right pane of the studio window as shown below is dedicated to changing details about UI elements such as colour, position, dimensions, background, interactions, etc.

We will move on to designing a dummy app UI with installing the InVision - Design & Prototype app on our mobile device for testing.

# Prototyping a dummy app

All the source files can be found at the following location -

For our dummy app we are going to design a social networking app prototype. We will start with adding another Artboard alongside the default one.

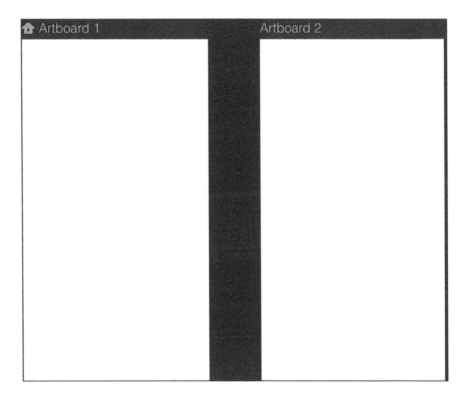

Artboard 1 as we may have guessed, will be our splash page. For its design we are going to use Oval and Rounded options from the list of components menu '+'.

First we will add colour and text to the button create with Rounded option, at the bottom, and add pictures in the Oval elements. To add colour to the button, it is selected and the properties panel on the right show values relevant to it. The colour is changed from the fill option, as shown below -

Some shadow effect is added to the button as well, with the blur property set to 10.

Here is the button after adding text, and setting the colour and font property of the text in the same way as before, from the right panel.

The contents of the Artboard 1 after adding the UI components are listed in the following way in the left Layers panel -

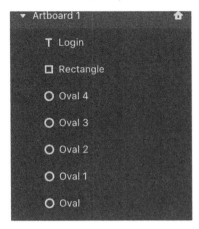

Now to add a picture to one of the Ovals, an image is downloaded and added to the Artboard.

As we can see the image is positioned right over the biggest Oval object. In the Layers panel, the respective Oval and the image objects are selected -

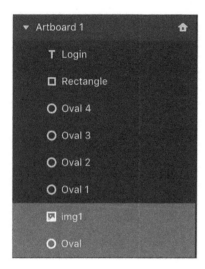

Then right from the menu on top of the window, we click the Toggle Mask option which we will find as highlighted as shown below in the rightmost option -

This will turn our selected items into the following visual -

The two elements have been grouped together as we can see in the Layers panel -

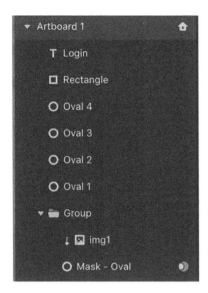

Now the rest of the view is designed the same way, which results into the following -

There is a slight shadow added to each of the Ovals and for this the individual oval element has to be selected from the Layer groups. The login button is comprised of the Text and the Rounded/Rectangle element but they exist as separate elements as shown below -

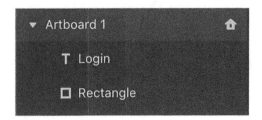

We are going to group them by selecting both and use *Toggle Mask* option as before or right mouse click on the selected items in the Layers panel to reveal a drop down menu.

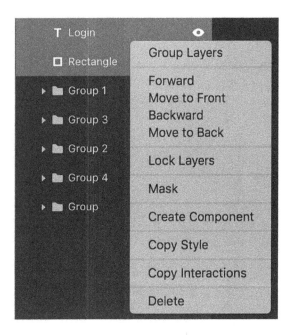

From here we will select the option *Group Layers* to group the selected items.

　　Now for the login button, we may want to use it further in this or other projects, so we can go ahead and designate the button as a component for our project. We select the button and click the *Create component* button at the top menu -

The name for this component will be set as the following -

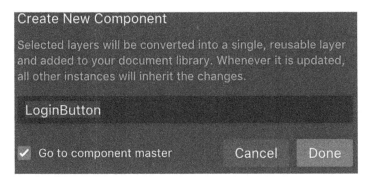

As the option '*Go to component master*' is selected, it would take us to a list of all custom created components. We may choose to uncheck the option and select *Done*. Our button has now become a component which can be reused across projects and so the entry in Layers panel has now changed for the button -

Now, the next Artboard is designed as the following -

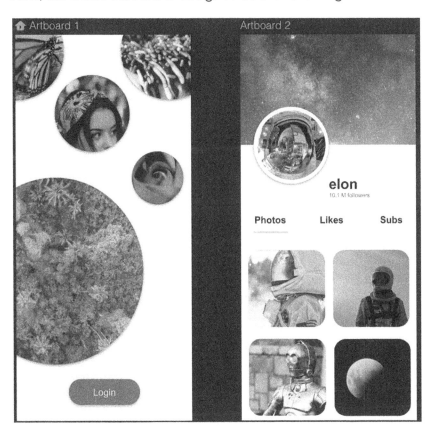

In the Artboard 2, we want to add a button using the LoginButton component we just created. Selecting the Artboard 2 from Layers panel, we click the '+' menu at the top to add a component. As the component we wish to add is a custom one, it will not be showing the list of fundamental components that come with InVision.

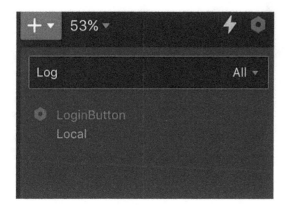

Typing the name of the component int he search bar shows the required element and from here on we can just drag and drop the component in our desired location on the Artboard.

Now as the button has been made into a component, it has a limited degree of edibility. We can change the text on the button by selecting the text element from the Layers panel, but other properties are not changeable such as colours, font, etc. Selecting the component button would show us the available set of properties in the right panel.

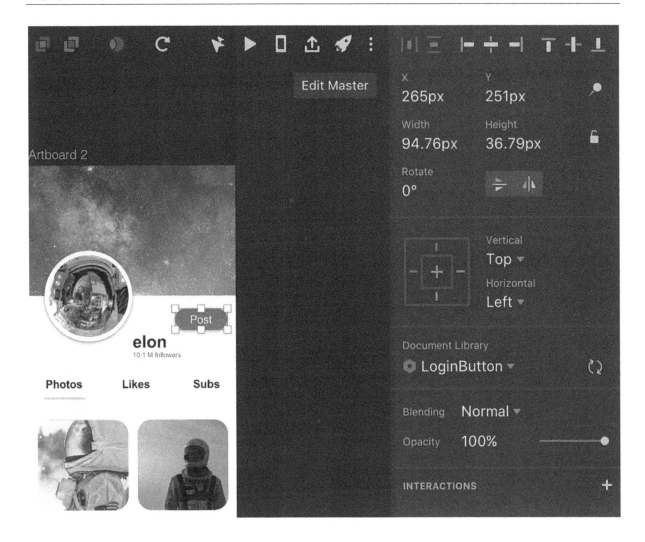

In comparison to the other UI elements, the *LoginButton* is designated as belonging to Document Library, as we can see on the right panel in the above image. The *LoginButton* component can also be found in the *Toggle libraries* option as shown below -

Next, we want to add an interaction between the two Artboards. A click on the *Login* button in Artboard 1, should navigate us to the Artboard 2. For this, we select the Login button, and click the Add interaction option at the top menu -

This would show a blue line floating along with our mouse cursor. With the floating blue line activated, we click on the Artboard 2 at any place.

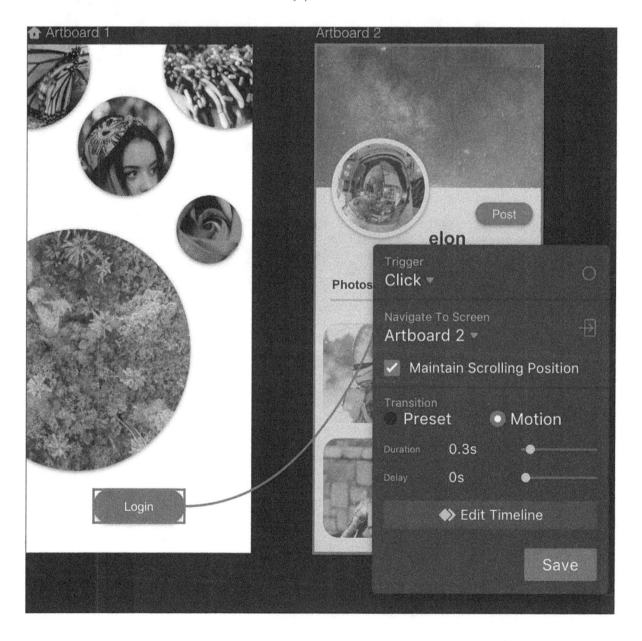

A floating menu would appear as shown in the above image and we would go ahead and select *Save*. The resultant is an interaction between the two Artboards and will be shown as a blue line according to the below image -

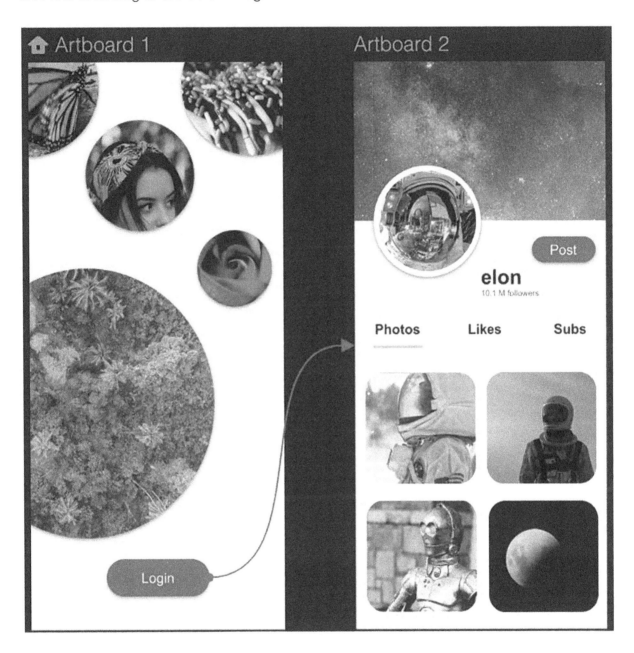

We can go ahead and run preview, which will open the emulator of the desired device size.

Next we want the contents in the Artboard 2 to be scrollable. The way animations and transitions work in InVision, is by letting a designer to draw only the beginning and the end frames of the animation. The intermediate states are automatically created by InVision. The designer also has individual access to the animation properties such as time, speed, delay, etc. For our scrolling action, we will create another Artboard and add elements to it w.r.t. the way the viewport of the app shall change upon scrolling. Here is the design of the new Artboard.

As we mentioned, for creating animations or transition effects in InVision, the first and the last frames have to be created, the following image shows the two Artboards that are those two frames.

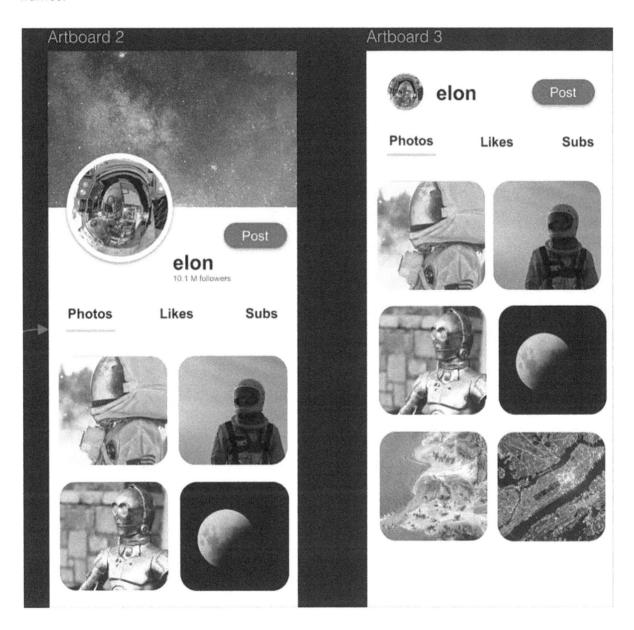

Now before we add a scrolling interaction to the Photos menu in the app, we will select all the photos in each of the Artboard and group them. Pressing hold the shift key, we select the four photos in Artboard 2 and click right mouse to reveal a drop down menu we saw earlier.

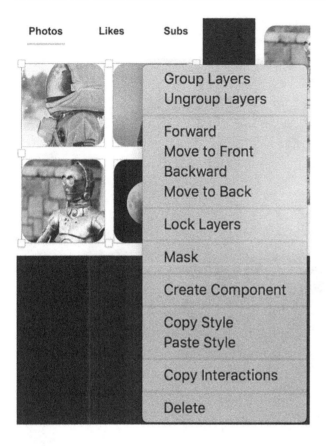

We select option *Group Layers* and perform the same action on Artboard 3 as well. Now we select the grouped photos in Artboard 2 and select Add interaction as before and apply the floating blue line to Artboard 3. But here in the floating interaction menu we will select a different trigger.

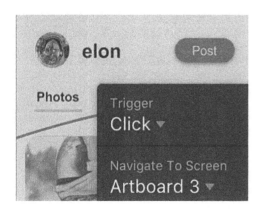

Instead of click we will use *Swipe Up*.

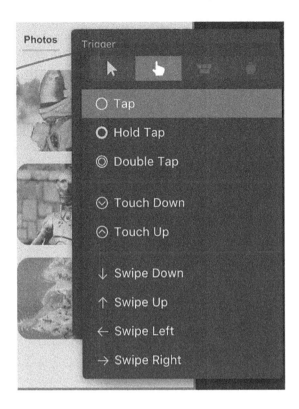

We also want to come back to the state as in Artboard 2 upon scrolling down from the state of animation as in Artboard 3. For this we will select the grouped photos in Artboard 3 and do Add interaction on Artboard 2, the same way as before, only this time the trigger would be set to *Swipe down*.

We can go ahead and check our current progress using the mobile app for InVision. For this, the test device has to be connected to the same WIFI network as the computer. A QR code will be shown on clicking the Mirror to device option from the top menu bar.

This QR code has to be scanned using the mobile app.

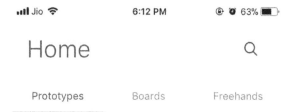

**No prototypes**

Sign In to InVision on your desktop to
create your first prototype.

In the above image the option pointed as 'Scan' opens the camera for scanning the QR code.

To explore how we can control animations, we will create another Artboard for the *Likes* button in the app and add interactions from Artboard 2 and 3 to the new Artboard, as the Likes button can be interacted from both of those Artboards.

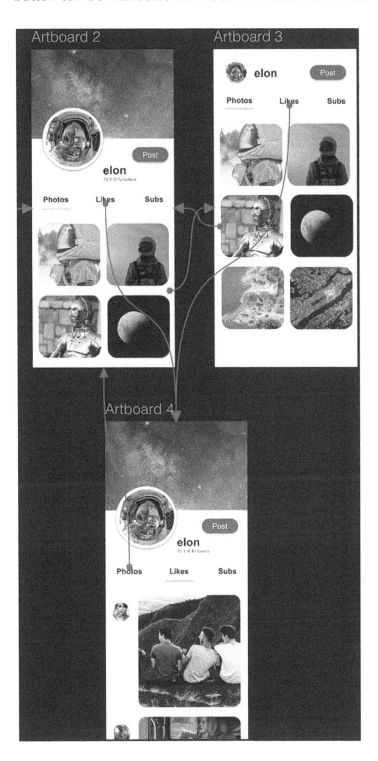

The app opens with the Photos option selected as the first screen, and the following image shows the selection marker -

# Photos

On clicking the *Likes* button, the selection marker slides from under *Photos* to *Likes*.

# Likes

We wish to edit the default sliding animation. First the Likes button on Artboard 2 is selected and from the right properties panel, we select *Edit Timeline* from under the interactions property.

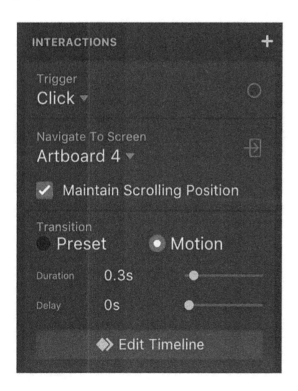

This changes InVision Studio's viewport into the following view -

On the left is the list of components involved in the transition between Artboard 2 and Artboard 4 and each component has its corresponding timeframe alongside, for the animation. The right side of the window is interactive and is reserved for playing the animation. InVision provides control over the timeline of each component involved in the animation for any interaction component.

The component of our interest is with the name *Rectangle 1*, and it will be highlighted in the timeline list on the left, upon selecting it on the right. Here is the image showing that -

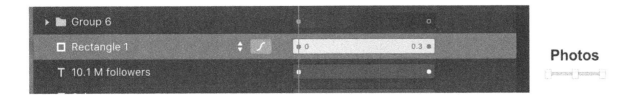

All the components begin animation from the same time and we want to start the animation for the selected component after a delay. The timeframe is slid by the required amount -

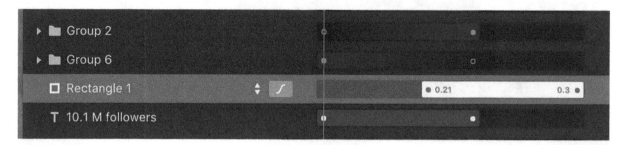

Each animation is defined by a Bezier function's curve and it can be chosen from the drop down menu as shown below -

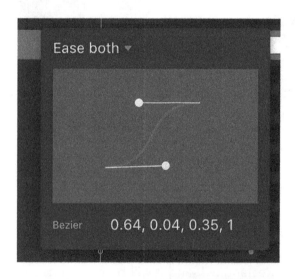

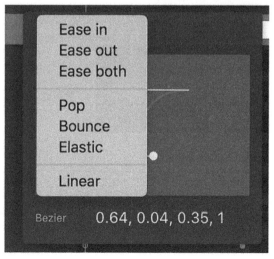

The Bezier curves can be customized as desired, thereby giving a designer, the full freedom to manipulate the change in animation frames over time. It can be done by dragging the ends of the curve as shown below -

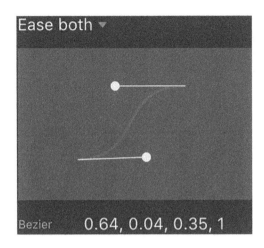

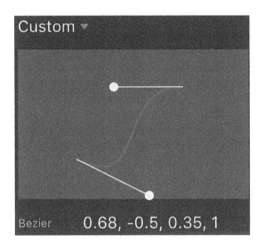

When the *Ease both* animation curve is manipulated by dragging the white pointers, the name of the animation type also changes to *Custom* as shown in the above images.

The speed of playing the animation can be controlled, which is by default set to 1X, as shown below -

# SECTION 10

# Building mobile app
# with FuseOpen

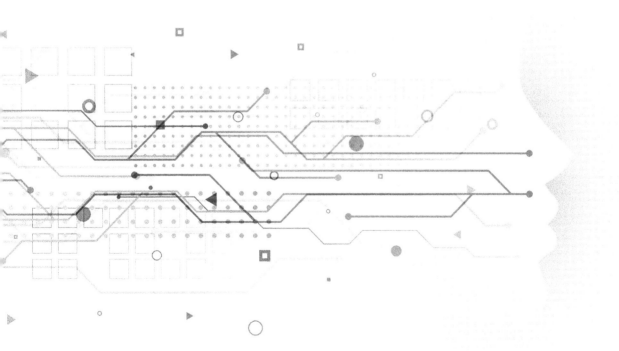

# Introduction

There was once a time when standalone application softwares were developed for being installed on a user's personal computer. The advent of web technologies saw a significant boom in adoption of a service based software distribution model. The web browser went on to become such an important and powerful tool, that its usage extended from just being a internet navigator to the only required application software in a computer. All types of standalone software applications started to be implemented in the web browser. Computing power intense applications such as, Photo/video editing applications from Adobe or console grade games, all were implemented as a web based application. The Chrome OS from Google is the focused completely on making the browser the only required application on a device and therefore showcase the true prowess of web based technologies.

The next significant technological breakthrough came in the form of smartphones. When majority of the applications in the standalone scope went on to become browser based, the introduction of smartphones brought about a new paradigm in application development. Companies that had web based applications such as Facebook, or Amazon started bringing out their array of features available on the web application to the smartphones as Apps from the introduction of the iPhone on 2007. From then on, apps and smartphones became powerful by the years and hence, almost every company has been coming out with the app version of their application software. The development of apps significantly added to the expenditure of companies, as they now have to maintain a separate team of developers for building apps. We can take the example of the widely popular video communication application Skype. It initially was a standalone application that a user can install on a personal computer. Then came the web browser based version on Skype in the form of a Chrome browser extension and then finally the smartphone version as app. The situation is such, that, these three types of applications currently co-exist and Skype has to come out with updates across all the platforms. Therefore, it can easily be estimated, how much a development costing and focus has to be distributed across multiple domains, and for a startup company, it is a real challenge.

The complexity increases even further because, unlike in a browser based application scenario, which did not require to develop different apps for different supported browsers, the app eco-system is further sub divided into heterogeneous operating systems. The smartphone marketplace is fragmented into three major segments - iOS, Android and others. The others section consists of niche operating systems for various phone manufacturers such as Windows Phone and BlackBerry. The current landscape of app development requires companies to have two separate development teams working on the respective versions of an app for the major two OS platforms - iOS and Android.

In the midst of such a fragmented app development scenario, it is a matter of great ease if a single code base can be maintained for both types of mobile OS. In this section of the book, we are going to learn such a technology. With FuseOpen not only we will be able to compile the same code base both for iOS and Android, but since FuseOpen uses NDK (Native Development Kit), the apps will even run faster. There are other tools such a NativeScript or React Native or Flutter, which like FuseOpen uses JavaScript or Dart (in case of Flutter) for programming the app. A developer coming from the background of web development will find an easy learning curve with FuseOpen. The clean and precise markup syntax encourages a developer to try out new features and do rapid prototyping, which is an extremely crucial requirement for any development team. FuseOpen uses the OpenGL native graphics library to render the app's UI, and so visually rich applications can be built with ease. Although the development community surrounding React Native and Flutter is ample and growing by the day, FuseOpen despite having a comparatively small community, is in no way less capable a tool.

The most noteworthy thing about FuseOpen as compared to React Native or Flutter, is that, it has been developed with the intent of bridging the gap between an app developer and a UI/UX developer. A development lifecycle usually comprises of the phase when a UI/UX designer builds the design of the app with all its animations and transitions and other shapes and effects. The next phase is usually a little more time consuming as the app developer has to go back and forth with the UI/UX developer, iterating over changes and adjustments, to give shape to the actual app exactly the way it was intended. FuseOpen addresses a fundamental problem there has been in implementing an app's UI design. FuseOpen is capable to remove the phase of design implementation and changes, between UI/UX developer and an app developer. The existing tools that are used by a designer to express the various visual elements in an app, are available only as designed models. An app developer has to go through the phase of building upon that design through coding and a substantial amount of actual development time can be consumed in coding an app design that is the most accurate to the designed model. FuseOpen takes in account this problem and through its clean and simple markup syntax, makes it possible for a UI/UX designer to write code that compiles to actual app's design. This drastically improves the development focus as both app developers and UI/UX developers can express their using the same toolset. FuseOpen makes it possible for a designer to express animation rich app designs through an intuitive markup syntax that requires the least learning curve.

# What is FuseOpen?

FuseOpen is an open source library of toolsets that enable creation of native mobile apps both for iOS and Android.

There are plenty of native app development frameworks but what makes FuseOpen special, is its simplicity.

For long, there has been a divide between app developers and UI/UX designers. The clean programming style is aimed at designers who can build apps with the minimal learning curve in programming. The FuseOpen framework takes care of all the peripheral complexities of building and managing code for two different OS platforms, and a person building an app, can focus just on coding the various functionalities of an app. With FuseOpen a single codebase compiles to both iOS and Android.

FuseOpen uses a declarative-reactive XML markup language for UI/UX elements. The UX markup provides access to an OS's native UI elements, ultra-fast OpenGL-based rendering and flexible vector-based graphics. The UX markup compiles to C++ for native performance on mobile devices. FuseOpen introduces a new language *Uno*, which is a lightweight dialect of C# and sits at the heart. It is Uno, that compiles the UX markup into C++ and has seamless interoperability with Java (for Android) and Objective-C (for iOS). The most powerful feature of Uno, it its ability to interface with legacy code of an app on either of the OS platforms, with minimal or no change to the actual code.

FuseOpen's unique technology stack makes app building most intuitive and easy for web developers. Building apps with FuseOpen does not come with a learning curve at all for web developers because along with the XML based markup for UI/UX, the business logic for an app is implemented with *Javascript*. The javascript framework FuseJS, is different from React Native and NativeScript. Both NativeScript and React Native run javascript in a VM, and provide access to a platform's native API and UI elements. The key difference with FuseJS is that, it uses javascript only for establishing business logic, unlike NativeScript and React Native, where the javascript is actually responsible for translation of the javascript calls to actual native API calls. Here is a blog that discusses in details about this -

FuseOpen comes with not just a framework but an application for Windows and Mac, called Fuse Studio, which is an IDE. FuseOpen also has a mobile app Fuse Preview in both App stores and Play store. Together with Fuse Studio and Fuse Preview, live changes to an app in development can be viewed on a mobile device of all form factors.

FuseOpen comes with plugins for Visual Studio Code editor, Atom editor and Sublime text 3 editor, which provides code completion, error listing, output logging and also the ability to launch FuseOpen apps right from the editor.

# Dummy: A sample app

All the source files are present in the following location -

We will start off by creating a simple app called dummy that displays a text on startup and for that, a new project is created in Fuse Studio.

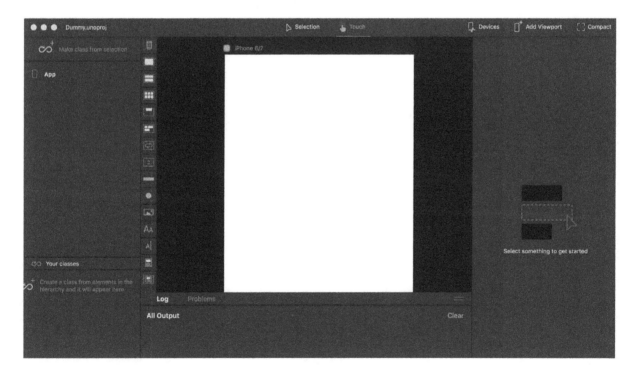

*A basic layout of Fuse development environment*

The left pane shows the different UI elements and their relationship with one another in a tree structure. Creating a new project will pre-load the project with some basic minimal code, but here we are starting with only one element - App, which is the topmost element in the hierarchy and represents an app object.

The strip next to the left pane -

is a listing of some of the fundamental UI elements, which can be added to the hierarchy in a drag and drop fashion.

On selecting the *App* element, the rightmost panel shows all the various properties associated with the element such as layout, size, position, color, etc. which can be configured in a clickable environment without requiring any coding.

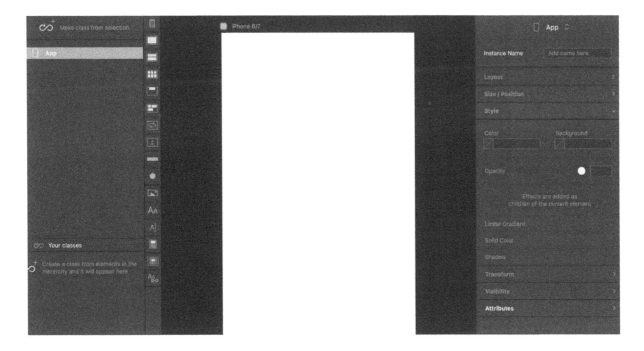

We will be using Atom text editor for coding the app. The code corresponding to the current state of the app, is as follows -

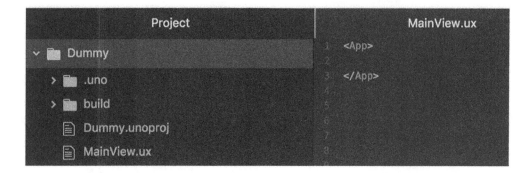

The App element in the UI hierarchy -

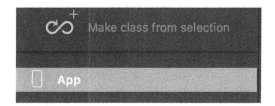

corresponds to *<App> </App>* markup. The changes made to the app, either from Fuse Studio or the Atom editor through coding, are always synced. When a <ClientPanel /> is added to the app hierarchy through drag and drop, it gets added to the code as well.

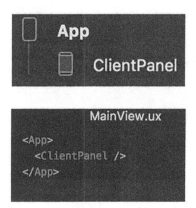

ClientPanel represents the space taken not by the app's UI elements but the OS' such as, the status bar, the keyboard, etc. A later upgrade to ClientPanel came in the form of <SafeEdgePanel /> which accounts for the notched displays in phones since iPhone X. We updated our code likewise and provided a background color that remains common throughout the app for all the *Views* that are to be added to the app moving forward.

```
<App>
  <SafeEdgePanel Color="#42f4bc">


  </SafeEdgePanel>
</App>
```

As the changes are reflected back to the preview of the app in Fuse Studio, we are going to have a live look of the app in iOS and Android devices using the Preview app.

In order to preview on a device, we have to make sure both the machine on which the coding is being done and the device to test upon, are connected to the same WIFI network. FuseOpen transfer data of the app's attributes to the Preview app over WIFI. Our *Dummy* project in Fuse Studio is represented by a unique QR code under the Devices button above the pane on right.

The Preview app has both options to connect to Fuse Studio, either through the IP and Code, or the QR code.

On previewing with the app, this is the current state of our app.

The FuseOpen design principle makes it the best candidate for rapid prototyping and building powerful and visually rich apps. The Fuse Studio, the Atom text editor (in our case), the Preview app, all can work in unison if connected to the same WIFI network. If the Preview app is running on multiple types of devices say an Android phone and tablet, an iOS phone and tablet and also Android and Apple watch devices, the live changes in the app will be visible and testable across all of these devices.

Before, going ahead with building the app, we will take a quick look at the various files and their significance in the project explorer in Atom editor.

*.uno* - Directory containing Uno modules and other files for project and is created automatically.

*build* - This directory contains the build files for Local preview, Android and iOS. This gets updated from the Preview > Rebuild menu and is handy when there is a requirement to purge the current build and rebuild from source.

*Dummy.unoproj* - This the manifest for our application and the primary file representing key properties of the project. Every FuseOpen app will have this file as all of FuseOpen projects are basically Uno projects, and its compiler complies the UX markup code and the business logic javascript into C++.

*MainView.ux* - This is a UX file containing the markup syntax for UI/UX of the app and also the location where from the app loads and starts.

## Initial building blocks of the app

Now getting back to adding UI elements to the app, here are the things we will build first into the app -

a) A Splash screen with animation
b) A login view
c) A home/landing view on successful login

Initially our requirement is to create three views/pages for the app and so we need to place a mechanism that navigates through the different views/pages. The <Navigator /> is a container for views/pages that are to be rendered at runtime of the actual app. A <Navigator /> tag is useful in cases where, for example, a list of hundred images have to the displayed in the fashion of turning from page to page like a book. Since all of the images are to be displayed in the same pattern inside a view/page, making hundred separate pages to hold those images increases the size the app. Instead, a template for such a page should be made and placed inside <Navigator /> tag. The template page will be rendered with all the other UX elements in it at runtime of the app, as and when required and for our case of hundred pages, it will be iterated a hundred times.

The splash screen page, the login page and the home page are to be rendered at runtime, since their usage is limited in the life-cycle of any app. Before placing the pages inside <Navigator /> tag, the pages have to be defined.

The splash page -

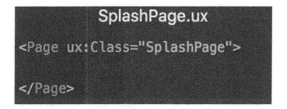

```
SplashPage.ux
<Page ux:Class="SplashPage">

</Page>
```

The login page -

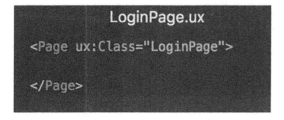

```
LoginPage.ux
<Page ux:Class="LoginPage">

</Page>
```

The home page -

```
HomePage.ux
<Page ux:Class="HomePage">

</Page>
```

We have created three new files named SplashPage.ux, LoginPage.ux and HomePage.ux in our project directory.

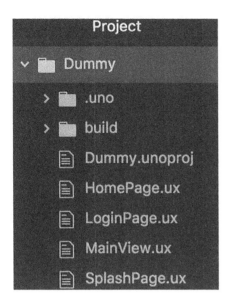

Each page is being defined as a class of UX markup element like <App/> or <SafeEdgePanel/>, which we have come across thus far. The *ux:Class* attribute defines an Uno class where the type of element is the base class.

Syntax –

```
<Base_class ux:Class="Class_name"/>
```

So, now our project has a new element by the name Class_name which we can use as <Class_name />.

The base class for defining pages is intuitively named in FuseOpen as <Page/>.

FuseOpen takes an object oriented approach toward all of the UX markup elements. Each element has set of properties such as Color, Value, Height, Width, etc. and actions such as OnClicked, KeyPressed, etc. just to name a few. The UX markup elements are basically Uno classes and have methods and properties accessible from Uno as well during writing scripts in Uno for an app project.

The *.ux file created for say splash has the same name as the Page class defined in it *(ux:Class="SplashPage")*. This is not a requirement and *.ux file names share no dependance. Even, we could have defined all of the classes - SplashPage, LoginPage and HomePage in a single *.ux file.

As the required three *Page classes* have been created, they can be listed under the <Navigator/> tag.

```
                    MainView.ux

<App>
  <SafeEdgePanel Color="#42f4bc">

    <Navigator DefaultPath="splash">
      <SplashPage ux:Template="splash" />
      <LoginPage ux:Template="login" />
      <HomePage ux:Template="home" />
    </Navigator>

  </SafeEdgePanel>
</App>
```

As mentioned earlier, *<Navigator/>* element is only able to work with pages that are dynamically rendered at runtime, and so, the instances of the Page classes - SplashPage, etc. bear the usage of *ux:Template* attribute. The *ux:Template* attribute tells Uno to treat the page objects <SplashPage />, <LoginPage/>, <HomePage/> as templates or blue-prints for actual pages that are to be rendered at runtime. Each of the templates are named *ux:Template="<template_name>"* and the name of the template set as the *DefaultPath* value in *<Navigator/>* becomes the first page.

Although *<Navigator/>* has the knowledge of the pages that has to be handled, and also the page to be treated as the starting point, there is still no way to instruct the *<Navigator/>* to route to a certain page from inside a page. For example, when the app starts, the first page the app opens is <SplashPage/>, and when the control is focussed on <SplashPage/>, there needs to be some mechanism to route to the next desired page. This routing functionality in an app is managed by a separate the UX element <Router/> and not by calling any function of *<Navigator/>*.

```
                    MainView.ux

<App>
  <SafeEdgePanel Color="#42f4bc">

    <Router ux:Name="nav_router" />

    <Navigator DefaultPath="splash">
      <SplashPage ux:Template="splash" router="nav_router" />
      <LoginPage ux:Template="login" router="nav_router" />
      <HomePage ux:Template="home" router="nav_router" />
    </Navigator>

  </SafeEdgePanel>
</App>
```

A <Router/> object is created with the name *nav_router* and passed along to an attribute named *router* in each of the pages. The attribute name *router* is user defined. Now inside a page, another <Router/> object has to be created that has a relation with *nav_router*.

We add a <Router/> object to all of the pages and here is the one for *SplashPage*.

```
<Page ux:Class="SplashPage">
  <Router ux:Dependency="router" />


</Page>
```

The *ux:Dependency* attribute is responsible for binding the relationship with the router object *nav_router* whose reference is passed to the SplashPage class' attribute named *router*. A diagrammatic representation of the control of the pages with <Router/> objects is as the following -

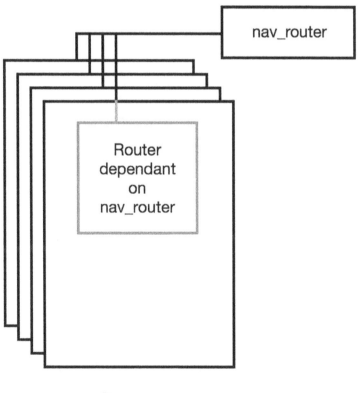

Pages

A user defined attribute *router* is created for the instance of SplashPage class and the reference to nav_router is passed to it -

```
<Router ux:Name="nav_router" />

<Navigator DefaultPath="splash">
  <SplashPage ux:Template="splash" router="nav_router" />
```

The reference to nav_router is accessed from another <Router/> in the SplashPage class by declaring a dependency on the referred object stored in the attribute *router*.

```
<Page ux:Class="SplashPage">
  <Router ux:Dependency="router" />
```

## *Designing the SplashPage*

In order for the splash page to look like the following -

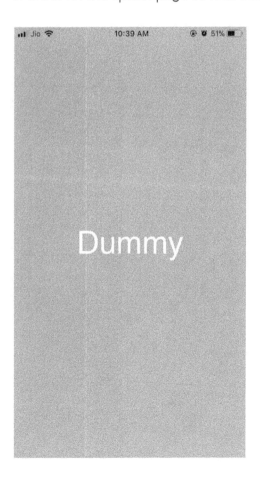

The corresponding code is -

```
SplashPage.ux

<Page ux:Class="SplashPage">
  <Router ux:Dependency="router" />

  <Rectangle>

  <LinearGradient AngleDegrees="45">
      <GradientStop Offset="0" Color="#42f489" />
      <GradientStop Offset="1" Color="#41f4eb" />
  </LinearGradient>

  <Text Value="Dummy" FontSize="50" Color="#fff" Alignment="Center" />
  </Rectangle>
</Page>
```

The SplashPage has a <LinearGradient/> element which is responsible for the beautiful colour gradient on the page. The AngleDegrees attribute states the angle of the colour brush. <GradientStop/> *Offset* values range from 0 to 1 and defines where from a particular colour will begin. If we want more colours in <LinearGradient/>, more *GradientStops* have to be added, such as -

```
<LinearGradient AngleDegrees="45">
  <GradientStop Offset="0" Color="#f00" />
  <GradientStop Offset="0.3" Color="#f0f" />
  <GradientStop Offset="0.6" Color="#00f" />
  <GradientStop Offset="1" Color="#0ff" />
</LinearGradient>
```

<LinearGradient/> is an element from the Fuse.Drawing namespace in Uno and can be applied to Rectangle, Circle, and other shapes. Therefore, in order to apply a gradient to the entire page, a <Rectangle/> element is added without any *Height* and *Width* properties set such that it takes up all the space available in the page. The <LinearGradient/> now when placed inside the <Rectangle/>, is applied to the entire page. All the other elements are to be now placed inside the <Rectangle> … <Rectangle/> tags, since it would provide the common gradient background to those UX elements.

The <Text/> element displays the text Dummy, has a font size of 50, Color attribute set to #fff (White) and Alignment set to the center of the page. If FontSize attribute is not explicitly set, it defaults to 11 and adjusts the size according to the device the page is viewed on.

Now we want to apply some styling to the text with custom fonts. For this we will first create a new Assets directory that would contain all external artefacts such as images, icons, font files, etc.

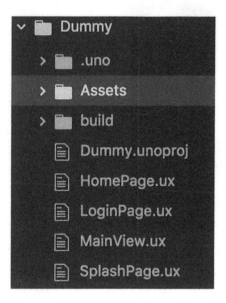

We download a free available Blobtastics.tff font file and place it in Assets directory.

Now to access the font in Assets/Blobtastics.tff, the path to the font file has to be registered as a <Font/> element. We want the *Assets* such as fonts and icons to be accessible throughout the app and so it will be easier if a particular artefact can be accessed with a globally referable name. This can be achieved in the following way for the font file introduced to the project -

```
<!-- Fonts -->
<Font File="Assets/Blobtastics.ttf" ux:Global="BigBanner" />
```

The ux:Global attribute exposes an element as a global static resource for a project. Now the font can be referred by the name *BigBanner*. We can add the <Font/> element to SplashPage. ux but for organisational purpose, all the global resources will be placed in a separate *.ux file named - AllGlobals.ux.

The AllGlobals.ux file -

```
                AllGlobals.ux
<Panel ux:Class="AllGlobals">
    <!-- Fonts -->
<Font File="Assets/Blobtastics.ttf" ux:Global="BigBanner" />

</Panel>
```

We cannot just declare the <Font/> element in a *.ux file, since each *.ux file has to have a root element. We simply create a new class *AllGlobals* from the base class *Panel* and declare the <Font/> element as a member of the class. Although <Panel/> is an element (a class defined in Uno) that is used for layout purposes, we are not going to use its derived class AllGlobals for defining any layout in our app. Its use in AllGlobals.ux file is purely for containment purposes and could also have been achieved in the following way -

```
                AllGlobals.ux
<Rectangle ux:Class="AllGlobals">
    <!-- Fonts -->
<Font File="Assets/Blobtastics.ttf" ux:Global="BigBanner" />

</Rectangle>
```

The class *AllGlobals* will contain all global resources as its members.

Now, that the font has been registered it can be accessed in <Text/> with the name *BigBanner*.

```
SplashPage.ux
<Page ux:Class="SplashPage">
  <Router ux:Dependency="router" />

  <Rectangle>

  <LinearGradient AngleDegrees="45">
      <GradientStop Offset="0" Color="#42f489" />
      <GradientStop Offset="1" Color="#41f4eb" />
  </LinearGradient>

  <Text Value="Dummy" Font="BigBanner" FontSize="50" Color="#fff" Alignment="Center" />
  </Rectangle>
</Page>
```

The corresponding preview with the font used -

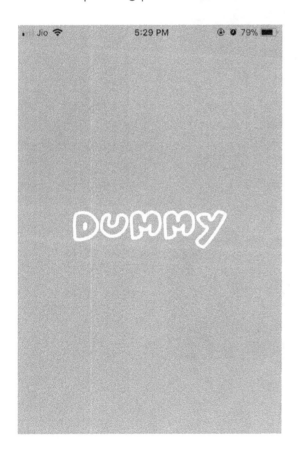

Now for decorative purposes we will add an emboss effect to the text with <DropShadow/>.

```
SplashPage.ux
<Page ux:Class="SplashPage">
  <Router ux:Dependency="router" />

  <Rectangle>

  <LinearGradient AngleDegrees="45">
      <GradientStop Offset="0" Color="#42f489" />
      <GradientStop Offset="1" Color="#41f4eb" />
  </LinearGradient>

  <Text Value="Dummy" Font="BigBanner" FontSize="50" Color="#fff" Alignment="Center">
    <DropShadow Color="#54665d" Angle="45" Size="2" Distance="3" Spread="0.1" />
  </Text>
  </Rectangle>
</Page>
```

*Angle* defines the incident angle of light that casts the shadow. *Distance* defines how far the shadow extends from the UX object, and *Spread* defines how smoothly the shadow drops off at the end.

We get the following result -

## Adding animation to the splash screen

We will add some animation to the text, as if the text emerges from a little lower position from the placed position, fading in and expanding to the original size.

```
<Text ux:Name="appName" Value="Dummy" Font="BigBanner" FontSize="50" Color="#fff" Alignment="Center">
  <DropShadow Color="#54665d" Angle="45" Size="2" Distance="3" Spread="0.1" />
  <AddingAnimation>
    <Change this.Opacity="0" Delay="0.2" Duration="0.8" />
    <Scale  Easing="BackOut" Duration="0.8" Factor="0.5"/>
    <Move RelativeTo="Size" Duration="0.4" Y="0.5" Easing="BackOut" />
  </AddingAnimation>
</Text>
```

FuseOpen provides a rather extensive ability to animate various elements on a page. Every animation is triggered as a result of some gesture, user interaction or event and so animations are performed by various types of *Trigger* classes. There is a huge collection of *Triggers* and <AddingAnimation /> is one of them. <AddingAnimation /> tag dictates that the enclosing transformations *Change*, *Scale* and *Move* are performed in the declared order when the element Text is added to the UX hierarchy. UX elements for animation creation and control will be discussed in detail later. The list of all *Triggers* are here -

<Change/> is an element of the *Animator* class, which here temporarily changes the value of Opacity from 1 to 0 and then back to 1 over a *Duration* of 0.8 seconds. The *Delay* of 0.2 seconds makes the *Change* animation wait after the *Trigger* has taken place.

The <Scale/> animation takes place right after *Change* and its behaviour is to display the element in a scaled down version along all its axes by the *Factor*. Scaling does not change the actual size of an element but displays the element with differential number of pixels. The *Easing* attribute defines how the animation progresses with time based on a list algebraic functions to choose from - QuadraticInOut, BackIn, BackOut, BounceInOut, etc. and plenty of other functions. Here is a list of all the *Easing* functions -

<Move/> animator gives an offset to the position of an element without changing the layout, thereby causing translation animation. The RelativeTo property is set to *Size*, which means the movement along Y axis will be by 0.5 times the size of the element. If RelativeTo property was omitted the element would have been moved simply 0.5 points along the Y axis. Here is a list of all the possible values for Move's RelativeTo property -

We have come across three animators Change, Move and Scale, and will find more interesting usage of these as we add more animations to the app. The list of all the other animation classes are -

The final change we will do to the SplashPage is globally naming the colours used. For this we will refer again to AllGlobals.ux file and name the colours - #42f489, #41f4eb and #54665d used so far.

```
<!-- Colors -->
<float4 ux:Value="#42f489" ux:Global="LightGreen"/>
<float4 ux:Value="#41f4eb" ux:Global="VibrantCyan"/>
<float4 ux:Value="#54665d" ux:Global="GreyShadow"/>
```

Accordingly, the Color attributes in SplashPage.ux is updated.

```
<LinearGradient AngleDegrees="45">
      <GradientStop Offset="0" Color="LightGreen" />
      <GradientStop Offset="1" Color="VibrantCyan" />
</LinearGradient>

<Text ux:Name="appName" Value="Dummy" Font="BigBanner" FontSize="50" Color="#fff" Alignment="Center">
  <DropShadow Color="GreyShadow" Angle="45" Size="2" Distance="3" Spread="0.1" />
```

The SplashPage's design is complete but we have not yet defined any business logic for this page. We want the SplashPage to load, halt for 3 seconds and then route to the next page, LoginPage. FuseJS is based on ECMA-6 javascript specification and almost all of the basic javascript functions are available. The setTimeout(…) javascript function will be placed inside <JavaScript/> tags to wait and then perform the task of routing to *login*.

```
SplashPage.ux

<Page ux:Class="SplashPage">
  <Router ux:Dependency="router" />

  <JavaScript>
  setTimeout(function()
  {
    router.goto("login");
  }, 3000);
  </JavaScript>

  <Rectangle>

  <LinearGradient AngleDegrees="45">
        <GradientStop Offset="0" Color="LightGreen" />
        <GradientStop Offset="1" Color="VibrantCyan" />
  </LinearGradient>

  <Text ux:Name="appName" Value="Dummy" Font="BigBanner"
    FontSize="50" Color="#fff" Alignment="Center">
    <DropShadow Color="GreyShadow" Angle="45" Size="2" Distance="3" Spread="0.1" />
    <AddingAnimation>
      <Change this.Opacity="0" Delay="0.2" Duration="0.8" />
      <Scale  Easing="BackOut" Duration="0.8" Factor="0.5"/>
      <Move RelativeTo="Size" Duration="0.4" Y="0.5" Easing="BackOut" />
    </AddingAnimation>
  </Text>

  </Rectangle>
</Page>
```

## Designing the login page

For the login page, we will have a login button like -

This button has a gradient component similar to that of the SplashPage. We want the design for this button to be available throughout all the pages of the app and so it will be defined as a class in a separate *.ux file of its own. A new directory is created to store all resources such as this button for the project.

The button class we are going to create will be called *ThemeButton* and defined in the file ThemeButton.ux.

```
ThemeButton.ux
<Rectangle ux:Class="ThemeButton" CornerRadius="30"
    Width="100" Height="50">
  <LinearGradient AngleDegrees="45">
      <GradientStop Offset="0" Color="LightGreen" />
      <GradientStop Offset="1" Color="VibrantCyan" />
  </LinearGradient>
</Rectangle>
```

The button is derived from *Rectangle* class and the *CornerRadius* attribute gives it the rounded edge look.

The login page is going to be designed as overlapping of multiple *Panel* elements in a single page which in this case is LoginPage class. One Panel will display the login form along with its other UX elements and another will hold the elements in a welcome screen.

A Panel is a container for other elements and the child elements defined inside <Panel/> tag, takes up all the available space of a Panel.

After adding a router similar as SplashPage, a root <Panel/> is created and the *Page* is painted the *Color* #fff.

```
                    LoginPage.ux
<Page ux:Class="LoginPage" Color="#fff">
  <Router ux:Dependency="router" />


  <Panel>

  </Panel>
</Page>
```

As stated, we will design this page in a way that after a successful login operation, a new set of visual elements will be displayed on the same page. This design logic behind creating such a visualisation is creation of two separate *Panels*, each of which contain the desired visual elements. One <Panel/> will be referred to as the - loggedOutView and another <Panel/> as loggedInView.

```
                    LoginPage.ux
<Page ux:Class="LoginPage" Color="#fff">
  <Router ux:Dependency="router" />

  <Panel>
    <!-- View for logged in state -->
    <Panel ux:Name="loggedInView">
    </Panel>


    <!-- View for logged out state -->
    <Panel ux:Name="loggedOutView">
    </Panel>



  </Panel>
</Page>
```

The Panels are stacked up in the order they are defined, with loggedOutView at the topmost element of the stack.

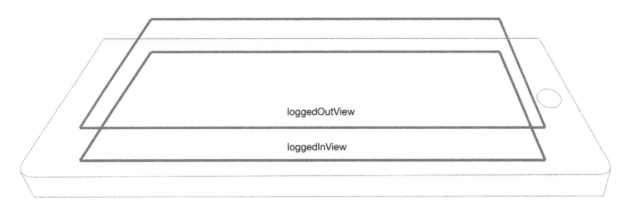

Here is the design of the loggedOutView -

Username

Password

Sign in

The "Sign in" button is to be animated such that it becomes a circle on clicking and does a loading animation on the button like -

Username


Password

When the loading animation is complete, the button has to scale up and fill up the entire screen with a view that has the colour of the "Sign in" button. It is then upon this coloured view, the contents of loggedInView is to be displayed.

Now, when the "Sign in" button is clicked and it fills the screen with the button's colour, it is not the colour of loggedOutView Panel is being changed. Another <Panel/> is placed underneath the loggedInView, and it is this Panel, that is flooded with the expanded button. We add a new Panel *superFillView* to the LoginPage -

```
                    LoginPage.ux

<Page ux:Class="LoginPage" Color="#fff">
  <Router ux:Dependency="router" />

  <Panel>
    <!-- Super Fill panel -->
    <Panel ux:Name="superFillView" Width="500%" Height="500%"
    Alignment="Center" HitTestMode="None" BoxSizing="FillAspect" Aspect="1" />
    <!-- -->

    <!-- View for logged in state -->
    <Panel ux:Name="loggedInView">
    </Panel>

    <!-- View for logged out state -->
    <Panel ux:Name="loggedOutView">
    </Panel>

  </Panel>
</Page>
```

The *Width* and *Height* attributes are set to 500% of the actual viewport dimensions of a device, thereby filling up an extra imaginary space. This is just to ensure that the button when expands and floods the screen, to take up all the space available to a device. *BoxSizing* tells how to calculate the size and position of a UX element. *HitTestMode* when set to None, make the Panel non-reactive to user interactions such as touch or tap. *Aspect* is the aspect ratio (X:Y) that an element must fill in a layout and the value 1 means uniform for height and width.

After adding the new <Panel/>, this is how the panels are stacked -

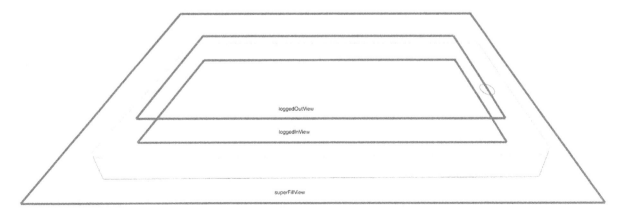

The superFillView takes extra logical space outside the available viewport of a device and the other two panels are stacked upon it. *The "Sign in" button on the loggedOutView after animation, scales up to take the entire space occupied by superFillView.*

We add the "Sign up" button -

```
<!-- View for logged out state -->
<Panel ux:Name="loggedOutView">
  <Grid Rows="1.5*,auto,1*" Padding="40,0">

  <Panel ux:Name="signupButton" Row="2" Width="150" Height="60">
     <Panel ux:Name="loadingCirclePanel">
        <Circle ux:Name="loadingCircle" Width="70%" Height="70%" Opacity="0"
           StartAngleDegrees="0" LengthAngleDegrees="90">
           <Stroke Width="1" Brush="#fff" />
        </Circle>
     </Panel>


     <ThemeButton ux:Name="rectNormalScale" CornerRadius="30" Width="200" Height="60">
        <Text ux:Name="text" Alignment="Center" Value="Sign in" FontSize="18" Color="#fff"/>
        <DropShadow Color="LightGreyShadow" Angle="100" Size="5" Distance="2" Spread="0.1" />
        <AddingAnimation>
           <Change rectNormalScale.Opacity="0" Delay="0.2" Duration="0.8" />
           <Move RelativeTo="Size" Y="0.5" DurationBack="0.3"
              Easing="ExponentialInOut" />
        </AddingAnimation>
     </ThemeButton>

     <Circle ux:Name="loadingButton" Opacity="0" Alignment="Center"
        Layer="Background" Width="240" Height="240">
        <LinearGradient AngleDegrees="45">
              <GradientStop Offset="0" Color="LightGreen" />
              <GradientStop Offset="1" Color="VibrantCyan" />
        </LinearGradient>
        <Scaling Factor="0.25" />
     </Circle>
  </Panel>
  </Grid>
</Panel>
```

The available space inside *loggedOutView* is mapped into a three row <Grid/>. The first and the third row is 1.5* and 1* respectively and remaining space available is allocated for the second row. This is proportional sizing of the *Rows*. For example, if the Rows or Columns were valued as "1*,1*,3*", the size calculation would be done w.r.t. the viewport size of a device, by first taking sum of all values i.e. (1+1+3) = 5 and then diving them as 1/5 = 20%, 1/5 = 20%, 1/5 = 60%. The Rows and Columns can also be sized with absolute values.

The <Panel/> signupButton is the overlapping of three UX elements - *loadingCirclePanel*, *rectNormalScale*, *loadingButton*. The *loadingCirclePanel* contains a <Circle/> element *loadingCircle*, which represents the circular button during animation of the loading spinner.

But *loadingCircle* isn't the one with this gradient colouring. Its Opacity is disabled with value 0. The only purpose of *loadingCircle* is to provide the <Stroke/> element which is visible in the above image as a thin white circular line on its circumference. The SliceAngleDegrees attribute is the degree where the circle is sliced and the LengthAngleDegrees is the offset of how long the gap from the cut will span. The effect of this is visible in the above image as well where the white outline of the circle is sliced.

The next element is *rectNormalScale*, which is the instance of class ThemeButton, which we created earlier. This represents the "Sign up" button with the text on the button provided by the <Text/> element inside it. The <AddingAnimation/> gives the button an effect of fading-in appearance from below.

The final element *loadingButton* is the one that is represented in the above image as the circle with the theme colour gradient of our app. The *Layer* attribute is set to *Background* which means the *superFillView* panel. This is because after the completion of the spinning loading animation, the *loadingButton* will be scaled and blown up to fill the entire area available to *superFillView*. It is also provided a <Scaling/> element where the Factor attribute defines the multiple of the target (*superFillView*) size to scale to.

Now that the "Sign up" button is added, the remaining elements - the topmost logo and the username-password form is added inside the loggedOutView panel.

```
<!-- Topmost circular logo -->
<Circle ux:Name="mark"  Row="0" Width="100" Height="100">
<ImageFill  File="Assets/Icons/user-trump.jpg"/>
  <AddingAnimation>
    <Scale Factor="0.8" Duration="0.5" />
  </AddingAnimation>
</Circle>
```

```
<!-- Signup form -->
<Grid ux:Name="loginArea" Row="1" Padding="0,20" RowCount="2" Height="160" MaxWidth="400">
  <TextInput Row="0" PlaceholderText="Username" PlaceholderColor="#999"
    Alignment="Center" TextColor="#000" CaretColor="LightGreen" />
  <TextInput Row="1" PlaceholderText="Password" PlaceholderColor="#999"
    Alignment="Center" TextColor="#000" CaretColor="LightGreen" IsPassword="true"/>
</Grid>
```

When the user focus is set to the form fields, the native keyboard comes up takes up space in the viewport. To compensate for the space taken up by the keyboard, without disturbing the arrangement of the other elements on the screen, the topmost logo and the signup form is shifted from their initial position. This is accomplished by adding a *WhileKeyboardVisible* Trigger to the loggedOutView panel.

```
<!-- View for logged out state -->
<Panel ux:Name="loggedOutView">
  <Grid Rows="1.5*,auto,1*" Padding="40,0">
  <WhileKeyboardVisible>
    <Move Target="mark" Y="-200" Duration=".6" Easing="ExponentialInOut"/>
    <Move Target="loginArea" Y="-200" Duration=".6" Easing="ExponentialInOut"/>
  </WhileKeyboardVisible>
```

The Target is set to *mark* and *loginArea*, which are the names of top logo and signup form respectively.

A click on "Sign up" button and routing to the next view involves a number of animations. All the animation are placed in conditional <WhiteTrue/> Trigger blocks.

```
<Page ux:Class="LoginPage" Color="#fff">
  <Router ux:Dependency="router" />

  <!-- Animations during loading and logging in -->
  <!-- # 1 -->
  <WhileTrue ux:Name="changeWidth">
  <Change rectNormalScale.Width="60" Duration=".5"
    DurationBack="0" Easing="CircularInOut"/>
  </WhileTrue>

  <!-- # 2 -->
  <WhileTrue ux:Name="loadCircle">
  <Change text.Opacity="0" Duration="0.2" DurationBack="0"/>
```

```
<Change loadingCircle.Opacity="1" Duration="0.3"
  Delay="0.2" DelayBack="0" DurationBack="0"/>
<Spin Target="loadingCircle" Frequency="2"/>
<Cycle Target="loadingCircle.LengthAngleDegrees"
  Low="30" High="300" Frequency="0.7" />
</WhileTrue>


<!-- # 3 -->
<WhileTrue ux:Name="scaleAndFade">
<Change loadingCirclePanel.Opacity="0" Duration="0.1" />
<Change loadingButton.Opacity="1" Duration="0.01" />
<Change rectNormalScale.Opacity="0" Duration="0.01" />
<Scale Target="loadingButton" Factor="3" RelativeTo="SizeFactor"
  RelativeNode="transitionScaleGuide"
      Delay="0.01" Duration="0.7" Easing="ExponentialInOut" DurationBack="0" />
</WhileTrue>


<!-- # 4 -->
<WhileTrue ux:Name="showLoggedIn">
  <Change loggedInView.Opacity="1" Delay="0.1" Duration="0.65"
    DurationBack="0.35" DelayBack="0.2" Easing="CubicInOut"/>
  <Change loggedInView.IsEnabled="true" />

</WhileTrue>
<!-- End of animations list during loading and logging in  -->
```

Each of these animation blocks and their respective activities are triggered by the click action of "Sign up" button and so all of the four <WhileTrue/> blocks must be sequenced and set into action by a single <WhileTrue/> Trigger block named *loading*.

```
<!--  Trigger for starting animations during logging in -->
<WhileTrue ux:Name="loading">
  <Change changeWidth.Value="true" DelayBack="0"/>
  <Change loadCircle.Value="true" DelayBack="0"/>

  <Change scaleAndFade.Value="true" Delay="2.5" DelayBack="0"/>
  <Change showLoggedIn.Value="true" Delay="2.9" />
</WhileTrue>
<!--  end of Trigger definition -->
```

This <WhileTrue/> block is a controller for all the animations following the "Sign up" operation and so the button will have a <Clicked/> Trigger that sets the *Value* attribute of *loading* to *true*.

```
<Panel Row="2" Width="150" Height="60">
    <Panel ux:Name="loadingCirclePanel">
      <Circle ux:Name="loadingCircle" Width="70%" Height="70%"
        Opacity="0" StartAngleDegrees="0" LengthAngleDegrees="90">
        <Stroke Width="1" Brush="#fff" />
      </Circle>
    </Panel>

    <Clicked>
      <Set loading.Value="true"/>
    </Clicked>

    <ThemeButton ux:Name="rectNormalScale" CornerRadius="30" Width="200" Height="60">
      <Text ux:Name="text" Alignment="Center" Value="Sign in" FontSize="18" Color="#fff"/>
      <DropShadow Color="LightGreyShadow" Angle="100" Size="5" Distance="2" Spread="0.1" />
      <AddingAnimation>
        <Change rectNormalScale.Opacity="0" Delay="0.2" Duration="0.8" />
        <Move RelativeTo="Size" Y="0.5" DurationBack="0.3"
          Easing="ExponentialInOut" />
      </AddingAnimation>
    </ThemeButton>

    <Circle ux:Name="loadingButton" Opacity="0" Alignment="Center"
      Layer="Background" Width="240" Height="240">
      <LinearGradient AngleDegrees="45">
          <GradientStop Offset="0" Color="LightGreen" />
          <GradientStop Offset="1" Color="VibrantCyan" />
      </LinearGradient>
      <Scaling Factor="0.25" />
    </Circle>
</Panel>
```

## *Designing the post login experience*

Next, the loggedInView is to be coded according to the following design -

#1.

#2.

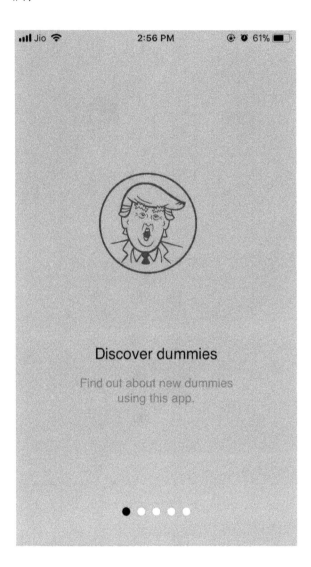

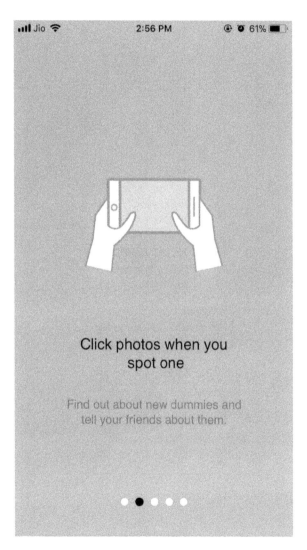

#3.

#4.

#5.

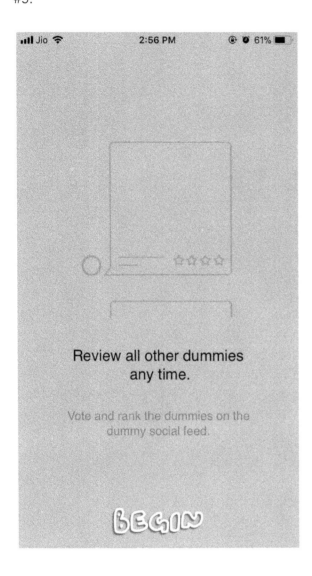

The loggedInView will consist of a collection of swipe-able content, each of which is listed in the above images. Although the views seem like separate pages but they are just contents inside <Panel/> tags. The coloured gradient background in the above views is the gradient that was applied to *superFillView* by *loadingButton*. With loggedInView panel and its swipe-able content collection a new form of page control UX element will be used called *PageControl*.

Unlike <Navigator/> element which we already used to route through dynamically created pages, <PageControl/> is used for routing through pages that are created during build of the app and not rendered at runtime.

```
<!-- View for logged in state -->
<Panel ux:Name="loggedInView">
  <Grid Rows="1*,60">
    <PageControl ux:Name="pageControl">
      <Panel>
      </Panel>

      <Panel>
      </Panel>

      <Panel>
      </Panel>

      <Panel>
      </Panel>

      <Panel>
      </Panel>
    </PageControl>
  </Grid>
</Panel>
```

We created five <Panel/> elements inside <PageControl/> and each <Panel/> represents the five swipe-able views. The <PageControl/> is the housed in the first row of the <Grid/>. The second row will be provided to the *Begin* text in the final the swipe-able view and the dotted page indicator in the rest of the view -

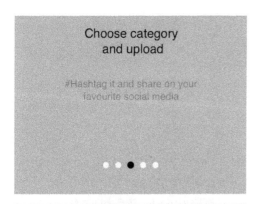

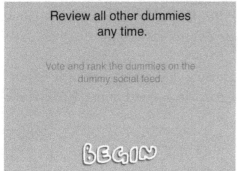

The page indicator design element is already present in FuseOpen as a ready to use class called <PageIndicator/>. The below code represents the *Begin* text and the page indicator.

```
<Panel>
  <Text ux:Name="getStartedText" Value="Begin" Font="BigBanner"
    Color="#fff" FontSize="34" Offset="0%,100%" Alignment="TopCenter">
    <DropShadow Color="GreyShadow" Angle="45" Size="2" Distance="3" Spread="0.1" />
  </Text>
  <PageIndicator ux:Name="pageIndicator" Navigation="pageControl"
    Dock="Bottom" Alignment="TopCenter">
    <Circle ux:Template="Dot" ux:Name="dotFac" Color="#fff" Margin="5" Width="10" Height="20">
      <ActivatingAnimation>
        <Scale Factor="1.1"/>
        <Change dotFac.Color="#000" />
      </ActivatingAnimation>
    </Circle>
  </PageIndicator>
</Panel>
```

The *Navigation* attribute is bound with <PageControl/> with its name *pageControl*. The <Circle/> element could be replaced by any other shape of choice such as <Rectangle/>.

For the text content in each swipe-able view, a class *PageContent* is created.

```
<!-- View for logged in state -->
<Panel ux:Name="loggedInView">
  <Grid ux:Class="PageContent" Padding="45,0" MinHeight="100">
    <string ux:Property="Title" />
    <string ux:Property="Content" />
    <Grid Rows="2*,3*">
      <Text Alignment="Top" Value="{ReadProperty this.Title}"
        FontSize="20" Color="#000" TextAlignment="Center" TextWrapping="Wrap" Margin="20,0" />
      <Text Alignment="Top" Value="{ReadProperty this.Content}"
        FontSize="16" Color="#777" TextAlignment="Center"  Margin="20,0" TextWrapping="Wrap"/>
    </Grid>
  </Grid>
```

The <string/> elements are member variables of the class PageContent and are referenced by the name set by *ux:Property*.

Now for the panels handled by <PageControl/> we will begin with the fifth and final panel. Here is the content representing the final panel -

```
<Panel>
  <Grid Rows="1*,200">
    <Feed Width="70%"/>
    <PageContent Title="Review all other dummies &#xA; any time."
      Content="Vote and rank the dummies on the dummy social feed." />
```

```
  </Grid>
  <ActivatingAnimation>
    <Move Target="getStartedText" Y="-1" RelativeTo="ParentSize"
      Delay="0.7" Duration="0.1"/>
    <Change getStartedText.Opacity="1" Duration="0.1" Delay="0.7"/>
    <Change pageIndicator.Opacity="0" Duration="0.3"/>
  </ActivatingAnimation>
</Panel>
```

The <Feed/> tag is a derived <Image/> class and is defined in ImagesAndIcons.ux file with other derivations of the <Image/> class for all the images to be used in the app.

```
          ImagesAndIcons.ux
<Panel ux:Class="ImagesAndIcons">
  <Image ux:Class="Chat" File="../Assets/Icons/chat.png"/>
  <Image ux:Class="Feed" File="../Assets/Icons/feed.png"/>
  <Image ux:Class="Marker" File="../Assets/Icons/marker.png"/>
  <Image ux:Class="Phone" File="../Assets/Icons/phone.png"/>
  <Image ux:Class="PhoneHands" File="../Assets/Icons/phoneHands.png"/>
  <Image ux:Class="Tags" File="../Assets/Icons/tags.png"/>
  <Image ux:Class="Map" File="../Assets/Icons/map.png" />
  <Image ux:Class="Trump" File="../Assets/Icons/user-trump.jpg"/>
  <Image ux:Class="TrumpWelcome1" File="../Assets/Icons/trump-welcome1.png"/>
  <Image ux:Class="TrumpWelcome2" File="../Assets/Icons/trump-welcome2.png"/>
</Panel>
```

The <ActivatingAnimation/> states that when the last panel in page control is active, the *getStartedText* object for the text *Begin* will have opacity 1 i.e. visible and *pageIndicator* object will go invisible with opacity 0.

The definition for the fourth <Panel/> -

```
<Panel>
  <Grid Rows="1*,4*,200">
    <Panel Row="1" Width="60%" Alignment="Center">
      <ActivatingAnimation>
        <Change markerTrans.Y="0" Delay="0.3" Duration="0.7" />
        <Change marker.Opacity="1" Delay="0.3" Duration="0.7"/>
        <Change faceLScaling.Vector="1,1,1" Delay="0.3" Duration="0.7"/>
        <Change faceRScaling.Vector="1,1,1" Delay="0.3" Duration="0.7"/>
        <Change faceL.Opacity="1" Delay="0.3" Duration="0.7"/>
        <Change faceR.Opacity="1" Delay="0.3" Duration="0.7"/>
      </ActivatingAnimation>
      <Marker ux:Name="marker" Width="30%" Alignment="Top" Opacity="0" Offset="2%,-15%">
        <Translation ux:Name="markerTrans" Y="-1" RelativeTo="Size" />
      </Marker>
      <TrumpWelcome2 ux:Name="faceL" Width="20%" Alignment="Left" Anchor="50%,50%" Opacity="0">
        <Scaling ux:Name="faceLScaling" Vector="0,1,1" />
```

```
    </TrumpWelcome2>
    <TrumpWelcome2 ux:Name="faceR" Width="26%" Alignment="Right" Offset="-5%,-5%" Opacity="0">
      <Scaling ux:Name="faceRScaling" Vector="0,1,1" />
    </TrumpWelcome2>
    <Map />
  </Panel>
  <PageContent Row="2" Title="Pin the location &#xA; when you discover a dummy"
    Content="Be notified when you visit a dummy spot." />
  </Grid>
</Panel>
```

The Vector attribute states the amount of size change to apply in each dimension while scaling and 0,1,1 addresses the directions left, top and right.

The first, second and third panels are as follows -

```
<Panel> <!-- #1 -->
  <Grid Rows="2*,200" >
    <PageContent ux:Name="page1Content" Alignment="Top" Row="1"
          Title="Discover dummies"
          Content="Find out about new dummies using this app." >
      <AddingAnimation>
        <Move Y="2" RelativeTo="Size" Duration="0.6" Easing="QuinticIn" />
        <Change  page1Content.Opacity="0" Duration="0.6" Easing="QuinticIn" />
      </AddingAnimation>
    </PageContent>
  </Grid>
</Panel>


<Panel> <!-- #2 -->
  <Grid Rows="1*,1*,200">
    <PhoneHands Row="1" Width="50%" Alignment="Top"/>
    <PageContent Row="2" Title="Click photos when you &#xA; spot one"
      Content="Find out about new dummies and tell your friends about them." />
  </Grid>
</Panel>


<Panel> <!-- #3 -->
  <Grid Rows="1*,200">
    <Panel Width="70%" Alignment="Center">
      <Tags Alignment="Bottom"/>
      <Phone Margin="5"/>
    </Panel>
    <PageContent Title="Choose category &#xA; and upload"
      Content="#Hashtag it and share on your favourite social media" />
  </Grid>
</Panel>
```

We have created one <Grid/> element in *loggedInView* that holds the <PageControl/> element. We will place another <Grid/> element in loggedInView which overlaps the other one and it would contain the following icon -

This overlapping in required because our design requirement is to reuse this icon on the third page of *pageControl* stacked on top of other images -

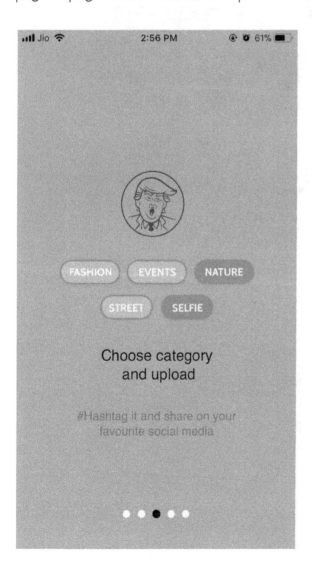

Here is the code for the same -

```
<Grid ux:Name="trumpGrid" Rows="3*,1*">
  <Panel ux:Name="trumps" Width="70%" HitTestMode="None" Alignment="Center">
    <TrumpWelcome1 ux:Name="trumpFill" Width="50%" Alignment="Bottom" Offset="~4.0%,-0.5%"/>
    <AddingAnimation>
      <Move Y="-2" RelativeTo="Size" Duration="0.6" Easing="QuinticIn" />
      <Change  trumps.Opacity="0" Duration="0.6" Easing="QuinticIn" />
    </AddingAnimation>
  </Panel>
</Grid>
```

We have used the terms panel and pages interchangeably in case of <PageControl/> despite of the fact <Panel/> element is used in our example. The loggedInView is has all the UX elements as per our requirements, and now although the loggedInView <Panel/> does not have a background colour to it, it will still displaying the contents overlapped on others. We take care of that by setting the Opacity attribute to 0 and also IsEnabled attribute to false, thereby disallowing any response for user interaction.

```
<!-- View for logged in state -->
<Panel ux:Name="loggedInView" Opacity="0" IsEnabled="false">
```

Now that the UX elements in loggedInView has been defined, we will code the animations using <Timeline/> class to group multiple animations.

```
<!-- Animations -->
<Timeline ux:Name="timeline" TargetProgress="1">
<Move Target="trumps" RelativeTo="Size">
 <Keyframe Y="-0.38"        Time="0.25"/>
 <Keyframe Y="-0.2"         Time="0.5"/>
 <Keyframe X="-0.3" Y="-0"  Time="0.75"/>
 <Keyframe X="0.2"  Y="-0.2" Time="0.98"/>
 <Keyframe X="0.08" Y="-0.2" Time="1.0"/>
</Move>

<Scale Target="trumps">
 <Keyframe Value="1"    Time="0.25"/>
 <Keyframe Value="0.65" Time="0.5"/>
 <Keyframe Value="0.2"  Time="0.75"/>
 <Keyframe Value="0.45" Time="0.98"/>
</Scale>

<Change Target="trumpFill.Opacity">
 <Keyframe Value="0.7" Time="0.0"/>
 <Keyframe Value="0"   Time="0.25"/>
 <Keyframe Value="0.7" Time="0.5"/>
 <Keyframe Value="0.7" Time="0.75"/>
 <Keyframe Value="0"   Time="1.0"/>
</Change>
```

```
<Change Target="trumps.Opacity">
 <Keyframe Value="0.25" Time="0.25"/>
 <Keyframe Value="1"    Time="0.5"/>
 <Keyframe Value="0"    Time="0.65"/>
 <Keyframe Value="0"    Time="0.85"/>
 <Keyframe Value="1"    Time="1.0"/>
</Change>
</Timeline>
```

The <Timeline/> element sets the course of animations that are to be done on the <Panel/> named *trumps* containing the following icon -

The <Timeline/> animations are to be started when the first panel of <PageControl/> is active. Therefore an <ActivatingAnimation/> Trigger is added to the <PageControl/> in the first <Panel/>.

```
<PageControl ux:Name="pageControl">
  <Panel> <!-- #1 -->
    <ActivatingAnimation Scale="0.25">
      <Change timeline.Progress="0"/>
    </ActivatingAnimation>
    <Grid Rows="2*,200" >
      <PageContent ux:Name="page1Content" Alignment="Top" Row="1"
            Title="Discover dummies"
            Content="Find out about new dummies using this app." >
        <AddingAnimation>
          <Move Y="2" RelativeTo="Size" Duration="0.6" Easing="QuinticIn" />
          <Change  page1Content.Opacity="0" Duration="0.6" Easing="QuinticIn" />
        </AddingAnimation>
      </PageContent>
    </Grid>
  </Panel>
```

The *Progress* attribute of <Timeline/> is set to 0, signifying the beginning of the animations.

Lastly, the the Begin text has to route to the home page. The javascript for this task -

```
<Panel>
  <JavaScript>
    function goto_home()
    {
      router.goto("home");
    }
    module.exports =
    {
      goto_home: goto_home,
    }
  </JavaScript>
  <Text ux:Name="getStartedText" Value="Begin" Font="BigBanner"
    Color="#fff" FontSize="34" Offset="0%,100%" Alignment="TopCenter" Clicked="{goto_home}">
    <DropShadow Color="GreyShadow" Angle="45" Size="2" Distance="3" Spread="0.1" />
  </Text>
```

The *Clicked* attribute of <Text/> is bound with the *goto_home* function such that it behaves as a button.

## Designing the home page

The HomePage is the landing view after login for a user of the app, and shall contain the pages that server the intent and functionalities of the app. A generic structure of most apps is about having a form a menu system that navigates a user through the various functionalities provided by the app. Here is the blueprint of how the app will sport a menu system -

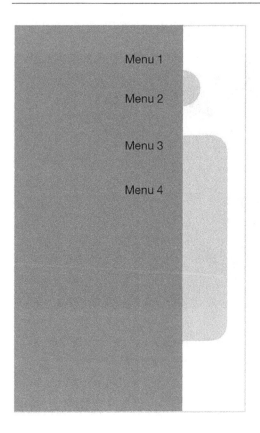

The HomePage is home to all other pages that are accessible through the menu. We will create a new directory UserPages in our project to contain these pages -

In order for these pages to be accessible from a menu bar drawable from the edge of a viewport, the <EdgeNavgator/> element is used.

```
                    HomePage.ux

  <Page ux:Class="HomePage" Color="#fff">
    <Router ux:Dependency="router" />



    <EdgeNavigator ClipToBounds="true">


    </EdgeNavigator>
  </Page>
```

The ClipToBounds attribute clips the child elements to the bounds of this UX element visually when set ot *true*. Suppose a child view has area say 10 units and extends beyond the area occupied by the parent element which is say 8 units. When ClipToBounds attribute is set to true, the overflowing amount of space which is 10 - 8 units will be clipped off.

The user pages defined by the classes First.ux and Second.ux are static pages and so have to navigated by <PageControl/>. Therefore, a <PageControl/> element is placed inside the <EdgeNavigator/> tags.

```
                 HomePage.ux

  <Page ux:Class="HomePage" Color="#fff">
    <Router ux:Dependency="router" />



    <EdgeNavigator ClipToBounds="true">

      <!-- Pages corresponding each edge menu panel option -->
      <PageControl ux:Name="userPageControl">
        <First ux:Name="firstPage"/>
        <Second ux:Name="secondPage"/>
      </PageControl>


    </EdgeNavigator>
  </Page>
```

The various menu items have to be created corresponding to the pages and so a class will be defined called MenuItem.

```
<!-- Side bar menu item class -->
<Rectangle ux:Class="MenuItem" MinHeight="20" >
  <string ux:Property="menuName"/>

  <Text ux:Name="menuText" Value="{Property menuName}"
    Padding="10" Alignment="CenterRight" FontSize="25"
    Font="Headings" TextColor="DarkCyan"/>

  <WhileSelected>
    <Change menuText.Color="#fff"/>
  </WhileSelected>

</Rectangle>
```

The <EdgeNavigator/> element will have two distinct sections, a) a definition of the entries in the edge menu, b) the corresponding pages to the menu items.

```
<EdgeNavigator ClipToBounds="true">
  <Rectangle ux:Name="sideMenuBar" Edge="Left" Width="60%">
    <Shadow ux:Name="shadow" Angle="180" Distance="8" Size="16" Color="#0000" />
     <ActivatingAnimation>
        <Change shadow.Color="#0004"/>
     </ActivatingAnimation>

     <LinearGradient AngleDegrees="45">
         <GradientStop Offset="0" Color="LightGreen" />
         <GradientStop Offset="1" Color="VibrantCyan" />
     </LinearGradient>

  <!-- Contents in edge menu panel -->
  <StackPanel ItemSpacing="5" Margin="5">
    <!-- Side Bar: Menu items -->
    <MenuItem  menuName="First"/>
    <MenuItem  menuName="Second"/>
  </StackPanel>
  </Rectangle>



  <!-- Pages corresponding each edge menu panel option -->
  <PageControl ux:Name="userPageControl">
    <First ux:Name="firstPage"/>
    <Second ux:Name="secondPage"/>
  </PageControl>

</EdgeNavigator>
```

The edge menu is defined with the rectangle *sideMenuBar* and the attribute *Edge* defines the menu will be drawable from the left of the viewport. A <Rectangle/> element is used in this case rather than <Panel/>, which would be our natural intuition, because, we have applied a <LinearGradient/> element in it.

The <MenuItem/> elements need to be connected to the pages in <PageControl/> such that the corresponding page is turned over to on selecting a menu item. We will require yet another router for routing through the pages in *userPageControl.*

```
<Router ux:Name="user_router"/>
<!-- Pages corresponding each edge menu panel option -->
<PageControl ux:Name="userPageControl">
  <First ux:Name="firstPage"/>
  <Second ux:Name="secondPage"/>
</PageControl>
```

*We* will create a separate *.js file to declare the functions to be called on selecting a menu item -

```
                HomePage.js
function goto_first()
{
  user_router.goto("firstPage");
}

function goto_second()
{
  user_router.goto("secondPage");
}

module.exports =
{
  goto_first: goto_first,
  goto_second: goto_second,
}
```

The functions are bound to the *Clicked* action -

```
<!-- Contents in edge menu panel -->
<StackPanel ItemSpacing="5" Margin="5">
  <!-- Side Bar: Menu items -->
  <MenuItem menuName="First" Clicked="{goto_first}"/>
  <MenuItem menuName="Second" Clicked="{goto_second}"/>
</StackPanel>
```

FuseOpen provides a *Selection API* that is to be used for purposes such as this, where a choice has to be made from a list of options and the selection in turn would trigger the execution some tasks. There are two major components in Selection class to be used - a) a <Selectable/> element to identify the UX elements that are a part of the list from which a option is to be selected, b) a <Selection/> element to define the properties such as maximum or minimum number of selection possible and also to provide a namespace to the selectable list.

　　Our app requires only one option to be selected from the list of menu items. Therefore, we create a <Selection/> element with MinCount and MaxCount set to 1, restricting selection of options to only one at a time.

```
<!-- Contents in edge menu panel -->
<StackPanel ItemSpacing="5" Margin="5">
  <Selection MaxCount="1" MinCount="1"/>
  <!-- Side Bar: Menu items -->
  <MenuItem menuName="First" Clicked="{goto_first}"/>
  <MenuItem menuName="Second" Clicked="{goto_second}"/>
</StackPanel>
```

The *MenuItem* class has to contain a <Selectable/> element that does the selection process based on any of the member variables of the class that will have a unique value.

```
<!-- Side bar menu item class -->
<Rectangle ux:Class="MenuItem" MinHeight="20" >
  <string ux:Property="menuId"/>
  <string ux:Property="menuName"/>
  <Selectable Value="{Property menuId}"/>

  <Text ux:Name="menuText" Value="{Property menuName}"
    Padding="10" Alignment="CenterRight" FontSize="25"
    Font="Headings" TextColor="DarkCyan"/>

  <WhileSelected>
    <Change menuText.Color="#fff"/>
  </WhileSelected>

</Rectangle>
<!-- -->
```

We create a new member variable *menuId* for using it as a unique value latched with the <Selectable/> element. The <Selection/> list will turn those items to the colour #fff (White) which have been selected but in our case we require only one item to be selected at once and the previous selection has to be modified. To achieve this a <ToggleSelection/> element will be added to the *menuItem* class.

```
<!-- Side bar menu item class  -->
<Rectangle ux:Class="MenuItem" MinHeight="20" >
  <string ux:Property="menuId"/>
  <string ux:Property="menuName"/>
  <Selectable Value="{Property menuId}"/>

  <Text ux:Name="menuText" Value="{Property menuName}"
    Padding="10" Alignment="CenterRight" FontSize="25"
    Font="Headings" TextColor="DarkCyan"/>

  <WhileSelected>
    <Change menuText.Color="#fff"/>
  </WhileSelected>

  <Clicked>
    <ToggleSelection />
  </Clicked>

</Rectangle>
```

The <Clicked/> Trigger deselects and toggles the previous selection.

The edge menu can be drawn from the left of the viewport by a swipe action but our design requires the menu to be visible by the click on a menu icon at the top left corner of user pages. This menu icon has to be a common UX element for all the pages, and so a custom status bar class will be defined that houses the menu. The status bar is defined in a separate file StatusBar.ux -

```
<Panel ux:Class="StatusBar">
  <string ux:Property="SideBarName"/>
  <StackPanel>
    <StatusBarBackground />

    <Panel Margin="5" >
      <Grid ColumnCount="6">
      <Circle Column="0" Margin="5" Height="30">
        <DropShadow Color="LightGreyShadow" Angle="120" Size="5"
          Distance="2" Spread="0.1" />
        <LinearGradient AngleDegrees="45">
            <GradientStop Offset="0" Color="LightGreen" />
            <GradientStop Offset="1" Color="VibrantCyan" />
        </LinearGradient>
        <Clicked>
          <NavigateToggle Target="{Property SideBarName}" />
        </Clicked>
      </Circle>
      </Grid>
    </Panel>

  </StackPanel>
</Panel>
```

The <StatusBarBackground/> element represents the default status bar for iOS and android containing cellular information and other notifications. It is stacked upon another panel that contains the menu icon.

The <NavigateToggle/> works only with *EdgeNavigator* class and when triggered with <Clicked/>, opens the side bar menu.

As we stated about the two distinct sections in EdgeNavigator class definition, the edge sidebar *sideMenuBar,* which has been defined and the corresponding pages given by *userPageControl*, the <StatusBar/> has to be placed at the top of each of the pages in <PageControl/>. The <PageControl/> and the <StatusBar/> will be placed inside a <DockPanel/> in the following way -

```
<DockPanel>
  <StatusBar Dock="Top" SideBarName="sideMenuBar"/>

  <Router ux:Name="user_router"/>
  <!-- Pages corresponding each edge menu panel option -->
  <PageControl ux:Name="userPageControl">
    <First ux:Name="firstPage"/>
    <Second ux:Name="secondPage"/>
  </PageControl>

  <Panel Dock="Bottom" Height="10" />
</DockPanel>
```

The Dock attribute places the <StatusBar/> at the top of the view port and the blank <Panel/> at the bottom. The remaining middle section is reserved for the user pages. Here is the schematic of the <DockPanel/> and its contents -

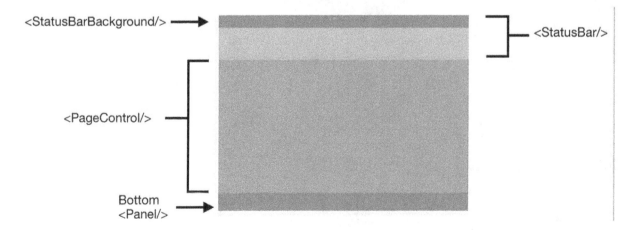

A final element is to be added to the HomePage, which is a shadow visualisation over the contents of HomePage when the edge menu is active and drawn upon the viewport. For this, we will place a <Rectangle/> in the <DockPanel/> that would sport a shadowy colour.

```
<DockPanel>
  <Rectangle ux:Name="sidebarFade" Layer="Overlay"
    Color="#0005" Opacity="0" HitTestMode="None" />
  <StatusBar Dock="Top" SideBarName="sideMenuBar"/>

  <Router ux:Name="user_router"/>
  <!-- Pages corresponding each edge menu panel option -->
  <PageControl ux:Name="userPageControl">
    <First ux:Name="firstPage"/>
    <Second ux:Name="secondPage"/>
  </PageControl>

  <Panel Dock="Bottom" Height="10" />
</DockPanel>
```

The <Rectangle/> *sideBarFade* has the *Layer* attribute set to *Overlay*, which means it will be spread over the visual stack. Now before previewing again on the Preview app, we will bind the HomePage.js file to HomePage.ux for the functions goto_first and goto_second to be accessible.

```
<Page ux:Class="HomePage" Color="#fff">
  <Router ux:Dependency="router" />
  <JavaScript File="HomePage.js"/>
```

Also, we will add a black panel before the first menu item in the edge menu bar so that the menu name list begins with an amount of space left on top and the status bar do not overlap.

```
<!-- Contents in edge menu panel -->
<StackPanel ItemSpacing="5" Margin="5">
  <!-- Side Bar: Menu items -->
  <Selection MaxCount="1" MinCount="1"/>
  <Panel Height="30"/>
  <MenuItem menuId="1" menuName="First" Clicked="{goto_first}"/>
  <MenuItem menuId="2" menuName="Second" Clicked="{goto_second}"/>
</StackPanel>
```

Here is how the side menu and the pages look in the Preview app -

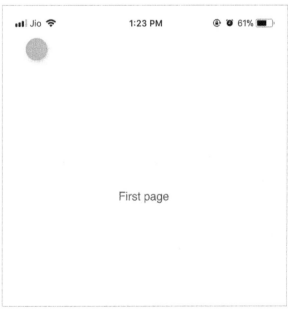

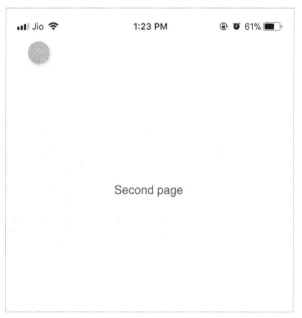

## *Designing pages navigable from side menu*

We will next add visual elements to these pages starting with the first page that will have following design -

There are two sections in First.ux - a) a fixed panel at the top of the page with circles, b) a scrollable continuous feed section with rounded rectangles. The array of <Circle/> elements at top panel is scrollable horizontally and the <Rectangle/> elements are scrollable vertically.

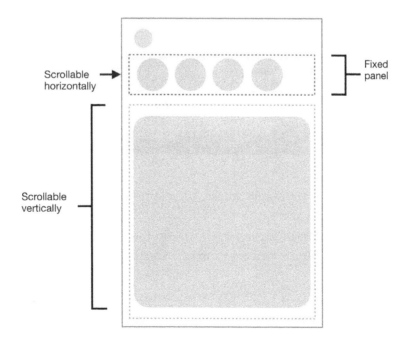

The panels marked by dotted red and green are stacked upon one another.

```
<Page ux:Class="First" Color="#fff">

  <StackPanel Margin="20">

    <Panel Margin="0,10,0,0" Height="70" >
    </Panel>

    <Panel Margin="0,10,0,0" Height="480" >
    </Panel>

  </StackPanel>

</Page>
```

Here are the two <Panel/> items which themselves are fixed and it is the contents within each of these panels that are going to be scrollable. Starting with the first <Panel/> a <ScrollView/> element is placed in it.

```
<Panel Margin="0,10,0,0" Height="70" >
  <ScrollView AllowedScrollDirections="Horizontal" >

  </ScrollView>
</Panel>
```

The default direction for a <ScrollView/> is vertical and so it is set to *Horizontal* with *AllowedScrollDirection* attribute. The <ScrollView/> element requires to have only one immediate child element and so the <Circle/> elements will be placed in <StackPanel/>.

```
<Panel Margin="0,10,0,0" Height="70" >
  <ScrollView AllowedScrollDirections="Horizontal" >
    <StackPanel Orientation="Horizontal"  ItemSpacing="5">

    </StackPanel>
  </ScrollView>
</Panel>
```

The <StackPanel/> element by default stacks UX elements vertically and it is changed to *Horizontal* with the *Orientation* attribute.

FuseOpen provides a looping mechanism in UX, in the form of <Each/> element. We will use this <Each/> element to repeat the creation of <Circle/> element.

```
<Panel Margin="0,10,0,0" Height="70" >
  <ScrollView AllowedScrollDirections="Horizontal" >
    <StackPanel Orientation="Horizontal"  ItemSpacing="5">
      <Each Count="{circles_count}">
        <Circle Height="60" Width="60" Color="LightGreyShadow"/>
      </Each>
    </StackPanel>
  </ScrollView>
</Panel>
```

The *Count* attribute is the loop counter and here the value is to be provided from the JavaScript scope.

Similarly, the code for the vertically scrollable <Rectangle/> panels is as follows -

```
<Panel Margin="0,10,0,0" Height="480" >
  <ScrollView>
    <StackPanel ItemSpacing="20">
      <Each Count="{rectangles_count}">
        <Rectangle Color="LightGreyShadow" CornerRadius="20" Height="400">
          <DropShadow Color="LightGreyShadow" Angle="120"
            Size="5" Distance="2" Spread="0.1" />
        </Rectangle>
      </Each>
    </StackPanel>
  </ScrollView>
</Panel>
```

We will create the First.js file and define *rectangles_count* and *circles_count* variables. We choose the same names for JavaScript files w.r.t. their *.ux counter part because of uniformity only.

```
var Observable = require("FuseJS/Observable");
var circles_count = Observable(5);
var rectangles_count = Observable(5);


module.exports =
{
  circles_count: circles_count,
  rectangles_count: rectangles_count,
}
```

A completely new module *Observable* has been used from the FuseJS library and the variables *circles_count* and *rectangles_count* have been instantiated with the values 5. The Observables API will be discussed later but for now we will test the FirstPage in the Preview app.

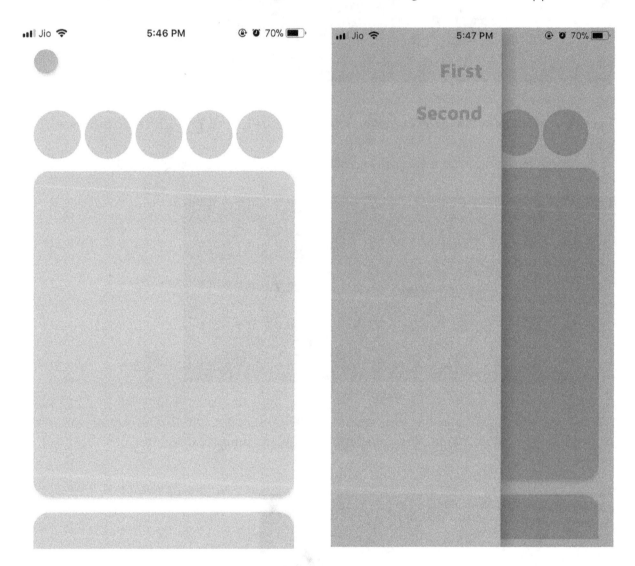

## Getting to know Observables

FuseOpen provides a vivid set of modules through FuseJS and the Observable API forms the key concept in dynamic handling of data described through javascript for establishing the business logic. Observables are rightly named because of the way it binds data with the UX views. Any instance of Observable type is observed for any changes in value(s) and it is updated in the UX dynamically.

Observables are appropriate to be used in case of those variables that may undergo changes. The Observable module in FuseJS in imported with *require* and can hold a single value or a list of values.

```
var Observable = require("FuseJS/Observable");
var foo = Observable(1);
var bar = Observable(1,2,3);
var spam = Observable("abc","def");
var ham = Observable(3.14);
var eggs = Observable(true);
var fum = Observable([1,1,1,1], [0,0,0,1]);
var qux = Observable({id: 1, text: "one" },{id: 2, text: "two" });
```

A UX element that is data bound to an Observable is basically a subscriber of that Observable and will be the recipient of changes to it.

The require(...) function returns a function and is stored in the function object *Observable*. The variables are created by calling this function object as shown in the above example and the value of a variable when accessed as - *.value*, the data value is computed by evaluating the function object.

```
var Observable = require("FuseJS/Observable");

var foo = Observable("Nikola");
var bar = Observable("Tesla");

var genius = Observable(function(){
  return foo.value + " " + bar.value;
})
```

In this snippet changes made to the values in foo and bar are reflected back to the value in genius since its value is generated from *.value*.

Observables can be segregated into two types - a) *state observables* that are created by the user such as the ones shown in the above snippets, and b) *derived observables* are the ones returned by various other API functions. The difference between the two is majorly regarding how data is populated and accessible in variables of either types. In state observables, data is synchronously available or readily accessible, whereas in the case of derived observables, data is generated by API functions and are not synchronous or readily available.

Data is state observables can be accessed and manipulated using Synchronous operators. Below are the few examples of the use of such operators -

```
//Returns a shallow copy of the list of values to array
var obs = Observable(1,2,3);
var obsArray = obs.toArray();

//Adding a value to the list
obs.add("4");

//Adding an array of items to the list
obs.addAll([5,6,7]);

// Insert an array of values at an index position
// obs.insertAll(index, array);
obs.insertAll(2,[98,99,100]);

// Insert a single value at an index position
//obs.insertAt(index, value);
obs.insertAt(4,42);
```

```
//Remove a particular value from the list
obs.remove(99);

//Remove the value at a particular index position
obs.removeAt(1);

//Remove n number of values from the index position
// obs.removeRange(index,n)
obs.removeRange(0,3);

// Remove values where function is true
obs.removeWhere(function(val){
  return val > 5;
});

//Replace all the values in an Observable
obs.replaceAll([1,2,3,5,7]);

// Replace value at an index
//obs.replaceAt(index,value)
obs.replaceAt(1,11);

//Tries to remove first occurrence of the value
obs.tryRemove(11);
```

```
//Clear the data in Observable
obs.clear();

// Get the length of list
obs.length;

// Returns true is value exists
obs.contains(3);

// Invoke function on each item of list
// Does not change the actual list
// Type 1
obs.forEach(function(item){
  console.log("values is: " + item);
});
// Type 2
// obs.forEach(function(item,index){ ... })
obs.forEach(function(item,index){
  console.log("values is: " + item + "at position: " + index);
});

// Get value at an index
obs.getAt(2);

//Get the index of an item
obs.indexOf(5);
```

The last function refreshAll, gives the ability to preform three types of function on the data as well as update a list with new values all with the same definition. It applies both synchronous and asynchronous functionality on the data.

```
// refreshAll(new values, compare function, update function, map function)
var items = Observable(
  {id: 1, text: "one" },
  {id: 2, text: "two" },
  {id: 3, text: "tres" }
);

var newItems = [
  {id: 3, text: "three" },
  {id: 4, text: "four" },
  {id: 5, text: "five" }
];

items.refreshAll(newItems,
  //Compare on ID
  function(oldItem, newItem){
    return oldItem.id == newItem.id;
```

```
},
// Update text
function(oldItem, newItem){
  oldItem.text.value = newItem.text;
},
// Map to object with an observable version of text
function(newItem){
  return {
    id: newItem.id,
    text: Observable(newItem.text)
  };
}
);
```

The result of the comparison function is forwarded to the next function which is updation of the value. In the above example, only the value {id: 3, text: "tres" } gets updated to {id: 3, test: "three"}. The last function for mapping is a *reactive* operator and it returns an *Observable* whenever a new item in the list is available.

## *Reactive operators*

FuseJS provides a number of reactive operators which return an Observable on execution on other Observable(s) and are called Derived Observable. If any changes are made to the original Observable variable, the changes are reflected back to the Observable variables that are created by invoking a reactive operator function on the original Observable item(s). This is called two-way binding in the realm of FuseJS.

The any operator -

```
var vehicles = Observable(
  {type: "car", name: "SuperSpeeder 2000"},
  {type: "car", name: "Initial Dash 2k00"},
  {type: "boat", name: "Floaty McFloatface"}
);

var hasBoats = vehicles.any({type: "boat"}); //true
var hasAircraft = vehicles.any({type: "aircraft"}); //false
var hasCar = veichles.any(function(x) { return x.type === "car"; }) //true
```

In the above example a filter is applied on the *type* field of the data tuples with any(...) function and an Observable is returned containing the tuple that has been found in the list.

The combine operator -

```
var foo = Observable(1);
var boo = Observable(2);
var moo = Observable(3);

var res = foo.combine(boo, moo, function(f, b, m) {
  // f holds the current .value of foo
  // b holds the current .value of boo
  // m holds the current .value of moo

  return f+b+m; // the resulting observable will yield the value 6
})
```

Here, changes in the value of *foo, boo* or *moo* variables are updated in the value of *res* variable. Suppose the values in *boo* and *moo* are not currently available (var boo = Observable()), the value of *res* will be updated when the values in *boo* and *moo* become available. The function in *combine(...,function(...))* will be invoked even if none of the values are present and it would return *undefined* as the value of *res*.

Another function combineLatest(...,function(...)) does the same thing as combine(..., function(...)) with the only difference that, in combineLatest the function waits to invoke until at least one value is available.

Arrays can also be combined in the similar way using combineArrays(...,function(...)) -

```
var foo = Observable(1);
var boo = Observable("a", "b", c);
var moo = Observable(3);

var res = foo.combineArrays(boo, moo, function(f, b, m) {
  // f holds [1]
  // b holds ["a", "b", "c"]
  // m holds [3]

  // the resulting observable will hold the values (1, 3, 3)
  return [f[0], m[0], b.length];
})
```

```
// Returns the size of the list as an Observable
obs.count();

// Counts a item in the list based on a condition
var tasks = Observable(
```

```
  { title: "Learn Fuse", isDone: true },
  { title: "Learn about Observables", isDone: true },
  { title: "Make awesome app", isDone: false }
);
var tasksDone = tasks.count(function(x){
  return x.isDone;
});

// Returns a list of values Observable from an array Observable
 var obs = Observable([1,2,3,4]);
obs.expand() // returns Observable(1,2,3,4);
```

Observables can also be nested and the functions inner() and innerTwoWay() -

```
var foo = Observable(Observable(4))
var bar = foo.inner(); // bar.value = 4
 foo.value.value = 9;    // bar.value = 9
```

The function innerTwoWay() does two-way binding with data and updates the derived observable on changes to the original.

```
var outerObs = Observable(Observable("John"));
var innerObs = outerObs.innerTwoWay();
 innerObs.value = "Jake"; // outerObs.value.value = "Jake"
```

The map functionality with all its variants are a way of performing operations on each element of an observables list and getting an observables list in return.
   map(function(item)) -

```
var numbers = Observable(1, 4, 9);
var roots = numbers.map(function(number) {
  return Math.sqrt(number);
});
```

map(function(index,item)) -

```
var numbers = Observable("this", "item", "is");
var roots = numbers.map(function(item, index) {
  return item + " has the index : " + index;
});
```

FuseJS has functions that enable execution of tasks when the value of an observable is changed. The onValueChanged() function creates a subscription to the observable and monitors the changes to invoke a user defined function.

```
someObservable.onValueChanged(module, function(x) {
  console.log("We got a new value: " + x);
});
```

There are several other specialised functions in the official documentation of FuseOpen.

## Building app logic using Observable data-binding

We will now get back to building our app after the walkthrough with Observables. Before adding any new UX element to the app we will establish some business logic the pages we already have created.

We will start with the login page and put in place the logic for user authentication.

Our code will undergo significant changes to accommodate authentication, and the subsequent animations that would follow upon clicking the "Sign up" button. The animations were set to motion by changing the value of the <WhileTrue/> element named *loading* to true.

```
<Clicked>
  <Set loading.Value="true"/>
</Clicked>
```

All the animations were triggered from the *loading* block as follows -

```
<!-- Trigger for starting animations during logging in -->
  <WhileTrue ux:Name="loading">
    <Change changeWidth.Value="true" DelayBack="0"/>
    <Change loadCircle.Value="true" DelayBack="0"/>

    <Change scaleAndFade.Value="true" Delay="2.5" DelayBack="0"/>
    <Change showLoggedIn.Value="true" Delay="2.9" />
  </WhileTrue>
<!-- end of Trigger definition -->
```

This block of animation triggers will be divided into two separate <WhileTrue/> blocks. The loading animation when the button turns to circle, should be triggered only when both username and password fields have data. If the authentication is successful then the spinning circle animation shall continue along with the rest of the animations. In case of an unsuccessful authentication, the spinning circle shall be set back to the initial state of a rounded rectangle.

The loading <WhileTrue/> block is broken into two blocks -

```
<!-- Trigger for starting animations during logging in -->
  <WhileTrue ux:Name="loading" Value="{start_load_animation}">
    <Change changeWidth.Value="true" DelayBack="0"/>
    <Change loadCircle.Value="true" DelayBack="0"/>
  </WhileTrue>
<!-- end of Trigger definition -->


<!-- authenticate and login -->
<WhileTrue ux:Name="authAndLogin" Value="{auth_success}">
  <Change scaleAndFade.Value="true" Delay="2.5" DelayBack="0"/>
  <Change showLoggedIn.Value="true" Delay="2.9" />
</WhileTrue>
<!-- -->
```

As we can see both of the <WhileTrue/> blocks' *Value* attribute has been subscribed to an observable that is to be managed from JavaScript.

Previously, the <Panel/> holding the login button had a <Clicked/> trigger that is going to be removed and a call to the function *authenticate* is to declared with the *Clicked* attribute.

```
<Panel Row="2" Width="150" Height="60" Clicked="{authenticate}">
    <Panel ux:Name="loadingCirclePanel">
      <Circle ux:Name="loadingCircle" Width="70%" Height="70%"
        Opacity="0" StartAngleDegrees="0" LengthAngleDegrees="90">
        <Stroke Width="1" Brush="#fff" />
      </Circle>
    </Panel>
  </Panel>
```

On an unsuccessful authentication, we want the rounded face icon to rotate.

Username

Password

Sign in

The animation for the round icon is as follows -

```
<!-- Animation for authentication failure -->
<WhileTrue ux:Name="authFailure" Value="{auth_fail}">
  <Rotate Target="mark" Degrees="180" Duration=".4" DurationBack=".2"
    Easing="ExponentialInOut" />
</WhileTrue>
<!-- -->
```

For authentication, the text entered in the <TextInput/> fields have to be accessible from JavaScript and so the *Value* attribute is subscribed to an *observable*.

```
<TextInput Row="0" PlaceholderText="Username" Value="{username}"
```

```
<TextInput Row="1" PlaceholderText="Password" Value="{password}"
```

In order for the authentication to be processed in *authenticate* function in JavaScript, the username and password observables have to be non empty. Here is the JavaScript laying down the vanilla business logic for login.

```
                LoginPage.js
var Observable = require("FuseJS/Observable");
var username = Observable("");
var password = Observable("");
var auth_success = Observable(false);
var auth_fail = Observable(false);
var start_load_animation = Observable(false);

function authenticate()
{
  if(username.value && password.value)
  {

  }
  else
  {


  }

}
```

```
module.exports =
{
  start_load_animation: start_load_animation,
  username: username,
  password: password,
  authenticate: authenticate,
  auth_success: auth_success,
  auth_fail: auth_fail,
}
```

auth_fail, auth_success and start_load_animation are the trigger values for the <WhileTrue/> blocks of animation.

If the username and password fields are empty and the "Sign up" button is clicked, the placeholder text for both the fields are turned to #f00 (Red).

```
<TextInput Row="0" PlaceholderText="Username" Value="{username}" PlaceholderColor="{user_pass_color}"
```

```
<TextInput Row="1" PlaceholderText="Password" Value="{password}" PlaceholderColor="{user_pass_color}"
```

The PlaceholderColor is subscribed to an observable and its value is changed in authenticate function.

```
var user_pass_color = Observable("#999");

function authenticate()
{
  if(username.value && password.value)
  {

  }
  else
  {
    user_pass_color.value = "#f00";
  }

}

module.exports =
{
  user_pass_color: user_pass_color,
```

Now when authenticate function is called the following tasks are done.

The loading animation is started -

```
if(username.value && password.value)
{
  // Set the loading animation to motion
  start_load_animation.value = true;

}
```

The username and password is checked -

```
if(username.value && password.value)
{
  // Set the loading animation to motion
  start_load_animation.value = true;


  // Check username and password
  if(username.value == "foo" && password.value == "fee")
  {
    auth_success.value = true;
  }
  else
  {
    auth_fail.value = true;
    setTimeout(function() {
        auth_fail.value = false;
      }, 0500);
    username.value = "";
    password.value = "";
    start_load_animation.value = false;
  }

}
```

On authentication success the animation trigger value *auth_success* is set to *true*. Upon failure of authentication, *auth_fail* animation trigger is set to *true* with a timer setTimeout(...) function. The setTimeout(...) function stops the auth_fail animation by setting the value to false. If not done, the <WhileTrue/> trigger will remain in active state. The spinner loading animation is stopped by setting start_load_animation to false.

Usually a login or sign up activity is accompanied by sending user's details to a remote server and storing back some response artefacts on the local database of the app. FuseJS uses Fetch API for HTTP(S) communication. Here is a reference for more details on fetch() -

FuseJS also supports XMLHTTPRequest but we are going to use fetch in our app. A typical fetch request looks like -

```
var status = 0;
var response_ok = false;

fetch('http://example.com', {
  method: 'POST',
  headers: { "Content-type": "application/json"},
  body: JSON.stringify(requestObject)
}).then(function(response) {
  status = response.status;    // Get the HTTP status code
  response_ok = response.ok;   // Is response.status in the 200-range?
  return response.json();      // This returns a promise
}).then(function(responseObject) {
  // Do something with the result
}).catch(function(err) {
  // An error occurred somewhere in the Promise chain
});
```

Since doing HTTP(S) requests can be a common activity in any app, we are going to create a wrapper around the fetch call for ease of use.

We create a separate file comm.js to define the wrapper function.

```
                comm.js
var baseurl = 'http://example.com';

function request(url,requestData,successCallback=null,failureCallback=null)
{
     fetch(baseurl+url,{
      method: POST,
      headers: { "Content-type": "application/json"},
      body: JSON.stringify(requestData)
      })
     .then(function(response)
     {
       if (!response.ok)
       {
         console.log("[ JS error response ]");
         console.log(response.statusText);
         throw Error(response.statusText);
       }
         return response.json();
     })
     .then(function(response)
     {
       if(successCallback)
       {
         successCallback(response);
       }
     })
     .catch(function(error)
     {
       if(failureCallback)
       {
         failureCallback(error)
       }

     });
}
```

SuccessCallback is a function object that is to be passed to the call to request upon a successful response for a request. Similarly, failureCallback is a function object that is to be passed on failure.

We will require this JavaScript into Login.js and use the function.

```
            LoginPage.js
var Request = require("JSLib/comm.js");
```

The authenticate function is re-written as -

```
function authenticate()
{
  if(username.value && password.value)
  {
    // Set the loading animation to motion
    start_load_animation.value = true;

    // Check username and password
      Request.request("/signup",{username: username.value, password: password.value},
      function(response)
      {
        appDB.setItem("user_key",response.user_key);
        auth_success.value = true;
      },
      function(error)
      {
        auth_fail.value = true;
        setTimeout(function() {
            auth_fail.value = false;
          }, 0500);
        username.value = "";
        password.value = "";
        start_load_animation.value = false;
      });

  }
  else
  {
    user_pass_color.value = "#f00";
  }
}
```

## Using a persistent data store

Here we use a key-value pair datastore for our app's local storage.

```
var appDB = localStorage;
```

appDB is an instance of JavaScript's own key-value store given by *localStorage*. We assume that a fictional remote app server responds to the request and sends back a *user_key* in JSON format and is accessed as *response.user_key*.

Data from the data store can be retrieved in the following way -

```
_key = appDB.getItem("user_key");
```

Data can be removed in the following way -

```
appDB.removeItem("user_key");
```

After a successful login/sign up activity, the user should be directly lead to the HomePage and so a conditional routing has to be introduced in SplashPage upon *user_key*. Here is a silly check applied, which is obviously not recommended in an actual app -

```
<JavaScript>
var appDB = localStorage;
if(appDB.getItem("user_key"))
{
  setTimeout(function()
  {
    router.goto("home");
  }, 3000);
}
else
{
  setTimeout(function()
  {
    router.goto("login");
  }, 3000);
}
```

Now that we have established a logic for authentication with server side communication, we will keep adding elements to the *HomePage*.

# Dummy app continued

## Adding elements to First.ux page

Starting with the page First, it will be used for camera and photos taken.

The <Circle/> elements at the top of the page are going to serve as buttons. The rounded <Rectangle/> elements beneath are going to showcase the pictures taken with the camera. For the sake of this example app we are going to use only one of the <Circle/> elements for opening the camera. The final render for the app is as follows -

Previously we had created the First page having a <StackPanel/> as the root element of the page and containing two <Panel/> elements stacked upon one another. Here is the code snippet -

```
<Page ux:Class="First" Color="#fff">

  <StackPanel Margin="20">

    <Panel Margin="0,10,0,0" Height="70" >
    </Panel>

    <Panel Margin="0,10,0,0" Height="480" >
    </Panel>

  </StackPanel>

</Page>
```

The first <Panel/> from top will contain the horizontally scrollable <Circle/> buttons. To accommodate the array of circles they are placed in <StackPanel/> inside a <ScrollView/> element as seen before -

```
<Panel Margin="0,10,0,0" Height="70" >
  <ScrollView AllowedScrollDirections="Horizontal" >
    <StackPanel Orientation="Horizontal"  ItemSpacing="5">

    </StackPanel>
  </ScrollView>
</Panel>
```

The first <Circle/> element is an active button and its corresponding code is as follows -

```
<Circle ux:Name="cameraIconShadow" Height="60" Width="60" Color="LightGreyShadow">
  <DropShadow Color="LightGreyShadow" Angle="120"
    Size="5" Distance="2" Spread="0.1" />
  <ImageFill ContentAlignment="Center" File="../Assets/Icons/camera.png"/>
  <Clicked>
    <Change cameraIconShadow.Color="GreyShadow" Duration="0.1" />
    <Set ModalCamera.IsEnabled="true" Delay="0.15" />
  </Clicked>
  <Stroke Color="#000" Width="3">
    <LinearGradient AngleDegrees="45">
```

```
        <GradientStop Offset="0" Color="LightGreen" />
        <GradientStop Offset="1" Color="VibrantCyan" />
    </LinearGradient>
  </Stroke>
</Circle>
```

The <ImageFill/> element fills the space occupied by its parent element which is the <Circle/> element *cameraIconShadow* with the image specified by the *File* attribute. The rest of the <Circle/> elements are just placeholders and will be created by iterating a loop over the <Circle/> element.

```
<Each Count="4">
 <Circle Height="60" Width="60" Color="LightGreyShadow">
   <Stroke Color="#000" Width="3">
     <LinearGradient AngleDegrees="45">
         <GradientStop Offset="0" Color="LightGreen" />
         <GradientStop Offset="1" Color="VibrantCyan" />
     </LinearGradient>
   </Stroke>
 </Circle>
</Each>
```

The <Circle/> element named *cameraIconShadow* for opening the camera has the following tasks defined for <Clicked/> event.

```
<Clicked>
   <Change cameraIconShadow.Color="GreyShadow" Duration="0.1" />
   <Set ModalCamera.IsEnabled="true" Delay="0.15" />
</Clicked>
```

The first animator <Change/>, applies a change in the button shadow upon click. The <Set/> animator the prime task of enabling the view or page that holds the camera viewport which is something named *ModalCamera* in our app. *ModalCamera* is an alternative root element which is basically a visual node that is to be inserted into the parent visual node at a designated position. The parent visual node to the page First as well as SecondPage is HomePage. Currently HomePage has the following visual definition -

```
<DockPanel>

  <Rectangle ux:Name="sidebarFade" Layer="Overlay"
    Color="#0005" Opacity="0" HitTestMode="None" />
  <StatusBar Dock="Top" SideBarName="sideMenuBar"/>
```

```
<DockPanel>

  <Rectangle ux:Name="sidebarFade" Layer="Overlay"
    Color="#0005" Opacity="0" HitTestMode="None" />
  <StatusBar Dock="Top" SideBarName="sideMenuBar"/>

<Router ux:Name="user_router"/>
<!-- Pages corresponding each edge menu panel option -->
<PageControl ux:Name="userPageControl">
  <First ux:Name="firstPage"/>
  <Second ux:Name="secondPage"/>
</PageControl>

<Panel Dock="Bottom" Height="10" />
</DockPanel>
```

The alternate root resource is to be placed according to the following layout of HomePage -

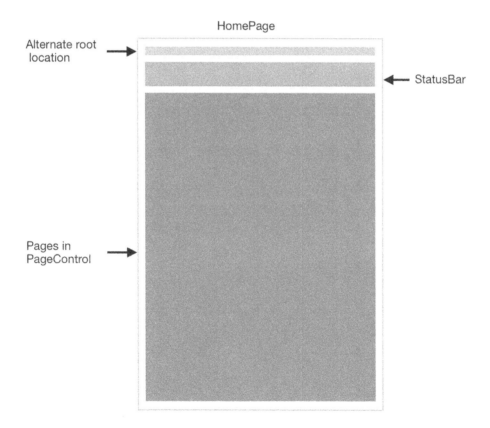

The alternate root is positioned at the top of the page in the form of a <Panel/>.

```
<DockPanel>
  <Panel ux:Name="FullWindow" Layer="Overlay"/>
  <ResourceObject Key="FullWindow" Value="FullWindow"/>

  <Rectangle ux:Name="sidebarFade" Layer="Overlay"
    Color="#0005" Opacity="0" HitTestMode="None" />
  <StatusBar Dock="Top" SideBarName="sideMenuBar"/>

  <Router ux:Name="user_router"/>
  <!-- Pages corresponding each edge menu panel option -->
  <PageControl ux:Name="userPageControl">
    <First ux:Name="firstPage"/>
    <Second ux:Name="secondPage"/>
  </PageControl>

  <Panel Dock="Bottom" Height="10" />
</DockPanel>
```

The <Panel/> named *FullWindow* is our placeholder for any alternate visual node to be inserted in the visual hierarchy. The <Panel/> is not assigned any actual space in the viewport as no *Height* is assigned to it and when a visual element is dynamically placed inside the <Panel/>, it expands the Height and the Width, to the values set for that new visual. The <ResourceObject/> element is responsible for binding the new visual resource to the visual tree and a relation is formed with the <Panel/> by setting the *Value* attribute to the name of the <Panel/>, i.e. *FullWindow*.

The visual element will be defined in the pages *firstPage* and *secondPage* and here is the container that will hold the *to-be-inserted* visual element.

```
<AlternateRoot IsEnabled="false" ParentNode="{Resource FullWindow}" ux:Name="ModalCamera">

</AlternateRoot>
```

The *ParentNode* attribute is set to the *Key* name as given to <ResourceObject/> element and so it is referenced as *Resource FullWindow*. It is this <AlternateRoot/> element named *ModalCamera* that is being called here -

```
<Clicked>
  <Change cameraIconShadow.Color="GreyShadow" Duration="0.1" />
  <Set ModalCamera.IsEnabled="true" Delay="0.15" />
</Clicked>
```

Therefore, on clicking the button, the *IsEnabled* attribute is set to *true* which is otherwise set to *false* in <AlternateRoot/> element.

Next, visual elements are going to be placed inside <AlternateRoot/> and the desired visual is of the form -

There are two visual components that make up the page - a) a viewport for the camera and b) a control bar at the bottom with controls.

The viewport for camera is created using the <CameraView/> element inside <NativeViewHost/> tags.

```
<NativeViewHost Dock="Fill">
  <Rectangle Layer="Background"  Color="#fff"/>

  <CameraView ux:Name="_cameraView" />
</NativeViewHost>
```

The <Rectangle/> element is there as a background layer just to provide a white surface upon which the camera is placed. As for the control bar at the bottom, the space inside a <Panel/> is divided into three columns.

```
<Panel Color="#fff" Dock="Bottom" Height="70">
  <ColumnLayout ColumnCount="3"/>

</Panel>
```

The element <ColumnLayout/> divides the space inside the <Panel/> equally into three columns as specified by the attribute ColumnCount and so each control placed after the <ColumnLayout/> element, will be allocated position starting from left to right by default.

First the close button is placed to close the view opened by <AlternateRoot/> named *ModalCamera*, by setting the IsEnabled attribute to *false*.

```
<Panel Color="#fff" Dock="Bottom" Height="70">
  <ColumnLayout ColumnCount="3"/>

  <Circle Height="50" Width="50" HitTestMode="LocalBoundsAndChildren">
    <DropShadow ux:Name="closeCameraIconShadow" Color="LightGreyShadow" Angle="120"
      Size="5" Distance="2" Spread="0.1" />
    <ImageFill File="../Assets/Icons/close.png"/>
    <Clicked>
      <Change closeCameraIconShadow.Color="GreyShadow" Duration="0.1" />
      <Set ModalCamera.IsEnabled="false" Delay="0.15"/>
    </Clicked>
  </Circle>

</Panel>
```

Next the button to capture the photo is placed.

```
<Circle Height="50" Width="50" HitTestMode="LocalBoundsAndChildren" Clicked="{capture_photo}">
  <DropShadow ux:Name="captureCameraIconShadow" Color="LightGreyShadow" Angle="120"
    Size="5" Distance="2" Spread="0.1" />
  <ImageFill ux:Name="capture" Opacity="1" File="../Assets/Icons/record.png"/>
  <Clicked>
    <Change captureCameraIconShadow.Color="GreyShadow" Duration="0.1" />
    <Change capture.Opacity="0.5"/>
  </Clicked>
</Circle>
```

The third and last button is for saving the image.

```
<Circle Height="50" Width="50" HitTestMode="LocalBoundsAndChildren" Clicked="{save_photo}">
  <DropShadow ux:Name="savePicIconShadow" Color="LightGreyShadow" Angle="120"
    Size="5" Distance="2" Spread="0.1" />
  <ImageFill File="../Assets/Icons/save.png"/>
  <Clicked>
    <Change savePicIconShadow.Color="GreyShadow" Duration="0.1" />
  </Clicked>
</Circle>
```

The two visual components inside <AlternateRoot/>, the camera viewport and the control bar at the bottom are placed inside a <DockPanel/> element.

```
<AlternateRoot IsEnabled="false" ParentNode="{Resource FullWindow}" ux:Name="ModalCamera">
  <DockPanel>

    <NativeViewHost Dock="Fill">
    </NativeViewHost>

    <Panel Color="#fff" Dock="Bottom" Height="70">
      <ColumnLayout ColumnCount="3"/>
    </Panel>

  </DockPanel>
</AlternateRoot>
```

The photos taken and saved will be showcased in the rounded rectangles -

The photos in these rounded rectangles are vertically scrollable and so they are stacked inside a <ScrollView/> element -

```
<Panel Margin="0,10,0,0" Height="480" >
  <ScrollView>
    <StackPanel ItemSpacing="20">
      <Each Items="{allFiles}">
        <Rectangle ux:Name="photoFrame" Color="LightGreyShadow" CornerRadius="20" Height="400">
          <DropShadow Color="LightGreyShadow" Angle="120"
            Size="5" Distance="2" Spread="0.1" />
            <ImageFill File="{=data()}" StretchMode="UniformToFill" />

        <AddingAnimation>
          <Change photoFrame.Opacity="0" Duration="0.3"/>
        </AddingAnimation>
        <RemovingAnimation>
          <Change photoFrame.Opacity="0" Duration="0.1"/>
        </RemovingAnimation>
        <LayoutAnimation>
          <Move Y="1" RelativeTo="PositionChange" Duration="0.15" Easing="CubicInOut"/>
        </LayoutAnimation>
        </Rectangle>
      </Each>

      <WhileEmpty Items="{allFiles}" >
        <Rectangle Color="LightGreyShadow" CornerRadius="20" Height="400">
          <DropShadow Color="LightGreyShadow" Angle="120"
            Size="5" Distance="2" Spread="0.1" />
            <Text Alignment="Center" Value="No images yet" Font="Headings"
              FontSize="25" Color="#fff" />
        </Rectangle>
      </WhileEmpty>
    </StackPanel>
  </ScrollView>
</Panel>
```

The <Each/> looping element iterates through the *Items* in the *Observable allFiles*. The *allFiles* variable is the one which is of list type whose items are the file path to the locations where the photo files are saved.

The <WhileEmpty/> tag is used on the same *allFiles* variable to declare the scheme of things when the list is empty. Here want to show the following card -

Now we will define the functions in First.js file for the corresponding UX elements created in firstPage.

Here is the function definition of the *capture_photo* which will be called upon clicking the capture button -

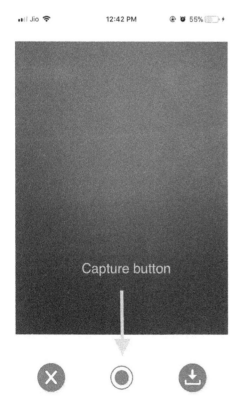

```
function capture_photo()
{
    Camera.capturePhoto(640,480)
        .then(function(photo)
        {
            photo.save()
                .then(function(path)
                {
                    console.log("Photo saved to: " + path);
                    photoPath.value = path;
                    photo.release();
                })
                .catch(function(error)
                {
                    console.log("Failed to save photo: " + error);
                    photo.release();
                });
        })
        .catch(function(error)
        {
            console.log("Failed to capture photo: " + error);
        });
}
```

The CameraView module is used here to take a picture with its instance *Camera* -

```
var Camera = _cameraView;
```

The <CameraView/> element is named *_cameraView* and it is with this reference, an instance is created to be controlled from JavaScript. The variable *photoPath* is used to store the file path of the saved location. The file path is set to a default location but for our app we will save the photo in a location of our choice. A directory *DummyImages* will be created during launch of the application and therefore will be defined in MainView.ux -

```
<App>
  <SafeEdgePanel Color="#42f4bc">
    <JavaScript>
      var FileSystem = require("FuseJS/FileSystem");
      FileSystem.createDirectory(FileSystem.dataDirectory + "/" + "DummyImages");
```

After an image is taken and saved at the default location, it is to be moved to the DummyImages directory upon clicking the save button -

The save_photo function will be called -

```
function save_photo()
{
  FileSystem.move(photoPath.value,savePath.value+photoCount.value+1+".jpg");
}
```

The filenames chosen for the photos are as - 1.jpg, 2.jpg ... and the *photoCount* variable as the name suggests keeps the count of the files present in the DummyImages directory.

A _init_() function will be called when the page firstPage is loaded and it is in this function the Observable *allFiles* is appended with the file locations of the images to showcase.

```
var allFiles = Observable();

function _init_()
{
  FileSystem.listFiles(FileSystem.dataDirectory + "/" + "DummyImages/")
  .then(function(files)
  {
      photoCount.value = files.length;
      allFiles.clear();
      allFiles.addAll(files);

      console.log(photoCount.value);
    }, function(error) {
        console.log("Unable to list files of directory: " + error);
    });

}
```

This function is to be called when the page is active as the visible page and so the <Activated/> trigger is used in First.ux.

```
First.ux
<Page ux:Class="First" Color="#fff">
  <JavaScript File="First.js"/>
  <Activated Handler="{_init_}"/>
```

Now here are a few screenshots of the gallery view of the photos captured by the camera -

## Adding elements to Second.ux page

As we have implemented camera and a gallery view in the page First.ux, the next page is going to be dedicated to videos. We are keeping the UI format almost identical to the page First.ux, as the gallery of captured videos will be accessible from the scrollable list of videos. The page formatting is same as that of before -

The <Circle/> elements at the top are the buttons same as before, so the corresponding code is as follows -

```
Second.ux

<Page ux:Class="Second" Color="#fff">
  <JavaScript File="Second.js"/>
  <Activated Handler="{_init_}"/>




  <StackPanel Margin="20">
    <Panel Margin="0,10,0,0" Height="70" >
      <ScrollView AllowedScrollDirections="Horizontal" >
        <StackPanel Orientation="Horizontal"  ItemSpacing="5">

          <Circle Height="60" Width="60" Color="LightGreyShadow">
            <DropShadow ux:Name="videoIconShadow" Color="LightGreyShadow" Angle="120"
              Size="5" Distance="2" Spread="0.1" />
            <ImageFill File="../Assets/Icons/video-camera.png"/>
            <Clicked>
```

```
                <Change videoIconShadow.Color="GreyShadow" Duration="0.1" />
                <Set ModalVideoCamera.IsEnabled="true" Delay="0.15" />
            </Clicked>
            <Stroke Color="#000" Width="3">
              <LinearGradient AngleDegrees="45">
                    <GradientStop Offset="0" Color="LightGreen" />
                    <GradientStop Offset="1" Color="VibrantCyan" />
              </LinearGradient>
            </Stroke>
          </Circle>

          <Each Count="4">
          <Circle Height="60" Width="60" Color="LightGreyShadow">
            <Stroke Color="#000" Width="3">
              <LinearGradient AngleDegrees="45">
                    <GradientStop Offset="0" Color="LightGreen" />
                    <GradientStop Offset="1" Color="VibrantCyan" />
              </LinearGradient>
            </Stroke>
          </Circle>
          </Each>

        </StackPanel>
      </ScrollView>
   </Panel>
```

The view for video camera gets opened in the same way as before, as we use an <AlternateRoot/> element -

```
    <AlternateRoot IsEnabled="false" ParentNode="{Resource FullWindow}" ux:Name="ModalVideoCamera">
        <DockPanel>
        <NativeViewHost Dock="Fill">
          <Rectangle Layer="Background"  Color="#fff"/>

          <CameraView ux:Name="_cameraViewForVideo" />

        </NativeViewHost>


      </DockPanel>
    </AlternateRoot>

  </StackPanel>


</Page>
```

Next, of course the visual elements are going to be placed in <AlternateRoot/>, and it is according to the following design -

The control buttons for video is placed at the bottom which are close button, record button, stop record button and save video button respectively from right.

The corresponding code for this view is as the following -

```
<AlternateRoot IsEnabled="false" ParentNode="{Resource FullWindow}" ux:Name="ModalVideoCamera">
    <DockPanel>
    <NativeViewHost Dock="Fill">
        <Rectangle Layer="Background"  Color="#fff"/>

        <CameraView ux:Name="_cameraViewForVideo" />

    </NativeViewHost>

    <Panel Color="#fff" Dock="Bottom" Height="70">
        <ColumnLayout ColumnCount="4"/>
        <Circle Height="50" Width="50" HitTestMode="LocalBoundsAndChildren" Clicked="{check_save_before_closing}">
            <DropShadow ux:Name="closeVideoIconShadow" Color="LightGreyShadow" Angle="120"
            Size="5" Distance="2" Spread="0.1" />
            <ImageFill File="../Assets/Icons/close.png"/>
            <Clicked>
                <Change closeVideoIconShadow.Color="GreyShadow" Duration="0.1" />
                <Set ModalVideoCamera.IsEnabled="false" Delay="0.15"/>
            </Clicked>
        </Circle>
```

```
    <Circle Height="50" Width="50" HitTestMode="LocalBoundsAndChildren" Clicked="{start_recording}">
      <DropShadow ux:Name="recordVideoIconShadow" Color="LightGreyShadow" Angle="120"
        Size="5" Distance="2" Spread="0.1" />
      <ImageFill ux:Name="startRecord" Opacity="1" File="../Assets/Icons/record.png"/>
      <Clicked>
        <Change recordVideoIconShadow.Color="GreyShadow" Duration="0.1" />
        <Set startRecord.Opacity="0.5"/>
        <Set stopText.Opacity="1"/>
      </Clicked>
    </Circle>

    <Circle Height="50" Width="50" HitTestMode="LocalBoundsAndChildren" Clicked="{stop_recording}">
      <Stroke Color="#f00"/>
      <DropShadow ux:Name="stopVideoIconShadow" Color="LightGreyShadow" Angle="120"
        Size="5" Distance="2" Spread="0.1" />
      <Text Alignment="Center" ux:Name="stopText" Opacity="0.5" Value="Stop" Font="Headings"/>
      <Clicked>
        <Change recordVideoIconShadow.Color="GreyShadow" Duration="0.1" />
        <Set stopText.Opacity="0.5"/>
        <Set startRecord.Opacity="1"/>
      </Clicked>
    </Circle>

    <Circle Height="50" Width="50" HitTestMode="LocalBoundsAndChildren" Clicked="{save_video}">
      <DropShadow ux:Name="saveVideoIconShadow" Color="LightGreyShadow" Angle="120"
        Size="5" Distance="2" Spread="0.1" />
      <ImageFill File="../Assets/Icons/save.png"/>
      <Clicked>
        <Change saveVideoIconShadow.Color="GreyShadow" Duration="0.1" />
      </Clicked>
    </Circle>
  </Panel>

  </DockPanel>
</AlternateRoot>
```

We will define the functions *start_recording*, *stop_recording*, *save_video* and *check_save_before_closing*. The CameraView is a powerful API that we are going to use for capturing video as well, and so we will instantiate the instance of CameraView element in JavaScript.

```
var VideoCamera = _cameraViewForVideo;
```

The definition for *start_recording* function -

```
function start_recording()
{

  console.log("Start record");
  VideoCamera.setCaptureMode(VideoCamera.CAPTURE_MODE_VIDEO)
    .then(function(newCaptureMode) { /* ready to record video */ })
    .catch(function(error) { /* failed */ });

  VideoCamera.startRecording()
      .then(function(session) {
          console.log("Video recording started!");
          recordingSession = session;
      })
      .catch(function(error) {
          console.log("Failed to start recording: " + error);
      });
}
```

The definition for stop_recording function -

```
function stop_recording()
{
  console.log("Stop record");
  if (recordingSession == null)
      return;

    recordingSession.stop()
      .then(function(recording) {
          videoPath = recording.filePath();
          console.log("Recording stopped, saved to: " + videoPath);
          recordingSession = null;
      })
      .catch(function(error) {
          console.log("Failed to stop recording: " + error);
          recordingSession = null;
      });
}
```

The CameraView API saves the recorded video into a temporary location when the *stop* function is invoked. The recordingSession variable stores the recorded video and so upon stopping the recording, the recorded content in recordingSession is saved to a temporary location, and the variable is again set to null.

The definition for *save_video* -

```
function save_video()
{
  console.log("Save video");
  FileSystem.move(videoPath,savePath+videoCount.value+1+".mov");
  saved = true;
}
```

The file path of the video saved temporarily is contained in the variable *videoPath*, which is used to move the content from that temporary location to our own set location of *DummyVideos* directory. We are using a flag variable with the name *saved*, that indicates if the captured video has been saved at our desired location.

The saved variable has its application in the *check_save_before_closing* function where the recorded and saved video from the temporary location is removed, if the flag variable *saved* is set to false. Here is the code for *check_save_before_closing* -

```
function check_save_before_closing()
{
  if(!saved && videoPath != "")
  {
    FileSystem.delete(videoPath).then(function(){
      console.log("Removed temporary saved video");
    },function(error){
      console.log("Failed to remove temporarily saved video: "+error);
    });
  }
}
```

Here is all the variables that are declared -

```
                  Second.js
var Observable = require("FuseJS/Observable");
var VideoCamera = _cameraViewForVideo;
var recordingSession = null;
var FileSystem = require("FuseJS/FileSystem");
var savePath = FileSystem.dataDirectory + "/" + "DummyVideos/";
```

```
var videoCount = Observable();
var videoPath = "";
var saved = false;
var allVideoFiles = Observable();
```

Next, we will all the gallery view of the saved videos and for which we will place a list of rectangular panels stacked right after the <Circle/> buttons at the top.

```
<Panel Margin="0,10,0,0" Height="480" >
  <ScrollView>
    <StackPanel ItemSpacing="20">
      <Each Items="{allVideoFiles}">
        <Rectangle ux:Name="videoFrame" Margin="10" CornerRadius="10" Height="400">
          <LinearGradient AngleDegrees="45">
              <GradientStop Offset="0" Color="LightGreyShadow" />
              <GradientStop Offset="1" Color="#fff" />
          </LinearGradient>

          <DockPanel Margin="10,10,10,20">
          <DropShadow Color="LightGreyShadow" Angle="120"
            Size="5" Distance="2" Spread="0.1" />

            <Video ux:Name="video" Dock="Fill" File="{=data()}" IsLooping="true" StretchMode="UniformToFill">
              <ProgressAnimation>
                <Change progressBar.Width="100" />
              </ProgressAnimation>
            </Video>

            <Grid Dock="Bottom" Margin="0,5,0,0" ColumnCount="2" RowCount="1">
              <ThemeButton>
                <Text Alignment="Center" Value="Play" FontSize="18" Color="#fff"/>
                <DropShadow Color="LightGreyShadow" Angle="100" Size="5" Distance="2" Spread="0.1" />
                <Clicked>
                  <Play Target="video" />
                </Clicked>
              </ThemeButton>

              <ThemeButton>
                <Text Alignment="Center" Value="Pause" FontSize="18" Color="#fff"/>
                <DropShadow Color="LightGreyShadow" Angle="100" Size="5" Distance="2" Spread="0.1" />
                <Clicked>
                  <Play Target="video" />
                </Clicked>
              </ThemeButton>
            </Grid>

            <Rectangle ux:Name="progressBar" Dock="Bottom" Fill="#f00" Width="0%" Height="10" />
          </DockPanel>
          </Rectangle>
      </Each>
```

```
    <WhileEmpty Items="{allVideoFiles}" >
      <Rectangle Color="LightGreyShadow" CornerRadius="20" Height="400">
        <DropShadow Color="LightGreyShadow" Angle="120"
          Size="5" Distance="2" Spread="0.1" />
          <Text Alignment="Center" Value="No videos yet" Font="Headings"
            FontSize="25" Color="#fff" />
      </Rectangle>
    </WhileEmpty>
  </StackPanel>
</ScrollView>
</Panel>
```

The *allVideoFiles* Observable will contain the file paths of all the saved videos and so, we will load the values from *DummyVideos* directory in the *_init_()* function.

```
function _init_()
{
  saved = false;
  var recordingSession = null;
  videoPath = "";

  FileSystem.listEntries(FileSystem.dataDirectory + "/" + "DummyVideos/")
  .then(function(files)
  {
      videoCount.value = files.length;
      allVideoFiles.clear();
      allVideoFiles.addAll(files);

    }, function(error) {
      console.log("Unable to list files of directory: " + error);
    });

}
```

Finally, the Second page has the following UI -

When the video is played, a progress bar is visible at the bottom of the video frame. The above screenshot shows the thumbnail of the saved video in the video frame.

We are going to end the development of our app here, and shift focus to packaging and generating the ready to deploy app file. In order to do so, we have to first prepare the Dummy. unoproj file -

```
Dummy.unoproj
{
  "RootNamespace":"",
  "Title": "Dummy",
  "Description": "The app is dummy, i.e. does nothing.",
  "Publisher": "Bhoson",
  "Copyright": "Copyright © 20018-infinity $(Publisher)",
  "VersionCode": 1,
  "Version": "0.1.0",
  "Android": {
    "VersionName": "$(Version)",
    "Key": {
      "Alias": "application",
      "AliasPassword": "apppass",
      "Store": "release.keystore",
      "StorePassword": "keypass"
    },
  },
  "iOS": {
    "BundleVersion": "$(Version)"
  },
  "Packages": [
    "Fuse",
    "FuseJS",
    "Fuse.Controls.CameraView",
    "Fuse.Camera",

  ],
  "Includes": [
    "*",
    "*.js:Bundle",
  ]
}
```

The values for Alias, AliasPassword, Store and StorePassword can all be set while signing the application. Our application will be identified in the Google Play store with a unique RSA key which is generated by executing the following command in the application root directory -

```
snehadeepbhowmick 05:55 PM:$ keytool -genkey -v -keystore release.keystore \
> -alias application -keyalg RSA -keysize 2048 -validity 10000
Enter keystore password:
Re-enter new password:
What is your first and last name?
  [Unknown]:  Bhoson
What is the name of your organizational unit?
  [Unknown]:  App Development
What is the name of your organization?
  [Unknown]:  Bhoson
What is the name of your City or Locality?
  [Unknown]:  Kolkata
What is the name of your State or Province?
  [Unknown]:  West Bengal
What is the two-letter country code for this unit?
  [Unknown]:  IN
Is CN=Bhoson, OU=App Development, O=Bhoson, L=Kolkata, ST=West Bengal, C=IN correct?
  [no]:  yes

Generating 2,048 bit RSA key pair and self-signed certificate (SHA256withRSA) with a validity of 10,000 days
        for: CN=Bhoson, OU=App Development, O=Bhoson, L=Kolkata, ST=West Bengal, C=IN
Enter key password for <application>
        (RETURN if same as keystore password):
Re-enter new password:
[Storing release.keystore]
```

We are prompted to create the *keystore* password as StorePassword in the beginning, and then for the application password as AliasPassword at the end. The execution of the command will result in creation of the *release.keystore* file in our project's root directory.

The *Packages* directive in Dummy.unoproj file states which of the Fuse APIs are being used for our project.

The *Includes* directive dictates which files are to be included in our project, which in this case is - * and *.js.

We are going to build our app for Android platform only as *.apk file will be available on building the app. In the case of iOS, the application has to be built with Xcode IDE, and the application will be installed on an iOS device. A complete description of the process can be found in the official documentation at -

A complete list of the remaining directives for *.unoproj file can be found at -

Finally we build the application for release using the following command in the root directory of the project -

```
snehadeepbhowmick 07:00 PM:$ fuse build --target=android --configuration=Release
Uno 1.9.0 (dev-build) macOS 10.12 x86_64 N/A
Copyright © 2015-2018 Fusetools


Configuring
  0.74 s
Compiling syntax tree
  2.22 s
Generating code and data
Fontconfig warning: no <cachedir> elements found. Check configuration.
Fontconfig warning: adding <cachedir>~/Library/Caches/com.xamarin.fontconfig</cachedir>
Fontconfig warning: adding <cachedir prefix="xdg">fontconfig</cachedir>

  7.18 s
Building Android app


Note: Some input files use or override a deprecated API.
Note: Recompile with -Xlint:deprecation for details.

2 m, 13.67 s

Build completed in 143.85 seconds
```

The *.apk file can be found at location build/Android/Release/Dummy.apk. This *.apk file is can be installed in any Android device, or in case of hosting in the Google Play store, will be uploaded to the Google Play account. Further details about building and exporting an app can be found at -

Our application's *.apk file will show the custom icon from FuseOpen when installed. In order to use an icon of our own, we have to create our own icons. Android apps require icon packs of five types - ldpi, mdpi, hdpi, xhdpi, xxhdpi, xxxhdpi, which can be generated from https://makeappicon.com/. The icons have to be listed in the Dummy.unoproj file.

# SECTION 11

# CI/CD with Jenkins

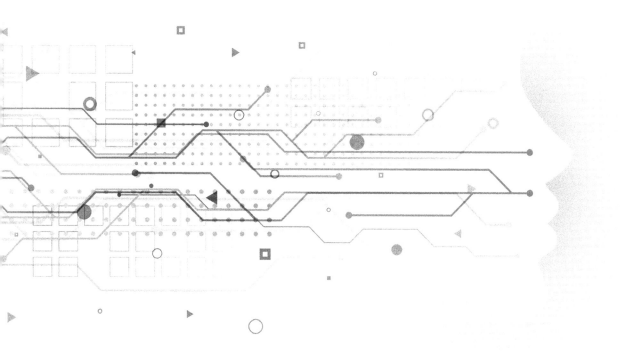

# Introduction

Our journey throughout this book has been about knowing those technologies that are required at some point during the building of a software product. This final section is about learning the way to optimise the continuous process of development of updates, testing of these updates and rolling out the changes.

For any software product whether it is for a paying customer or an open-source licensed or free software, there can be multiple developers who work on various areas of the software. Almost all software companies maintain a testing and/or QA team whose task is to keep writing tests for new code, ensure the successful building of the software, and running it under different scenarios. It is not that a test which ran successfully before, will continue to successfully build always. It is seen as a common case when an update to the shared library used by the application is causing the build to break for any particular active version of the software. Therefore, it becomes the task of the testing and QA team to keep track of the effects a change has on various acting versions. Previously, a testing team had to manually carry out tests and generate test reports to be passed along to the responsible development teams.

For startup companies, it is less feasible to maintain elaborate teams for testing and QA tasks and so, it becomes important to embrace an automated mechanism. The intent for incorporating automation in this phase of software development, is to be able to keep track of the solidarity of all active versions of a software such that there is no dependence between the developer and the testing team to get a feed back on the status of a build. This reduction in dependence allows a developer to respond quickly to an issue and come out with fixes, when working in a time constrained environment.

# What is Jenkins?

*Jenkins* is an open source automation server program that can be used to automate all kinds of tasks related to building, testing and delivering or deploying of an application.

In this book we have already discussed about implementing automation with Ansible, so it becomes important to outline the difference between the two. But before that, we will learn about our intention with Jenkins and the meaning of *Continuous Integration and Continuous Deployment (CI/CD)*.

For an application that undergoes updates always goes through a constant set of phases which are - building of the application, the various types of testing on the application and then deploying of that application to be ultimately used by its users. The phase of building of the application does not mean development of the app through writing of code, but the set of steps that prepares the source code to be made execution ready. Since an application goes through evolution, there comes the need to automate the unchanged set of steps.

Let us take the example of the Linux kernel development which is the biggest software development project. Every time a change is added to the source code, the software has to be run and tested before publishing. The term *continuous integration* is used to describe the continuous process of development and addition/integration of either bug fixes or new features into a software. Almost all software projects, which are aimed at a user base, is version controlled and therefore, before being rolled out to the user base, it has to be executed in an environment same as that of its users'. The earlier process of software development used to include manual effort each time a new release had to be tested. The developers behind a particular version of the software had to setup the desired environment where all kinds of tests were run and obviously based on the reports of the tests, delivery of the software was decided. A software project that has a substantial number of developers, usually has the trend where groups of developers work on separate features or bugs of different supported versions of the software. That means these developers would be working on different types of software and hardware environments and committing these source code changes in frequent intervals. The complexity of maintaining and managing the process of setting up a target environment and run tests increases to a point when it is difficult for an individual to keep track of all the changes reports per development branch in the source code tree. We have stated how the pre-steps before rolling out a new release of a software is mostly constant and consists of the following generic steps -

a)  Preparing the target hardware environment for the software.
b)  Installing the required libraries that are used by the software.
c)  Running the software.

d) Running tests on the software.
e) Generating and logging the test reports.
f) Going forward with releasing the software or going back to the development phase to fix the problems.

The term *continuous deployment* represents the process of building (as in compiling) and running the application on test environments for every change in the code made.

It should be noted, that any production software before being released usually goes through the four execution environments - development, staging, pre-production and production. Each of the environment emulates a particular stress situation on the application. For reference, a mobile application when run in the production environment, represents the actual ground truth scenario of how it performs alongside all other applications on a user's device. The pre-production and staging environments are environments that emulate a more suitable environment for an application with less throttling of the resources. The pre-production and staging environments are sometimes similar in description and so they are clubbed as just staging. Therefore, every time a new release has to go through the same set of steps in all these four environments. Under such circumstances of repeating stages and steps for multiple environment, it only makes sense to have some sort of programmed solution rather than manual.

Ansible as we have already come across in this book is an automator of tasks, so quite naturally we can be inclined toward it to be used for the task of continuous integration and deployment. Ansible although is pretty easy in terms of implementation of automation tasks, but it is only limited to execution on remote machines. As for our

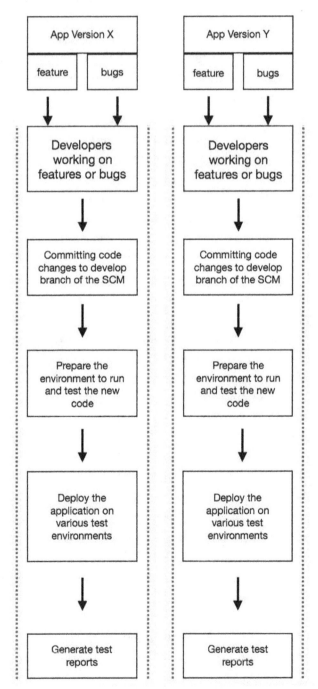

purpose we require an advanced set of tools that make the whole process GUI oriented and also extensible for other toolchains to be added to make CI/CD more informative. As a result this would make the development and release phases much more organised and reliably robust.

Jenkins addresses these requirements and provides an easy solution. Let us generically visualise the way we wish to automate the whole process from development to deployment and finally delivery.

In the above diagram, we take a example situation of a particular application that has two active versions. These two versions therefore, correspond to specific development channels. The generic steps in each of the channels represent a sequence of activities that can be arranged only in a particular order forming a pipeline. It is this logical pipeline that is represented in the above diagram through dotted red lines and we are going to define the steps to be automated with Jenkins and refer to them as pipelines.

# Interacting with Jenkins

All the source files can be found in the following location -

The first thing we are going to do is install Jenkins. We are using a Centos 7 VM where we install Docker and Java 8.

```
yum install epel-release
yum install docker-ce
yum install java
```

Jenkins application is written in Java and so we download the jenkins war file -

```
wget http://mirrors.jenkins.io/war-stable/latest/jenkins.war
```

The application is started -

```
[root@jenkins ~]# java -jar jenkins.war --httpPort=8080
Running from: /root/jenkins.war
webroot: $user.home/.jenkins
Jan 16, 2019 10:56:16 AM org.eclipse.jetty.util.log.Log initialized
INFO: Logging initialized @1082ms to org.eclipse.jetty.util.log.JavaUtilLog
Jan 16, 2019 10:56:17 AM winstone.Logger logInternal
INFO: Beginning extraction from war file
```

The initial run shows the admin password for the jenkins dashboard -

Jenkins initial setup is required. An admin user has been created and a password generated.
Please use the following password to proceed to installation:

0a003d9ab33b49bea9a19ed51560e0c3

This may also be found at: /root/.jenkins/secrets/initialAdminPassword

Here is the dashboard -

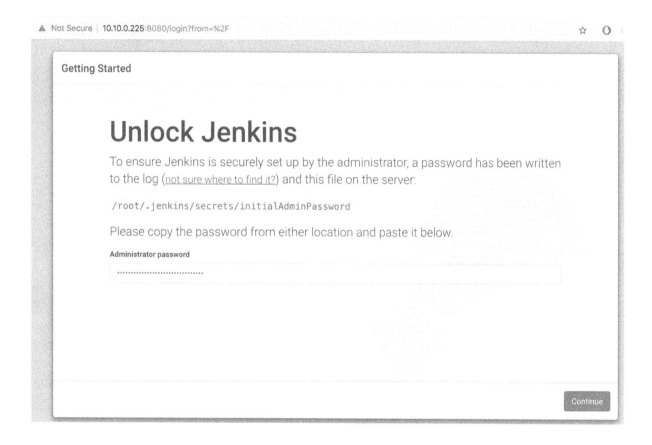

The next page after logging in with the admin password prompts us to install a list of pre-suggested plugins. Upon going forward with the installation, we will see the following status of the plugin installation -

# Customize Jenkins

Plugins extend Jenkins with additional features to support many different needs.

### Install suggested plugins

Install plugins the Jenkins community finds most useful.

### Select plugins to install

Select and install plugins most suitable for your needs.

Jenkins 2.150.1

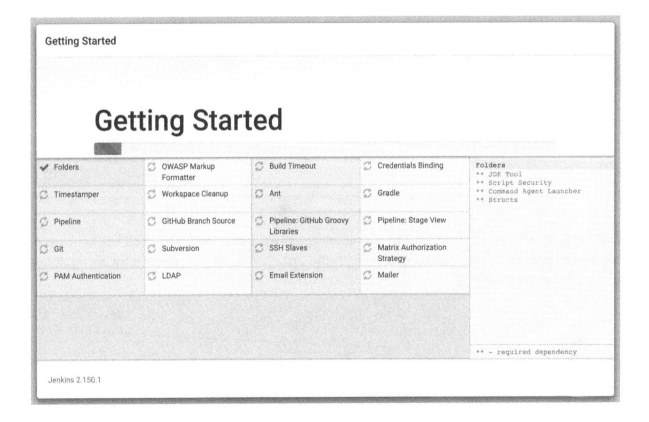

Getting Started

# Getting Started

| ✔ Folders | ↻ OWASP Markup Formatter | ↻ Build Timeout | ↻ Credentials Binding | Folders |
|---|---|---|---|---|
| ↻ Timestamper | ↻ Workspace Cleanup | ↻ Ant | ↻ Gradle | ** JDK Tool<br>** Script Security<br>** Command Agent Launcher<br>** Structs |
| ↻ Pipeline | ↻ GitHub Branch Source | ↻ Pipeline: GitHub Groovy Libraries | ↻ Pipeline: Stage View | |
| ↻ Git | ↻ Subversion | ↻ SSH Slaves | ↻ Matrix Authorization Strategy | |
| ↻ PAM Authentication | ↻ LDAP | ↻ Email Extension | ↻ Mailer | |

** - required dependency

Jenkins 2.150.1

Next, we will be prompted to create a new administrative user.

We will keep the url of the dashboard with the IP only, and so, the next page is kept as is and we select *Save and Finish*.

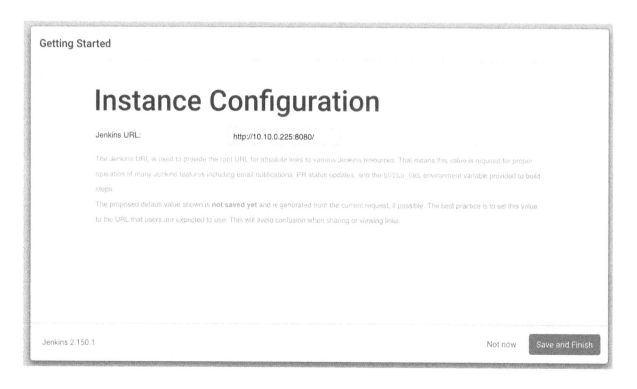

Here is the landing page of the Jenkins dashboard where from we will be managing every job.

The pipeline that we mention in the last chapter is represented with a *Jenkinsfile* that we will create. This Jenkinsfile will contain the declared set of steps for a continuous delivery pipeline. Here is a sample Jenkinsfile -

```
pipeline {
    agent { docker { image 'python:3.5.1' } }
    stages {
        stage('build') {
            steps {
                sh 'python --version'
            }
        }
    }
}
```

The first directive *agent* defines the base environment to use upon which the application will be running. Here the docker image for python is used. The next directive *stage* is used to group a set of steps under a namespace, that are defined inside the *steps* directive.

With our GUI dashboard ready, we create our first pipeline by selecting the option *New item*.

Entering a name for our pipeline, we select a multi-branch pipeline -

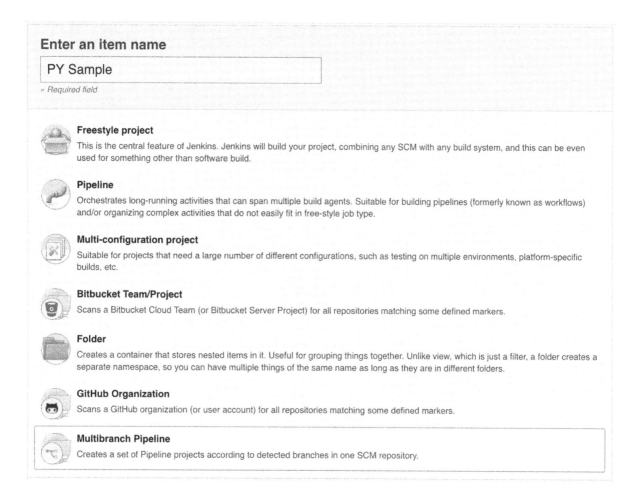

There are several options in the next page but initially we only mention the SCM repository from which the source code will be pulled to build the application.

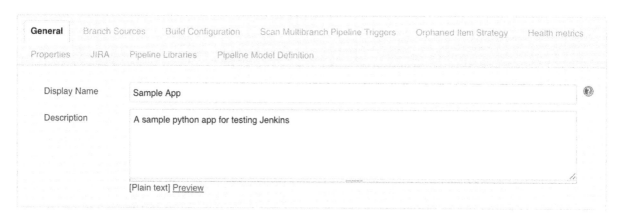

The sample repository that we will be using is *https://bhoson@bitbucket.org/bhoson/jenkins_ sample_project.git*

In the build configuration section, the path of the Jenkinsfile has to be mentioned. The Jenkinsfile is in the root location of our sample project, so the field is set to the following -

When the pipeline is *saved*, it runs the pipeline for the first time and the status of the pipeline is shown in the dashboard as the following -

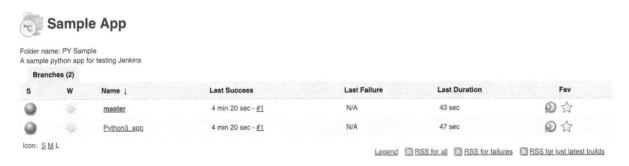

The above image shows a successful run of the pipeline. Jenkins provides a whole repository of plugins where from we can add to our Jenkins installation. It is accessible from the *Manage Plugins* option from *Manage Jenkins* -

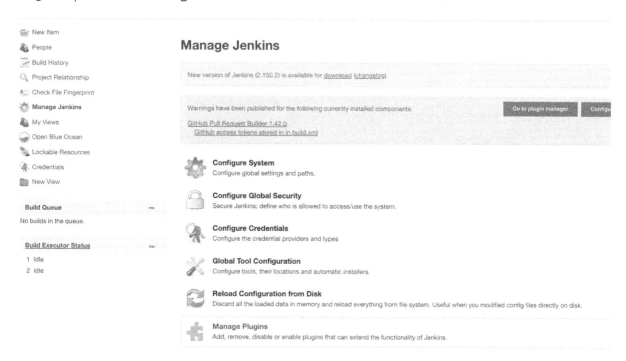

The one plugin which gets installed by default is the Blue Ocean plugin which provides a modern looking UI for the dashboard. The Blue Ocean dashboard can be switched on from the Open Blue Ocean option from the list of options of the left of the dashboard -

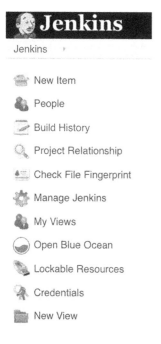

Here is the Blue Ocean dashboard which we will be using going forward -

Selecting a particular branch's run in the pipeline shows the following output of the various stages in the pipeline -

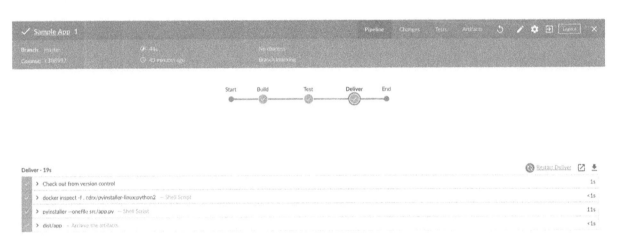

Our first pipeline has had a successful run and so next we are going to learn about the Jenkinsfile. Each software project, that we want to use with Jenkins, has to contain a Jenkinsfile. The following is the Jenkinsfile definition for our sample project -

```
pipeline {
    agent none
    stages {
        stage('Build') {
            agent {
                docker {
                    image 'python:2-alpine'
                }
            }
            steps {
                sh 'python -m py_compile src/app.py'
            }
        }
```

This the *Build* stage which uses the *python2* docker image for compiling the source code in *app.py*. Our pipeline will contain multiple stages which will require different environments. That is why the *agent* directive at the beginning of the pipeline is set to none and is explicitly mentioned in each of the stages.

The next stage is the *Test* phase which is defined as the following -

```
stage('Test') {
    agent {
        docker {
            image 'qnib/pytest'
        }
    }
    steps {
        sh 'py.test --verbose --junit-xml test-reports/results.xml src/test_app.py'
    }
    post {
        always {
            junit 'test-reports/results.xml'
        }
    }
}
```

The post directive tells Jenkins the action to perform after the completion of the *Test* stage.

And the final stage is the Deliver stage in which we use *pyinstaller* to compile our python script app.py to a deployable executable file.

```
stage('Deliver') {
    agent {
        docker {
            image 'cdrx/pyinstaller-linux:python2'
        }
    }
    steps {
        sh 'pyinstaller --onefile src/app.py'
    }
    post {
        success {
            archiveArtifacts 'dist/app'
        }
    }
}
```

The success directive is pretty self explanatory as the task to perform on a successful delivery ready build of the application in the *dist* directory as an executable.

# BIBLIOGRAPHY

- www.wikipedia.com
- www.analyticsvidhya.com
- www.superdatascience.com

Apart from these helpful resources, the official documentation for each of the technology used in this book, have been good sources of information.

9 789389 085938